A KISS ON THE NOSE TURNS ANGER ASIDE

Copr. © 1952, 1958 United Feature Syndicate, Inc.

Peanuts® Parade Paperbacks

1. Who's the Funny-Looking Kid with the Big Nose?
2. It's a Long Way to Tipperary
3. There's a Vulture Outside
4. What's Wrong with Being Crabby?
5. What Makes You Think You're Happy?
6. Fly, You Stupid Kite, Fly!
7. The Mad Punter Strikes Again
8. A Kiss on the Nose Turns Anger Aside
9. Thank Goodness for People
10. What Makes Musicians So Sarcastic?
11. Speak Softly, and Carry a Beagle
12. Don't Hassle Me with Your Sighs, Chuck

A KISS ON THE NOSE TURNS ANGER ASIDE

Cartoons from *You Can't Win, Charlie Brown* and *You Can Do It, Charlie Brown*

by Charles M. Schulz

Holt, Rinehart and Winston / New York

"Peanuts" comic strips from *You Can't Win, Charlie Brown*
Copyright © 1960, 1961, 1962 by United Feature Syndicate, Inc.

"Peanuts" comic strips from *You Can Do It, Charlie Brown*
Copyright © 1962, 1963 by United Feature Syndicate, Inc.

Published simultaneously in Canada by Holt, Rinehart
and Winston of Canada, Limited.

First published in this form in 1976.

Library of Congress Catalog Card Number: 76-8676

ISBN: 0-03-018101-1

Printed in the United States of America

10 9 8 7 6 5 4 3 2

Copr. © 1958 United Feature Syndicate, Inc.

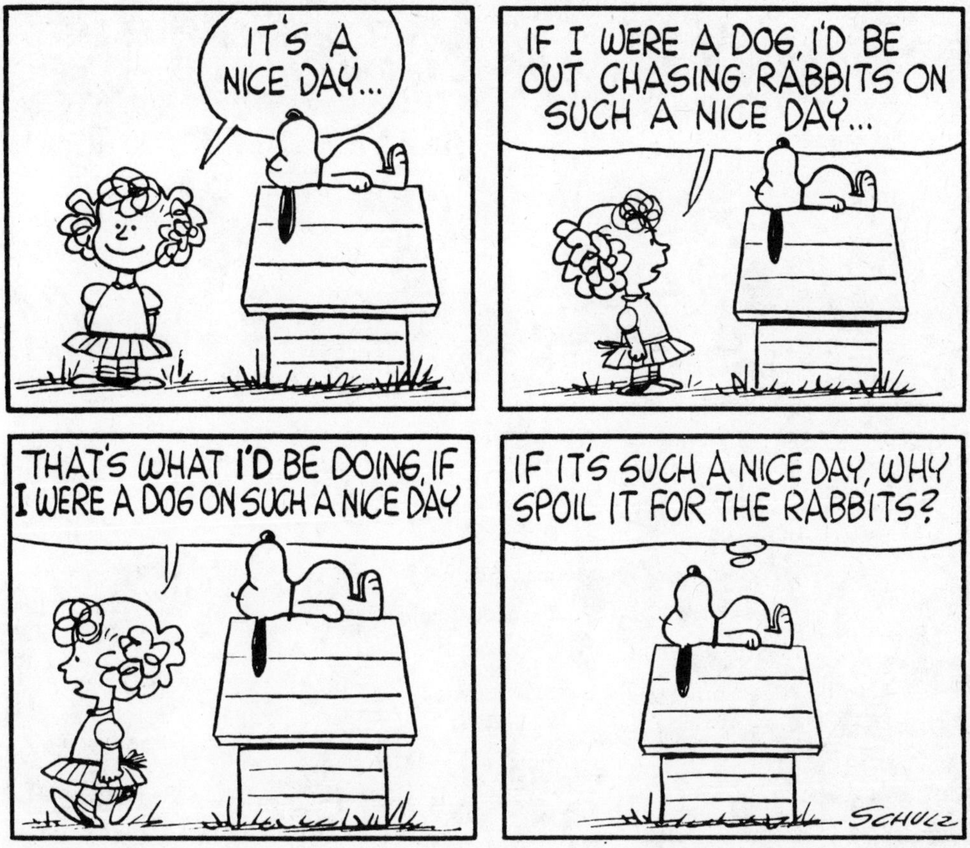
IT'S A NICE DAY...
IF I WERE A DOG, I'D BE OUT CHASING RABBITS ON SUCH A NICE DAY...
THAT'S WHAT **I'D** BE DOING, IF I WERE A DOG ON SUCH A NICE DAY
IF IT'S SUCH A NICE DAY, WHY SPOIL IT FOR THE RABBITS?
SCHULZ

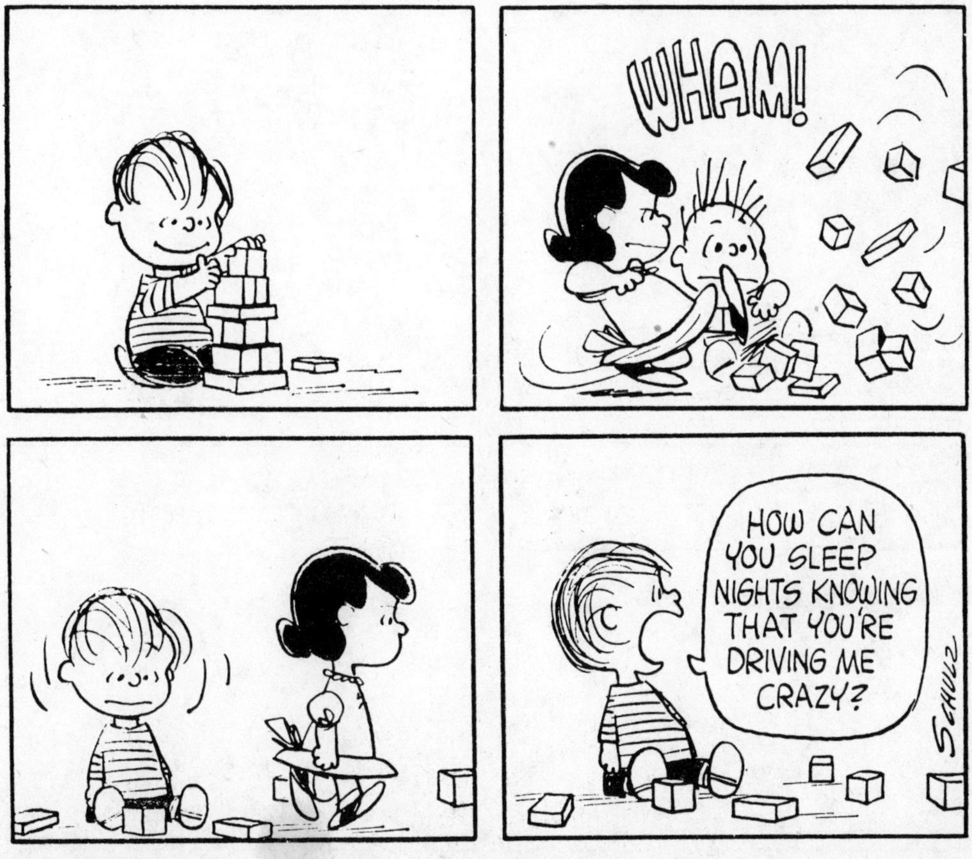
WHAM!
HOW CAN YOU SLEEP NIGHTS KNOWING THAT YOU'RE DRIVING ME CRAZY?
SCHULZ

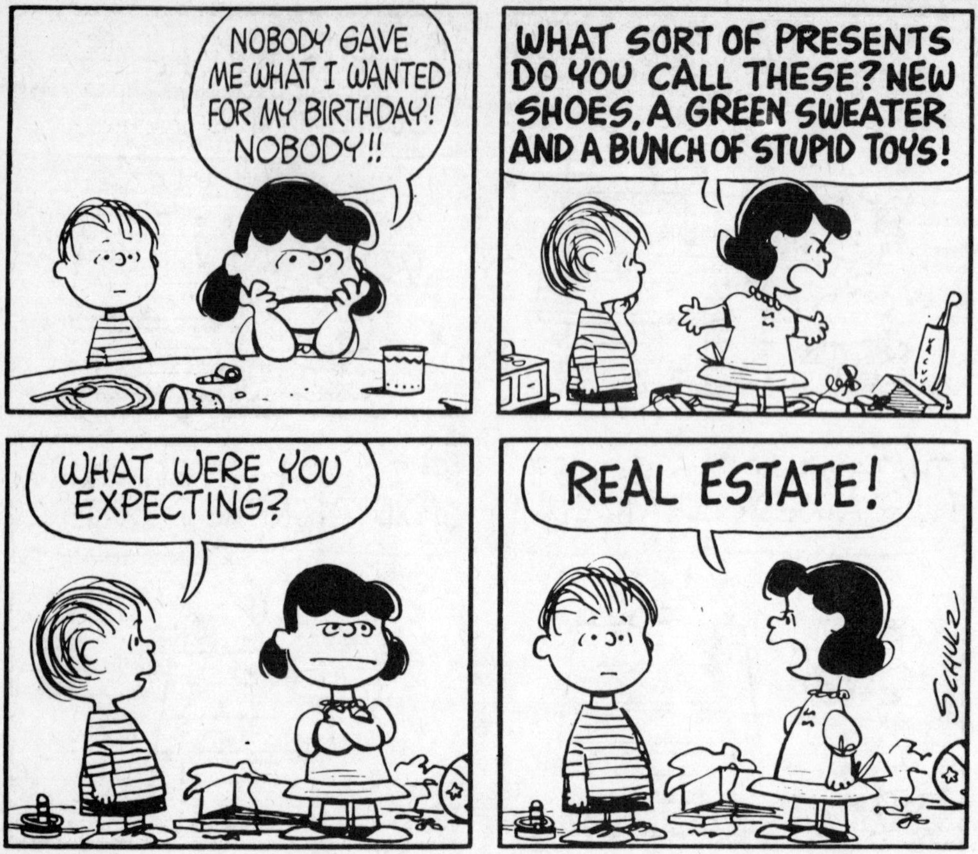
NOBODY GAVE ME WHAT I WANTED FOR MY BIRTHDAY! NOBODY!!
WHAT SORT OF PRESENTS DO YOU CALL THESE? NEW SHOES, A GREEN SWEATER AND A BUNCH OF STUPID TOYS!
WHAT WERE YOU EXPECTING?
REAL ESTATE!
SCHULZ

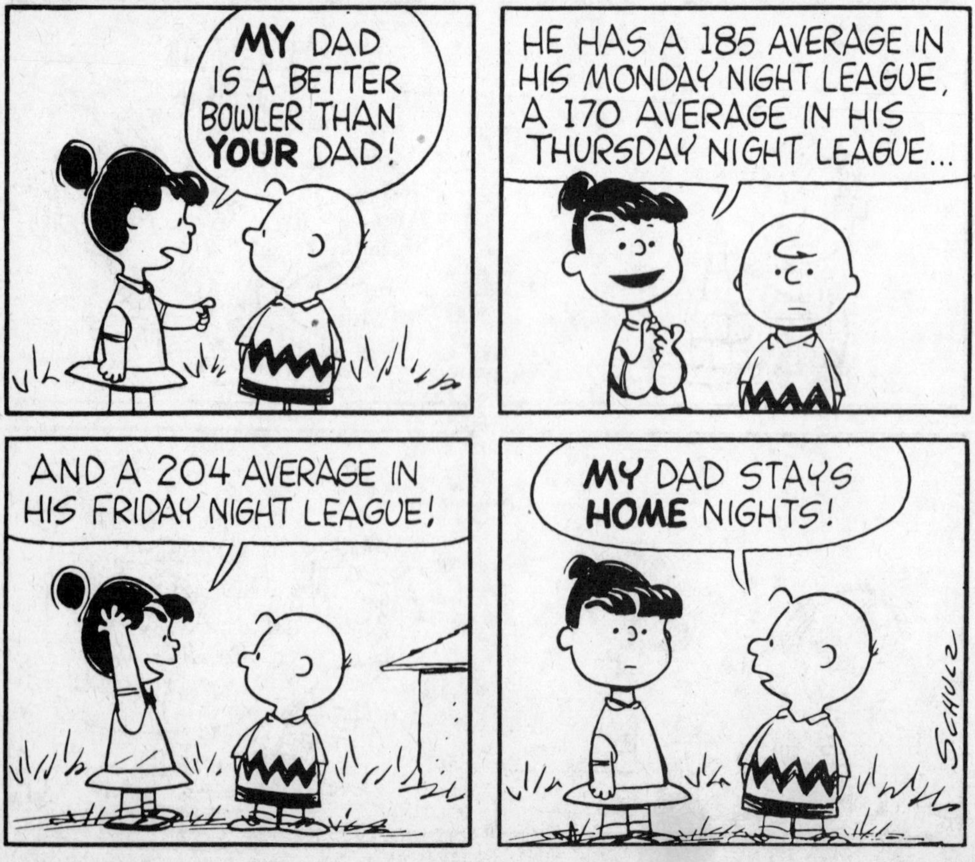
MY DAD IS A BETTER BOWLER THAN YOUR DAD!
HE HAS A 185 AVERAGE IN HIS MONDAY NIGHT LEAGUE, A 170 AVERAGE IN HIS THURSDAY NIGHT LEAGUE...
AND A 204 AVERAGE IN HIS FRIDAY NIGHT LEAGUE!
MY DAD STAYS HOME NIGHTS!
SCHULZ

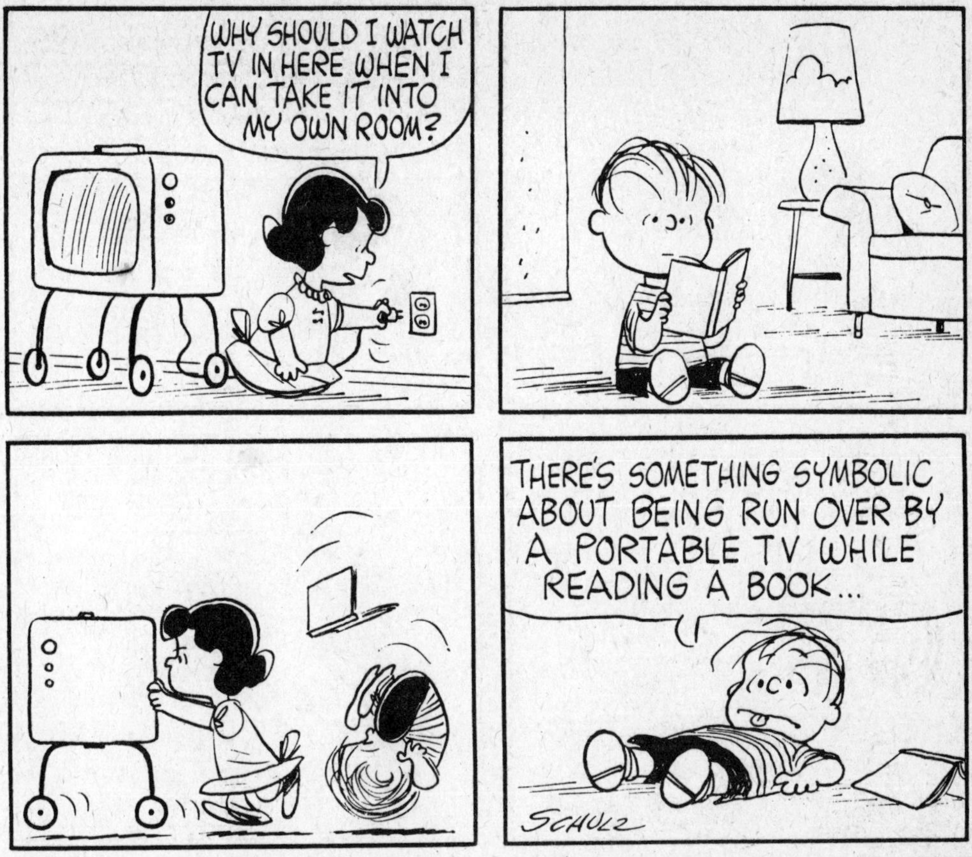
WHY SHOULD I WATCH TV IN HERE WHEN I CAN TAKE IT INTO MY OWN ROOM?
THERE'S SOMETHING SYMBOLIC ABOUT BEING RUN OVER BY A PORTABLE TV WHILE READING A BOOK...
SCHULZ

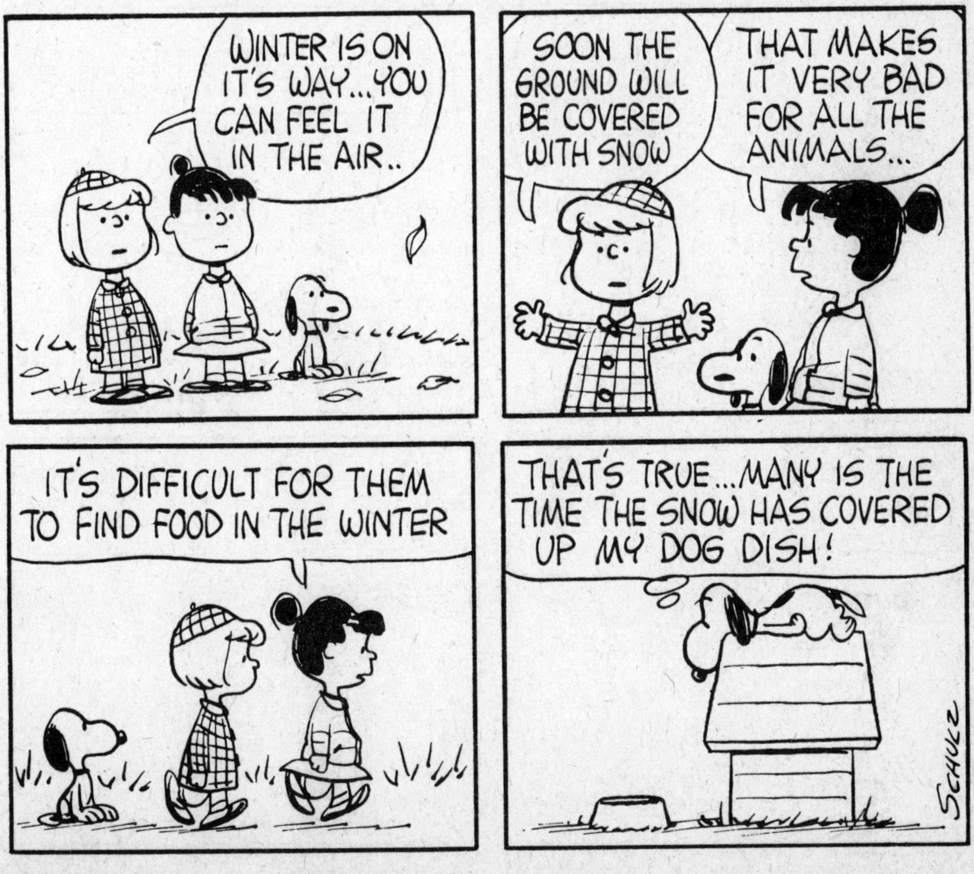
WINTER IS ON IT'S WAY...YOU CAN FEEL IT IN THE AIR..
SOON THE GROUND WILL BE COVERED WITH SNOW
THAT MAKES IT VERY BAD FOR ALL THE ANIMALS...
IT'S DIFFICULT FOR THEM TO FIND FOOD IN THE WINTER
THAT'S TRUE...MANY IS THE TIME THE SNOW HAS COVERED UP MY DOG DISH!
SCHULZ

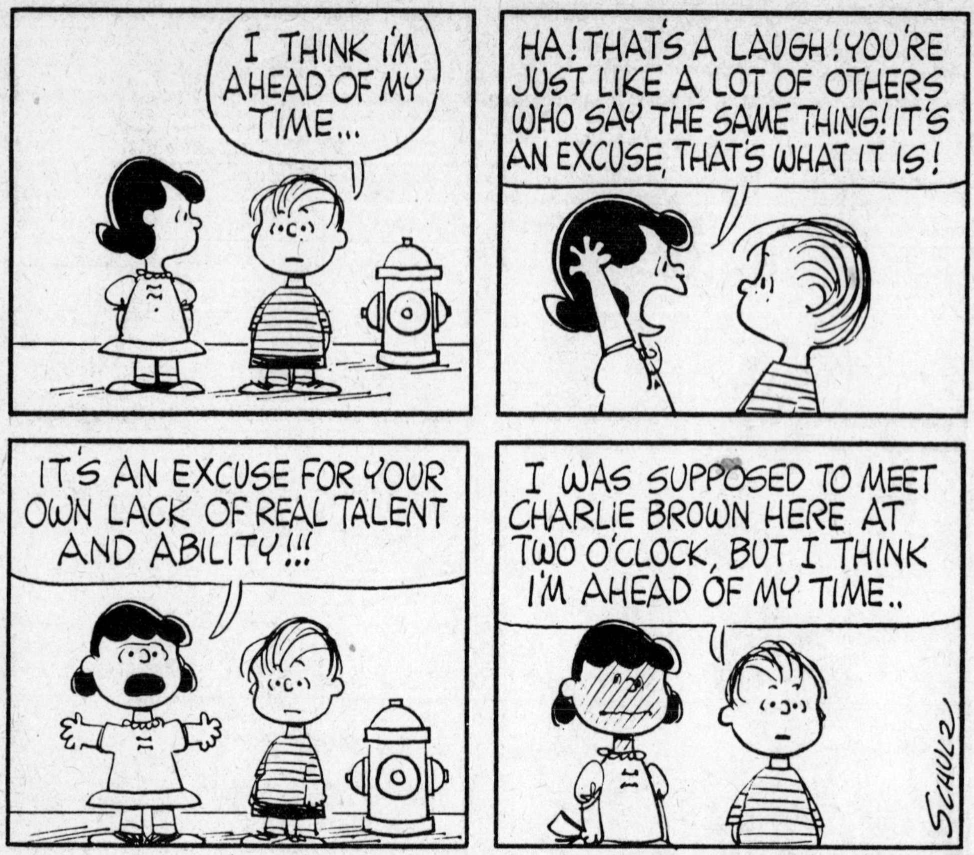
I THINK I'M AHEAD OF MY TIME...
HA! THAT'S A LAUGH! YOU'RE JUST LIKE A LOT OF OTHERS WHO SAY THE SAME THING! IT'S AN EXCUSE, THAT'S WHAT IT IS!
IT'S AN EXCUSE FOR YOUR OWN LACK OF REAL TALENT AND ABILITY!!!
I WAS SUPPOSED TO MEET CHARLIE BROWN HERE AT TWO O'CLOCK, BUT I THINK I'M AHEAD OF MY TIME..
SCHULZ

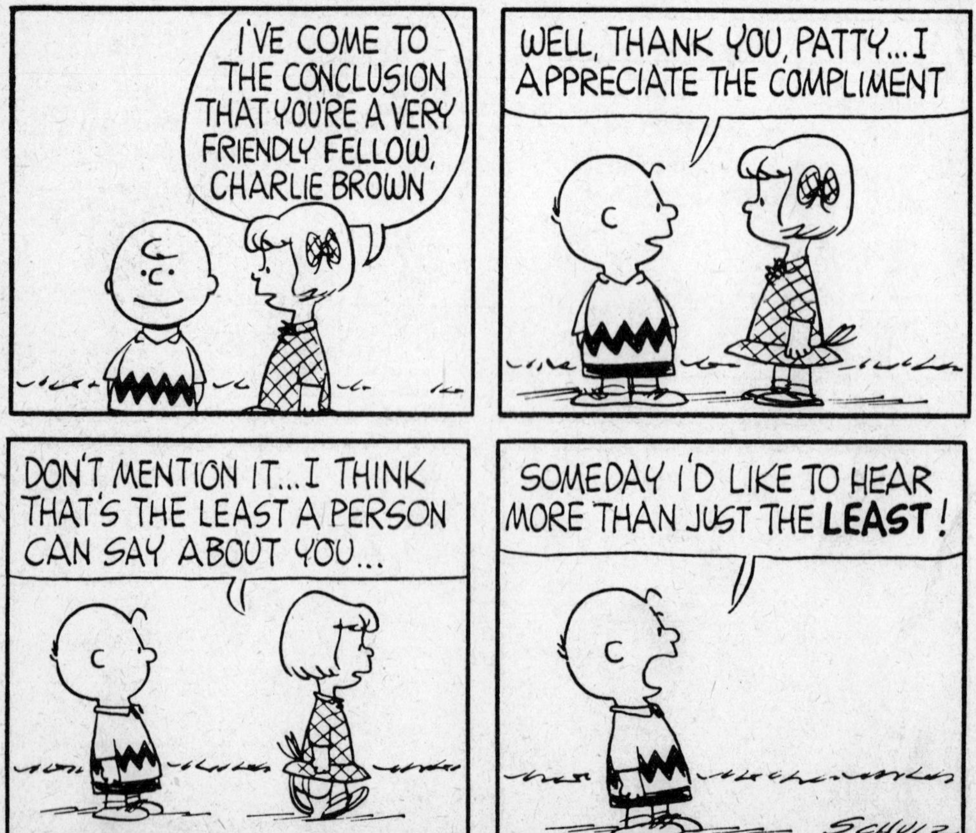
I'VE COME TO THE CONCLUSION THAT YOU'RE A VERY FRIENDLY FELLOW, CHARLIE BROWN
WELL, THANK YOU, PATTY...I APPRECIATE THE COMPLIMENT
DON'T MENTION IT...I THINK THAT'S THE LEAST A PERSON CAN SAY ABOUT YOU...
SOMEDAY I'D LIKE TO HEAR MORE THAN JUST THE **LEAST**!
SCHULZ

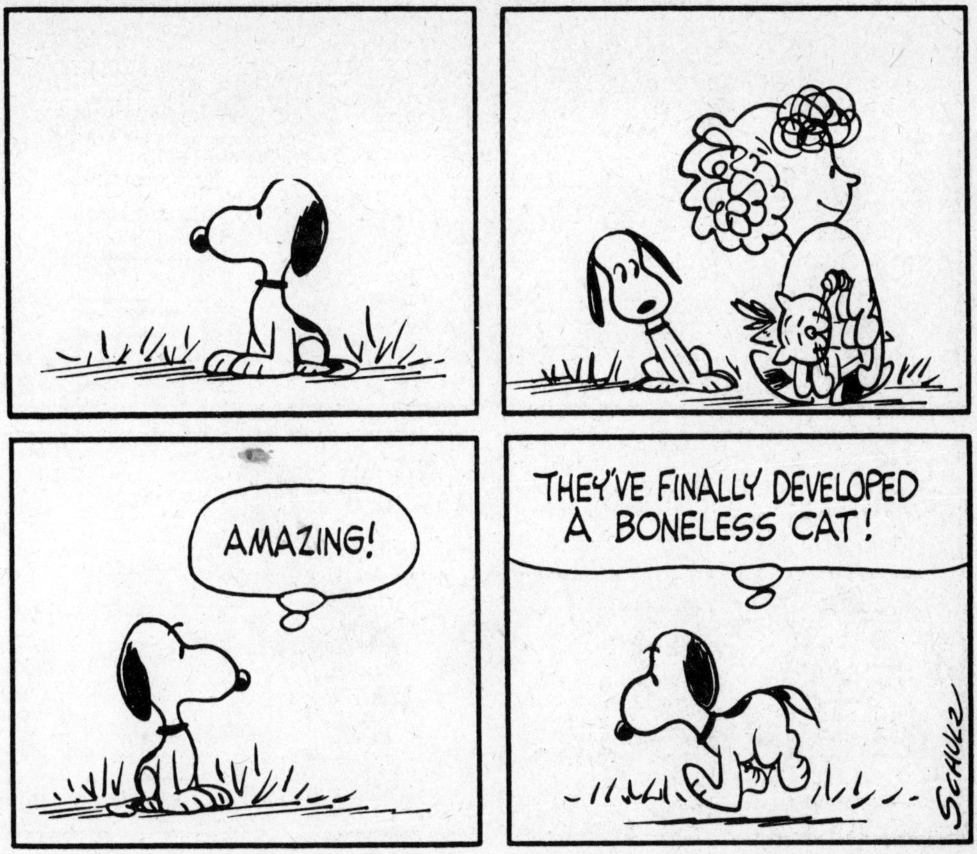
AMAZING!
THEY'VE FINALLY DEVELOPED A BONELESS CAT!
SCHULZ

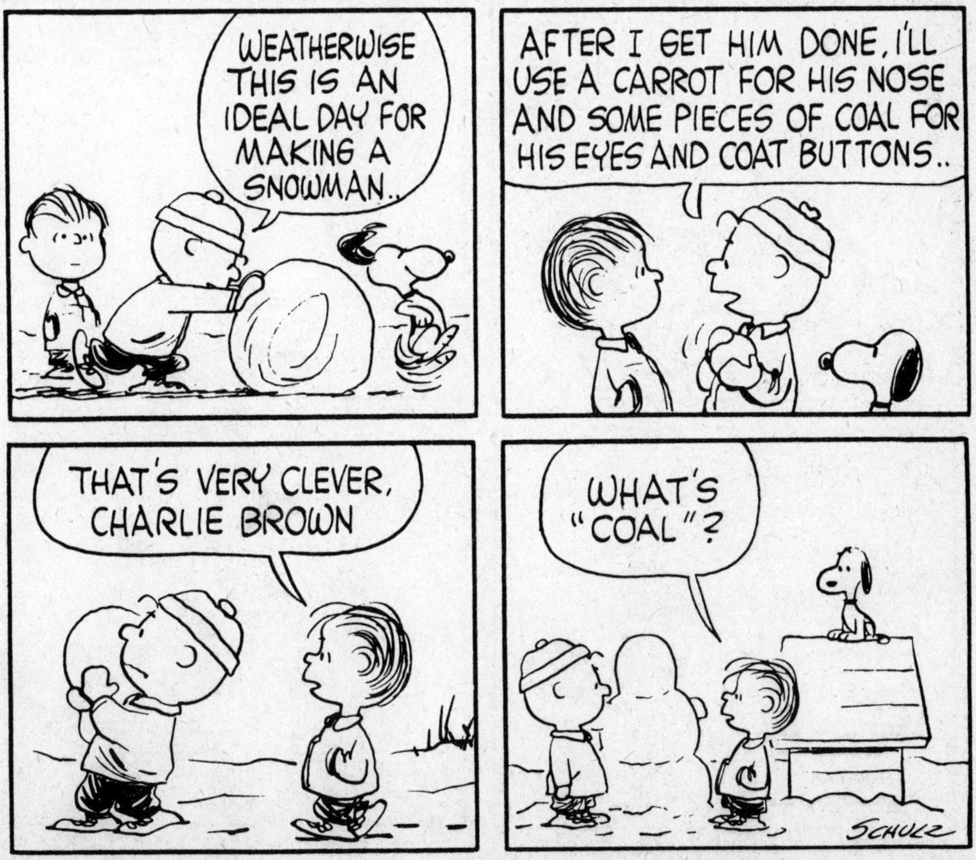
WEATHERWISE THIS IS AN IDEAL DAY FOR MAKING A SNOWMAN..
AFTER I GET HIM DONE, I'LL USE A CARROT FOR HIS NOSE AND SOME PIECES OF COAL FOR HIS EYES AND COAT BUTTONS..
THAT'S VERY CLEVER, CHARLIE BROWN
WHAT'S "COAL"?
SCHULZ

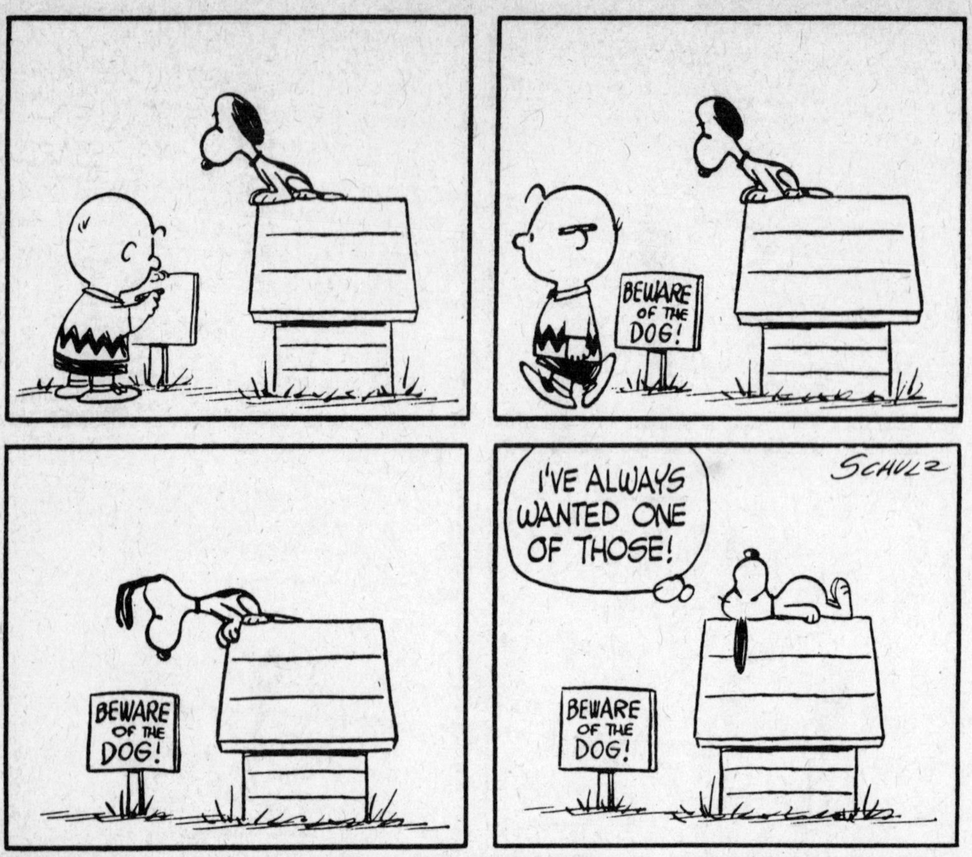
BEWARE OF THE DOG!
BEWARE OF THE DOG!
SCHULZ
I'VE ALWAYS WANTED ONE OF THOSE!
BEWARE OF THE DOG!

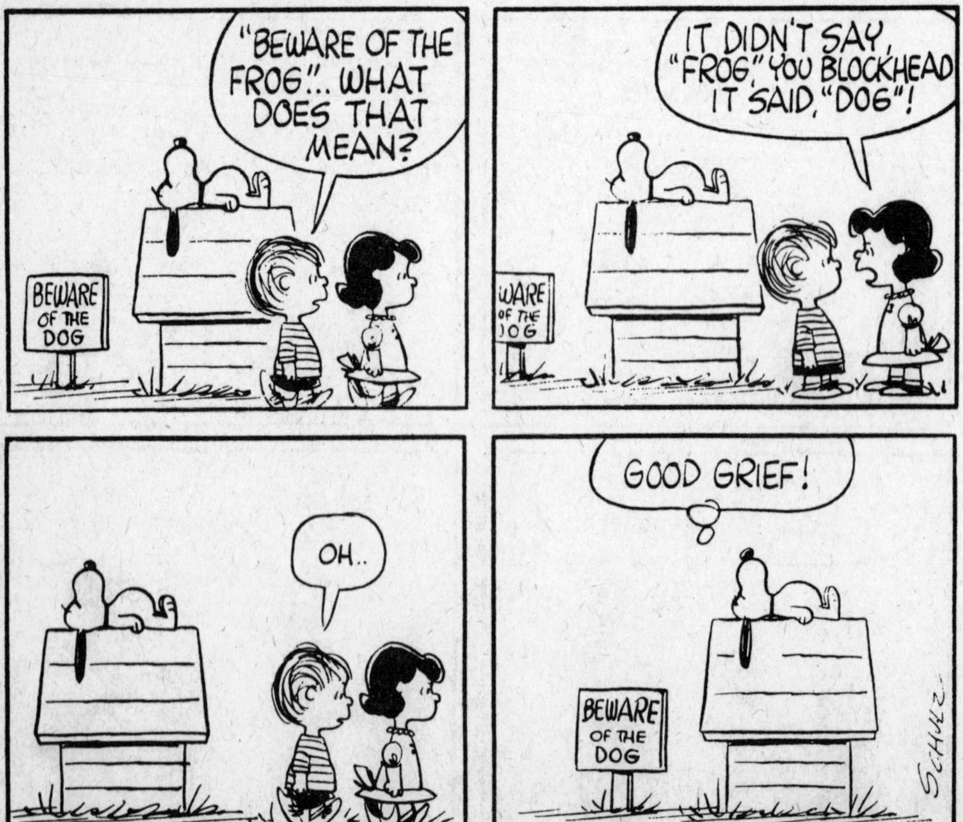
BEWARE OF THE DOG
"BEWARE OF THE FROG"... WHAT DOES THAT MEAN?
IT DIDN'T SAY, "FROG," YOU BLOCKHEAD IT SAID, "DOG"!
WARE OF THE OG
OH..
GOOD GRIEF!
BEWARE OF THE DOG
SCHULZ

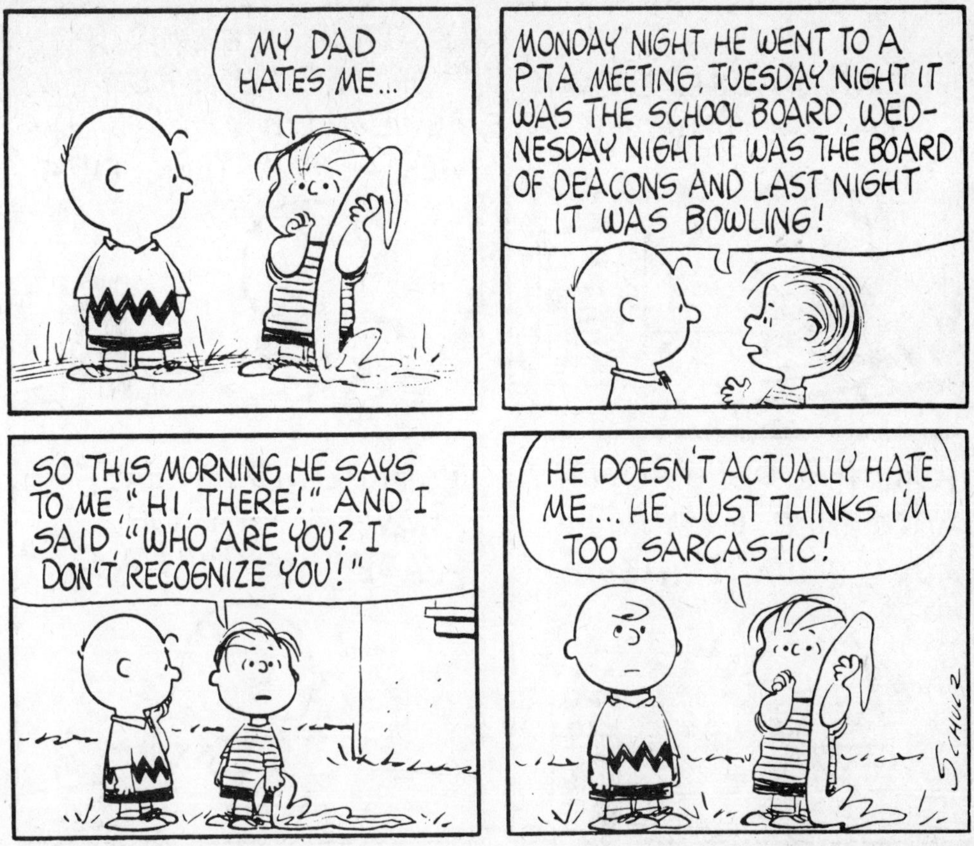
MY DAD HATES ME...
MONDAY NIGHT HE WENT TO A PTA MEETING, TUESDAY NIGHT IT WAS THE SCHOOL BOARD, WEDNESDAY NIGHT IT WAS THE BOARD OF DEACONS AND LAST NIGHT IT WAS BOWLING!
SO THIS MORNING HE SAYS TO ME, "HI, THERE!" AND I SAID, "WHO ARE YOU? I DON'T RECOGNIZE YOU!"
HE DOESN'T ACTUALLY HATE ME... HE JUST THINKS I'M TOO SARCASTIC!
SCHULZ

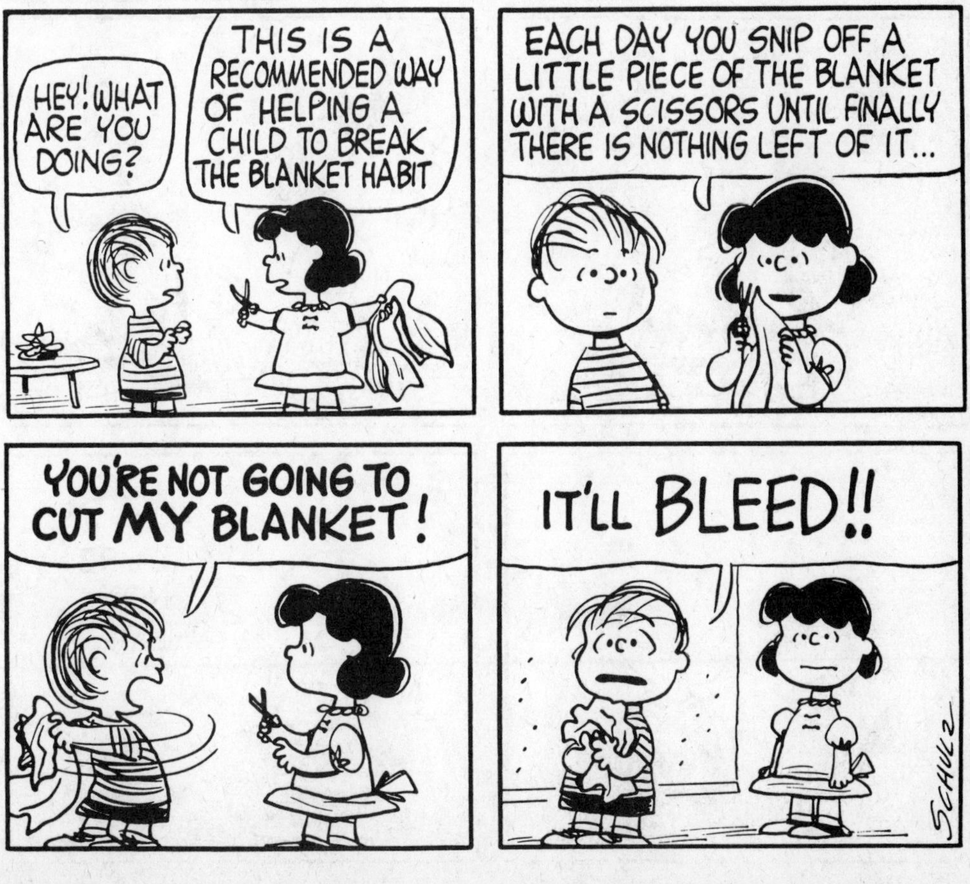
HEY! WHAT ARE YOU DOING?
THIS IS A RECOMMENDED WAY OF HELPING A CHILD TO BREAK THE BLANKET HABIT
EACH DAY YOU SNIP OFF A LITTLE PIECE OF THE BLANKET WITH A SCISSORS UNTIL FINALLY THERE IS NOTHING LEFT OF IT...
YOU'RE NOT GOING TO CUT MY BLANKET!
IT'LL BLEED!!
SCHULZ

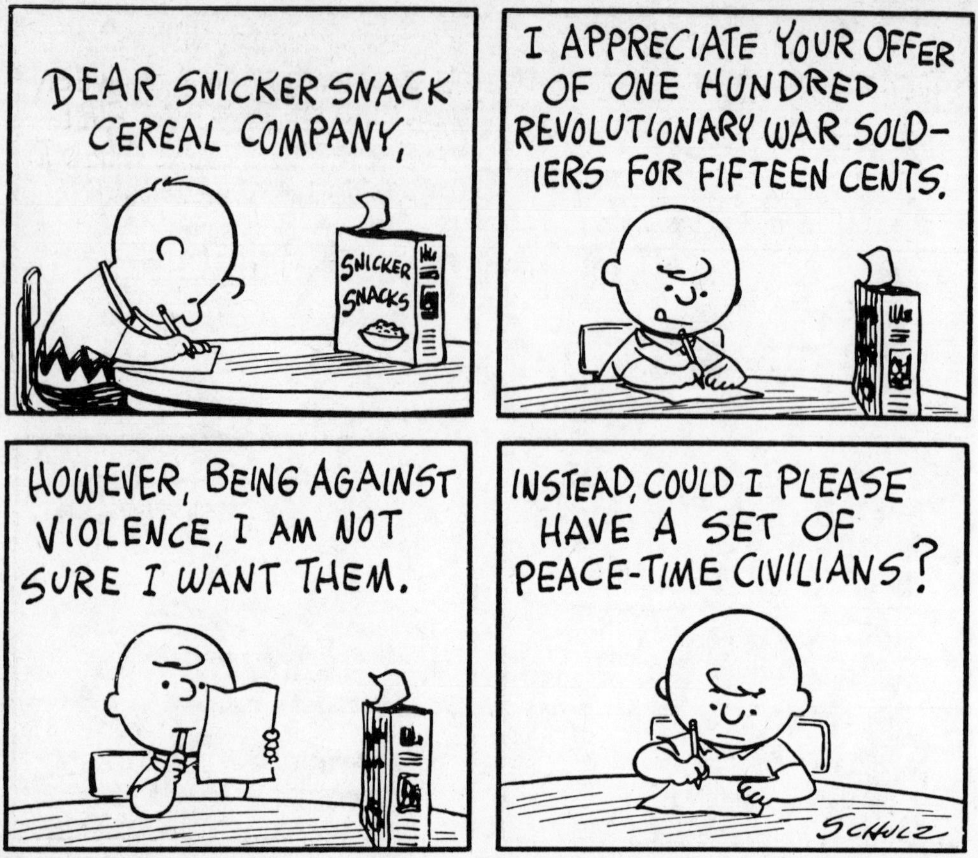
DEAR SNICKER SNACK CEREAL COMPANY,
SNICKER SNACKS
I APPRECIATE YOUR OFFER OF ONE HUNDRED REVOLUTIONARY WAR SOLD-IERS FOR FIFTEEN CENTS.
HOWEVER, BEING AGAINST VIOLENCE, I AM NOT SURE I WANT THEM.
INSTEAD, COULD I PLEASE HAVE A SET OF PEACE-TIME CIVILIANS?
SCHULZ

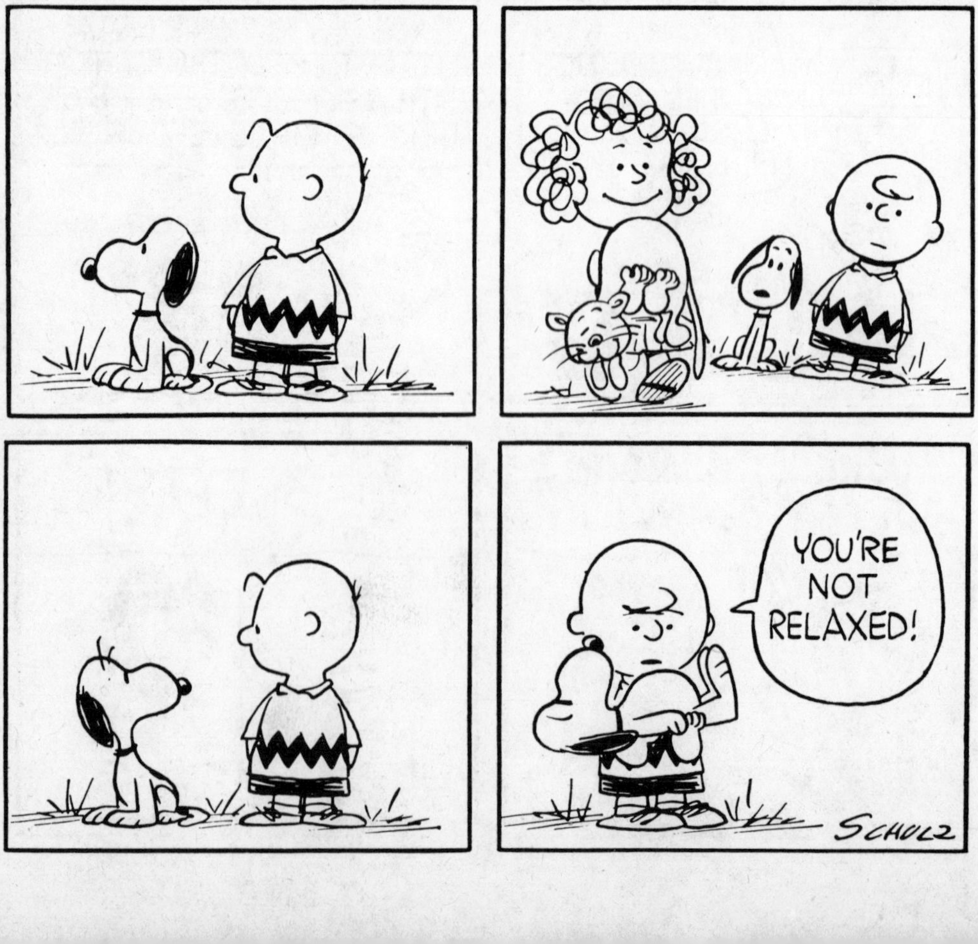
YOU'RE NOT RELAXED!
SCHULZ

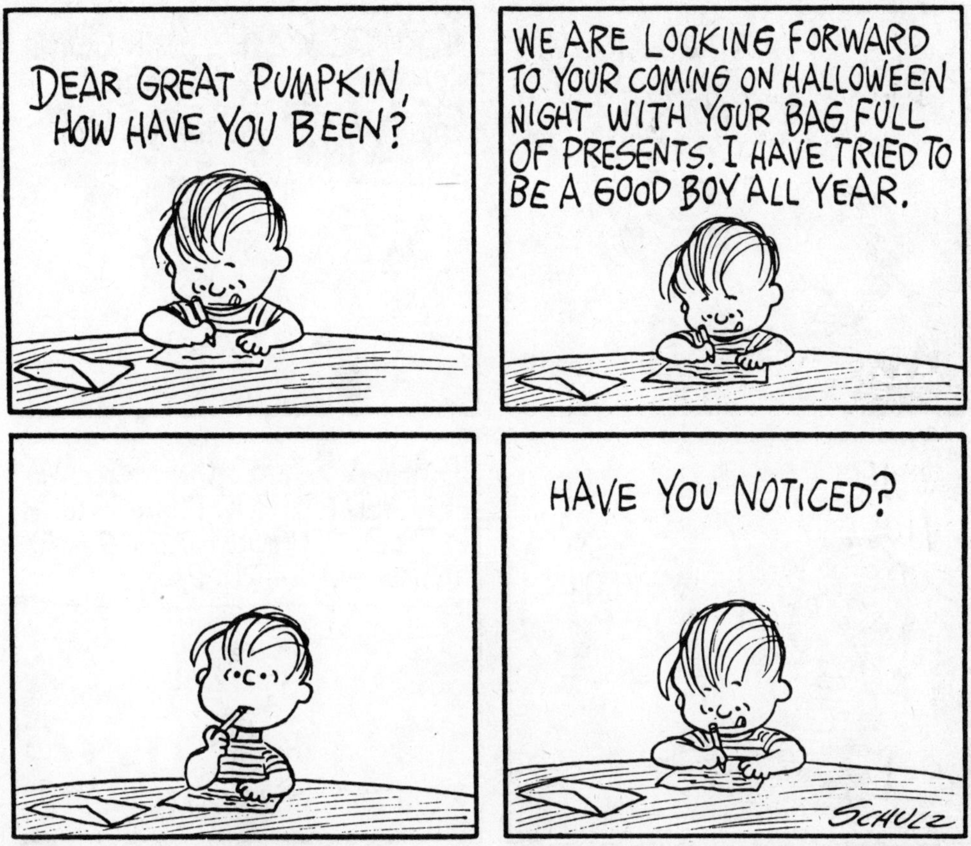
DEAR GREAT PUMPKIN, HOW HAVE YOU BEEN?
WE ARE LOOKING FORWARD TO YOUR COMING ON HALLOWEEN NIGHT WITH YOUR BAG FULL OF PRESENTS. I HAVE TRIED TO BE A GOOD BOY ALL YEAR.
HAVE YOU NOTICED?
SCHULZ

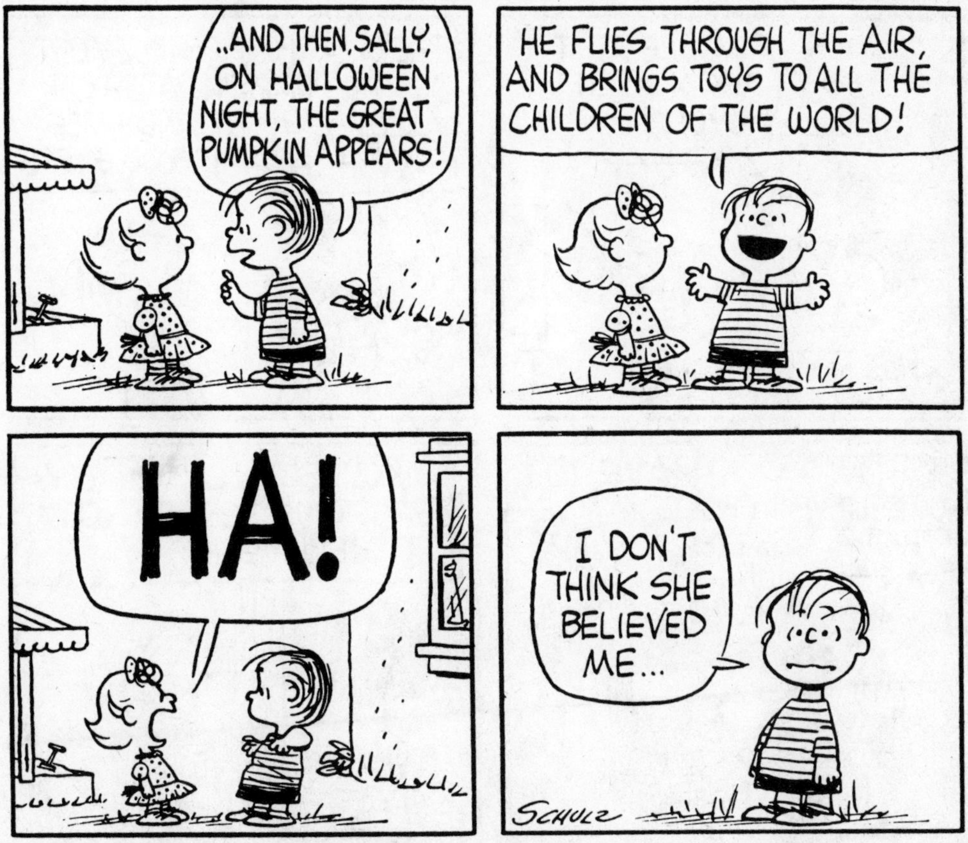
..AND THEN, SALLY, ON HALLOWEEN NIGHT, THE GREAT PUMPKIN APPEARS!
HE FLIES THROUGH THE AIR, AND BRINGS TOYS TO ALL THE CHILDREN OF THE WORLD!
HA!
I DON'T THINK SHE BELIEVED ME...
SCHULZ

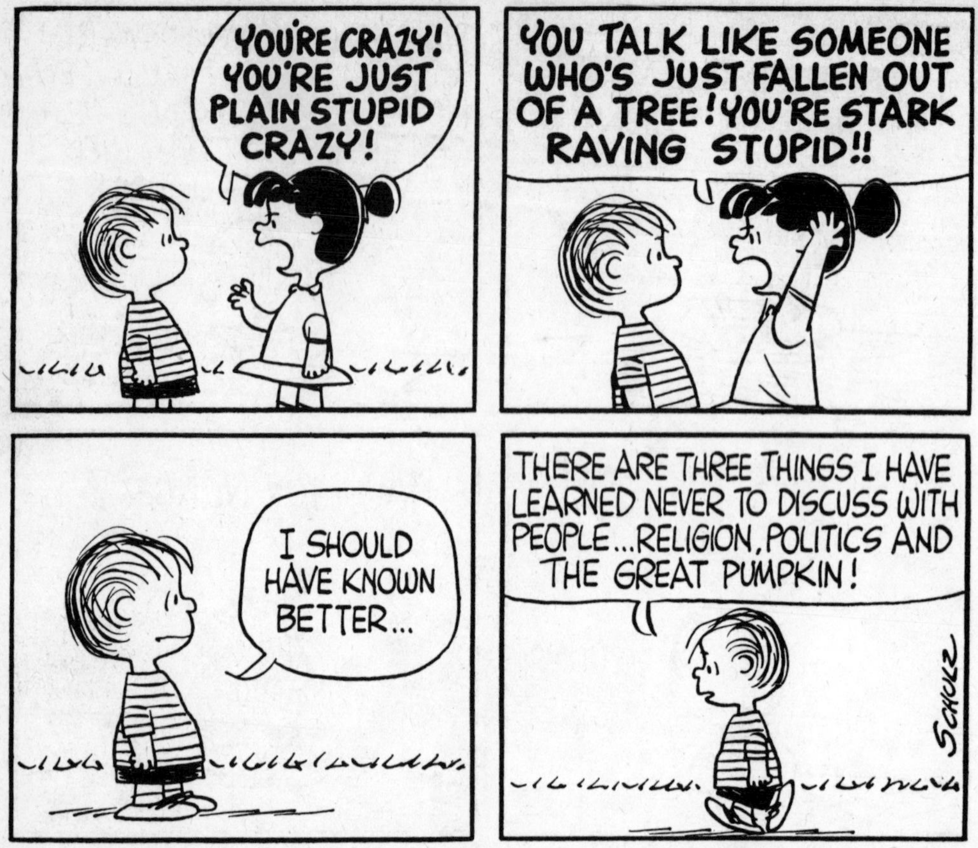
YOU'RE CRAZY! YOU'RE JUST PLAIN STUPID CRAZY!
YOU TALK LIKE SOMEONE WHO'S JUST FALLEN OUT OF A TREE! YOU'RE STARK RAVING STUPID!!
I SHOULD HAVE KNOWN BETTER...
THERE ARE THREE THINGS I HAVE LEARNED NEVER TO DISCUSS WITH PEOPLE...RELIGION, POLITICS AND THE GREAT PUMPKIN!
SCHULZ

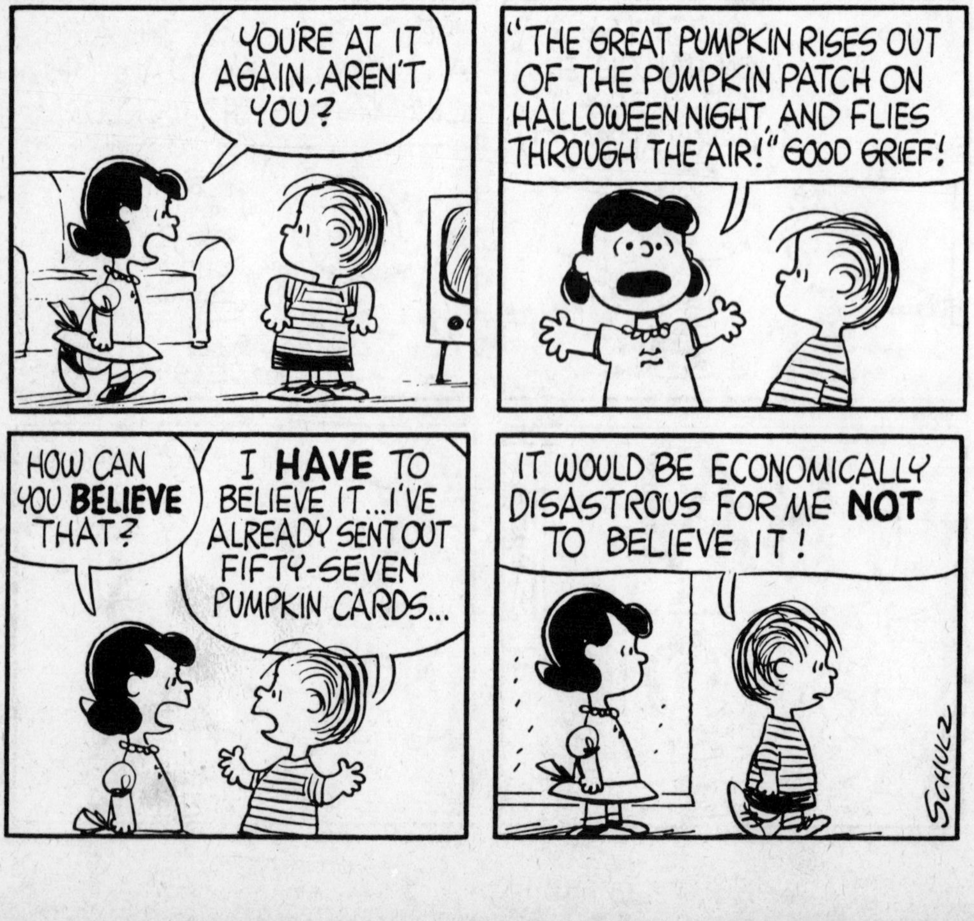
YOU'RE AT IT AGAIN, AREN'T YOU?
"THE GREAT PUMPKIN RISES OUT OF THE PUMPKIN PATCH ON HALLOWEEN NIGHT, AND FLIES THROUGH THE AIR!" GOOD GRIEF!
HOW CAN YOU BELIEVE THAT?
I HAVE TO BELIEVE IT...I'VE ALREADY SENT OUT FIFTY-SEVEN PUMPKIN CARDS...
IT WOULD BE ECONOMICALLY DISASTROUS FOR ME NOT TO BELIEVE IT!
SCHULZ

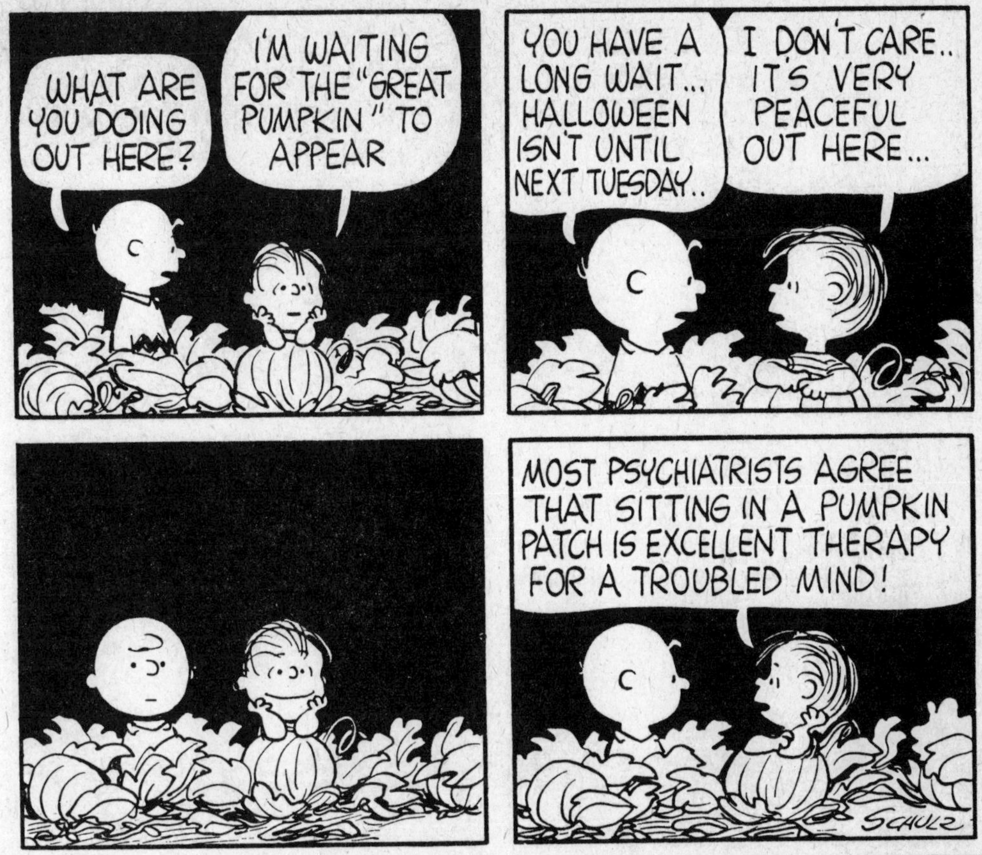
WHAT ARE YOU DOING OUT HERE?
I'M WAITING FOR THE "GREAT PUMPKIN" TO APPEAR
YOU HAVE A LONG WAIT... HALLOWEEN ISN'T UNTIL NEXT TUESDAY..
I DON'T CARE.. IT'S VERY PEACEFUL OUT HERE...
MOST PSYCHIATRISTS AGREE THAT SITTING IN A PUMPKIN PATCH IS EXCELLENT THERAPY FOR A TROUBLED MIND!
SCHULZ

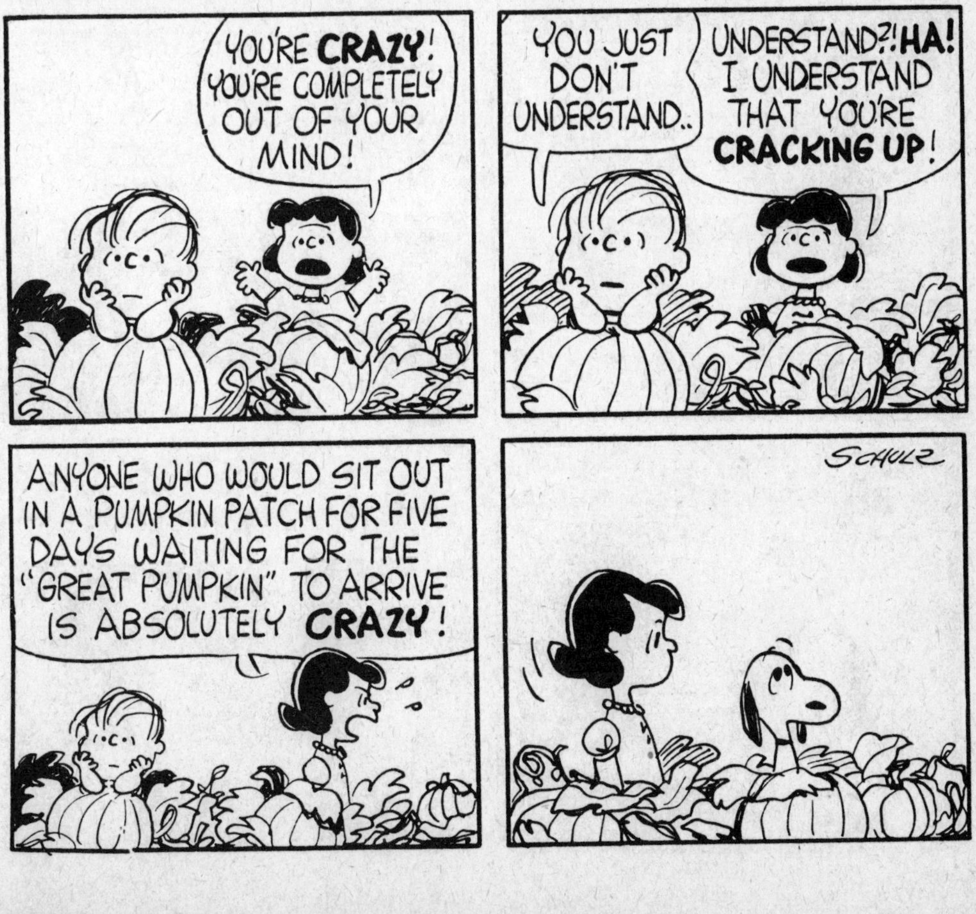
YOU'RE **CRAZY**! YOU'RE COMPLETELY OUT OF YOUR MIND!
YOU JUST DON'T UNDERSTAND..
UNDERSTAND?! **HA!** I UNDERSTAND THAT YOU'RE **CRACKING UP**!
ANYONE WHO WOULD SIT OUT IN A PUMPKIN PATCH FOR FIVE DAYS WAITING FOR THE "GREAT PUMPKIN" TO ARRIVE IS ABSOLUTELY **CRAZY**!
SCHULZ

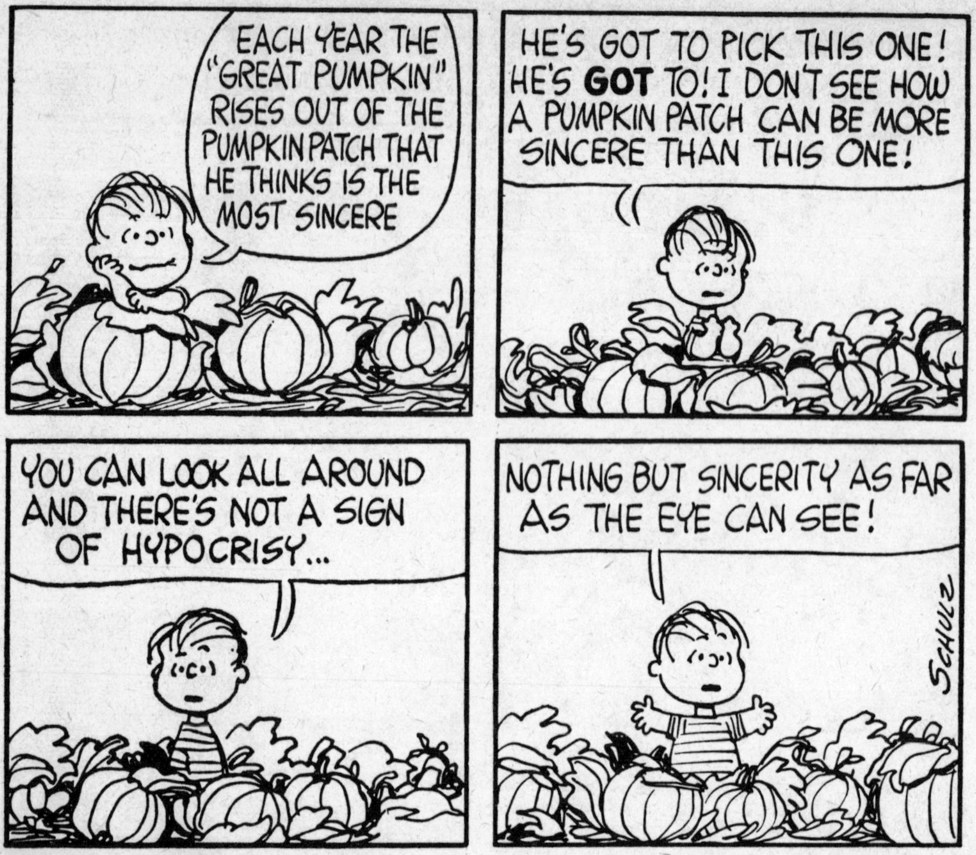
EACH YEAR THE "GREAT PUMPKIN" RISES OUT OF THE PUMPKIN PATCH THAT HE THINKS IS THE MOST SINCERE
HE'S GOT TO PICK THIS ONE! HE'S **GOT** TO! I DON'T SEE HOW A PUMPKIN PATCH CAN BE MORE SINCERE THAN THIS ONE!
YOU CAN LOOK ALL AROUND AND THERE'S NOT A SIGN OF HYPOCRISY...
NOTHING BUT SINCERITY AS FAR AS THE EYE CAN SEE!
SCHULZ

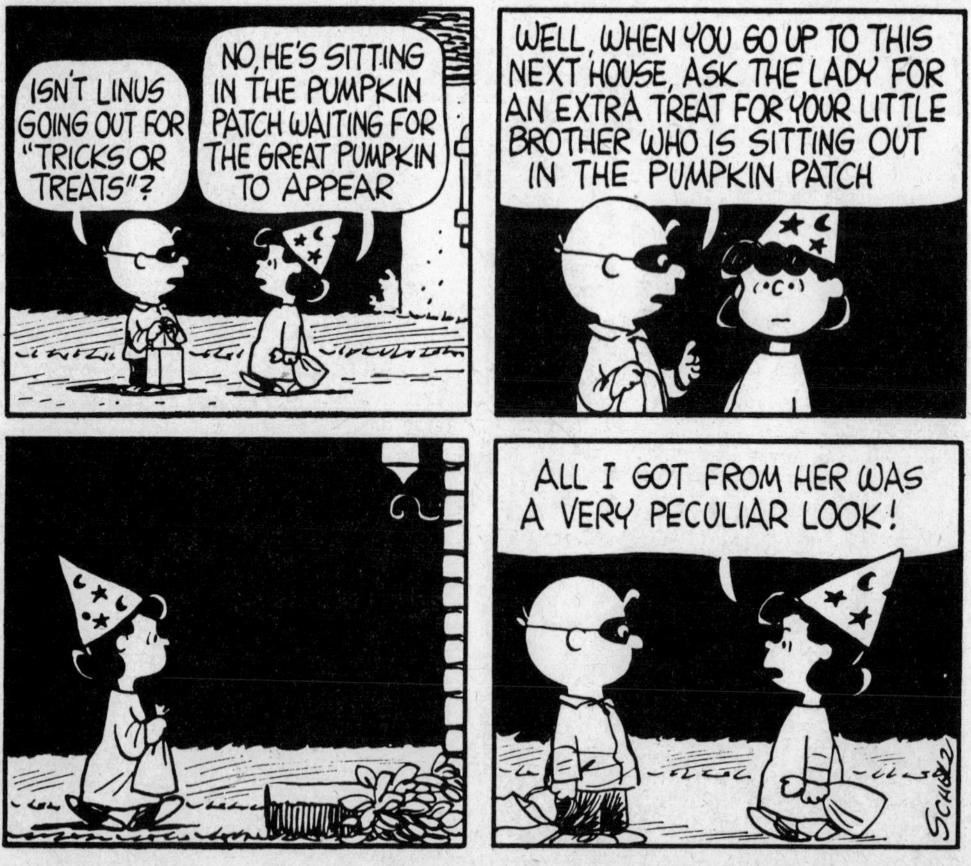
ISN'T LINUS GOING OUT FOR "TRICKS OR TREATS"?
NO, HE'S SITTING IN THE PUMPKIN PATCH WAITING FOR THE GREAT PUMPKIN TO APPEAR
WELL, WHEN YOU GO UP TO THIS NEXT HOUSE, ASK THE LADY FOR AN EXTRA TREAT FOR YOUR LITTLE BROTHER WHO IS SITTING OUT IN THE PUMPKIN PATCH
ALL I GOT FROM HER WAS A VERY PECULIAR LOOK!
SCHULZ

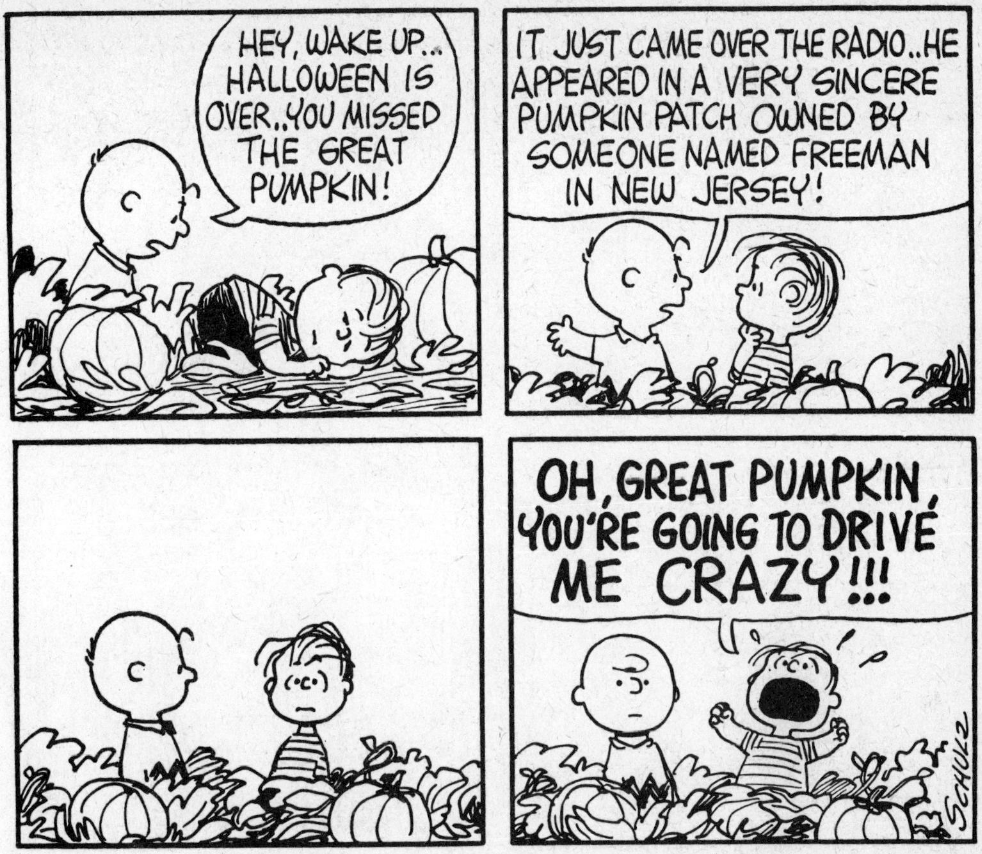
HEY, WAKE UP.. HALLOWEEN IS OVER..YOU MISSED THE GREAT PUMPKIN!
IT JUST CAME OVER THE RADIO..HE APPEARED IN A VERY SINCERE PUMPKIN PATCH OWNED BY SOMEONE NAMED FREEMAN IN NEW JERSEY!
OH, GREAT PUMPKIN, YOU'RE GOING TO DRIVE ME CRAZY!!!
SCHULZ

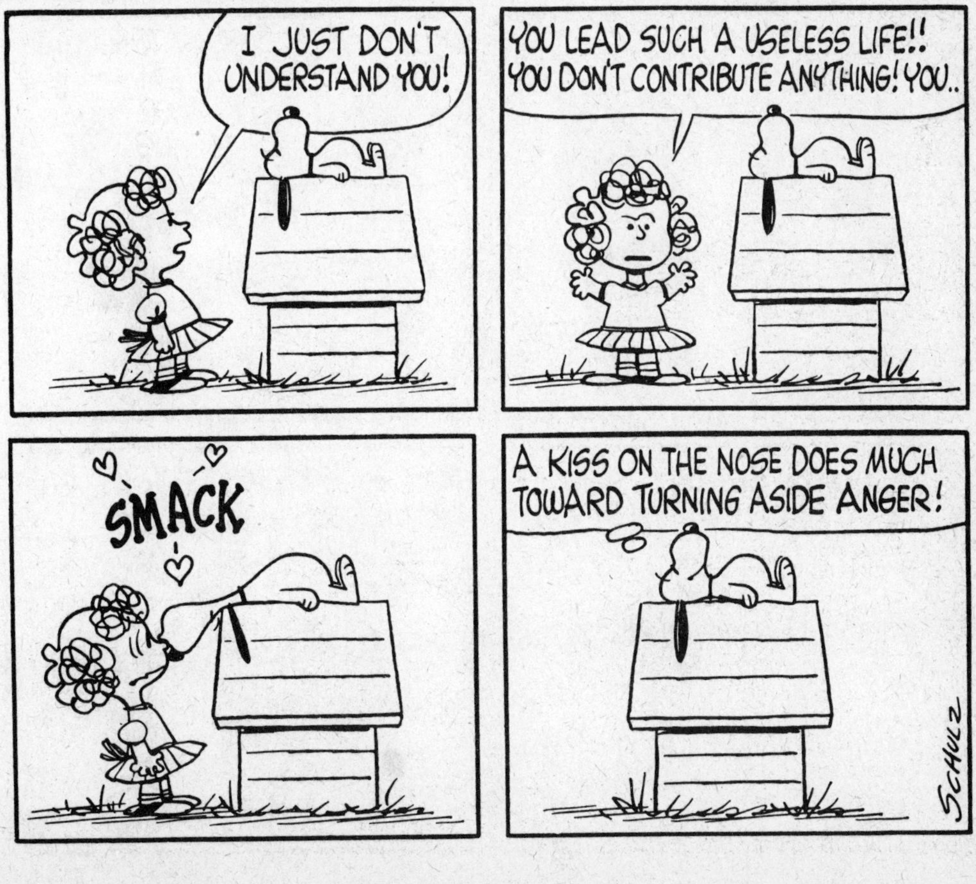
I JUST DON'T UNDERSTAND YOU!
YOU LEAD SUCH A USELESS LIFE!! YOU DON'T CONTRIBUTE ANYTHING! YOU..
SMACK
A KISS ON THE NOSE DOES MUCH TOWARD TURNING ASIDE ANGER!
SCHULZ

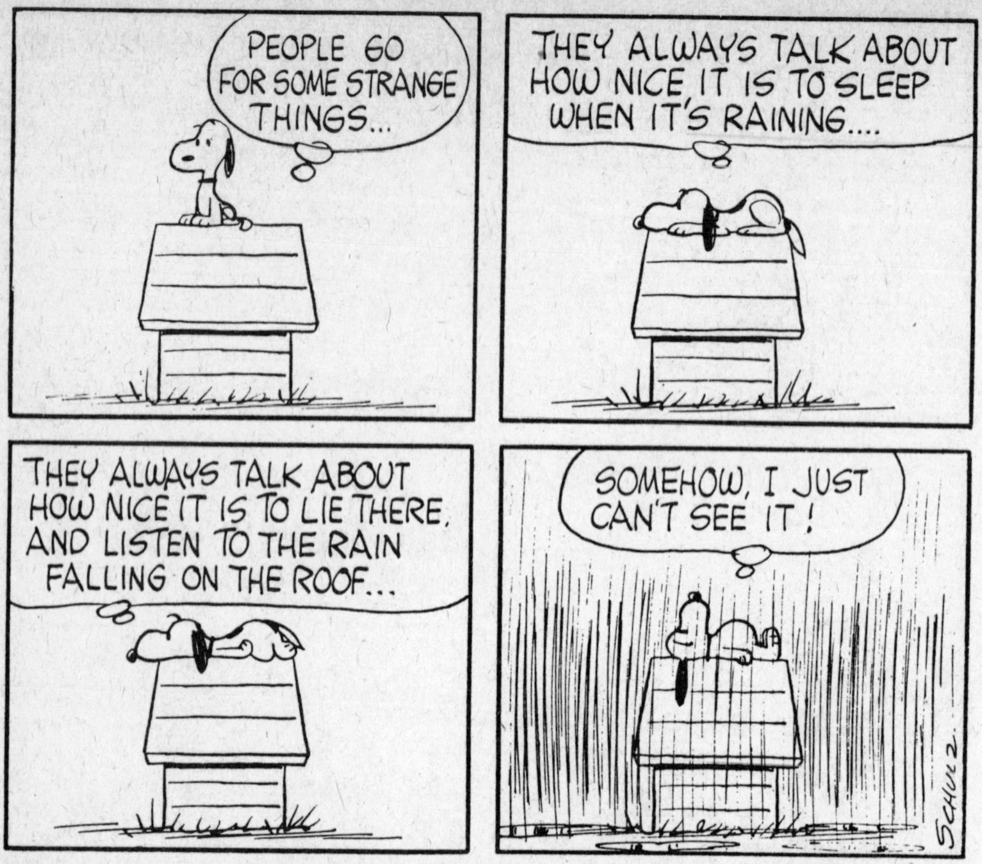
PEOPLE GO FOR SOME STRANGE THINGS...
THEY ALWAYS TALK ABOUT HOW NICE IT IS TO SLEEP WHEN IT'S RAINING....
THEY ALWAYS TALK ABOUT HOW NICE IT IS TO LIE THERE, AND LISTEN TO THE RAIN FALLING ON THE ROOF...
SOMEHOW, I JUST CAN'T SEE IT!
SCHULZ

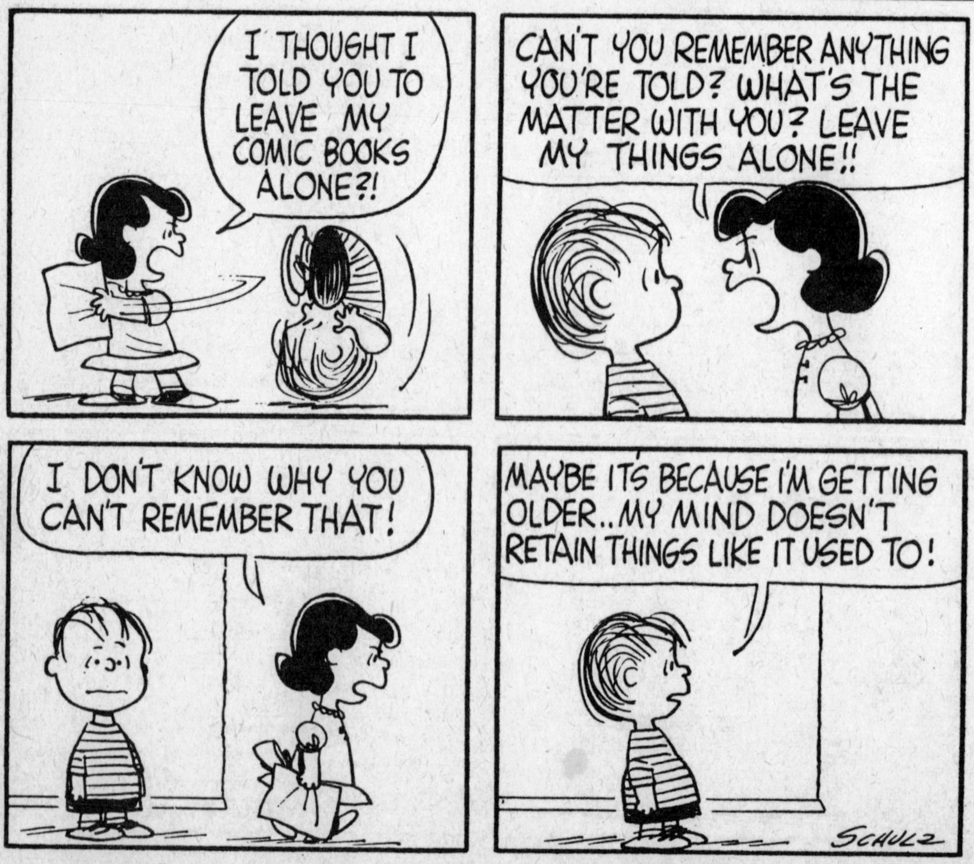
I THOUGHT I TOLD YOU TO LEAVE MY COMIC BOOKS ALONE?!
CAN'T YOU REMEMBER ANYTHING YOU'RE TOLD? WHAT'S THE MATTER WITH YOU? LEAVE MY THINGS ALONE!!
I DON'T KNOW WHY YOU CAN'T REMEMBER THAT!
MAYBE IT'S BECAUSE I'M GETTING OLDER..MY MIND DOESN'T RETAIN THINGS LIKE IT USED TO!
SCHULZ

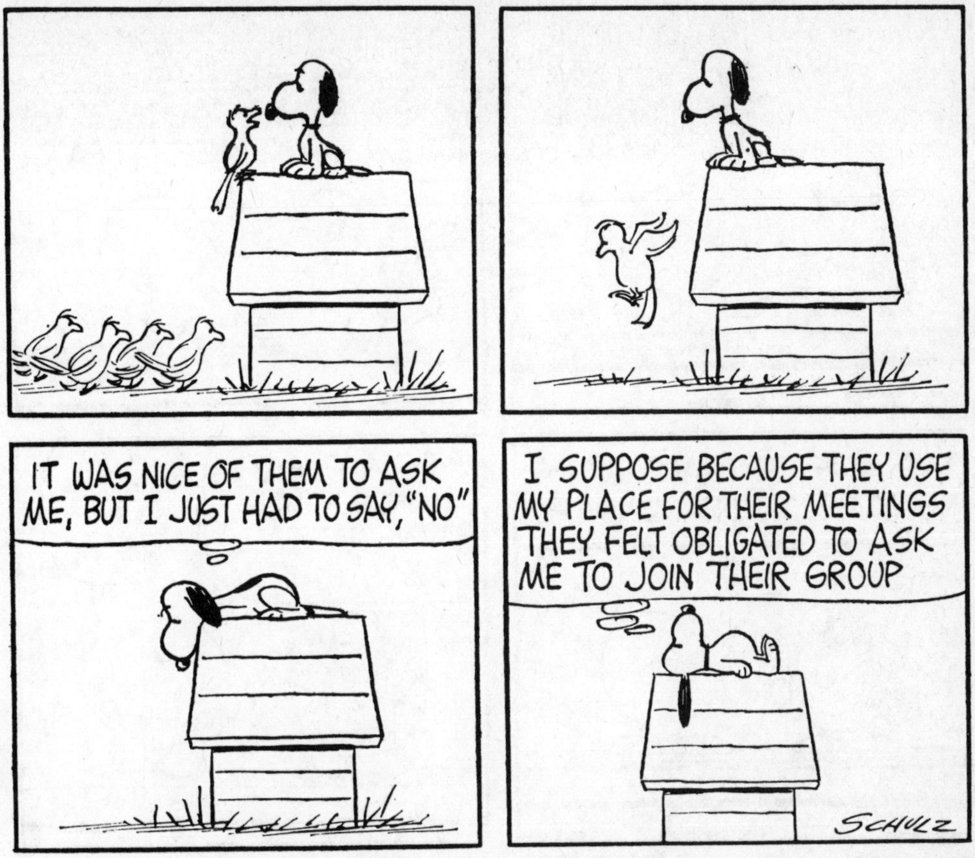
IT WAS NICE OF THEM TO ASK ME, BUT I JUST HAD TO SAY, "NO"
I SUPPOSE BECAUSE THEY USE MY PLACE FOR THEIR MEETINGS THEY FELT OBLIGATED TO ASK ME TO JOIN THEIR GROUP
SCHULZ

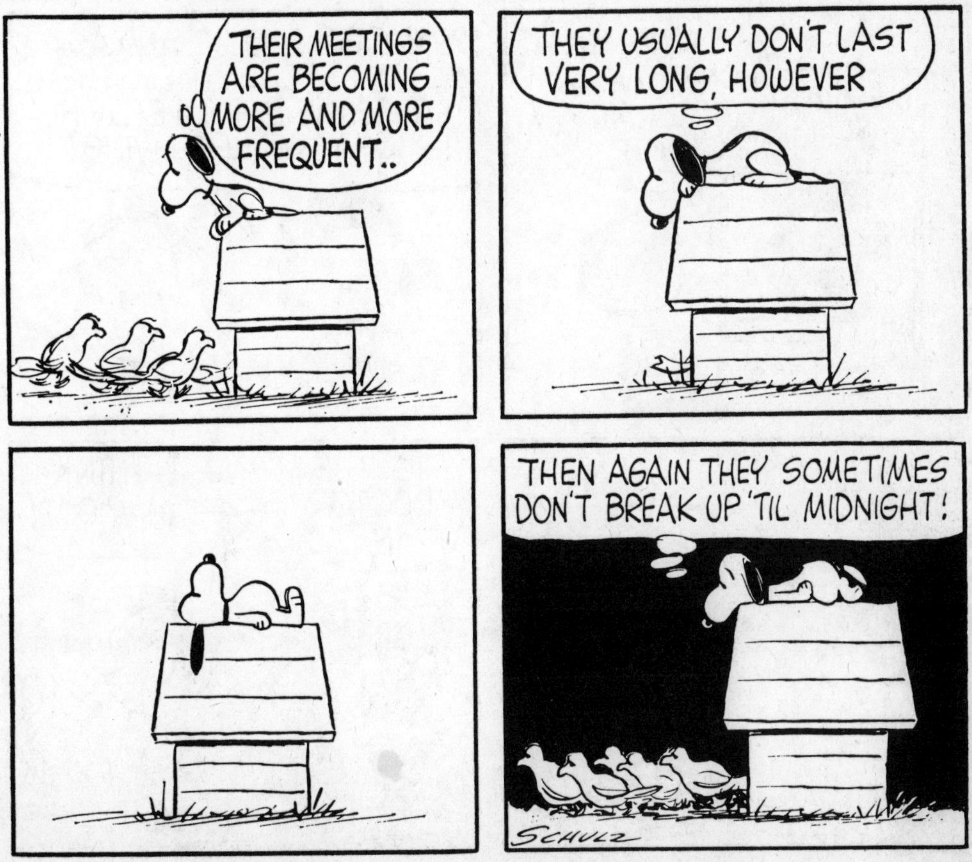
THEIR MEETINGS ARE BECOMING MORE AND MORE FREQUENT..
THEY USUALLY DON'T LAST VERY LONG, HOWEVER
THEN AGAIN THEY SOMETIMES DON'T BREAK UP 'TIL MIDNIGHT!
SCHULZ

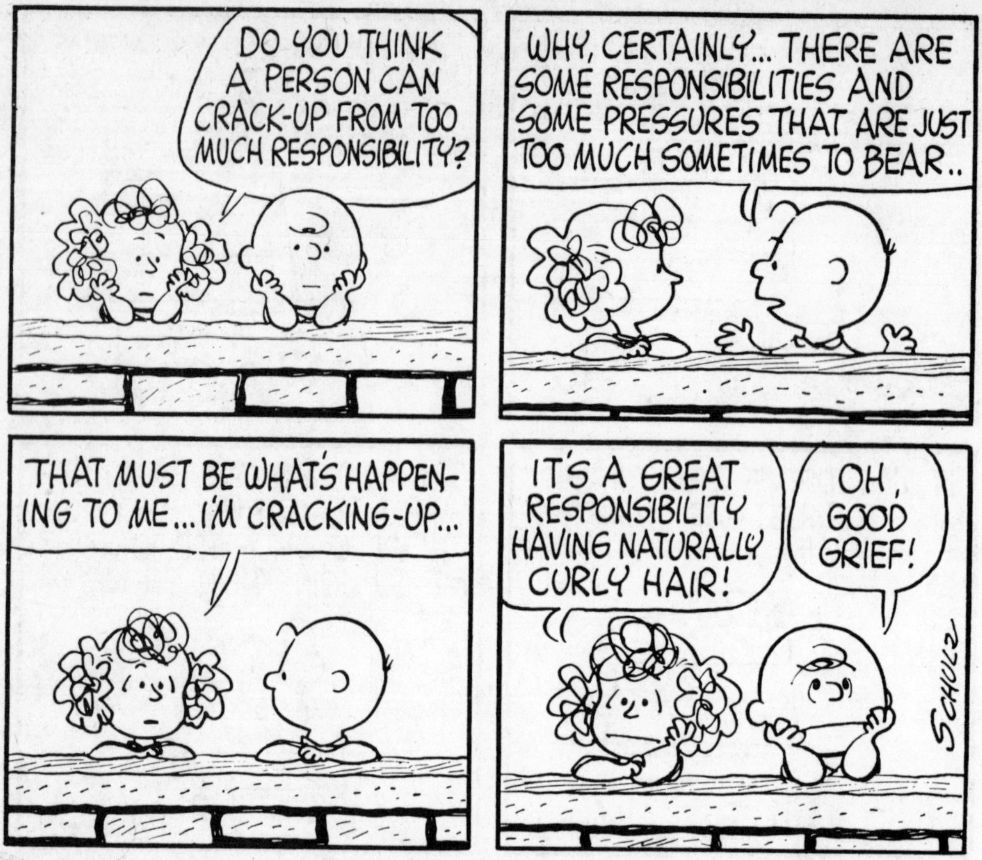
DO YOU THINK A PERSON CAN CRACK-UP FROM TOO MUCH RESPONSIBILITY?
WHY, CERTAINLY... THERE ARE SOME RESPONSIBILITIES AND SOME PRESSURES THAT ARE JUST TOO MUCH SOMETIMES TO BEAR..
THAT MUST BE WHAT'S HAPPENING TO ME...I'M CRACKING-UP...
IT'S A GREAT RESPONSIBILITY HAVING NATURALLY CURLY HAIR!
OH, GOOD GRIEF!
SCHULZ

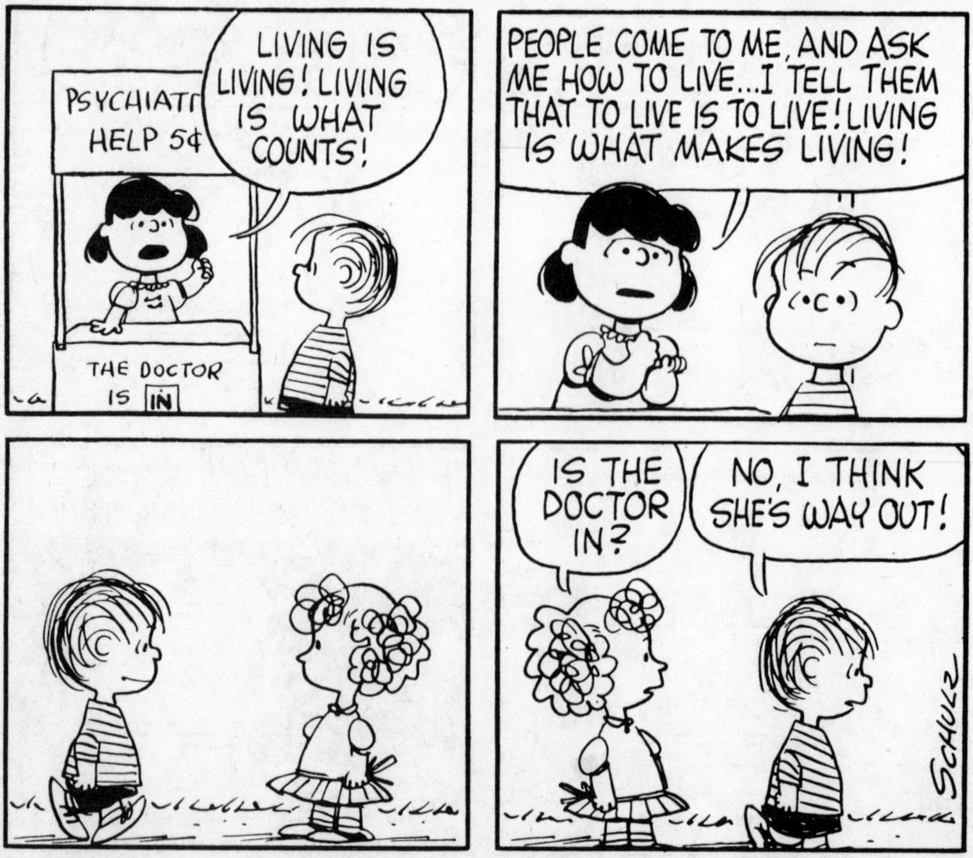
PSYCHIATRIC HELP 5¢
LIVING IS LIVING! LIVING IS WHAT COUNTS!
THE DOCTOR IS IN
PEOPLE COME TO ME, AND ASK ME HOW TO LIVE...I TELL THEM THAT TO LIVE IS TO LIVE! LIVING IS WHAT MAKES LIVING!
IS THE DOCTOR IN?
NO, I THINK SHE'S WAY OUT!
SCHULZ

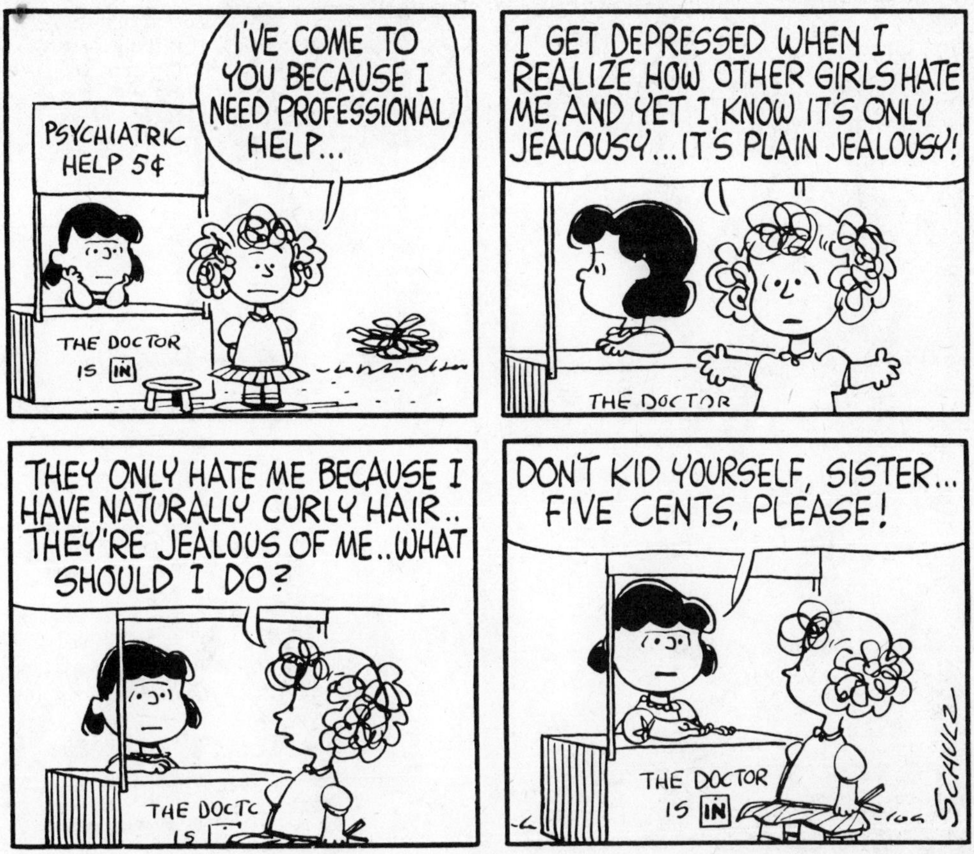
PSYCHIATRIC HELP 5¢
I'VE COME TO YOU BECAUSE I NEED PROFESSIONAL HELP...
THE DOCTOR IS IN
I GET DEPRESSED WHEN I REALIZE HOW OTHER GIRLS HATE ME, AND YET I KNOW IT'S ONLY JEALOUSY...IT'S PLAIN JEALOUSY!
THE DOCTOR
THEY ONLY HATE ME BECAUSE I HAVE NATURALLY CURLY HAIR.. THEY'RE JEALOUS OF ME..WHAT SHOULD I DO?
DON'T KID YOURSELF, SISTER... FIVE CENTS, PLEASE!
THE DOCTOR IS IN
SCHULZ

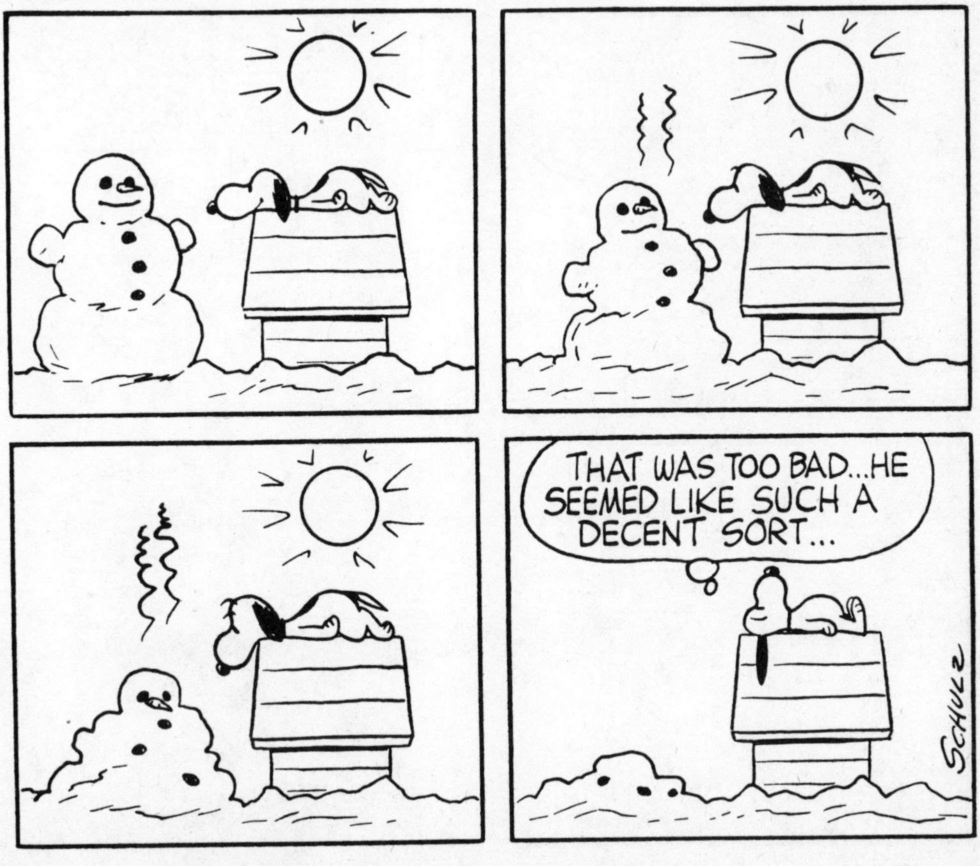
THAT WAS TOO BAD...HE SEEMED LIKE SUCH A DECENT SORT...
SCHULZ

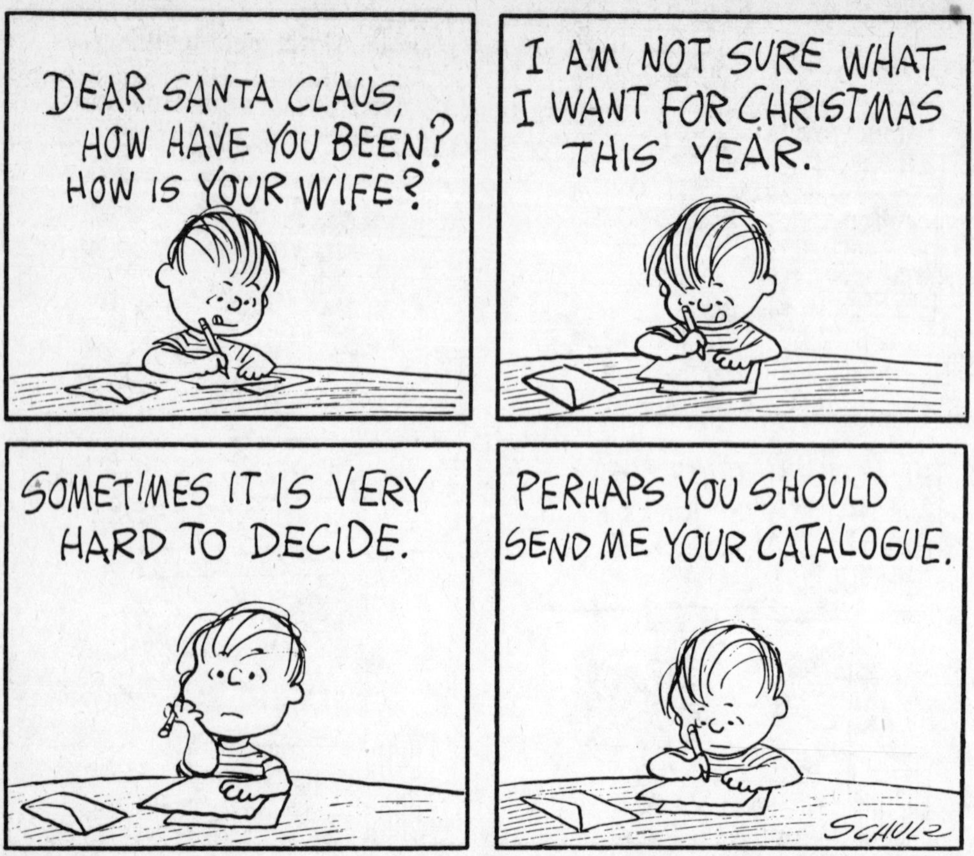
DEAR SANTA CLAUS, HOW HAVE YOU BEEN? HOW IS YOUR WIFE?
I AM NOT SURE WHAT I WANT FOR CHRISTMAS THIS YEAR.
SOMETIMES IT IS VERY HARD TO DECIDE.
PERHAPS YOU SHOULD SEND ME YOUR CATALOGUE.
SCHULZ

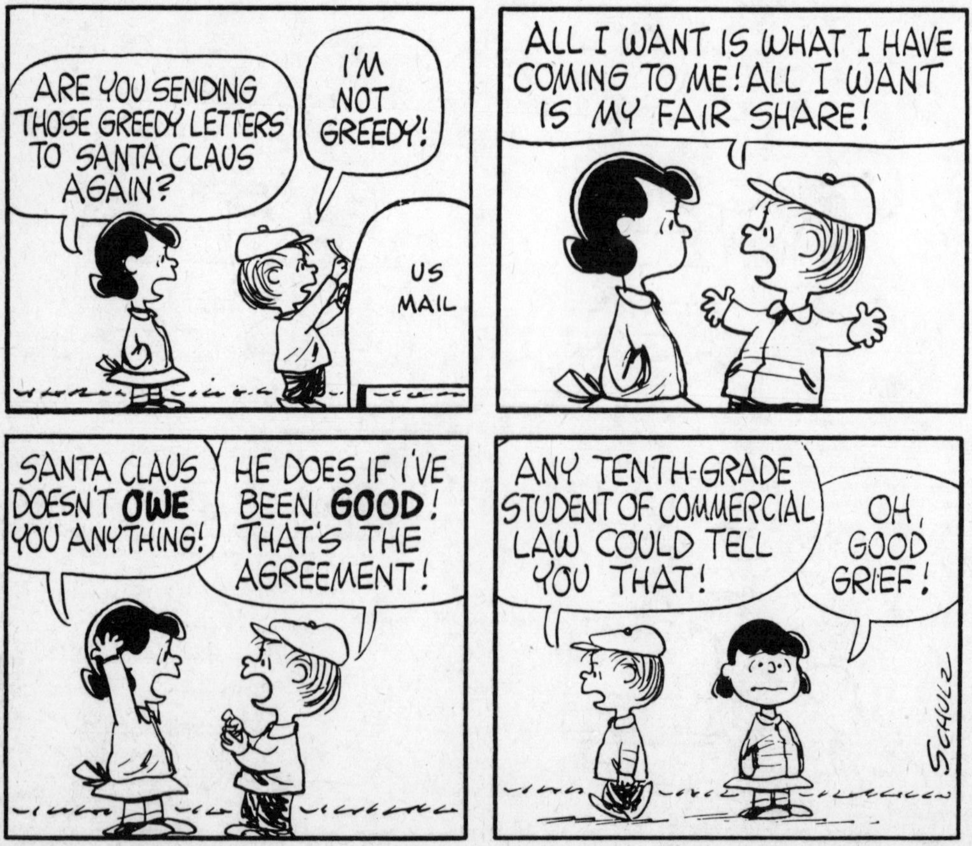
ARE YOU SENDING THOSE GREEDY LETTERS TO SANTA CLAUS AGAIN?
I'M NOT GREEDY!
US MAIL
ALL I WANT IS WHAT I HAVE COMING TO ME! ALL I WANT IS MY FAIR SHARE!
SANTA CLAUS DOESN'T **OWE** YOU ANYTHING!
HE DOES IF I'VE BEEN **GOOD**! THAT'S THE AGREEMENT!
ANY TENTH-GRADE STUDENT OF COMMERCIAL LAW COULD TELL YOU THAT!
OH, GOOD GRIEF!
SCHULZ

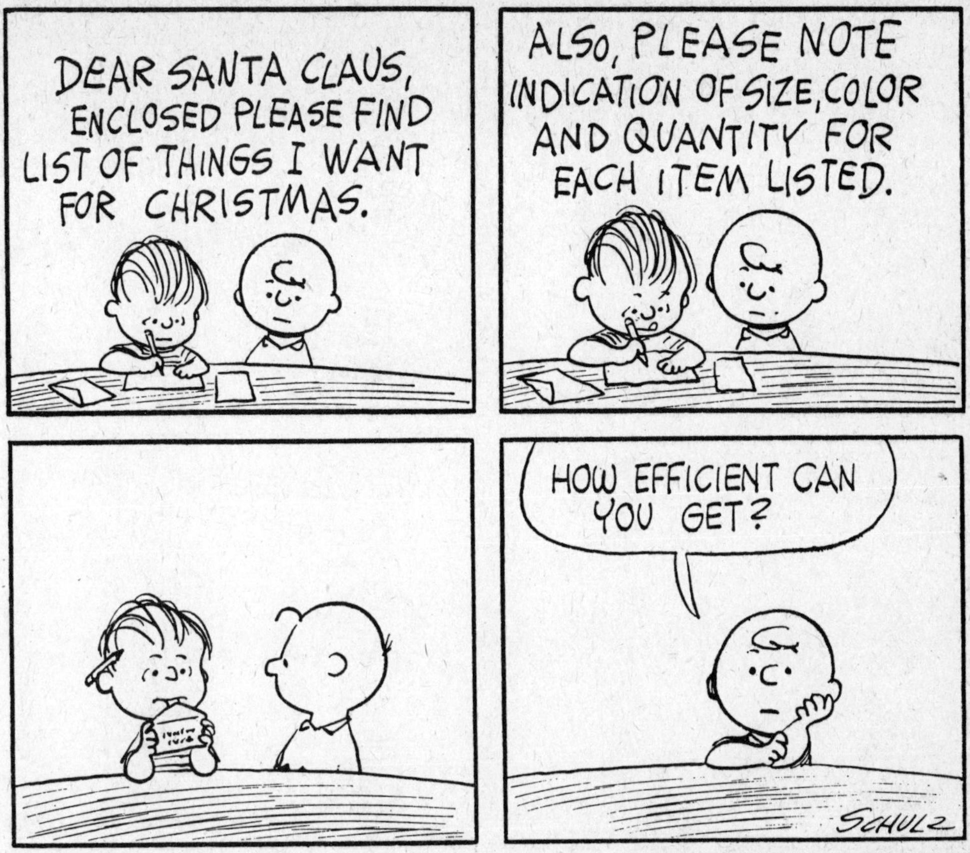
DEAR SANTA CLAUS,
ENCLOSED PLEASE FIND LIST OF THINGS I WANT FOR CHRISTMAS.
ALSO, PLEASE NOTE INDICATION OF SIZE, COLOR AND QUANTITY FOR EACH ITEM LISTED.
HOW EFFICIENT CAN YOU GET?
SCHULZ

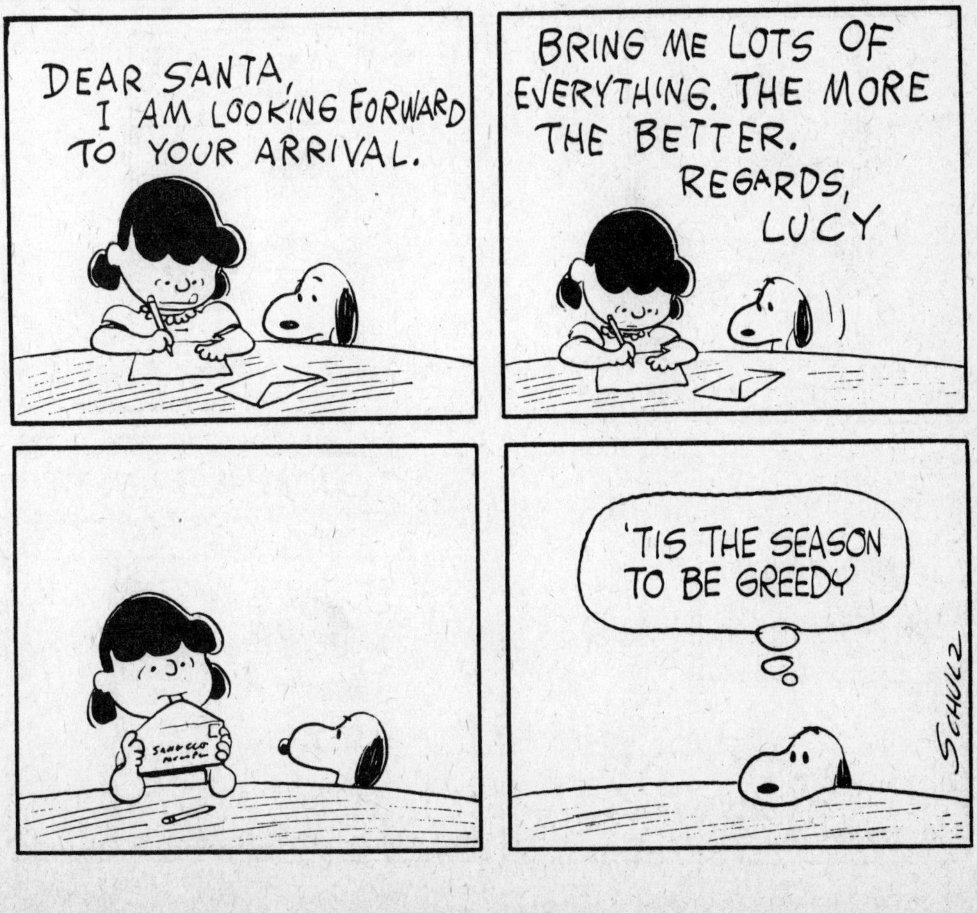
DEAR SANTA,
I AM LOOKING FORWARD TO YOUR ARRIVAL.
BRING ME LOTS OF EVERYTHING. THE MORE THE BETTER.
REGARDS,
LUCY
'TIS THE SEASON TO BE GREEDY
SCHULZ

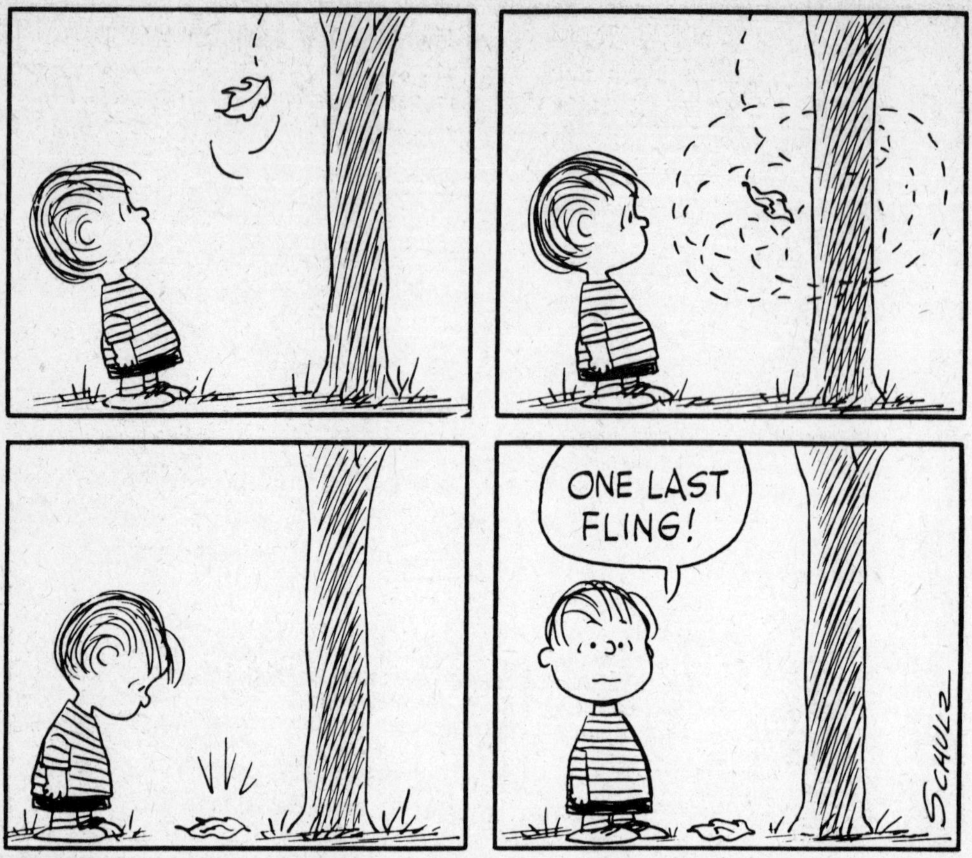
ONE LAST FLING!
SCHULZ

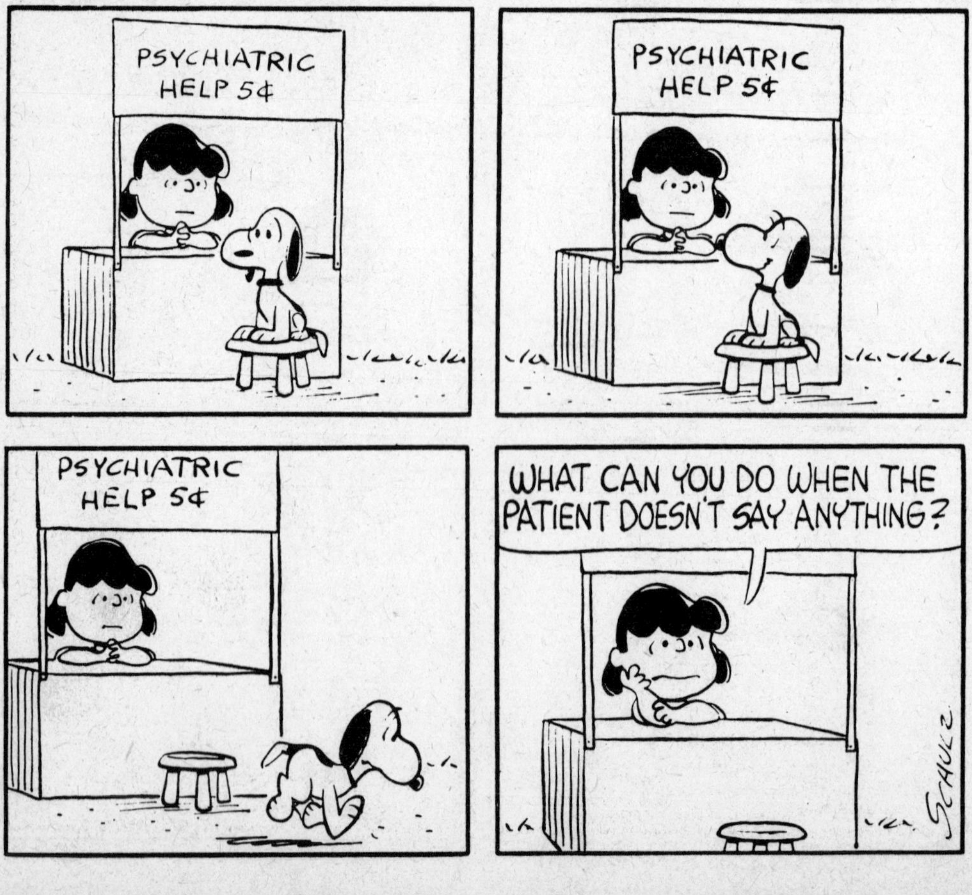
PSYCHIATRIC HELP 5¢
PSYCHIATRIC HELP 5¢
PSYCHIATRIC HELP 5¢
WHAT CAN YOU DO WHEN THE PATIENT DOESN'T SAY ANYTHING?
SCHULZ

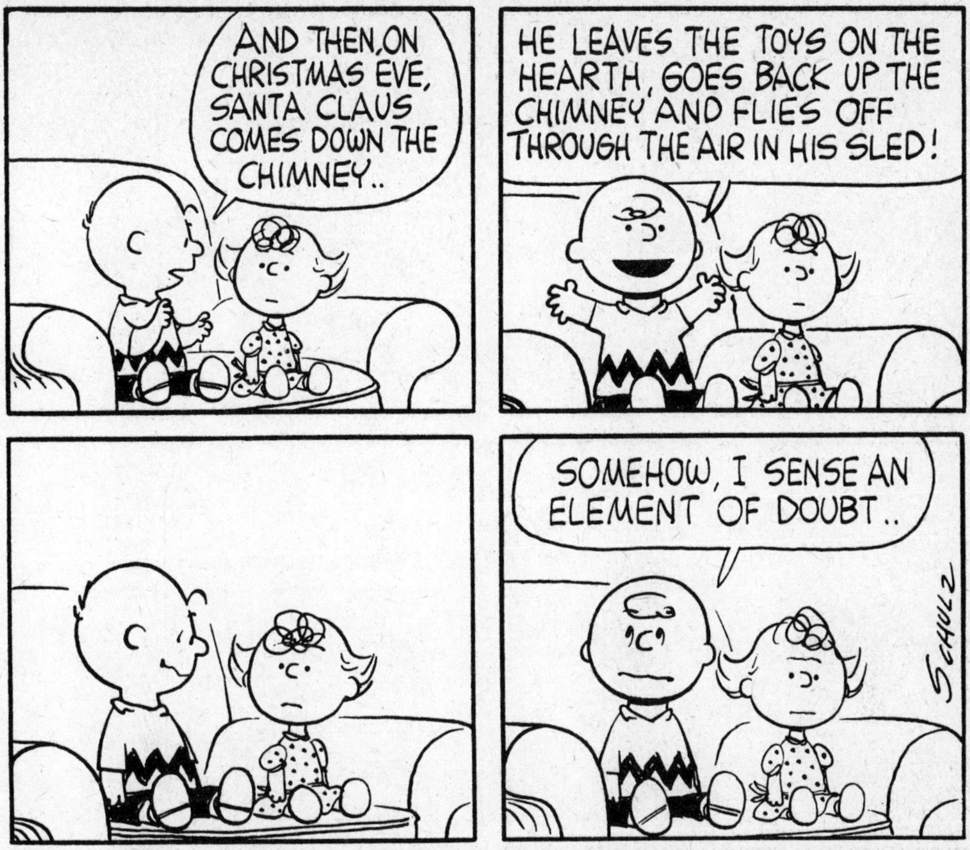
AND THEN, ON CHRISTMAS EVE, SANTA CLAUS COMES DOWN THE CHIMNEY..
HE LEAVES THE TOYS ON THE HEARTH, GOES BACK UP THE CHIMNEY AND FLIES OFF THROUGH THE AIR IN HIS SLED!
SOMEHOW, I SENSE AN ELEMENT OF DOUBT..
SCHULZ

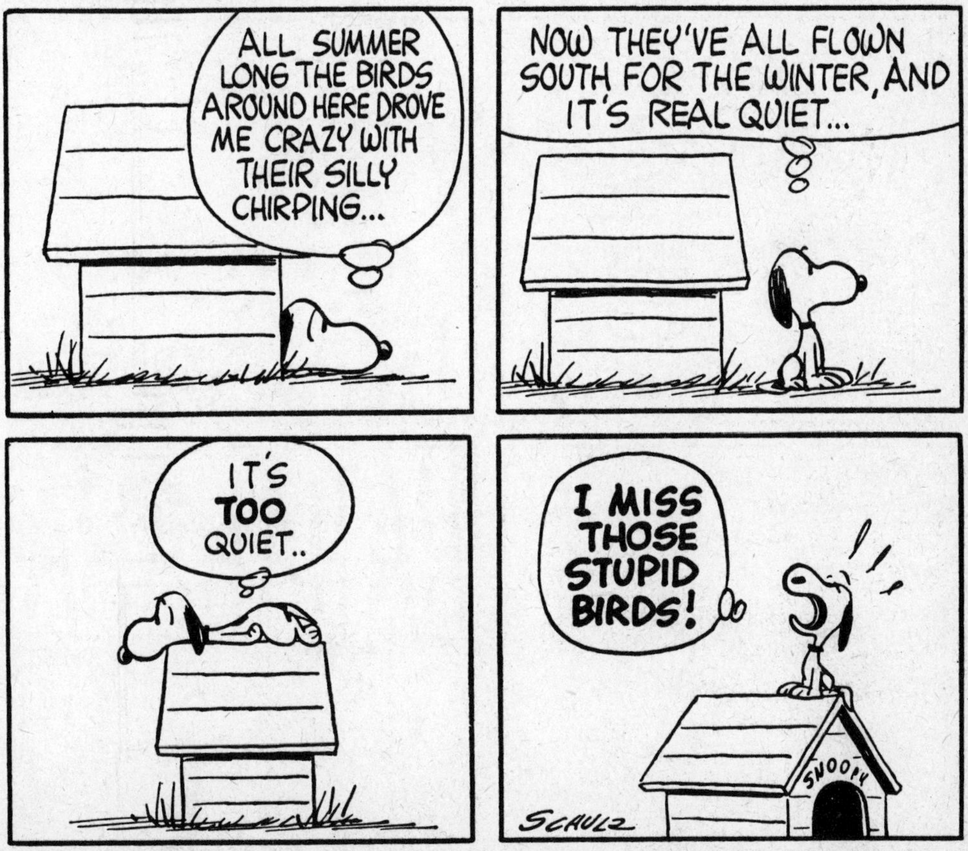
ALL SUMMER LONG THE BIRDS AROUND HERE DROVE ME CRAZY WITH THEIR SILLY CHIRPING...
NOW THEY'VE ALL FLOWN SOUTH FOR THE WINTER, AND IT'S REAL QUIET...
IT'S TOO QUIET..
I MISS THOSE STUPID BIRDS!
SNOOPY
SCHULZ

YOU HATE ME, DON'T YOU?
YOU HATE ME BECAUSE YOU WANTED TO BE AN "ONLY CHILD"! WHEN I WAS BORN, YOUR PLANS WERE SPOILED, WEREN'T THEY? HUH? HUH?
POW!
ACTUALLY, I THINK IT WOULD BE KIND OF NICE TO BE AN "ONLY CHILD"!
SCHULZ
I THINK IT'S DISGRACEFUL THE WAY YOU AND LINUS FIGHT ALL THE TIME!
YOU'RE REALLY LUCKY YOU HAVE EACH OTHER! BROTHERS AND SISTERS SHOULD LEARN TO GET ALONG...
YOU'RE RIGHT, CHARLIE BROWN..YOUR LITTLE SPEECH HAS OPENED MY EYES...
WELL, I'M VERY GLAD..
HAHAHAHA
SCHULZ

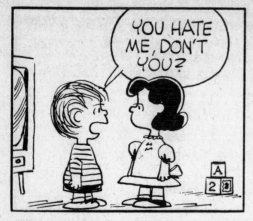

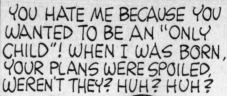

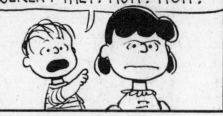

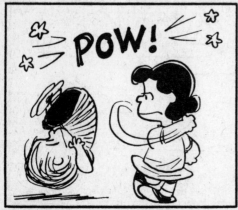

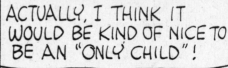

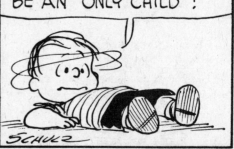

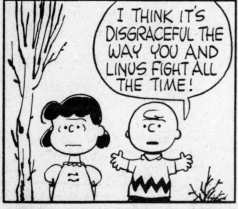

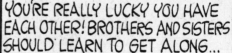

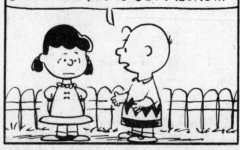

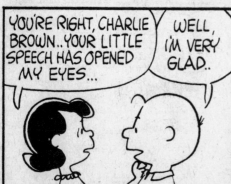

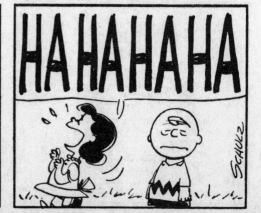

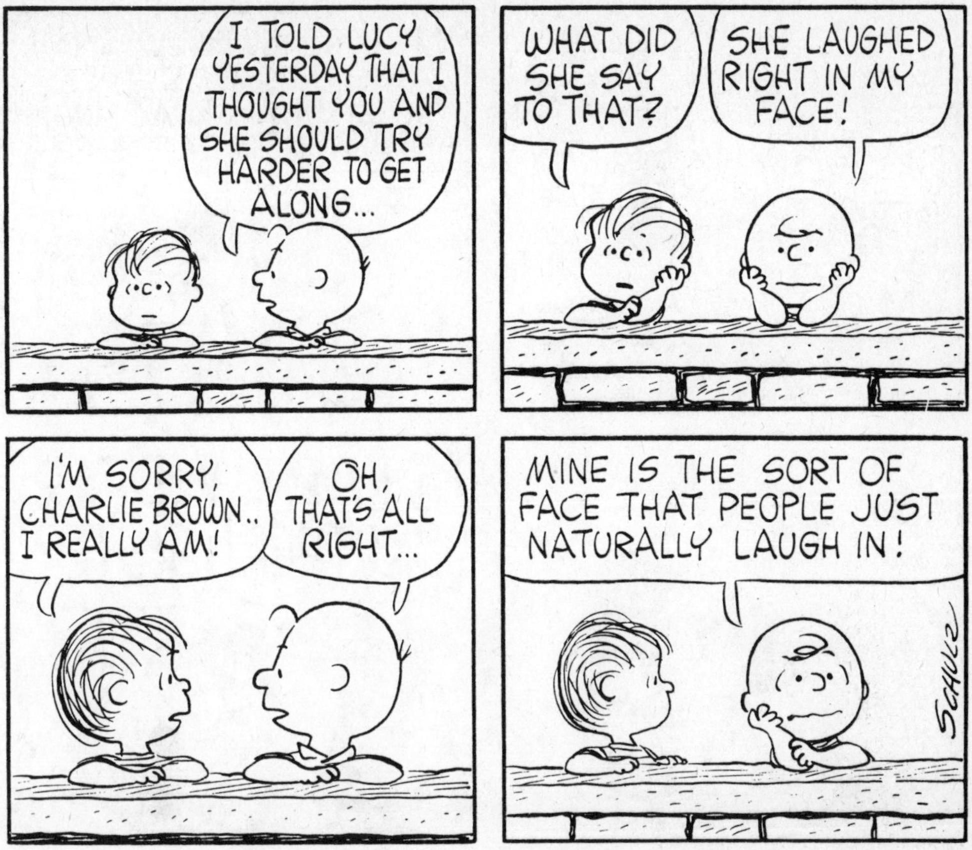
I TOLD LUCY YESTERDAY THAT I THOUGHT YOU AND SHE SHOULD TRY HARDER TO GET ALONG...
WHAT DID SHE SAY TO THAT?
SHE LAUGHED RIGHT IN MY FACE!
I'M SORRY, CHARLIE BROWN.. I REALLY AM!
OH, THAT'S ALL RIGHT...
MINE IS THE SORT OF FACE THAT PEOPLE JUST NATURALLY LAUGH IN!
SCHULZ

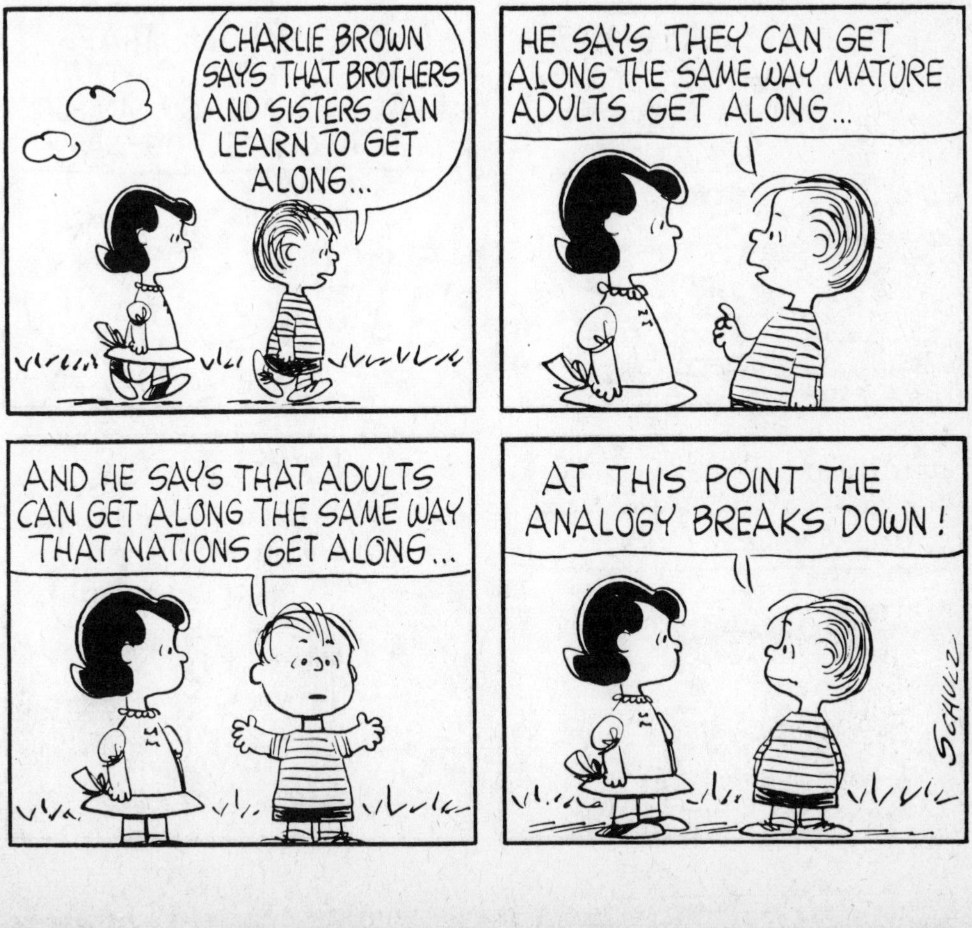
CHARLIE BROWN SAYS THAT BROTHERS AND SISTERS CAN LEARN TO GET ALONG...
HE SAYS THEY CAN GET ALONG THE SAME WAY MATURE ADULTS GET ALONG...
AND HE SAYS THAT ADULTS CAN GET ALONG THE SAME WAY THAT NATIONS GET ALONG...
AT THIS POINT THE ANALOGY BREAKS DOWN!
SCHULZ

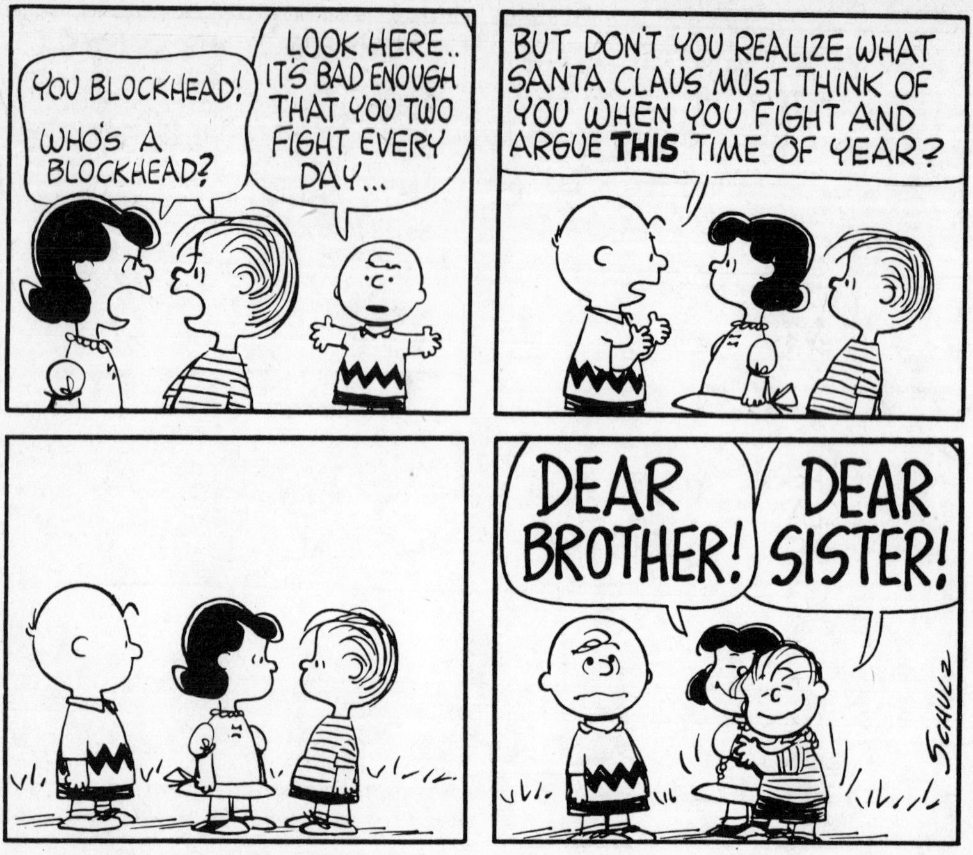
YOU BLOCKHEAD!
WHO'S A BLOCKHEAD?
LOOK HERE.. IT'S BAD ENOUGH THAT YOU TWO FIGHT EVERY DAY...
BUT DON'T YOU REALIZE WHAT SANTA CLAUS MUST THINK OF YOU WHEN YOU FIGHT AND ARGUE **THIS** TIME OF YEAR?
DEAR BROTHER!
DEAR SISTER!
SCHULZ

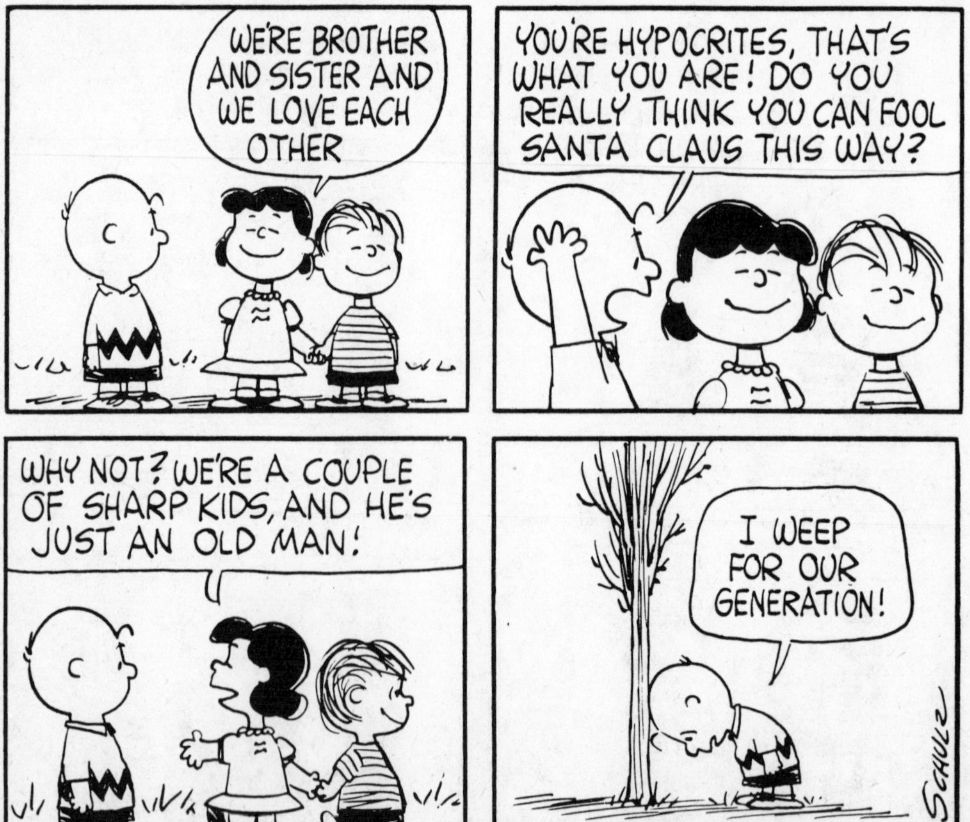
WE'RE BROTHER AND SISTER AND WE LOVE EACH OTHER
YOU'RE HYPOCRITES, THAT'S WHAT YOU ARE! DO YOU REALLY THINK YOU CAN FOOL SANTA CLAUS THIS WAY?
WHY NOT? WE'RE A COUPLE OF SHARP KIDS, AND HE'S JUST AN OLD MAN!
I WEEP FOR OUR GENERATION!
SCHULZ

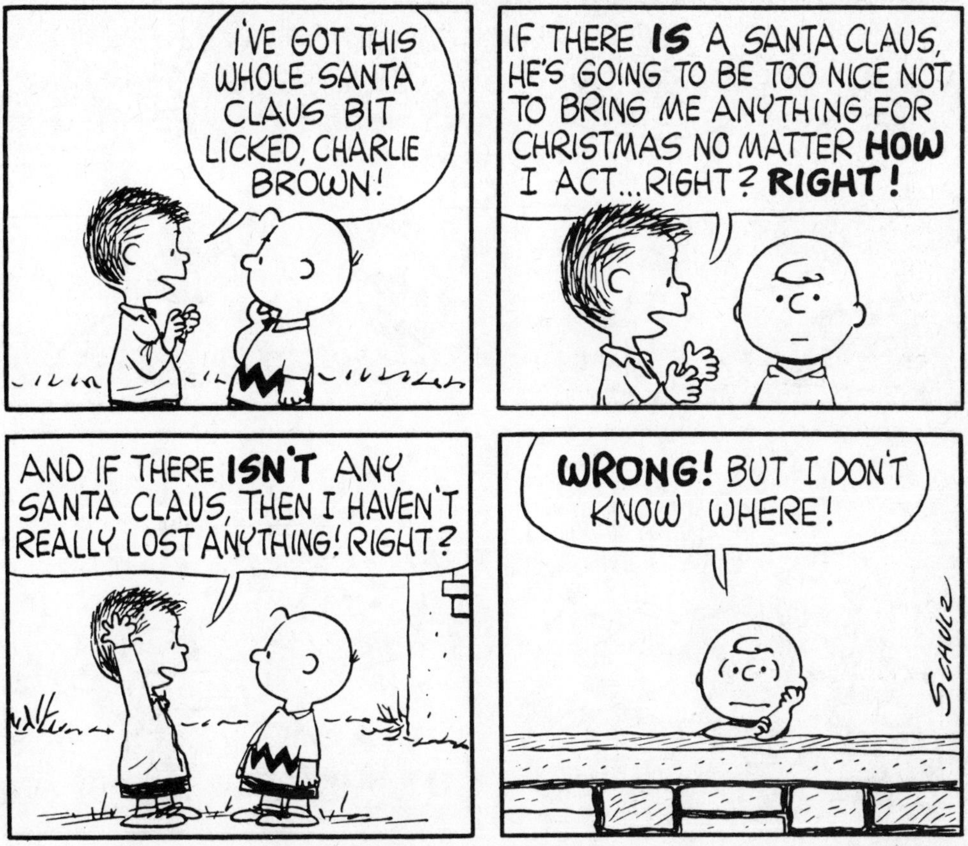
I'VE GOT THIS WHOLE SANTA CLAUS BIT LICKED, CHARLIE BROWN!
IF THERE **IS** A SANTA CLAUS, HE'S GOING TO BE TOO NICE NOT TO BRING ME ANYTHING FOR CHRISTMAS NO MATTER **HOW** I ACT...RIGHT? **RIGHT!**
AND IF THERE **ISN'T** ANY SANTA CLAUS, THEN I HAVEN'T REALLY LOST ANYTHING! RIGHT?
WRONG! BUT I DON'T KNOW WHERE!
SCHULZ

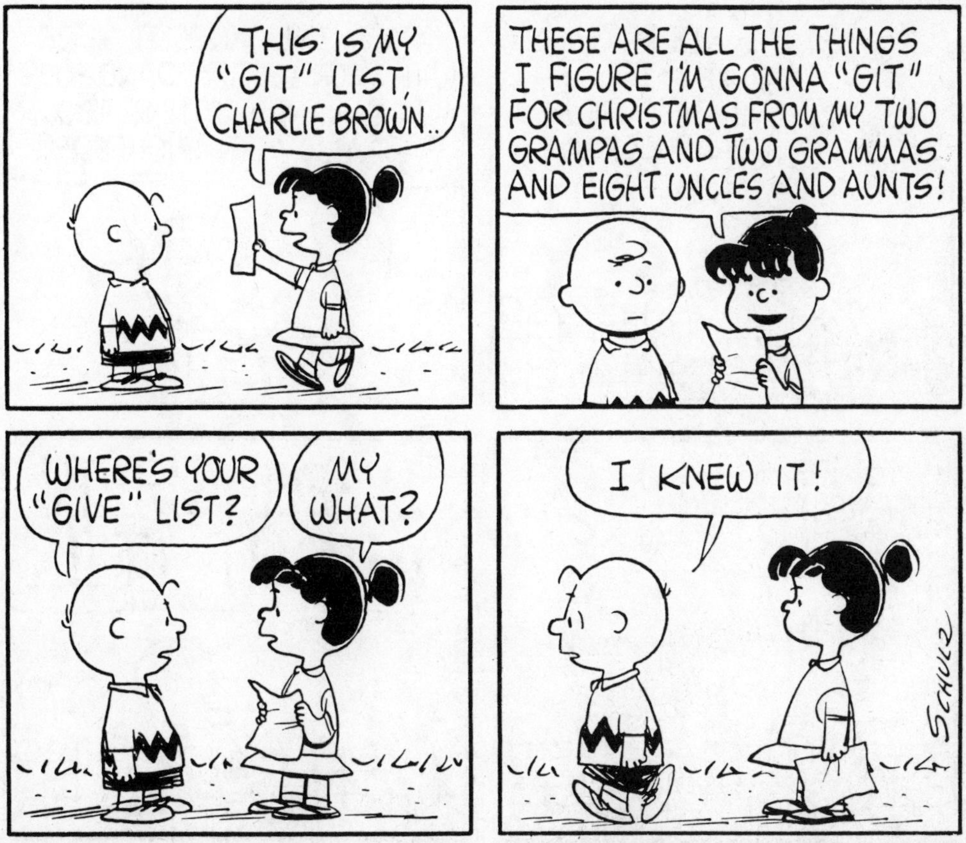
THIS IS MY "GIT" LIST, CHARLIE BROWN..
THESE ARE ALL THE THINGS I FIGURE I'M GONNA "GIT" FOR CHRISTMAS FROM MY TWO GRAMPAS AND TWO GRAMMAS AND EIGHT UNCLES AND AUNTS!
WHERE'S YOUR "GIVE" LIST?
MY WHAT?
I KNEW IT!
SCHULZ

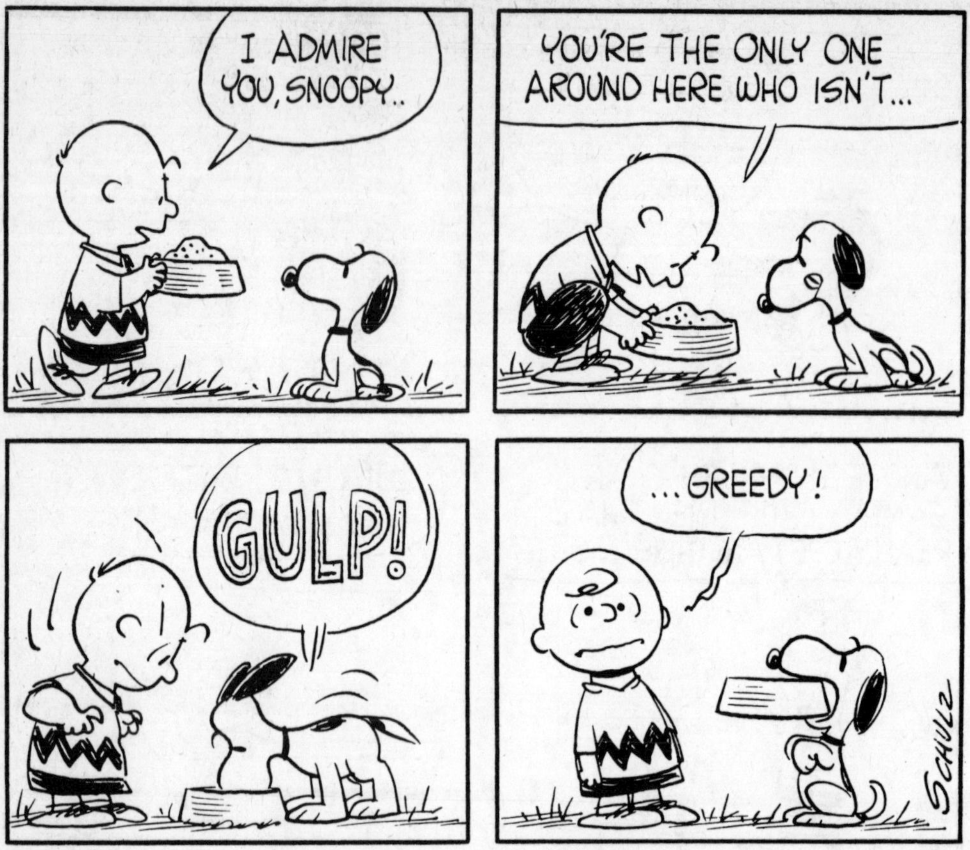
I ADMIRE YOU, SNOOPY..
YOU'RE THE ONLY ONE AROUND HERE WHO ISN'T...
GULP!
...GREEDY!
SCHULZ

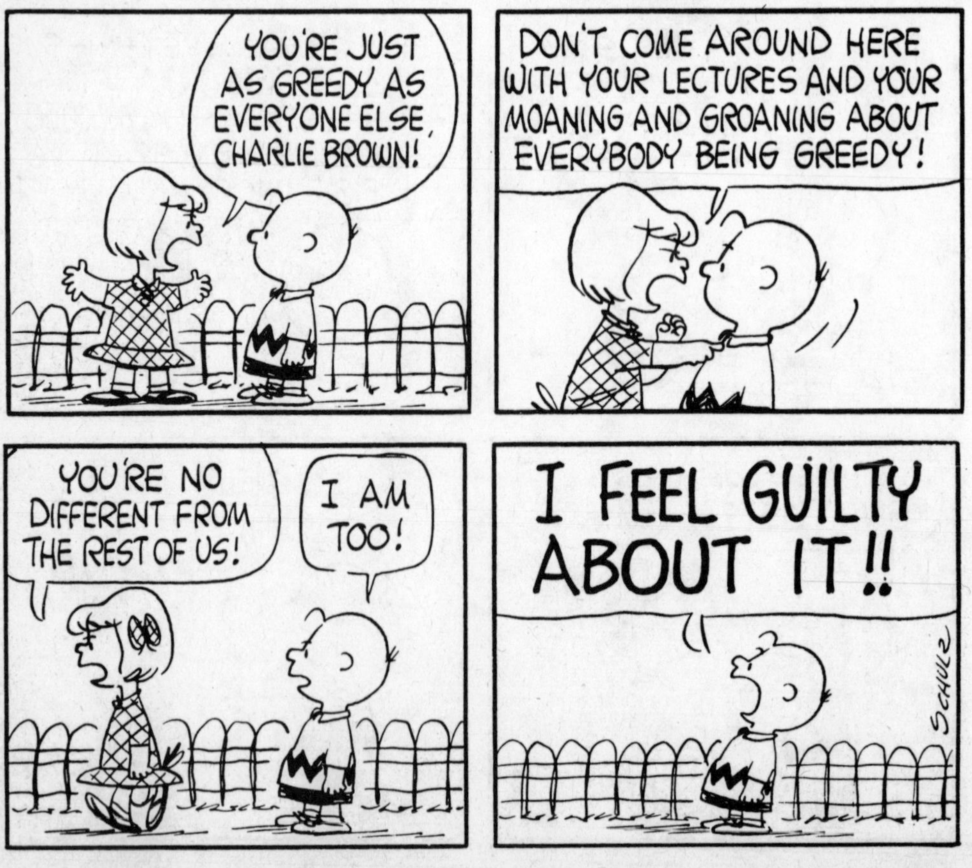
YOU'RE JUST AS GREEDY AS EVERYONE ELSE, CHARLIE BROWN!
DON'T COME AROUND HERE WITH YOUR LECTURES AND YOUR MOANING AND GROANING ABOUT EVERYBODY BEING GREEDY!
YOU'RE NO DIFFERENT FROM THE REST OF US!
I AM TOO!
I FEEL GUILTY ABOUT IT!!
SCHULZ

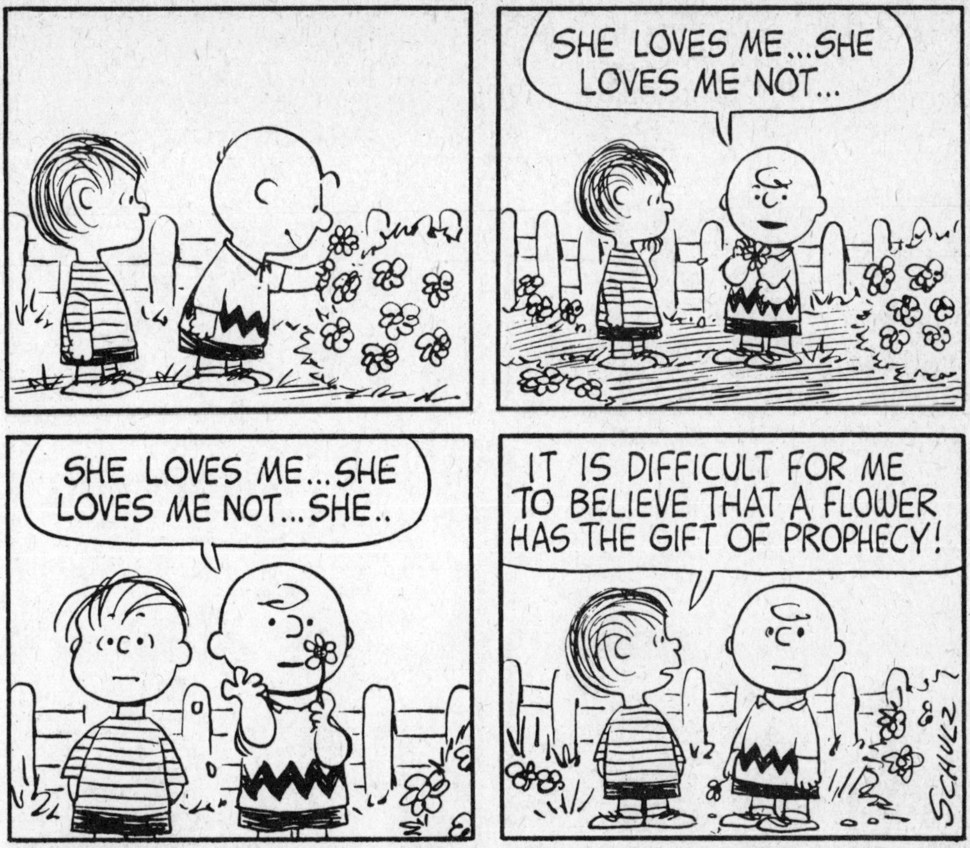
SHE LOVES ME...SHE LOVES ME NOT...
SHE LOVES ME...SHE LOVES ME NOT...SHE..
IT IS DIFFICULT FOR ME TO BELIEVE THAT A FLOWER HAS THE GIFT OF PROPHECY!
SCHULZ

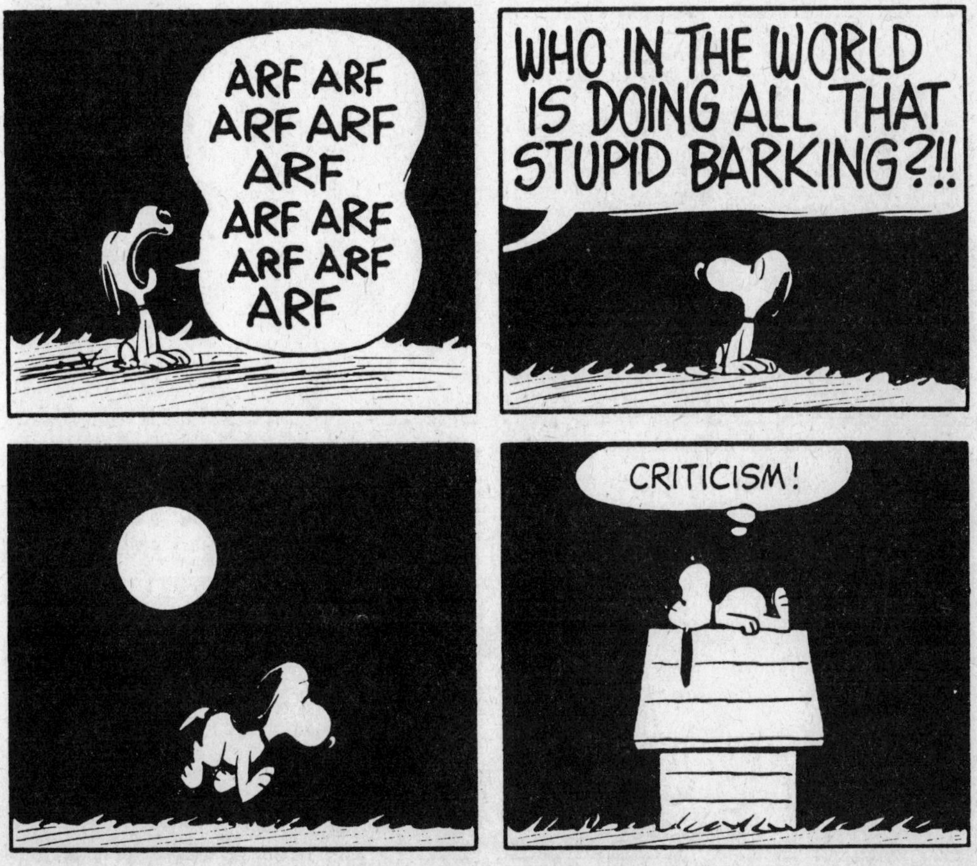
ARF ARF ARF ARF ARF ARF ARF ARF ARF ARF
WHO IN THE WORLD IS DOING ALL THAT STUPID BARKING?!!
CRITICISM!

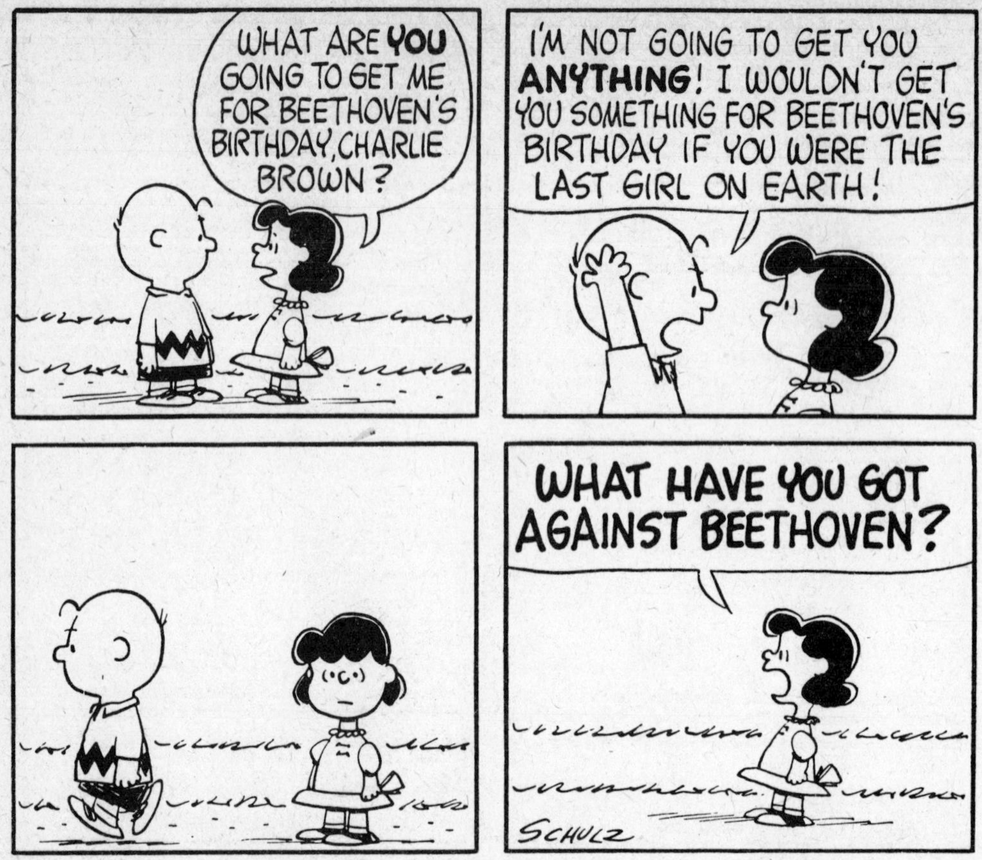
WHAT ARE **YOU** GOING TO GET ME FOR BEETHOVEN'S BIRTHDAY, CHARLIE BROWN?
I'M NOT GOING TO GET YOU **ANYTHING**! I WOULDN'T GET YOU SOMETHING FOR BEETHOVEN'S BIRTHDAY IF YOU WERE THE LAST GIRL ON EARTH!
WHAT HAVE YOU GOT AGAINST BEETHOVEN?
SCHULZ

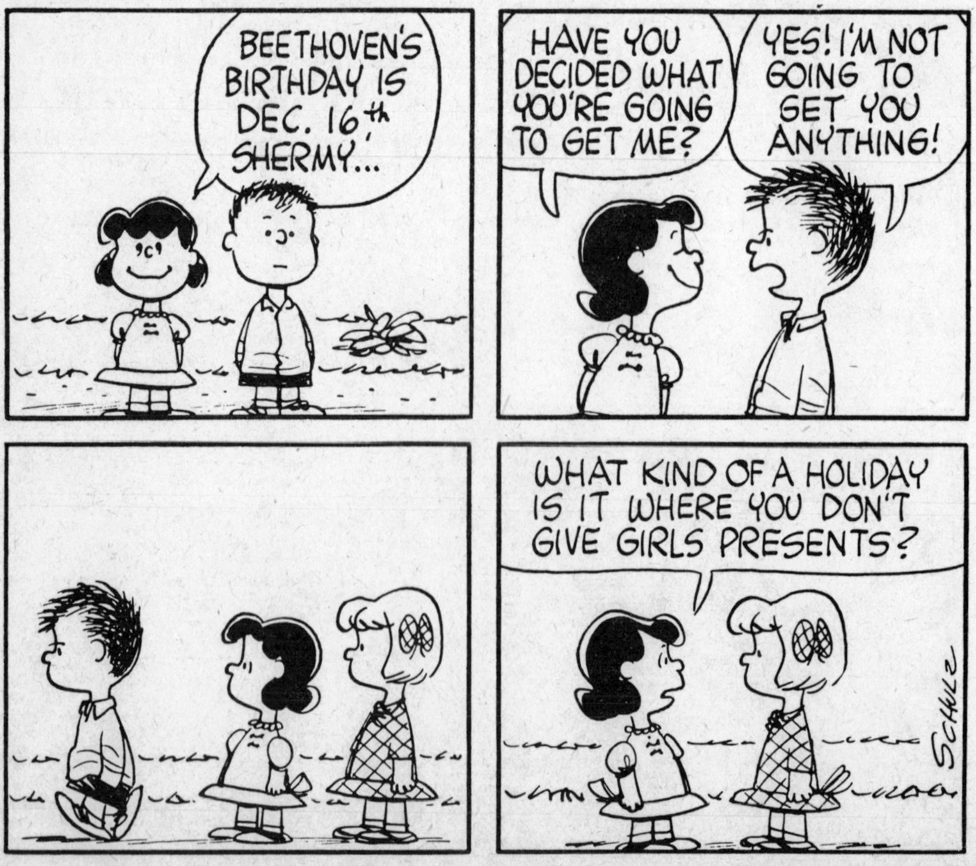
BEETHOVEN'S BIRTHDAY IS DEC. 16th, SHERMY...
HAVE YOU DECIDED WHAT YOU'RE GOING TO GET ME?
YES! I'M NOT GOING TO GET YOU ANYTHING!
WHAT KIND OF A HOLIDAY IS IT WHERE YOU DON'T GIVE GIRLS PRESENTS?
SCHULZ

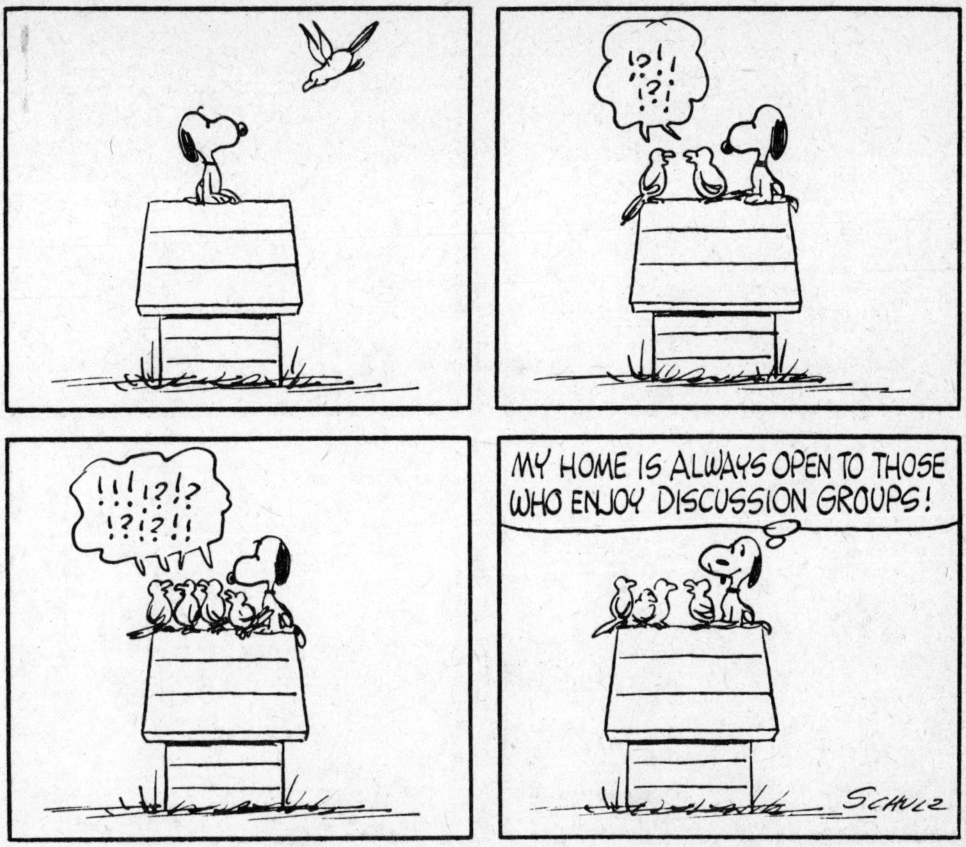
MY HOME IS ALWAYS OPEN TO THOSE WHO ENJOY DISCUSSION GROUPS!
SCHULZ

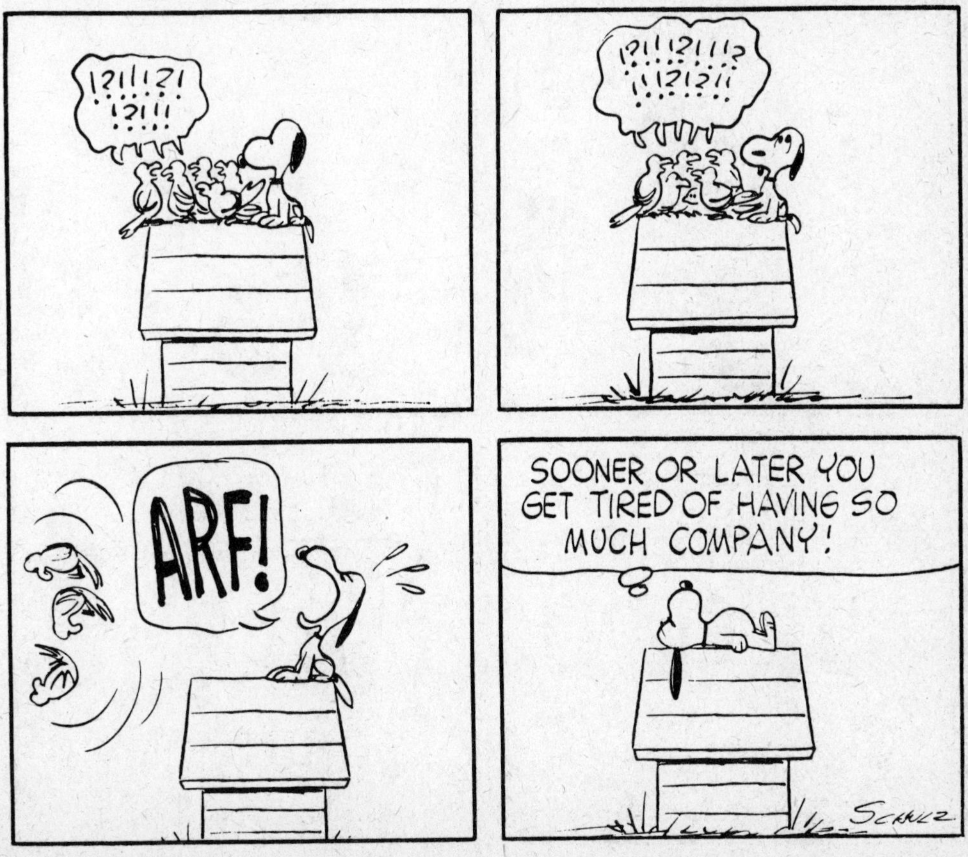
ARF!
SOONER OR LATER YOU GET TIRED OF HAVING SO MUCH COMPANY!
SCHULZ

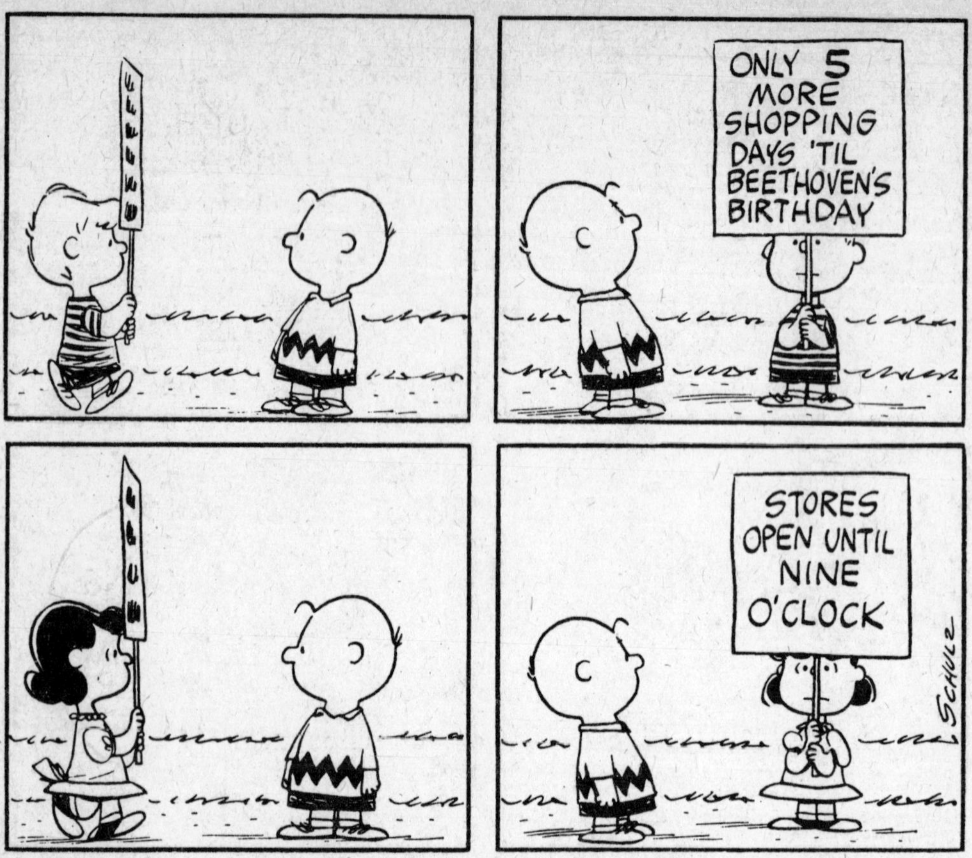
ONLY 5 MORE SHOPPING DAYS 'TIL BEETHOVEN'S BIRTHDAY
STORES OPEN UNTIL NINE O'CLOCK
SCHULZ

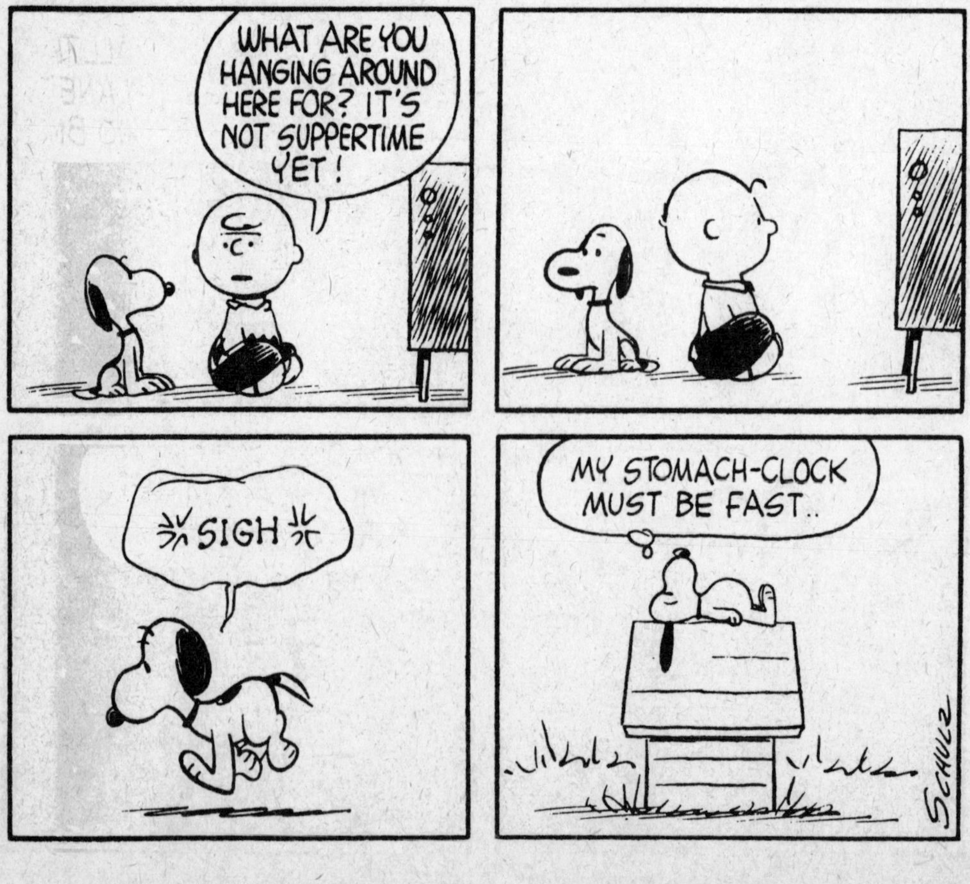
WHAT ARE YOU HANGING AROUND HERE FOR? IT'S NOT SUPPERTIME YET!
SIGH
MY STOMACH-CLOCK MUST BE FAST..
SCHULZ

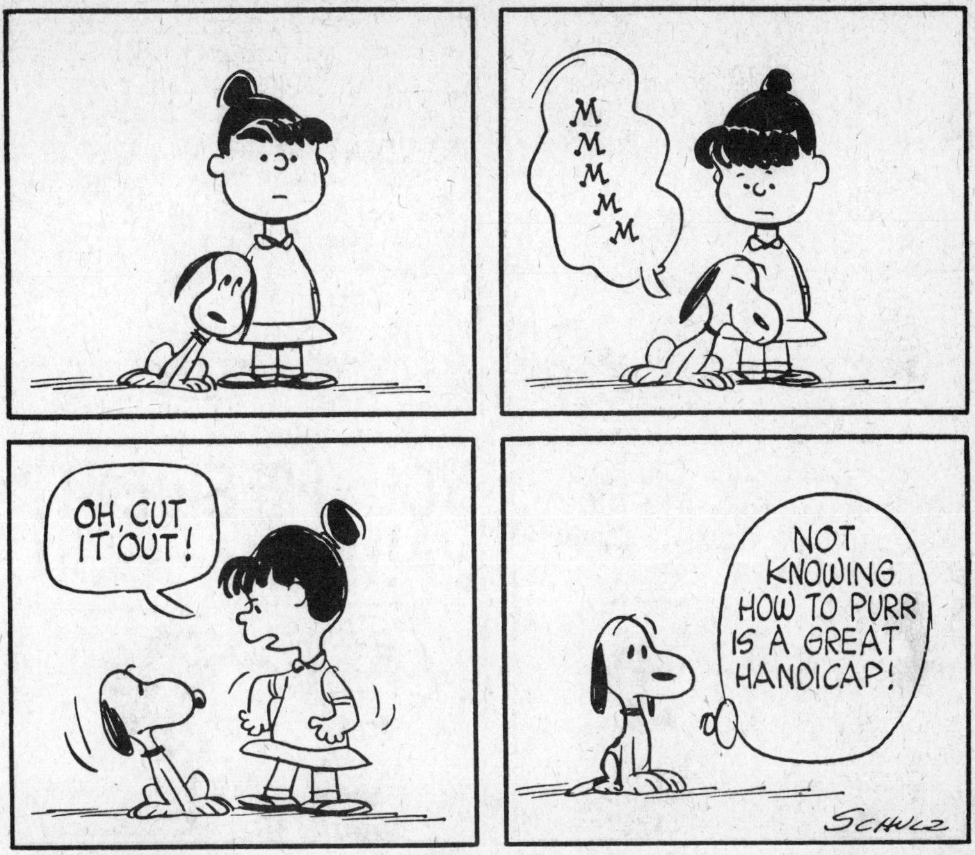
M M M M M
OH, CUT IT OUT!
NOT KNOWING HOW TO PURR IS A GREAT HANDICAP!
SCHULZ

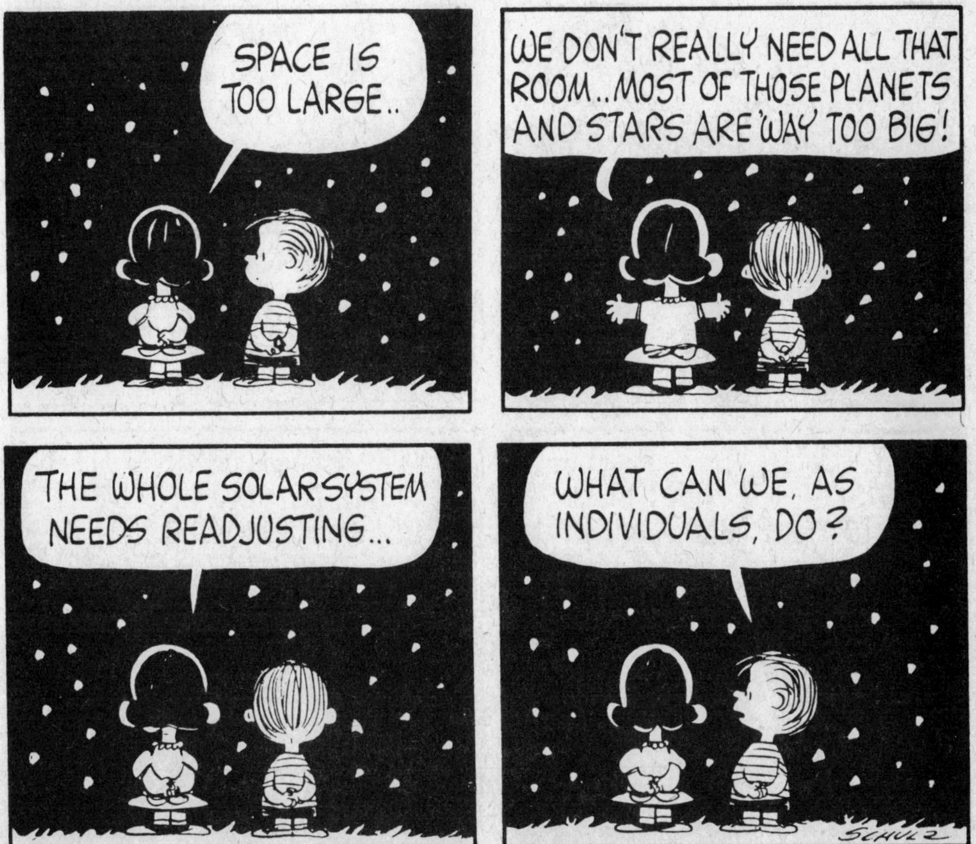
SPACE IS TOO LARGE..
WE DON'T REALLY NEED ALL THAT ROOM..MOST OF THOSE PLANETS AND STARS ARE 'WAY TOO BIG!
THE WHOLE SOLAR SYSTEM NEEDS READJUSTING...
WHAT CAN WE, AS INDIVIDUALS, DO?
SCHULZ

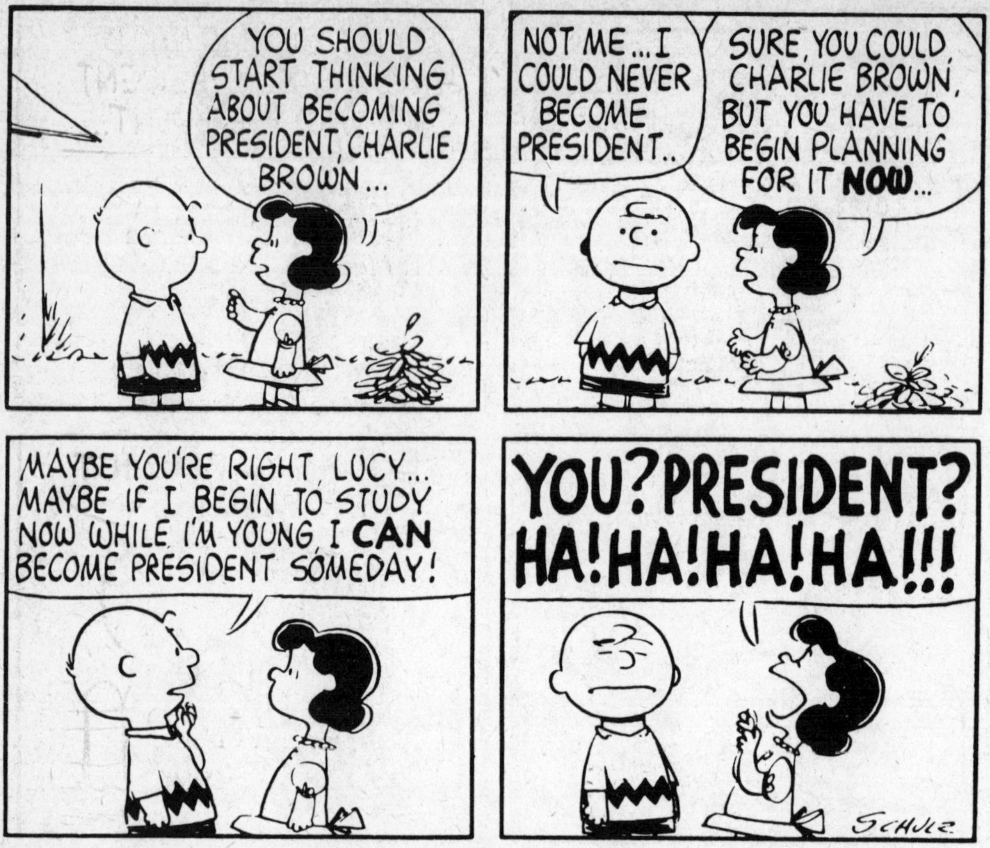
YOU SHOULD START THINKING ABOUT BECOMING PRESIDENT, CHARLIE BROWN...
NOT ME...I COULD NEVER BECOME PRESIDENT..
SURE, YOU COULD, CHARLIE BROWN, BUT YOU HAVE TO BEGIN PLANNING FOR IT NOW...
MAYBE YOU'RE RIGHT, LUCY... MAYBE IF I BEGIN TO STUDY NOW WHILE I'M YOUNG, I CAN BECOME PRESIDENT SOMEDAY!
YOU? PRESIDENT? HA!HA!HA!HA!!!
SCHULZ

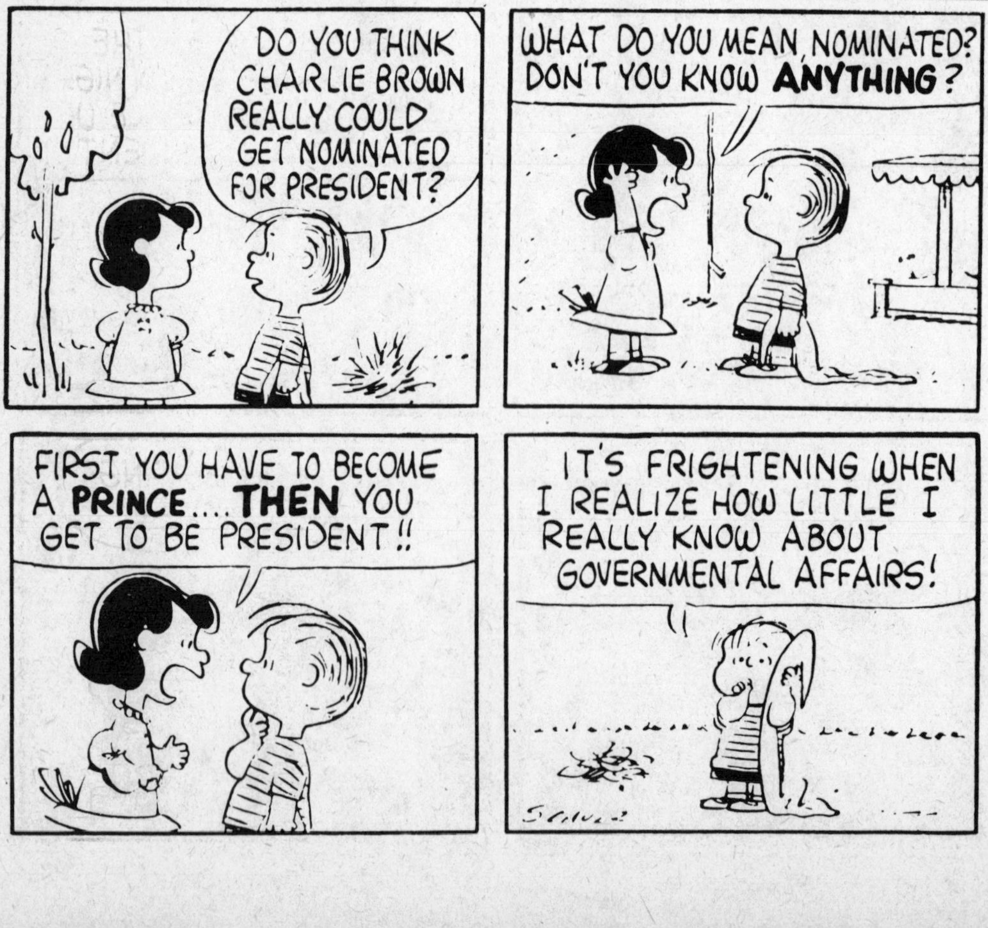
DO YOU THINK CHARLIE BROWN REALLY COULD GET NOMINATED FOR PRESIDENT?
WHAT DO YOU MEAN, NOMINATED? DON'T YOU KNOW ANYTHING?
FIRST YOU HAVE TO BECOME A PRINCE....THEN YOU GET TO BE PRESIDENT!!
IT'S FRIGHTENING WHEN I REALIZE HOW LITTLE I REALLY KNOW ABOUT GOVERNMENTAL AFFAIRS!
SCHULZ

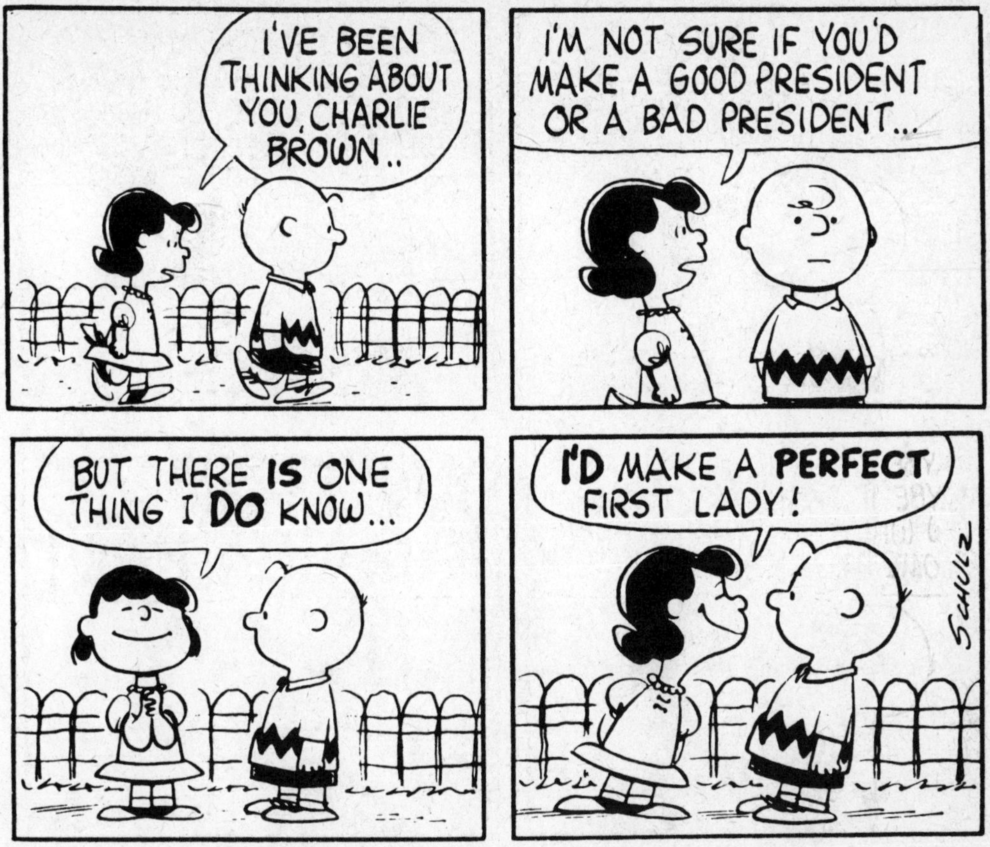
I'VE BEEN THINKING ABOUT YOU, CHARLIE BROWN..
I'M NOT SURE IF YOU'D MAKE A GOOD PRESIDENT OR A BAD PRESIDENT...
BUT THERE **IS** ONE THING I **DO** KNOW...
I'D MAKE A **PERFECT** FIRST LADY!
SCHULZ

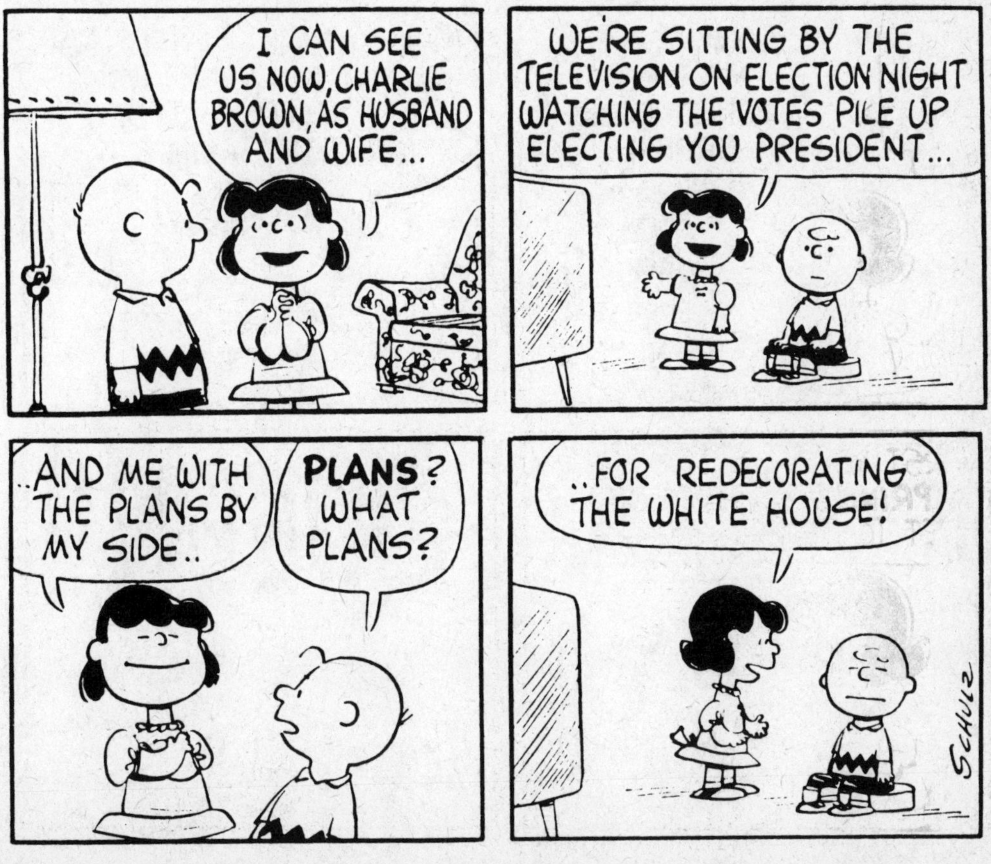
I CAN SEE US NOW, CHARLIE BROWN, AS HUSBAND AND WIFE...
WE'RE SITTING BY THE TELEVISION ON ELECTION NIGHT WATCHING THE VOTES PILE UP ELECTING YOU PRESIDENT...
..AND ME WITH THE PLANS BY MY SIDE..
PLANS? WHAT PLANS?
...FOR REDECORATING THE WHITE HOUSE!
SCHULZ

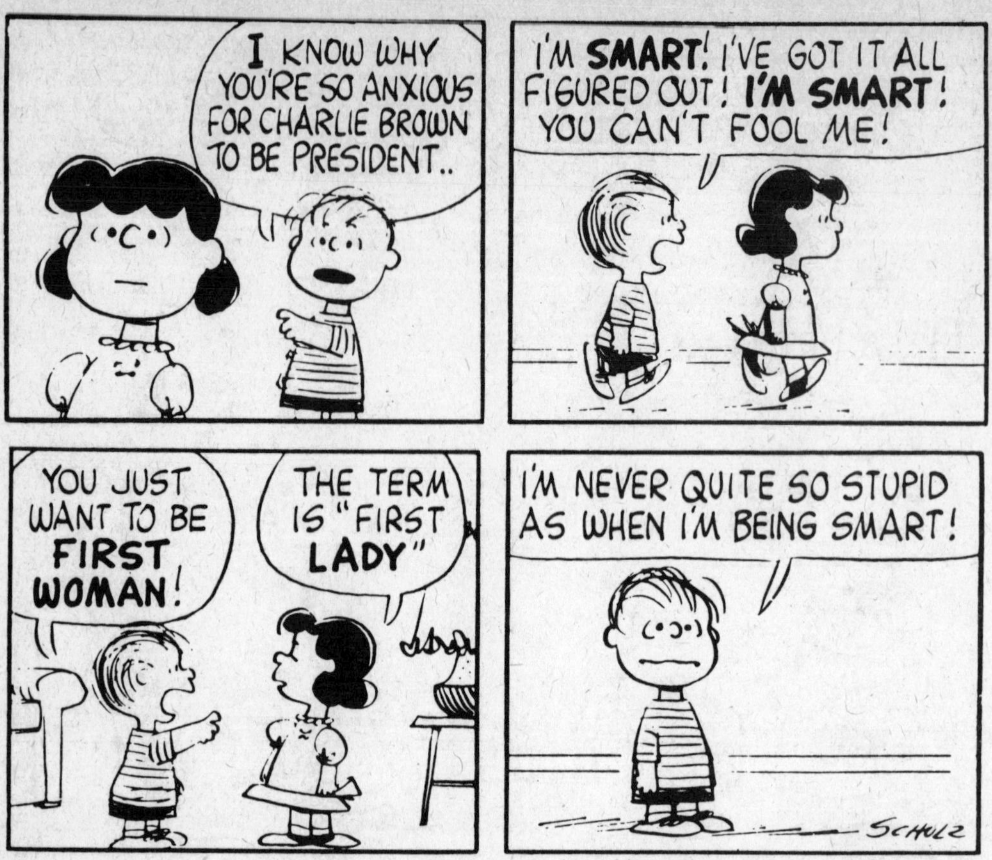
I KNOW WHY YOU'RE SO ANXIOUS FOR CHARLIE BROWN TO BE PRESIDENT..
I'M SMART! I'VE GOT IT ALL FIGURED OUT! I'M SMART! YOU CAN'T FOOL ME!
YOU JUST WANT TO BE FIRST WOMAN!
THE TERM IS "FIRST LADY"
I'M NEVER QUITE SO STUPID AS WHEN I'M BEING SMART!
SCHULZ

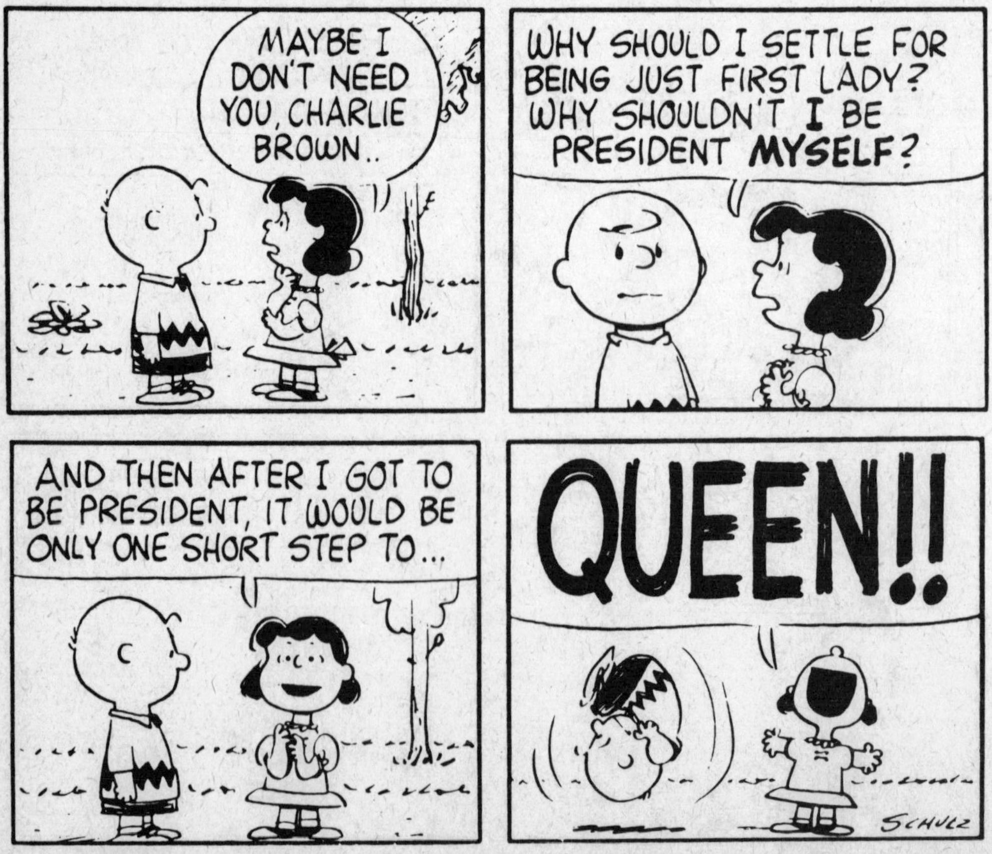
MAYBE I DON'T NEED YOU, CHARLIE BROWN..
WHY SHOULD I SETTLE FOR BEING JUST FIRST LADY? WHY SHOULDN'T I BE PRESIDENT MYSELF?
AND THEN AFTER I GOT TO BE PRESIDENT, IT WOULD BE ONLY ONE SHORT STEP TO...
QUEEN!!
SCHULZ

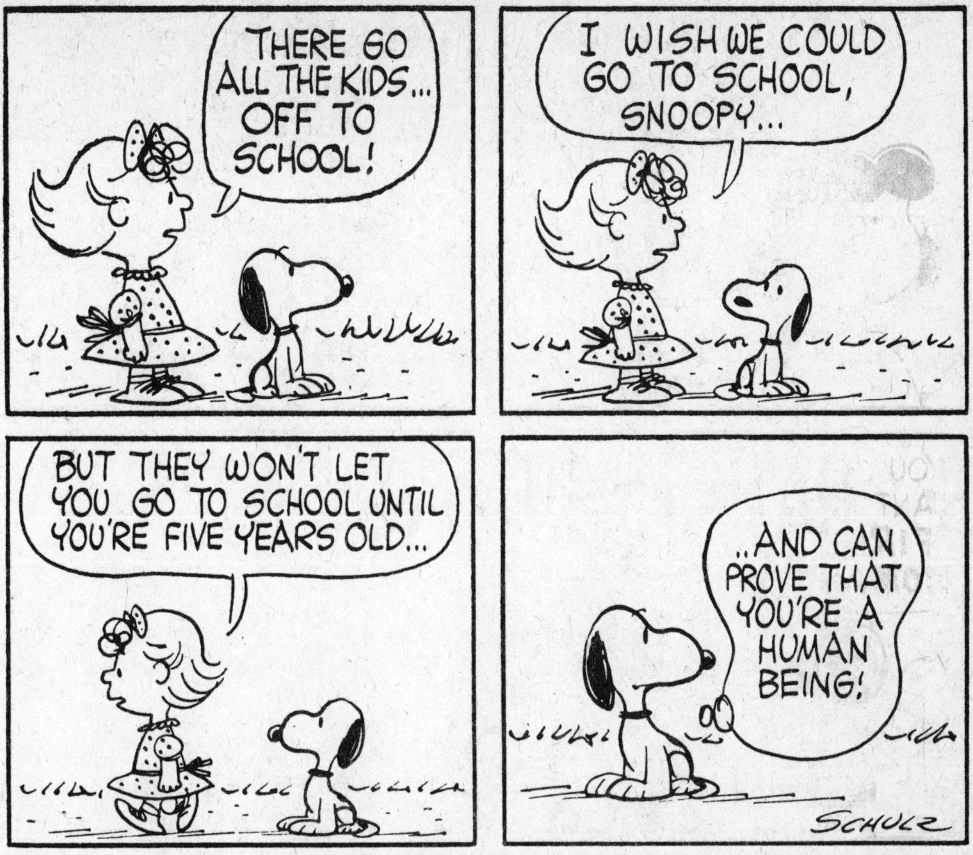
THERE GO ALL THE KIDS... OFF TO SCHOOL!
I WISH WE COULD GO TO SCHOOL, SNOOPY...
BUT THEY WON'T LET YOU GO TO SCHOOL UNTIL YOU'RE FIVE YEARS OLD...
..AND CAN PROVE THAT YOU'RE A HUMAN BEING!
SCHULZ

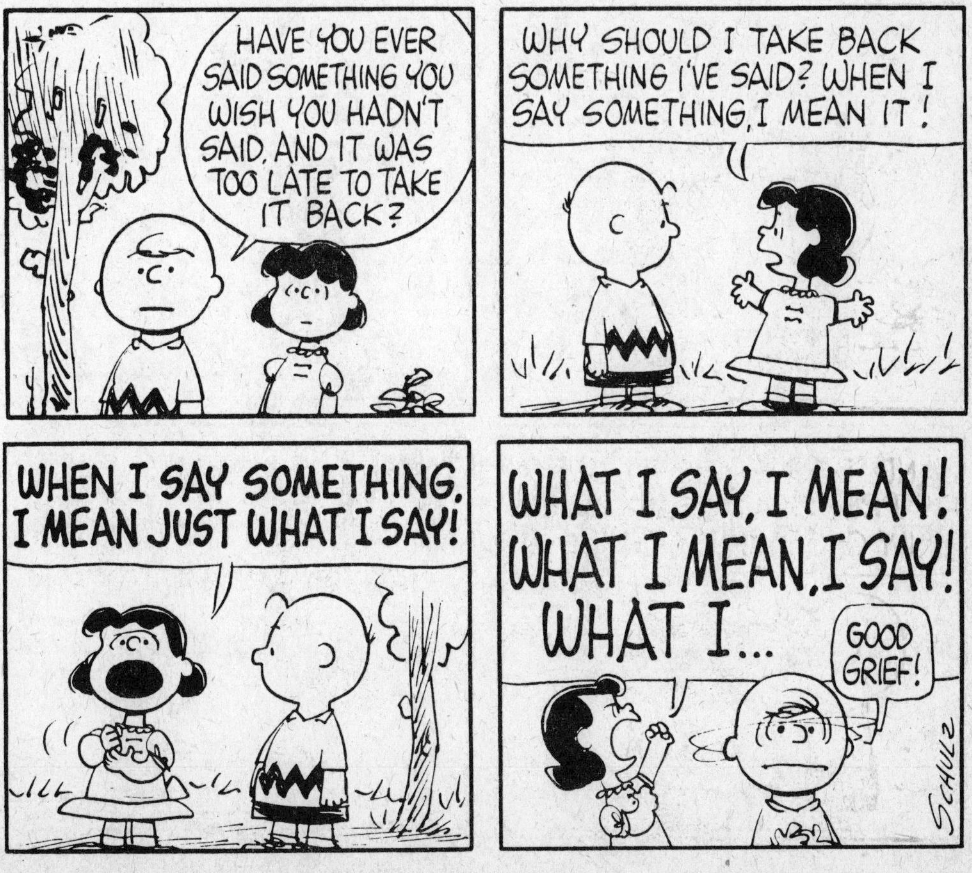
HAVE YOU EVER SAID SOMETHING YOU WISH YOU HADN'T SAID, AND IT WAS TOO LATE TO TAKE IT BACK?
WHY SHOULD I TAKE BACK SOMETHING I'VE SAID? WHEN I SAY SOMETHING, I MEAN IT!
WHEN I SAY SOMETHING, I MEAN JUST WHAT I SAY!
WHAT I SAY, I MEAN! WHAT I MEAN, I SAY! WHAT I...
GOOD GRIEF!
SCHULZ

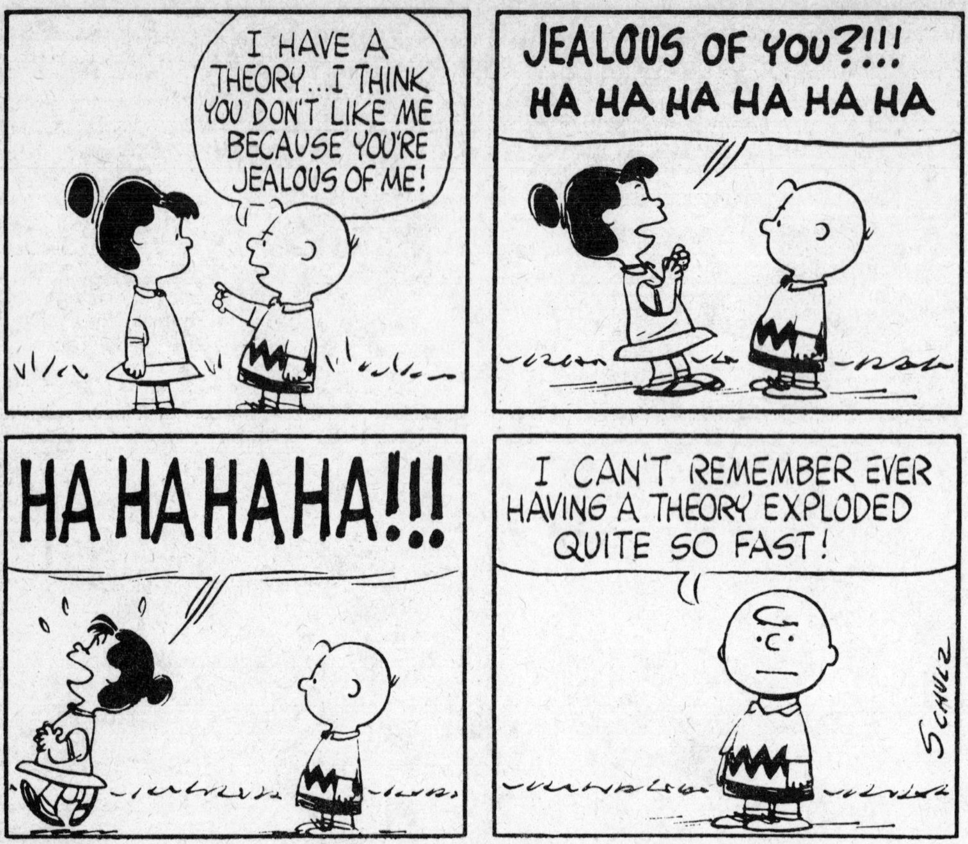
I HAVE A THEORY...I THINK YOU DON'T LIKE ME BECAUSE YOU'RE JEALOUS OF ME!
JEALOUS OF YOU?!!! HA HA HA HA HA HA
HA HA HA HA!!!
I CAN'T REMEMBER EVER HAVING A THEORY EXPLODED QUITE SO FAST!
SCHULZ

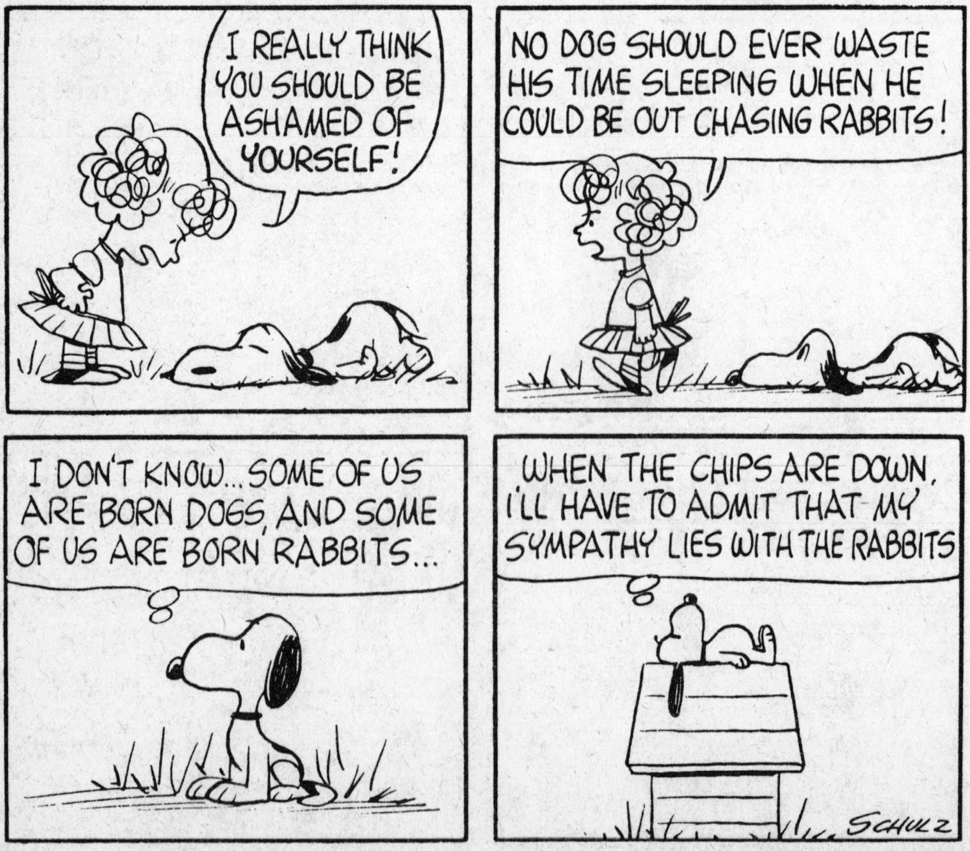
I REALLY THINK YOU SHOULD BE ASHAMED OF YOURSELF!
NO DOG SHOULD EVER WASTE HIS TIME SLEEPING WHEN HE COULD BE OUT CHASING RABBITS!
I DON'T KNOW... SOME OF US ARE BORN DOGS, AND SOME OF US ARE BORN RABBITS...
WHEN THE CHIPS ARE DOWN, I'LL HAVE TO ADMIT THAT MY SYMPATHY LIES WITH THE RABBITS
SCHULZ

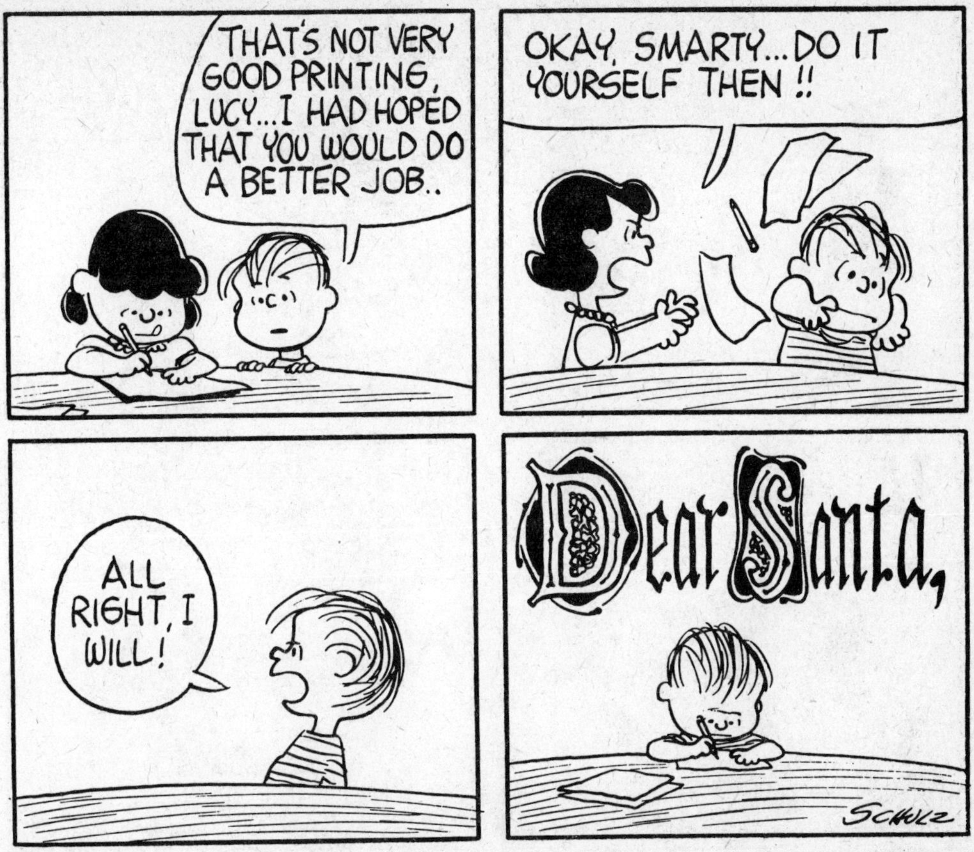
THAT'S NOT VERY GOOD PRINTING, LUCY...I HAD HOPED THAT YOU WOULD DO A BETTER JOB..
OKAY, SMARTY...DO IT YOURSELF THEN !!
ALL RIGHT, I WILL!
Dear Santa,
SCHULZ

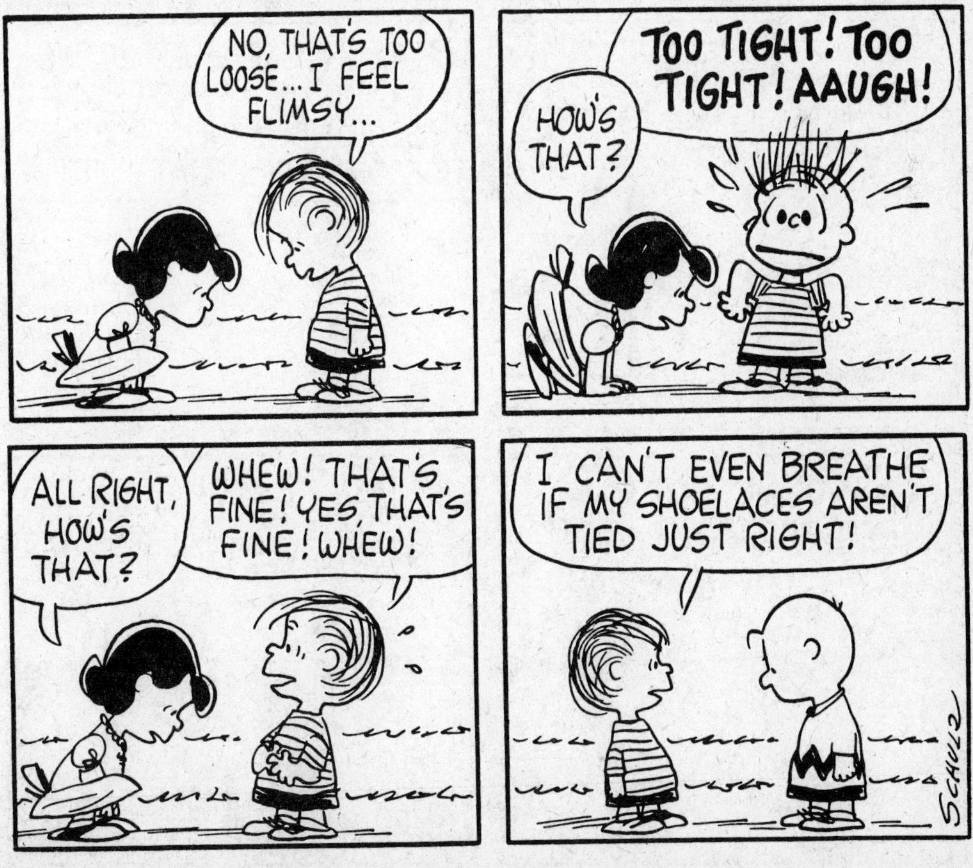
NO, THAT'S TOO LOOSE...I FEEL FLIMSY...
HOW'S THAT?
TOO TIGHT! TOO TIGHT! AAUGH!
ALL RIGHT, HOW'S THAT?
WHEW! THAT'S FINE! YES, THAT'S FINE! WHEW!
I CAN'T EVEN BREATHE IF MY SHOELACES AREN'T TIED JUST RIGHT!
SCHULZ

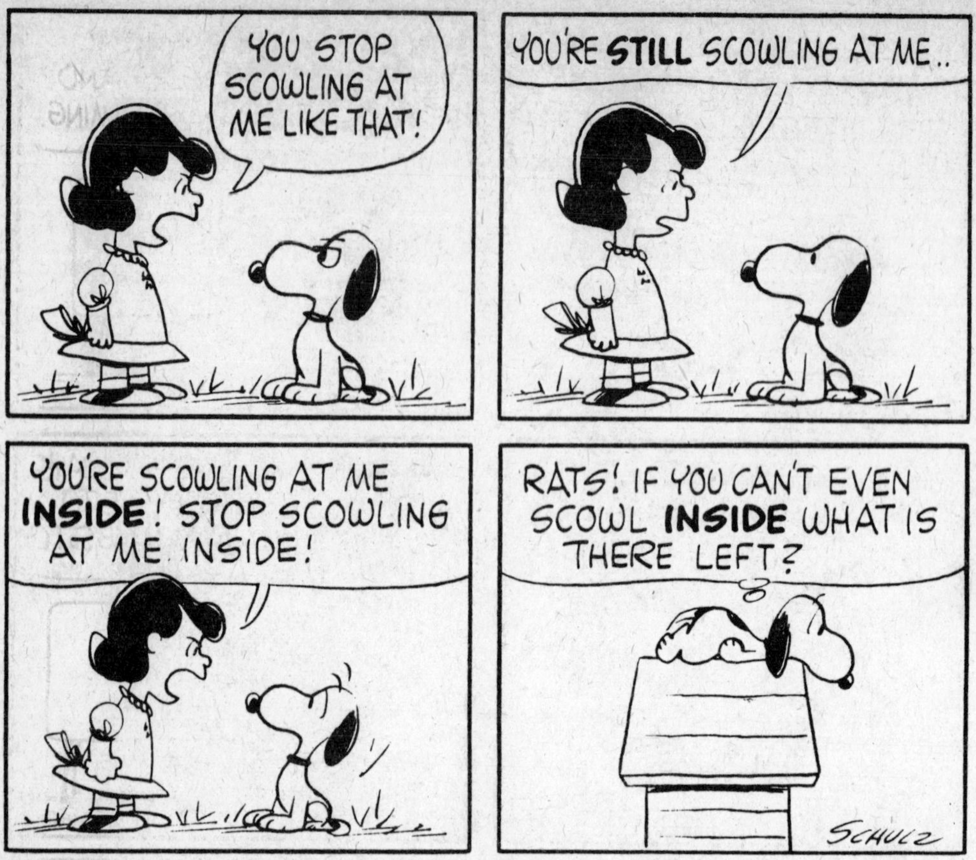
YOU STOP SCOWLING AT ME LIKE THAT!
YOU'RE STILL SCOWLING AT ME..
YOU'RE SCOWLING AT ME INSIDE! STOP SCOWLING AT ME INSIDE!
RATS! IF YOU CAN'T EVEN SCOWL INSIDE WHAT IS THERE LEFT?
SCHULZ

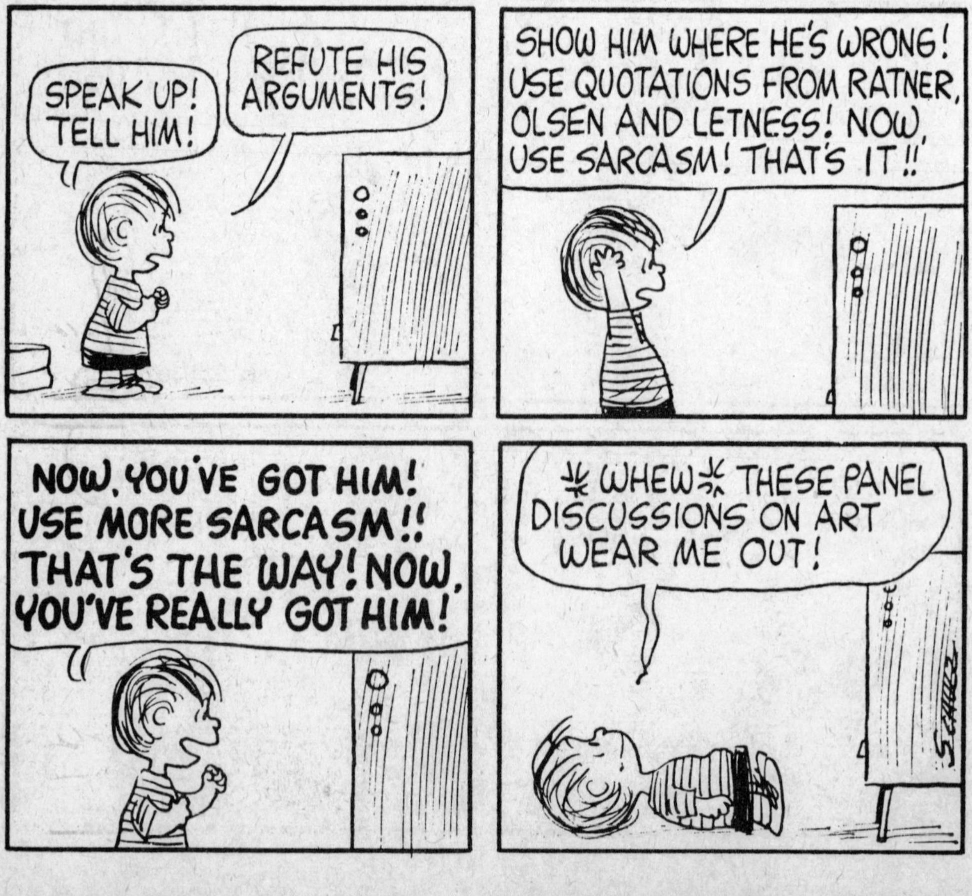
SPEAK UP! TELL HIM!
REFUTE HIS ARGUMENTS!
SHOW HIM WHERE HE'S WRONG! USE QUOTATIONS FROM RATNER, OLSEN AND LETNESS! NOW, USE SARCASM! THAT'S IT!!
NOW, YOU'VE GOT HIM! USE MORE SARCASM!! THAT'S THE WAY! NOW, YOU'VE REALLY GOT HIM!
WHEW THESE PANEL DISCUSSIONS ON ART WEAR ME OUT!
SCHULZ

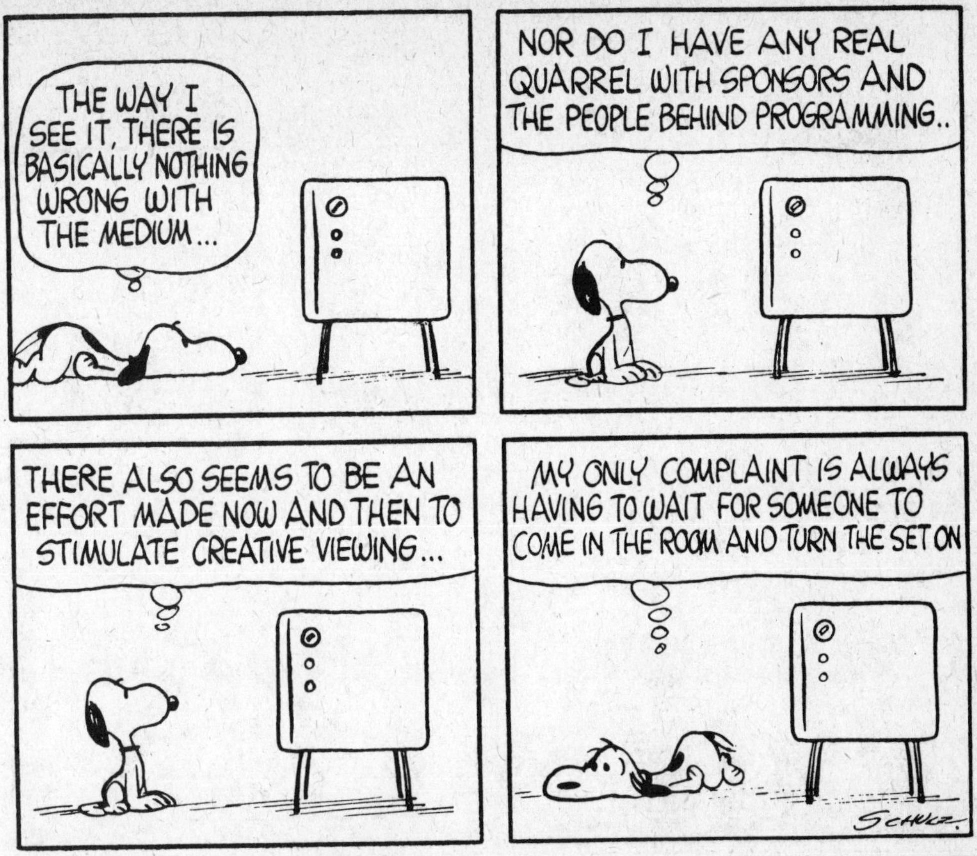
THE WAY I SEE IT, THERE IS BASICALLY NOTHING WRONG WITH THE MEDIUM...
NOR DO I HAVE ANY REAL QUARREL WITH SPONSORS AND THE PEOPLE BEHIND PROGRAMMING..
THERE ALSO SEEMS TO BE AN EFFORT MADE NOW AND THEN TO STIMULATE CREATIVE VIEWING...
MY ONLY COMPLAINT IS ALWAYS HAVING TO WAIT FOR SOMEONE TO COME IN THE ROOM AND TURN THE SET ON
SCHULZ

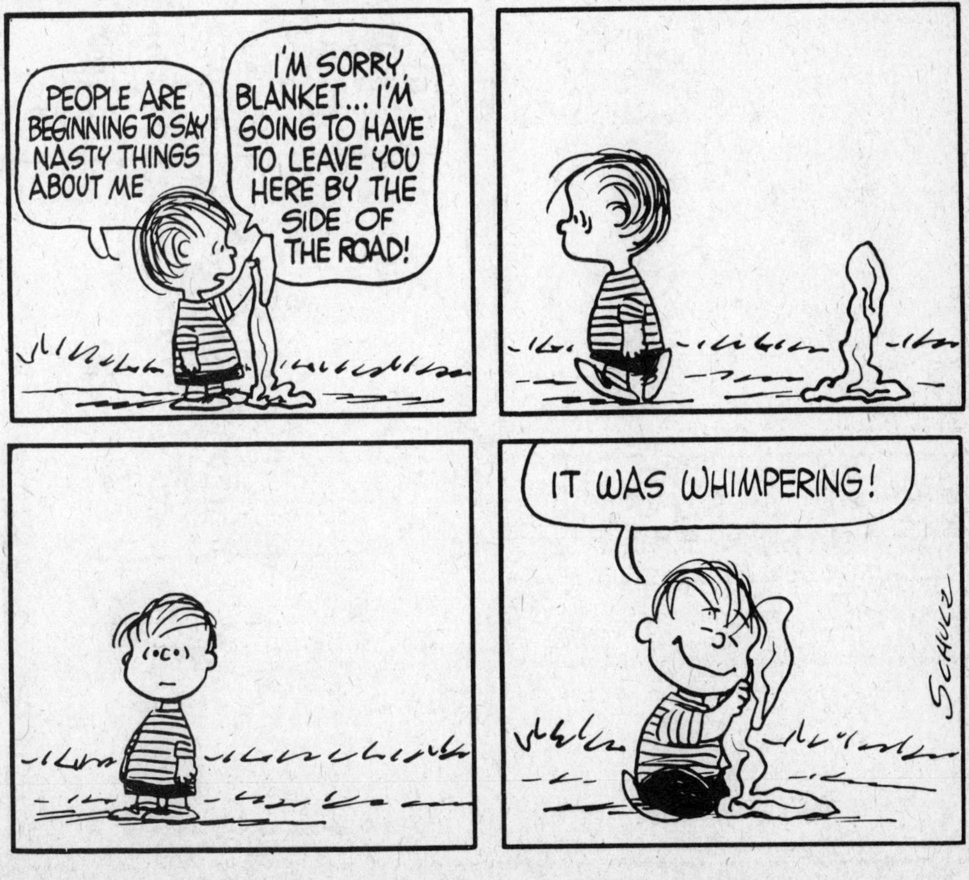
PEOPLE ARE BEGINNING TO SAY NASTY THINGS ABOUT ME
I'M SORRY, BLANKET... I'M GOING TO HAVE TO LEAVE YOU HERE BY THE SIDE OF THE ROAD!
IT WAS WHIMPERING!
SCHULZ

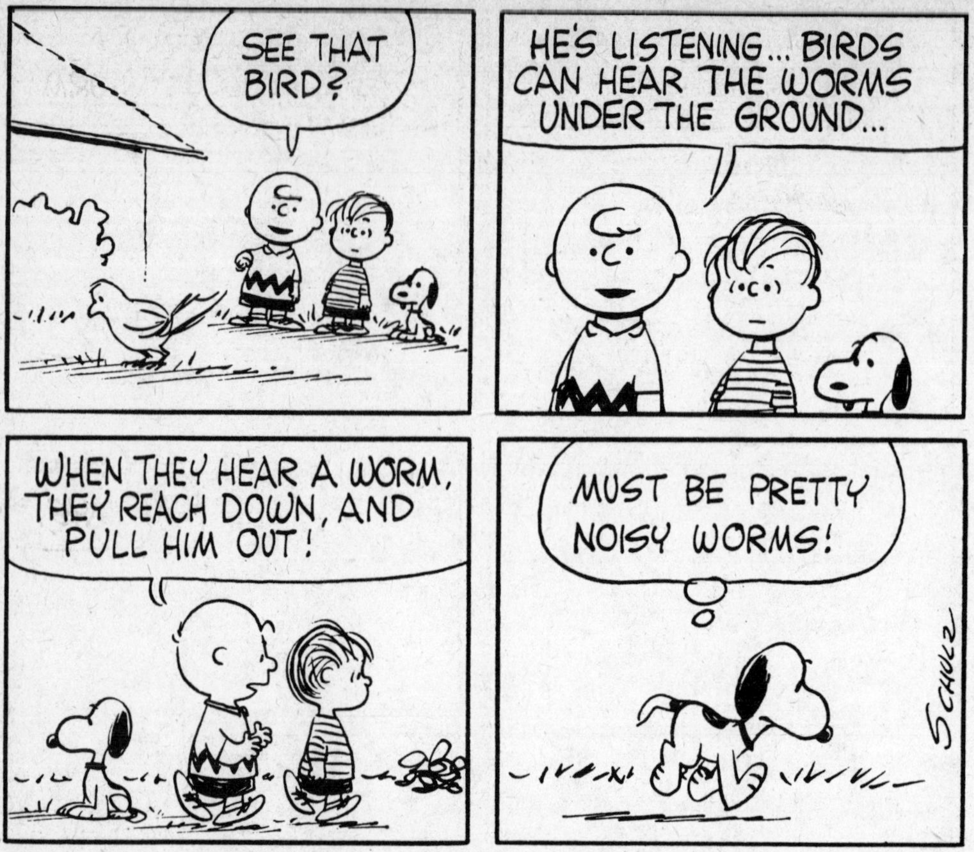
SEE THAT BIRD?
HE'S LISTENING... BIRDS CAN HEAR THE WORMS UNDER THE GROUND...
WHEN THEY HEAR A WORM, THEY REACH DOWN, AND PULL HIM OUT!
MUST BE PRETTY NOISY WORMS!
SCHULZ

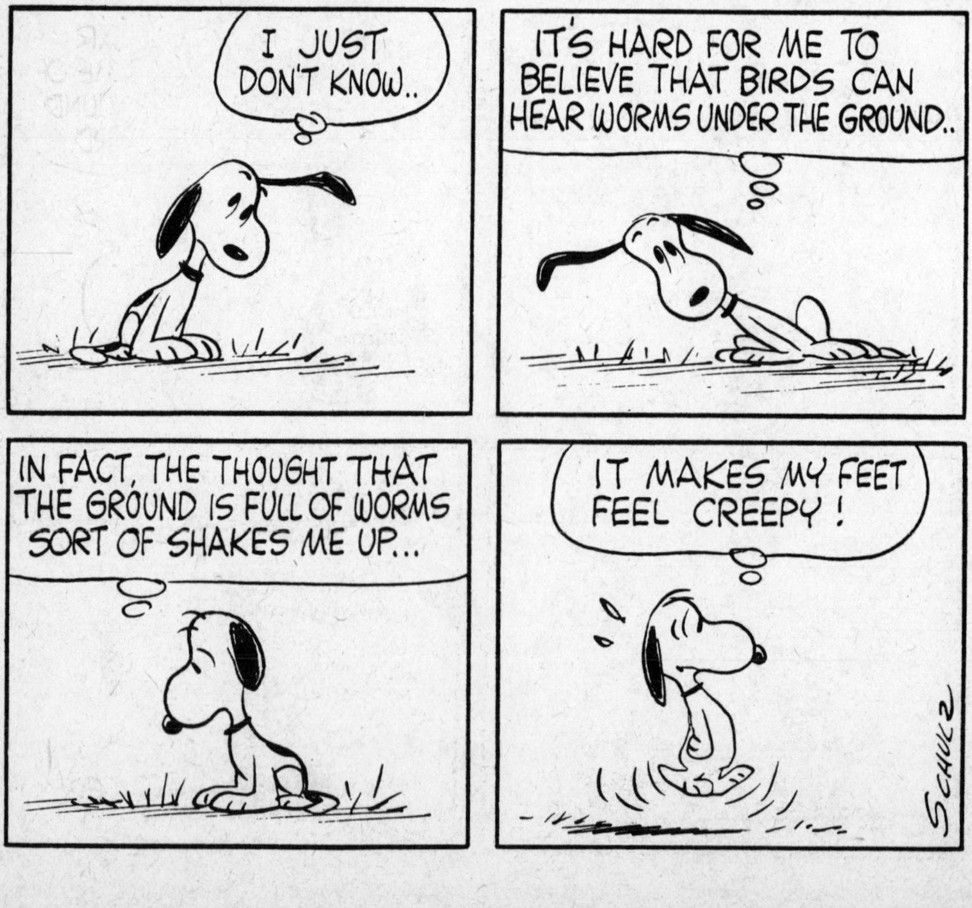
I JUST DON'T KNOW..
IT'S HARD FOR ME TO BELIEVE THAT BIRDS CAN HEAR WORMS UNDER THE GROUND..
IN FACT, THE THOUGHT THAT THE GROUND IS FULL OF WORMS SORT OF SHAKES ME UP...
IT MAKES MY FEET FEEL CREEPY!
SCHULZ

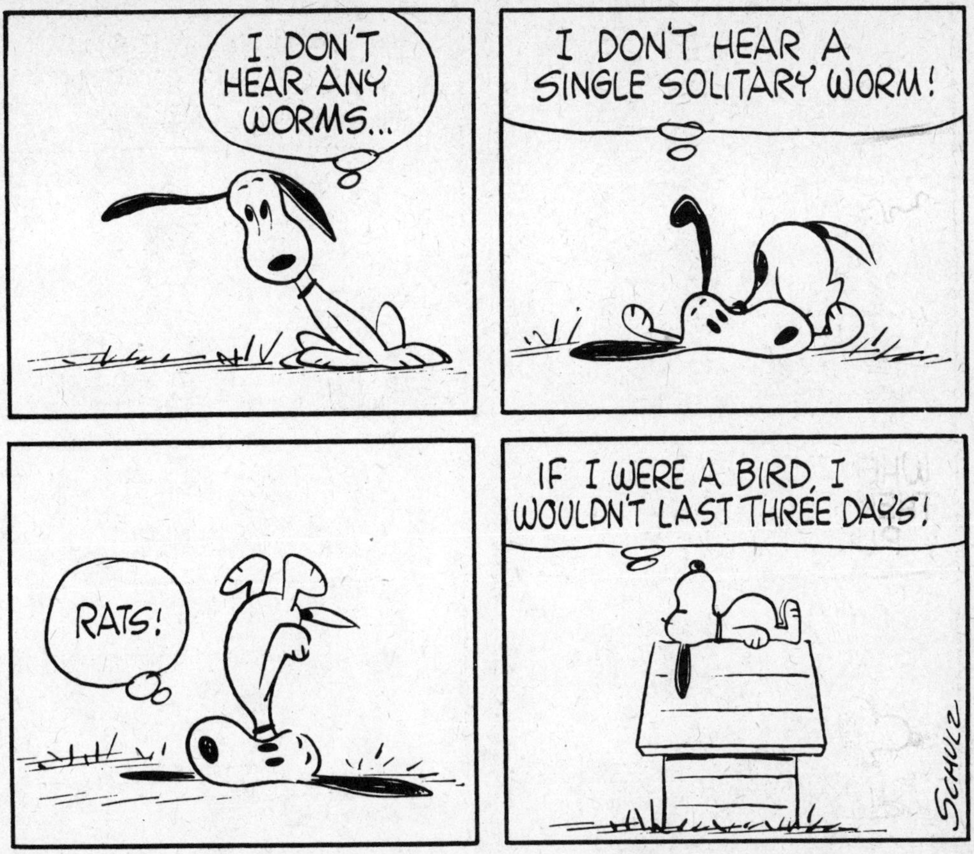
I DON'T HEAR ANY WORMS...
I DON'T HEAR A SINGLE SOLITARY WORM!
RATS!
IF I WERE A BIRD, I WOULDN'T LAST THREE DAYS!
SCHULZ

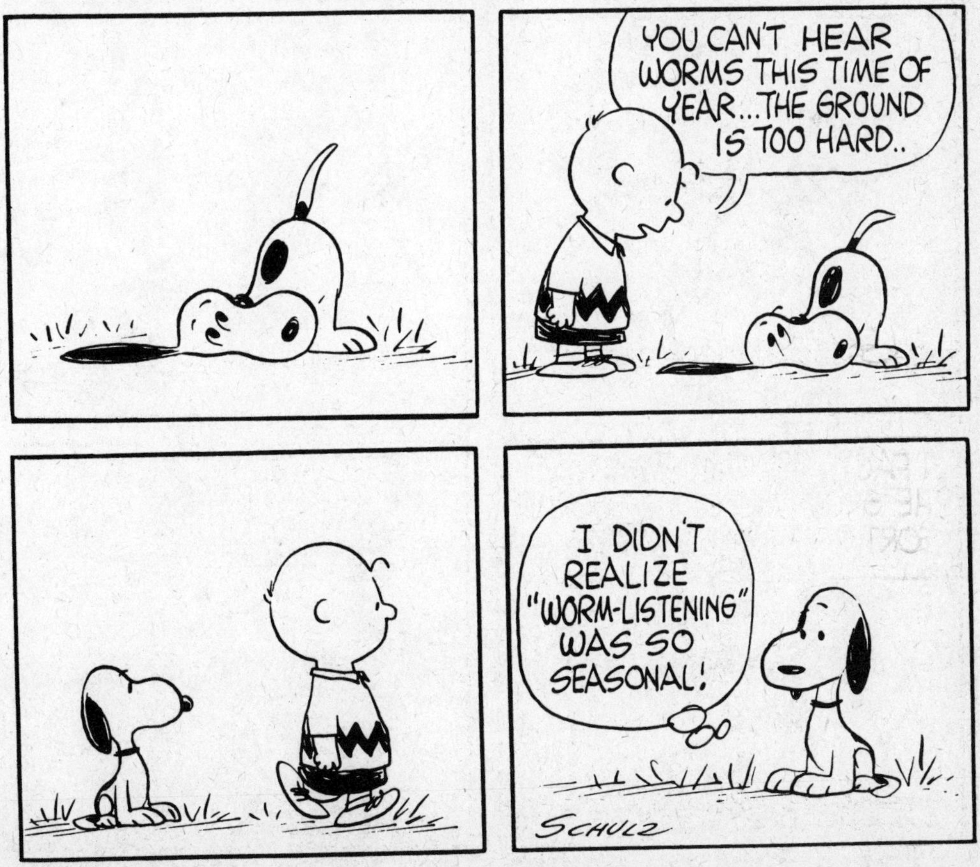
YOU CAN'T HEAR WORMS THIS TIME OF YEAR...THE GROUND IS TOO HARD..
I DIDN'T REALIZE "WORM-LISTENING" WAS SO SEASONAL!
SCHULZ

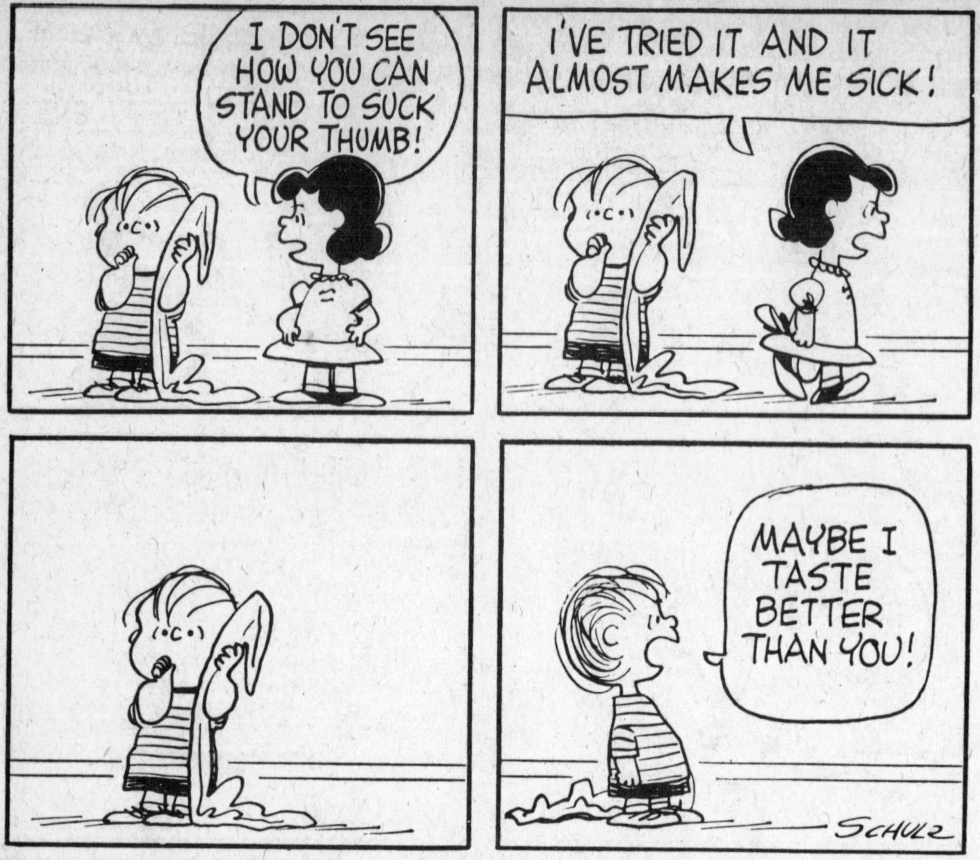
I DON'T SEE HOW YOU CAN STAND TO SUCK YOUR THUMB!
I'VE TRIED IT AND IT ALMOST MAKES ME SICK!
MAYBE I TASTE BETTER THAN YOU!
SCHULZ

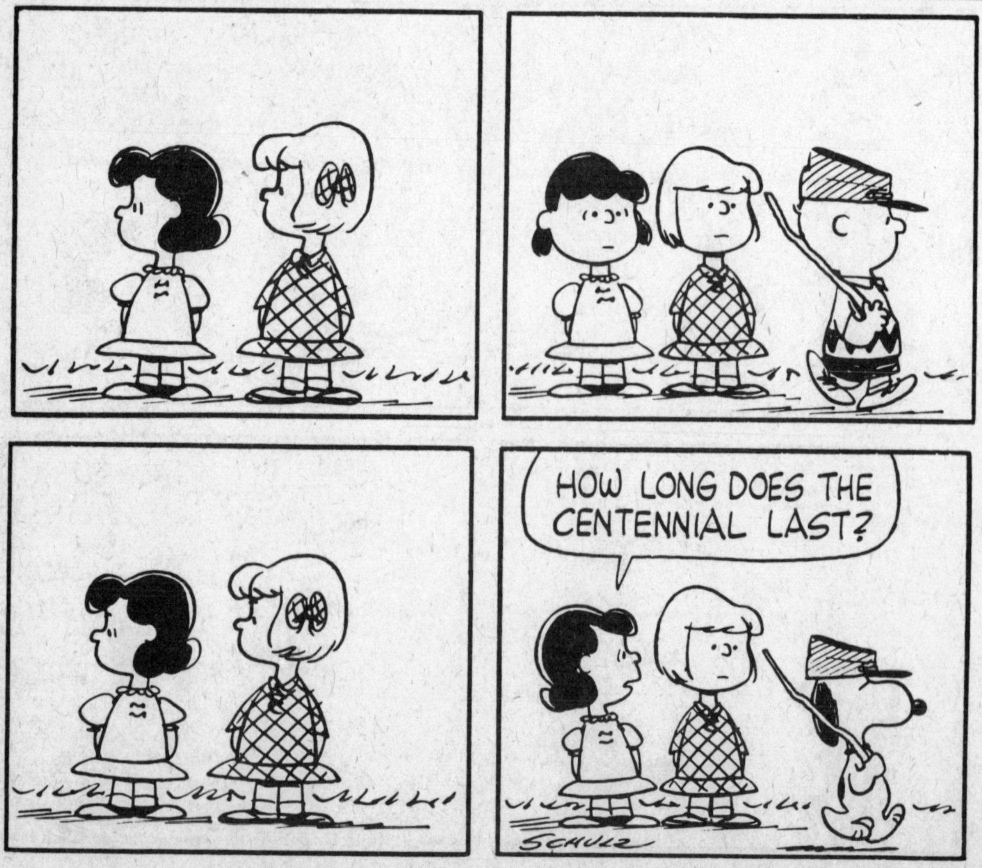
HOW LONG DOES THE CENTENNIAL LAST?
SCHULZ

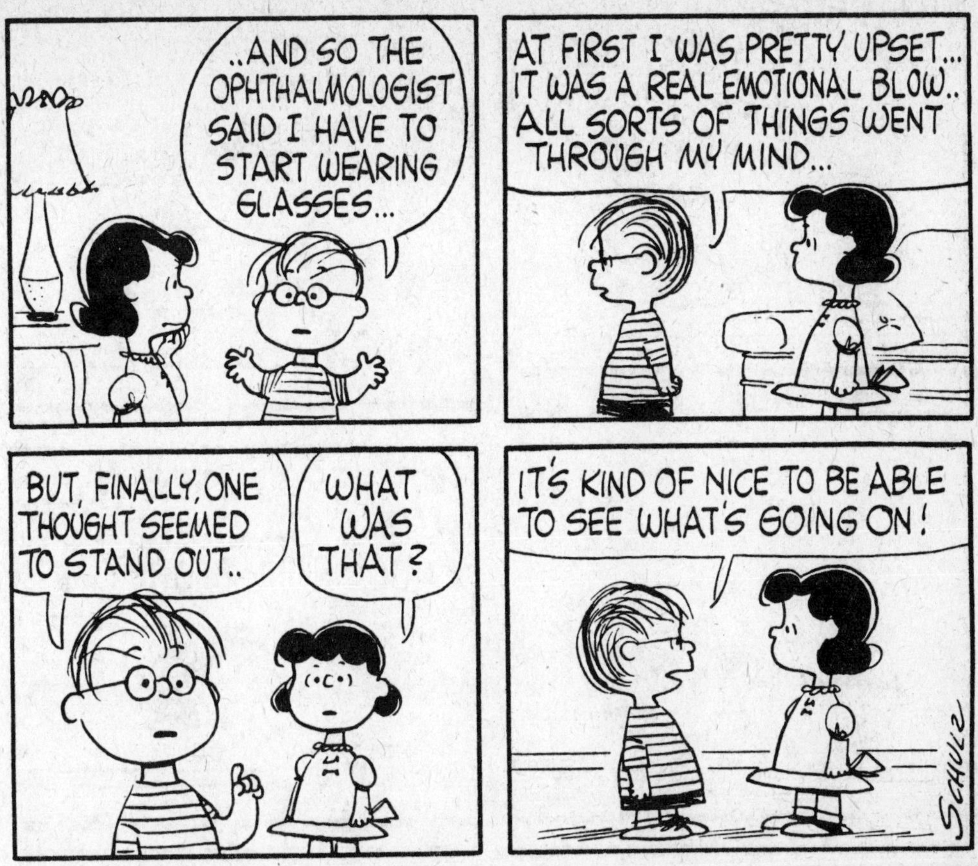
..AND SO THE OPHTHALMOLOGIST SAID I HAVE TO START WEARING GLASSES...
AT FIRST I WAS PRETTY UPSET... IT WAS A REAL EMOTIONAL BLOW.. ALL SORTS OF THINGS WENT THROUGH MY MIND...
BUT, FINALLY, ONE THOUGHT SEEMED TO STAND OUT..
WHAT WAS THAT?
IT'S KIND OF NICE TO BE ABLE TO SEE WHAT'S GOING ON!
SCHULZ

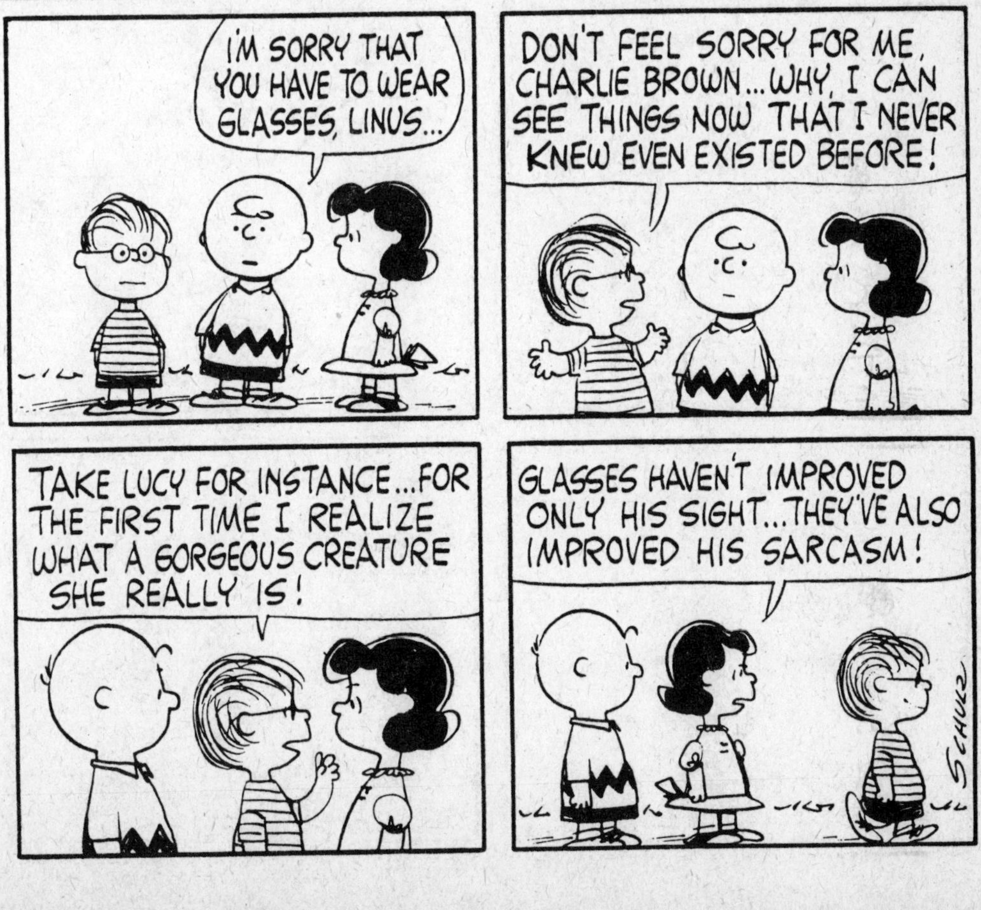
I'M SORRY THAT YOU HAVE TO WEAR GLASSES, LINUS...
DON'T FEEL SORRY FOR ME, CHARLIE BROWN... WHY, I CAN SEE THINGS NOW THAT I NEVER KNEW EVEN EXISTED BEFORE!
TAKE LUCY FOR INSTANCE...FOR THE FIRST TIME I REALIZE WHAT A GORGEOUS CREATURE SHE REALLY IS!
GLASSES HAVEN'T IMPROVED ONLY HIS SIGHT...THEY'VE ALSO IMPROVED HIS SARCASM!
SCHULZ

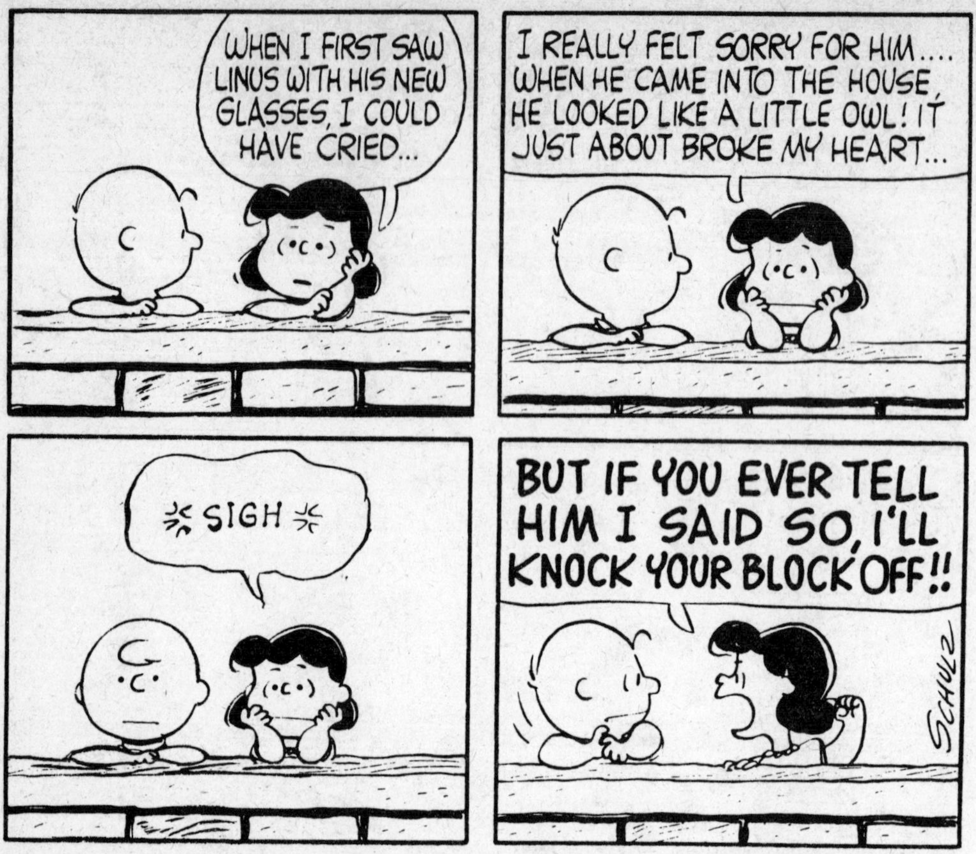
WHEN I FIRST SAW LINUS WITH HIS NEW GLASSES, I COULD HAVE CRIED...
I REALLY FELT SORRY FOR HIM.... WHEN HE CAME INTO THE HOUSE, HE LOOKED LIKE A LITTLE OWL! IT JUST ABOUT BROKE MY HEART...
SIGH
BUT IF YOU EVER TELL HIM I SAID SO, I'LL KNOCK YOUR BLOCK OFF!!
SCHULZ

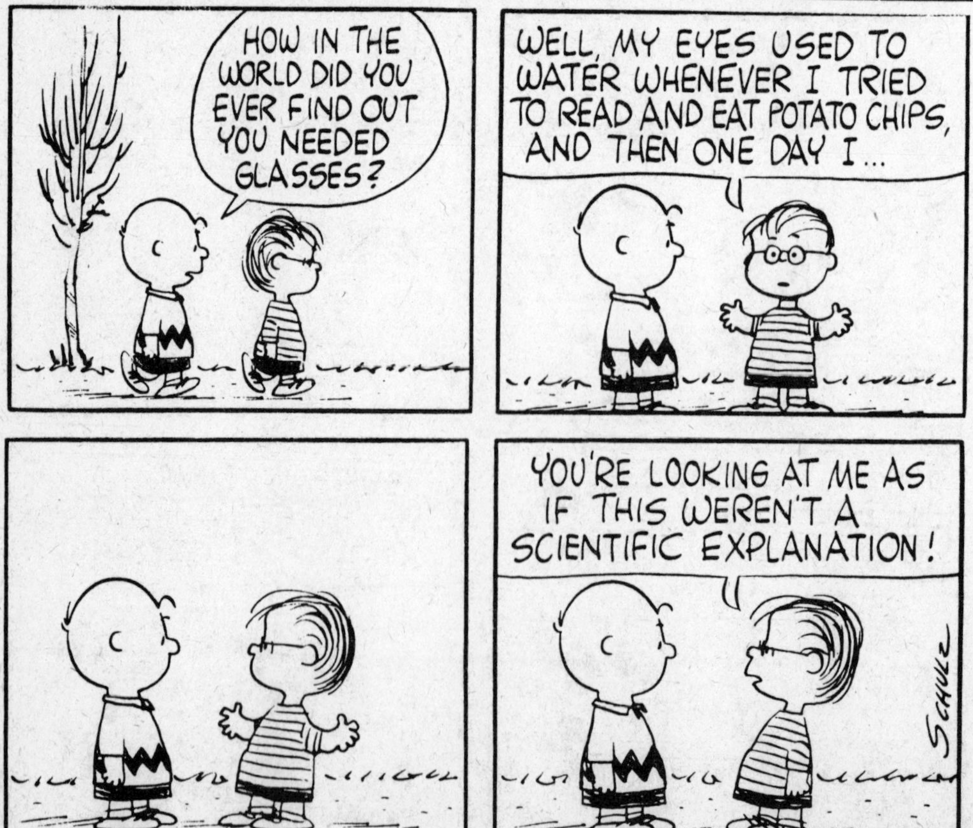
HOW IN THE WORLD DID YOU EVER FIND OUT YOU NEEDED GLASSES?
WELL, MY EYES USED TO WATER WHENEVER I TRIED TO READ AND EAT POTATO CHIPS, AND THEN ONE DAY I...
YOU'RE LOOKING AT ME AS IF THIS WEREN'T A SCIENTIFIC EXPLANATION!
SCHULZ

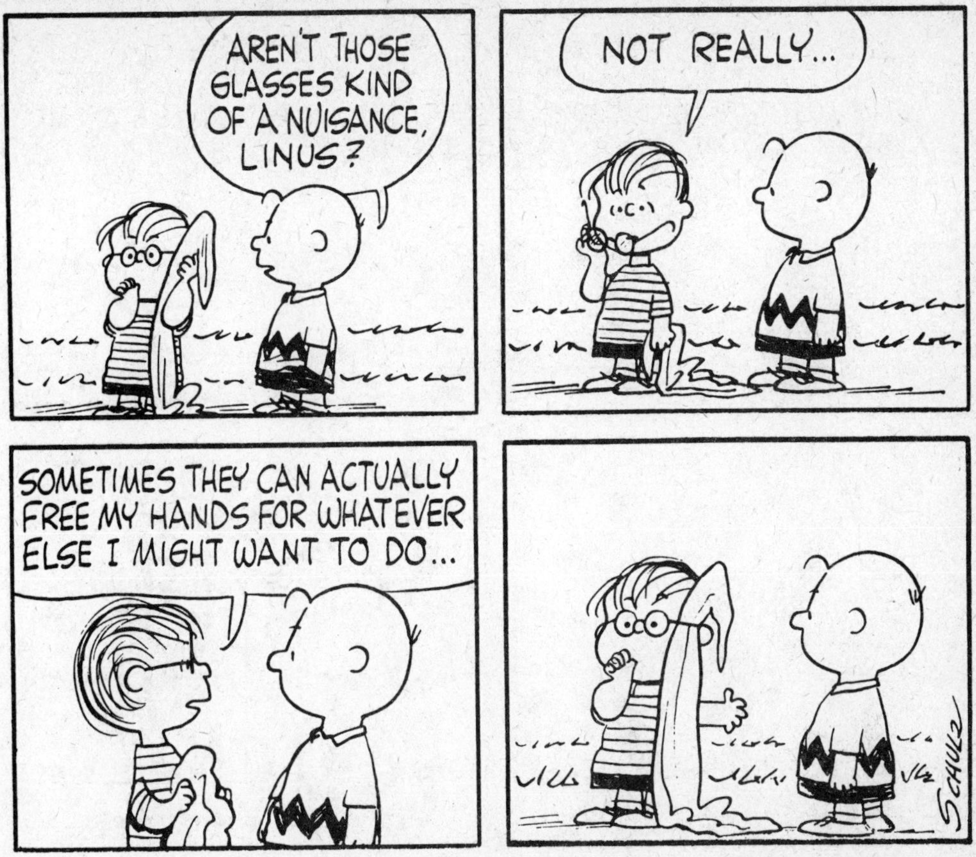
AREN'T THOSE GLASSES KIND OF A NUISANCE, LINUS?
NOT REALLY...
SOMETIMES THEY CAN ACTUALLY FREE MY HANDS FOR WHATEVER ELSE I MIGHT WANT TO DO...
SCHULZ

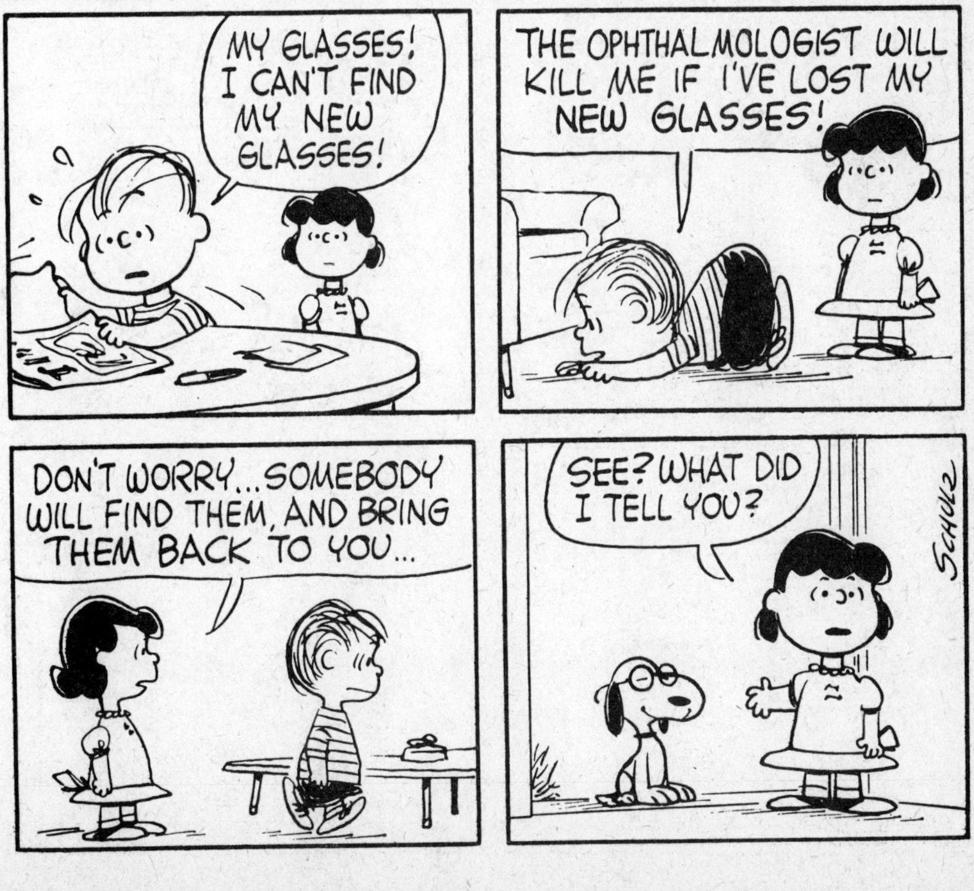
MY GLASSES! I CAN'T FIND MY NEW GLASSES!
THE OPHTHALMOLOGIST WILL KILL ME IF I'VE LOST MY NEW GLASSES!
DON'T WORRY...SOMEBODY WILL FIND THEM, AND BRING THEM BACK TO YOU...
SEE? WHAT DID I TELL YOU?
SCHULZ

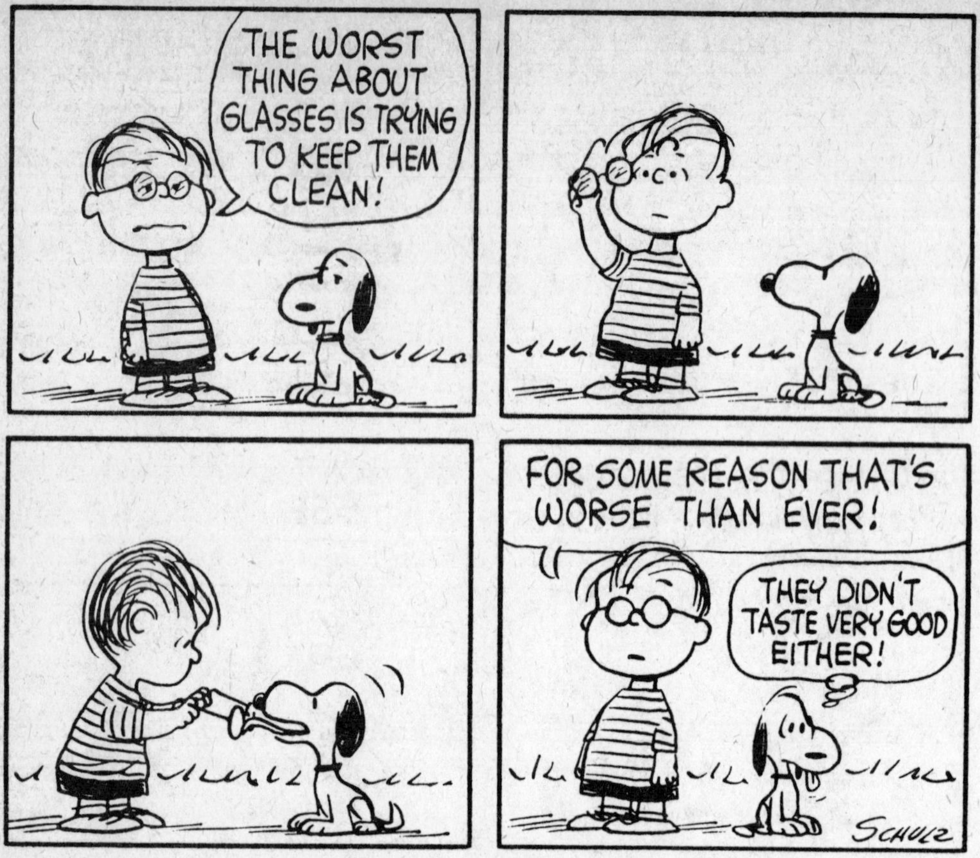
THE WORST THING ABOUT GLASSES IS TRYING TO KEEP THEM CLEAN!
FOR SOME REASON THAT'S WORSE THAN EVER!
THEY DIDN'T TASTE VERY GOOD EITHER!
SCHULZ

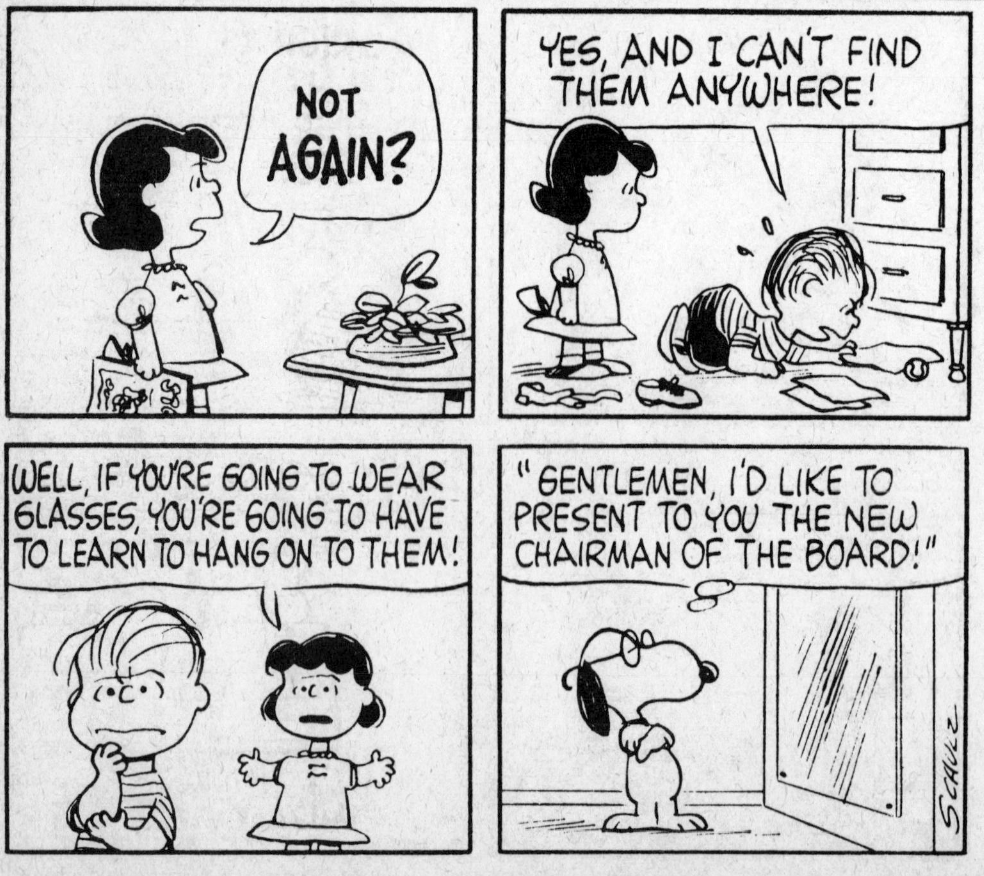
NOT AGAIN?
YES, AND I CAN'T FIND THEM ANYWHERE!
WELL, IF YOU'RE GOING TO WEAR GLASSES, YOU'RE GOING TO HAVE TO LEARN TO HANG ON TO THEM!
"GENTLEMEN, I'D LIKE TO PRESENT TO YOU THE NEW CHAIRMAN OF THE BOARD!"
SCHULZ

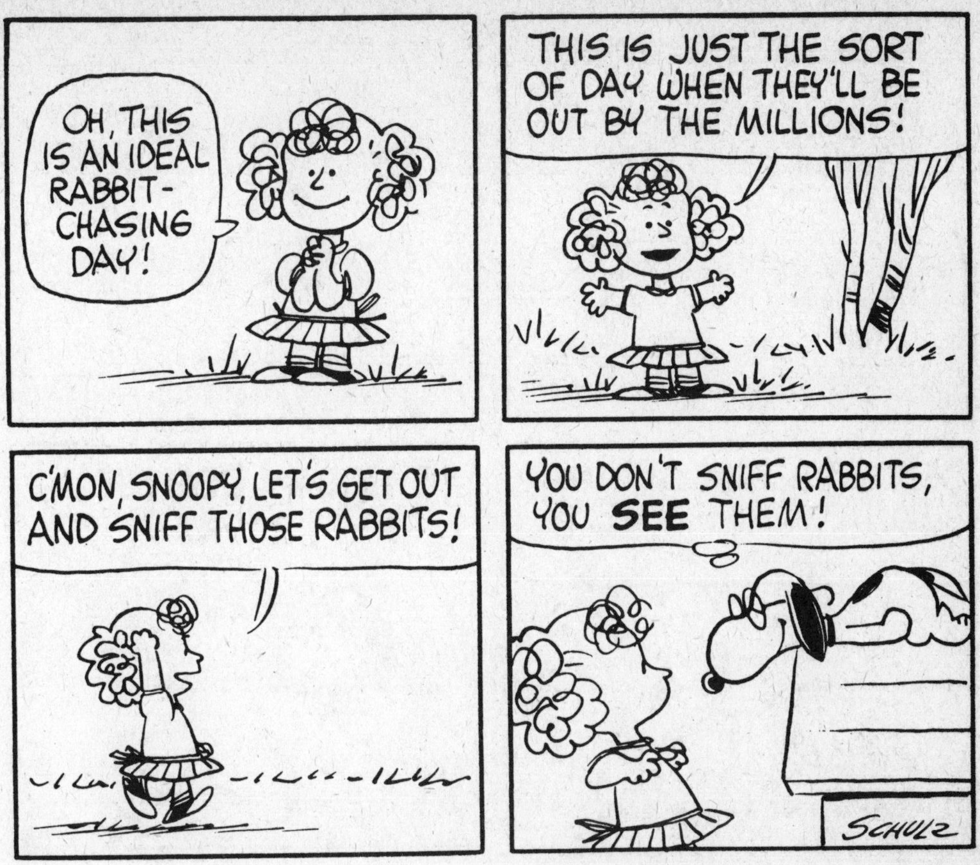
OH, THIS IS AN IDEAL RABBIT-CHASING DAY!
THIS IS JUST THE SORT OF DAY WHEN THEY'LL BE OUT BY THE MILLIONS!
C'MON, SNOOPY, LET'S GET OUT AND SNIFF THOSE RABBITS!
YOU DON'T SNIFF RABBITS, YOU **SEE** THEM!
SCHULZ

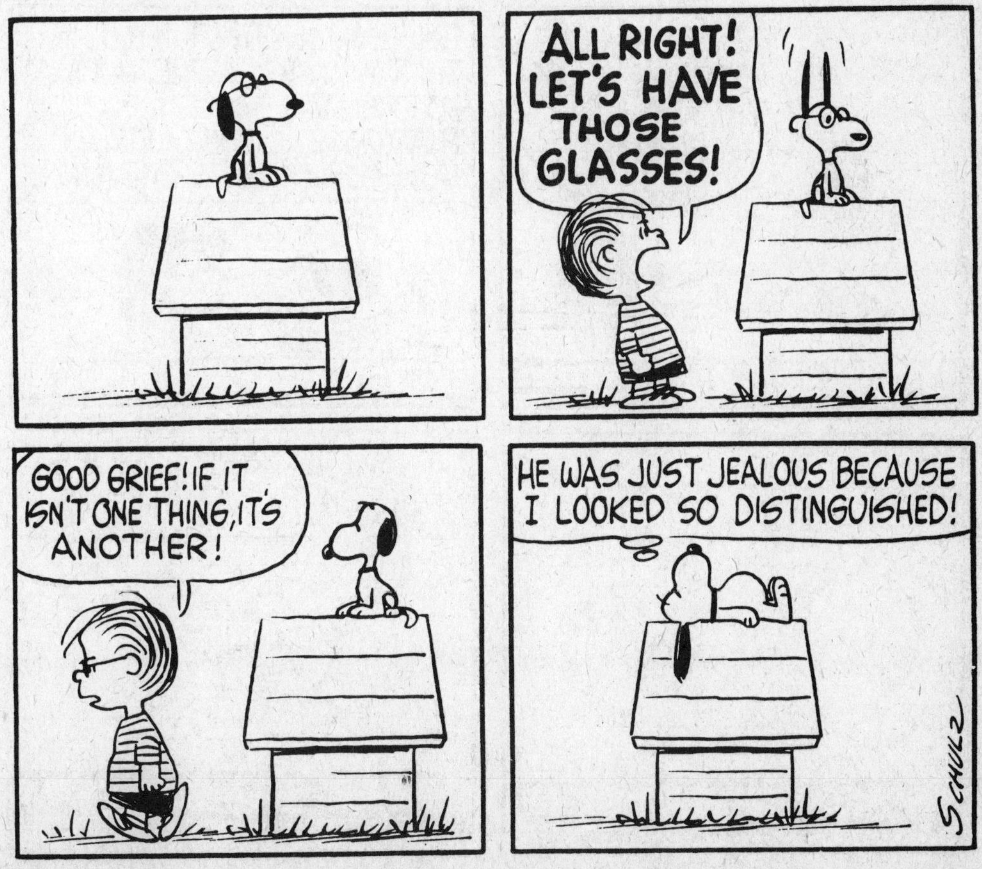
ALL RIGHT! LET'S HAVE THOSE GLASSES!
GOOD GRIEF! IF IT ISN'T ONE THING, IT'S ANOTHER!
HE WAS JUST JEALOUS BECAUSE I LOOKED SO DISTINGUISHED!
SCHULZ

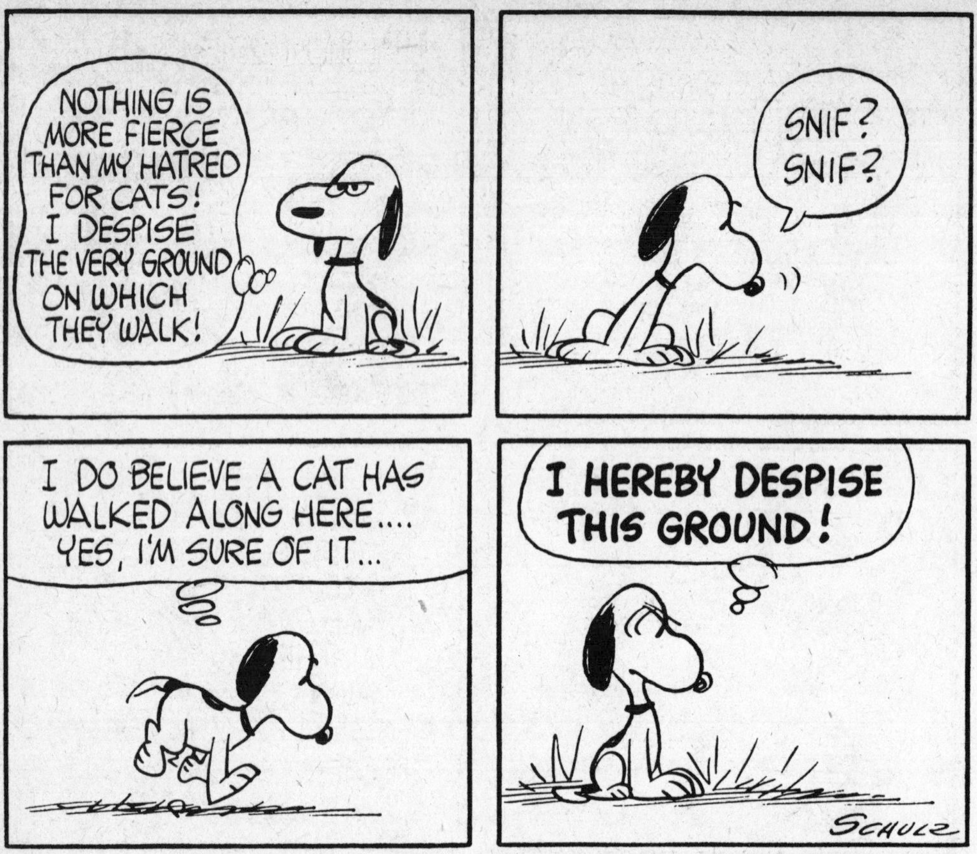
NOTHING IS MORE FIERCE THAN MY HATRED FOR CATS! I DESPISE THE VERY GROUND ON WHICH THEY WALK!
SNIF? SNIF?
I DO BELIEVE A CAT HAS WALKED ALONG HERE.... YES, I'M SURE OF IT...
I HEREBY DESPISE THIS GROUND!
SCHULZ

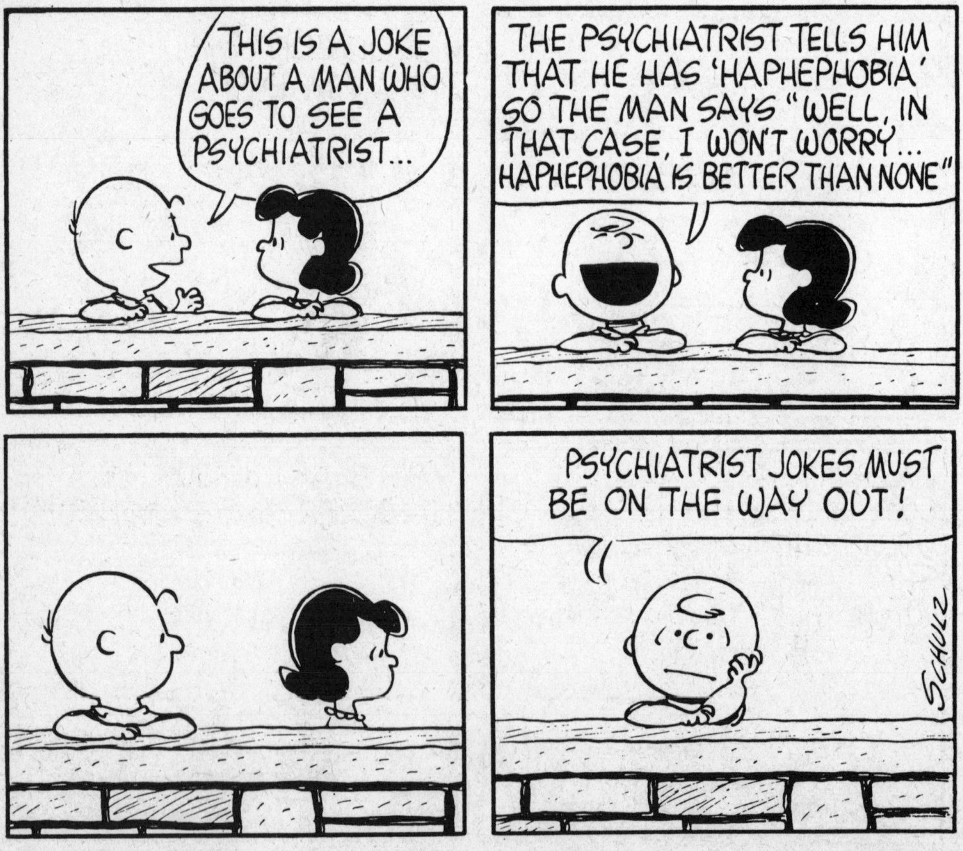
THIS IS A JOKE ABOUT A MAN WHO GOES TO SEE A PSYCHIATRIST...
THE PSYCHIATRIST TELLS HIM THAT HE HAS 'HAPHEPHOBIA' SO THE MAN SAYS "WELL, IN THAT CASE, I WON'T WORRY... HAPHEPHOBIA IS BETTER THAN NONE"
PSYCHIATRIST JOKES MUST BE ON THE WAY OUT!
SCHULZ

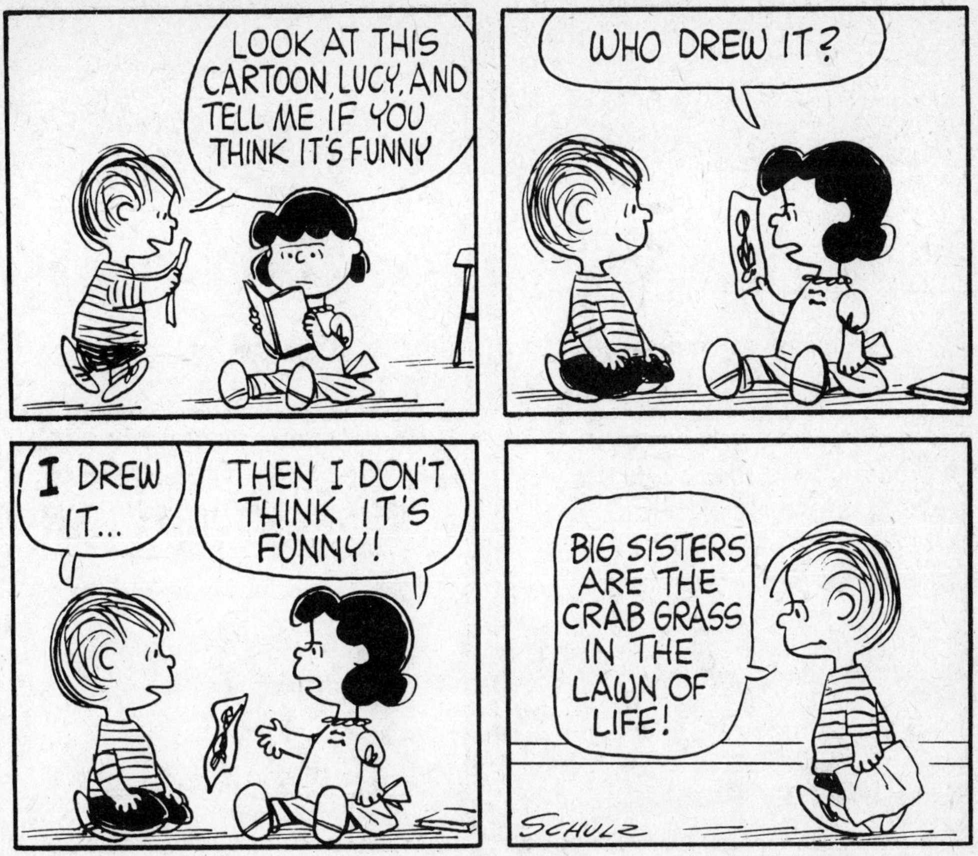
LOOK AT THIS CARTOON, LUCY, AND TELL ME IF YOU THINK IT'S FUNNY
WHO DREW IT?
I DREW IT...
THEN I DON'T THINK IT'S FUNNY!
BIG SISTERS ARE THE CRAB GRASS IN THE LAWN OF LIFE!
SCHULZ

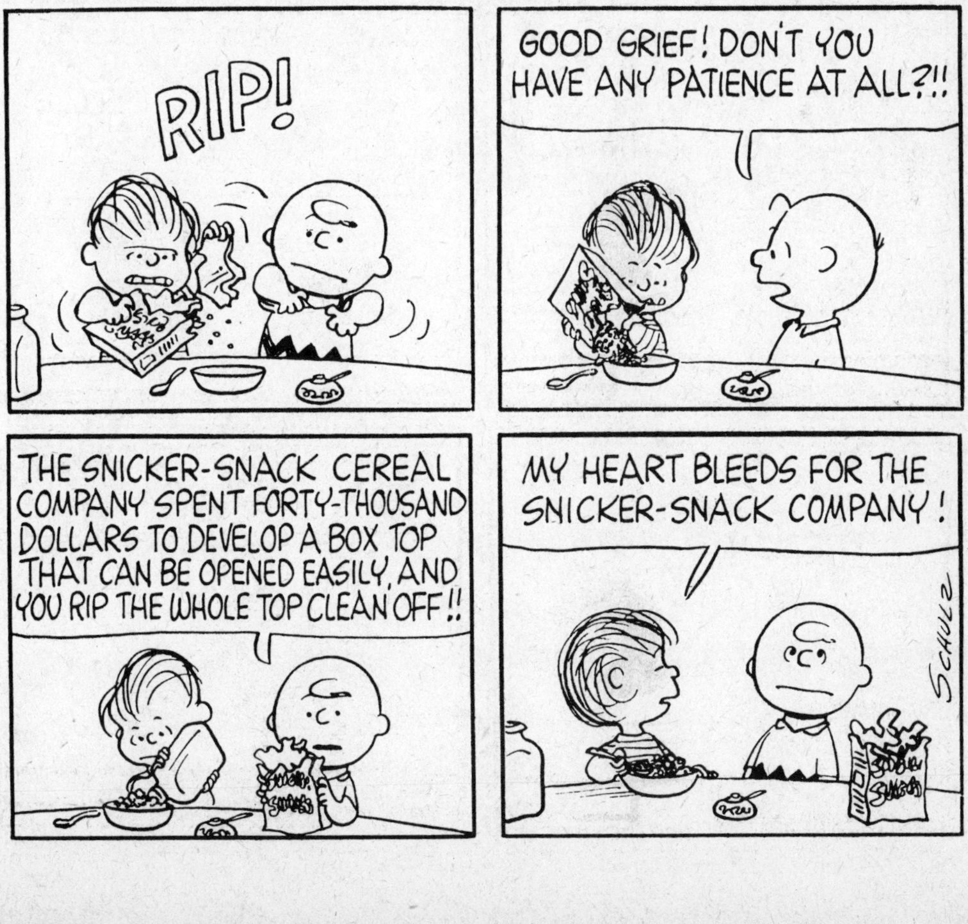
RIP!
GOOD GRIEF! DON'T YOU HAVE ANY PATIENCE AT ALL?!!
THE SNICKER-SNACK CEREAL COMPANY SPENT FORTY-THOUSAND DOLLARS TO DEVELOP A BOX TOP THAT CAN BE OPENED EASILY, AND YOU RIP THE WHOLE TOP CLEAN OFF!!
MY HEART BLEEDS FOR THE SNICKER-SNACK COMPANY!
SCHULZ

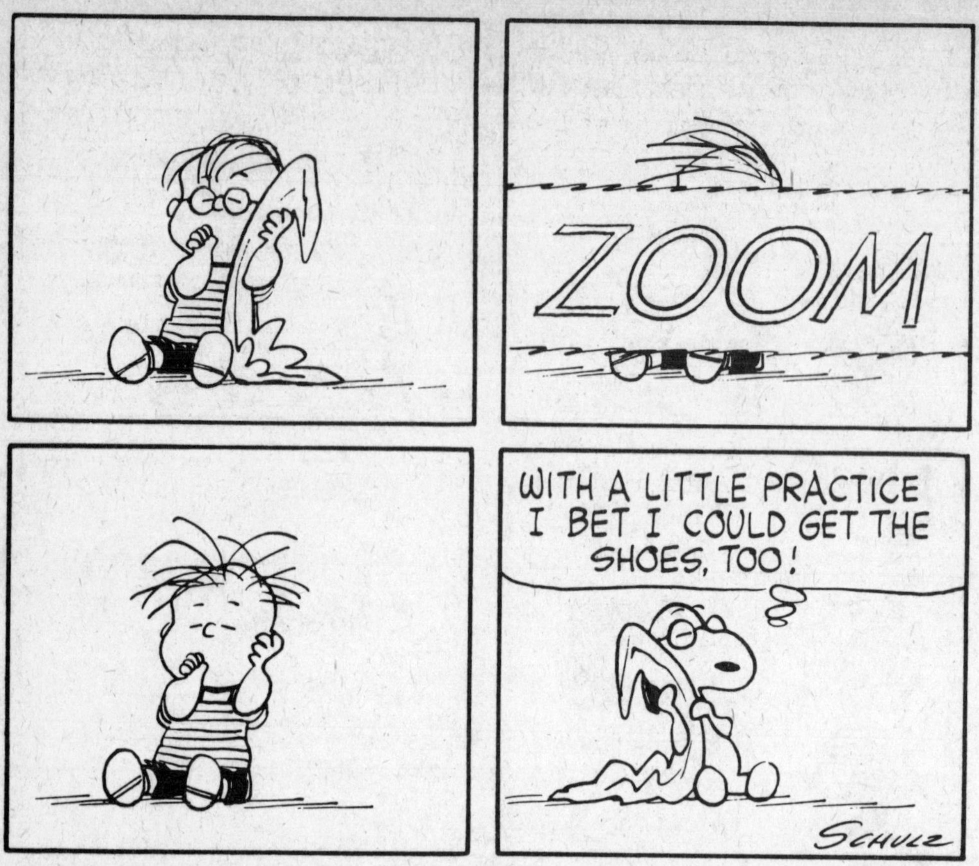
ZOOM
WITH A LITTLE PRACTICE I BET I COULD GET THE SHOES, TOO!
SCHULZ

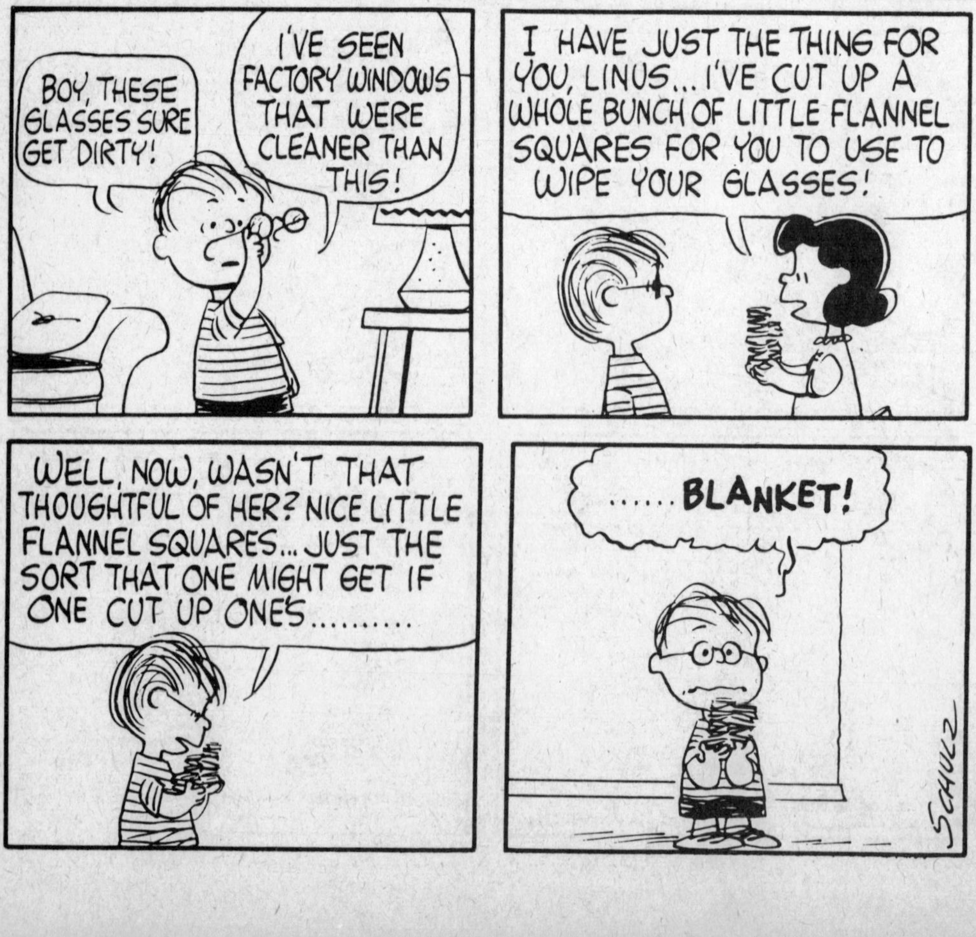
BOY, THESE GLASSES SURE GET DIRTY!
I'VE SEEN FACTORY WINDOWS THAT WERE CLEANER THAN THIS!
I HAVE JUST THE THING FOR YOU, LINUS... I'VE CUT UP A WHOLE BUNCH OF LITTLE FLANNEL SQUARES FOR YOU TO USE TO WIPE YOUR GLASSES!
WELL, NOW, WASN'T THAT THOUGHTFUL OF HER? NICE LITTLE FLANNEL SQUARES... JUST THE SORT THAT ONE MIGHT GET IF ONE CUT UP ONE'S.........
......BLANKET!
SCHULZ

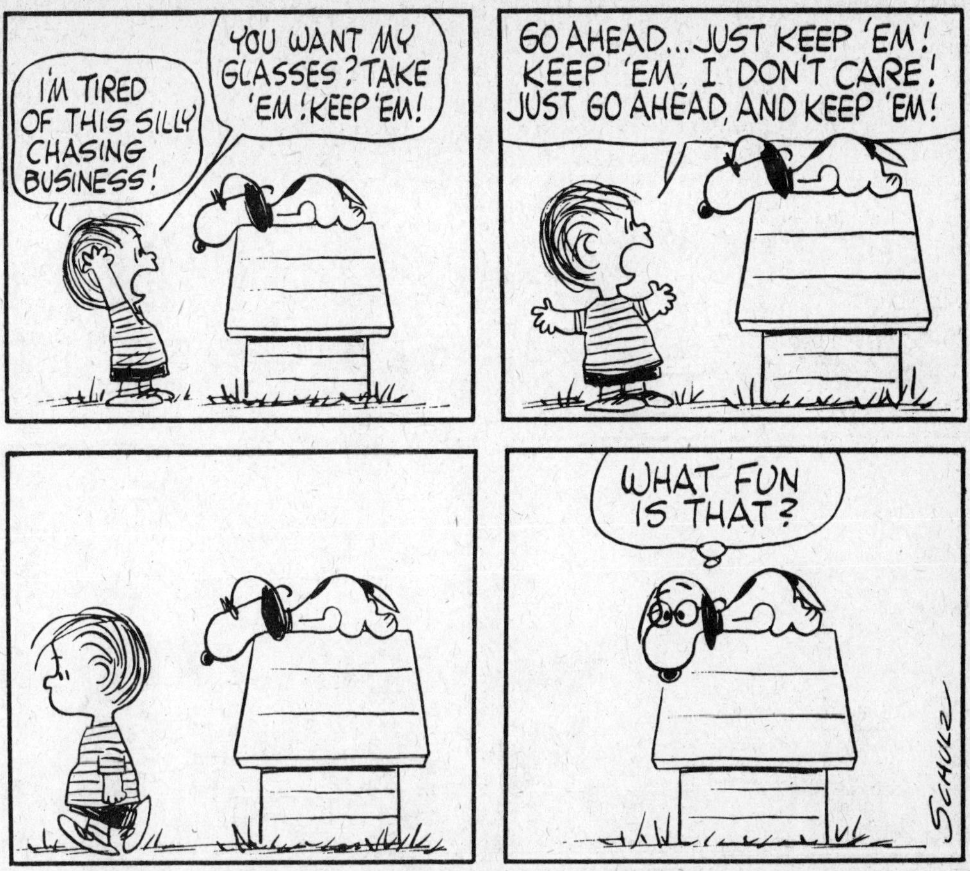
I'M TIRED OF THIS SILLY CHASING BUSINESS!
YOU WANT MY GLASSES? TAKE 'EM! KEEP 'EM!
GO AHEAD... JUST KEEP 'EM! KEEP 'EM, I DON'T CARE! JUST GO AHEAD, AND KEEP 'EM!
WHAT FUN IS THAT?
SCHULZ

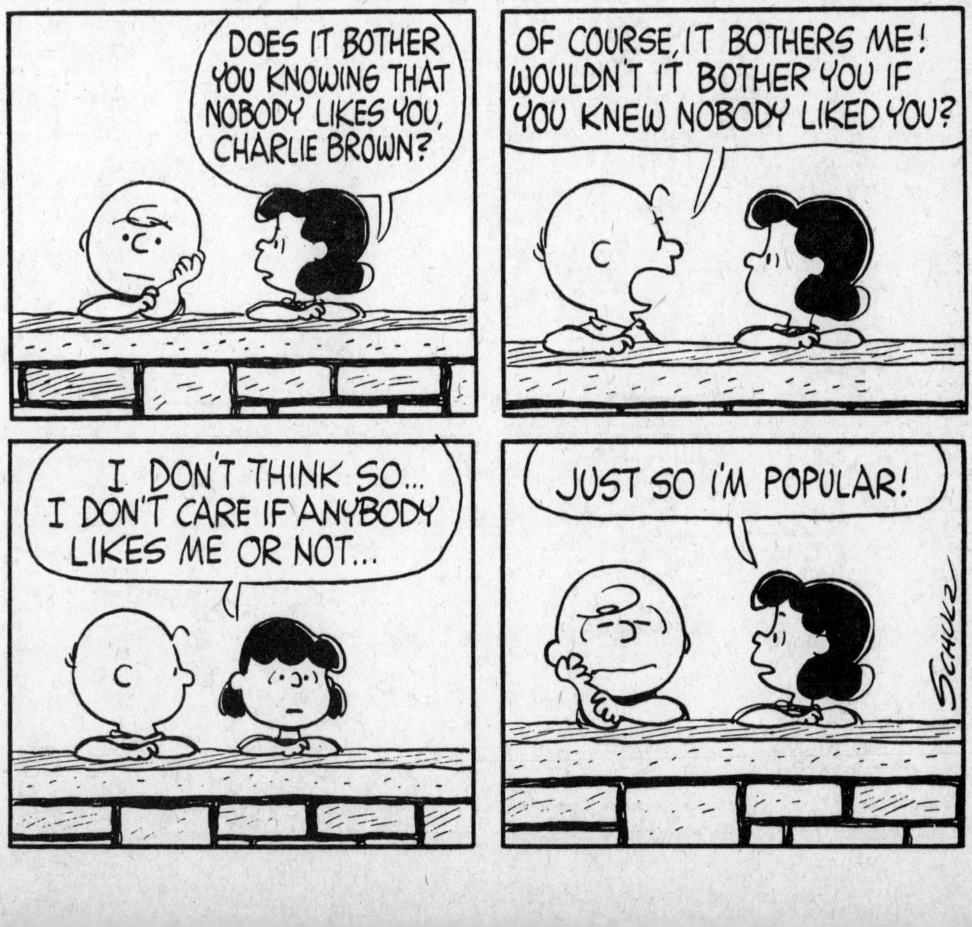
DOES IT BOTHER YOU KNOWING THAT NOBODY LIKES YOU, CHARLIE BROWN?
OF COURSE, IT BOTHERS ME! WOULDN'T IT BOTHER YOU IF YOU KNEW NOBODY LIKED YOU?
I DON'T THINK SO... I DON'T CARE IF ANYBODY LIKES ME OR NOT...
JUST SO I'M POPULAR!
SCHULZ

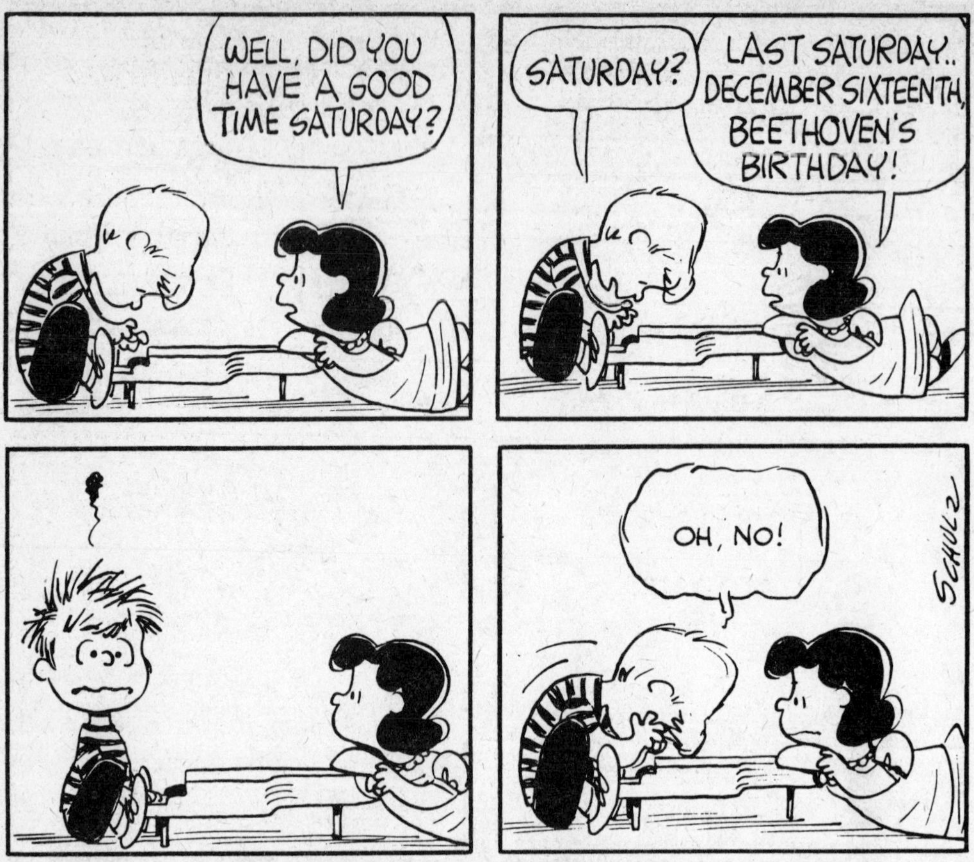
WELL, DID YOU HAVE A GOOD TIME SATURDAY?
SATURDAY?
LAST SATURDAY.. DECEMBER SIXTEENTH, BEETHOVEN'S BIRTHDAY!
OH, NO!
SCHULZ

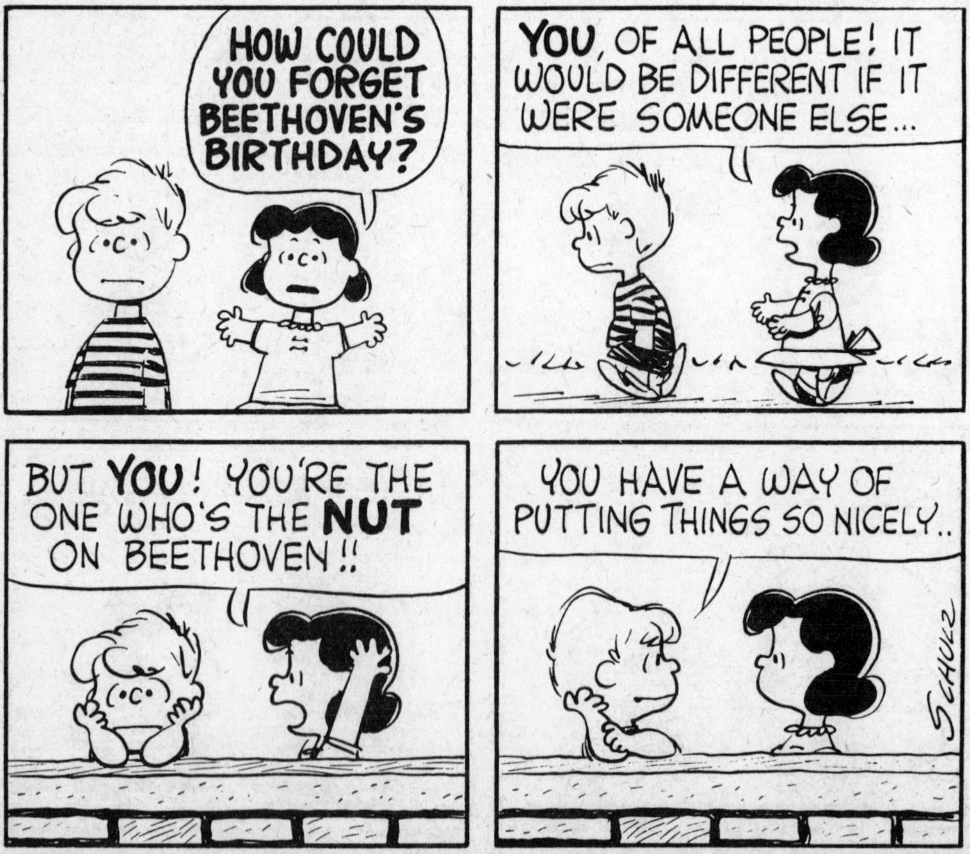
HOW COULD YOU FORGET BEETHOVEN'S BIRTHDAY?
YOU, OF ALL PEOPLE! IT WOULD BE DIFFERENT IF IT WERE SOMEONE ELSE...
BUT YOU! YOU'RE THE ONE WHO'S THE NUT ON BEETHOVEN!!
YOU HAVE A WAY OF PUTTING THINGS SO NICELY..
SCHULZ

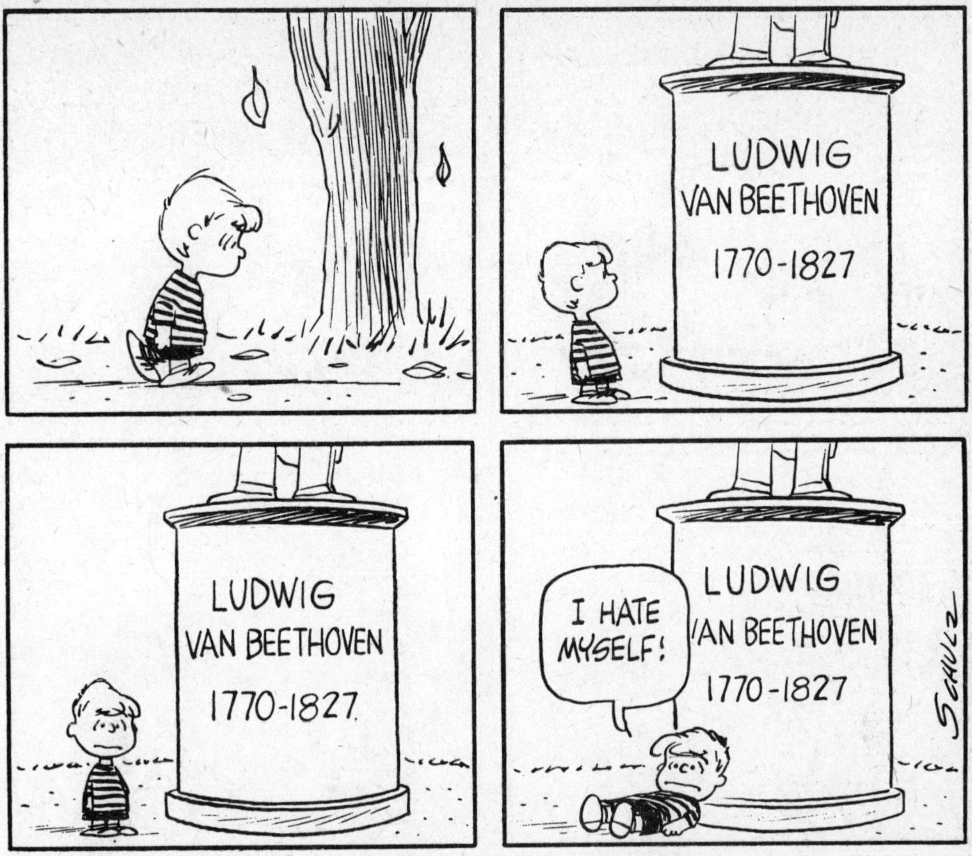
LUDWIG
VAN BEETHOVEN
1770-1827
LUDWIG
VAN BEETHOVEN
1770-1827
I HATE MYSELF!
LUDWIG
VAN BEETHOVEN
1770-1827
SCHULZ

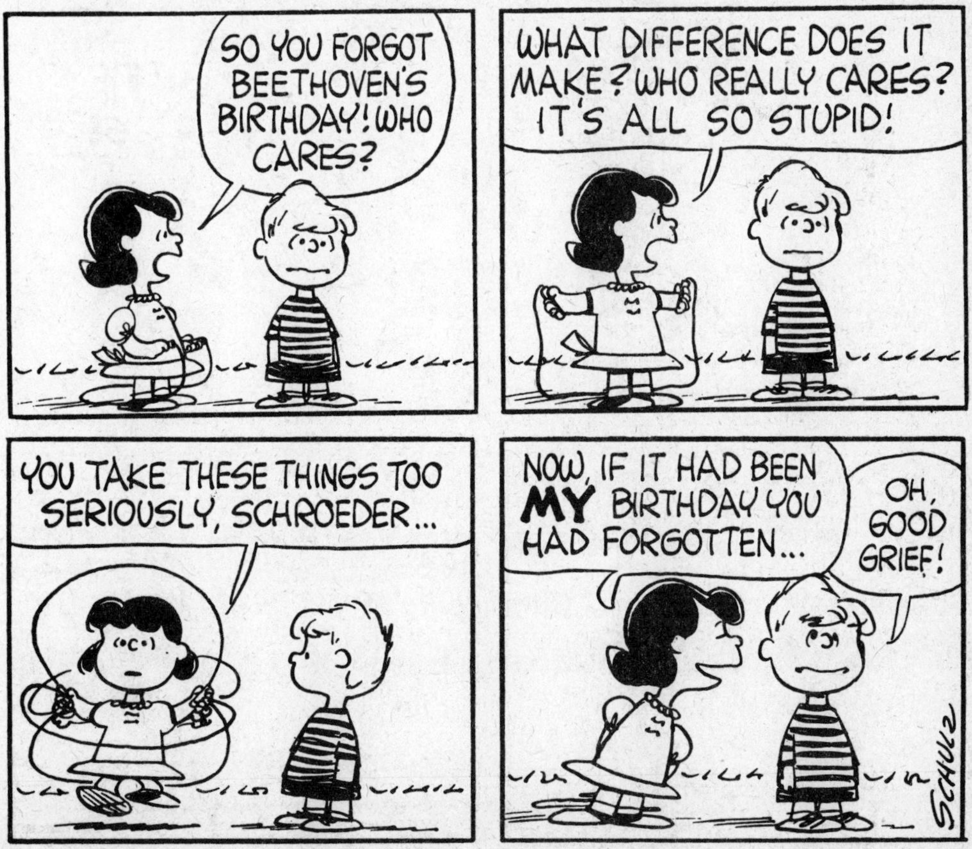
SO YOU FORGOT BEETHOVEN'S BIRTHDAY! WHO CARES?
WHAT DIFFERENCE DOES IT MAKE? WHO REALLY CARES? IT'S ALL SO STUPID!
YOU TAKE THESE THINGS TOO SERIOUSLY, SCHROEDER...
NOW, IF IT HAD BEEN **MY** BIRTHDAY YOU HAD FORGOTTEN...
OH, GOOD GRIEF!
SCHULZ

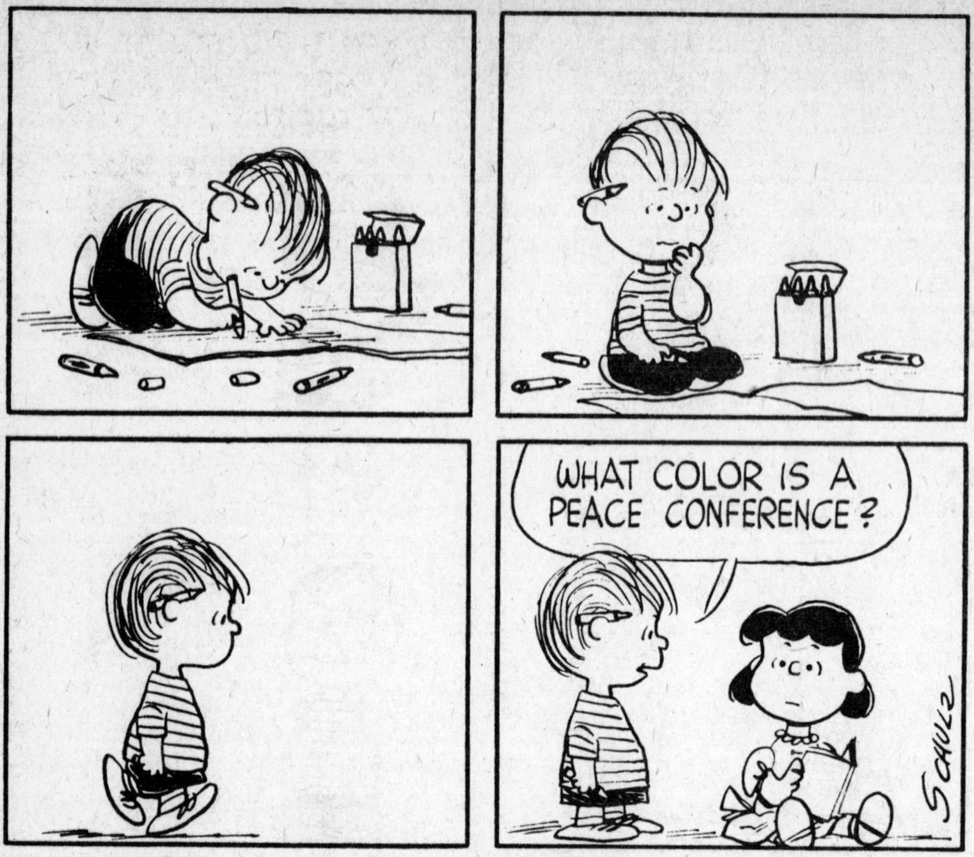
WHAT COLOR IS A PEACE CONFERENCE?
SCHULZ

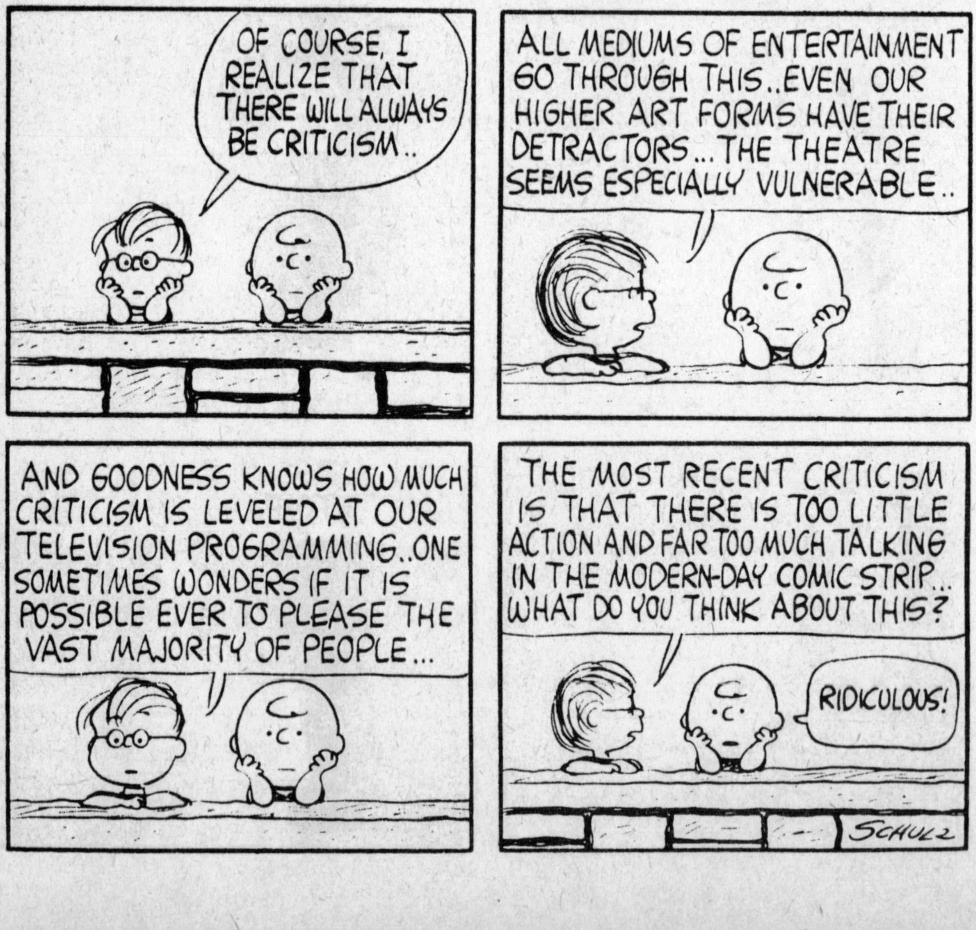
OF COURSE, I REALIZE THAT THERE WILL ALWAYS BE CRITICISM..
ALL MEDIUMS OF ENTERTAINMENT GO THROUGH THIS..EVEN OUR HIGHER ART FORMS HAVE THEIR DETRACTORS...THE THEATRE SEEMS ESPECIALLY VULNERABLE..
AND GOODNESS KNOWS HOW MUCH CRITICISM IS LEVELED AT OUR TELEVISION PROGRAMMING..ONE SOMETIMES WONDERS IF IT IS POSSIBLE EVER TO PLEASE THE VAST MAJORITY OF PEOPLE...
THE MOST RECENT CRITICISM IS THAT THERE IS TOO LITTLE ACTION AND FAR TOO MUCH TALKING IN THE MODERN-DAY COMIC STRIP... WHAT DO YOU THINK ABOUT THIS?
RIDICULOUS!
SCHULZ

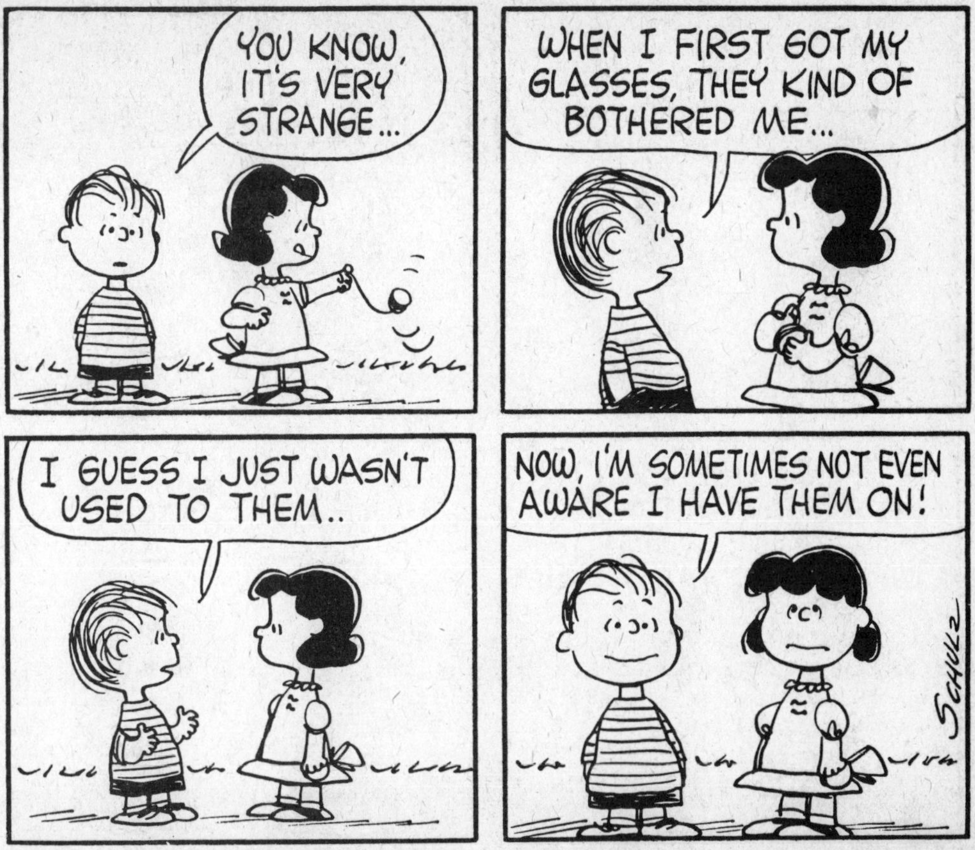
YOU KNOW, IT'S VERY STRANGE...
WHEN I FIRST GOT MY GLASSES, THEY KIND OF BOTHERED ME...
I GUESS I JUST WASN'T USED TO THEM..
NOW, I'M SOMETIMES NOT EVEN AWARE I HAVE THEM ON!
SCHULZ

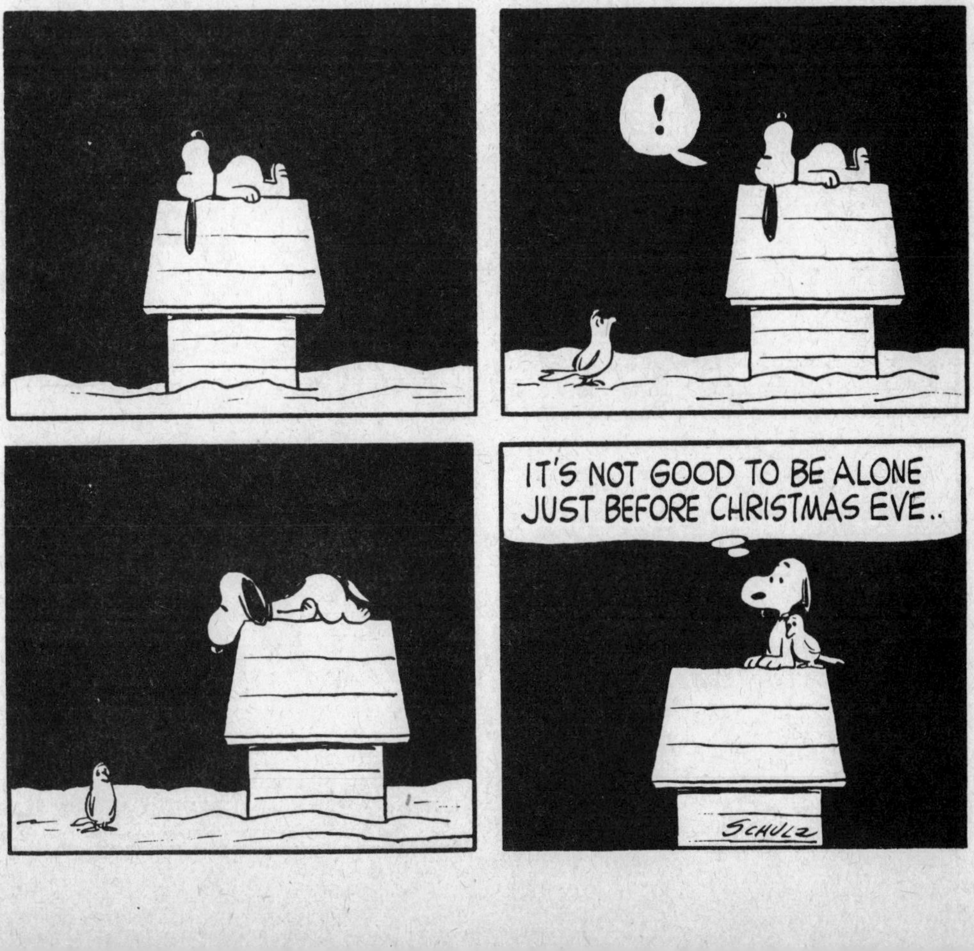
!
IT'S NOT GOOD TO BE ALONE JUST BEFORE CHRISTMAS EVE..
SCHULZ

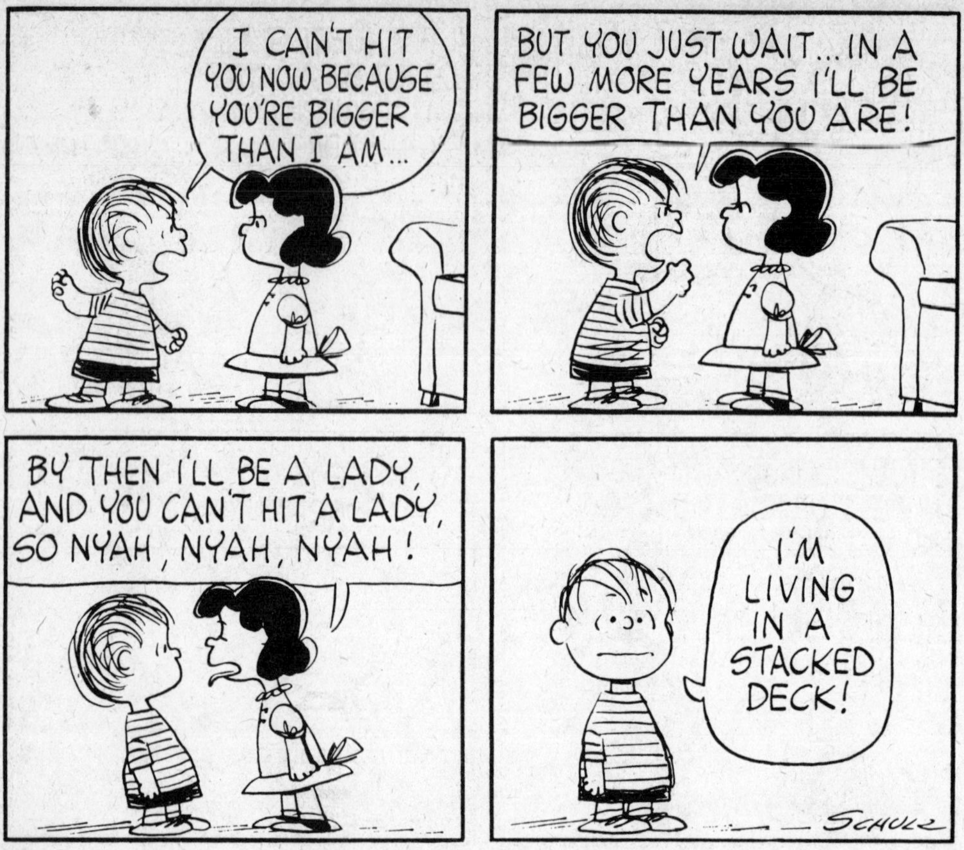
I CAN'T HIT YOU NOW BECAUSE YOU'RE BIGGER THAN I AM...
BUT YOU JUST WAIT... IN A FEW MORE YEARS I'LL BE BIGGER THAN YOU ARE!
BY THEN I'LL BE A LADY, AND YOU CAN'T HIT A LADY, SO NYAH, NYAH, NYAH!
I'M LIVING IN A STACKED DECK!
SCHULZ

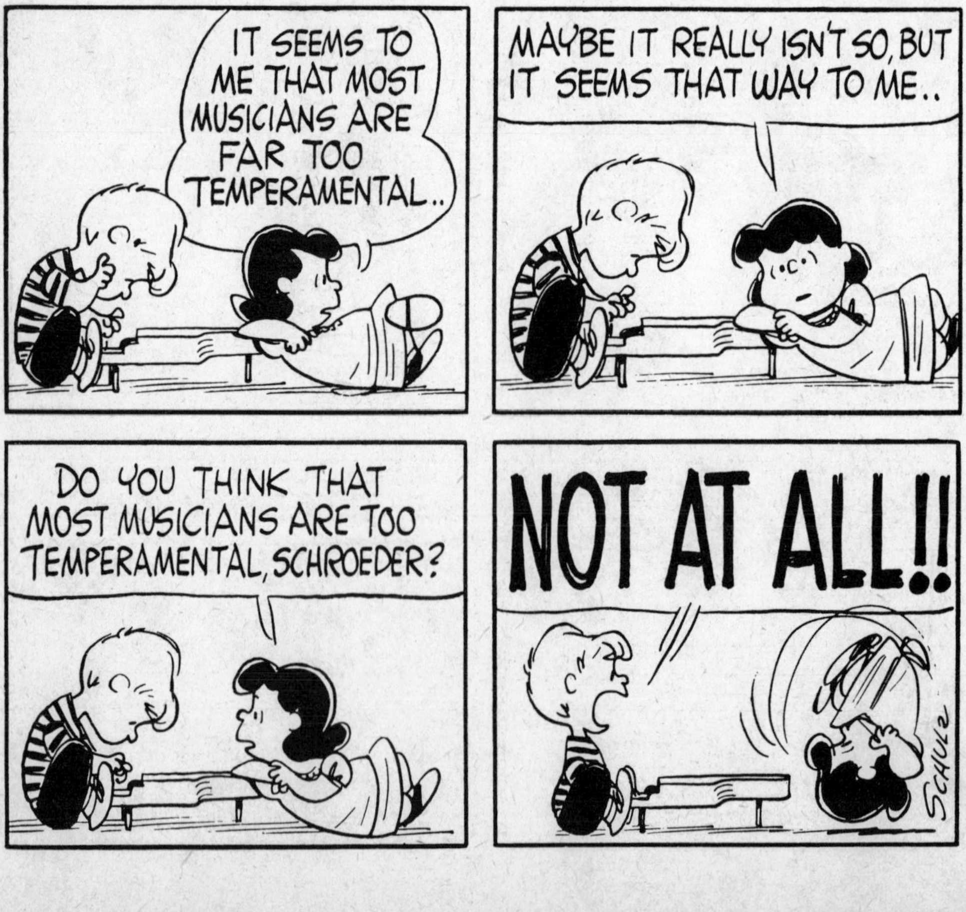
IT SEEMS TO ME THAT MOST MUSICIANS ARE FAR TOO TEMPERAMENTAL..
MAYBE IT REALLY ISN'T SO, BUT IT SEEMS THAT WAY TO ME..
DO YOU THINK THAT MOST MUSICIANS ARE TOO TEMPERAMENTAL, SCHROEDER?
NOT AT ALL!!
SCHULZ

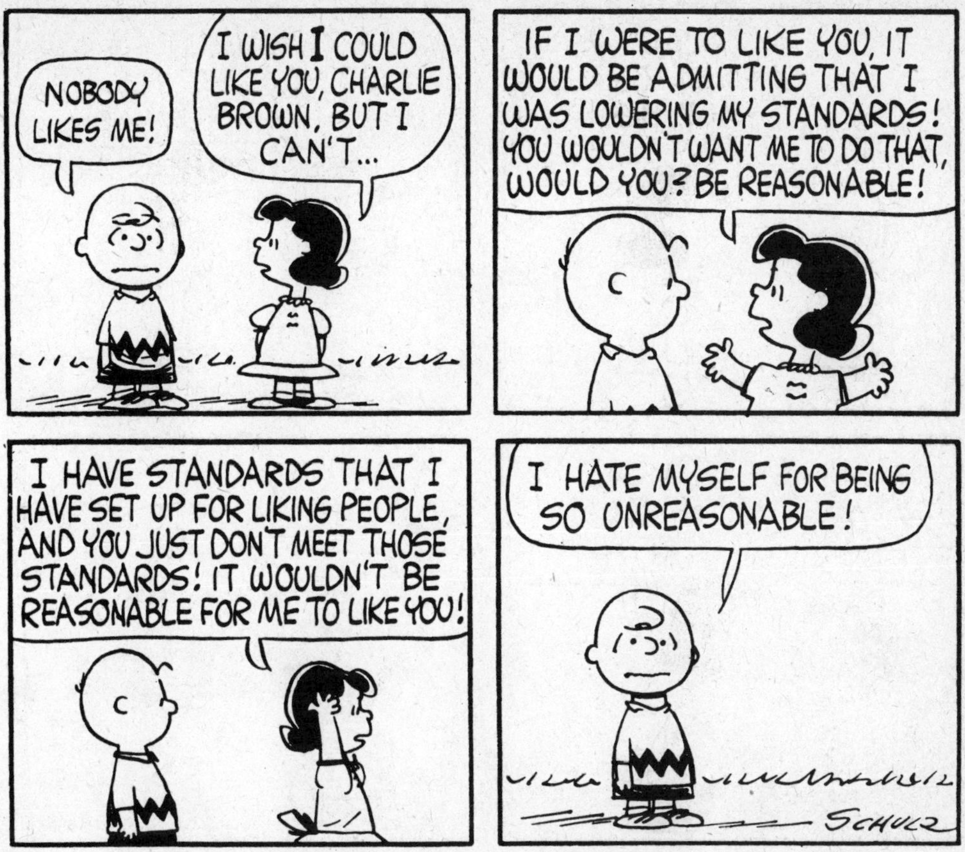
NOBODY LIKES ME!
I WISH I COULD LIKE YOU, CHARLIE BROWN, BUT I CAN'T...
IF I WERE TO LIKE YOU, IT WOULD BE ADMITTING THAT I WAS LOWERING MY STANDARDS! YOU WOULDN'T WANT ME TO DO THAT, WOULD YOU? BE REASONABLE!
I HAVE STANDARDS THAT I HAVE SET UP FOR LIKING PEOPLE, AND YOU JUST DON'T MEET THOSE STANDARDS! IT WOULDN'T BE REASONABLE FOR ME TO LIKE YOU!
I HATE MYSELF FOR BEING SO UNREASONABLE!
SCHULZ

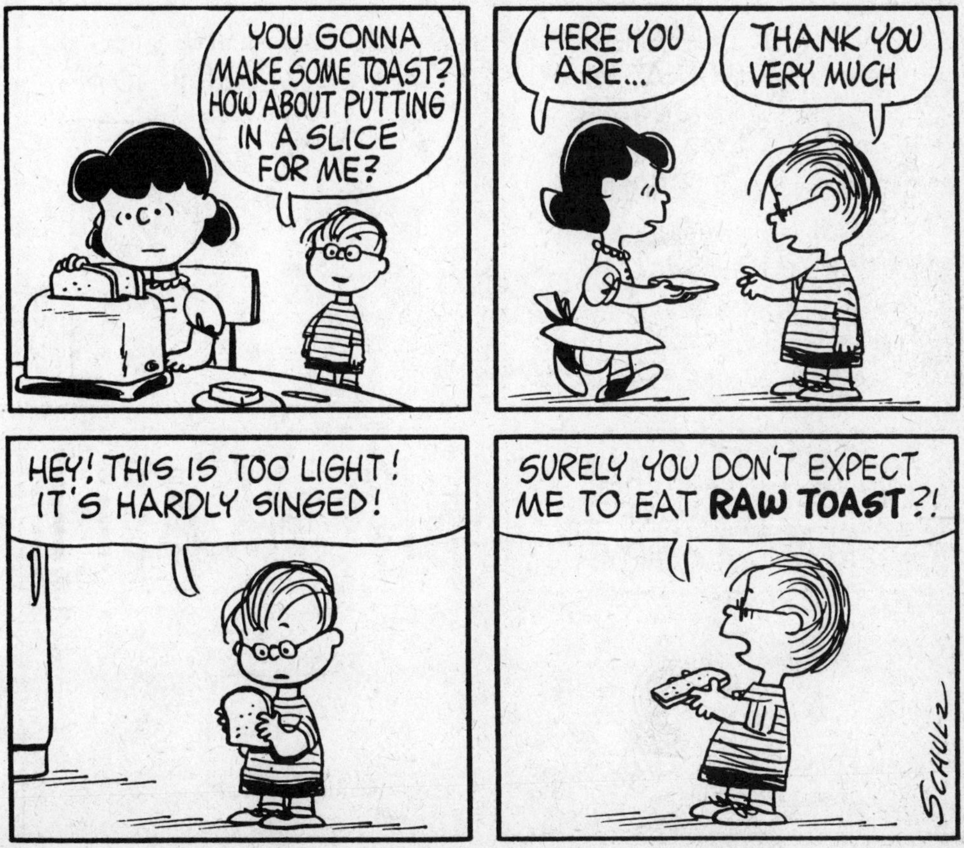
YOU GONNA MAKE SOME TOAST? HOW ABOUT PUTTING IN A SLICE FOR ME?
HERE YOU ARE...
THANK YOU VERY MUCH
HEY! THIS IS TOO LIGHT! IT'S HARDLY SINGED!
SURELY YOU DON'T EXPECT ME TO EAT **RAW TOAST**?!
SCHULZ

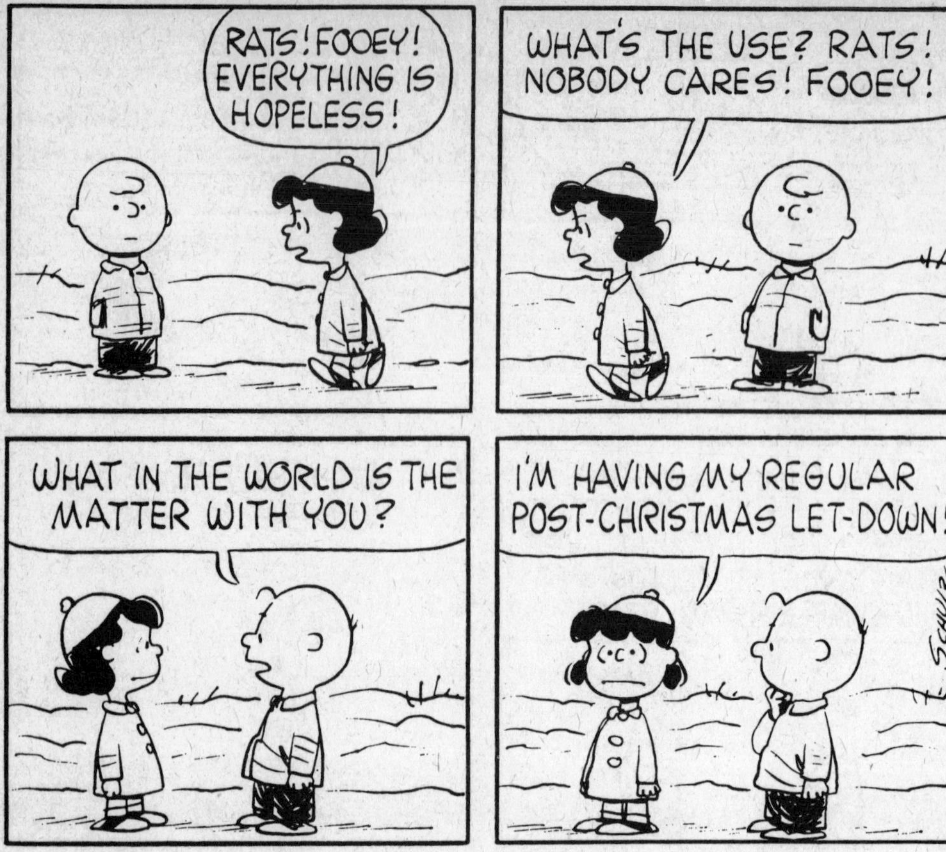
RATS! FOOEY! EVERYTHING IS HOPELESS!
WHAT'S THE USE? RATS! NOBODY CARES! FOOEY!
WHAT IN THE WORLD IS THE MATTER WITH YOU?
I'M HAVING MY REGULAR POST-CHRISTMAS LET-DOWN!
SCHULZ

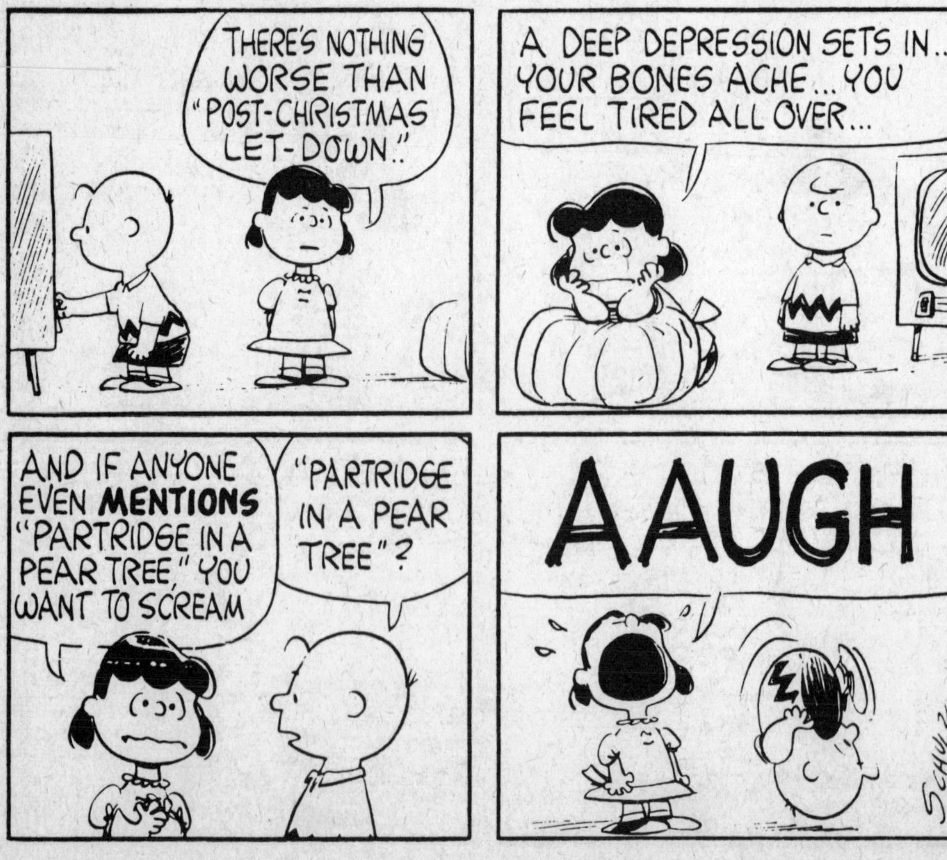
THERE'S NOTHING WORSE THAN "POST-CHRISTMAS LET-DOWN."
A DEEP DEPRESSION SETS IN.. YOUR BONES ACHE... YOU FEEL TIRED ALL OVER...
AND IF ANYONE EVEN **MENTIONS** "PARTRIDGE IN A PEAR TREE," YOU WANT TO SCREAM
"PARTRIDGE IN A PEAR TREE"?
AAUGH
SCHULZ

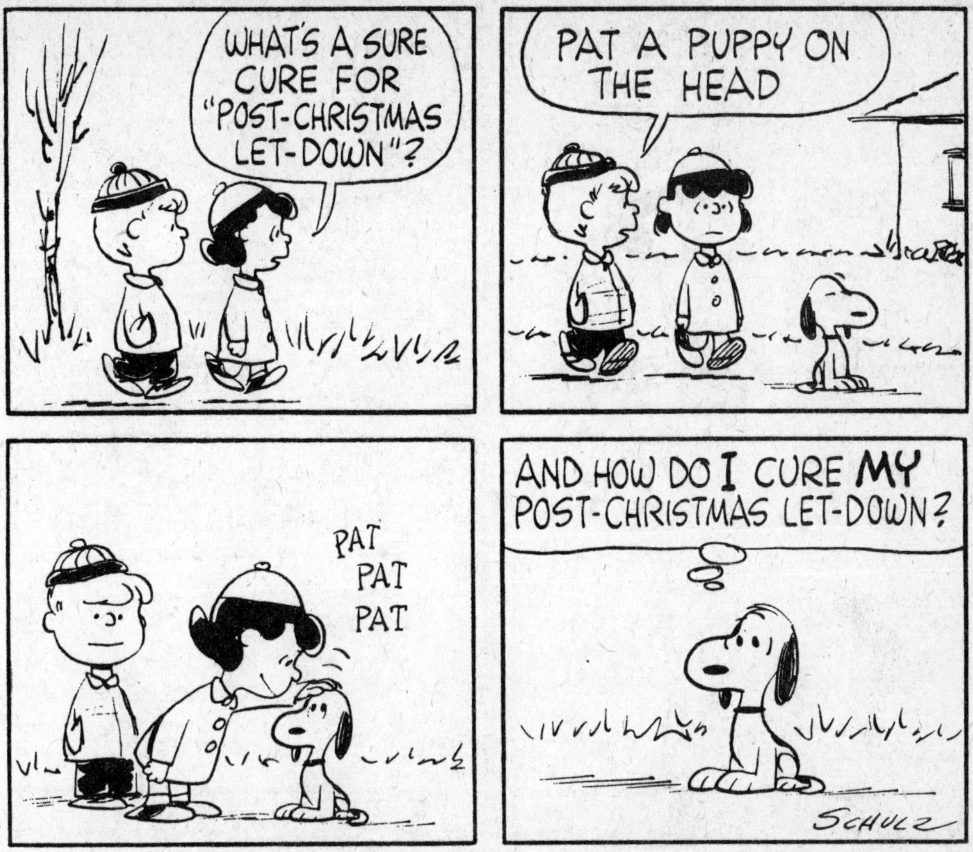
WHAT'S A SURE CURE FOR "POST-CHRISTMAS LET-DOWN"?
PAT A PUPPY ON THE HEAD
PAT PAT PAT
AND HOW DO I CURE MY POST-CHRISTMAS LET-DOWN?
SCHULZ

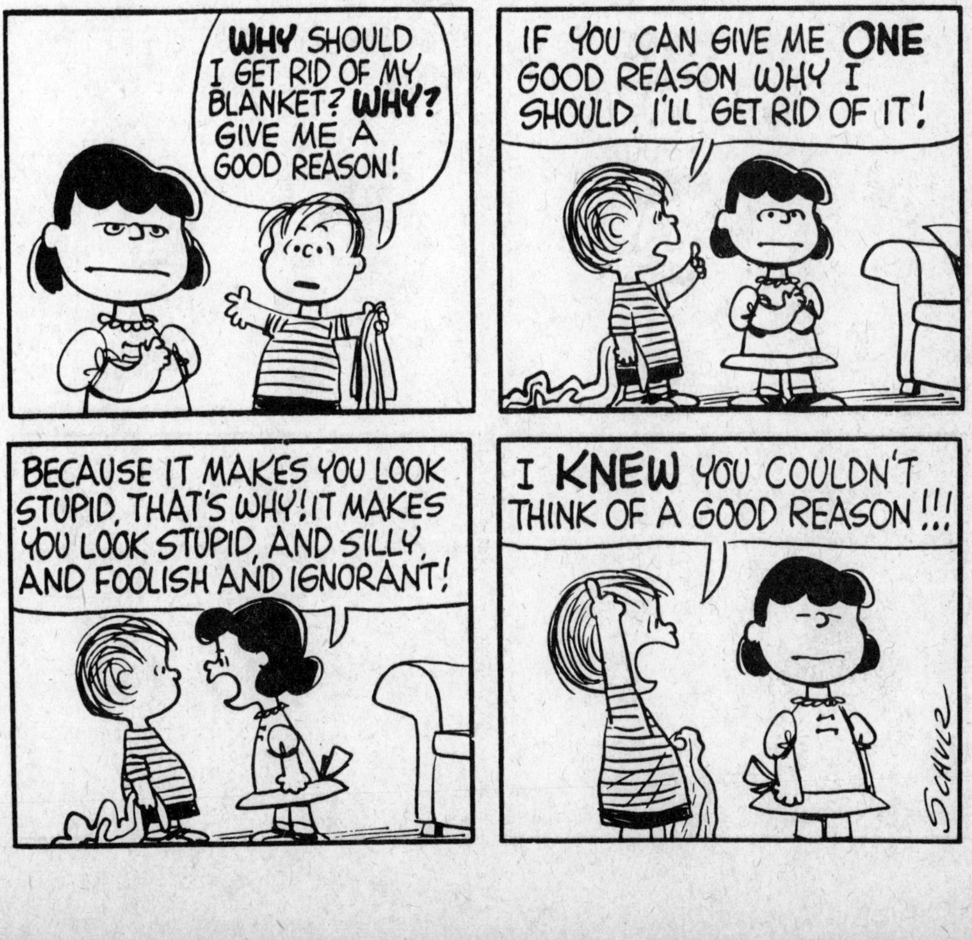
WHY SHOULD I GET RID OF MY BLANKET? WHY? GIVE ME A GOOD REASON!
IF YOU CAN GIVE ME ONE GOOD REASON WHY I SHOULD, I'LL GET RID OF IT!
BECAUSE IT MAKES YOU LOOK STUPID, THAT'S WHY! IT MAKES YOU LOOK STUPID, AND SILLY, AND FOOLISH AND IGNORANT!
I KNEW YOU COULDN'T THINK OF A GOOD REASON!!!
SCHULZ

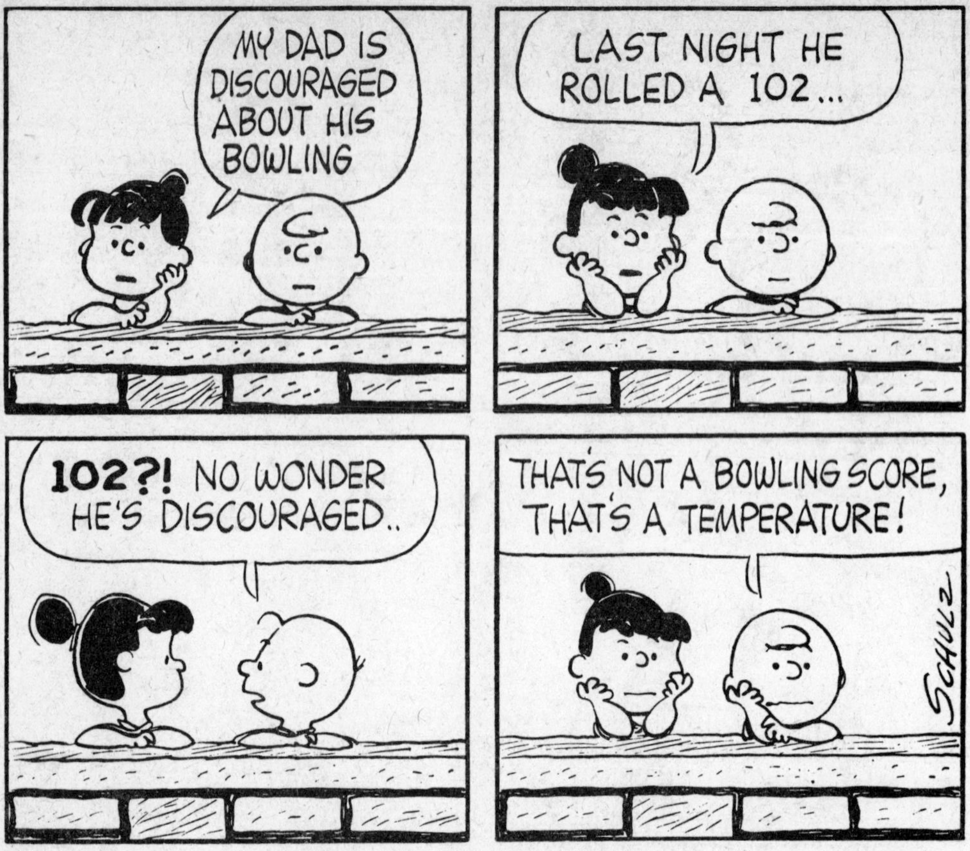
MY DAD IS DISCOURAGED ABOUT HIS BOWLING
LAST NIGHT HE ROLLED A 102...
102?! NO WONDER HE'S DISCOURAGED..
THAT'S NOT A BOWLING SCORE, THAT'S A TEMPERATURE!
SCHULZ

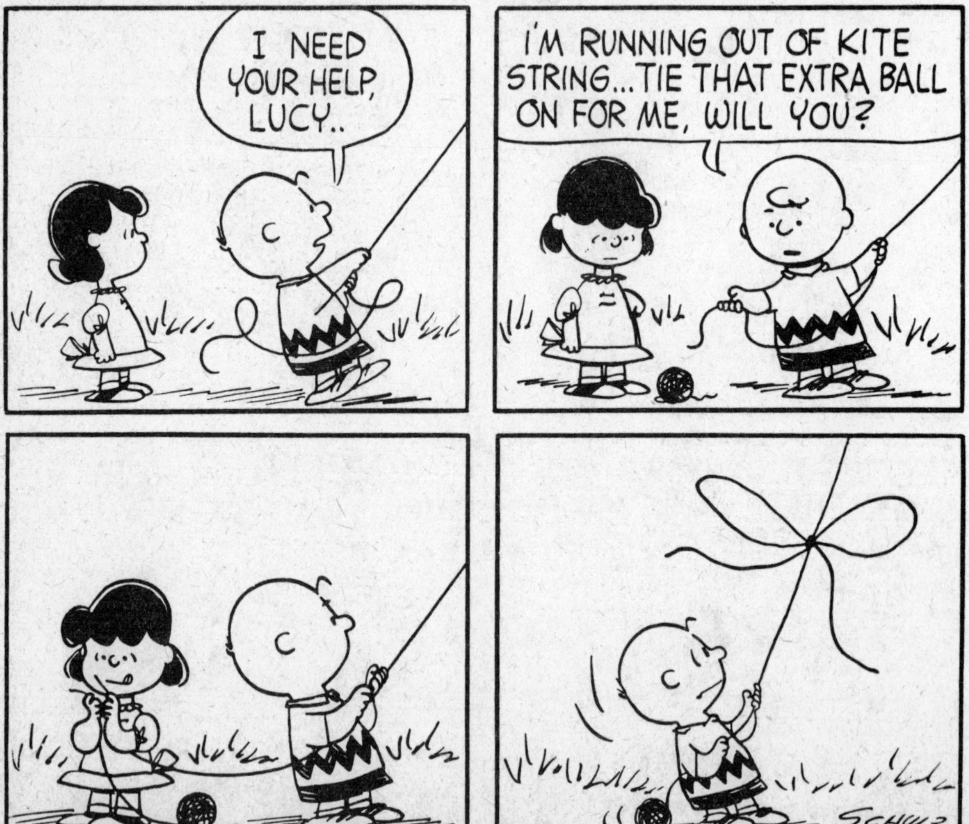
I NEED YOUR HELP, LUCY..
I'M RUNNING OUT OF KITE STRING...TIE THAT EXTRA BALL ON FOR ME, WILL YOU?
SCHULZ

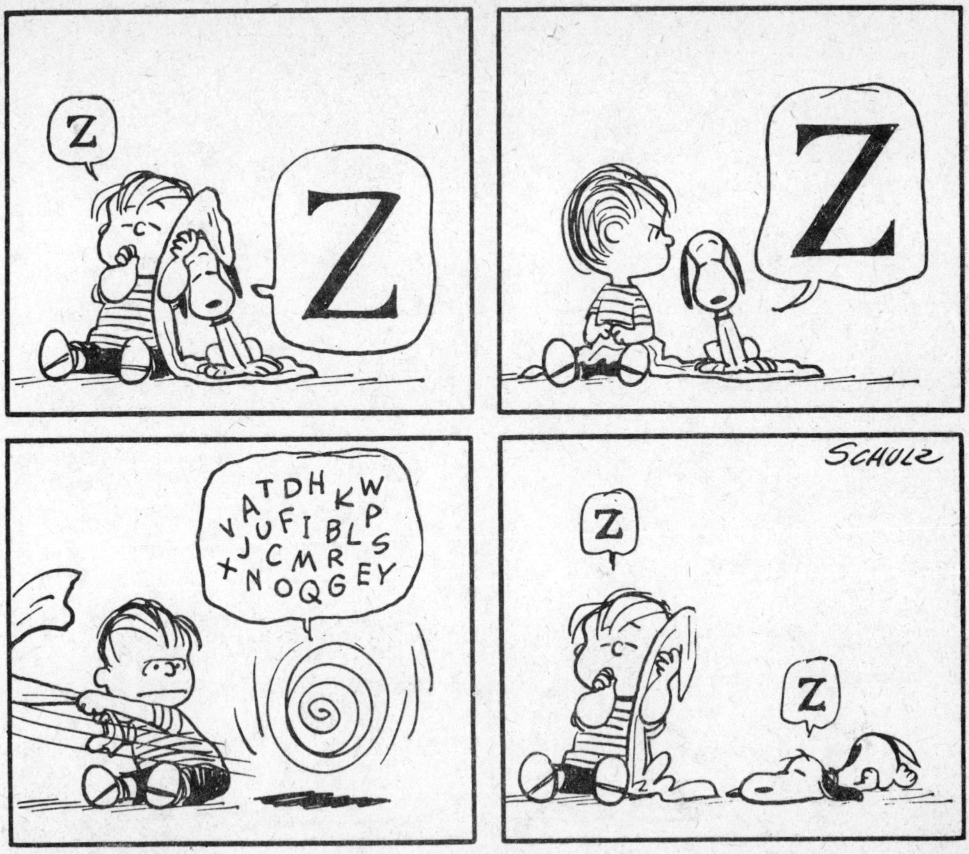
Z
Z
Z
ATDH KW
VUFIBLP
JCMRLS
XNOQGEY
SCHULZ
Z
Z

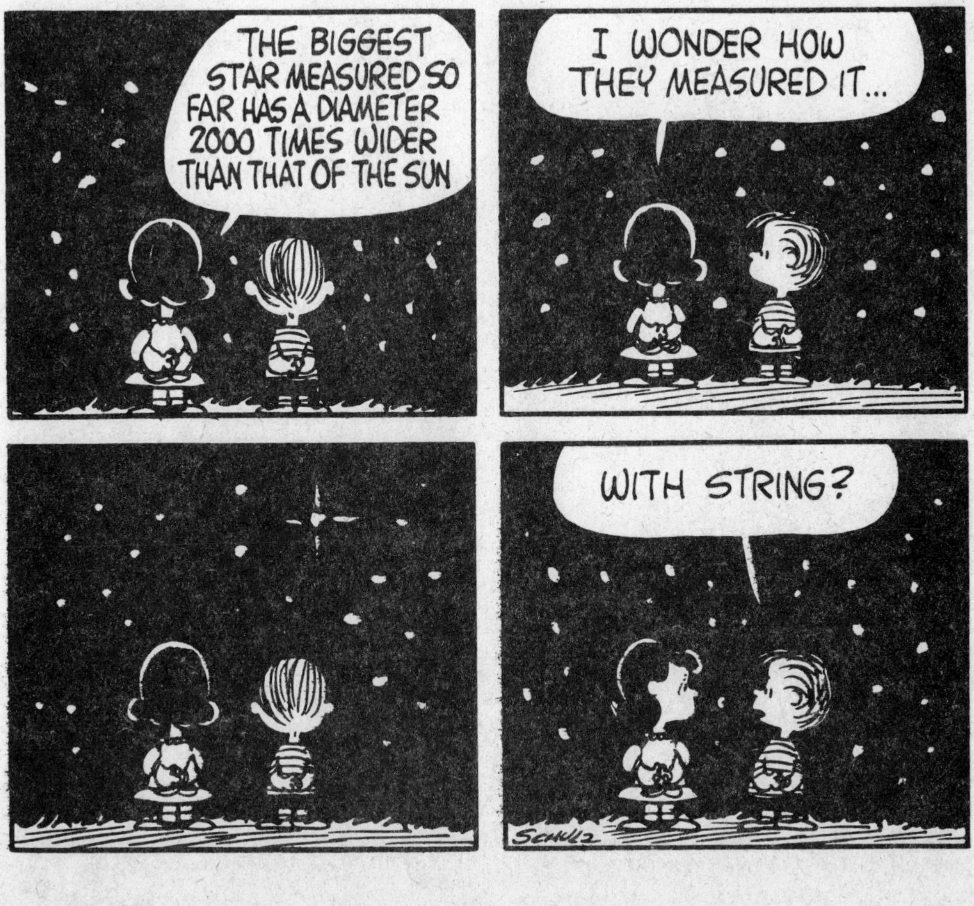
THE BIGGEST STAR MEASURED SO FAR HAS A DIAMETER 2000 TIMES WIDER THAN THAT OF THE SUN
I WONDER HOW THEY MEASURED IT...
WITH STRING?
SCHULZ

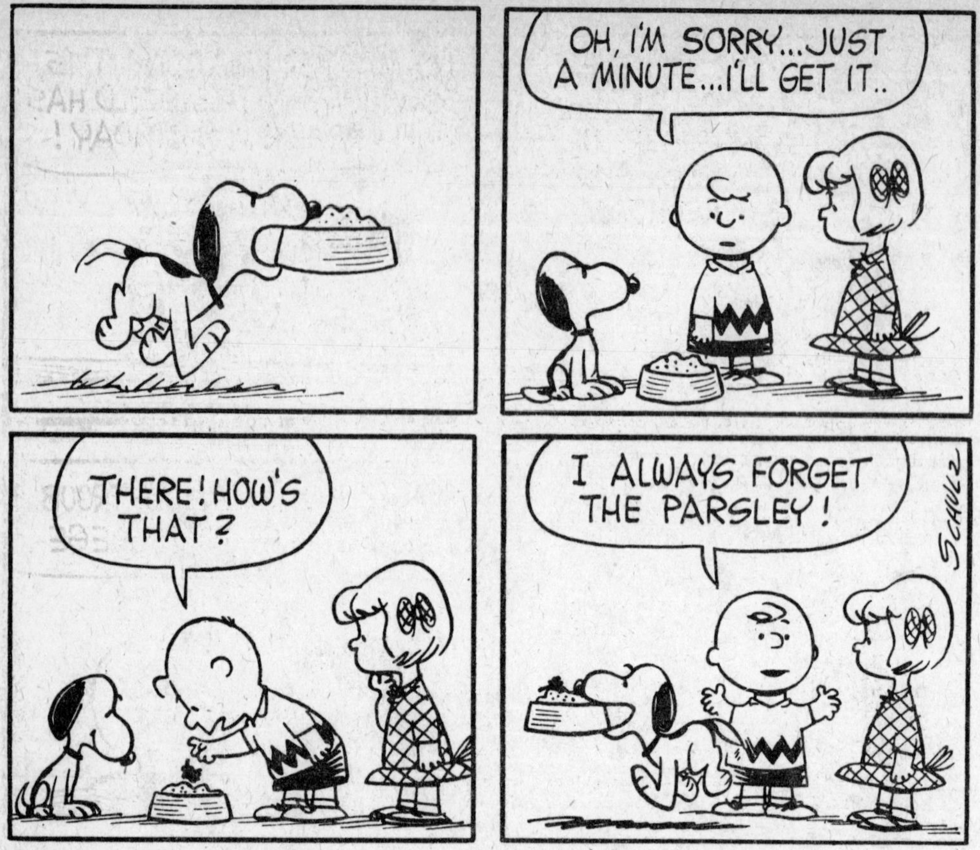
OH, I'M SORRY...JUST A MINUTE...I'LL GET IT..
THERE! HOW'S THAT?
I ALWAYS FORGET THE PARSLEY!
SCHULZ

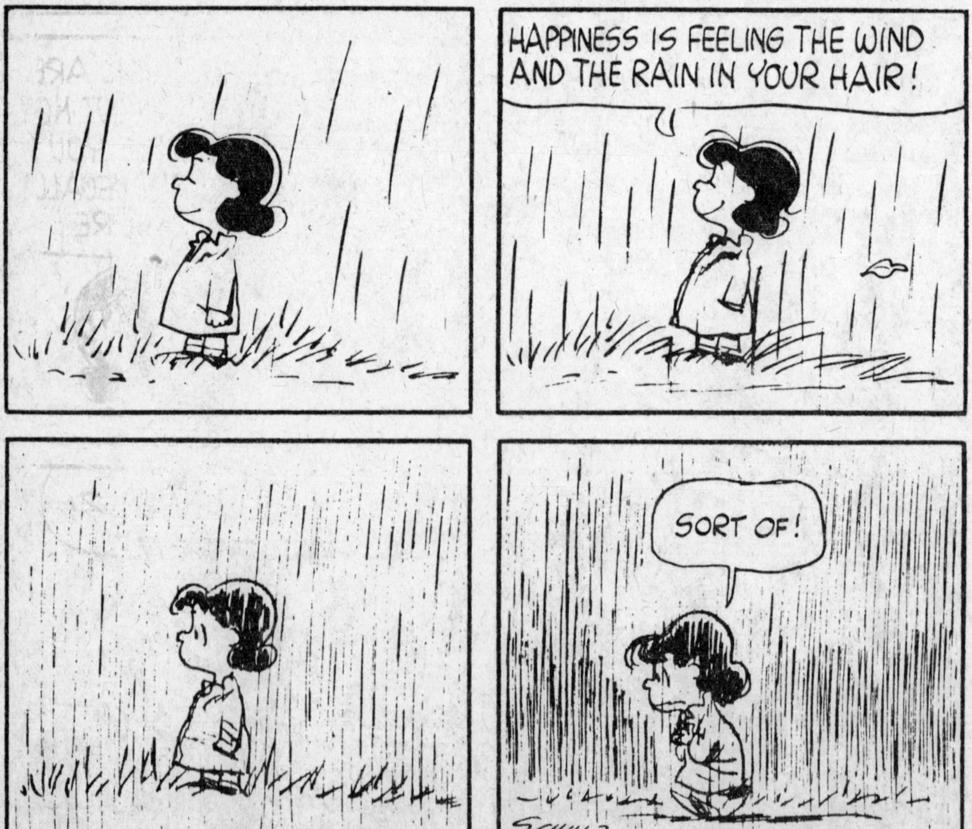
HAPPINESS IS FEELING THE WIND AND THE RAIN IN YOUR HAIR!
SORT OF!
SCHULZ

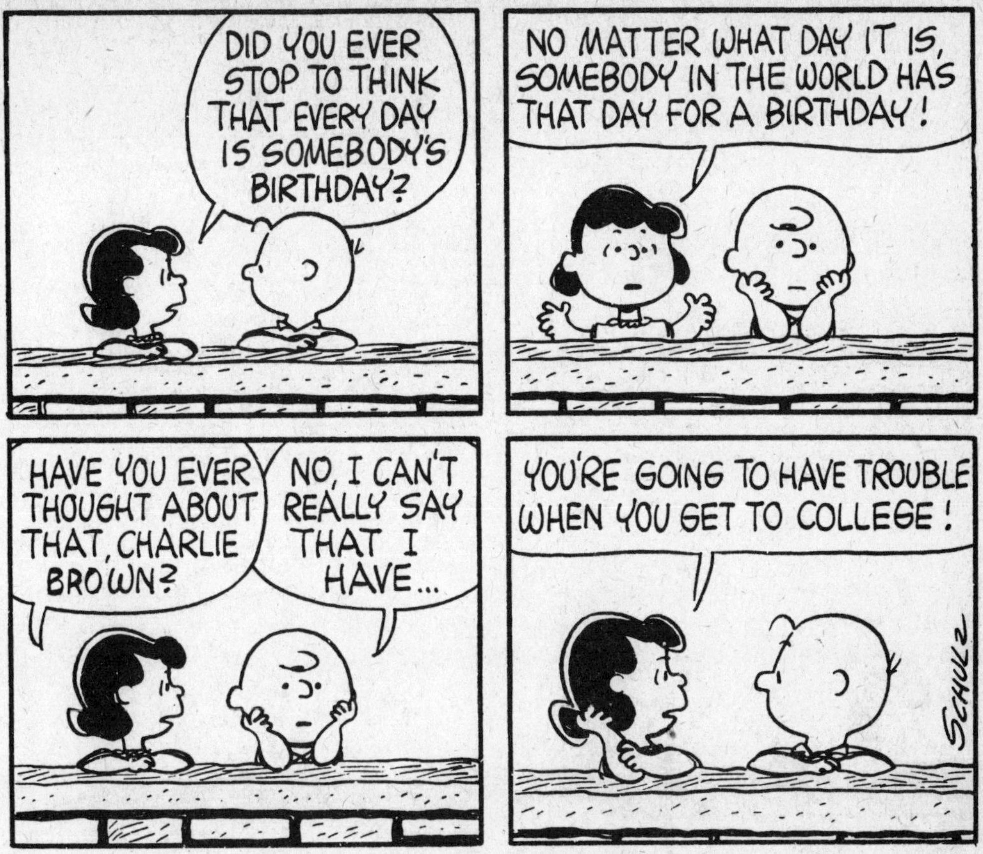
DID YOU EVER STOP TO THINK THAT EVERY DAY IS SOMEBODY'S BIRTHDAY?
NO MATTER WHAT DAY IT IS, SOMEBODY IN THE WORLD HAS THAT DAY FOR A BIRTHDAY!
HAVE YOU EVER THOUGHT ABOUT THAT, CHARLIE BROWN?
NO, I CAN'T REALLY SAY THAT I HAVE...
YOU'RE GOING TO HAVE TROUBLE WHEN YOU GET TO COLLEGE!
SCHULZ

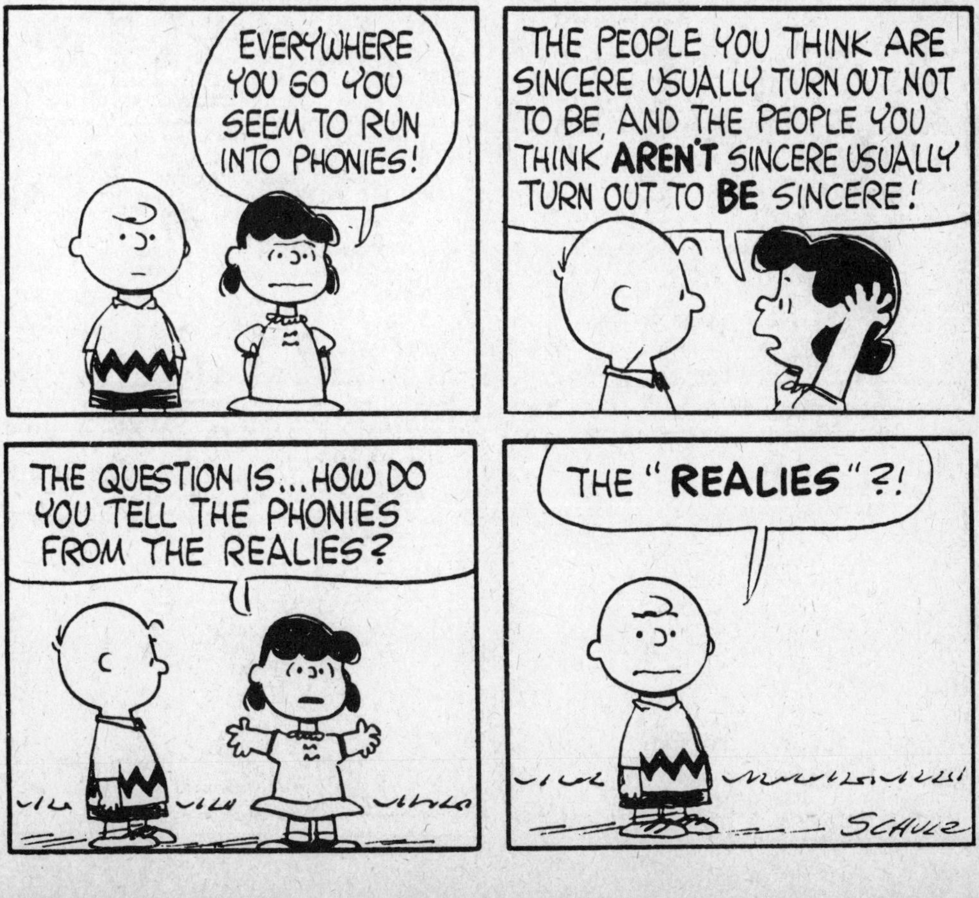
EVERYWHERE YOU GO YOU SEEM TO RUN INTO PHONIES!
THE PEOPLE YOU THINK ARE SINCERE USUALLY TURN OUT NOT TO BE, AND THE PEOPLE YOU THINK **AREN'T** SINCERE USUALLY TURN OUT TO **BE** SINCERE!
THE QUESTION IS...HOW DO YOU TELL THE PHONIES FROM THE REALIES?
THE "**REALIES**"?!
SCHULZ

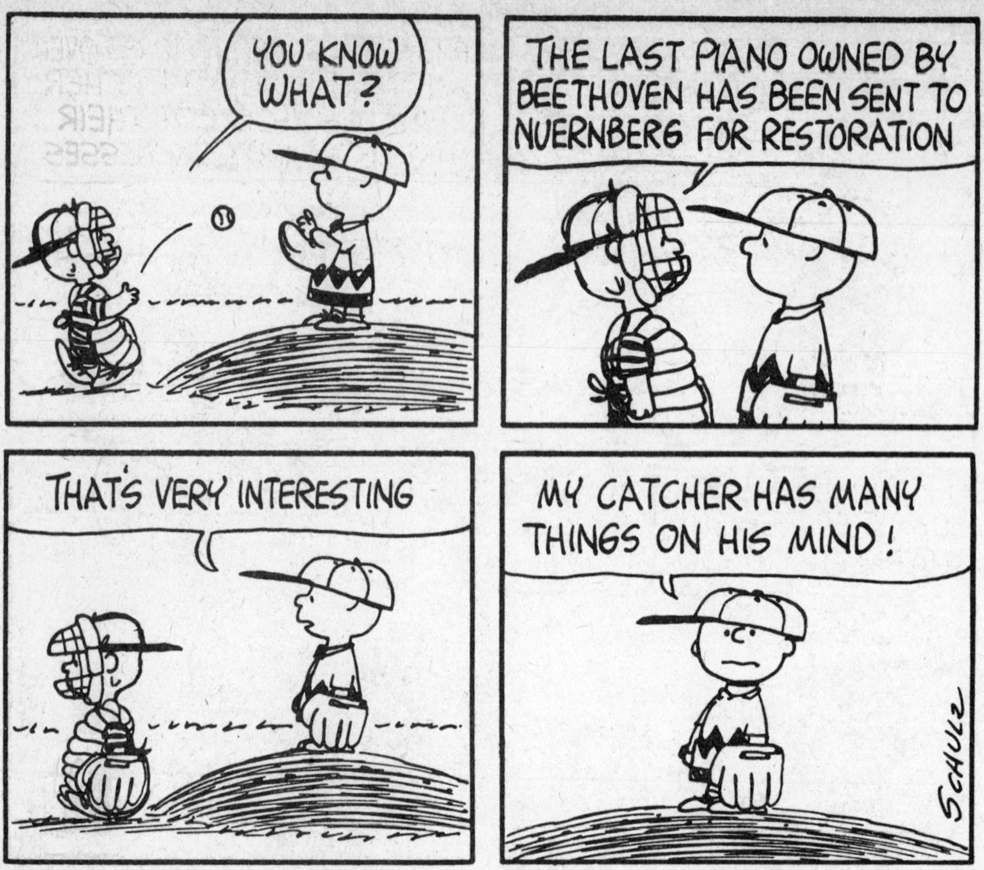
YOU KNOW WHAT?
THE LAST PIANO OWNED BY BEETHOVEN HAS BEEN SENT TO NUERNBERG FOR RESTORATION
THAT'S VERY INTERESTING
MY CATCHER HAS MANY THINGS ON HIS MIND!
SCHULZ

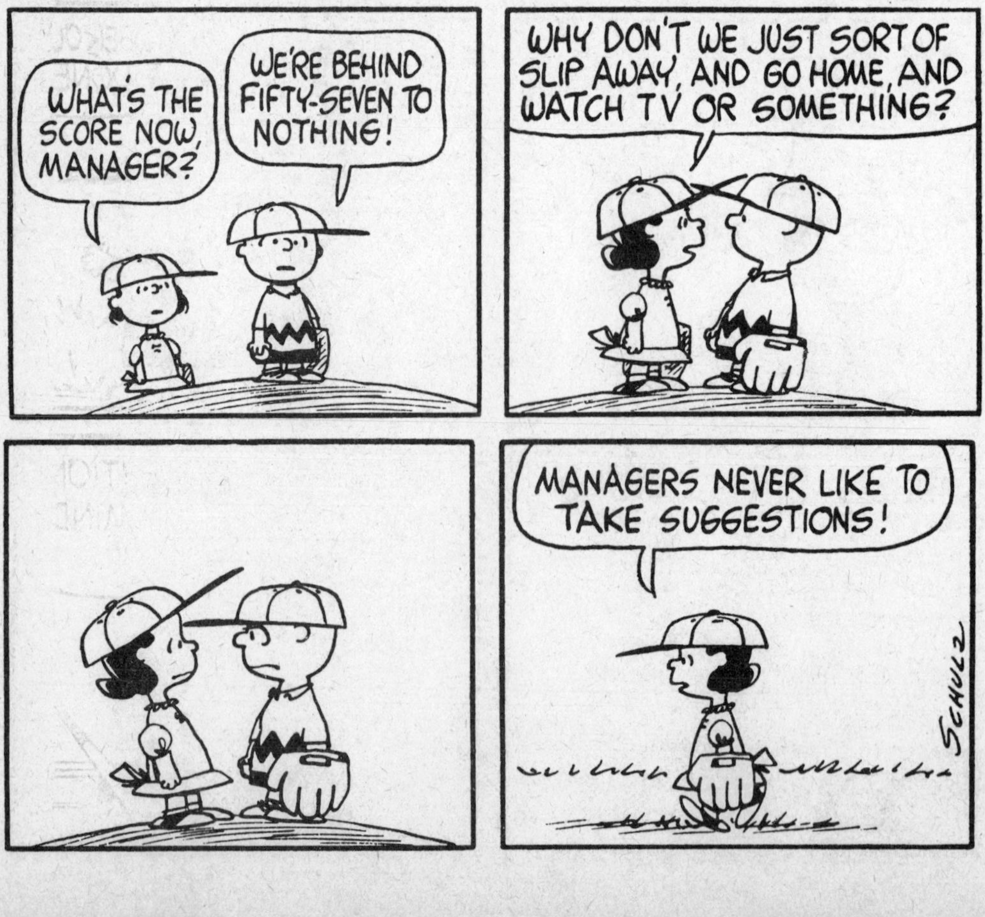
WHAT'S THE SCORE NOW, MANAGER?
WE'RE BEHIND FIFTY-SEVEN TO NOTHING!
WHY DON'T WE JUST SORT OF SLIP AWAY, AND GO HOME, AND WATCH TV OR SOMETHING?
MANAGERS NEVER LIKE TO TAKE SUGGESTIONS!
SCHULZ

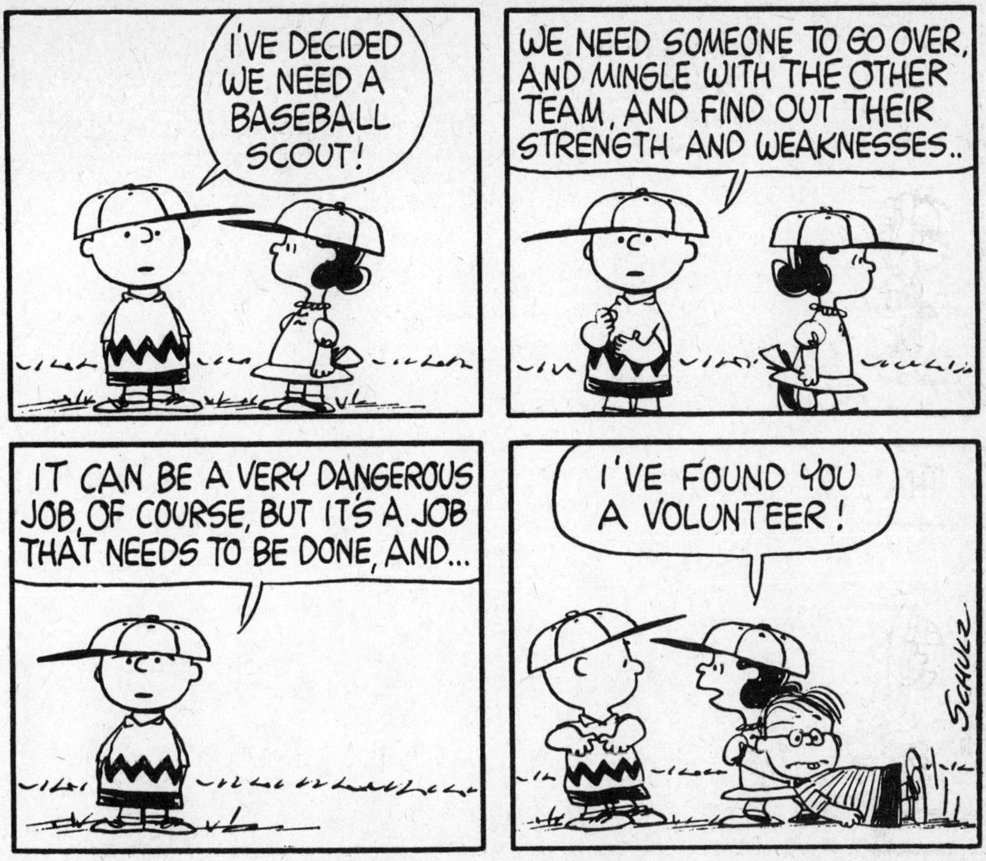
I'VE DECIDED WE NEED A BASEBALL SCOUT!
WE NEED SOMEONE TO GO OVER, AND MINGLE WITH THE OTHER TEAM, AND FIND OUT THEIR STRENGTH AND WEAKNESSES..
IT CAN BE A VERY DANGEROUS JOB, OF COURSE, BUT IT'S A JOB THAT NEEDS TO BE DONE, AND...
I'VE FOUND YOU A VOLUNTEER!
SCHULZ

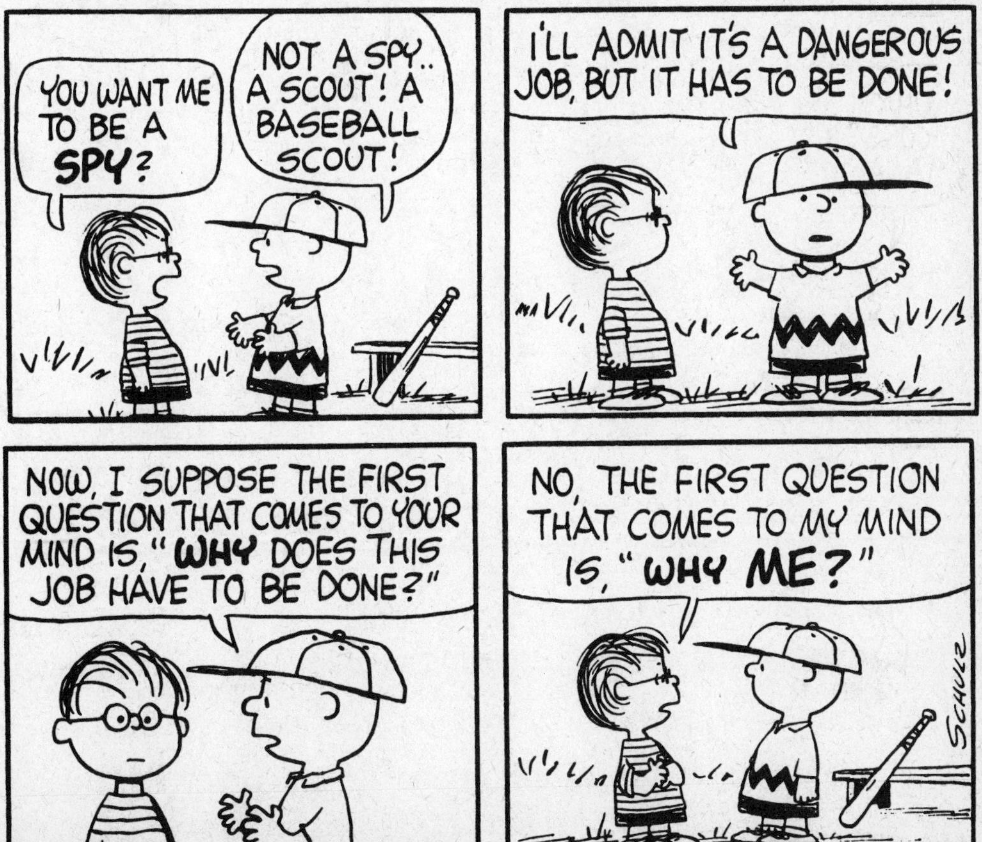
YOU WANT ME TO BE A **SPY**?
NOT A SPY.. A SCOUT! A BASEBALL SCOUT!
I'LL ADMIT IT'S A DANGEROUS JOB, BUT IT HAS TO BE DONE!
NOW, I SUPPOSE THE FIRST QUESTION THAT COMES TO YOUR MIND IS, "**WHY** DOES THIS JOB HAVE TO BE DONE?"
NO, THE FIRST QUESTION THAT COMES TO MY MIND IS, "**WHY ME?**"
SCHULZ

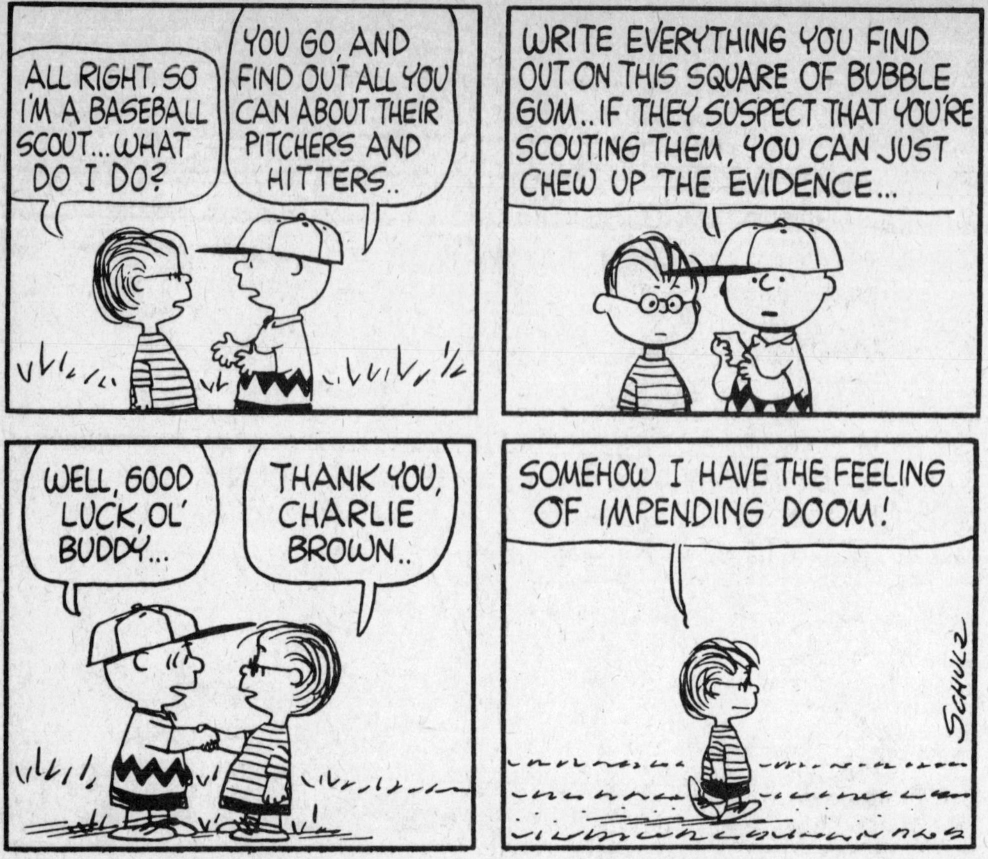
ALL RIGHT, SO I'M A BASEBALL SCOUT...WHAT DO I DO?
YOU GO, AND FIND OUT ALL YOU CAN ABOUT THEIR PITCHERS AND HITTERS..
WRITE EVERYTHING YOU FIND OUT ON THIS SQUARE OF BUBBLE GUM..IF THEY SUSPECT THAT YOU'RE SCOUTING THEM, YOU CAN JUST CHEW UP THE EVIDENCE...
WELL, GOOD LUCK, OL' BUDDY...
THANK YOU, CHARLIE BROWN..
SOMEHOW I HAVE THE FEELING OF IMPENDING DOOM!
SCHULZ

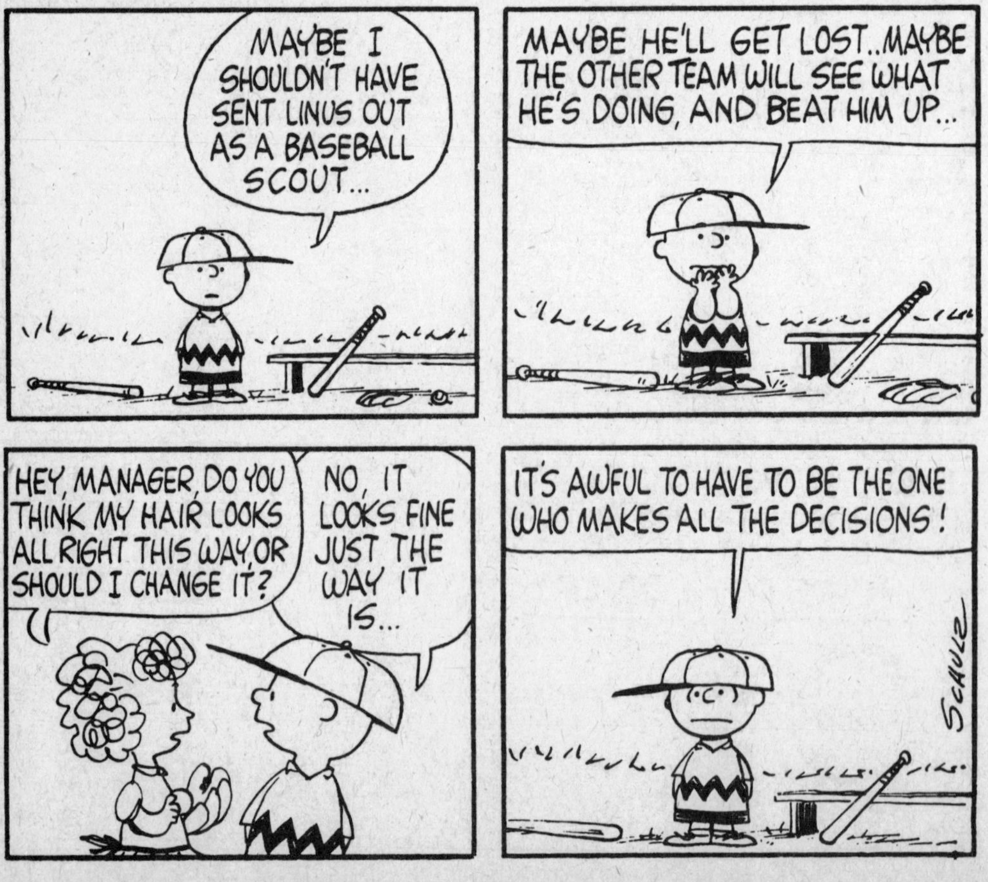
MAYBE I SHOULDN'T HAVE SENT LINUS OUT AS A BASEBALL SCOUT...
MAYBE HE'LL GET LOST..MAYBE THE OTHER TEAM WILL SEE WHAT HE'S DOING, AND BEAT HIM UP...
HEY, MANAGER, DO YOU THINK MY HAIR LOOKS ALL RIGHT THIS WAY, OR SHOULD I CHANGE IT?
NO, IT LOOKS FINE JUST THE WAY IT IS...
IT'S AWFUL TO HAVE TO BE THE ONE WHO MAKES ALL THE DECISIONS!
SCHULZ

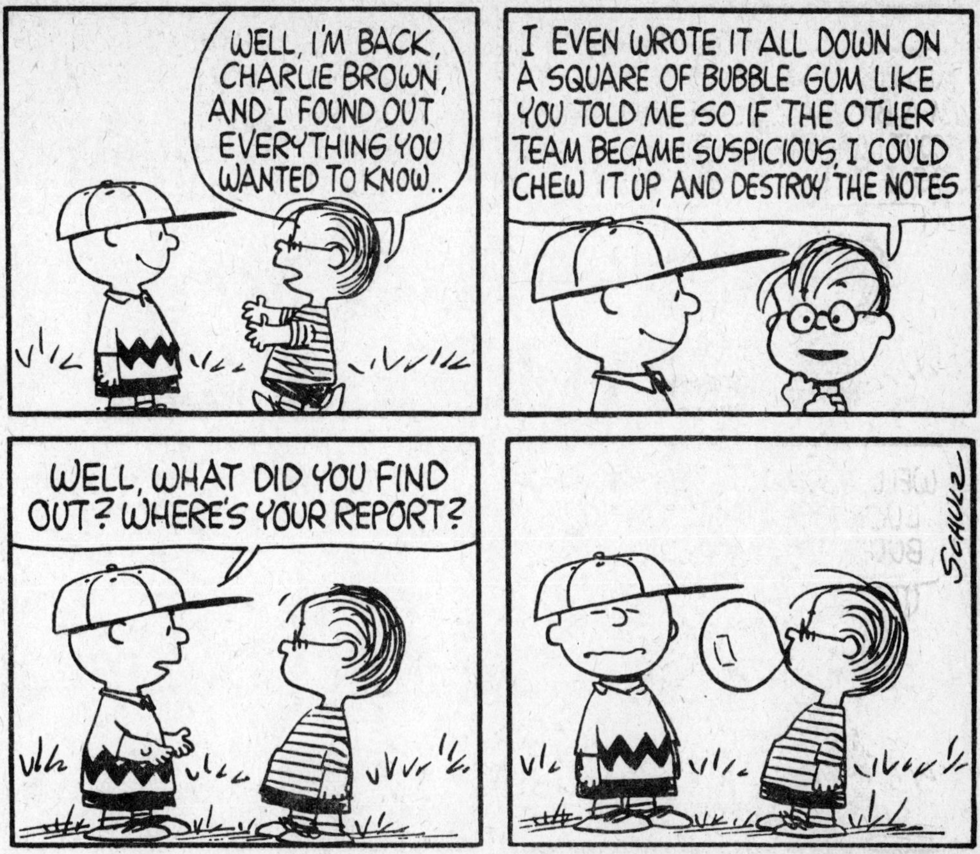
WELL, I'M BACK, CHARLIE BROWN, AND I FOUND OUT EVERYTHING YOU WANTED TO KNOW..
I EVEN WROTE IT ALL DOWN ON A SQUARE OF BUBBLE GUM LIKE YOU TOLD ME SO IF THE OTHER TEAM BECAME SUSPICIOUS, I COULD CHEW IT UP, AND DESTROY THE NOTES
WELL, WHAT DID YOU FIND OUT? WHERE'S YOUR REPORT?
SCHULZ

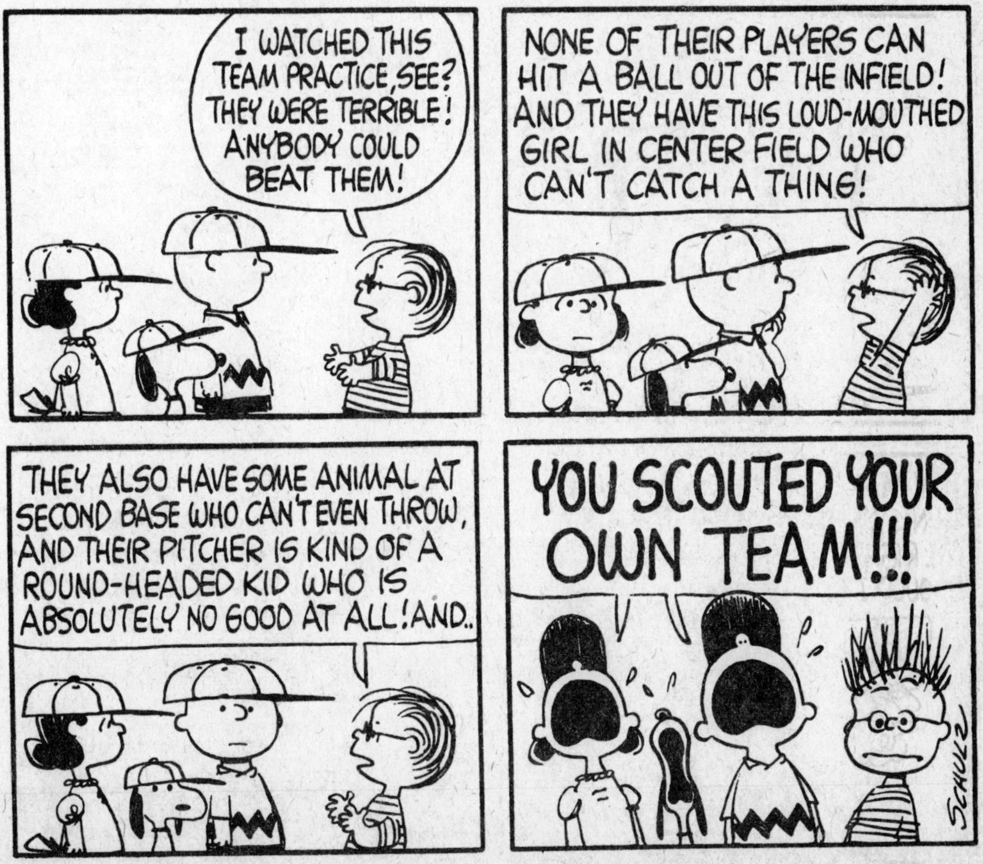
I WATCHED THIS TEAM PRACTICE, SEE? THEY WERE TERRIBLE! ANYBODY COULD BEAT THEM!
NONE OF THEIR PLAYERS CAN HIT A BALL OUT OF THE INFIELD! AND THEY HAVE THIS LOUD-MOUTHED GIRL IN CENTER FIELD WHO CAN'T CATCH A THING!
THEY ALSO HAVE SOME ANIMAL AT SECOND BASE WHO CAN'T EVEN THROW, AND THEIR PITCHER IS KIND OF A ROUND-HEADED KID WHO IS ABSOLUTELY NO GOOD AT ALL! AND..
YOU SCOUTED YOUR OWN TEAM!!!
SCHULZ

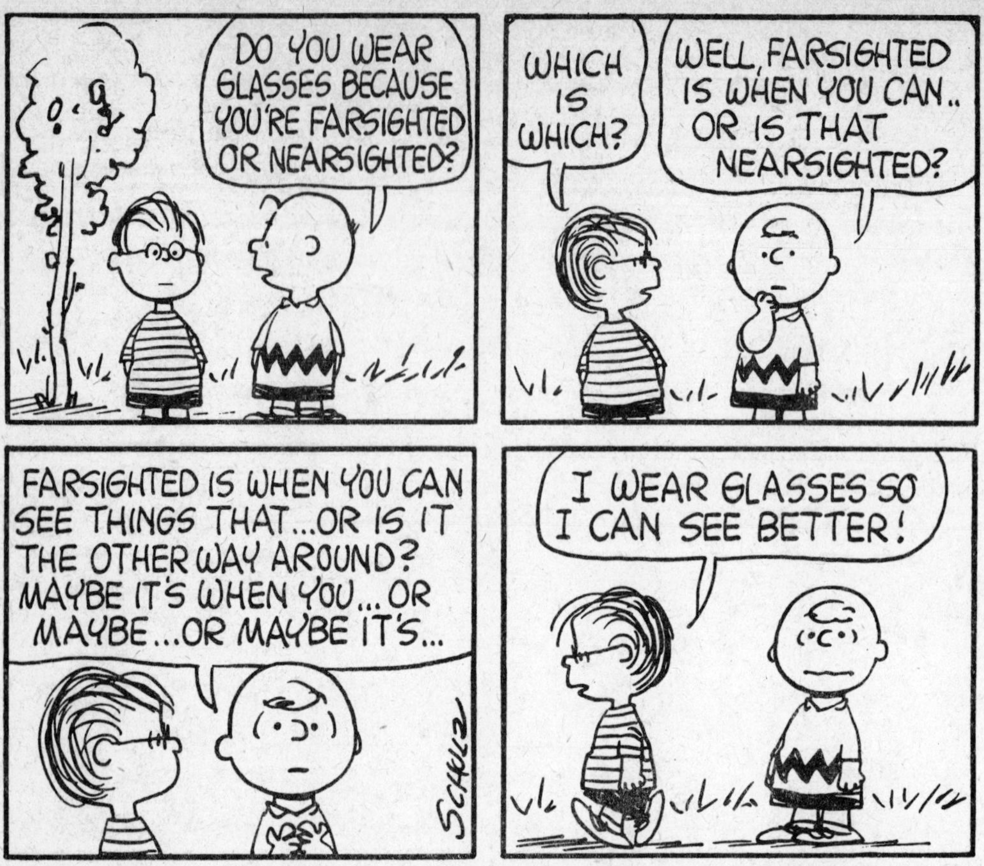
DO YOU WEAR GLASSES BECAUSE YOU'RE FARSIGHTED OR NEARSIGHTED?
WHICH IS WHICH?
WELL, FARSIGHTED IS WHEN YOU CAN.. OR IS THAT NEARSIGHTED?
FARSIGHTED IS WHEN YOU CAN SEE THINGS THAT...OR IS IT THE OTHER WAY AROUND? MAYBE IT'S WHEN YOU... OR MAYBE...OR MAYBE IT'S...
SCHULZ
I WEAR GLASSES SO I CAN SEE BETTER!

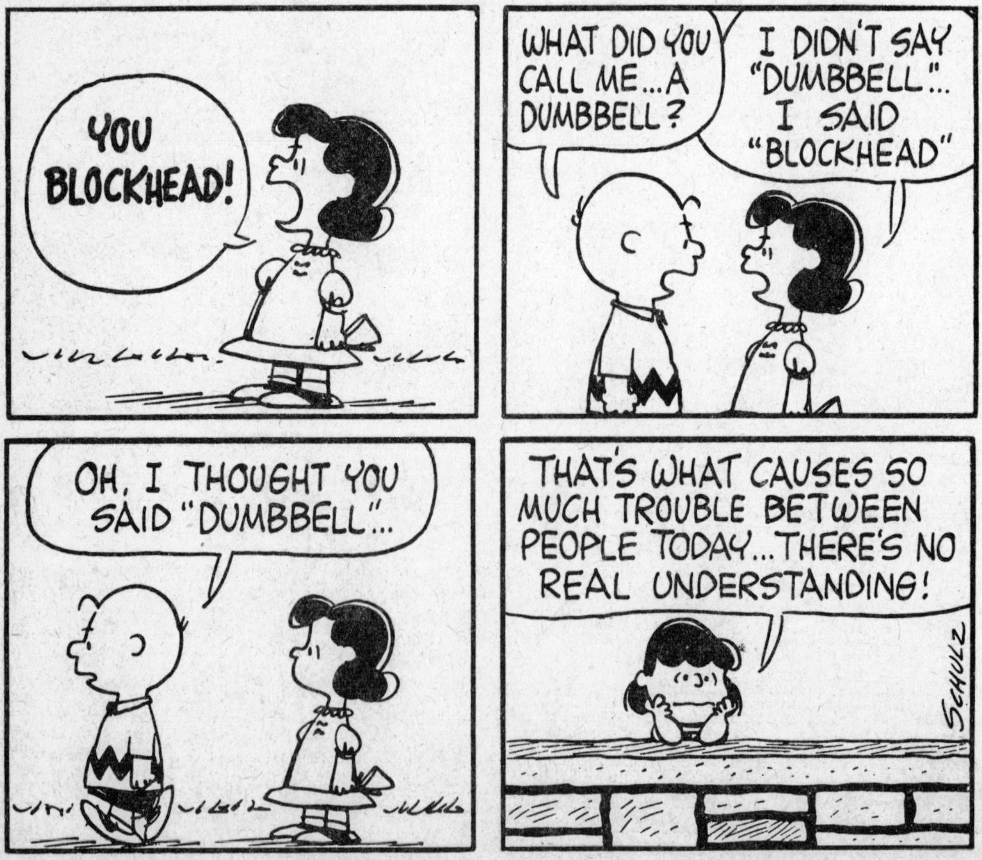
YOU BLOCKHEAD!
WHAT DID YOU CALL ME...A DUMBBELL?
I DIDN'T SAY "DUMBBELL"... I SAID "BLOCKHEAD"
OH, I THOUGHT YOU SAID "DUMBBELL"...
THAT'S WHAT CAUSES SO MUCH TROUBLE BETWEEN PEOPLE TODAY...THERE'S NO REAL UNDERSTANDING!
SCHULZ

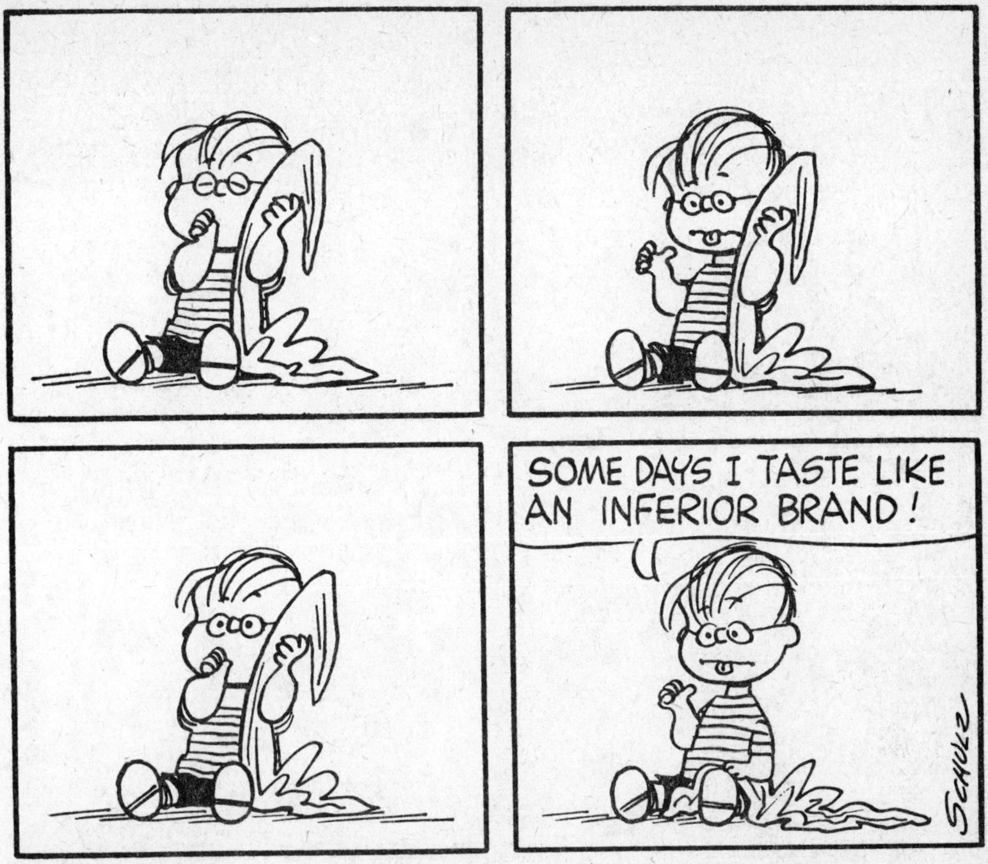
SOME DAYS I TASTE LIKE AN INFERIOR BRAND!
SCHULZ

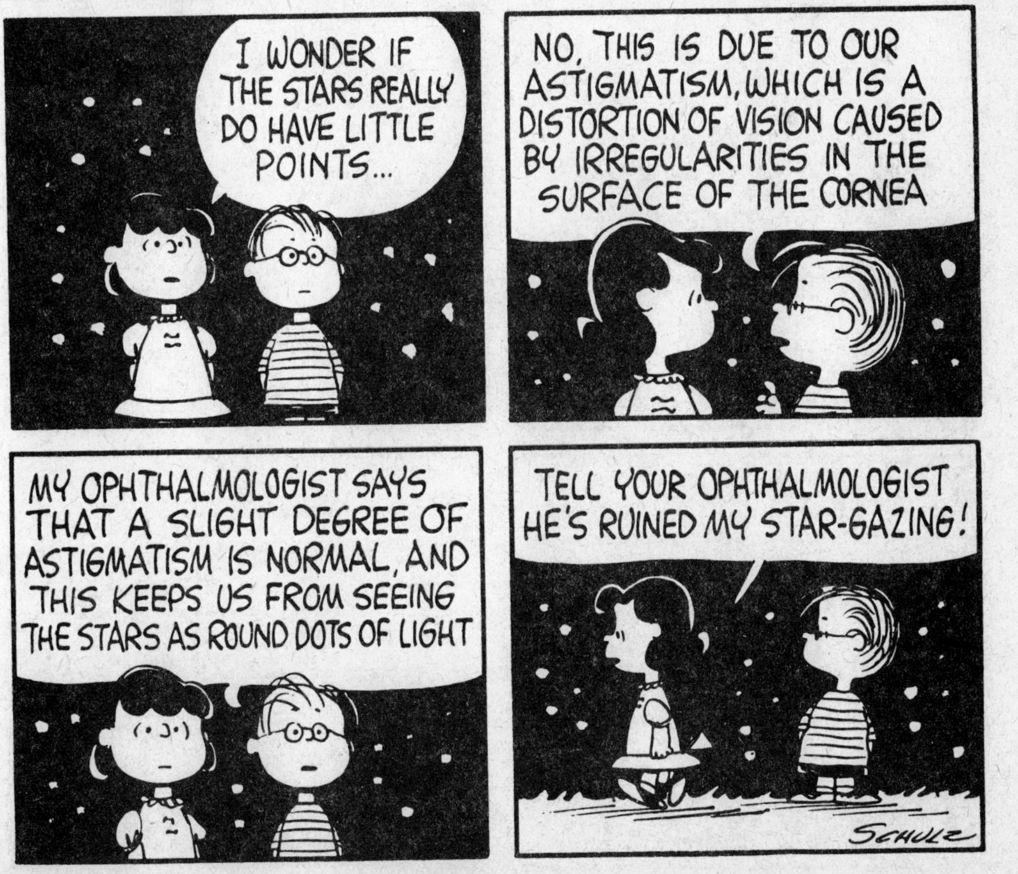
I WONDER IF THE STARS REALLY DO HAVE LITTLE POINTS...
NO, THIS IS DUE TO OUR ASTIGMATISM, WHICH IS A DISTORTION OF VISION CAUSED BY IRREGULARITIES IN THE SURFACE OF THE CORNEA
MY OPHTHALMOLOGIST SAYS THAT A SLIGHT DEGREE OF ASTIGMATISM IS NORMAL, AND THIS KEEPS US FROM SEEING THE STARS AS ROUND DOTS OF LIGHT
TELL YOUR OPHTHALMOLOGIST HE'S RUINED MY STAR-GAZING!
SCHULZ

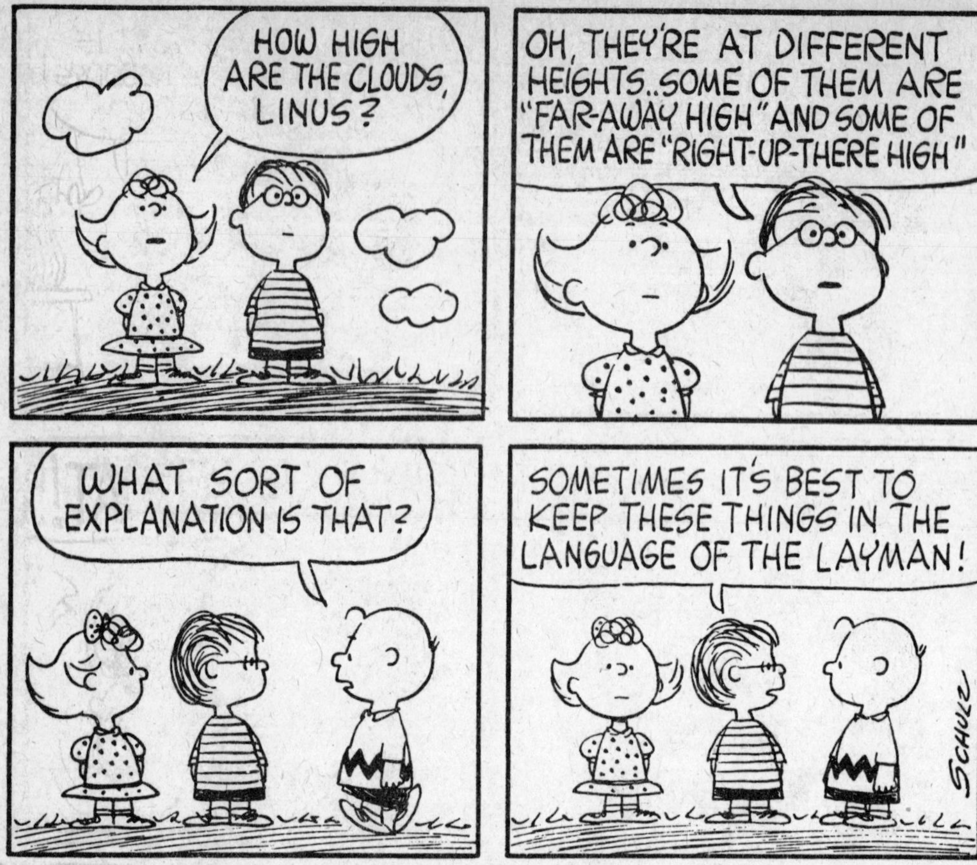
HOW HIGH ARE THE CLOUDS, LINUS?
OH, THEY'RE AT DIFFERENT HEIGHTS..SOME OF THEM ARE "FAR-AWAY HIGH" AND SOME OF THEM ARE "RIGHT-UP-THERE HIGH"
WHAT SORT OF EXPLANATION IS THAT?
SOMETIMES IT'S BEST TO KEEP THESE THINGS IN THE LANGUAGE OF THE LAYMAN!
SCHULZ

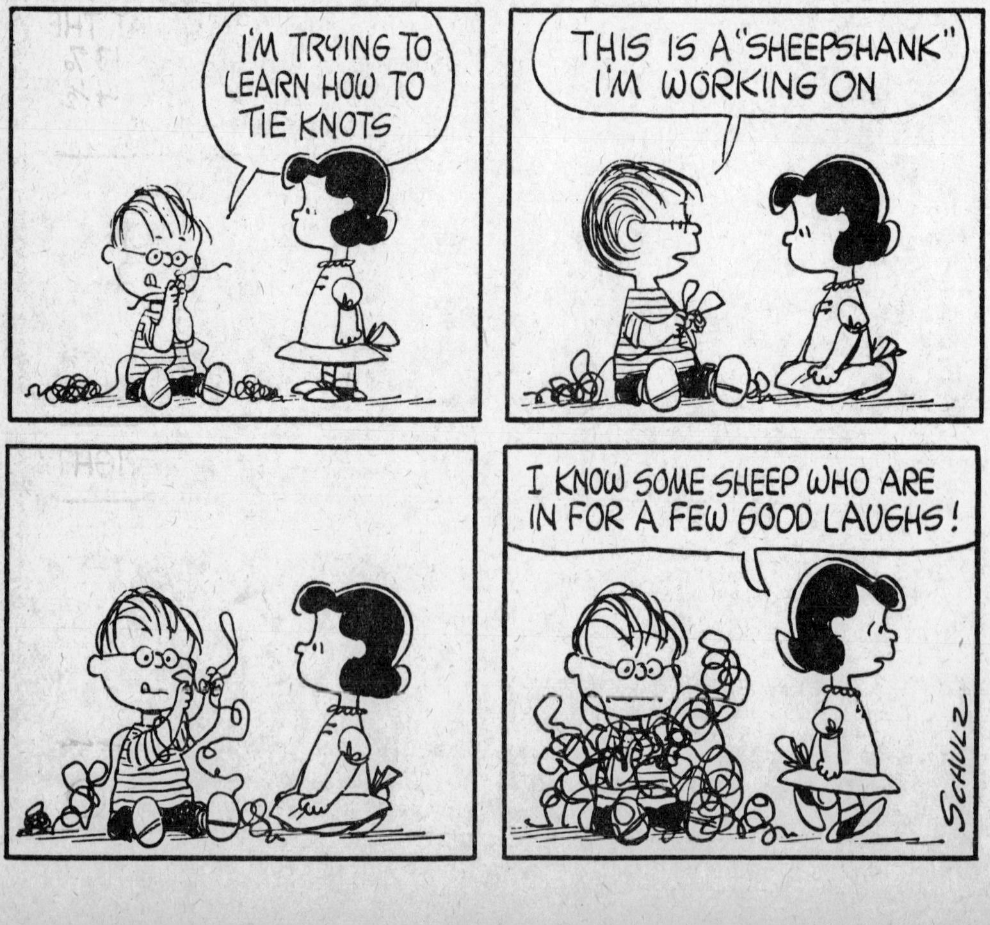
I'M TRYING TO LEARN HOW TO TIE KNOTS
THIS IS A "SHEEPSHANK" I'M WORKING ON
I KNOW SOME SHEEP WHO ARE IN FOR A FEW GOOD LAUGHS!
SCHULZ

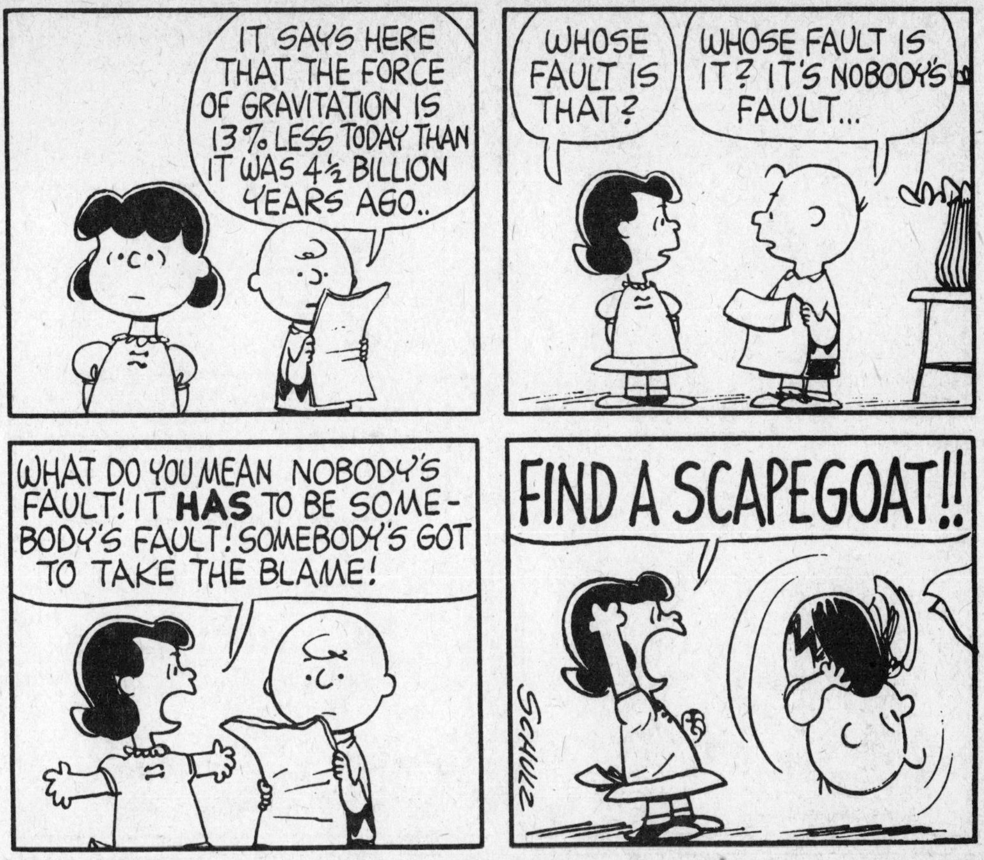
IT SAYS HERE THAT THE FORCE OF GRAVITATION IS 13% LESS TODAY THAN IT WAS 4½ BILLION YEARS AGO..
WHOSE FAULT IS THAT?
WHOSE FAULT IS IT? IT'S NOBODY'S FAULT...
WHAT DO YOU MEAN NOBODY'S FAULT! IT **HAS** TO BE SOMEBODY'S FAULT! SOMEBODY'S GOT TO TAKE THE BLAME!
FIND A SCAPEGOAT!!
SCHULZ

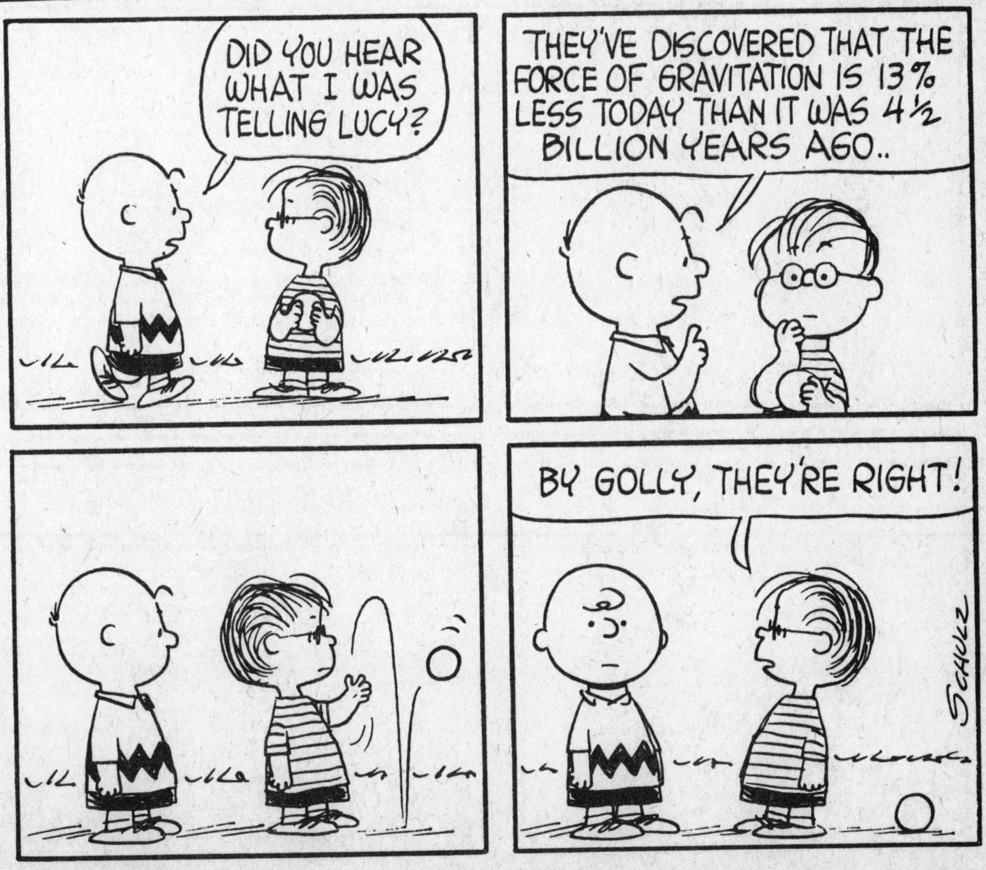
DID YOU HEAR WHAT I WAS TELLING LUCY?
THEY'VE DISCOVERED THAT THE FORCE OF GRAVITATION IS 13% LESS TODAY THAN IT WAS 4½ BILLION YEARS AGO..
BY GOLLY, THEY'RE RIGHT!
SCHULZ

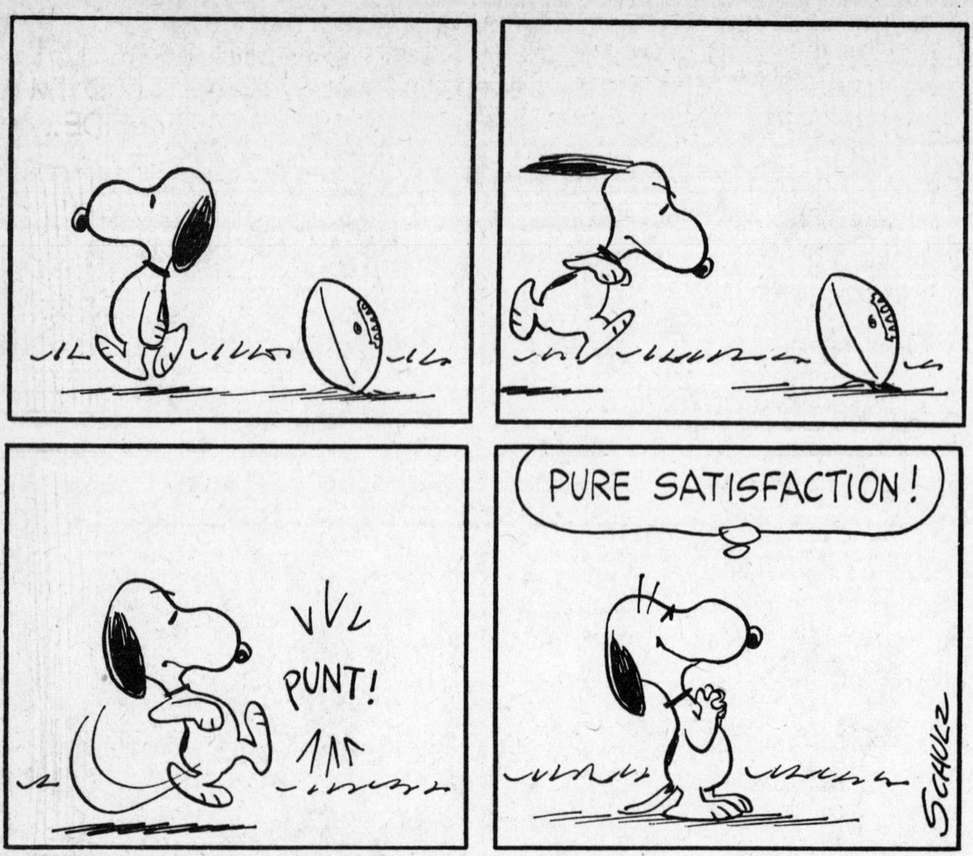

PUNT!
PURE SATISFACTION!
SCHULZ

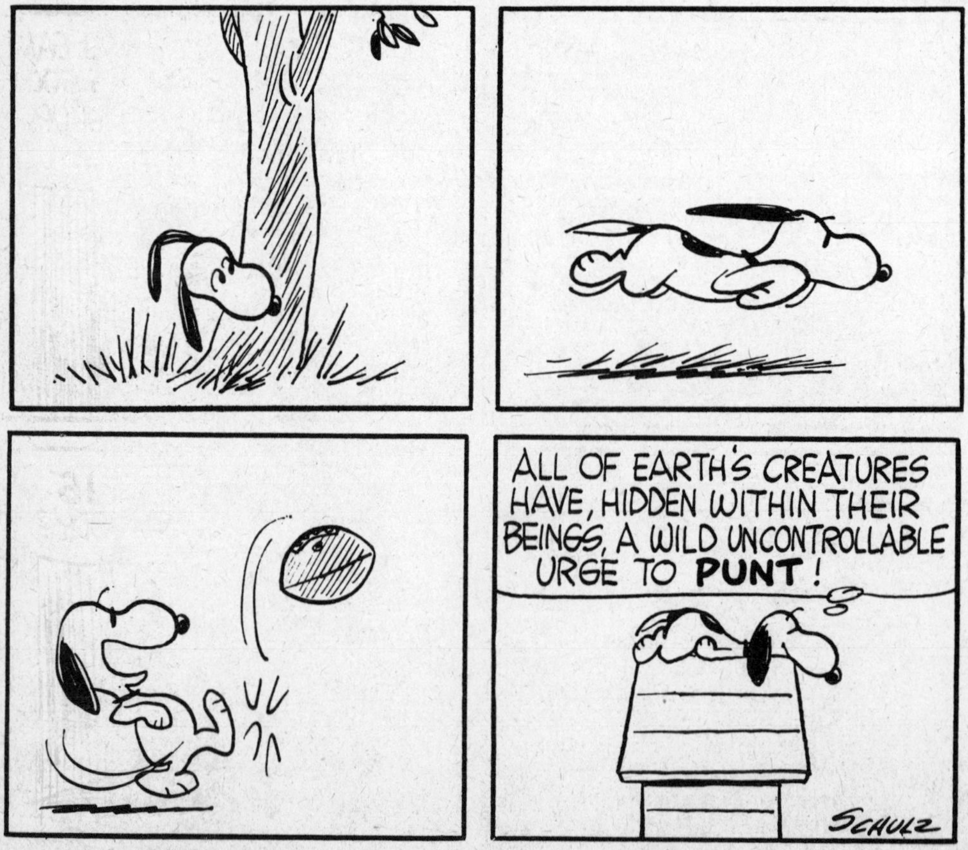

ALL OF EARTH'S CREATURES HAVE, HIDDEN WITHIN THEIR BEINGS, A WILD UNCONTROLLABLE URGE TO **PUNT**!
SCHULZ

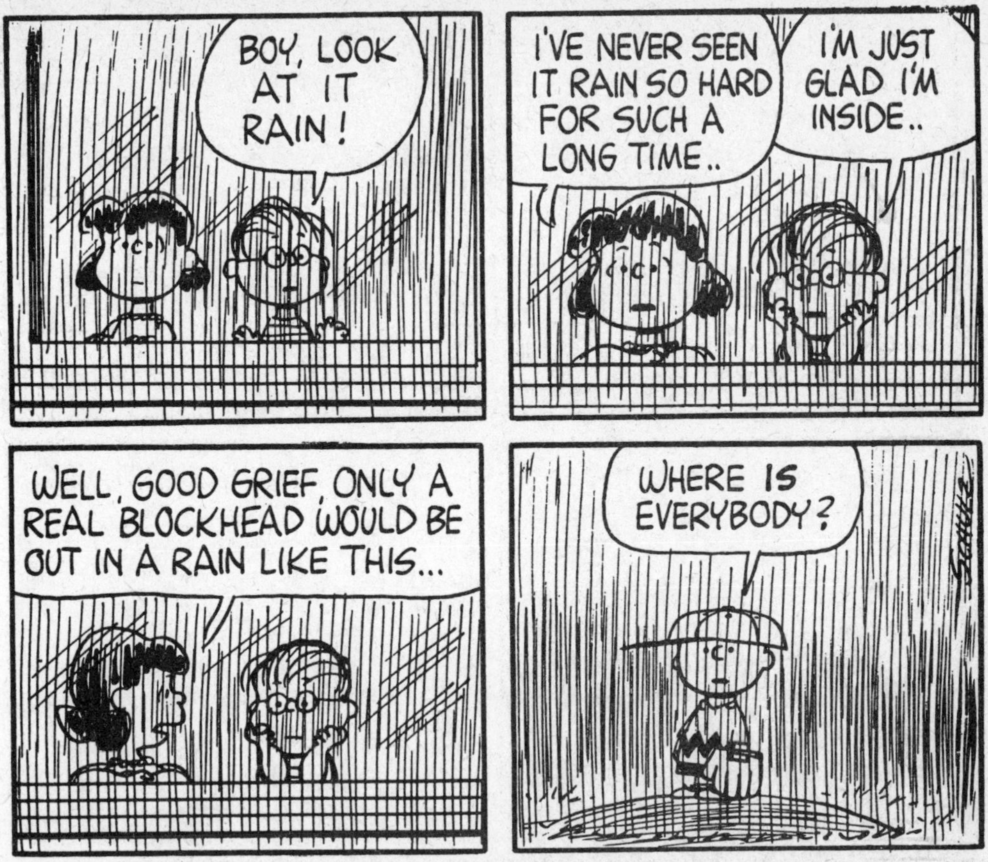
BOY, LOOK AT IT RAIN!
I'VE NEVER SEEN IT RAIN SO HARD FOR SUCH A LONG TIME..
I'M JUST GLAD I'M INSIDE..
WELL, GOOD GRIEF, ONLY A REAL BLOCKHEAD WOULD BE OUT IN A RAIN LIKE THIS...
WHERE IS EVERYBODY?
SCHULZ

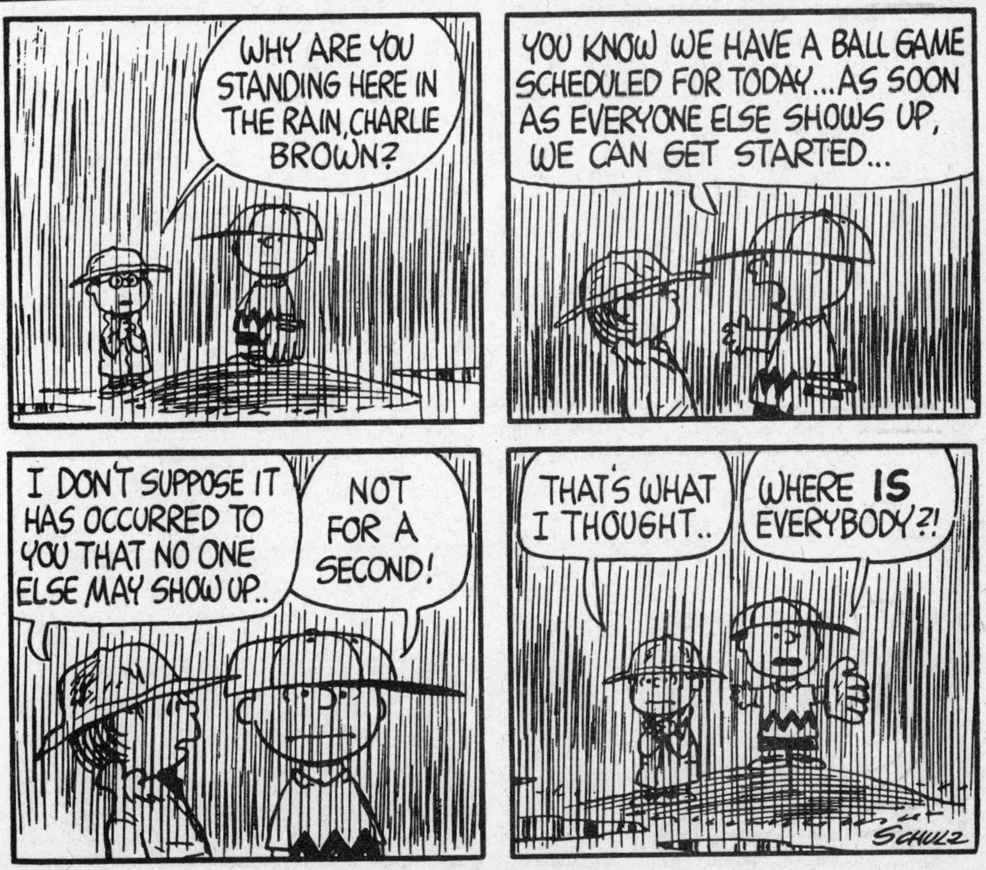
WHY ARE YOU STANDING HERE IN THE RAIN, CHARLIE BROWN?
YOU KNOW WE HAVE A BALL GAME SCHEDULED FOR TODAY...AS SOON AS EVERYONE ELSE SHOWS UP, WE CAN GET STARTED...
I DON'T SUPPOSE IT HAS OCCURRED TO YOU THAT NO ONE ELSE MAY SHOW UP..
NOT FOR A SECOND!
THAT'S WHAT I THOUGHT..
WHERE IS EVERYBODY?!
SCHULZ

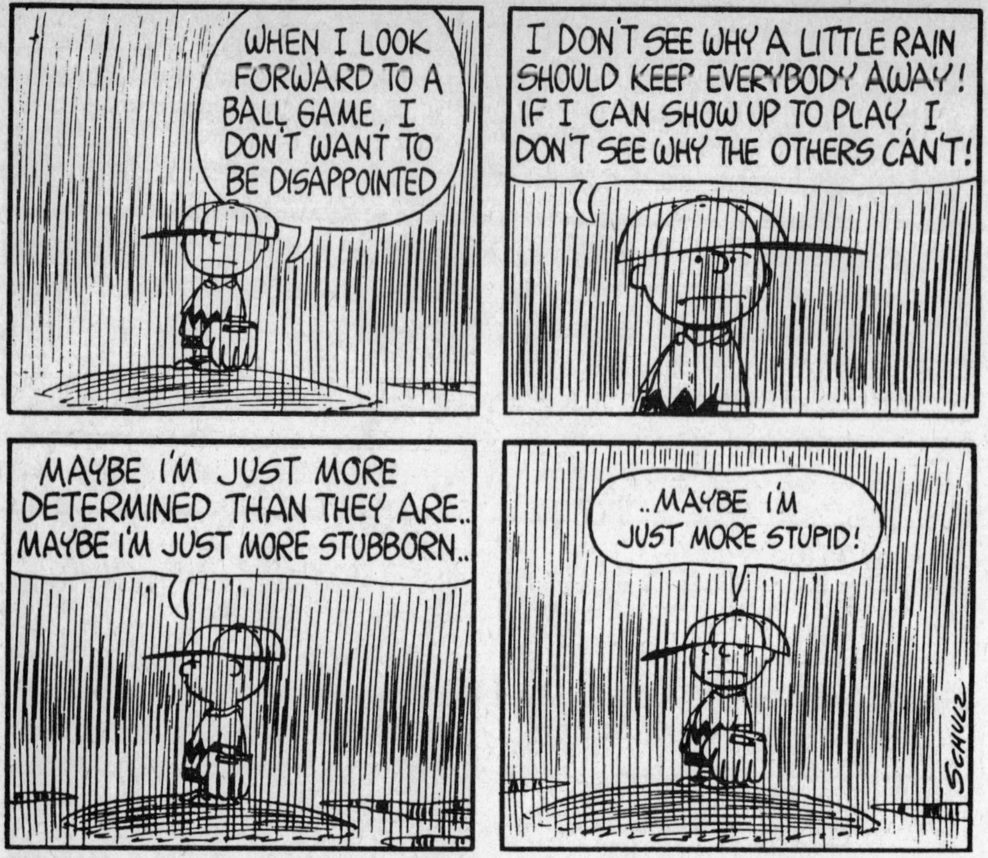
WHEN I LOOK FORWARD TO A BALL GAME, I DON'T WANT TO BE DISAPPOINTED
I DON'T SEE WHY A LITTLE RAIN SHOULD KEEP EVERYBODY AWAY! IF I CAN SHOW UP TO PLAY, I DON'T SEE WHY THE OTHERS CAN'T!
MAYBE I'M JUST MORE DETERMINED THAN THEY ARE.. MAYBE I'M JUST MORE STUBBORN..
..MAYBE I'M JUST MORE STUPID!
SCHULZ

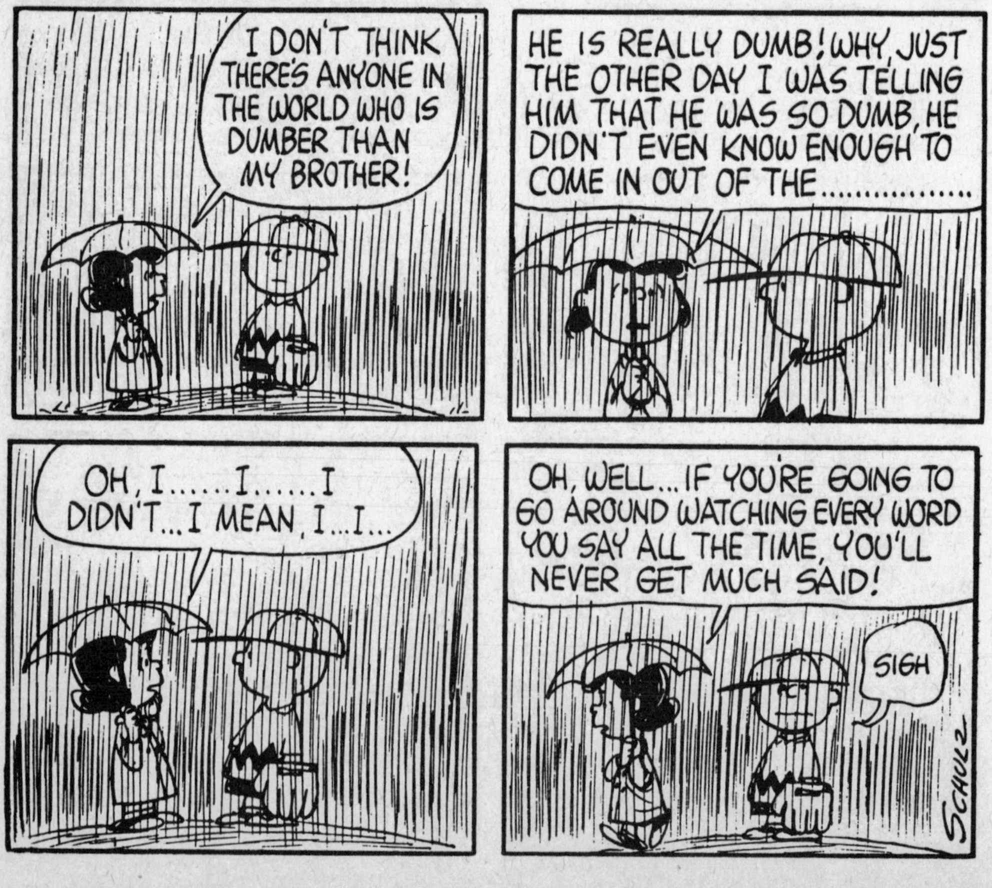
I DON'T THINK THERE'S ANYONE IN THE WORLD WHO IS DUMBER THAN MY BROTHER!
HE IS REALLY DUMB! WHY, JUST THE OTHER DAY I WAS TELLING HIM THAT HE WAS SO DUMB, HE DIDN'T EVEN KNOW ENOUGH TO COME IN OUT OF THE..............
OH, I......I......I DIDN'T...I MEAN, I...I...
OH, WELL...IF YOU'RE GOING TO GO AROUND WATCHING EVERY WORD YOU SAY ALL THE TIME, YOU'LL NEVER GET MUCH SAID!
SIGH
SCHULZ

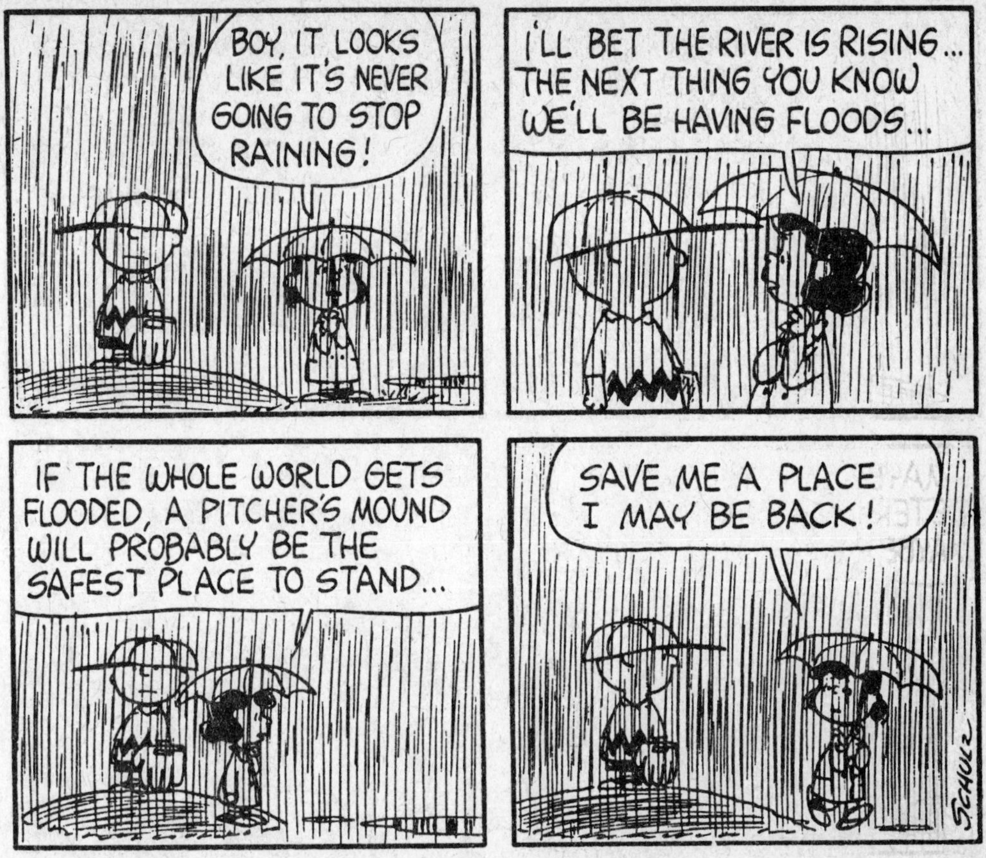
BOY, IT LOOKS LIKE IT'S NEVER GOING TO STOP RAINING!
I'LL BET THE RIVER IS RISING... THE NEXT THING YOU KNOW WE'LL BE HAVING FLOODS...
IF THE WHOLE WORLD GETS FLOODED, A PITCHER'S MOUND WILL PROBABLY BE THE SAFEST PLACE TO STAND...
SAVE ME A PLACE I MAY BE BACK!
SCHULZ

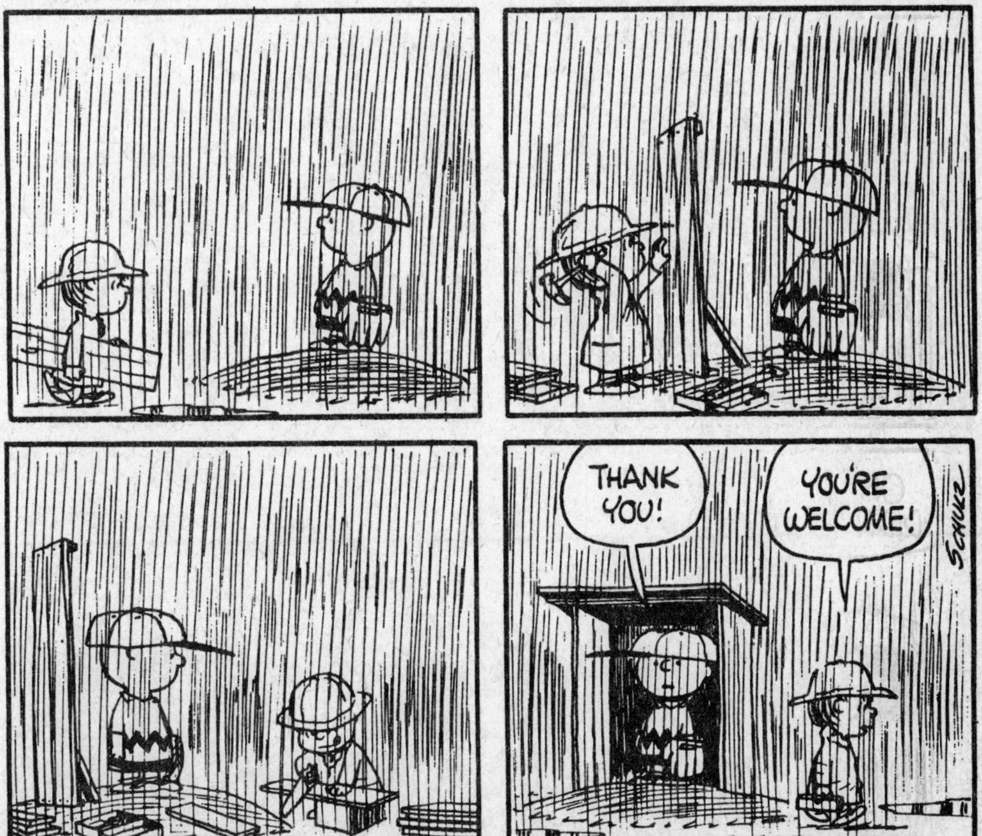
THANK YOU!
YOU'RE WELCOME!
SCHULZ

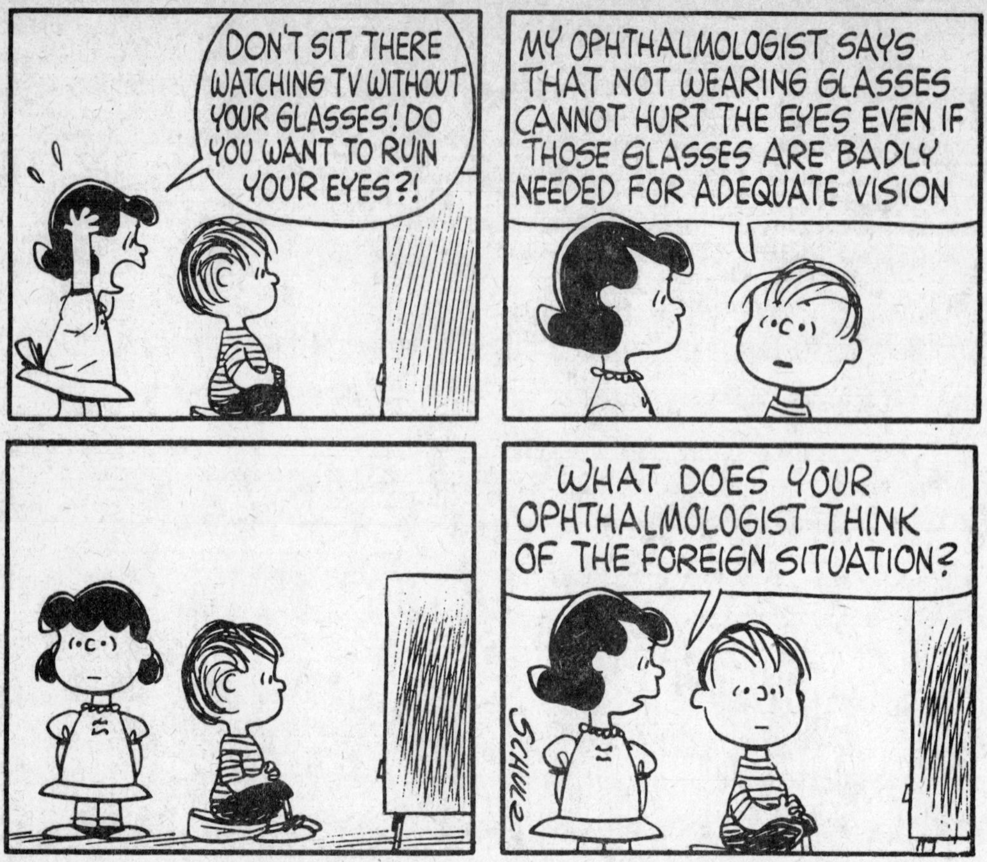
DON'T SIT THERE WATCHING TV WITHOUT YOUR GLASSES! DO YOU WANT TO RUIN YOUR EYES?!
MY OPHTHALMOLOGIST SAYS THAT NOT WEARING GLASSES CANNOT HURT THE EYES EVEN IF THOSE GLASSES ARE BADLY NEEDED FOR ADEQUATE VISION
WHAT DOES YOUR OPHTHALMOLOGIST THINK OF THE FOREIGN SITUATION?
SCHULZ

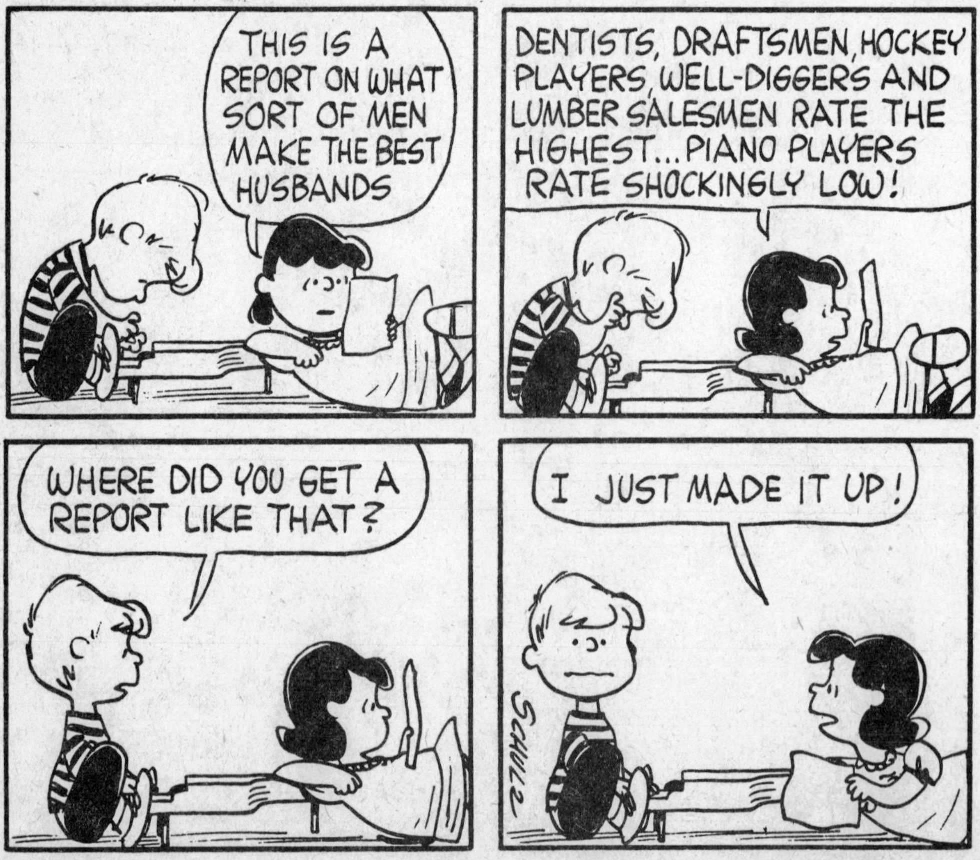
THIS IS A REPORT ON WHAT SORT OF MEN MAKE THE BEST HUSBANDS
DENTISTS, DRAFTSMEN, HOCKEY PLAYERS, WELL-DIGGERS AND LUMBER SALESMEN RATE THE HIGHEST...PIANO PLAYERS RATE SHOCKINGLY LOW!
WHERE DID YOU GET A REPORT LIKE THAT?
I JUST MADE IT UP!
SCHULZ

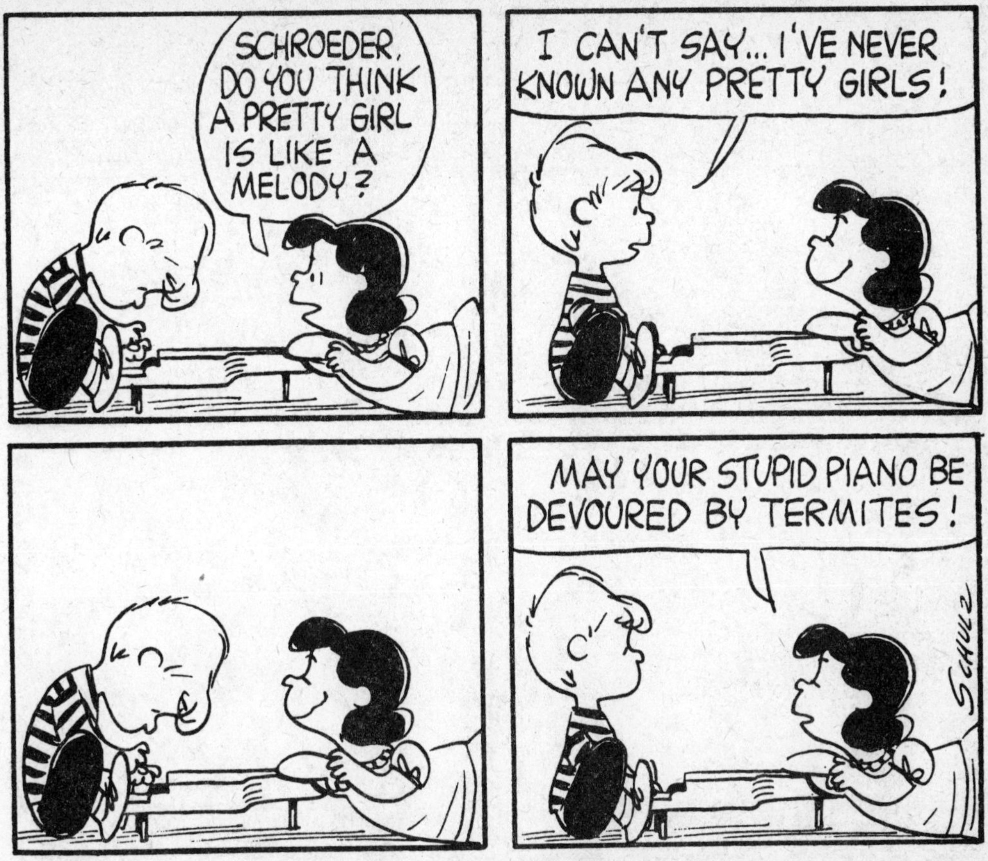
SCHROEDER, DO YOU THINK A PRETTY GIRL IS LIKE A MELODY?
I CAN'T SAY... I'VE NEVER KNOWN ANY PRETTY GIRLS!
MAY YOUR STUPID PIANO BE DEVOURED BY TERMITES!
SCHULZ

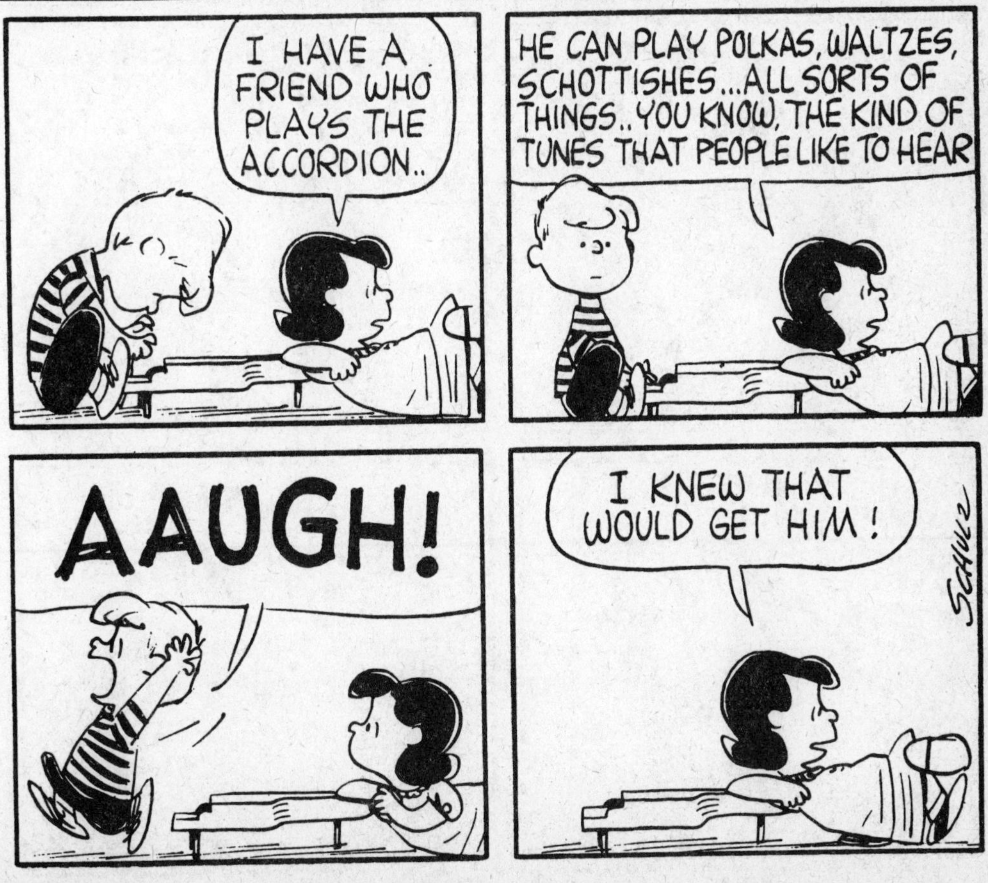
I HAVE A FRIEND WHO PLAYS THE ACCORDION..
HE CAN PLAY POLKAS, WALTZES, SCHOTTISHES...ALL SORTS OF THINGS.. YOU KNOW, THE KIND OF TUNES THAT PEOPLE LIKE TO HEAR
AAUGH!
I KNEW THAT WOULD GET HIM!
SCHULZ

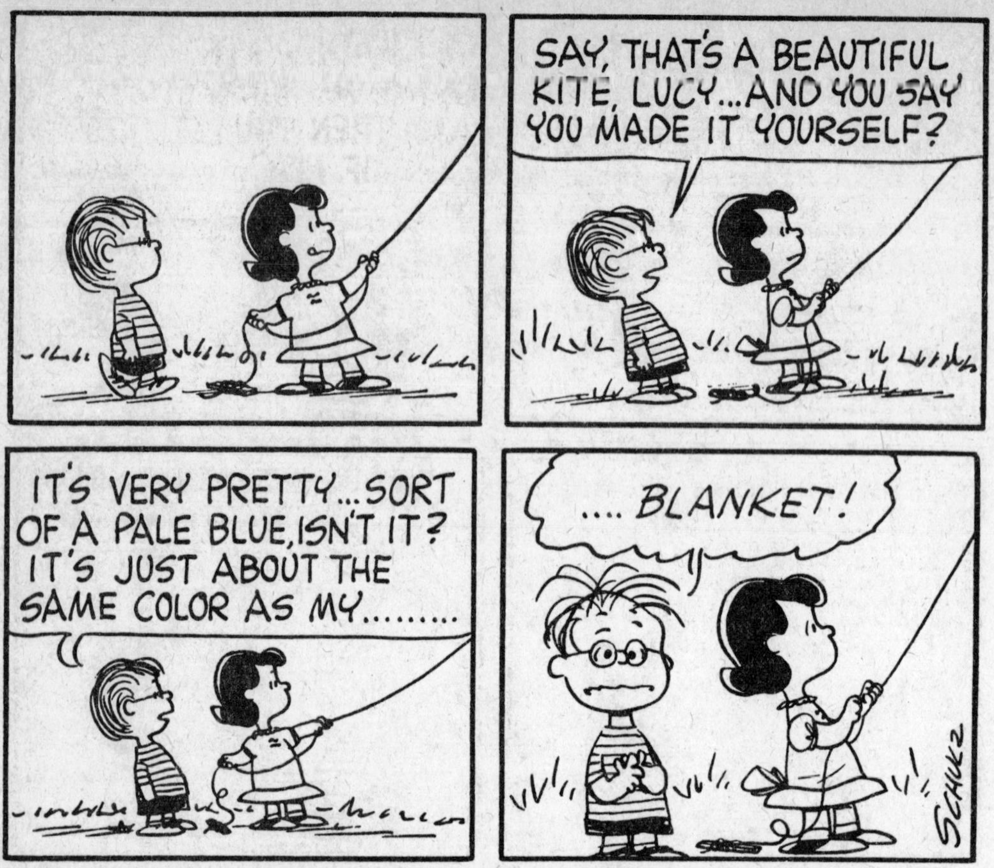
SAY, THAT'S A BEAUTIFUL KITE, LUCY...AND YOU SAY YOU MADE IT YOURSELF?
IT'S VERY PRETTY...SORT OF A PALE BLUE, ISN'T IT? IT'S JUST ABOUT THE SAME COLOR AS MY.........
.... BLANKET!
SCHULZ

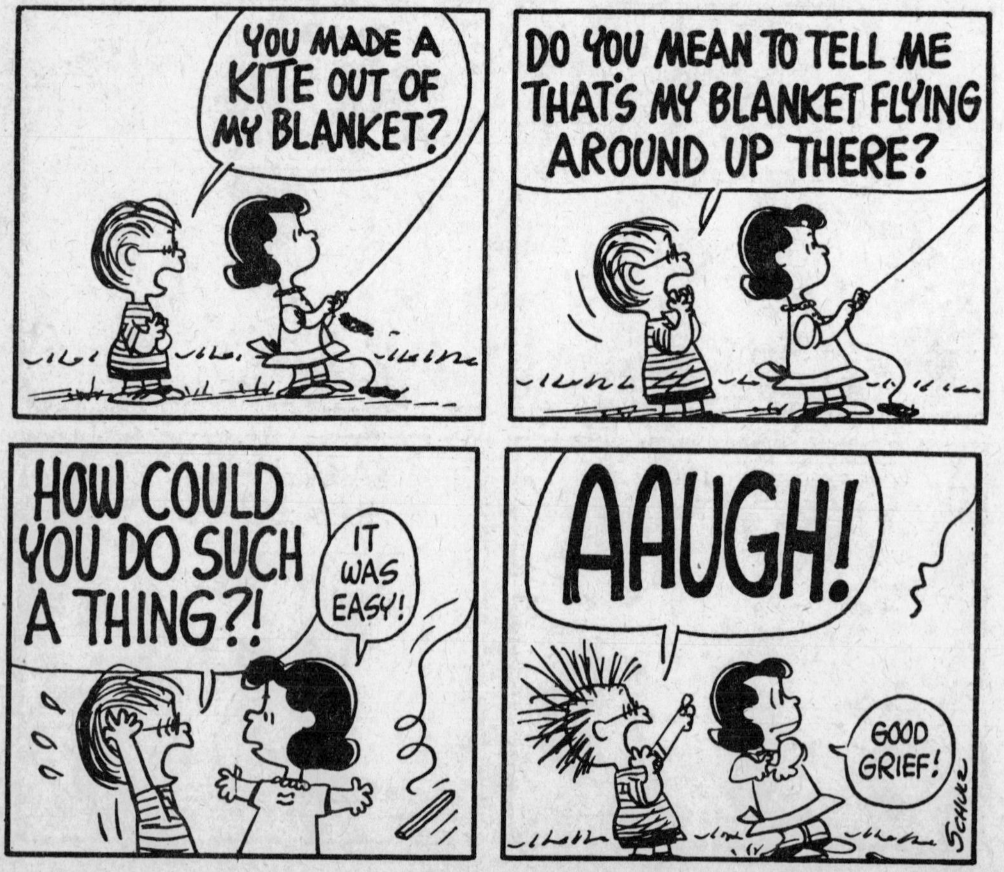
YOU MADE A KITE OUT OF MY BLANKET?
DO YOU MEAN TO TELL ME THAT'S MY BLANKET FLYING AROUND UP THERE?
HOW COULD YOU DO SUCH A THING?!
IT WAS EASY!
AAUGH!
GOOD GRIEF!
SCHULZ

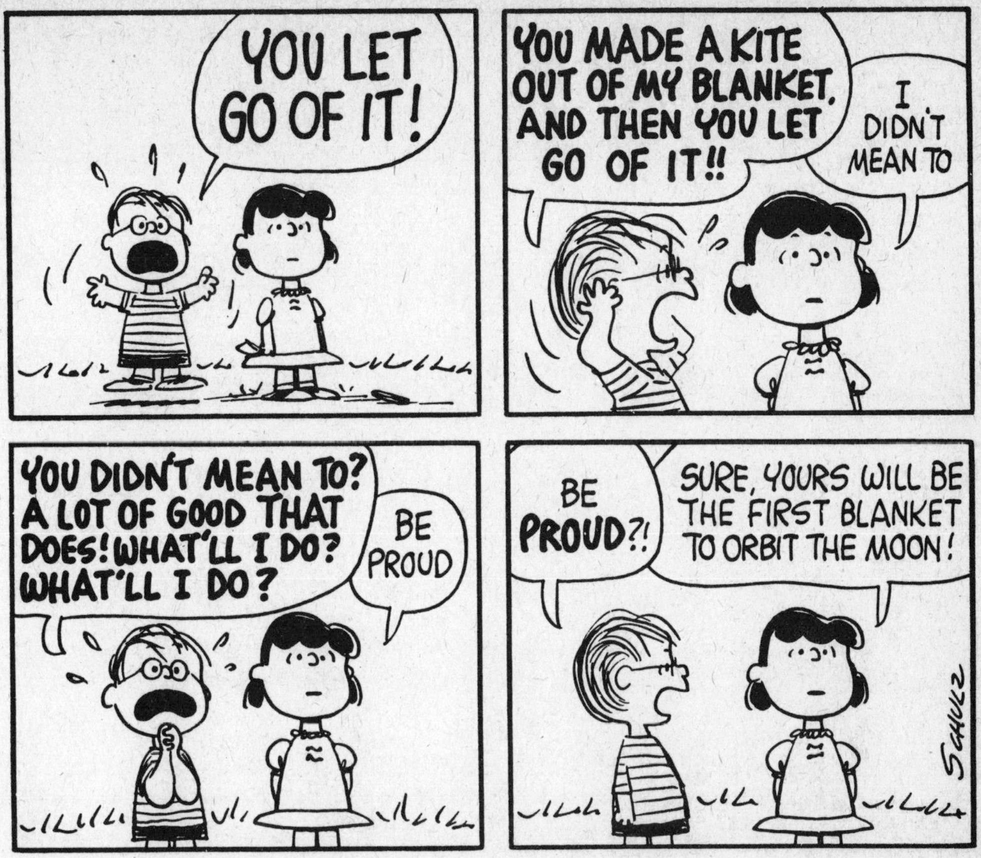
YOU LET GO OF IT!
YOU MADE A KITE OUT OF MY BLANKET, AND THEN YOU LET GO OF IT!!
I DIDN'T MEAN TO
YOU DIDN'T MEAN TO? A LOT OF GOOD THAT DOES! WHAT'LL I DO? WHAT'LL I DO?
BE PROUD
BE PROUD?!
SURE, YOURS WILL BE THE FIRST BLANKET TO ORBIT THE MOON!
SCHULZ

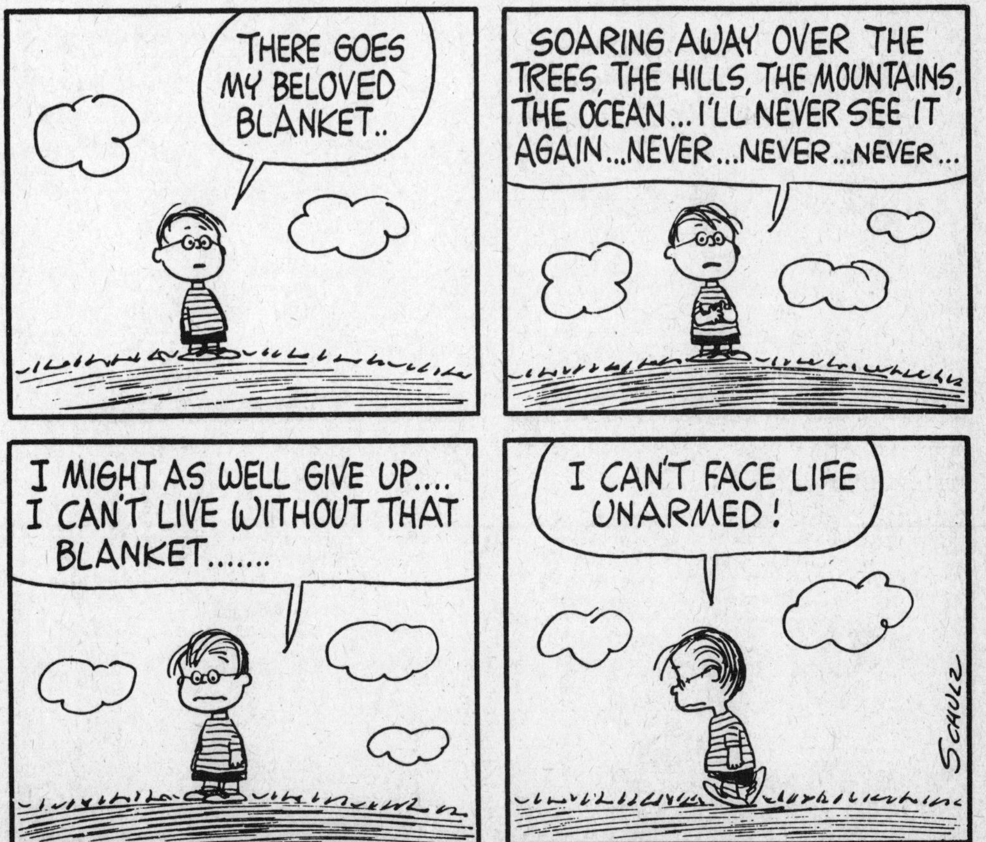
THERE GOES MY BELOVED BLANKET..
SOARING AWAY OVER THE TREES, THE HILLS, THE MOUNTAINS, THE OCEAN... I'LL NEVER SEE IT AGAIN...NEVER...NEVER...NEVER...
I MIGHT AS WELL GIVE UP.... I CAN'T LIVE WITHOUT THAT BLANKET.......
I CAN'T FACE LIFE UNARMED!
SCHULZ

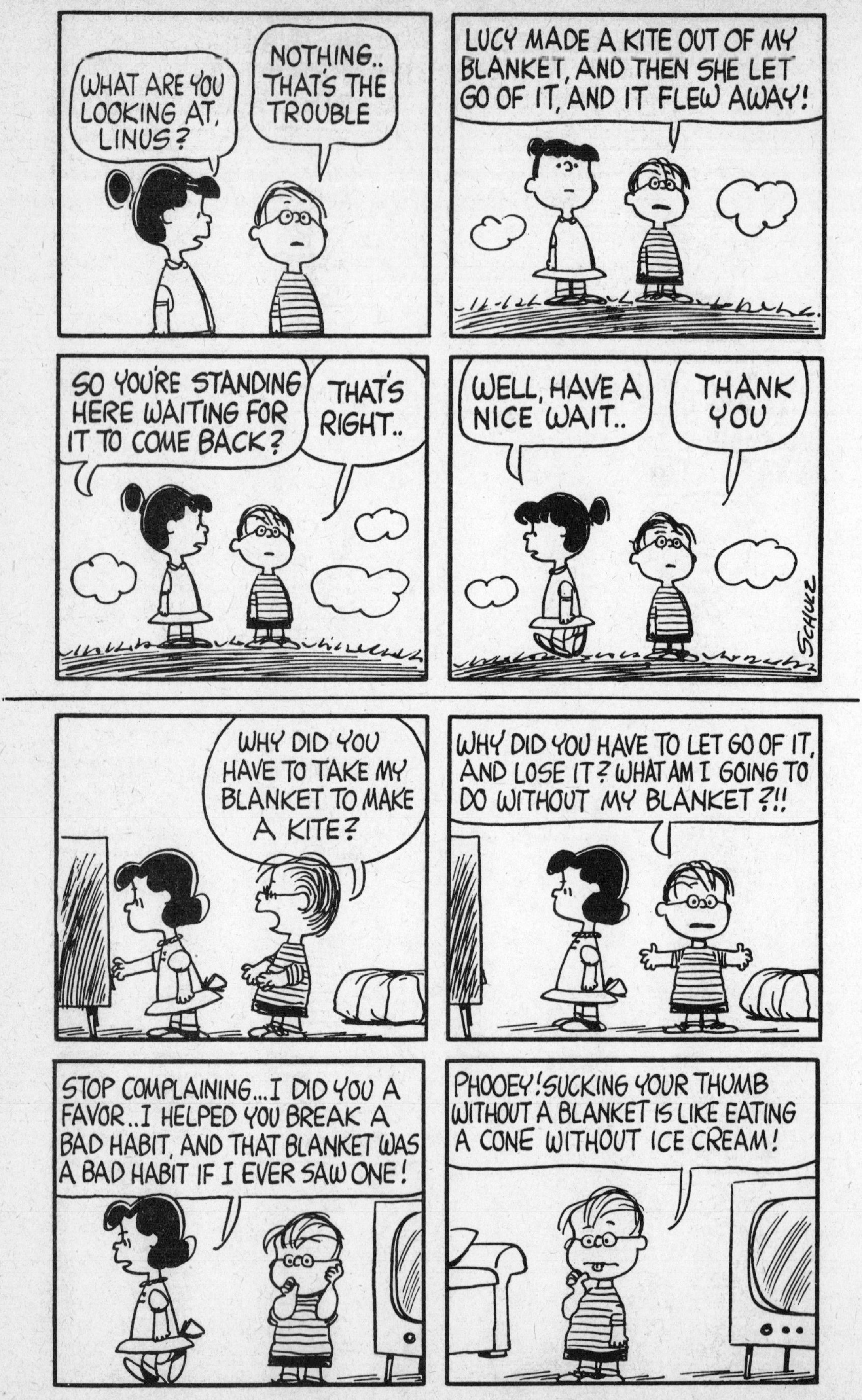
WHAT ARE YOU LOOKING AT, LINUS?
NOTHING.. THAT'S THE TROUBLE
LUCY MADE A KITE OUT OF MY BLANKET, AND THEN SHE LET GO OF IT, AND IT FLEW AWAY!
SO YOU'RE STANDING HERE WAITING FOR IT TO COME BACK?
THAT'S RIGHT..
WELL, HAVE A NICE WAIT..
THANK YOU
SCHULZ
WHY DID YOU HAVE TO TAKE MY BLANKET TO MAKE A KITE?
WHY DID YOU HAVE TO LET GO OF IT, AND LOSE IT? WHAT AM I GOING TO DO WITHOUT MY BLANKET?!!
STOP COMPLAINING...I DID YOU A FAVOR..I HELPED YOU BREAK A BAD HABIT, AND THAT BLANKET WAS A BAD HABIT IF I EVER SAW ONE!
PHOOEY! SUCKING YOUR THUMB WITHOUT A BLANKET IS LIKE EATING A CONE WITHOUT ICE CREAM!

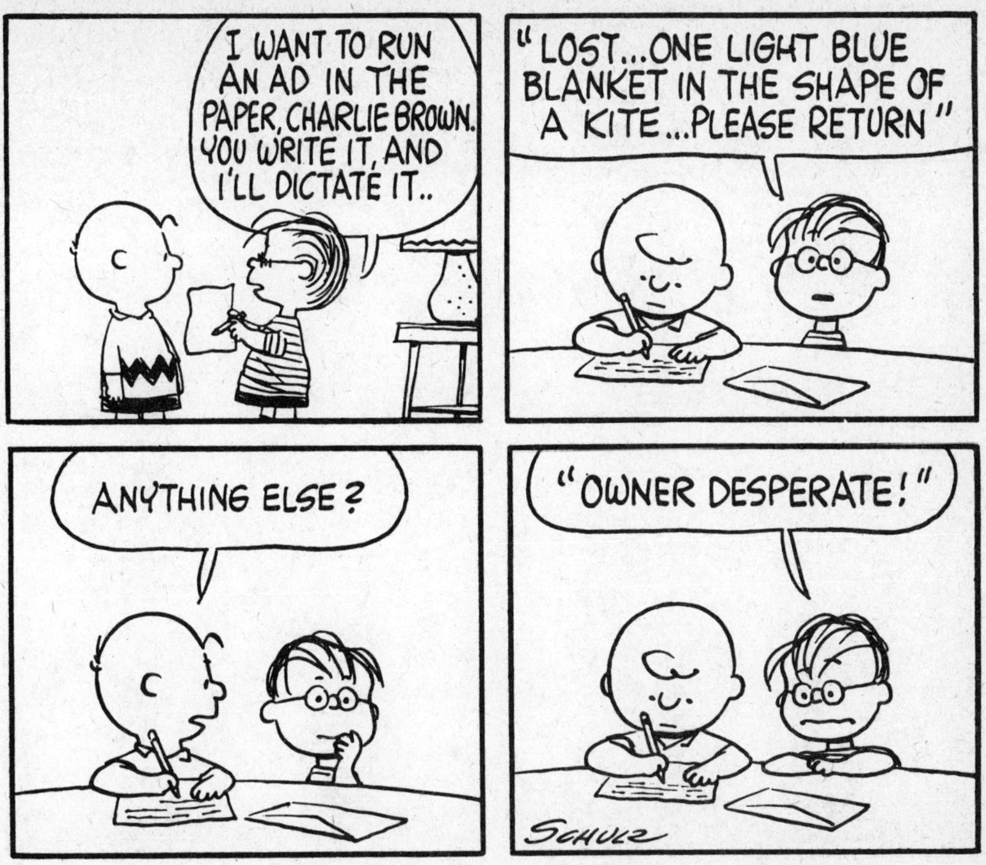
I WANT TO RUN AN AD IN THE PAPER, CHARLIE BROWN. YOU WRITE IT, AND I'LL DICTATE IT..
"LOST...ONE LIGHT BLUE BLANKET IN THE SHAPE OF A KITE...PLEASE RETURN"
ANYTHING ELSE?
"OWNER DESPERATE!"
SCHULZ

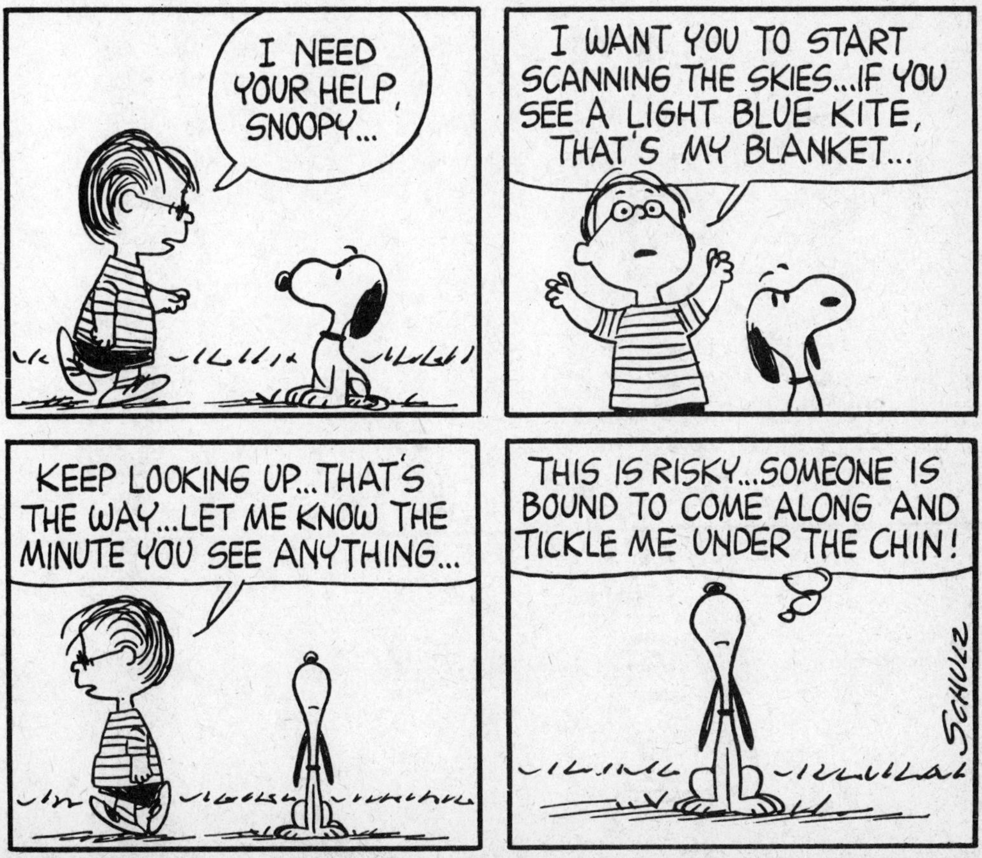
I NEED YOUR HELP, SNOOPY...
I WANT YOU TO START SCANNING THE SKIES...IF YOU SEE A LIGHT BLUE KITE, THAT'S MY BLANKET...
KEEP LOOKING UP...THAT'S THE WAY...LET ME KNOW THE MINUTE YOU SEE ANYTHING...
THIS IS RISKY...SOMEONE IS BOUND TO COME ALONG AND TICKLE ME UNDER THE CHIN!
SCHULZ

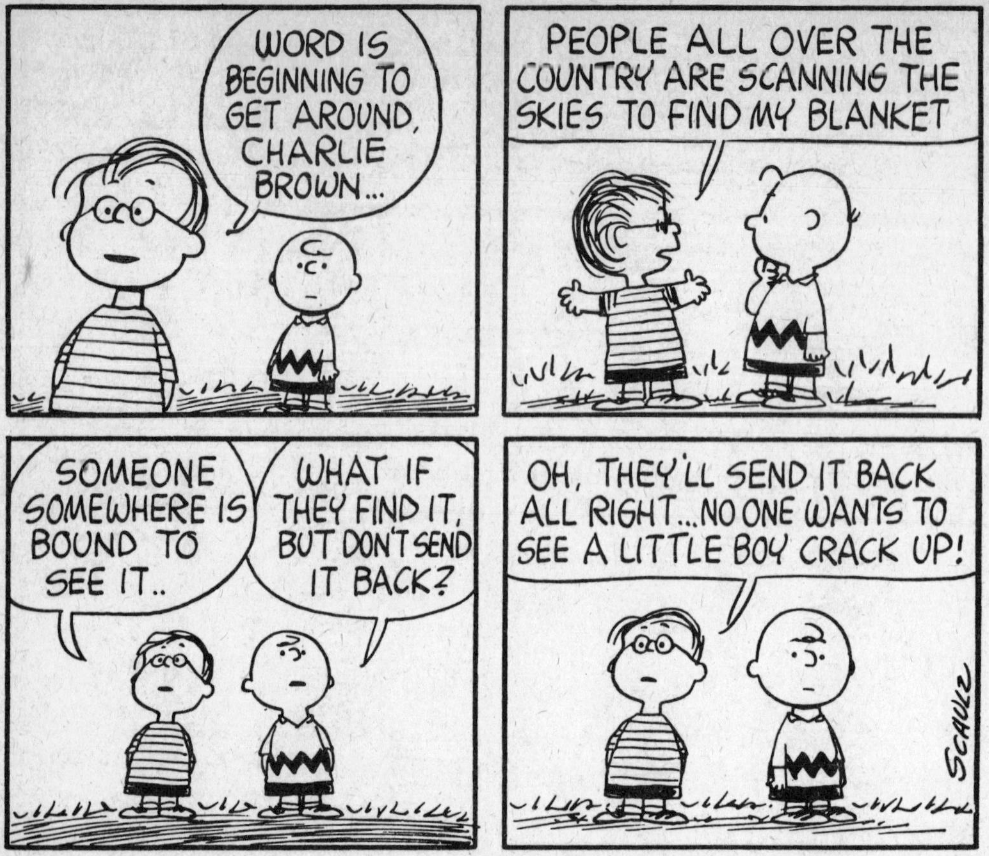
WORD IS BEGINNING TO GET AROUND, CHARLIE BROWN...
PEOPLE ALL OVER THE COUNTRY ARE SCANNING THE SKIES TO FIND MY BLANKET
SOMEONE SOMEWHERE IS BOUND TO SEE IT..
WHAT IF THEY FIND IT, BUT DON'T SEND IT BACK?
OH, THEY'LL SEND IT BACK ALL RIGHT...NO ONE WANTS TO SEE A LITTLE BOY CRACK UP!
SCHULZ

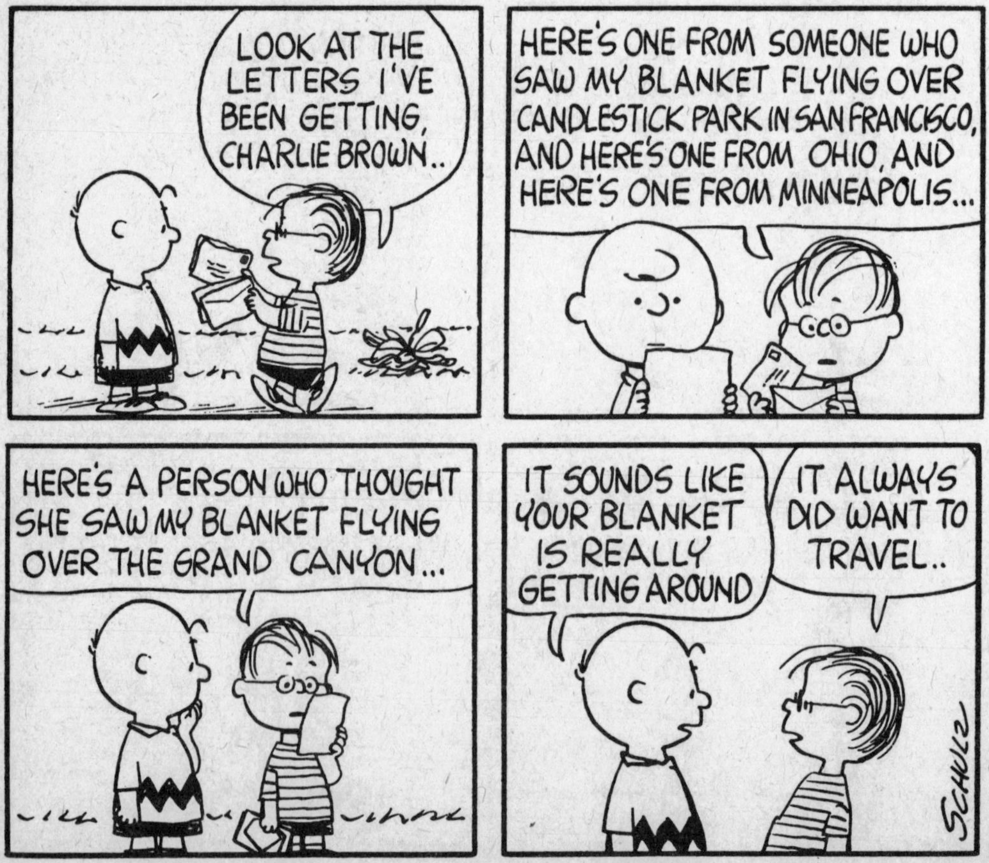
LOOK AT THE LETTERS I'VE BEEN GETTING, CHARLIE BROWN..
HERE'S ONE FROM SOMEONE WHO SAW MY BLANKET FLYING OVER CANDLESTICK PARK IN SAN FRANCISCO, AND HERE'S ONE FROM OHIO, AND HERE'S ONE FROM MINNEAPOLIS...
HERE'S A PERSON WHO THOUGHT SHE SAW MY BLANKET FLYING OVER THE GRAND CANYON...
IT SOUNDS LIKE YOUR BLANKET IS REALLY GETTING AROUND
IT ALWAYS DID WANT TO TRAVEL..
SCHULZ

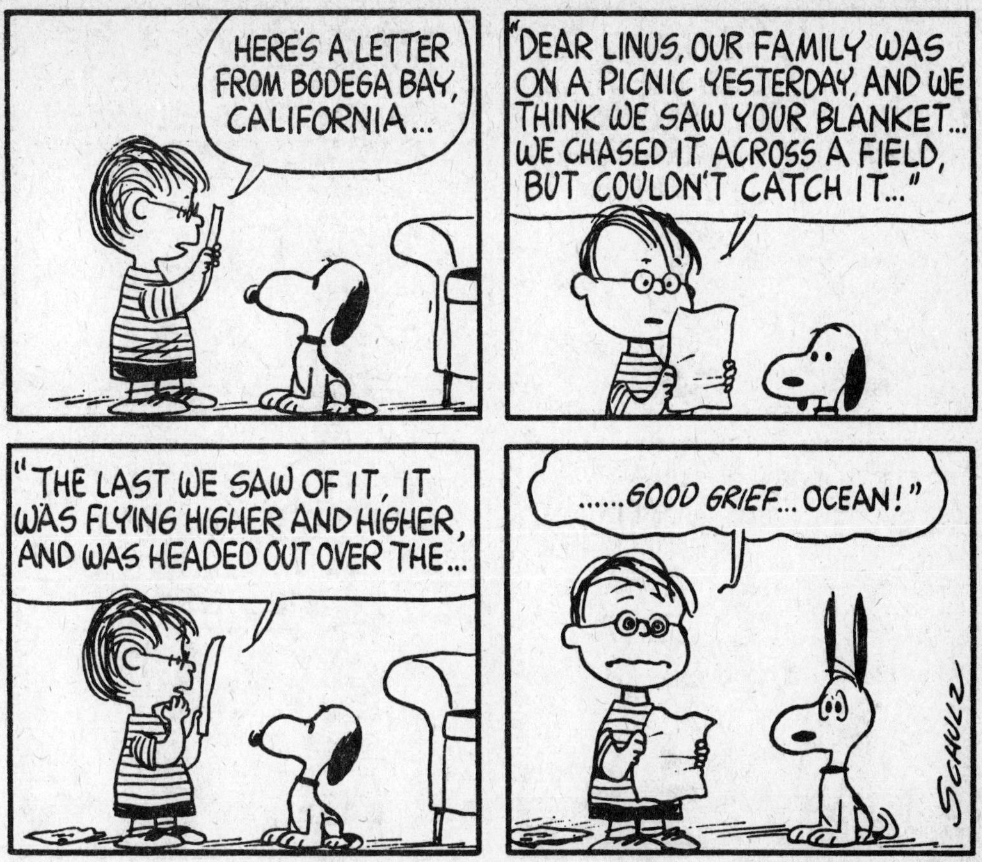
HERE'S A LETTER FROM BODEGA BAY, CALIFORNIA...
"DEAR LINUS, OUR FAMILY WAS ON A PICNIC YESTERDAY, AND WE THINK WE SAW YOUR BLANKET... WE CHASED IT ACROSS A FIELD, BUT COULDN'T CATCH IT..."
"THE LAST WE SAW OF IT, IT WAS FLYING HIGHER AND HIGHER, AND WAS HEADED OUT OVER THE...
......GOOD GRIEF... OCEAN!"
SCHULZ

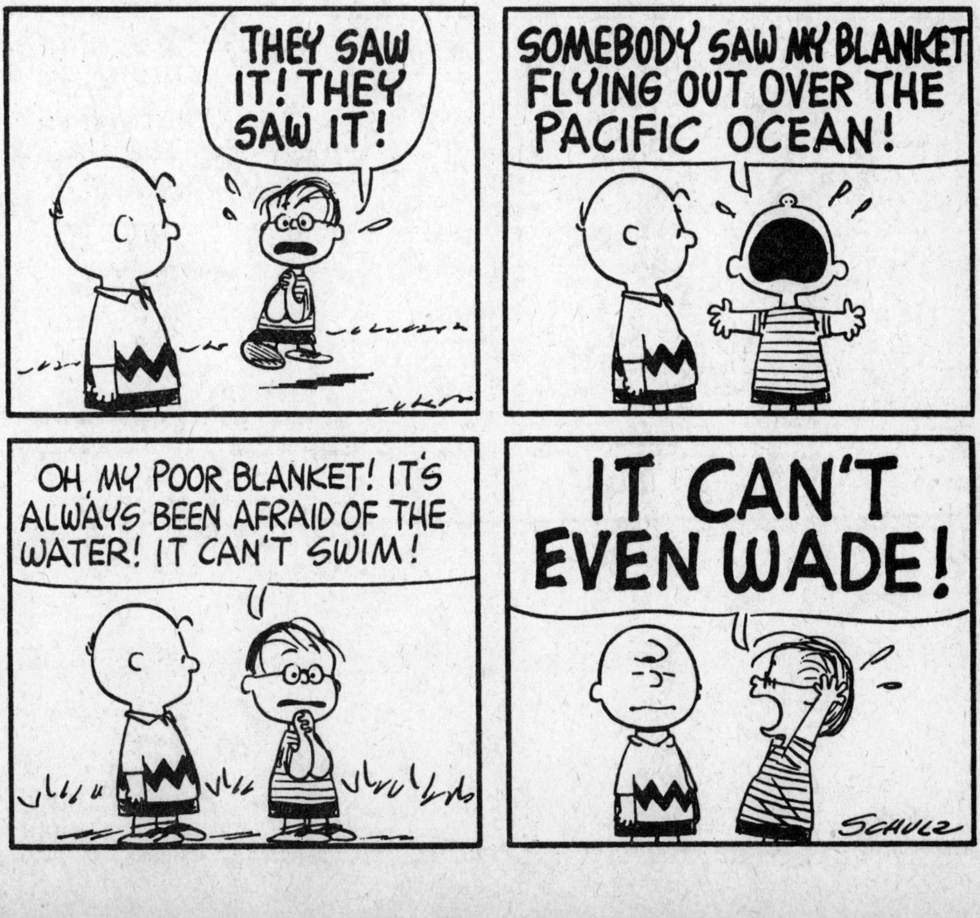
THEY SAW IT! THEY SAW IT!
SOMEBODY SAW MY BLANKET FLYING OUT OVER THE PACIFIC OCEAN!
OH, MY POOR BLANKET! IT'S ALWAYS BEEN AFRAID OF THE WATER! IT CAN'T SWIM!
IT CAN'T EVEN WADE!
SCHULZ

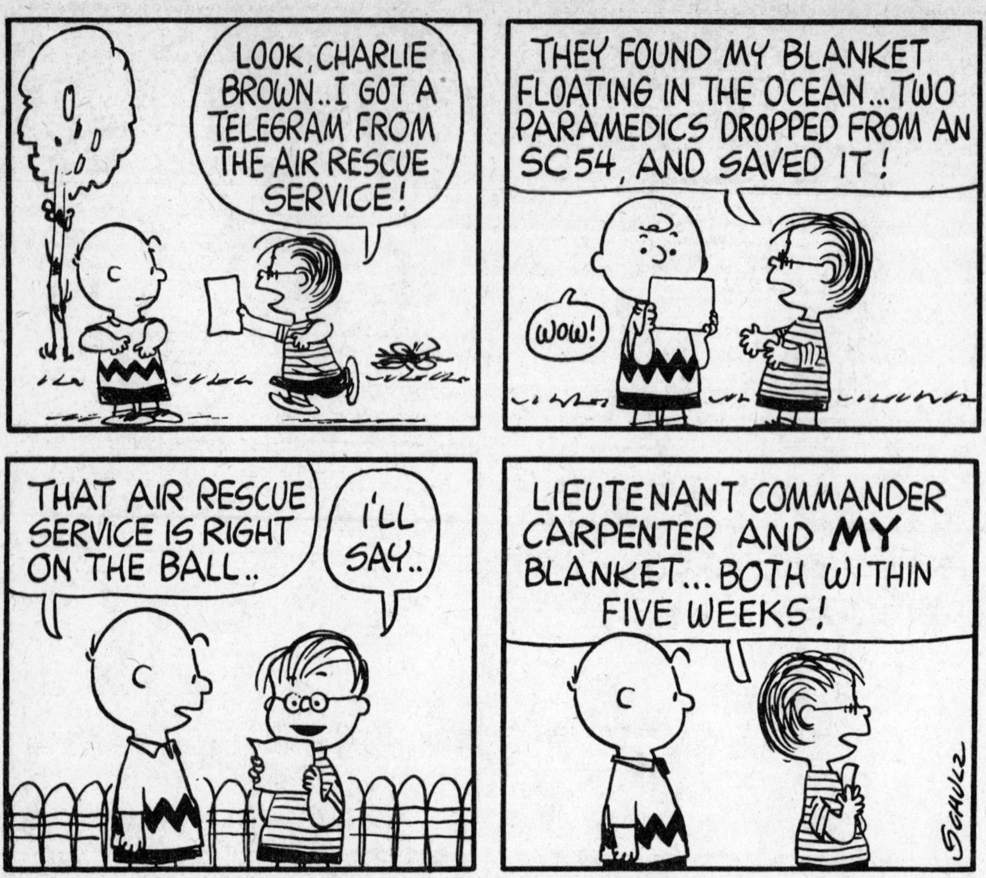
LOOK, CHARLIE BROWN..I GOT A TELEGRAM FROM THE AIR RESCUE SERVICE!
THEY FOUND MY BLANKET FLOATING IN THE OCEAN...TWO PARAMEDICS DROPPED FROM AN SC54, AND SAVED IT!
WOW!
THAT AIR RESCUE SERVICE IS RIGHT ON THE BALL..
I'LL SAY..
LIEUTENANT COMMANDER CARPENTER AND MY BLANKET... BOTH WITHIN FIVE WEEKS!
SCHULZ

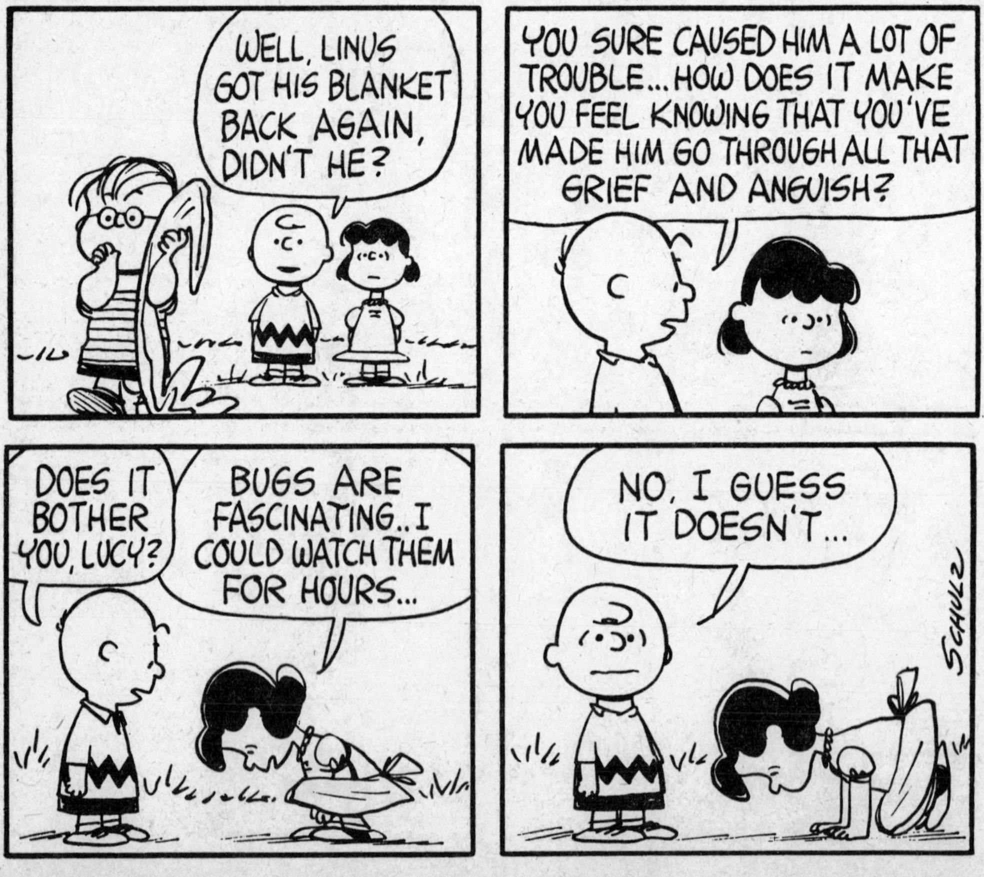
WELL, LINUS GOT HIS BLANKET BACK AGAIN, DIDN'T HE?
YOU SURE CAUSED HIM A LOT OF TROUBLE... HOW DOES IT MAKE YOU FEEL KNOWING THAT YOU'VE MADE HIM GO THROUGH ALL THAT GRIEF AND ANGUISH?
DOES IT BOTHER YOU, LUCY?
BUGS ARE FASCINATING..I COULD WATCH THEM FOR HOURS...
NO, I GUESS IT DOESN'T...
SCHULZ

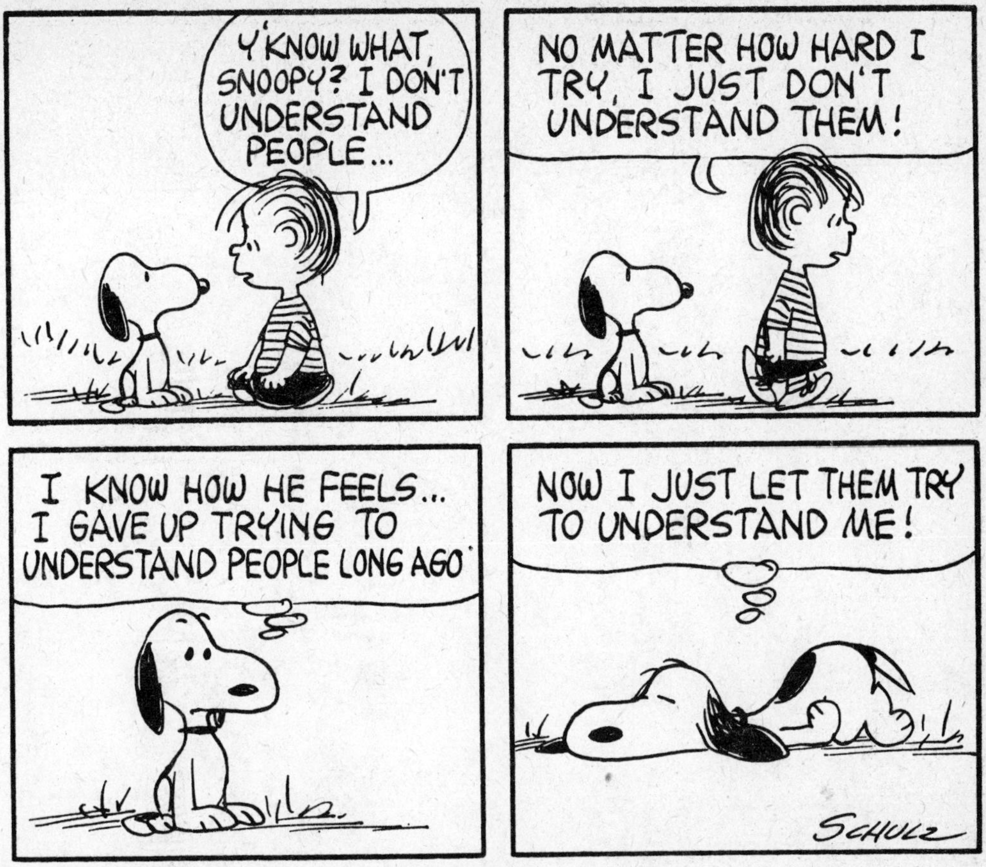
Y'KNOW WHAT, SNOOPY? I DON'T UNDERSTAND PEOPLE...
NO MATTER HOW HARD I TRY, I JUST DON'T UNDERSTAND THEM!
I KNOW HOW HE FEELS... I GAVE UP TRYING TO UNDERSTAND PEOPLE LONG AGO
NOW I JUST LET THEM TRY TO UNDERSTAND ME!
SCHULZ

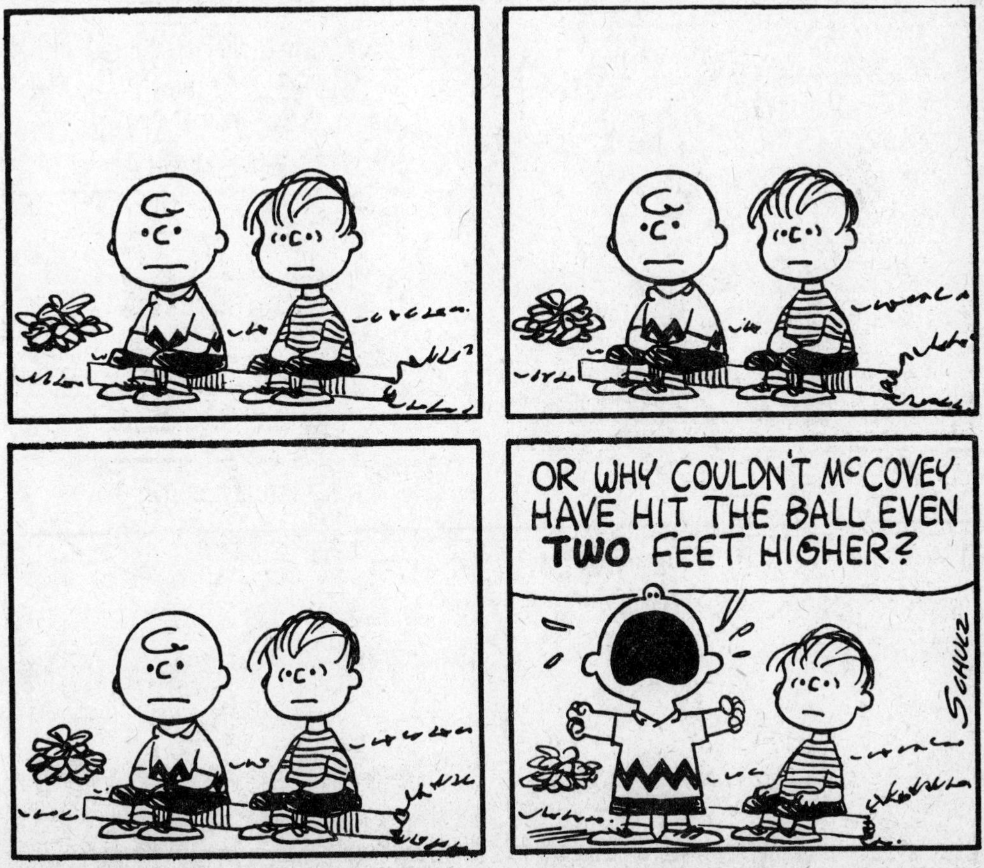
OR WHY COULDN'T McCOVEY HAVE HIT THE BALL EVEN **TWO** FEET HIGHER?
SCHULZ

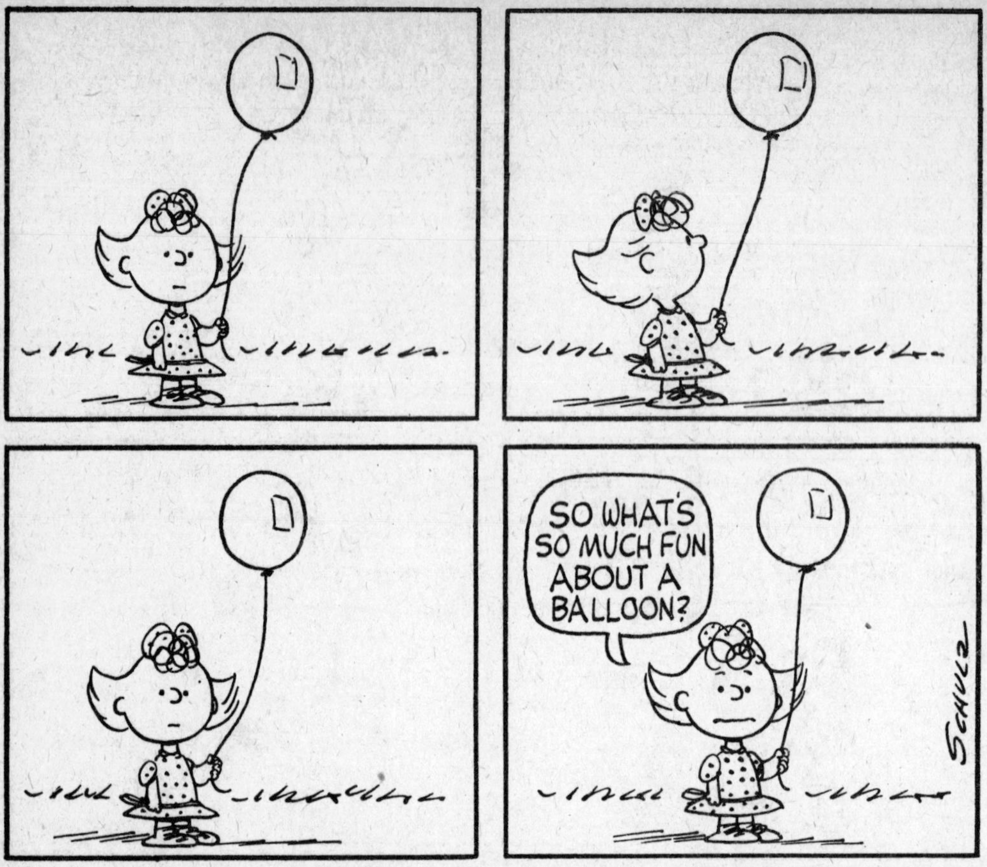
SO WHAT'S SO MUCH FUN ABOUT A BALLOON?
SCHULZ

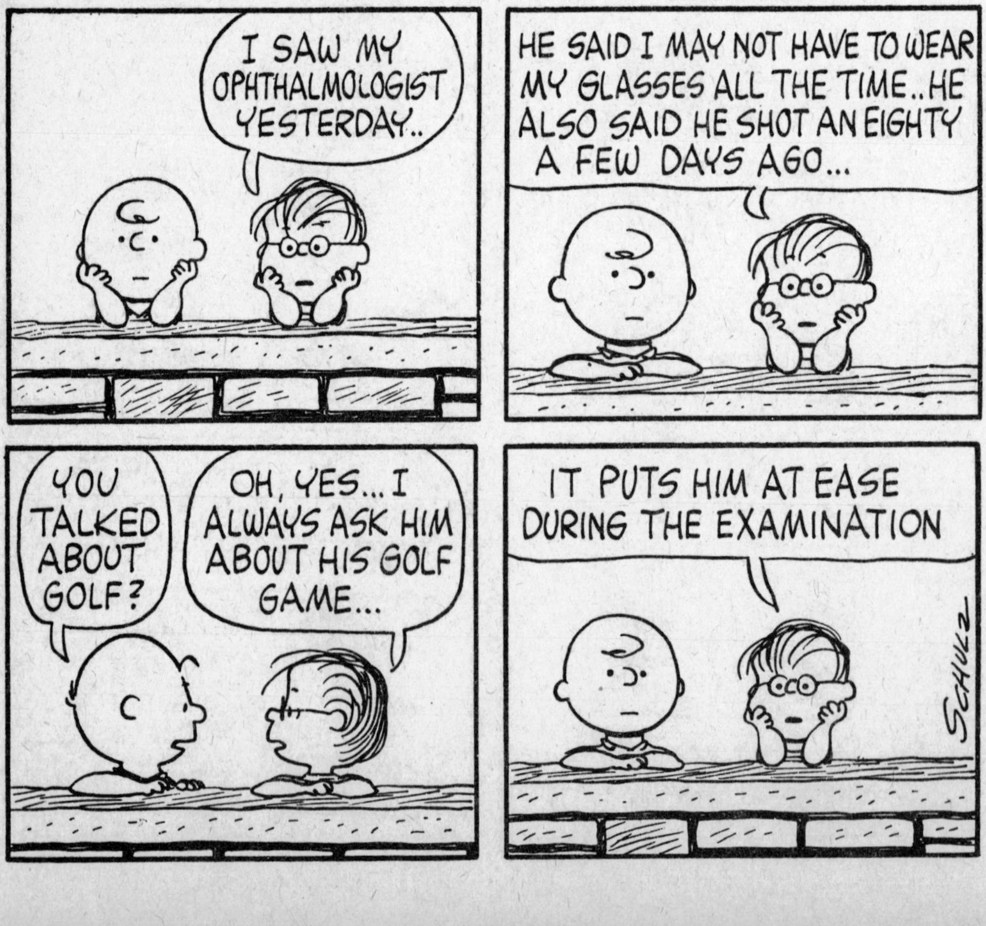
I SAW MY OPHTHALMOLOGIST YESTERDAY..
HE SAID I MAY NOT HAVE TO WEAR MY GLASSES ALL THE TIME..HE ALSO SAID HE SHOT AN EIGHTY A FEW DAYS AGO...
YOU TALKED ABOUT GOLF?
OH, YES...I ALWAYS ASK HIM ABOUT HIS GOLF GAME...
IT PUTS HIM AT EASE DURING THE EXAMINATION
SCHULZ

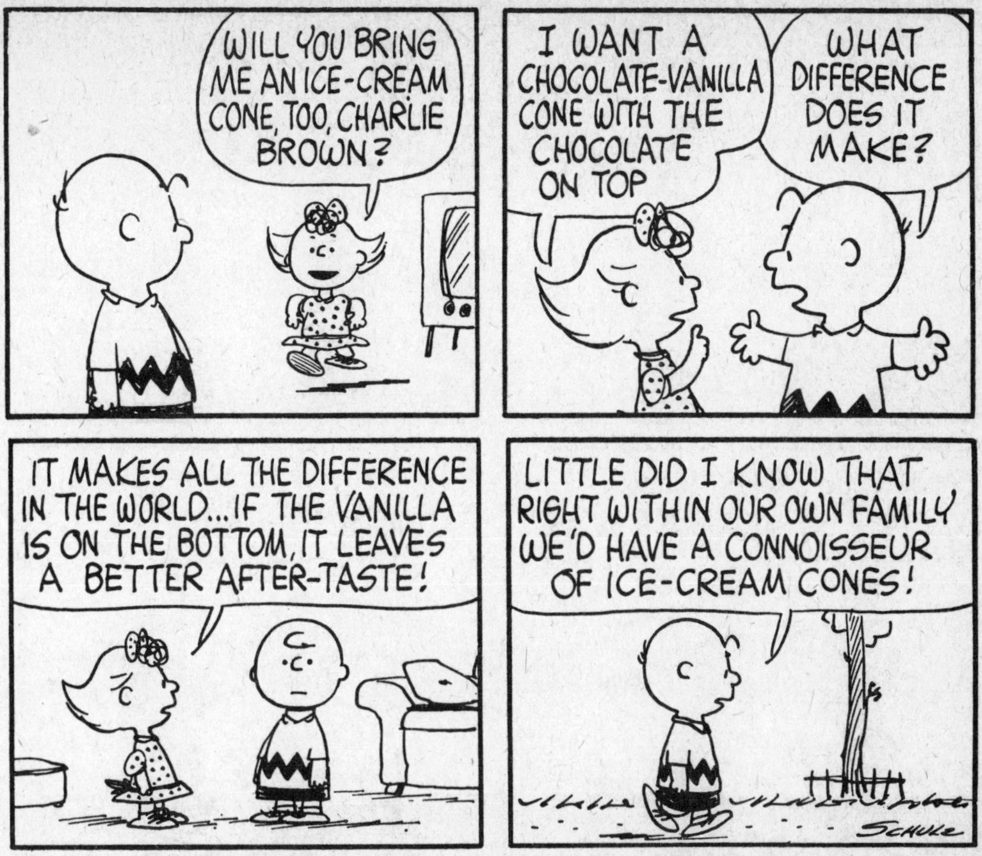
WILL YOU BRING ME AN ICE-CREAM CONE, TOO, CHARLIE BROWN?
I WANT A CHOCOLATE-VANILLA CONE WITH THE CHOCOLATE ON TOP
WHAT DIFFERENCE DOES IT MAKE?
IT MAKES ALL THE DIFFERENCE IN THE WORLD...IF THE VANILLA IS ON THE BOTTOM, IT LEAVES A BETTER AFTER-TASTE!
LITTLE DID I KNOW THAT RIGHT WITHIN OUR OWN FAMILY WE'D HAVE A CONNOISSEUR OF ICE-CREAM CONES!
SCHULZ

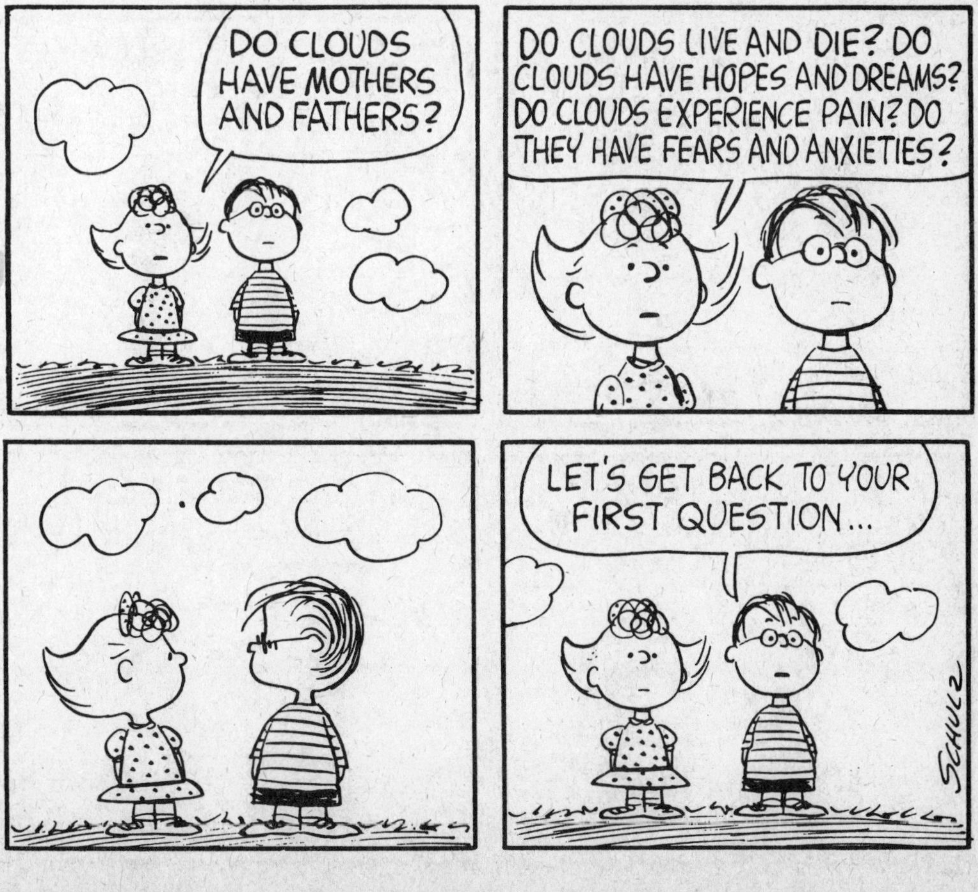
DO CLOUDS HAVE MOTHERS AND FATHERS?
DO CLOUDS LIVE AND DIE? DO CLOUDS HAVE HOPES AND DREAMS? DO CLOUDS EXPERIENCE PAIN? DO THEY HAVE FEARS AND ANXIETIES?
LET'S GET BACK TO YOUR FIRST QUESTION...
SCHULZ

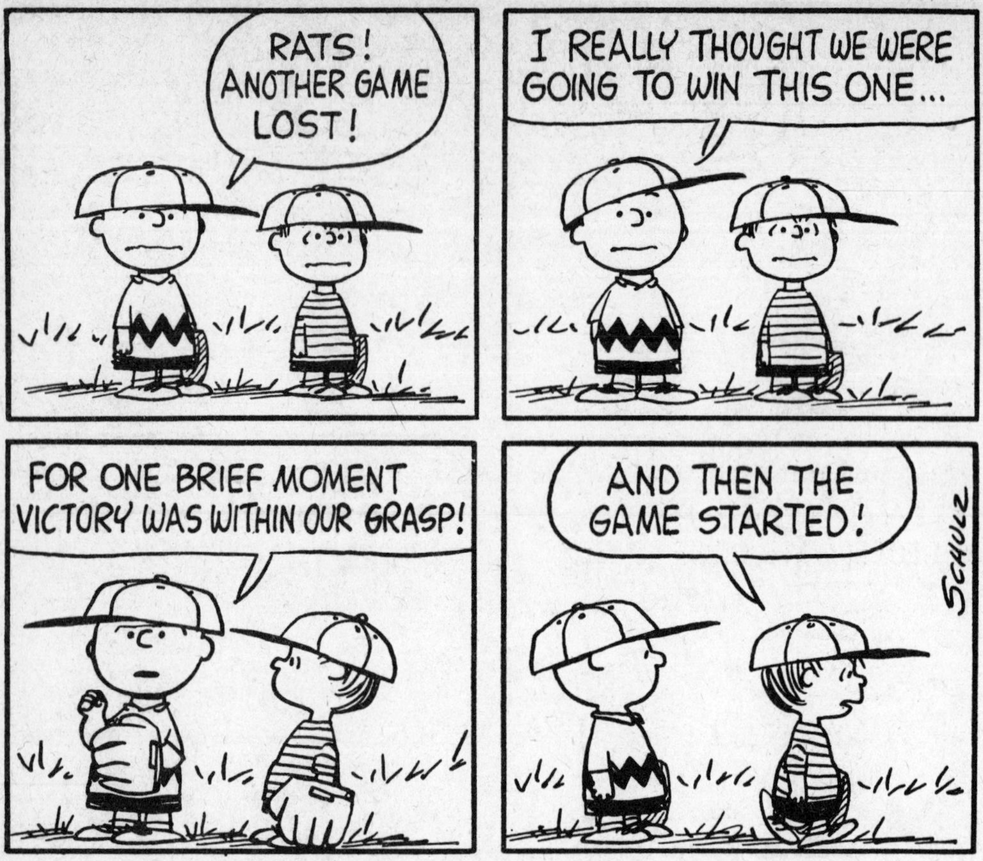
RATS! ANOTHER GAME LOST!
I REALLY THOUGHT WE WERE GOING TO WIN THIS ONE...
FOR ONE BRIEF MOMENT VICTORY WAS WITHIN OUR GRASP!
AND THEN THE GAME STARTED!
SCHULZ

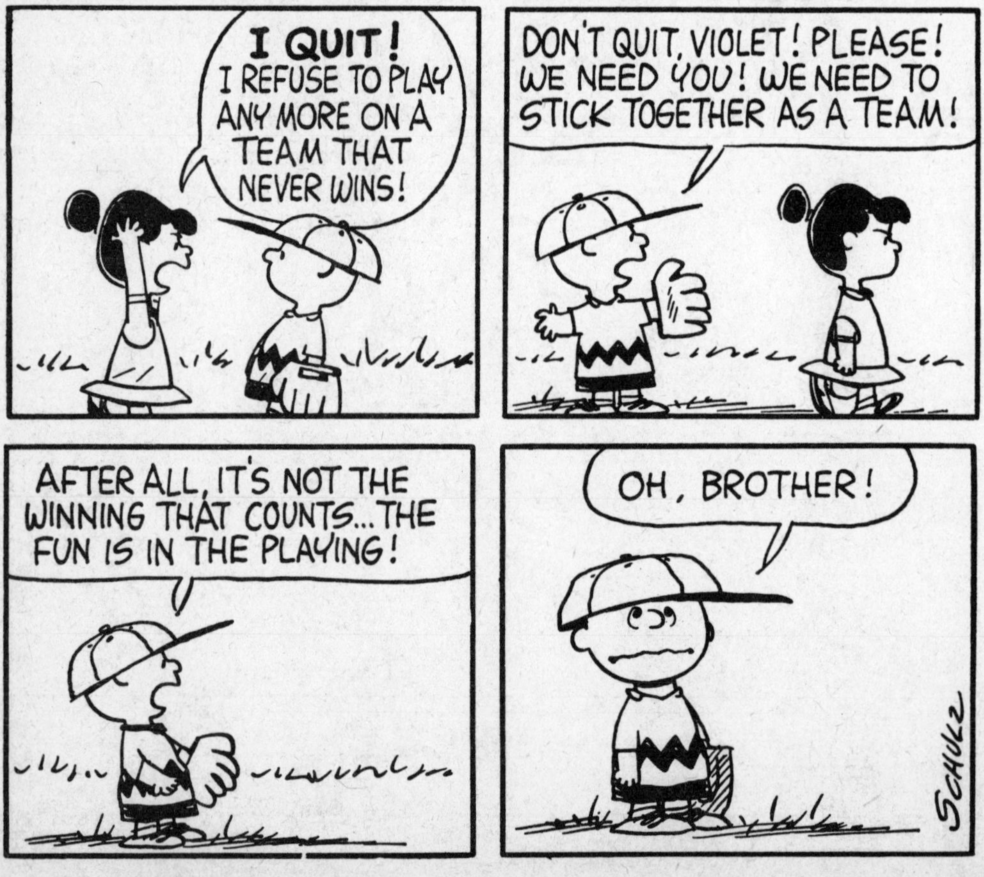
I QUIT! I REFUSE TO PLAY ANY MORE ON A TEAM THAT NEVER WINS!
DON'T QUIT, VIOLET! PLEASE! WE NEED YOU! WE NEED TO STICK TOGETHER AS A TEAM!
AFTER ALL, IT'S NOT THE WINNING THAT COUNTS...THE FUN IS IN THE PLAYING!
OH, BROTHER!
SCHULZ

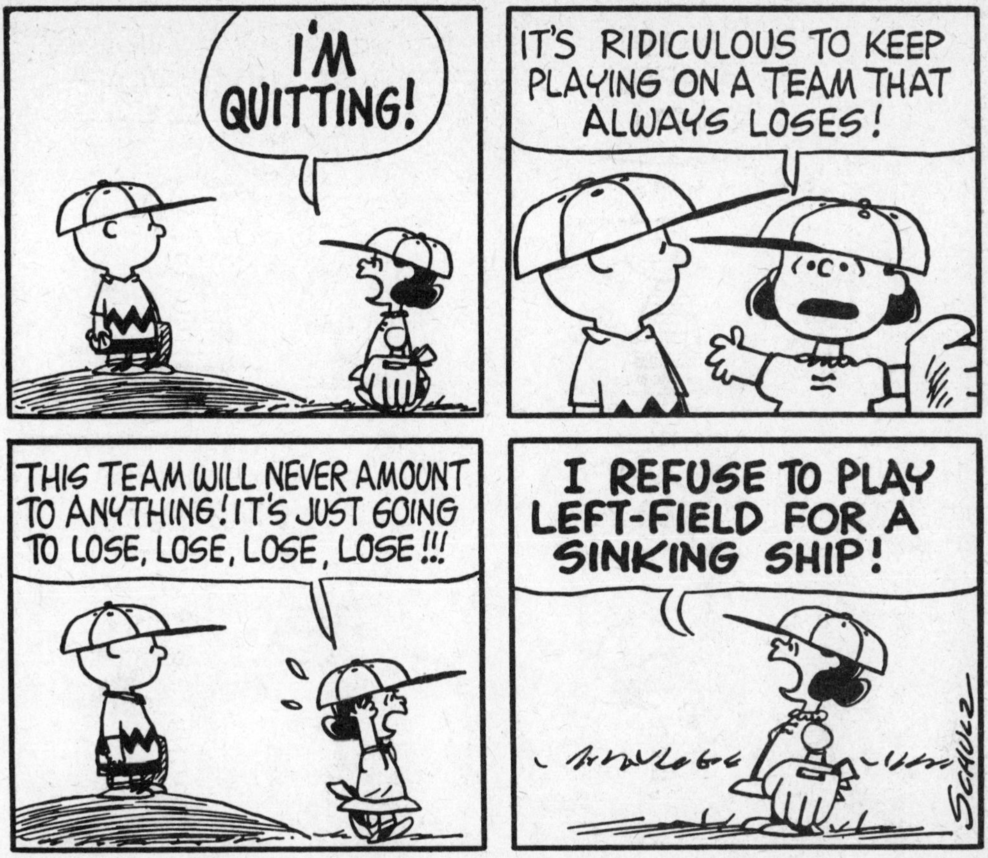
I'M QUITTING!
IT'S RIDICULOUS TO KEEP PLAYING ON A TEAM THAT ALWAYS LOSES!
THIS TEAM WILL NEVER AMOUNT TO ANYTHING! IT'S JUST GOING TO LOSE, LOSE, LOSE, LOSE!!!
I REFUSE TO PLAY LEFT-FIELD FOR A SINKING SHIP!
SCHULZ

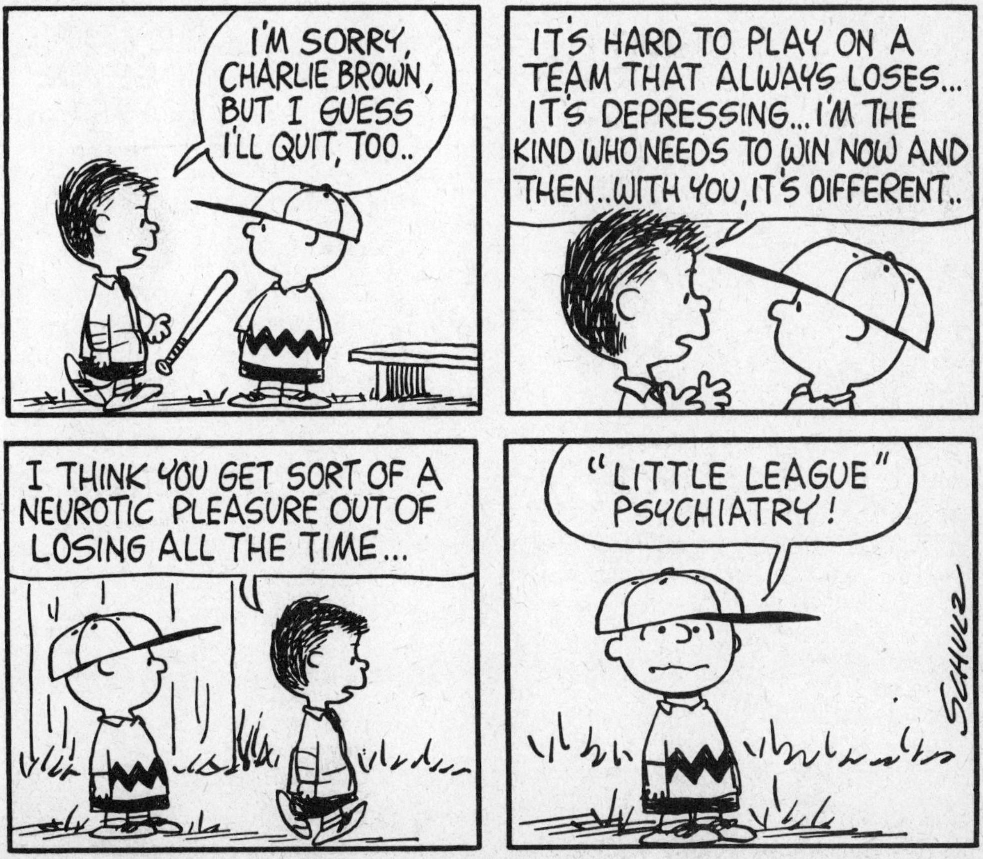
I'M SORRY, CHARLIE BROWN, BUT I GUESS I'LL QUIT, TOO..
IT'S HARD TO PLAY ON A TEAM THAT ALWAYS LOSES... IT'S DEPRESSING... I'M THE KIND WHO NEEDS TO WIN NOW AND THEN.. WITH YOU, IT'S DIFFERENT..
I THINK YOU GET SORT OF A NEUROTIC PLEASURE OUT OF LOSING ALL THE TIME...
"LITTLE LEAGUE" PSYCHIATRY!
SCHULZ

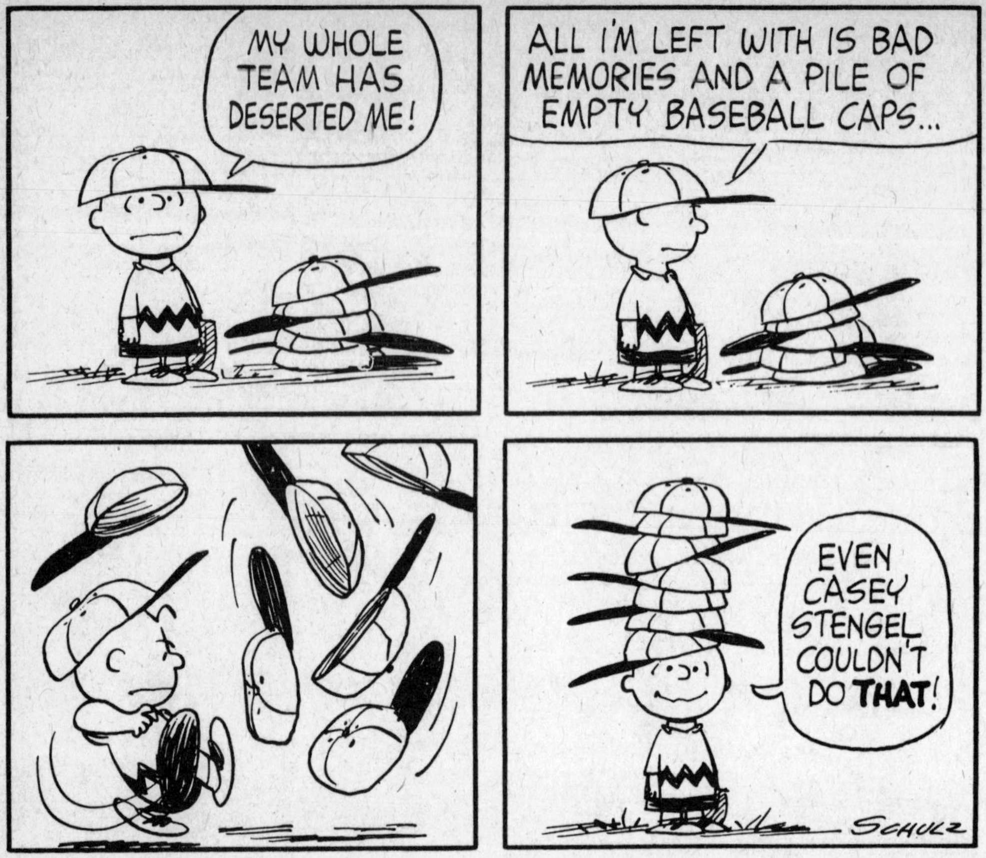
MY WHOLE TEAM HAS DESERTED ME!
ALL I'M LEFT WITH IS BAD MEMORIES AND A PILE OF EMPTY BASEBALL CAPS...
EVEN CASEY STENGEL COULDN'T DO **THAT**!
SCHULZ

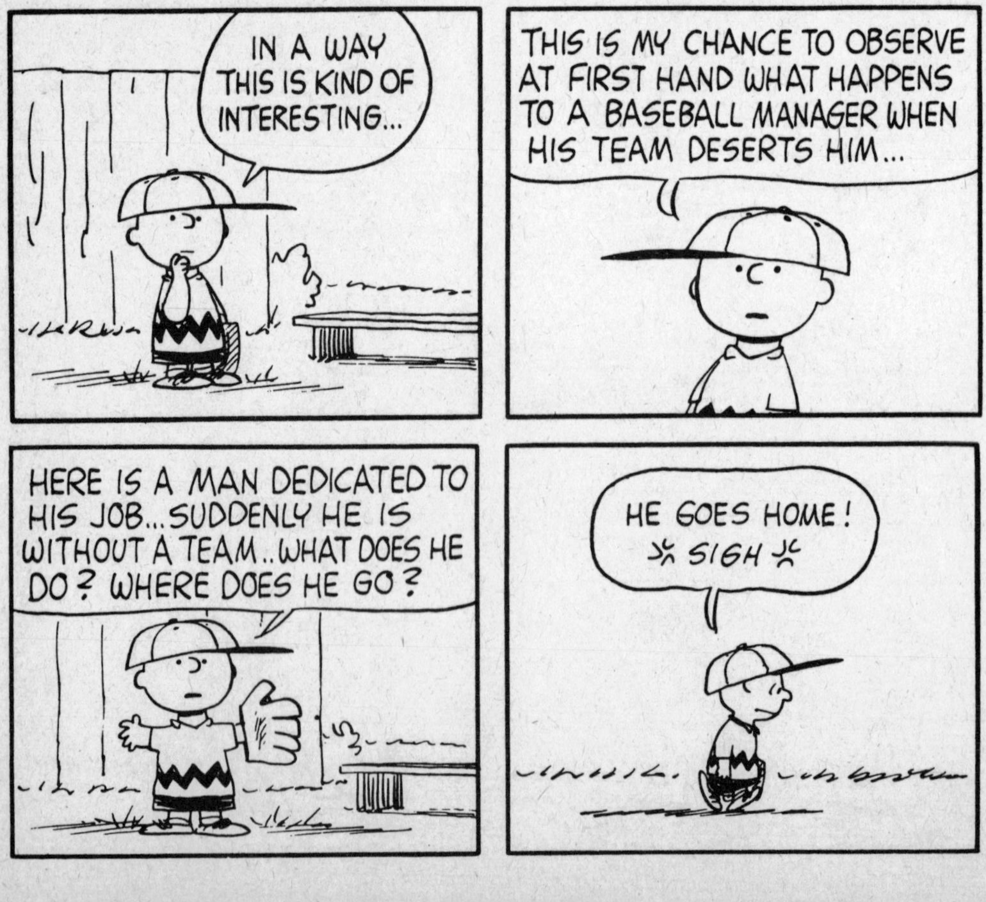
IN A WAY THIS IS KIND OF INTERESTING...
THIS IS MY CHANCE TO OBSERVE AT FIRST HAND WHAT HAPPENS TO A BASEBALL MANAGER WHEN HIS TEAM DESERTS HIM...
HERE IS A MAN DEDICATED TO HIS JOB...SUDDENLY HE IS WITHOUT A TEAM..WHAT DOES HE DO? WHERE DOES HE GO?
HE GOES HOME!
SIGH

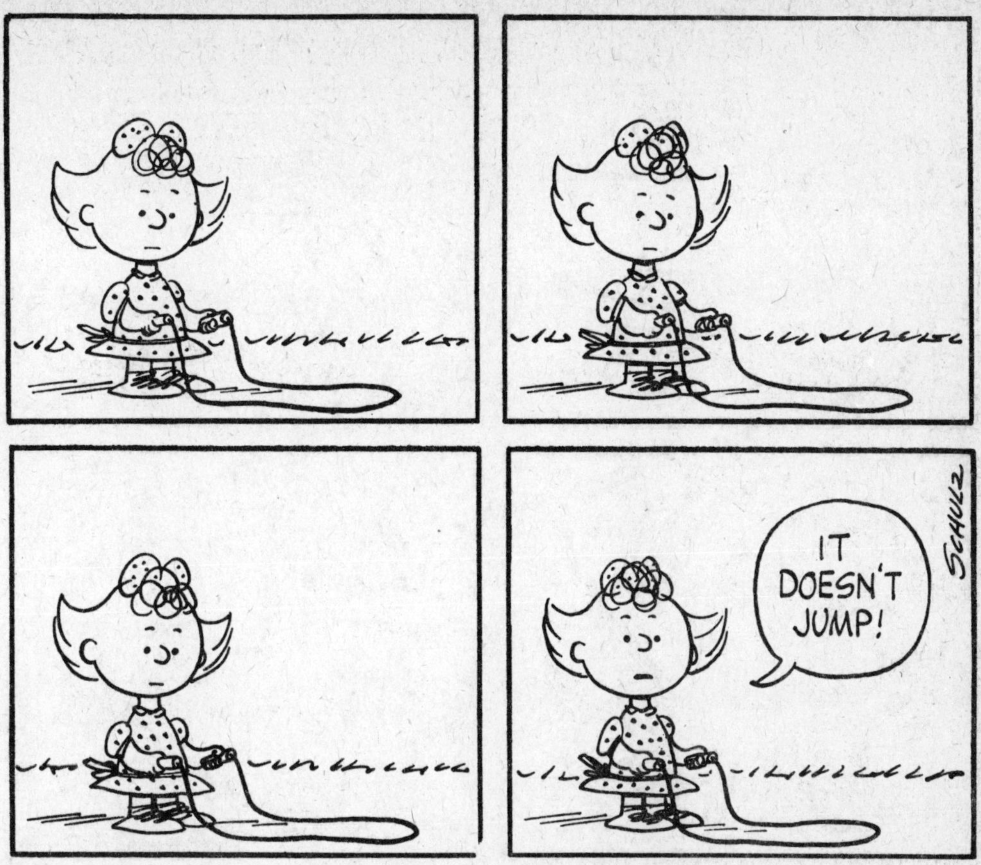
IT DOESN'T JUMP!
SCHULZ

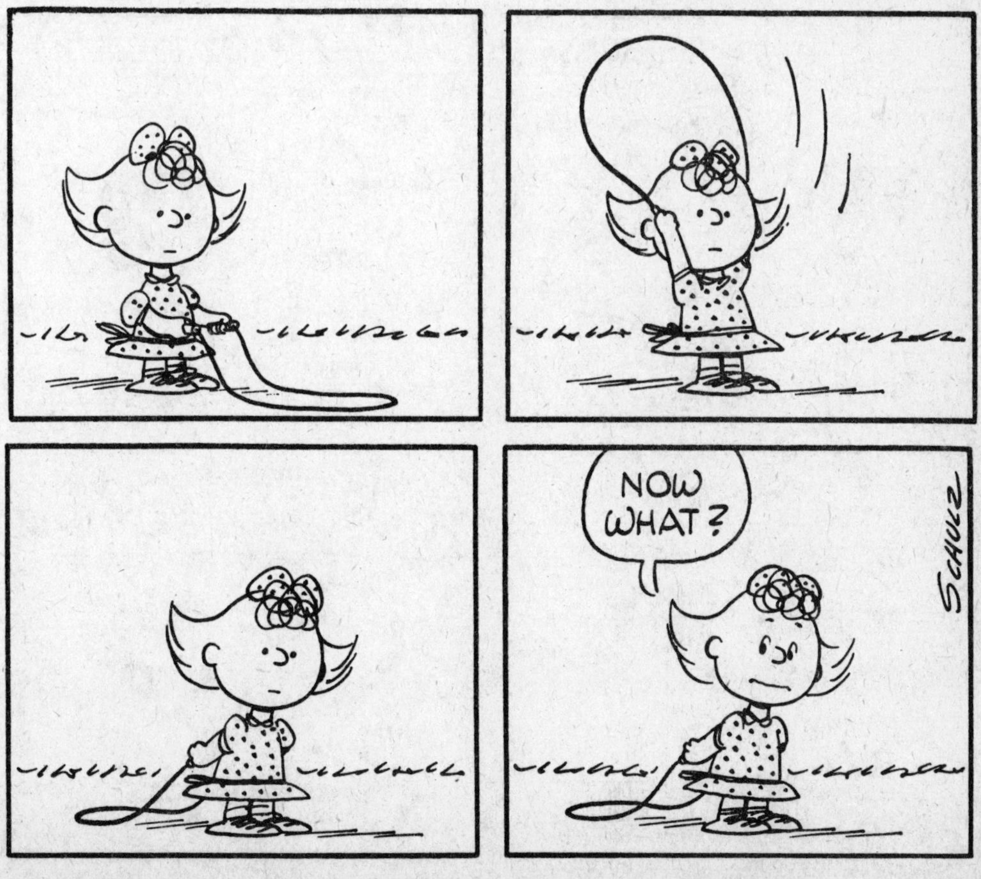
NOW WHAT?
SCHULZ

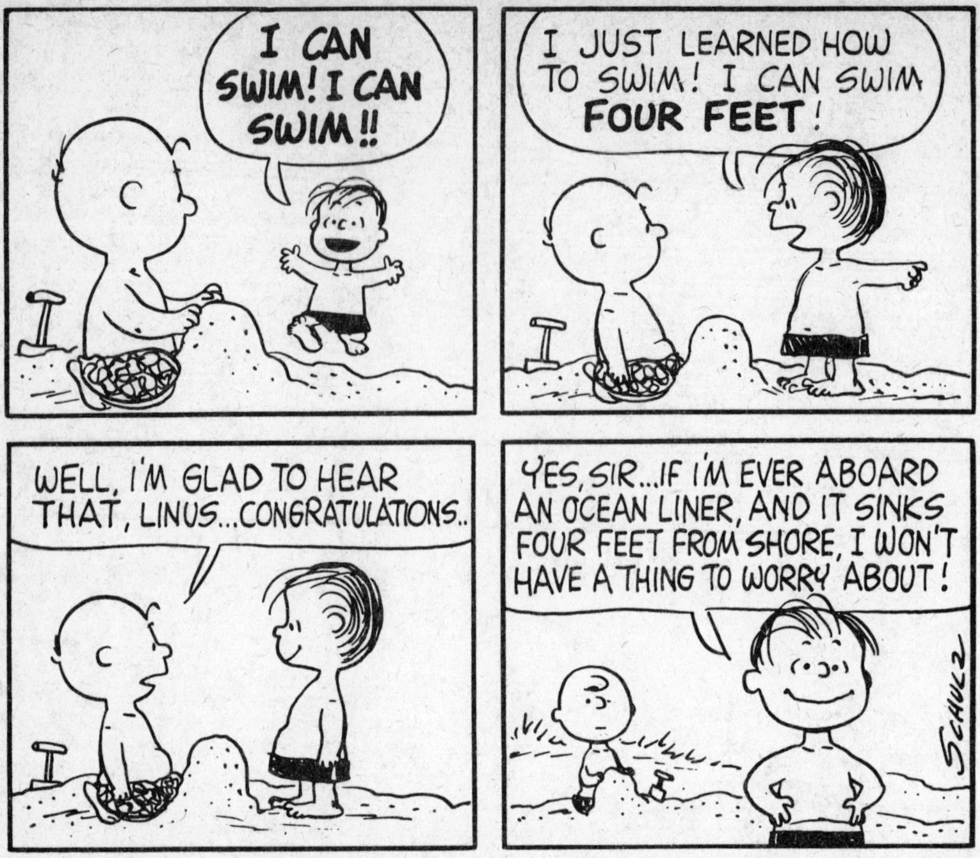
I CAN SWIM! I CAN SWIM!!
I JUST LEARNED HOW TO SWIM! I CAN SWIM **FOUR FEET**!
WELL, I'M GLAD TO HEAR THAT, LINUS...CONGRATULATIONS..
YES, SIR...IF I'M EVER ABOARD AN OCEAN LINER, AND IT SINKS FOUR FEET FROM SHORE, I WON'T HAVE A THING TO WORRY ABOUT!
SCHULZ

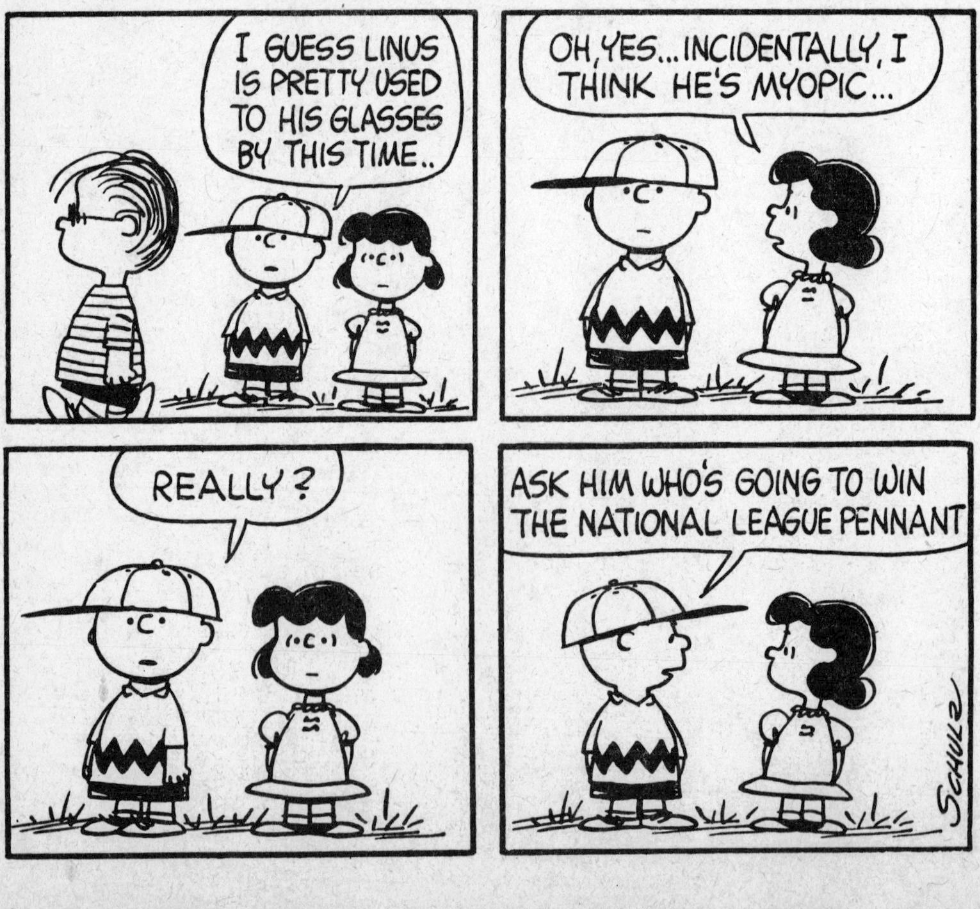
I GUESS LINUS IS PRETTY USED TO HIS GLASSES BY THIS TIME..
OH, YES...INCIDENTALLY, I THINK HE'S MYOPIC...
REALLY?
ASK HIM WHO'S GOING TO WIN THE NATIONAL LEAGUE PENNANT
SCHULZ

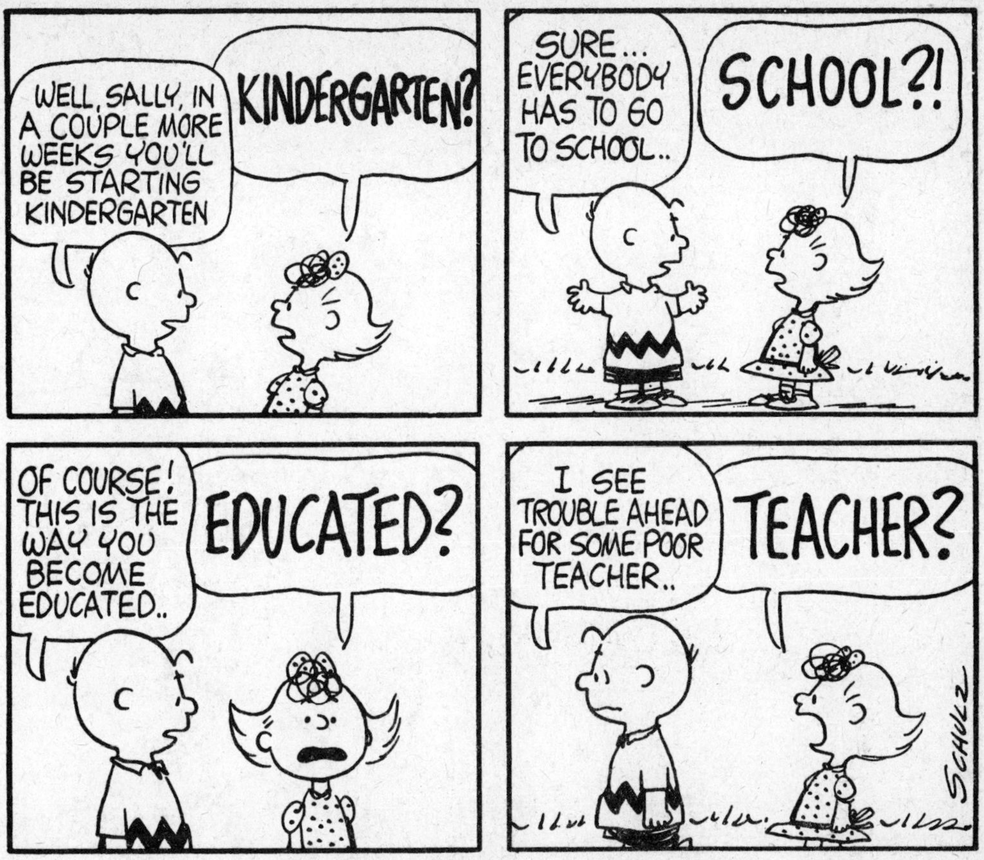
WELL, SALLY, IN A COUPLE MORE WEEKS YOU'LL BE STARTING KINDERGARTEN
KINDERGARTEN?
SURE... EVERYBODY HAS TO GO TO SCHOOL..
SCHOOL?!
OF COURSE! THIS IS THE WAY YOU BECOME EDUCATED..
EDUCATED?
I SEE TROUBLE AHEAD FOR SOME POOR TEACHER..
TEACHER?
SCHULZ

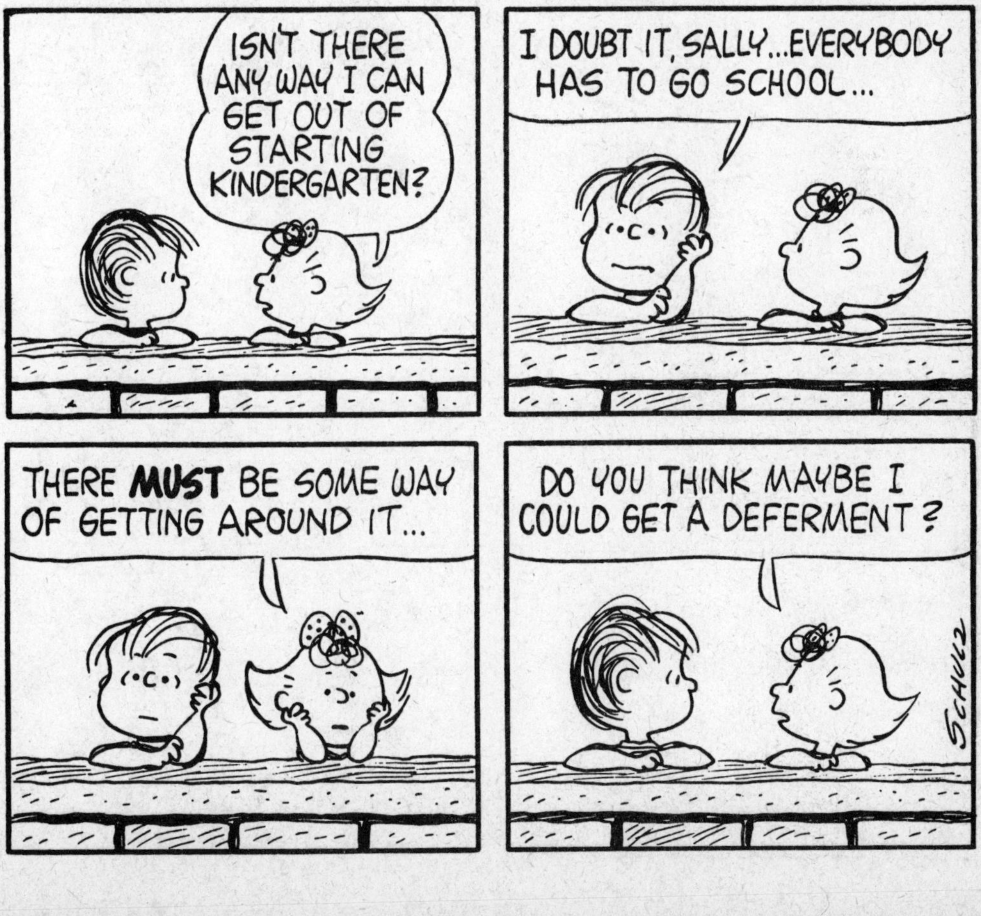
ISN'T THERE ANY WAY I CAN GET OUT OF STARTING KINDERGARTEN?
I DOUBT IT, SALLY...EVERYBODY HAS TO GO SCHOOL...
THERE **MUST** BE SOME WAY OF GETTING AROUND IT...
DO YOU THINK MAYBE I COULD GET A DEFERMENT?
SCHULZ

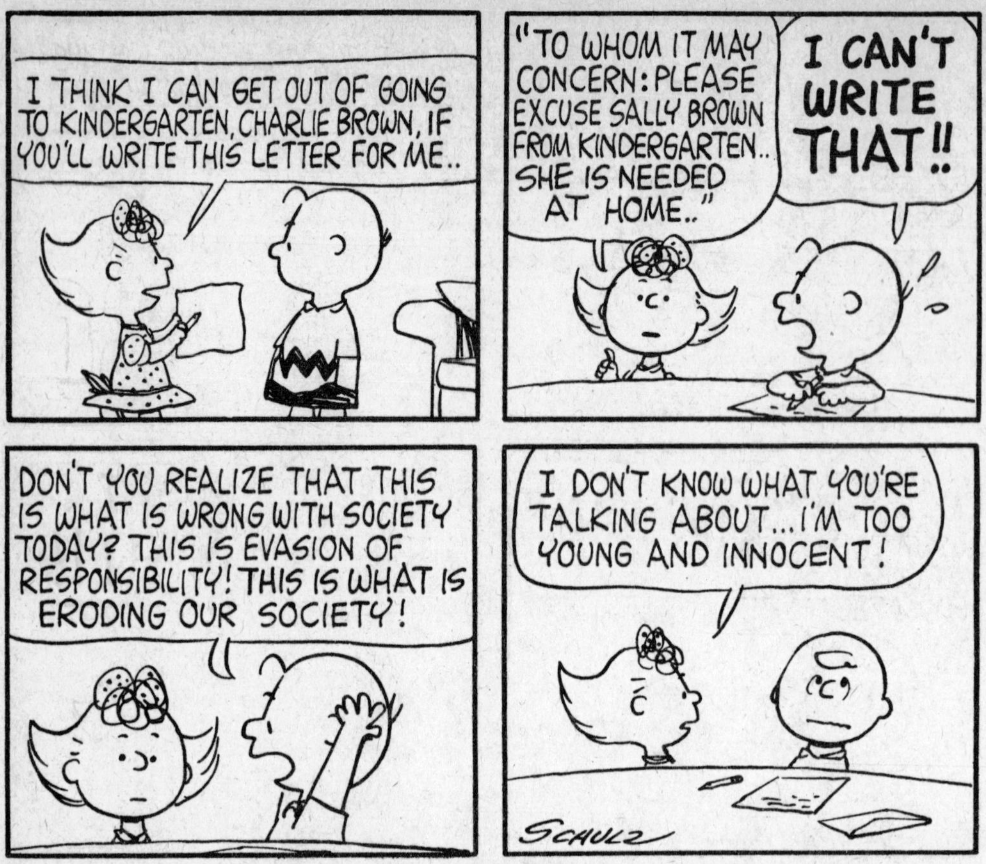
I THINK I CAN GET OUT OF GOING TO KINDERGARTEN, CHARLIE BROWN, IF YOU'LL WRITE THIS LETTER FOR ME..
"TO WHOM IT MAY CONCERN: PLEASE EXCUSE SALLY BROWN FROM KINDERGARTEN.. SHE IS NEEDED AT HOME.."
I CAN'T WRITE THAT!!
DON'T YOU REALIZE THAT THIS IS WHAT IS WRONG WITH SOCIETY TODAY? THIS IS EVASION OF RESPONSIBILITY! THIS IS WHAT IS ERODING OUR SOCIETY!
I DON'T KNOW WHAT YOU'RE TALKING ABOUT... I'M TOO YOUNG AND INNOCENT!
SCHULZ

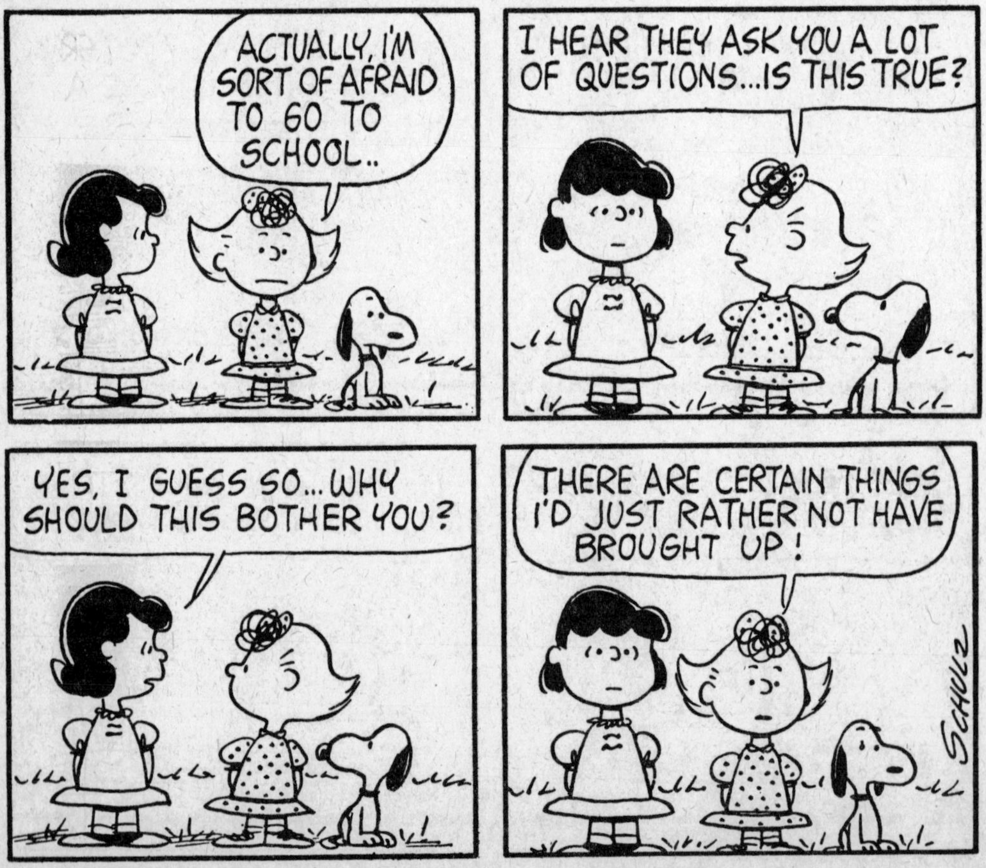
ACTUALLY, I'M SORT OF AFRAID TO GO TO SCHOOL..
I HEAR THEY ASK YOU A LOT OF QUESTIONS... IS THIS TRUE?
YES, I GUESS SO... WHY SHOULD THIS BOTHER YOU?
THERE ARE CERTAIN THINGS I'D JUST RATHER NOT HAVE BROUGHT UP!
SCHULZ

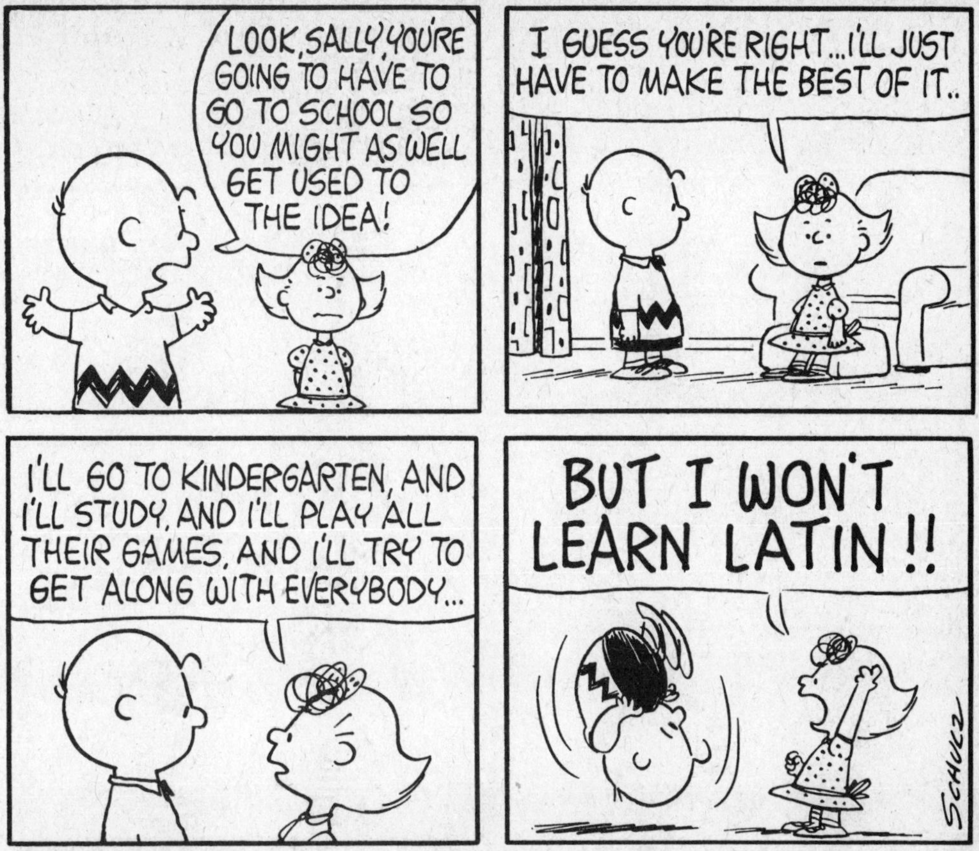
LOOK, SALLY, YOU'RE GOING TO HAVE TO GO TO SCHOOL SO YOU MIGHT AS WELL GET USED TO THE IDEA!
I GUESS YOU'RE RIGHT...I'LL JUST HAVE TO MAKE THE BEST OF IT..
I'LL GO TO KINDERGARTEN, AND I'LL STUDY, AND I'LL PLAY ALL THEIR GAMES, AND I'LL TRY TO GET ALONG WITH EVERYBODY...
BUT I WON'T LEARN LATIN !!
SCHULZ

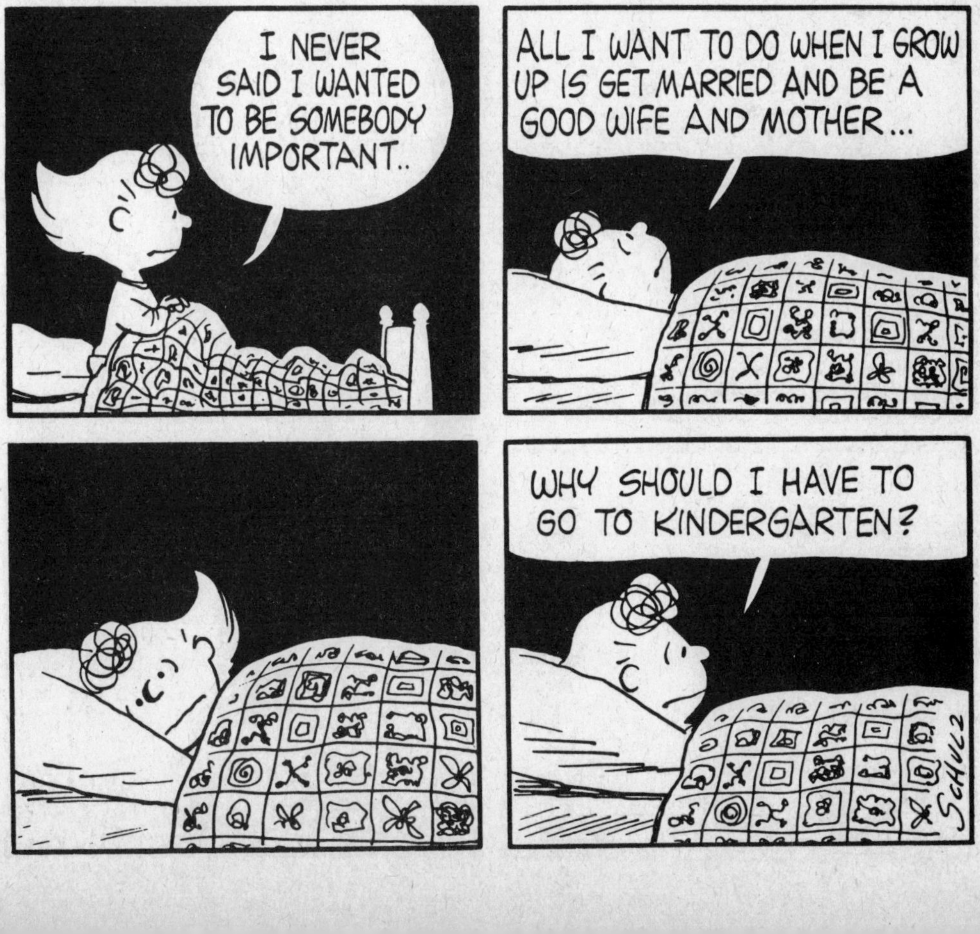
I NEVER SAID I WANTED TO BE SOMEBODY IMPORTANT..
ALL I WANT TO DO WHEN I GROW UP IS GET MARRIED AND BE A GOOD WIFE AND MOTHER...
WHY SHOULD I HAVE TO GO TO KINDERGARTEN?
SCHULZ

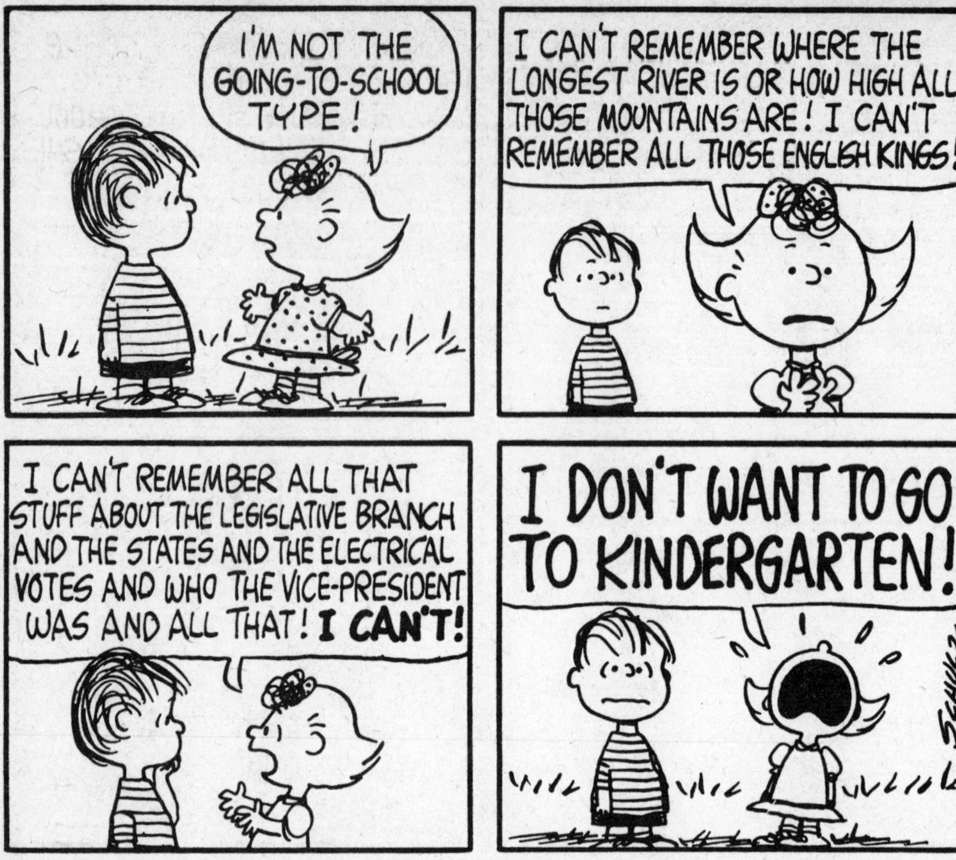
I'M NOT THE GOING-TO-SCHOOL TYPE!
I CAN'T REMEMBER WHERE THE LONGEST RIVER IS OR HOW HIGH ALL THOSE MOUNTAINS ARE! I CAN'T REMEMBER ALL THOSE ENGLISH KINGS!
I CAN'T REMEMBER ALL THAT STUFF ABOUT THE LEGISLATIVE BRANCH AND THE STATES AND THE ELECTRICAL VOTES AND WHO THE VICE-PRESIDENT WAS AND ALL THAT! I CAN'T!
I DON'T WANT TO GO TO KINDERGARTEN!
SCHULZ

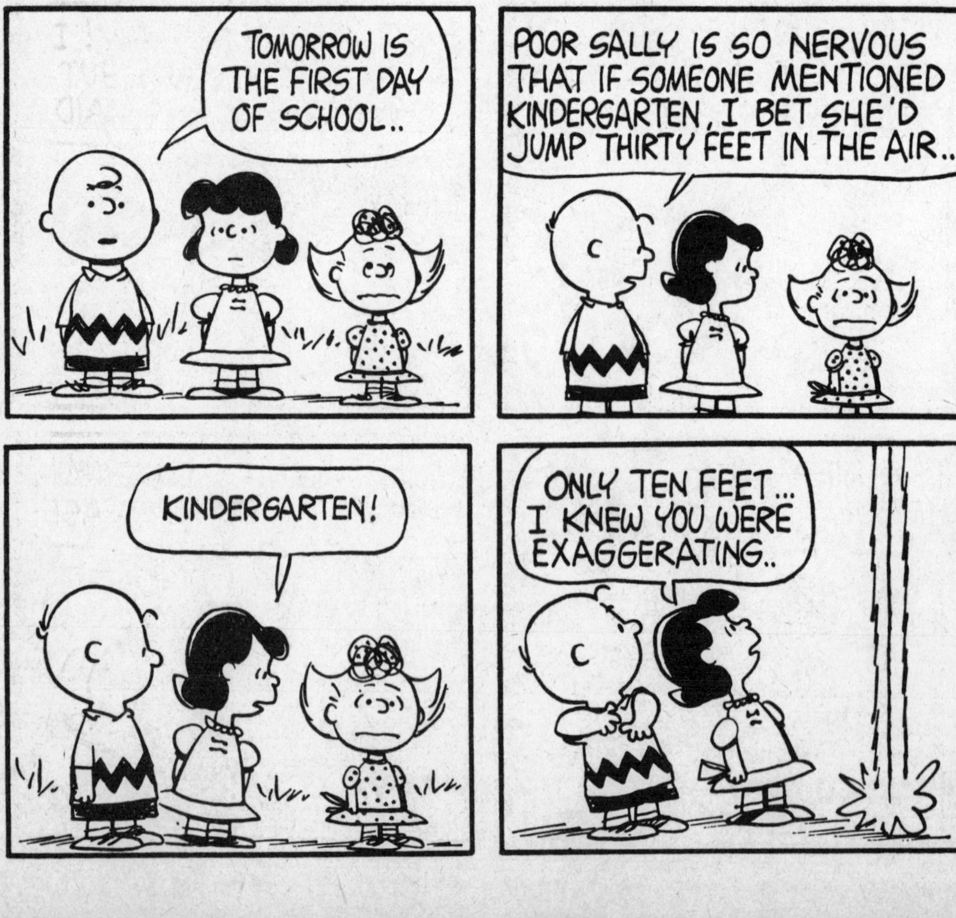
TOMORROW IS THE FIRST DAY OF SCHOOL..
POOR SALLY IS SO NERVOUS THAT IF SOMEONE MENTIONED KINDERGARTEN, I BET SHE'D JUMP THIRTY FEET IN THE AIR..
KINDERGARTEN!
ONLY TEN FEET... I KNEW YOU WERE EXAGGERATING..

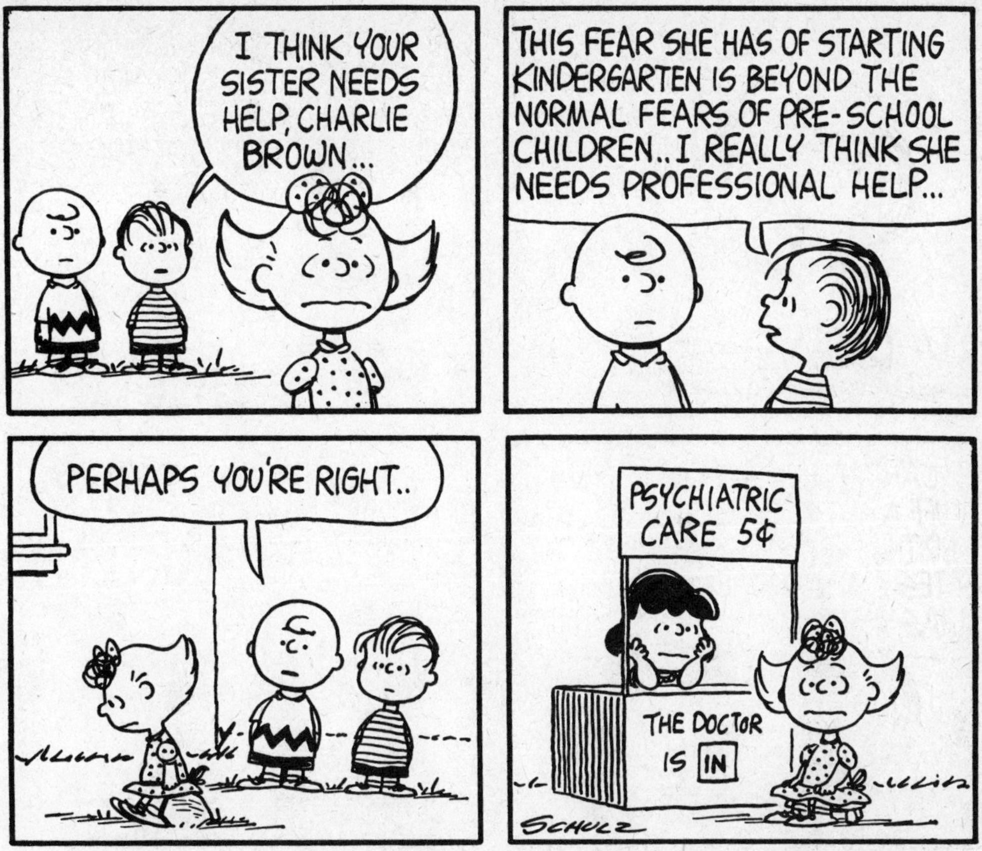
I THINK YOUR SISTER NEEDS HELP, CHARLIE BROWN...
THIS FEAR SHE HAS OF STARTING KINDERGARTEN IS BEYOND THE NORMAL FEARS OF PRE-SCHOOL CHILDREN.. I REALLY THINK SHE NEEDS PROFESSIONAL HELP...
PERHAPS YOU'RE RIGHT..
PSYCHIATRIC CARE 5¢
THE DOCTOR IS IN
SCHULZ

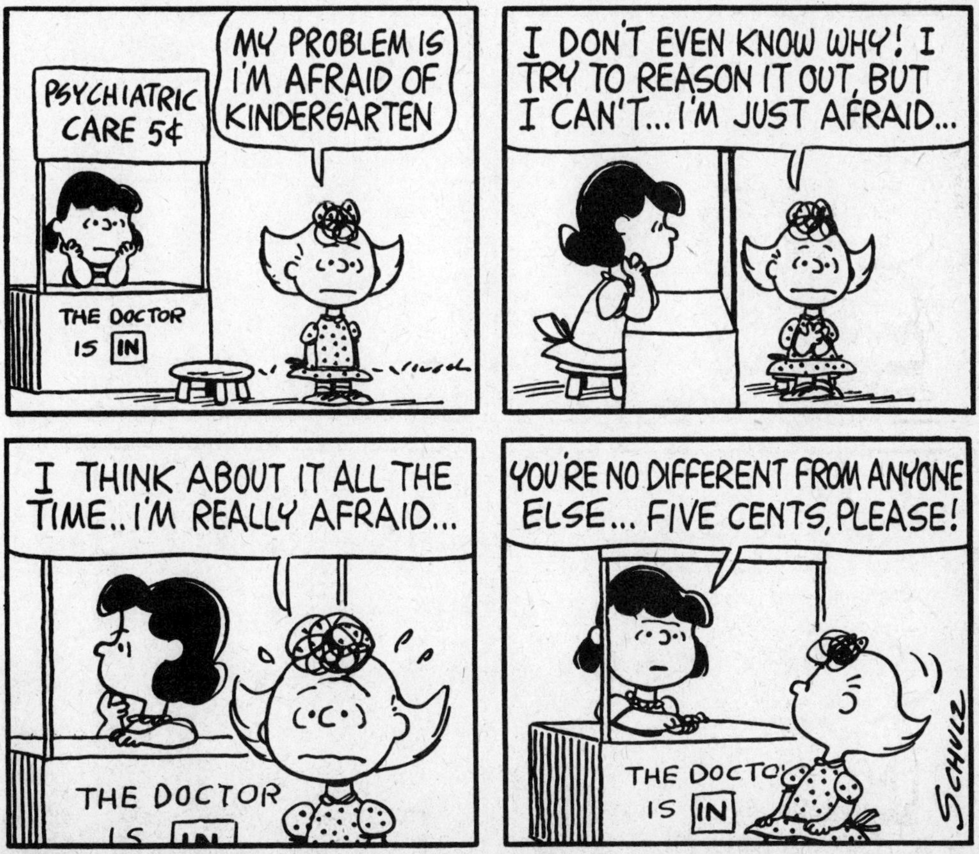
PSYCHIATRIC CARE 5¢
THE DOCTOR IS IN
MY PROBLEM IS I'M AFRAID OF KINDERGARTEN
I DON'T EVEN KNOW WHY! I TRY TO REASON IT OUT, BUT I CAN'T... I'M JUST AFRAID...
I THINK ABOUT IT ALL THE TIME.. I'M REALLY AFRAID...
THE DOCTOR
YOU'RE NO DIFFERENT FROM ANYONE ELSE... FIVE CENTS, PLEASE!
IS IN
SCHULZ

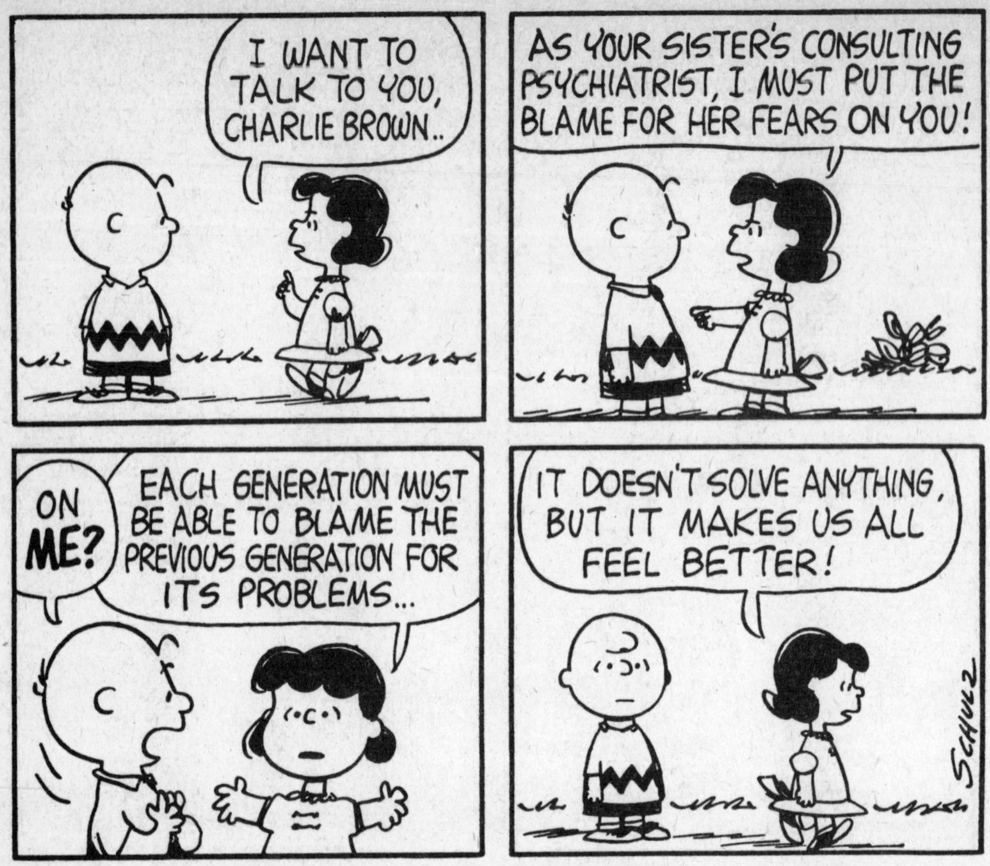
I WANT TO TALK TO YOU, CHARLIE BROWN..
AS YOUR SISTER'S CONSULTING PSYCHIATRIST, I MUST PUT THE BLAME FOR HER FEARS ON YOU!
ON ME?
EACH GENERATION MUST BE ABLE TO BLAME THE PREVIOUS GENERATION FOR ITS PROBLEMS...
IT DOESN'T SOLVE ANYTHING, BUT IT MAKES US ALL FEEL BETTER!
SCHULZ

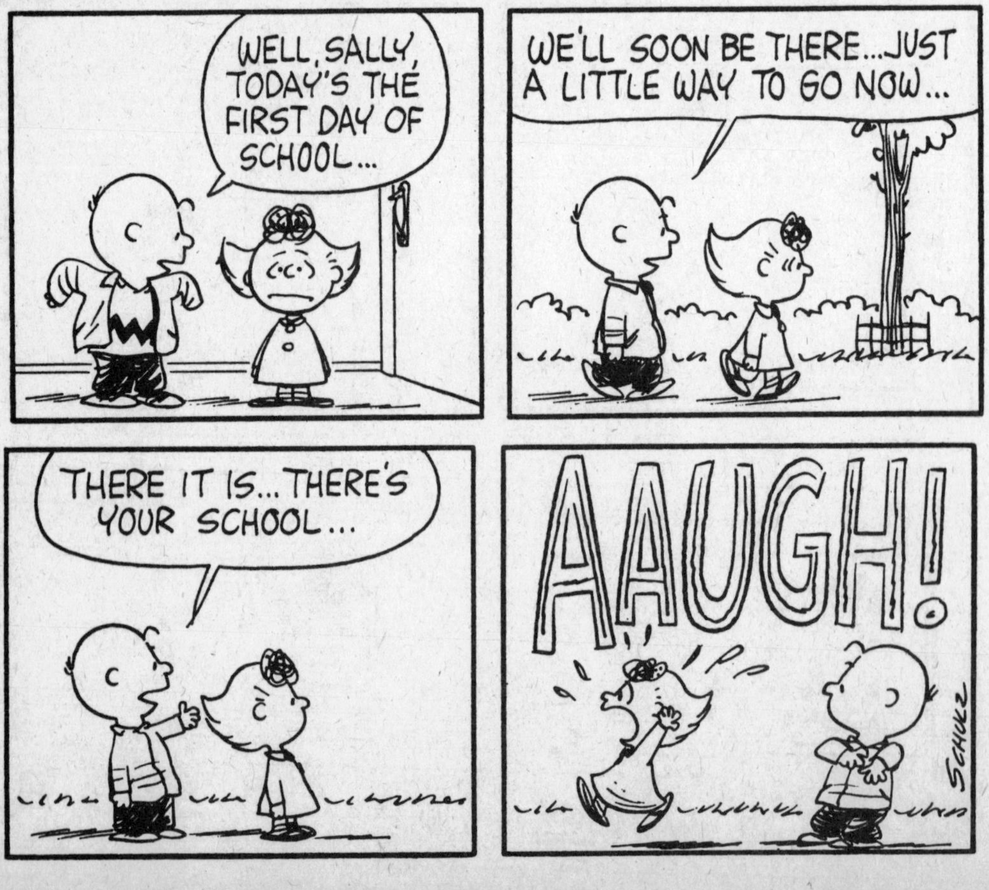
WELL, SALLY, TODAY'S THE FIRST DAY OF SCHOOL...
WE'LL SOON BE THERE....JUST A LITTLE WAY TO GO NOW...
THERE IT IS... THERE'S YOUR SCHOOL...
AAUGH!
SCHULZ

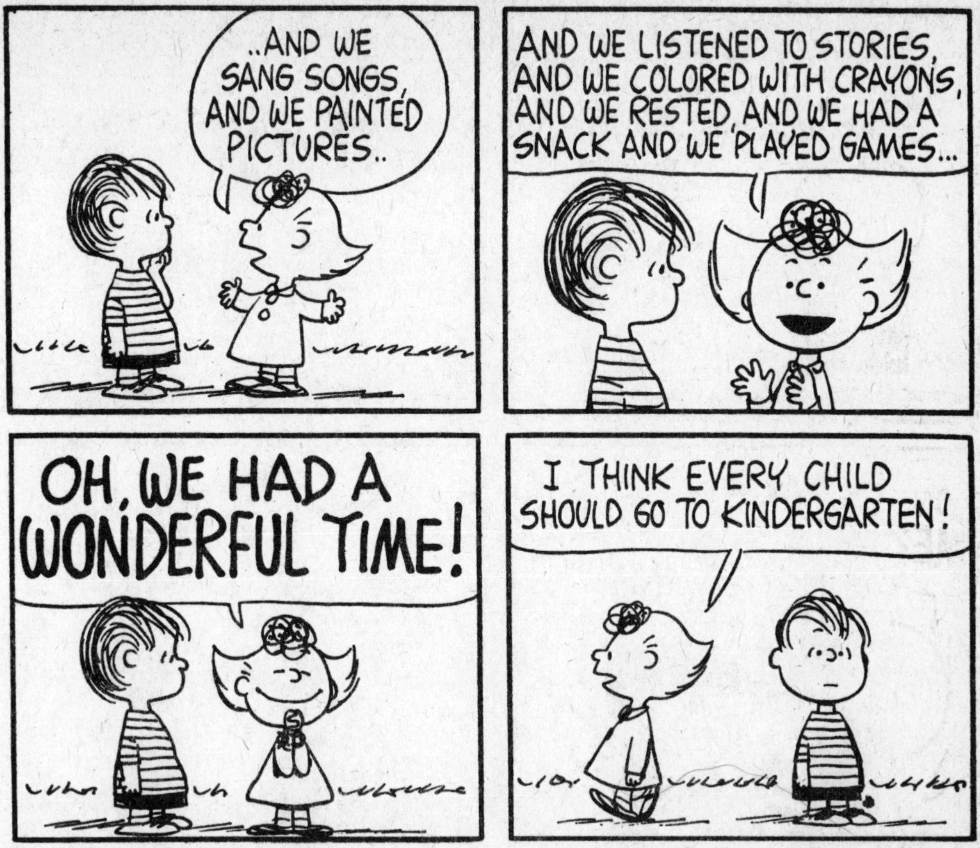
..AND WE SANG SONGS, AND WE PAINTED PICTURES..
AND WE LISTENED TO STORIES, AND WE COLORED WITH CRAYONS, AND WE RESTED, AND WE HAD A SNACK AND WE PLAYED GAMES...
OH, WE HAD A WONDERFUL TIME!
I THINK EVERY CHILD SHOULD GO TO KINDERGARTEN!

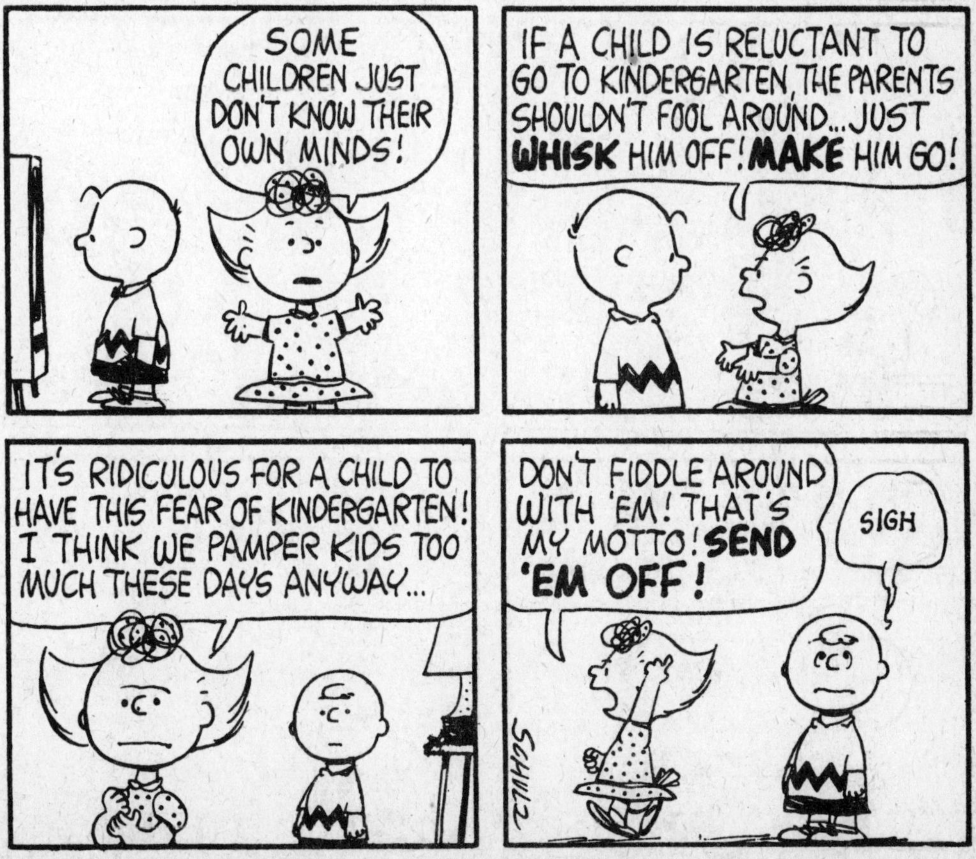
SOME CHILDREN JUST DON'T KNOW THEIR OWN MINDS!
IF A CHILD IS RELUCTANT TO GO TO KINDERGARTEN, THE PARENTS SHOULDN'T FOOL AROUND... JUST WHISK HIM OFF! MAKE HIM GO!
IT'S RIDICULOUS FOR A CHILD TO HAVE THIS FEAR OF KINDERGARTEN! I THINK WE PAMPER KIDS TOO MUCH THESE DAYS ANYWAY...
DON'T FIDDLE AROUND WITH 'EM! THAT'S MY MOTTO! SEND 'EM OFF!
SIGH
SCHULZ

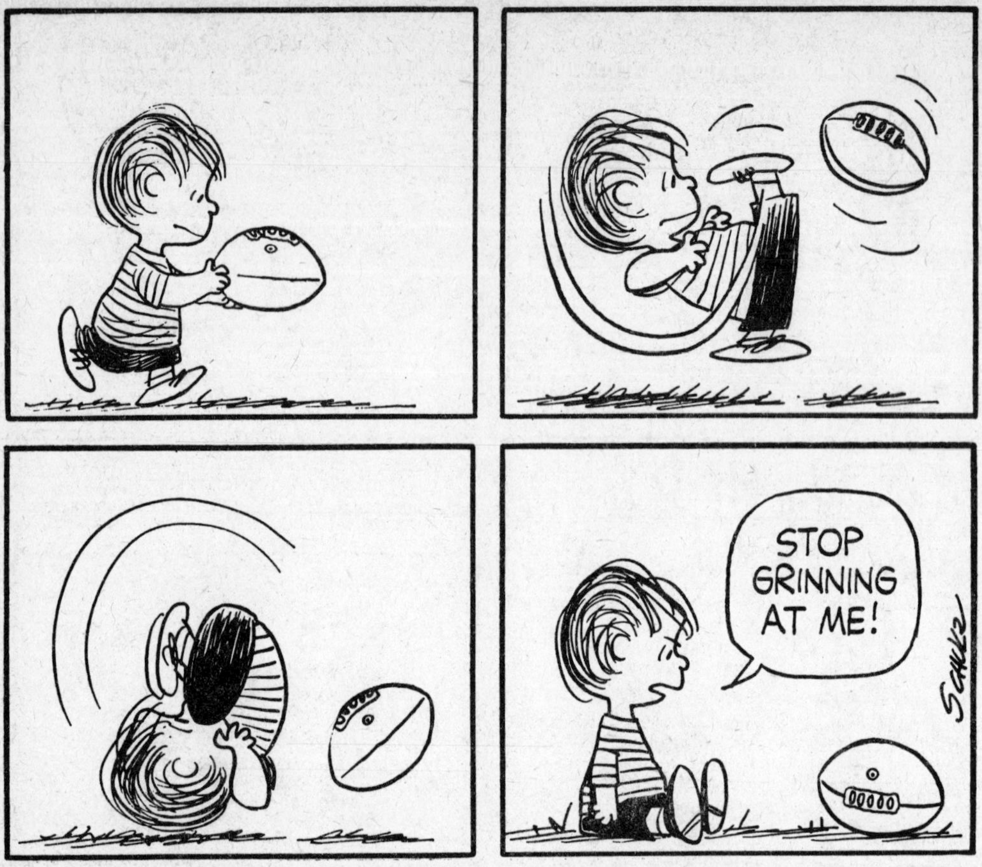
STOP GRINNING AT ME!
SCHULZ

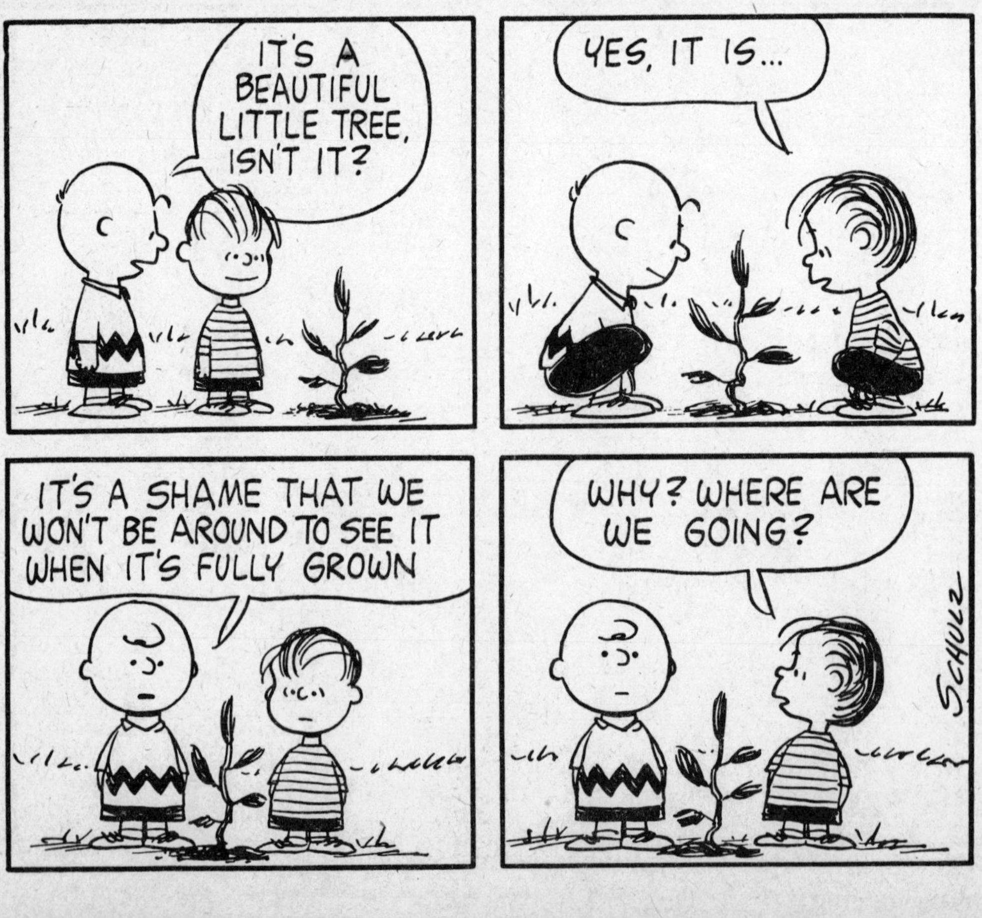
IT'S A BEAUTIFUL LITTLE TREE, ISN'T IT?
YES, IT IS...
IT'S A SHAME THAT WE WON'T BE AROUND TO SEE IT WHEN IT'S FULLY GROWN
WHY? WHERE ARE WE GOING?
SCHULZ

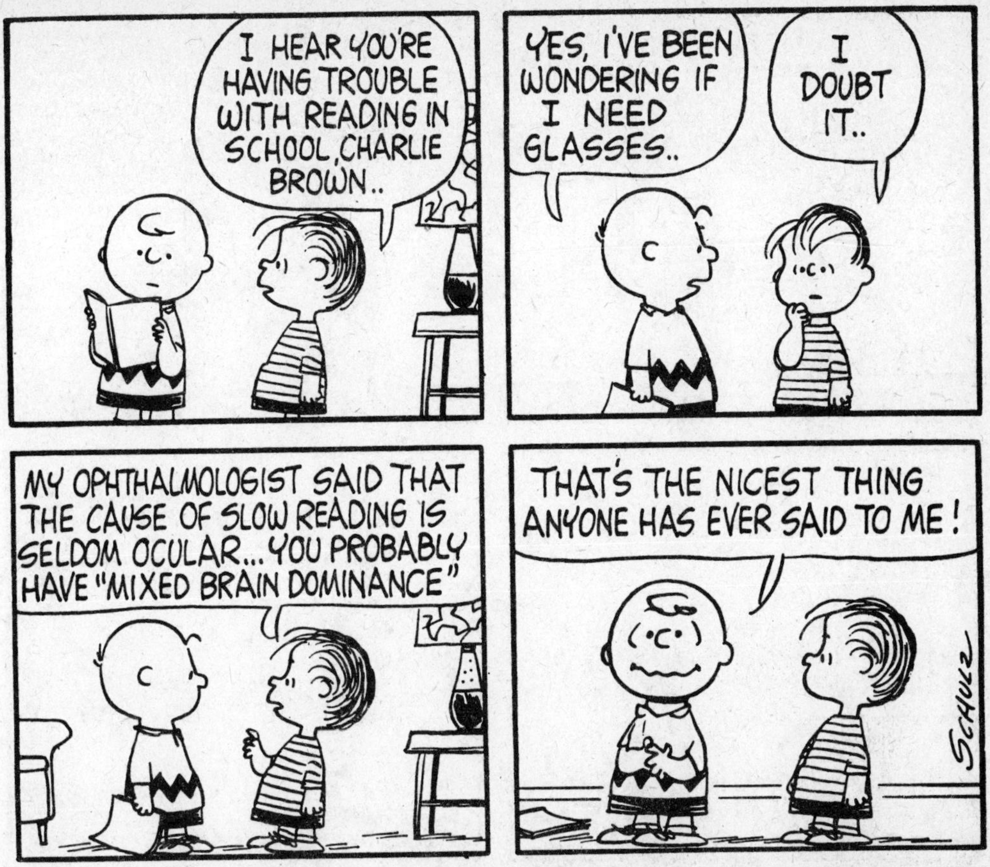
I HEAR YOU'RE HAVING TROUBLE WITH READING IN SCHOOL, CHARLIE BROWN..
YES, I'VE BEEN WONDERING IF I NEED GLASSES..
I DOUBT IT..
MY OPHTHALMOLOGIST SAID THAT THE CAUSE OF SLOW READING IS SELDOM OCULAR... YOU PROBABLY HAVE "MIXED BRAIN DOMINANCE"
THAT'S THE NICEST THING ANYONE HAS EVER SAID TO ME!
SCHULZ

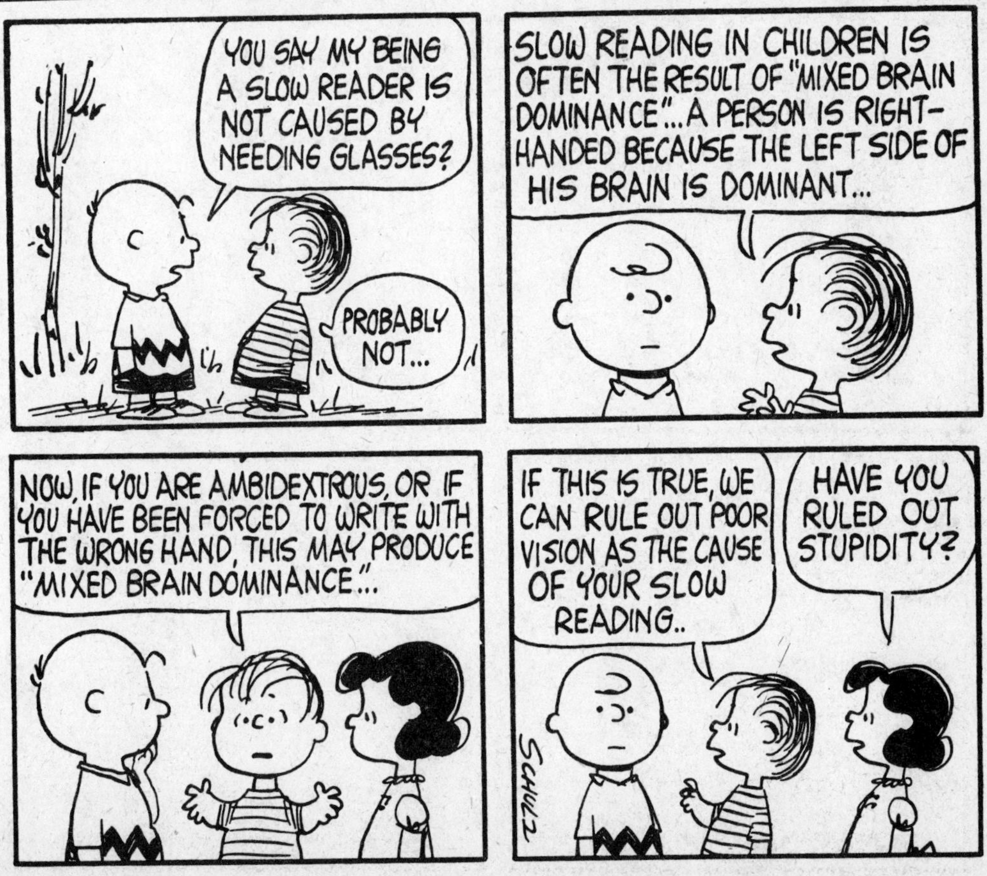
YOU SAY MY BEING A SLOW READER IS NOT CAUSED BY NEEDING GLASSES?
PROBABLY NOT...
SLOW READING IN CHILDREN IS OFTEN THE RESULT OF "MIXED BRAIN DOMINANCE"... A PERSON IS RIGHT-HANDED BECAUSE THE LEFT SIDE OF HIS BRAIN IS DOMINANT...
NOW, IF YOU ARE AMBIDEXTROUS, OR IF YOU HAVE BEEN FORCED TO WRITE WITH THE WRONG HAND, THIS MAY PRODUCE "MIXED BRAIN DOMINANCE"...
IF THIS IS TRUE, WE CAN RULE OUT POOR VISION AS THE CAUSE OF YOUR SLOW READING..
HAVE YOU RULED OUT STUPIDITY?
SCHULZ

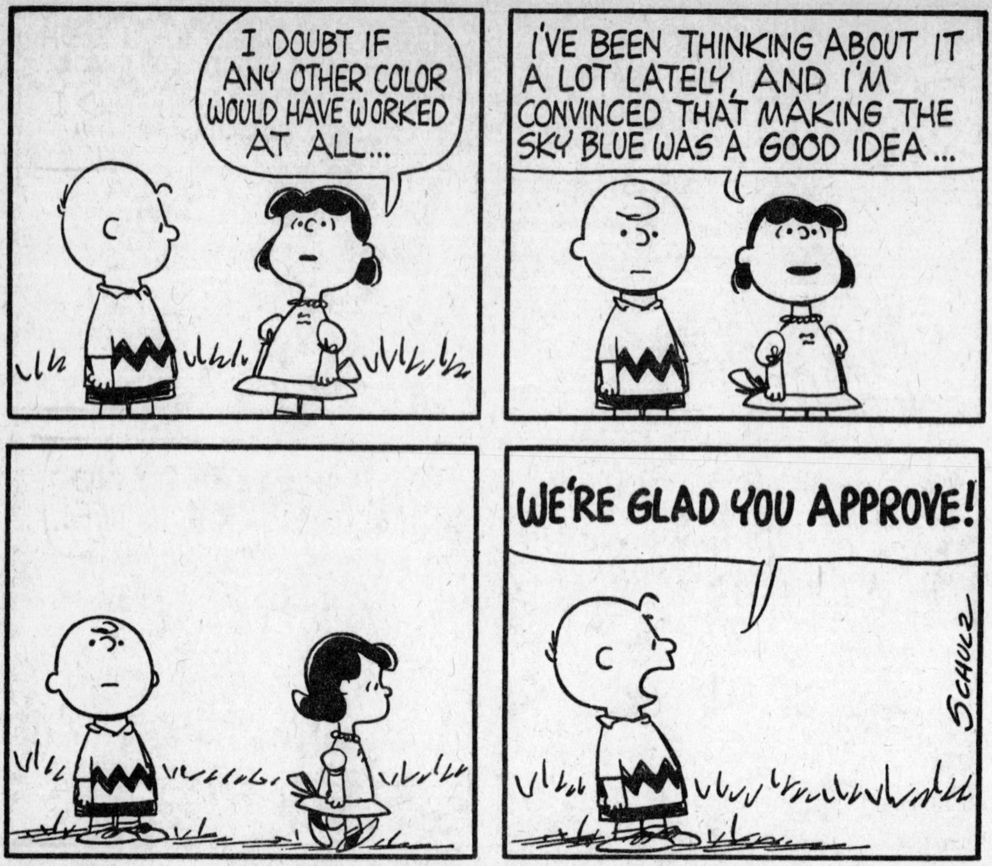
I DOUBT IF ANY OTHER COLOR WOULD HAVE WORKED AT ALL...
I'VE BEEN THINKING ABOUT IT A LOT LATELY, AND I'M CONVINCED THAT MAKING THE SKY BLUE WAS A GOOD IDEA...
WE'RE GLAD YOU APPROVE!
SCHULZ

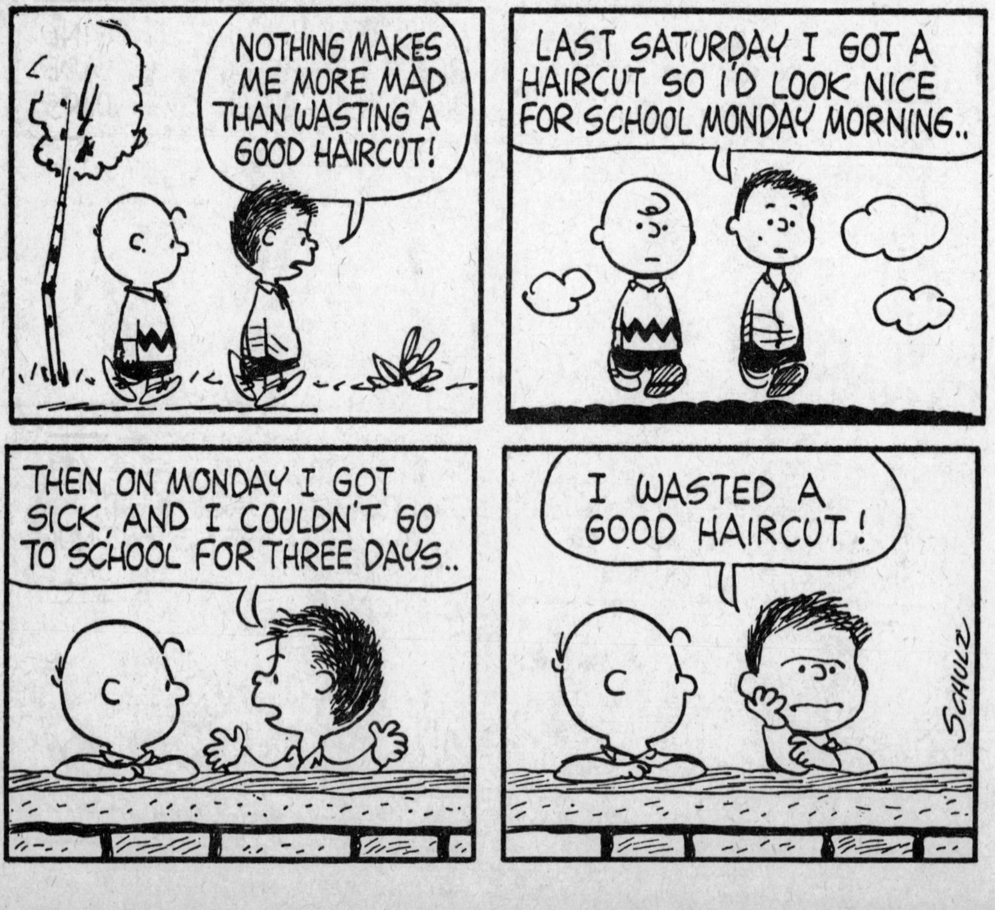
NOTHING MAKES ME MORE MAD THAN WASTING A GOOD HAIRCUT!
LAST SATURDAY I GOT A HAIRCUT SO I'D LOOK NICE FOR SCHOOL MONDAY MORNING..
THEN ON MONDAY I GOT SICK, AND I COULDN'T GO TO SCHOOL FOR THREE DAYS..
I WASTED A GOOD HAIRCUT!
SCHULZ

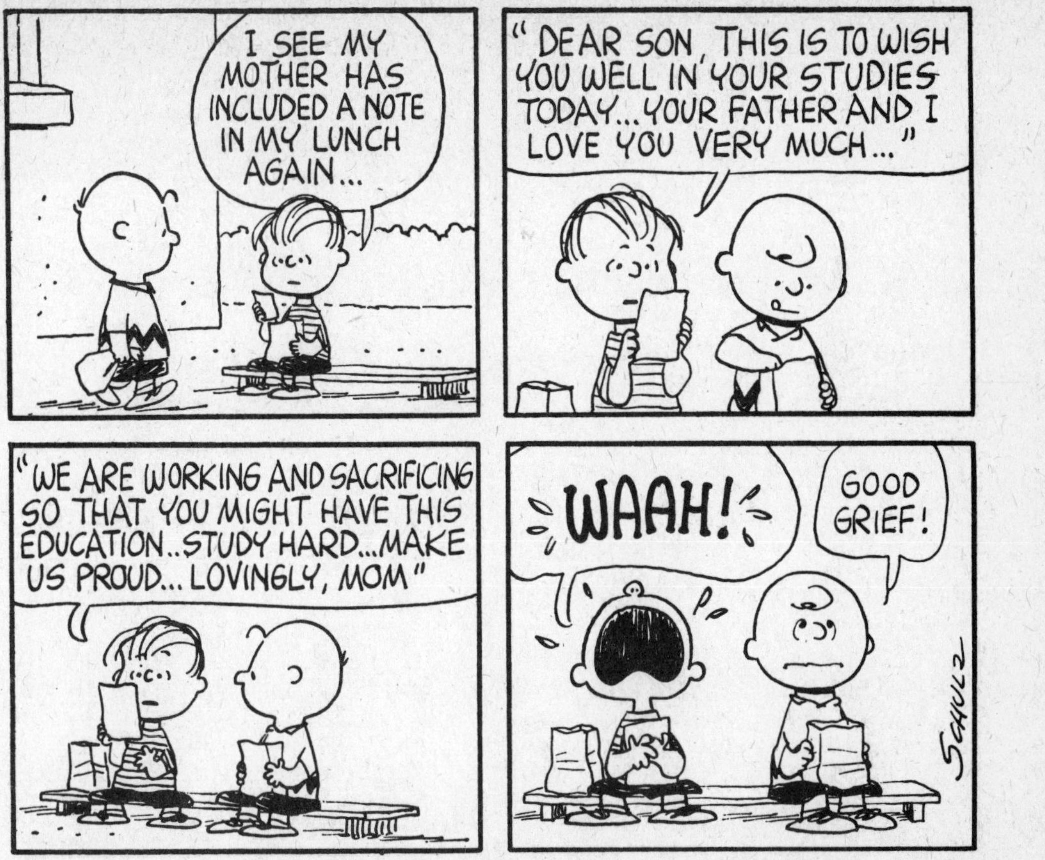
I SEE MY MOTHER HAS INCLUDED A NOTE IN MY LUNCH AGAIN...
"DEAR SON, THIS IS TO WISH YOU WELL IN YOUR STUDIES TODAY...YOUR FATHER AND I LOVE YOU VERY MUCH..."
"WE ARE WORKING AND SACRIFICING SO THAT YOU MIGHT HAVE THIS EDUCATION..STUDY HARD...MAKE US PROUD... LOVINGLY, MOM"
WAAH!
GOOD GRIEF!
SCHULZ

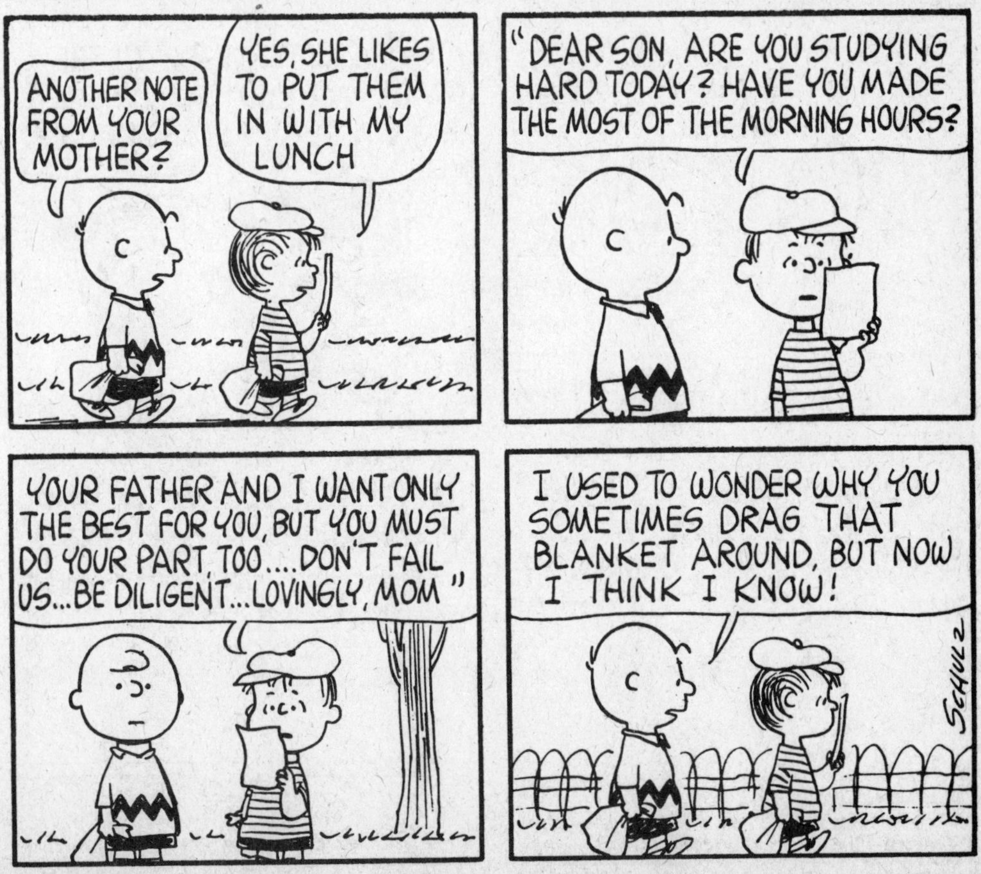
ANOTHER NOTE FROM YOUR MOTHER?
YES, SHE LIKES TO PUT THEM IN WITH MY LUNCH
"DEAR SON, ARE YOU STUDYING HARD TODAY? HAVE YOU MADE THE MOST OF THE MORNING HOURS?
YOUR FATHER AND I WANT ONLY THE BEST FOR YOU, BUT YOU MUST DO YOUR PART, TOO....DON'T FAIL US...BE DILIGENT...LOVINGLY, MOM"
I USED TO WONDER WHY YOU SOMETIMES DRAG THAT BLANKET AROUND, BUT NOW I THINK I KNOW!
SCHULZ

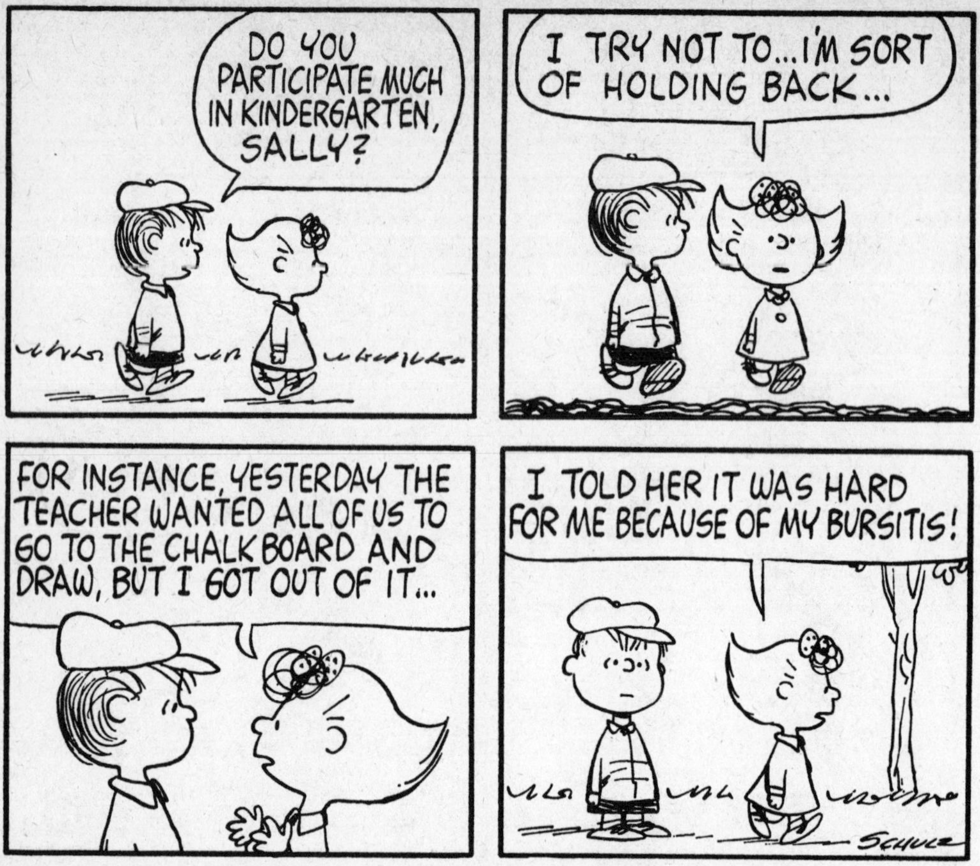
DO YOU PARTICIPATE MUCH IN KINDERGARTEN, SALLY?
I TRY NOT TO...I'M SORT OF HOLDING BACK...
FOR INSTANCE, YESTERDAY THE TEACHER WANTED ALL OF US TO GO TO THE CHALK BOARD AND DRAW, BUT I GOT OUT OF IT...
I TOLD HER IT WAS HARD FOR ME BECAUSE OF MY BURSITIS!
SCHULZ

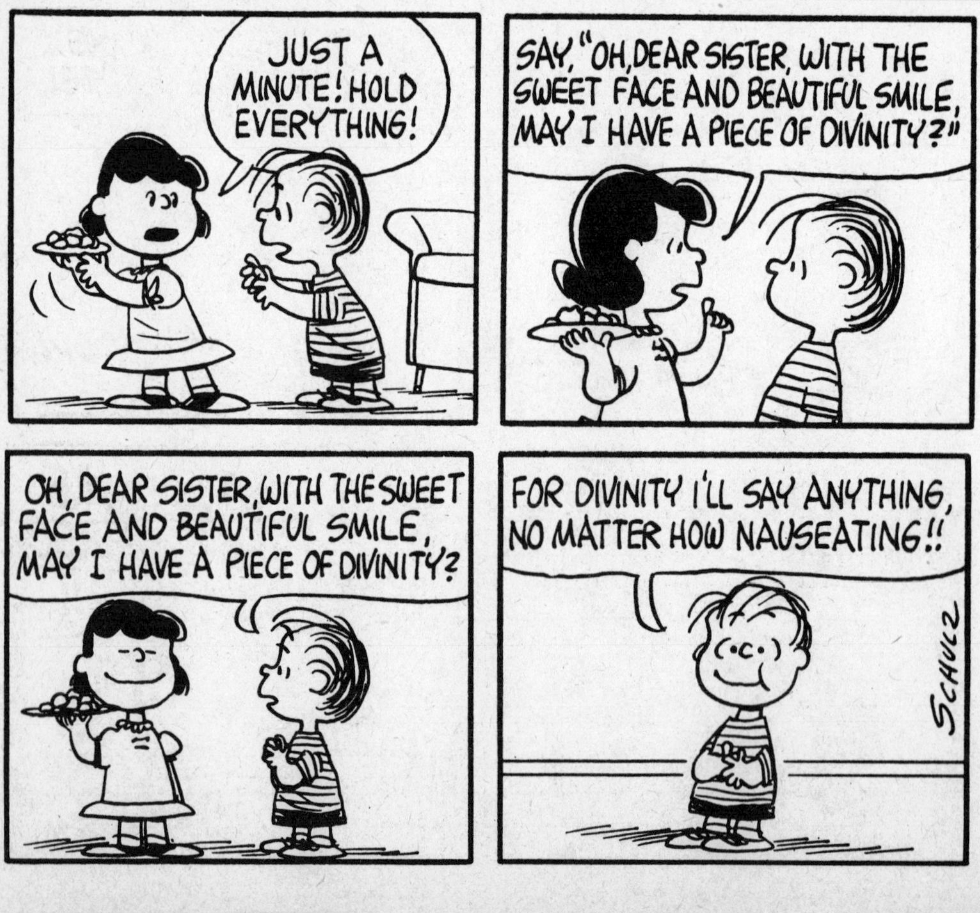
JUST A MINUTE! HOLD EVERYTHING!
SAY, "OH, DEAR SISTER, WITH THE SWEET FACE AND BEAUTIFUL SMILE, MAY I HAVE A PIECE OF DIVINITY?"
OH, DEAR SISTER, WITH THE SWEET FACE AND BEAUTIFUL SMILE, MAY I HAVE A PIECE OF DIVINITY?
FOR DIVINITY I'LL SAY ANYTHING, NO MATTER HOW NAUSEATING!!
SCHULZ

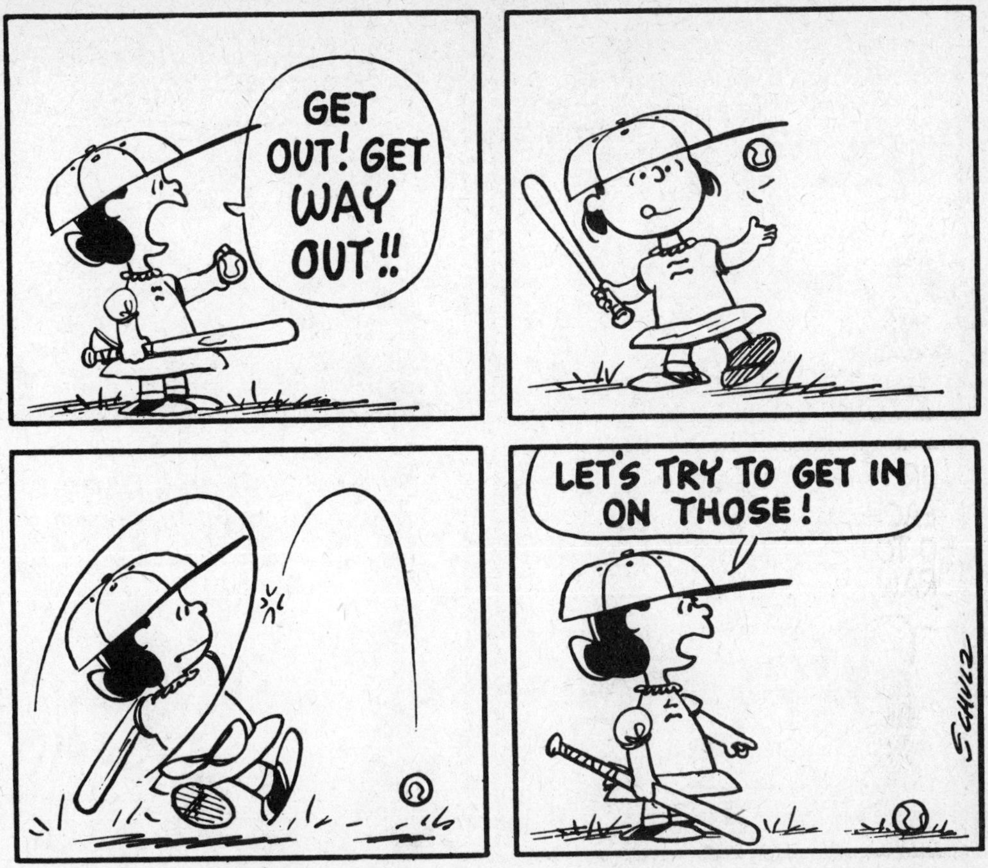
GET OUT! GET WAY OUT!!
LET'S TRY TO GET IN ON THOSE!
SCHULZ

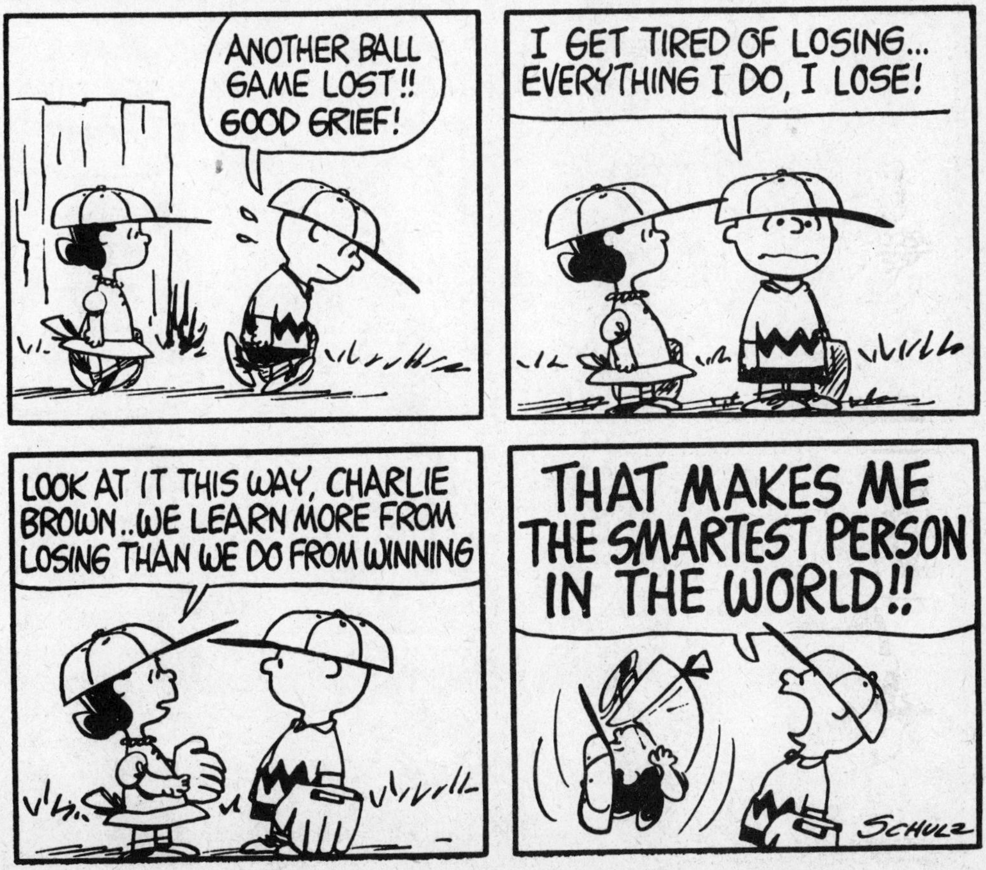
ANOTHER BALL GAME LOST!! GOOD GRIEF!
I GET TIRED OF LOSING... EVERYTHING I DO, I LOSE!
LOOK AT IT THIS WAY, CHARLIE BROWN..WE LEARN MORE FROM LOSING THAN WE DO FROM WINNING
THAT MAKES ME THE SMARTEST PERSON IN THE WORLD!!
SCHULZ

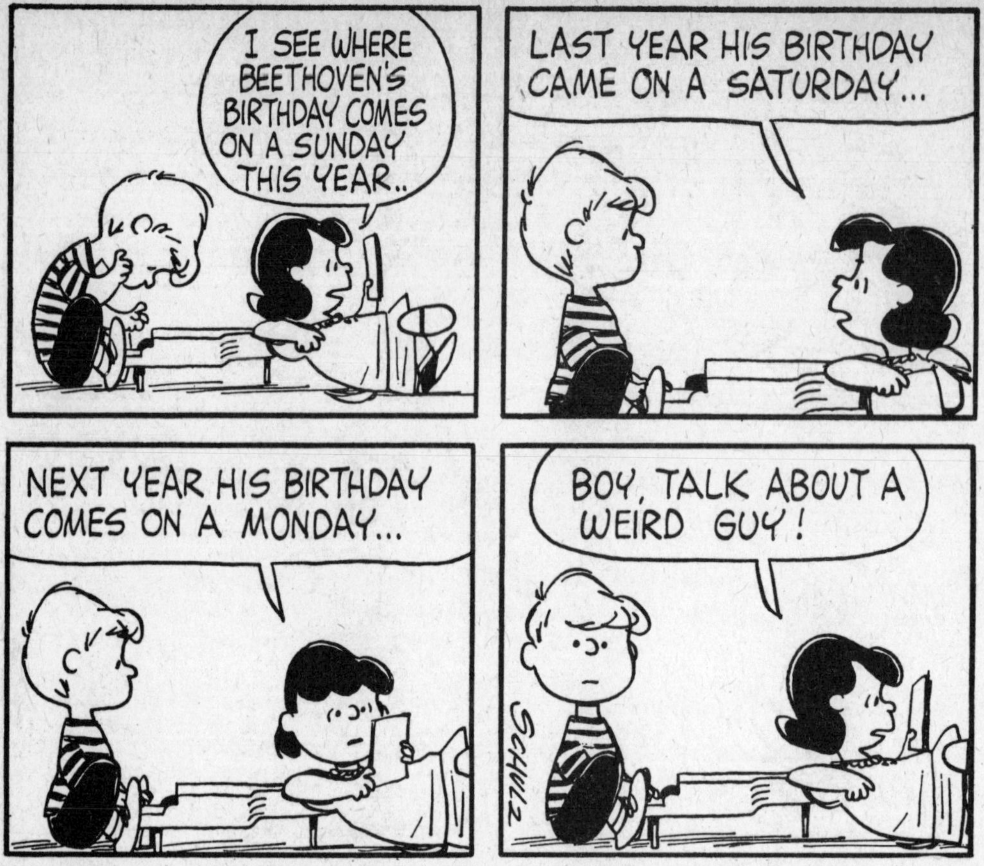
I SEE WHERE BEETHOVEN'S BIRTHDAY COMES ON A SUNDAY THIS YEAR..
LAST YEAR HIS BIRTHDAY CAME ON A SATURDAY...
NEXT YEAR HIS BIRTHDAY COMES ON A MONDAY...
BOY, TALK ABOUT A WEIRD GUY!
SCHULZ

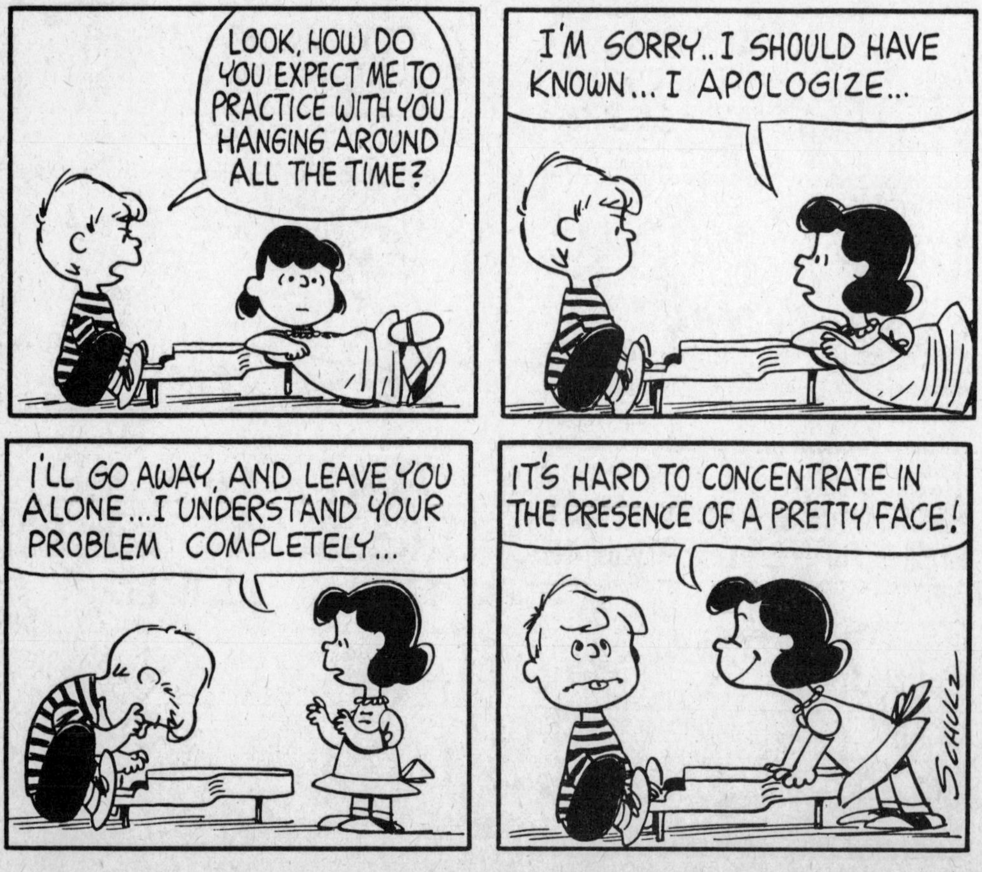
LOOK, HOW DO YOU EXPECT ME TO PRACTICE WITH YOU HANGING AROUND ALL THE TIME?
I'M SORRY..I SHOULD HAVE KNOWN... I APOLOGIZE...
I'LL GO AWAY, AND LEAVE YOU ALONE...I UNDERSTAND YOUR PROBLEM COMPLETELY...
IT'S HARD TO CONCENTRATE IN THE PRESENCE OF A PRETTY FACE!
SCHULZ

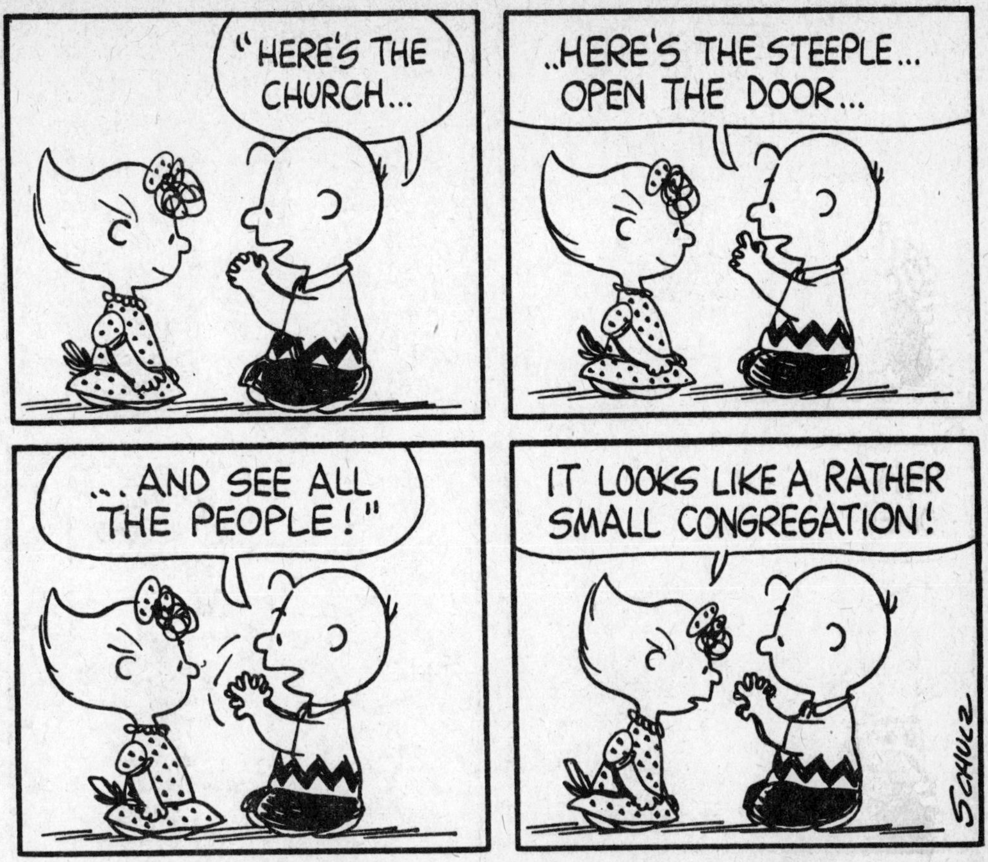
"HERE'S THE CHURCH...
..HERE'S THE STEEPLE... OPEN THE DOOR...
...AND SEE ALL THE PEOPLE!"
IT LOOKS LIKE A RATHER SMALL CONGREGATION!
SCHULZ

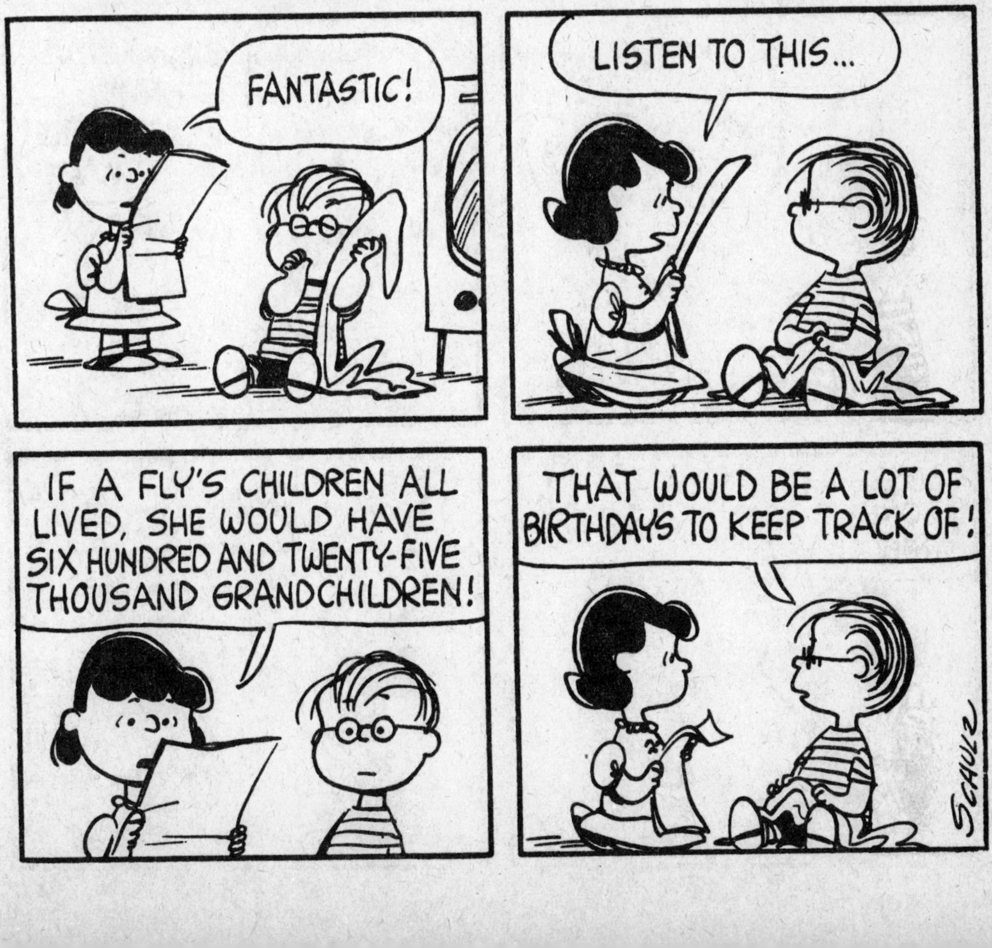
FANTASTIC!
LISTEN TO THIS...
IF A FLY'S CHILDREN ALL LIVED, SHE WOULD HAVE SIX HUNDRED AND TWENTY-FIVE THOUSAND GRANDCHILDREN!
THAT WOULD BE A LOT OF BIRTHDAYS TO KEEP TRACK OF!
SCHULZ

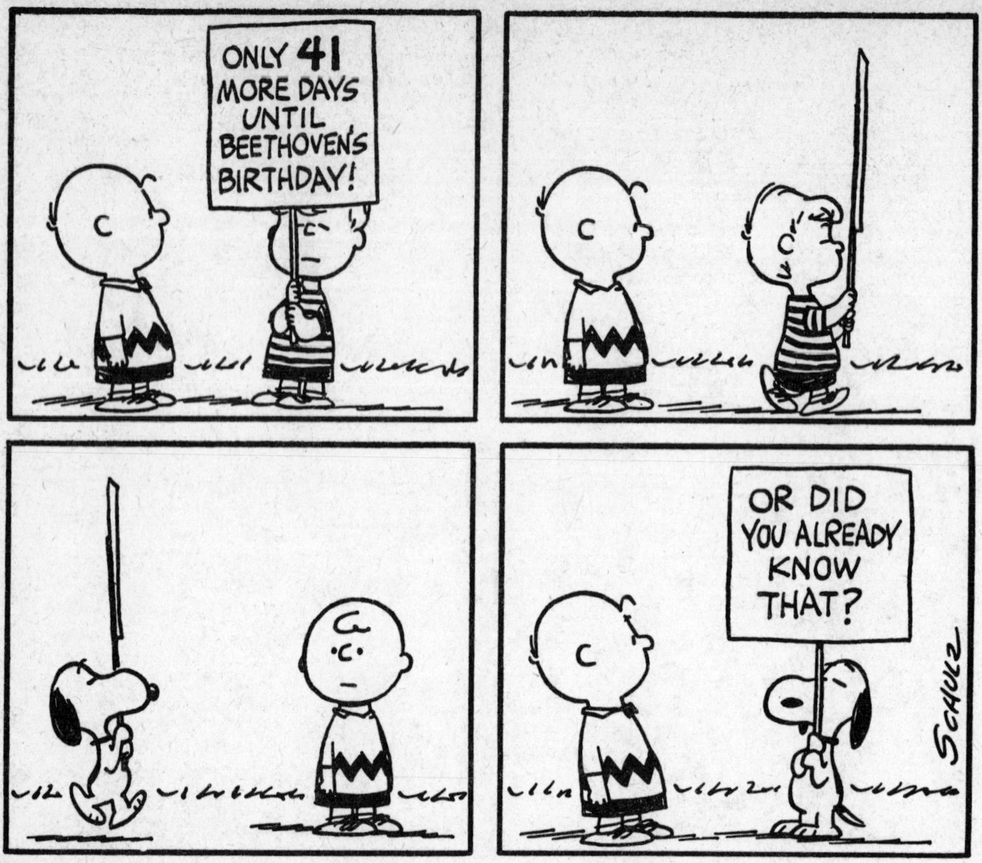
ONLY 41 MORE DAYS UNTIL BEETHOVEN'S BIRTHDAY!
OR DID YOU ALREADY KNOW THAT?
SCHULZ

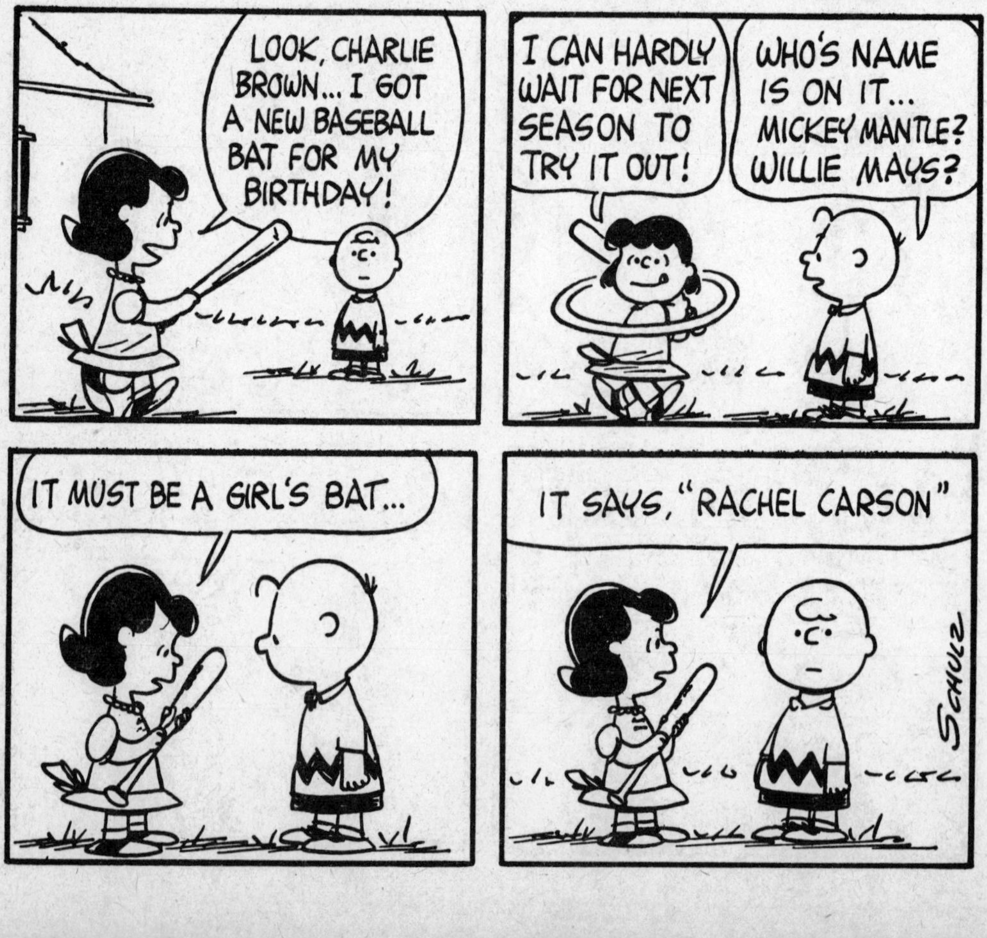
LOOK, CHARLIE BROWN... I GOT A NEW BASEBALL BAT FOR MY BIRTHDAY!
I CAN HARDLY WAIT FOR NEXT SEASON TO TRY IT OUT!
WHO'S NAME IS ON IT... MICKEY MANTLE? WILLIE MAYS?
IT MUST BE A GIRL'S BAT...
IT SAYS, "RACHEL CARSON"
SCHULZ

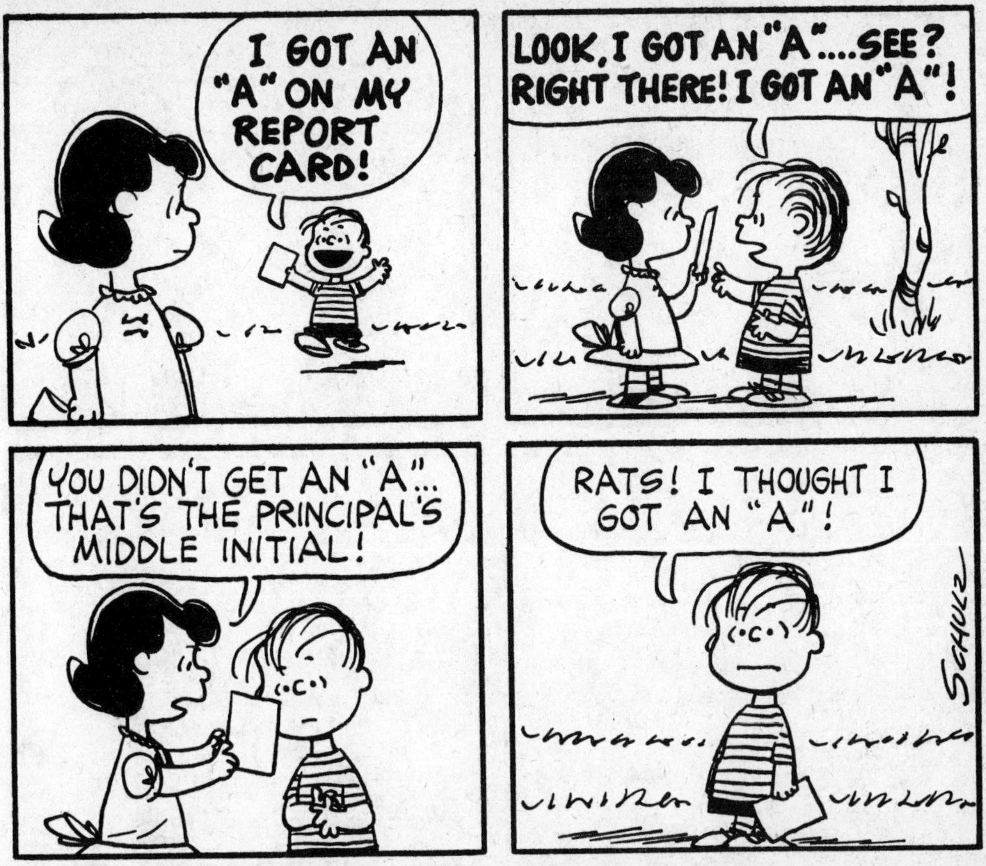
I GOT AN "A" ON MY REPORT CARD!
LOOK, I GOT AN "A"....SEE? RIGHT THERE! I GOT AN "A"!
YOU DIDN'T GET AN "A"... THAT'S THE PRINCIPAL'S MIDDLE INITIAL!
RATS! I THOUGHT I GOT AN "A"!
SCHULZ

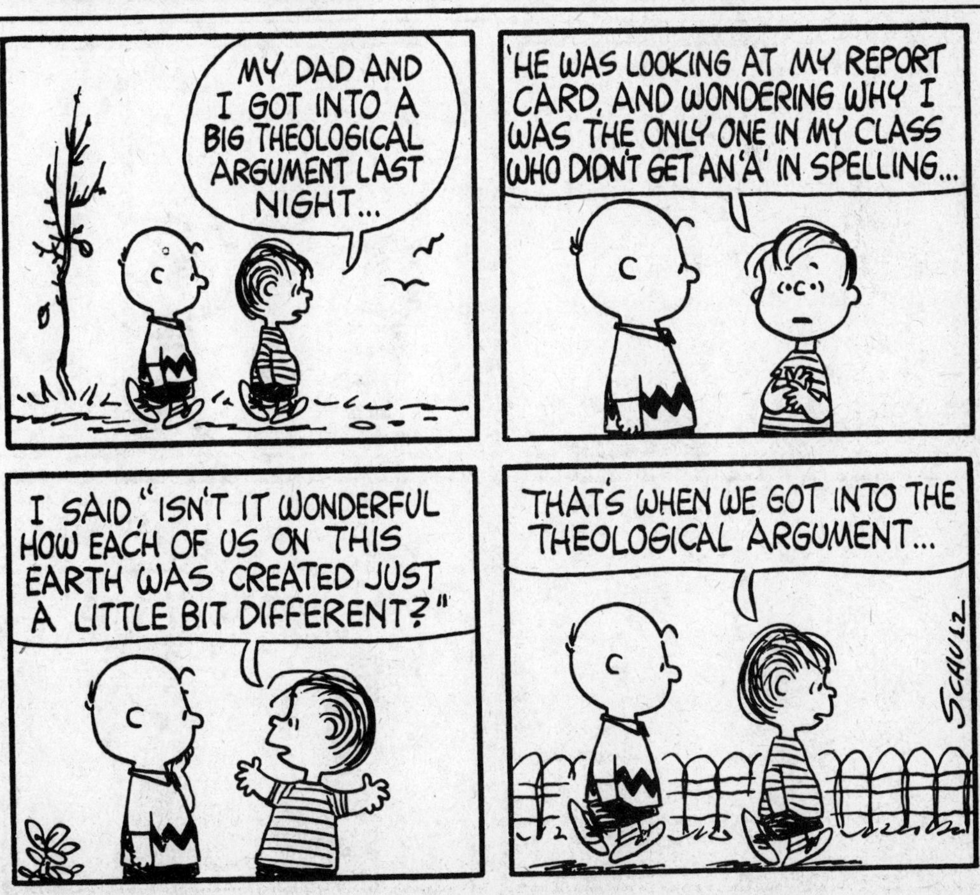
MY DAD AND I GOT INTO A BIG THEOLOGICAL ARGUMENT LAST NIGHT...
HE WAS LOOKING AT MY REPORT CARD, AND WONDERING WHY I WAS THE ONLY ONE IN MY CLASS WHO DIDN'T GET AN 'A' IN SPELLING...
I SAID, "ISN'T IT WONDERFUL HOW EACH OF US ON THIS EARTH WAS CREATED JUST A LITTLE BIT DIFFERENT?"
THAT'S WHEN WE GOT INTO THE THEOLOGICAL ARGUMENT...
SCHULZ

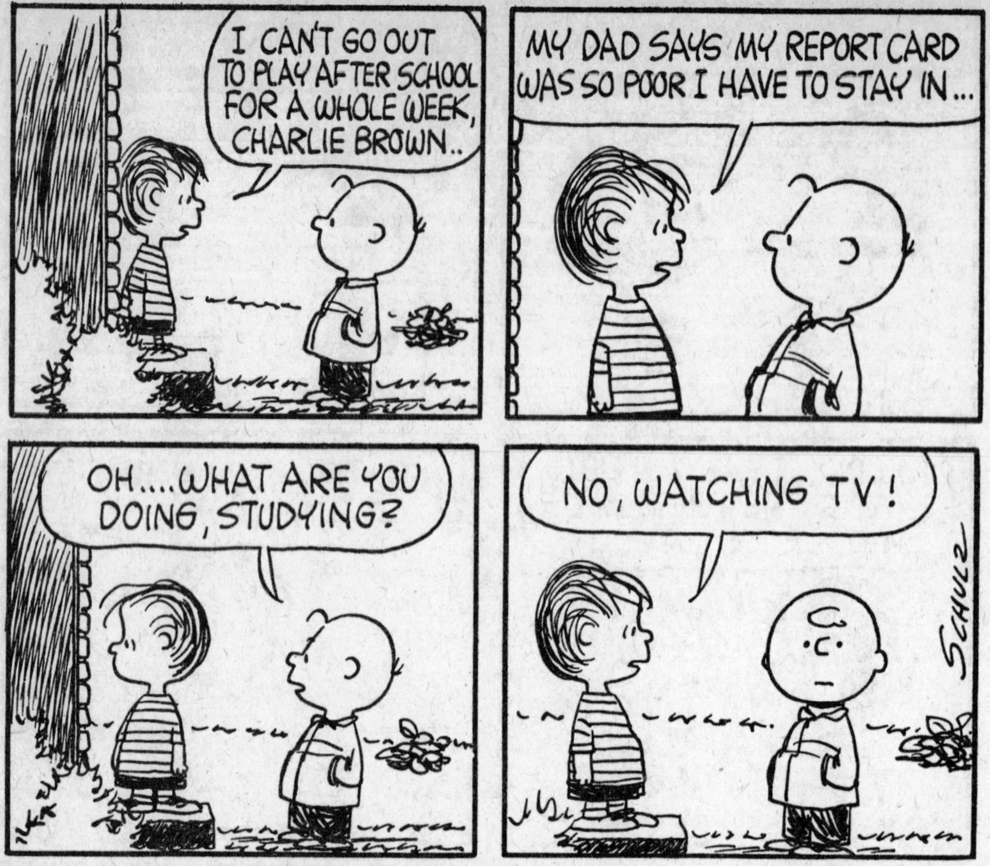
I CAN'T GO OUT TO PLAY AFTER SCHOOL FOR A WHOLE WEEK, CHARLIE BROWN..
MY DAD SAYS MY REPORT CARD WAS SO POOR I HAVE TO STAY IN...
OH....WHAT ARE YOU DOING, STUDYING?
NO, WATCHING TV!
SCHULZ

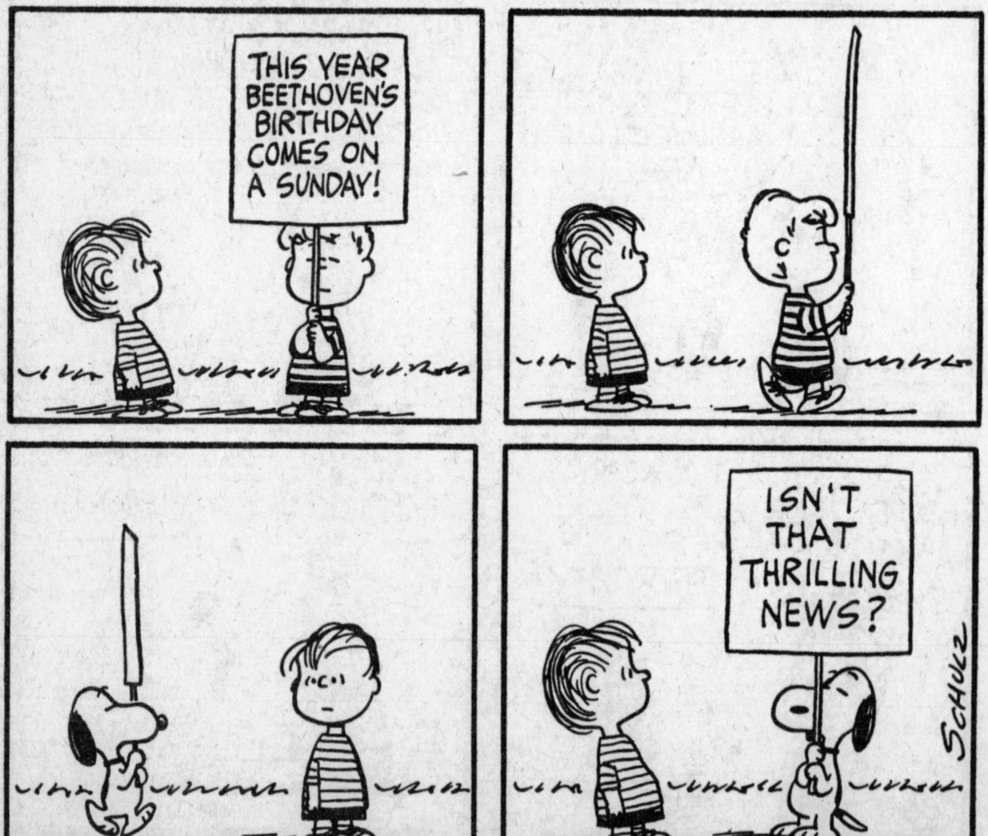
THIS YEAR BEETHOVEN'S BIRTHDAY COMES ON A SUNDAY!
ISN'T THAT THRILLING NEWS?
SCHULZ

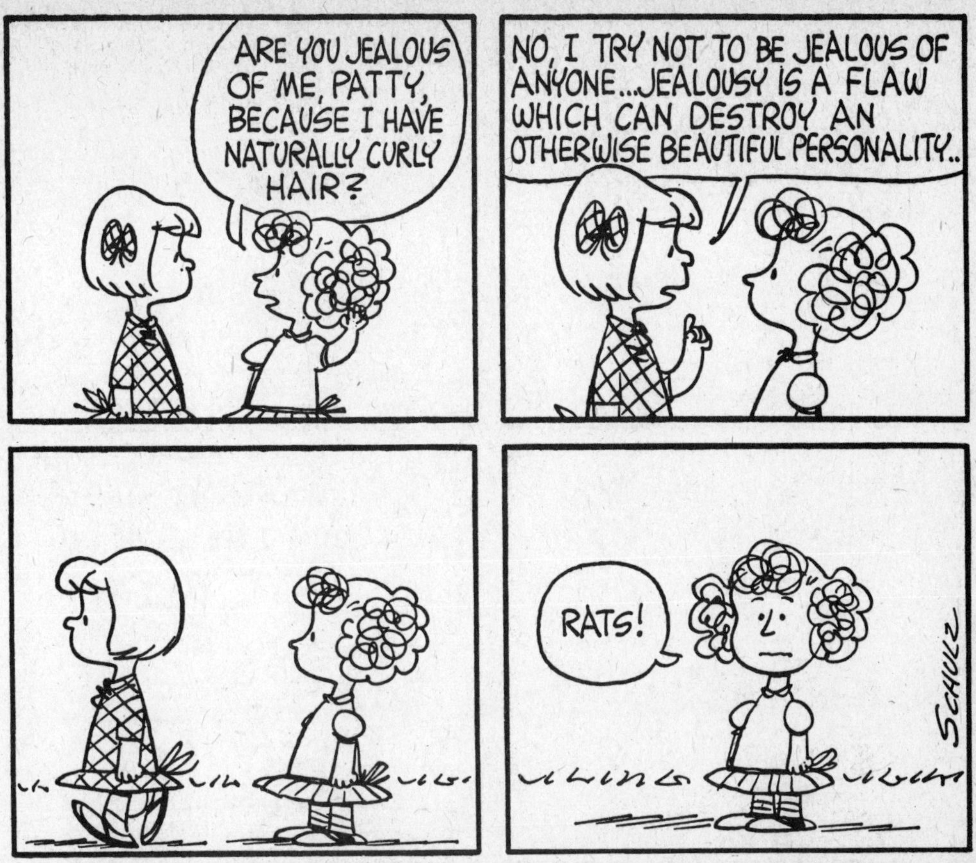
ARE YOU JEALOUS OF ME, PATTY, BECAUSE I HAVE NATURALLY CURLY HAIR?
NO, I TRY NOT TO BE JEALOUS OF ANYONE...JEALOUSY IS A FLAW WHICH CAN DESTROY AN OTHERWISE BEAUTIFUL PERSONALITY..
RATS!
SCHULZ

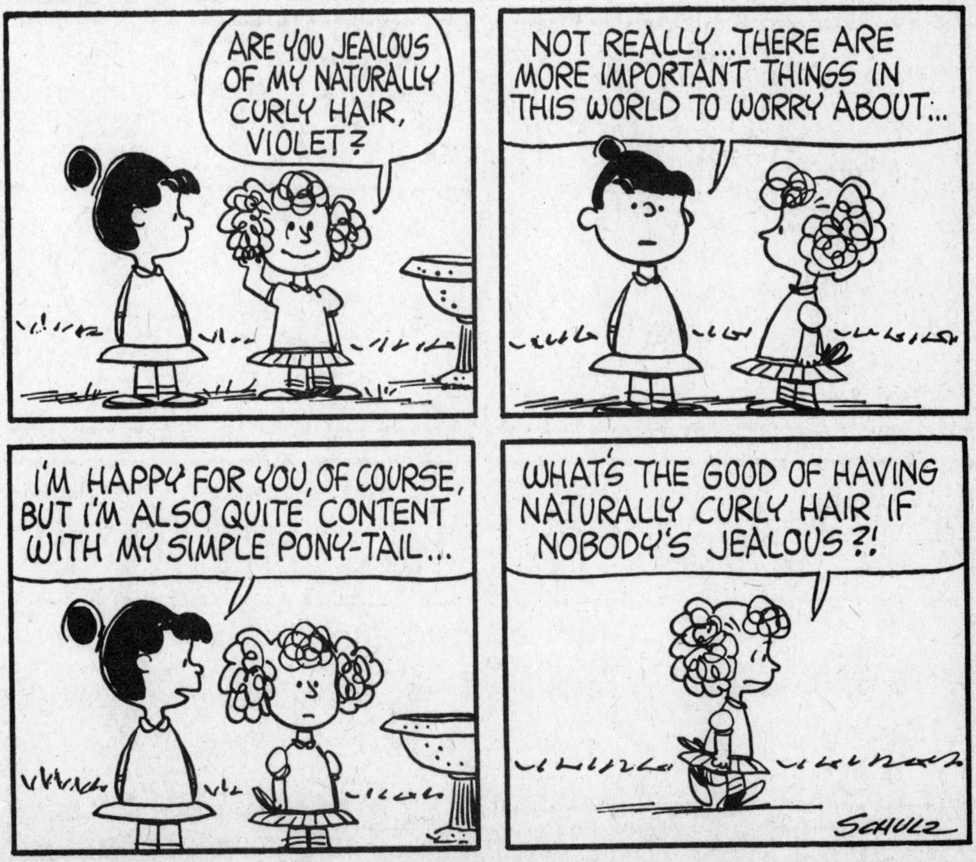
ARE YOU JEALOUS OF MY NATURALLY CURLY HAIR, VIOLET?
NOT REALLY...THERE ARE MORE IMPORTANT THINGS IN THIS WORLD TO WORRY ABOUT...
I'M HAPPY FOR YOU, OF COURSE, BUT I'M ALSO QUITE CONTENT WITH MY SIMPLE PONY-TAIL...
WHAT'S THE GOOD OF HAVING NATURALLY CURLY HAIR IF NOBODY'S JEALOUS?!
SCHULZ

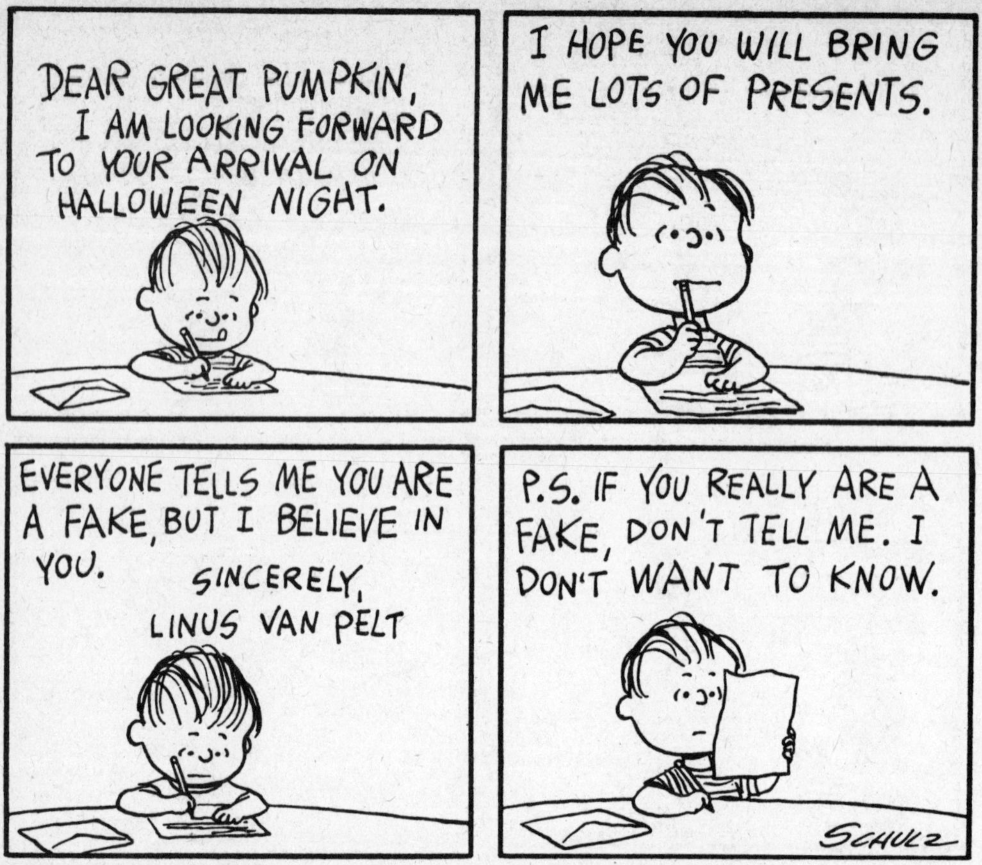
DEAR GREAT PUMPKIN, I AM LOOKING FORWARD TO YOUR ARRIVAL ON HALLOWEEN NIGHT.
I HOPE YOU WILL BRING ME LOTS OF PRESENTS.
EVERYONE TELLS ME YOU ARE A FAKE, BUT I BELIEVE IN YOU. SINCERELY, LINUS VAN PELT
P.S. IF YOU REALLY ARE A FAKE, DON'T TELL ME. I DON'T WANT TO KNOW.
SCHULZ

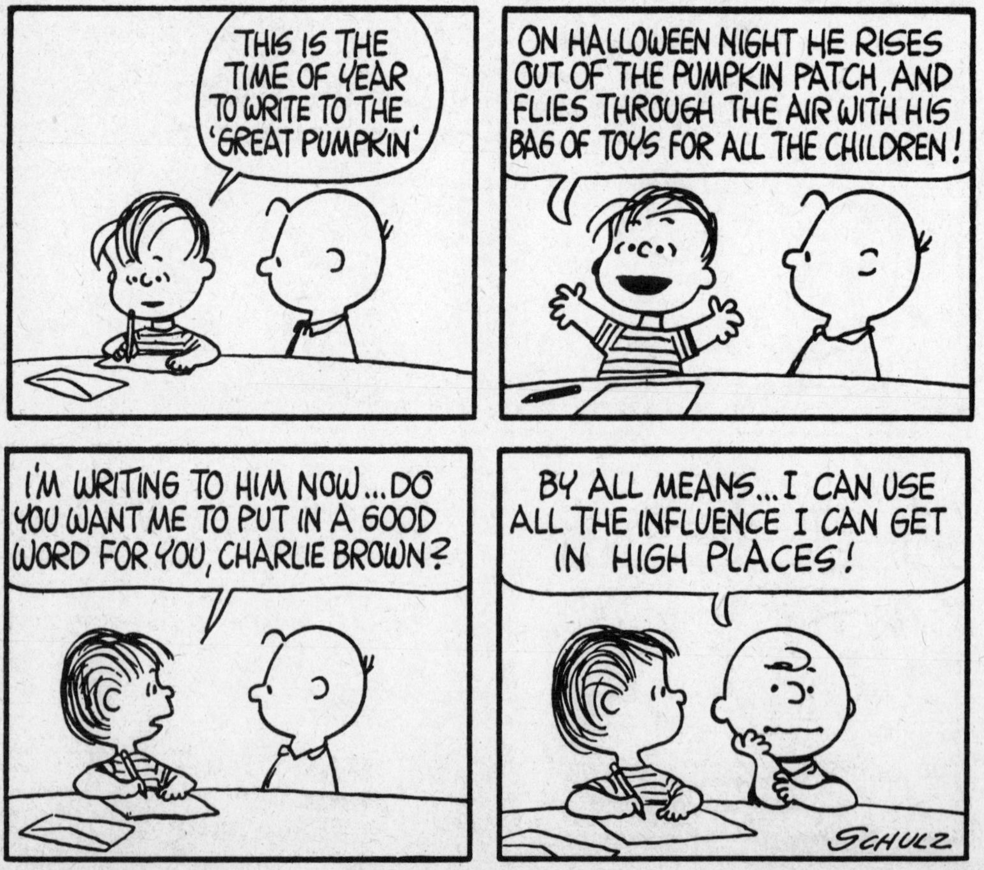
THIS IS THE TIME OF YEAR TO WRITE TO THE 'GREAT PUMPKIN'
ON HALLOWEEN NIGHT HE RISES OUT OF THE PUMPKIN PATCH, AND FLIES THROUGH THE AIR WITH HIS BAG OF TOYS FOR ALL THE CHILDREN!
I'M WRITING TO HIM NOW...DO YOU WANT ME TO PUT IN A GOOD WORD FOR YOU, CHARLIE BROWN?
BY ALL MEANS...I CAN USE ALL THE INFLUENCE I CAN GET IN HIGH PLACES!
SCHULZ

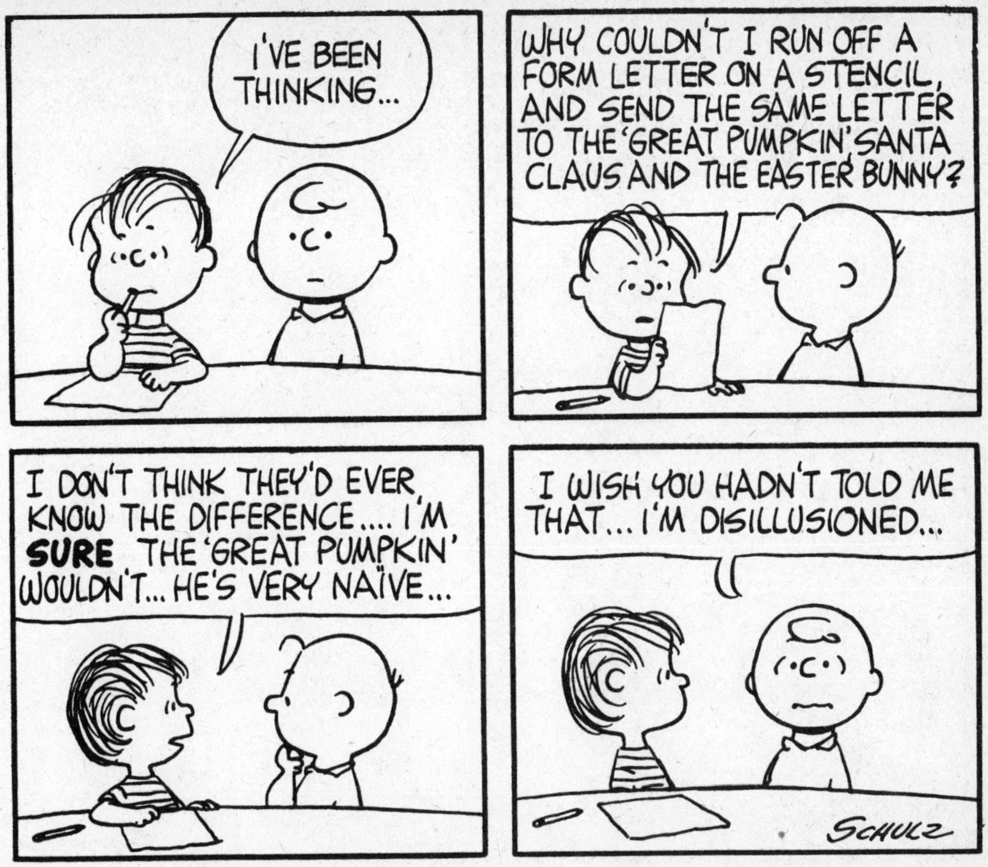
I'VE BEEN THINKING...
WHY COULDN'T I RUN OFF A FORM LETTER ON A STENCIL, AND SEND THE SAME LETTER TO THE 'GREAT PUMPKIN,' SANTA CLAUS AND THE EASTER BUNNY?
I DON'T THINK THEY'D EVER KNOW THE DIFFERENCE.... I'M **SURE** THE 'GREAT PUMPKIN' WOULDN'T... HE'S VERY NAÏVE...
I WISH YOU HADN'T TOLD ME THAT... I'M DISILLUSIONED...
SCHULZ

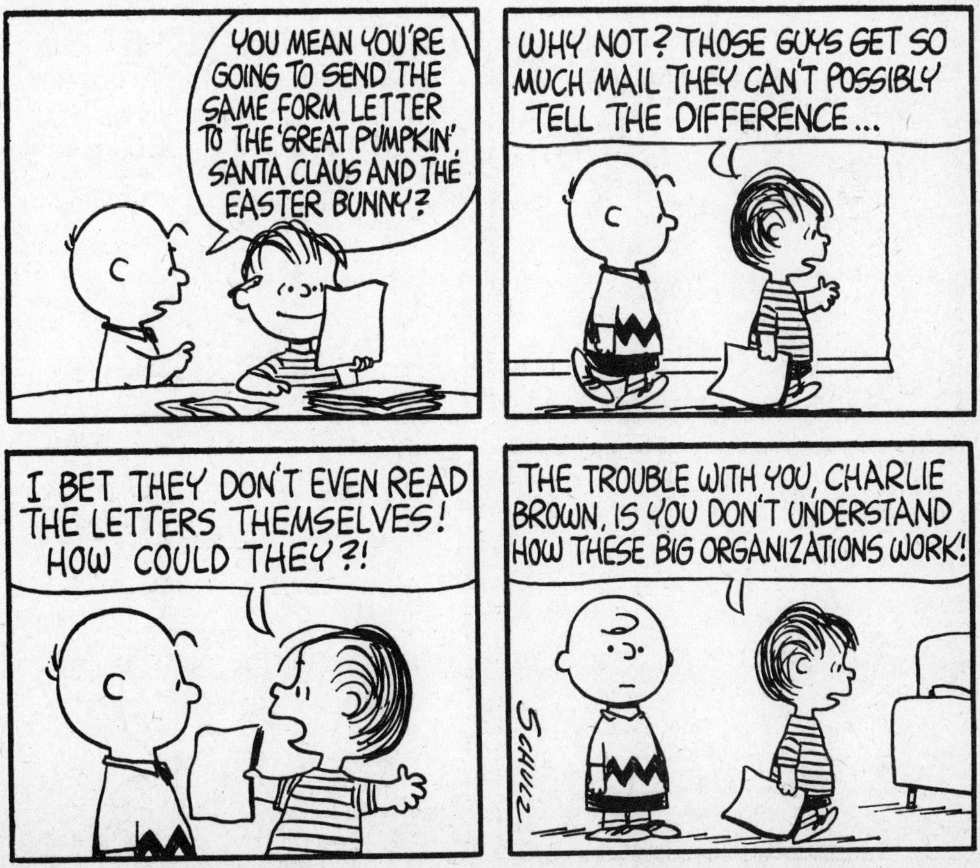
YOU MEAN YOU'RE GOING TO SEND THE SAME FORM LETTER TO THE 'GREAT PUMPKIN', SANTA CLAUS AND THE EASTER BUNNY?
WHY NOT? THOSE GUYS GET SO MUCH MAIL THEY CAN'T POSSIBLY TELL THE DIFFERENCE...
I BET THEY DON'T EVEN READ THE LETTERS THEMSELVES! HOW COULD THEY?!
THE TROUBLE WITH YOU, CHARLIE BROWN, IS YOU DON'T UNDERSTAND HOW THESE BIG ORGANIZATIONS WORK!
SCHULZ

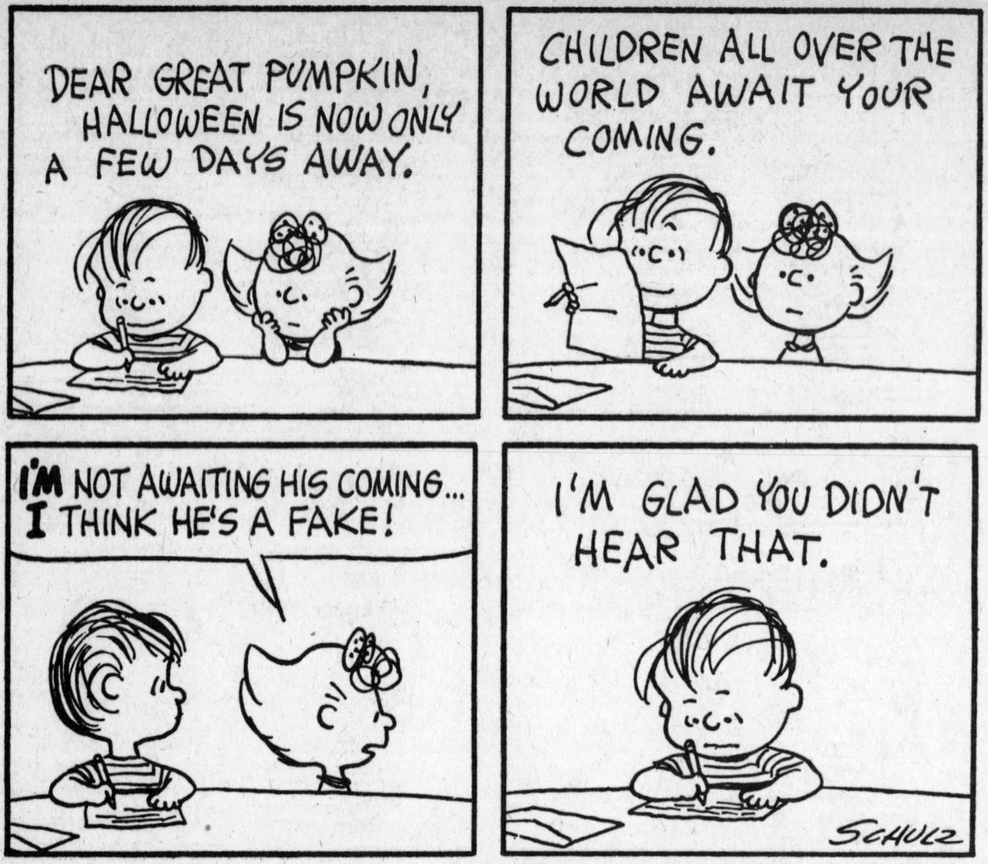
DEAR GREAT PUMPKIN, HALLOWEEN IS NOW ONLY A FEW DAYS AWAY.
CHILDREN ALL OVER THE WORLD AWAIT YOUR COMING.
I'M NOT AWAITING HIS COMING... I THINK HE'S A FAKE!
I'M GLAD YOU DIDN'T HEAR THAT.
SCHULZ

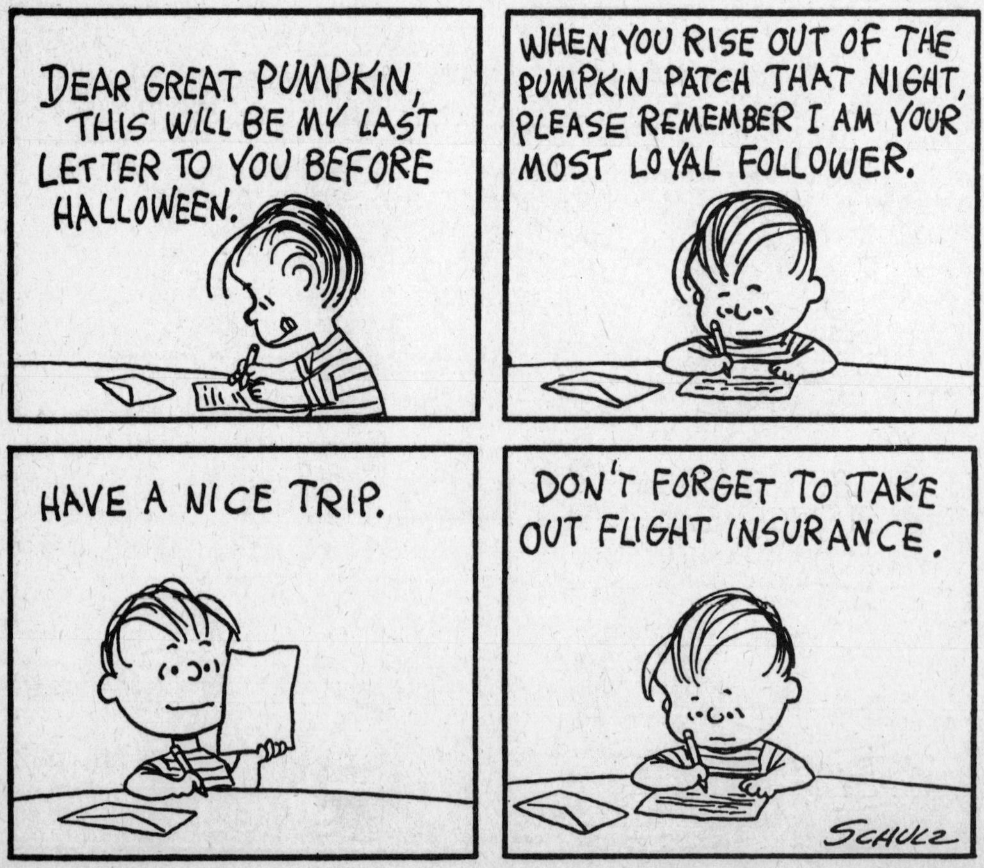
DEAR GREAT PUMPKIN, THIS WILL BE MY LAST LETTER TO YOU BEFORE HALLOWEEN.
WHEN YOU RISE OUT OF THE PUMPKIN PATCH THAT NIGHT, PLEASE REMEMBER I AM YOUR MOST LOYAL FOLLOWER.
HAVE A NICE TRIP.
DON'T FORGET TO TAKE OUT FLIGHT INSURANCE.
SCHULZ

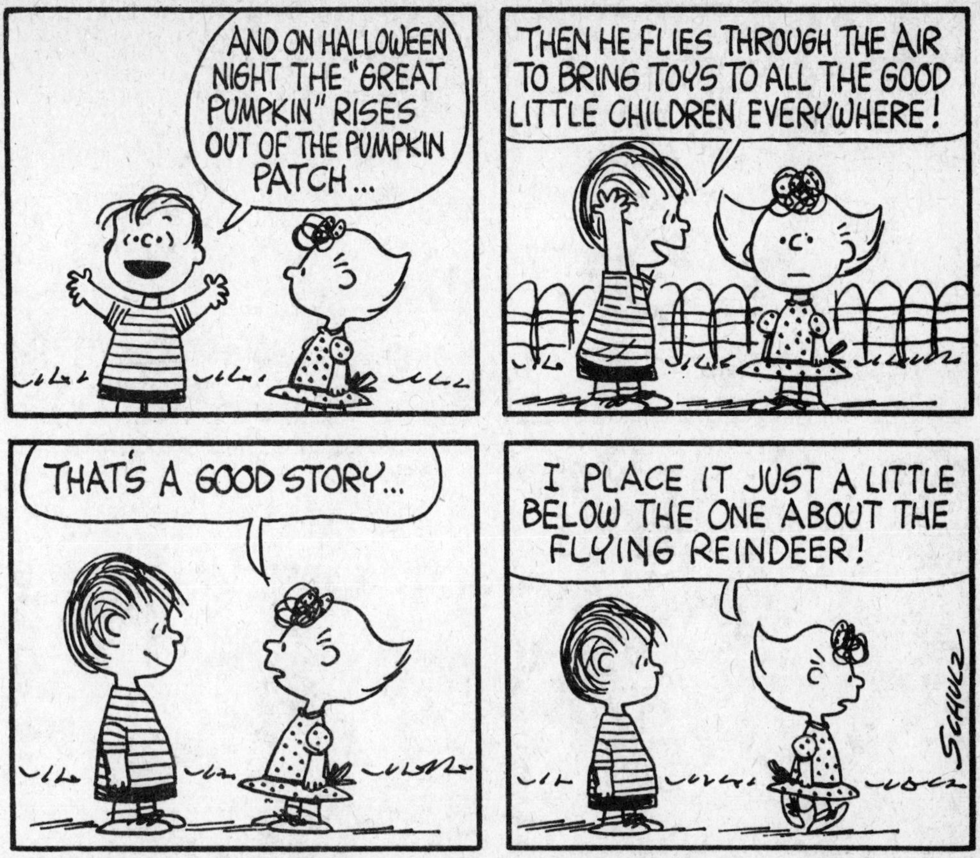
AND ON HALLOWEEN NIGHT THE "GREAT PUMPKIN" RISES OUT OF THE PUMPKIN PATCH...
THEN HE FLIES THROUGH THE AIR TO BRING TOYS TO ALL THE GOOD LITTLE CHILDREN EVERYWHERE!
THAT'S A GOOD STORY...
I PLACE IT JUST A LITTLE BELOW THE ONE ABOUT THE FLYING REINDEER!
SCHULZ

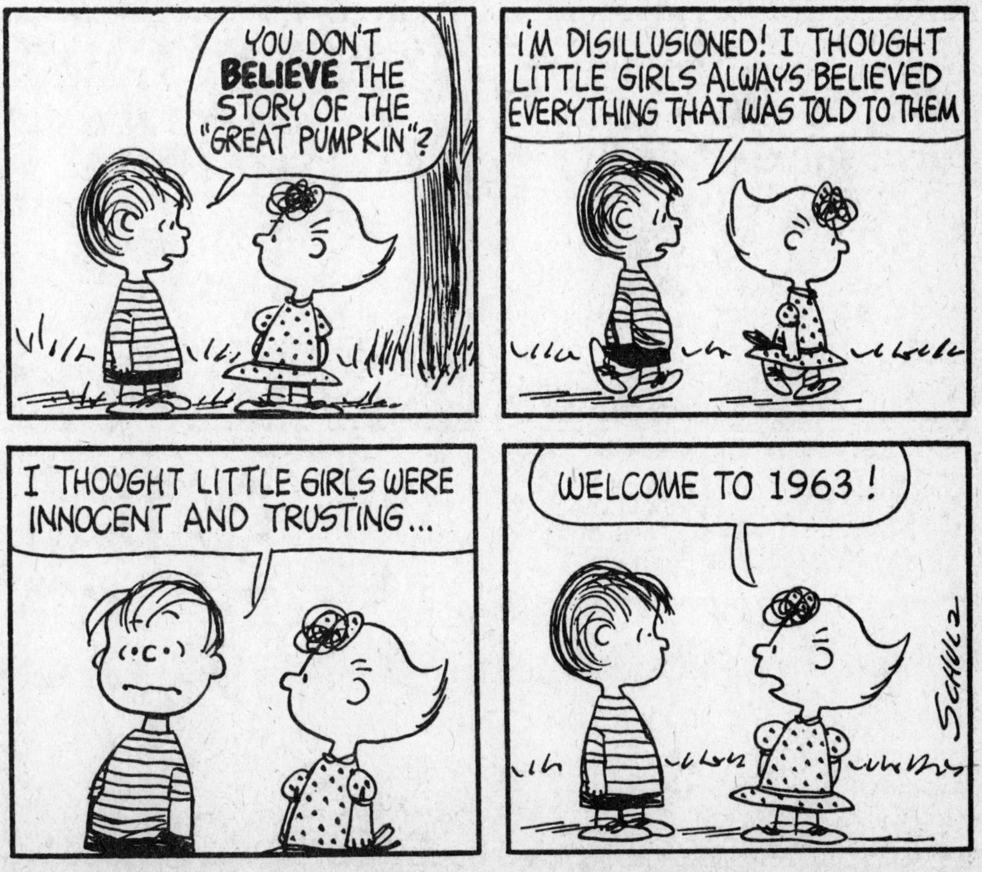
YOU DON'T **BELIEVE** THE STORY OF THE "GREAT PUMPKIN"?
I'M DISILLUSIONED! I THOUGHT LITTLE GIRLS ALWAYS BELIEVED EVERYTHING THAT WAS TOLD TO THEM
I THOUGHT LITTLE GIRLS WERE INNOCENT AND TRUSTING...
WELCOME TO 1963!
SCHULZ

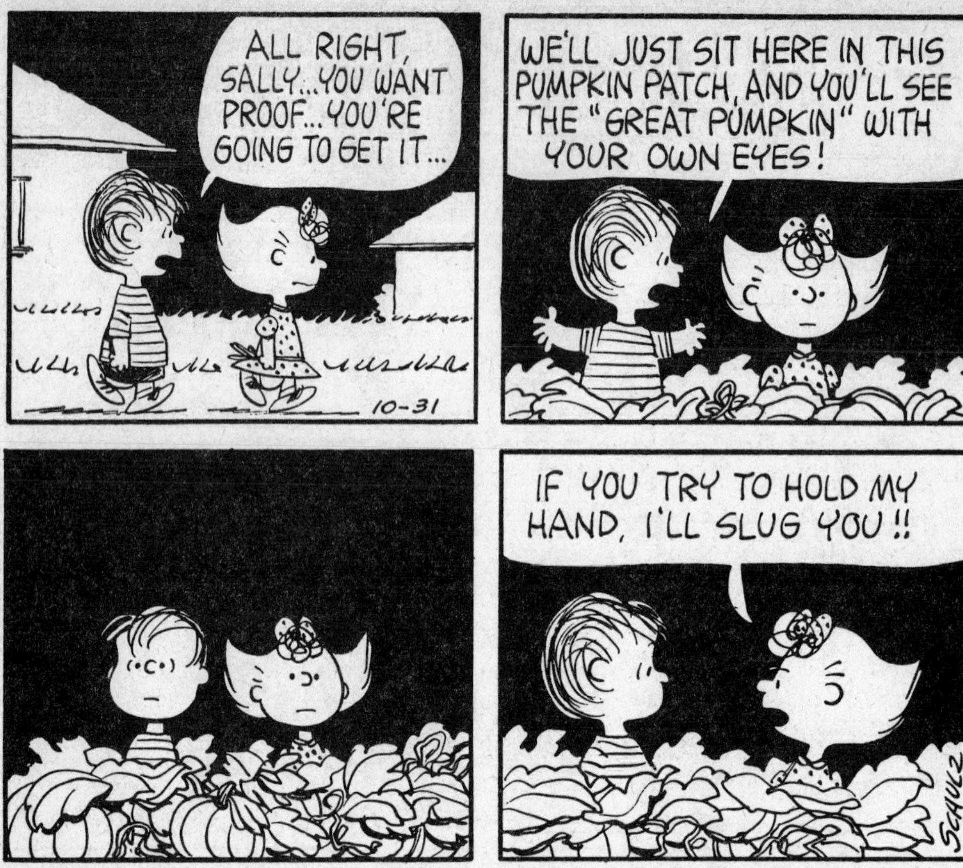
ALL RIGHT, SALLY...YOU WANT PROOF...YOU'RE GOING TO GET IT...
10-31
WE'LL JUST SIT HERE IN THIS PUMPKIN PATCH, AND YOU'LL SEE THE "GREAT PUMPKIN" WITH YOUR OWN EYES!
IF YOU TRY TO HOLD MY HAND, I'LL SLUG YOU!!
SCHULZ

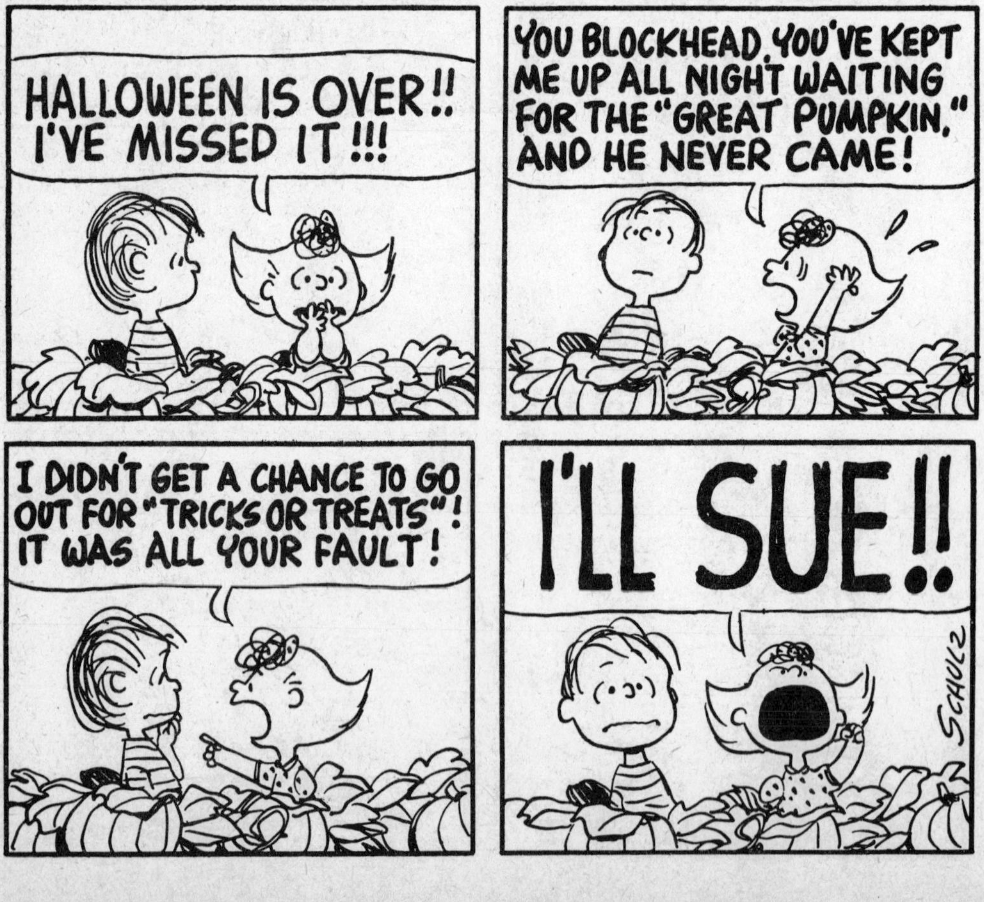
HALLOWEEN IS OVER!! I'VE MISSED IT!!!
YOU BLOCKHEAD, YOU'VE KEPT ME UP ALL NIGHT WAITING FOR THE "GREAT PUMPKIN," AND HE NEVER CAME!
I DIDN'T GET A CHANCE TO GO OUT FOR "TRICKS OR TREATS"! IT WAS ALL YOUR FAULT!
I'LL SUE!!
SCHULZ

I WAS ROBBED!

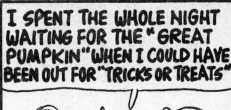

I SPENT THE WHOLE NIGHT WAITING FOR THE "GREAT PUMPKIN" WHEN I COULD HAVE BEEN OUT FOR "TRICKS OR TREATS"

YOU'VE HEARD ABOUT FURY AND A WOMAN SCORNED, HAVEN'T YOU?

YES, I GUESS I HAVE...

WELL, THAT'S NOTHING COMPARED TO THE FURY OF A WOMAN WHO HAS BEEN CHEATED OUT OF "TRICKS OR TREATS"!

WHAT A FOOL I WAS!

I COULD HAVE HAD CANDY AND APPLES AND GUM AND COOKIES AND MONEY AND ALL SORTS OF THINGS, BUT, NO! I HAD TO LISTEN TO YOU! WHAT A FOOL I WAS!

"TRICKS OR TREATS" COMES ONLY ONCE A YEAR, AND I MISS IT BY SITTING IN A PUMPKIN PATCH WITH A BLOCKHEAD!

YOU OWE ME RESTITUTION!!!

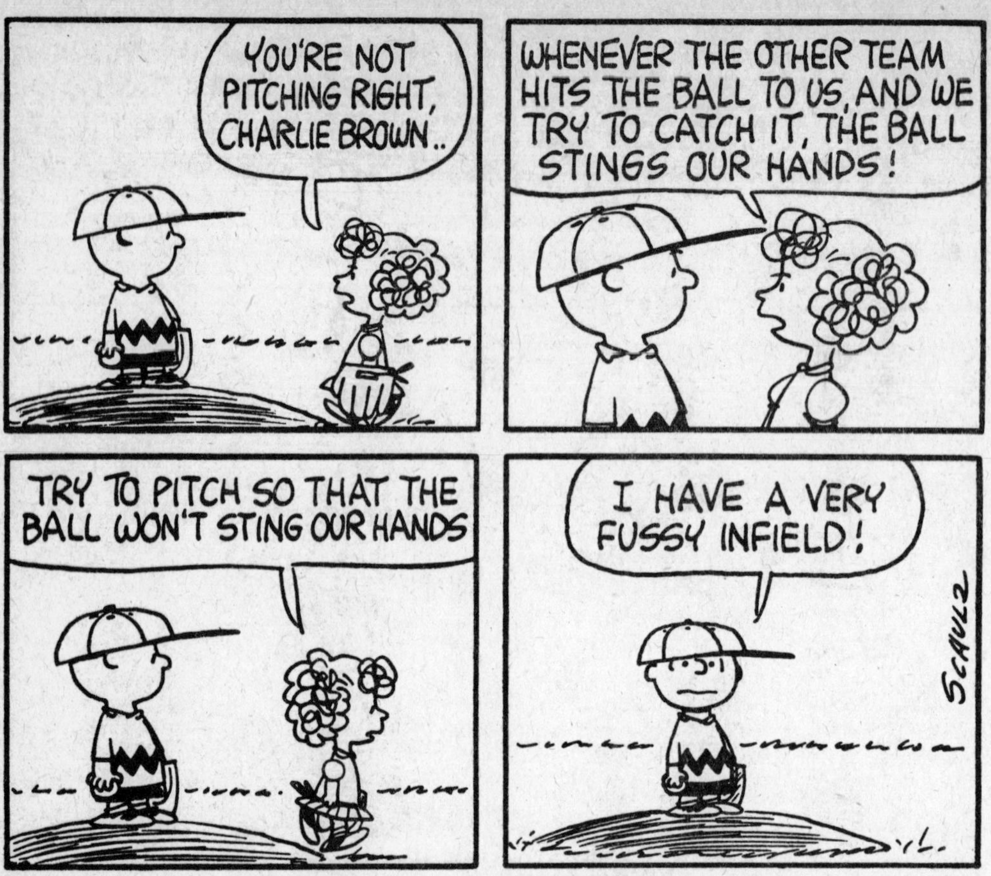
YOU'RE NOT PITCHING RIGHT, CHARLIE BROWN..
WHENEVER THE OTHER TEAM HITS THE BALL TO US, AND WE TRY TO CATCH IT, THE BALL STINGS OUR HANDS!
TRY TO PITCH SO THAT THE BALL WON'T STING OUR HANDS
I HAVE A VERY FUSSY INFIELD!
SCHULZ

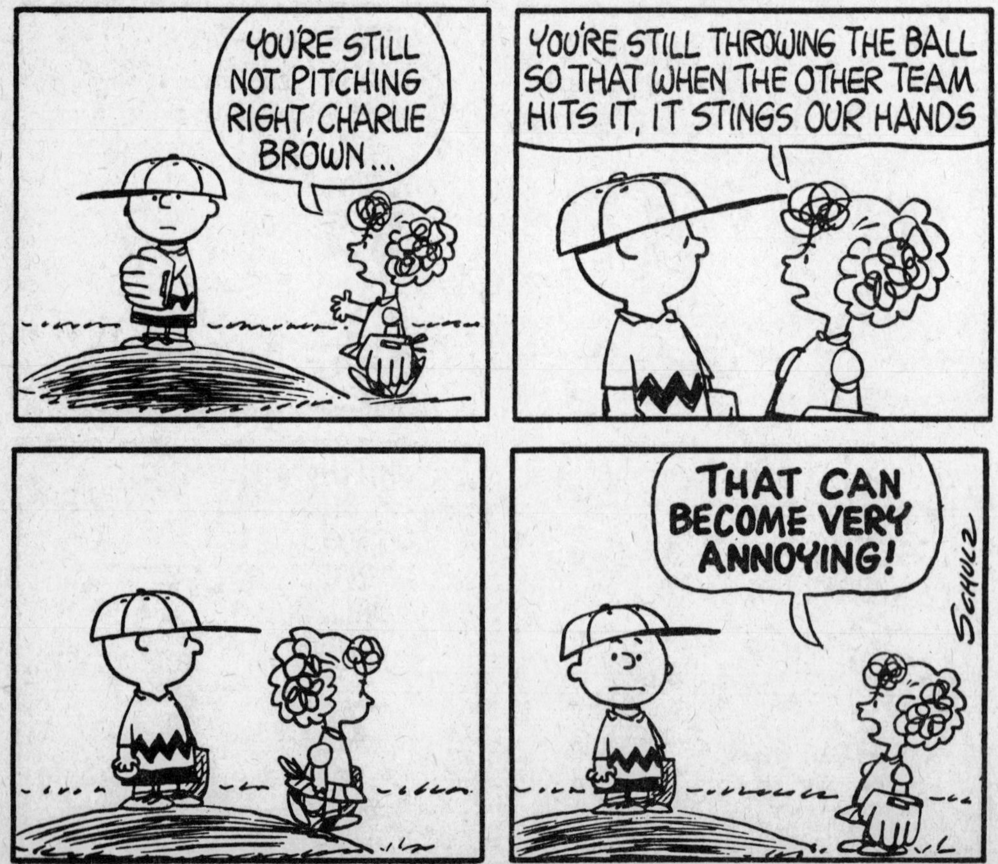
YOU'RE STILL NOT PITCHING RIGHT, CHARLIE BROWN...
YOU'RE STILL THROWING THE BALL SO THAT WHEN THE OTHER TEAM HITS IT, IT STINGS OUR HANDS
THAT CAN BECOME VERY ANNOYING!
SCHULZ

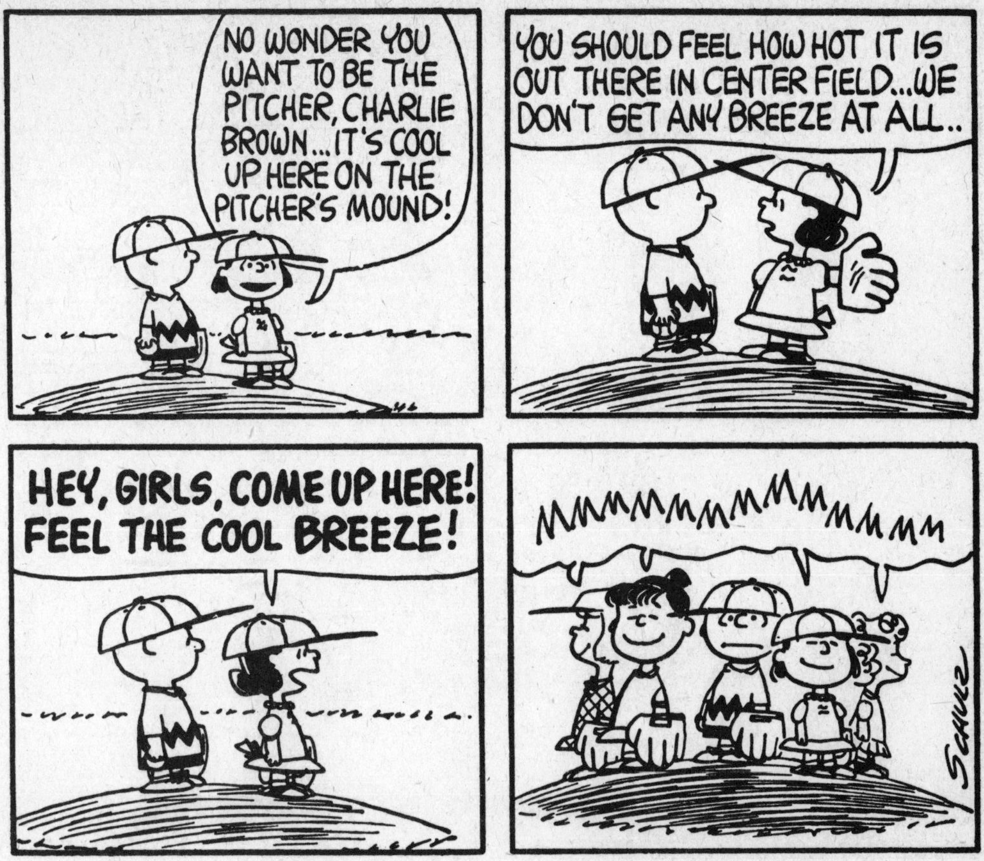
NO WONDER YOU WANT TO BE THE PITCHER, CHARLIE BROWN...IT'S COOL UP HERE ON THE PITCHER'S MOUND!
YOU SHOULD FEEL HOW HOT IT IS OUT THERE IN CENTER FIELD...WE DON'T GET ANY BREEZE AT ALL..
HEY, GIRLS, COME UP HERE! FEEL THE COOL BREEZE!
MMMMMMMMMMMMMMMMMMM
SCHULZ

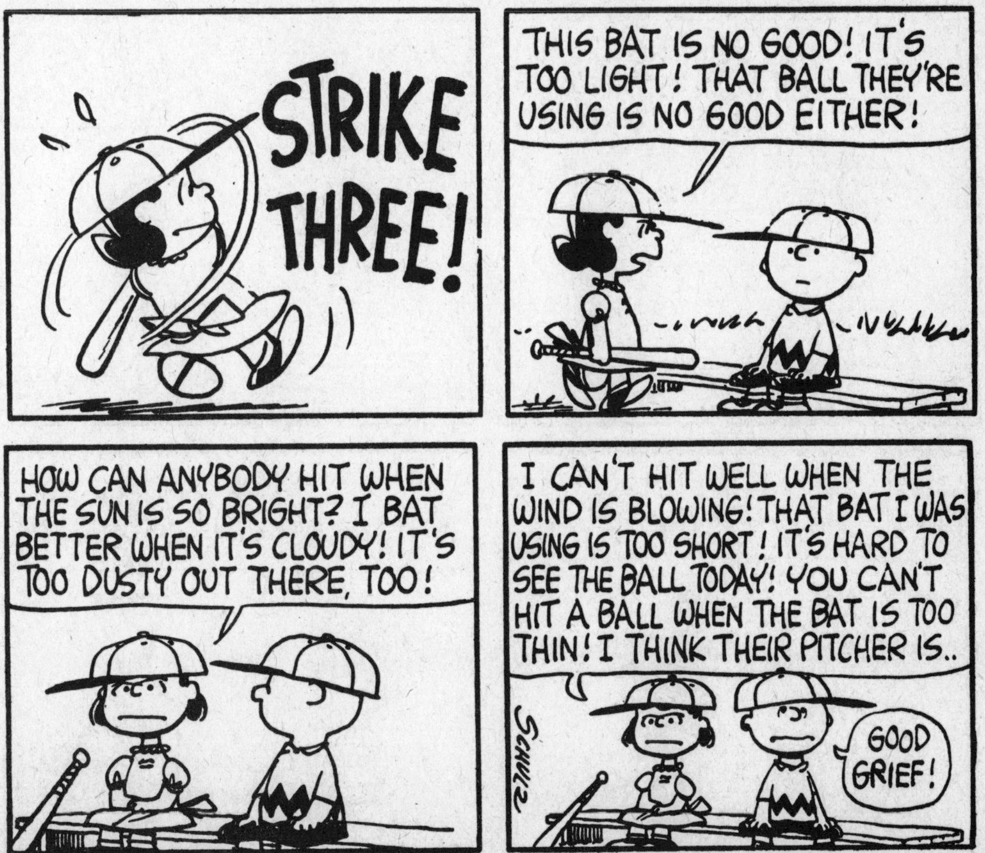
STRIKE THREE!
THIS BAT IS NO GOOD! IT'S TOO LIGHT! THAT BALL THEY'RE USING IS NO GOOD EITHER!
HOW CAN ANYBODY HIT WHEN THE SUN IS SO BRIGHT? I BAT BETTER WHEN IT'S CLOUDY! IT'S TOO DUSTY OUT THERE, TOO!
I CAN'T HIT WELL WHEN THE WIND IS BLOWING! THAT BAT I WAS USING IS TOO SHORT! IT'S HARD TO SEE THE BALL TODAY! YOU CAN'T HIT A BALL WHEN THE BAT IS TOO THIN! I THINK THEIR PITCHER IS..
GOOD GRIEF!
SCHULZ

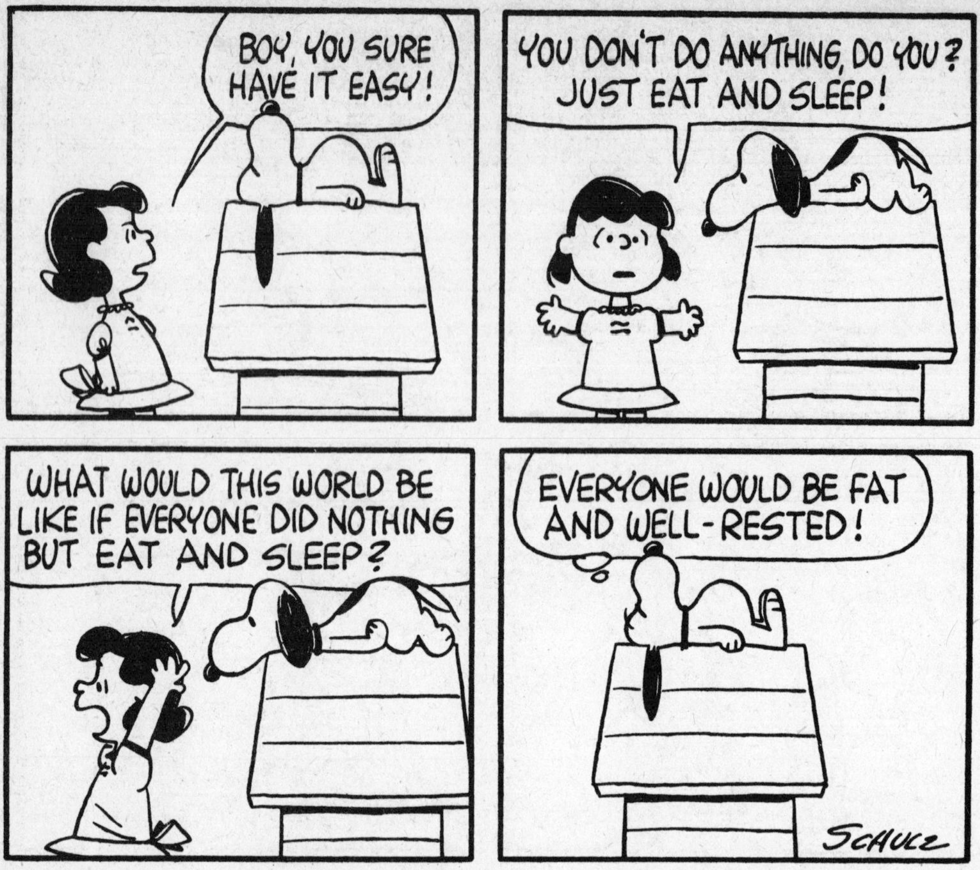
BOY, YOU SURE HAVE IT EASY!
YOU DON'T DO ANYTHING, DO YOU? JUST EAT AND SLEEP!
WHAT WOULD THIS WORLD BE LIKE IF EVERYONE DID NOTHING BUT EAT AND SLEEP?
EVERYONE WOULD BE FAT AND WELL-RESTED!

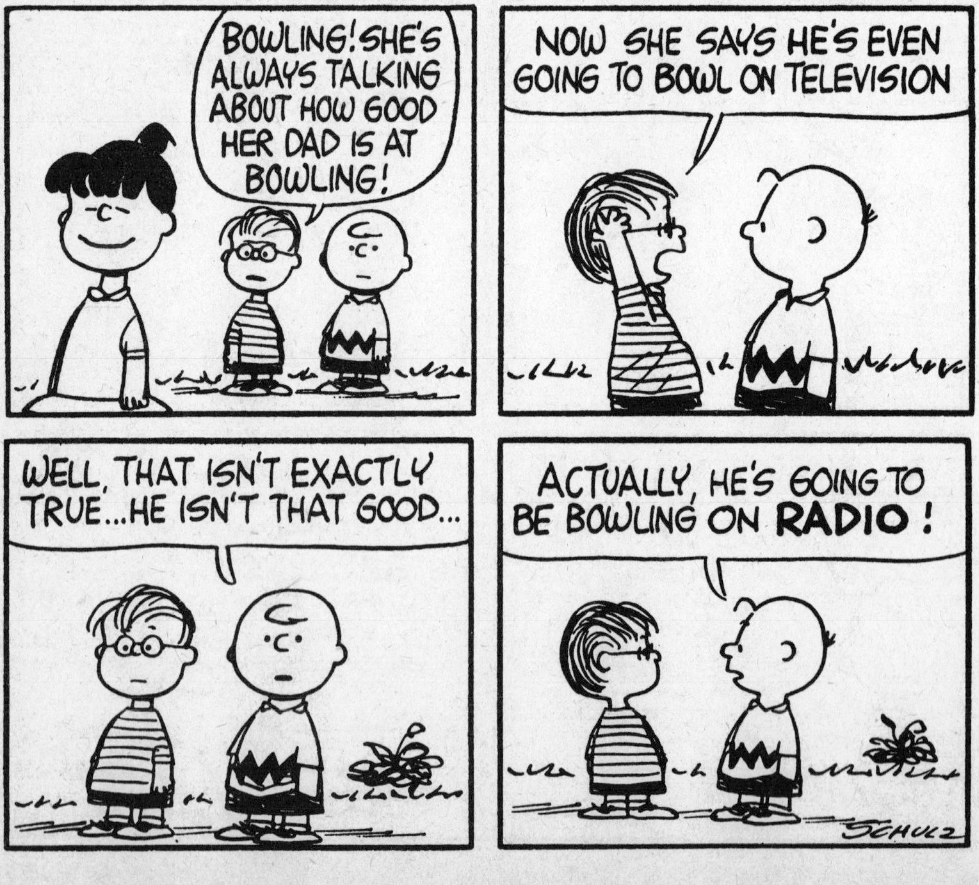
BOWLING! SHE'S ALWAYS TALKING ABOUT HOW GOOD HER DAD IS AT BOWLING!
NOW SHE SAYS HE'S EVEN GOING TO BOWL ON TELEVISION
WELL, THAT ISN'T EXACTLY TRUE...HE ISN'T THAT GOOD...
ACTUALLY, HE'S GOING TO BE BOWLING ON **RADIO**!

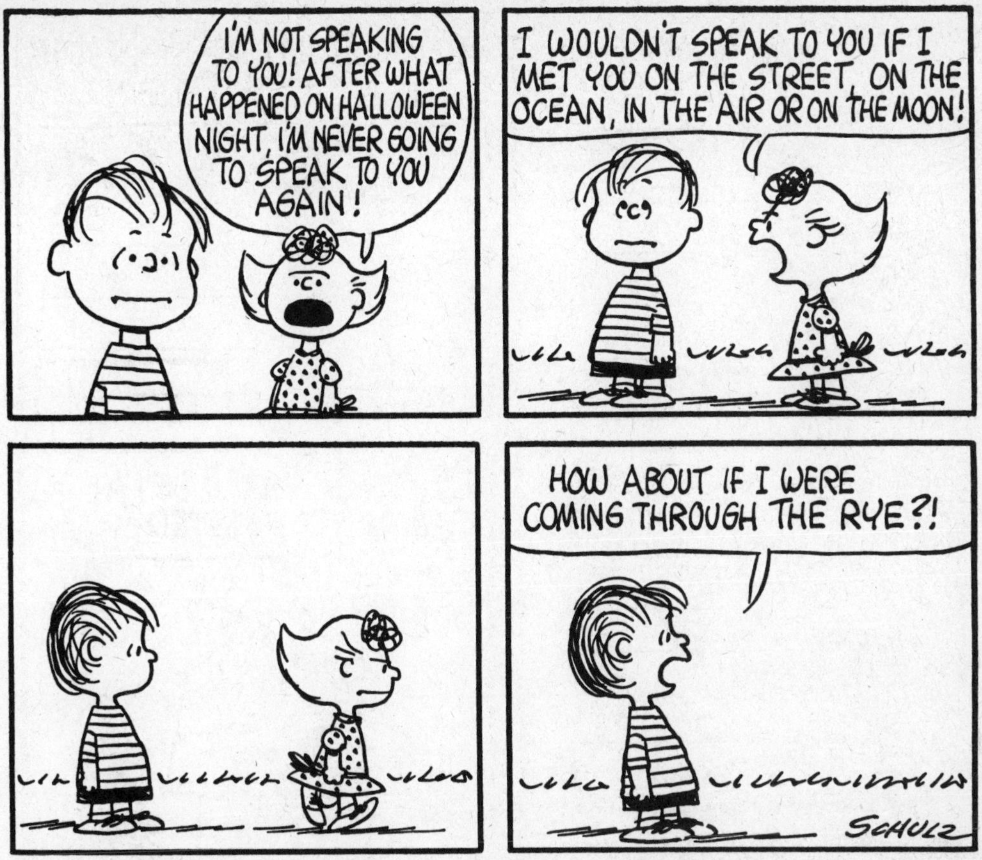
I'M NOT SPEAKING TO YOU! AFTER WHAT HAPPENED ON HALLOWEEN NIGHT, I'M NEVER GOING TO SPEAK TO YOU AGAIN!
I WOULDN'T SPEAK TO YOU IF I MET YOU ON THE STREET, ON THE OCEAN, IN THE AIR OR ON THE MOON!
HOW ABOUT IF I WERE COMING THROUGH THE RYE?!
SCHULZ

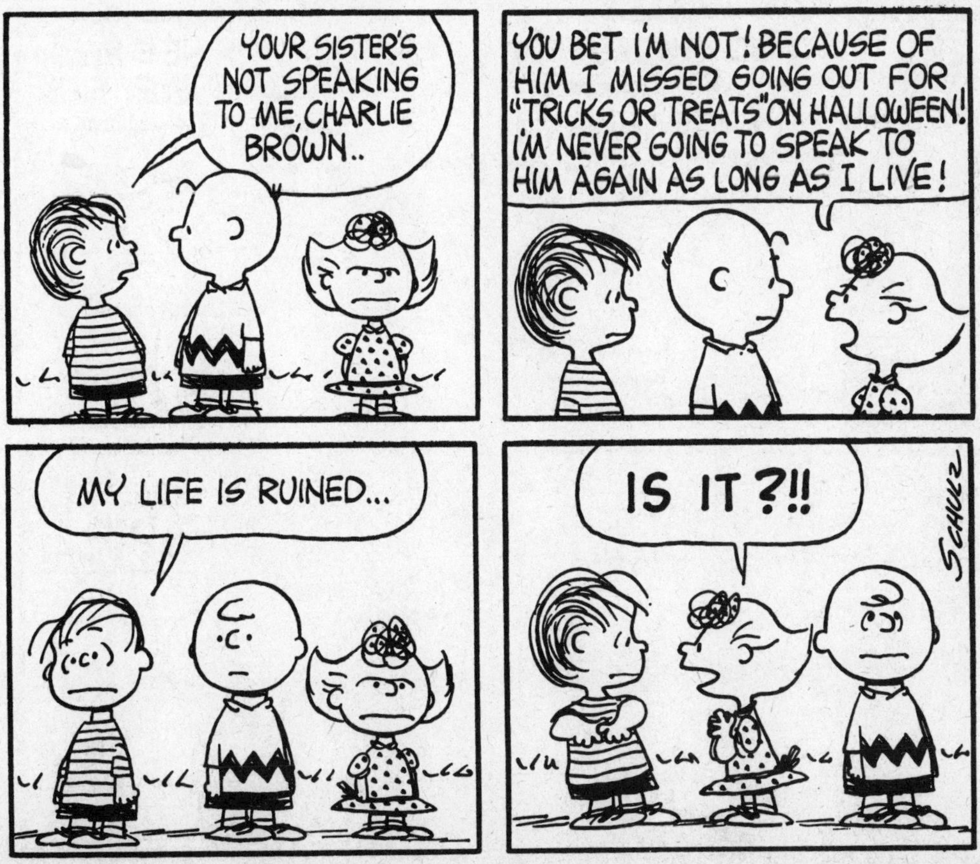
YOUR SISTER'S NOT SPEAKING TO ME, CHARLIE BROWN..
YOU BET I'M NOT! BECAUSE OF HIM I MISSED GOING OUT FOR "TRICKS OR TREATS" ON HALLOWEEN! I'M NEVER GOING TO SPEAK TO HIM AGAIN AS LONG AS I LIVE!
MY LIFE IS RUINED...
IS IT?!!
SCHULZ

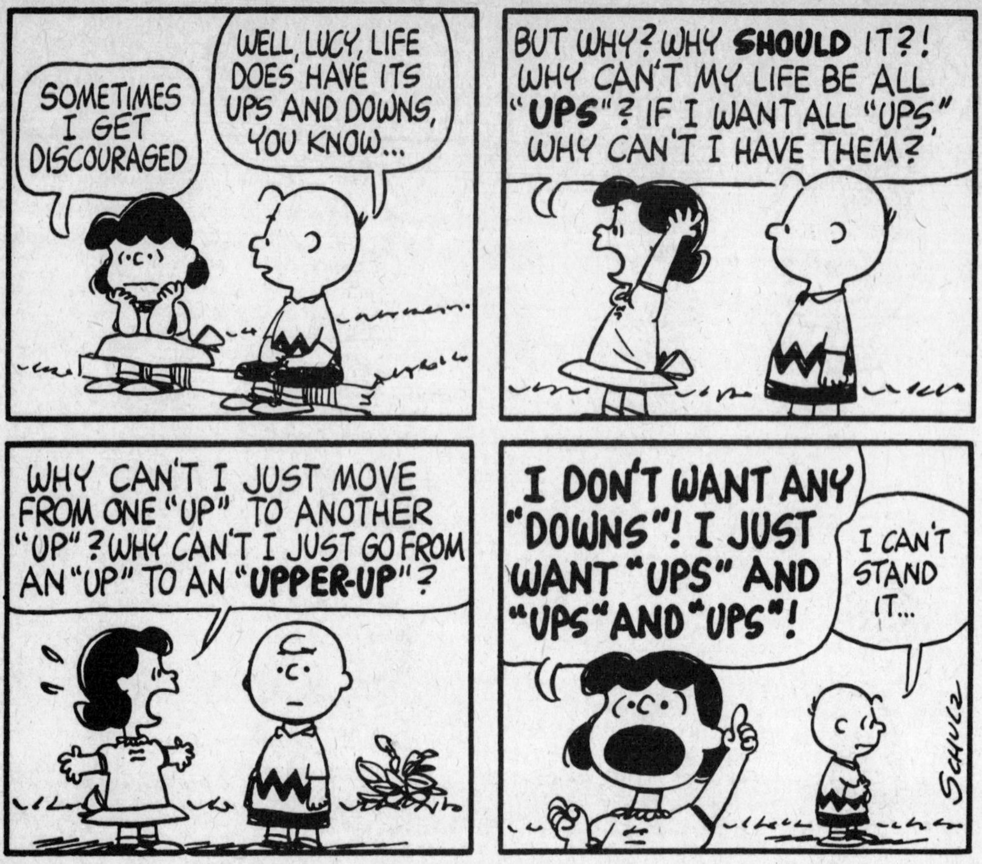
SOMETIMES I GET DISCOURAGED
WELL, LUCY, LIFE DOES HAVE ITS UPS AND DOWNS, YOU KNOW...
BUT WHY? WHY **SHOULD** IT?! WHY CAN'T MY LIFE BE ALL "**UPS**"? IF I WANT ALL "UPS," WHY CAN'T I HAVE THEM?
WHY CAN'T I JUST MOVE FROM ONE "UP" TO ANOTHER "UP"? WHY CAN'T I JUST GO FROM AN "UP" TO AN "**UPPER-UP**"?
I DON'T WANT ANY "DOWNS"! I JUST WANT "UPS" AND "UPS" AND "UPS"!
I CAN'T STAND IT...
SCHULZ

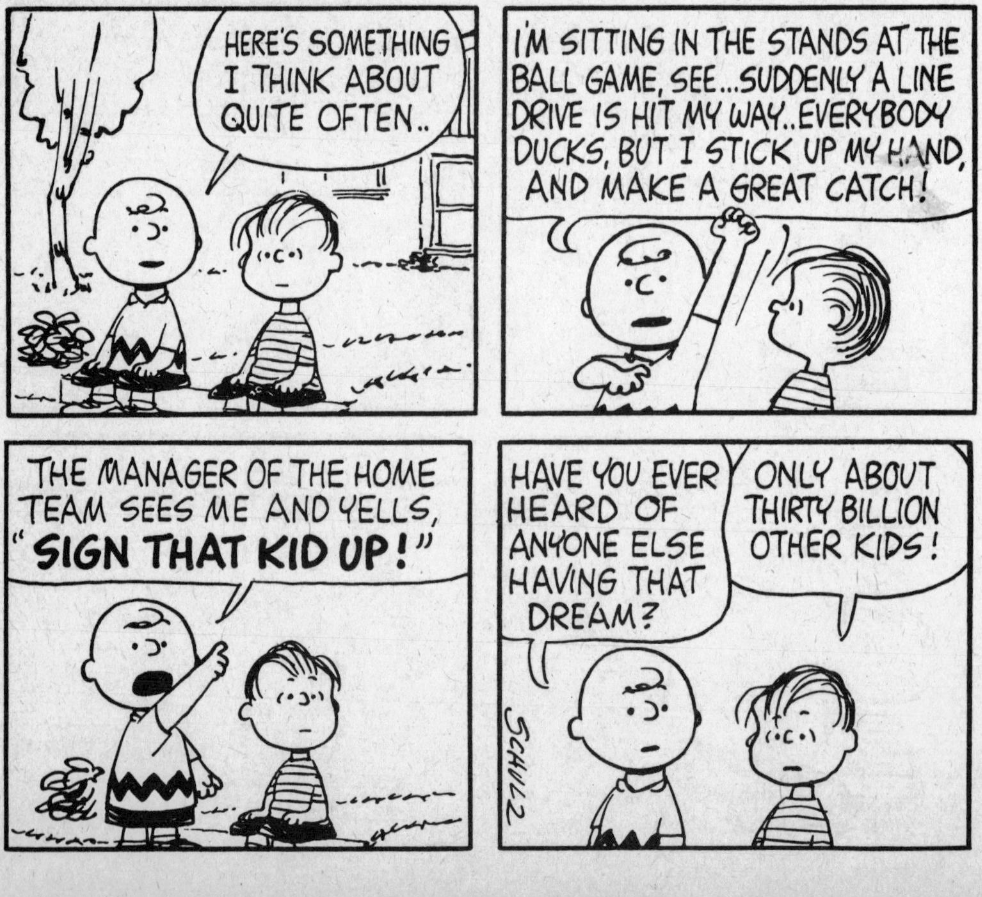
HERE'S SOMETHING I THINK ABOUT QUITE OFTEN..
I'M SITTING IN THE STANDS AT THE BALL GAME, SEE...SUDDENLY A LINE DRIVE IS HIT MY WAY..EVERYBODY DUCKS, BUT I STICK UP MY HAND, AND MAKE A GREAT CATCH!
THE MANAGER OF THE HOME TEAM SEES ME AND YELLS, "**SIGN THAT KID UP!**"
HAVE YOU EVER HEARD OF ANYONE ELSE HAVING THAT DREAM?
ONLY ABOUT THIRTY BILLION OTHER KIDS!
SCHULZ

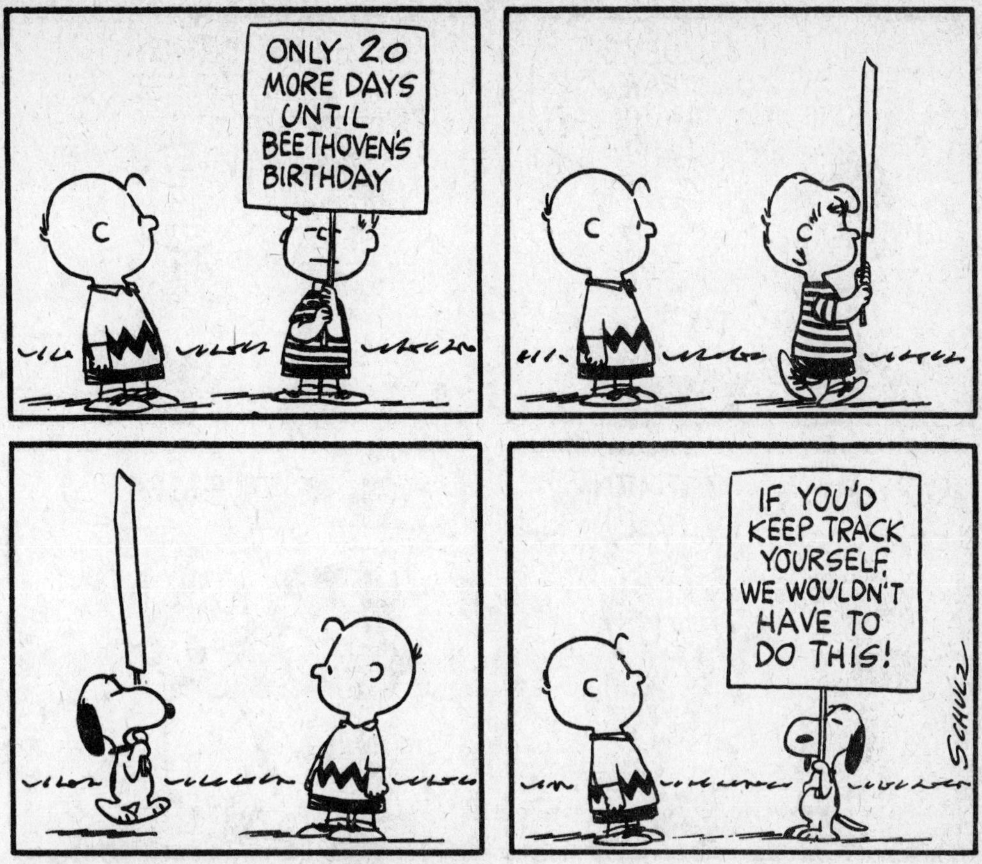
ONLY 20 MORE DAYS UNTIL BEETHOVEN'S BIRTHDAY
IF YOU'D KEEP TRACK YOURSELF, WE WOULDN'T HAVE TO DO THIS!
SCHULZ

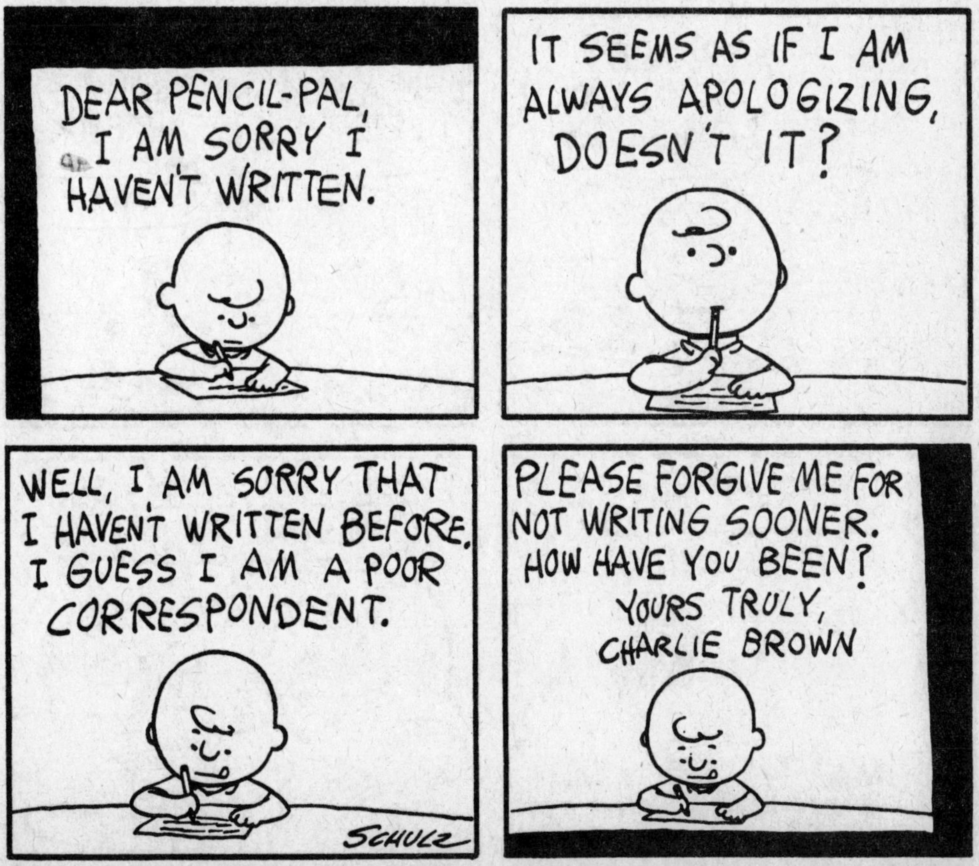
DEAR PENCIL-PAL, I AM SORRY I HAVEN'T WRITTEN.
IT SEEMS AS IF I AM ALWAYS APOLOGIZING, DOESN'T IT?
WELL, I AM SORRY THAT I HAVEN'T WRITTEN BEFORE. I GUESS I AM A POOR CORRESPONDENT.
SCHULZ
PLEASE FORGIVE ME FOR NOT WRITING SOONER. HOW HAVE YOU BEEN?
YOURS TRULY, CHARLIE BROWN

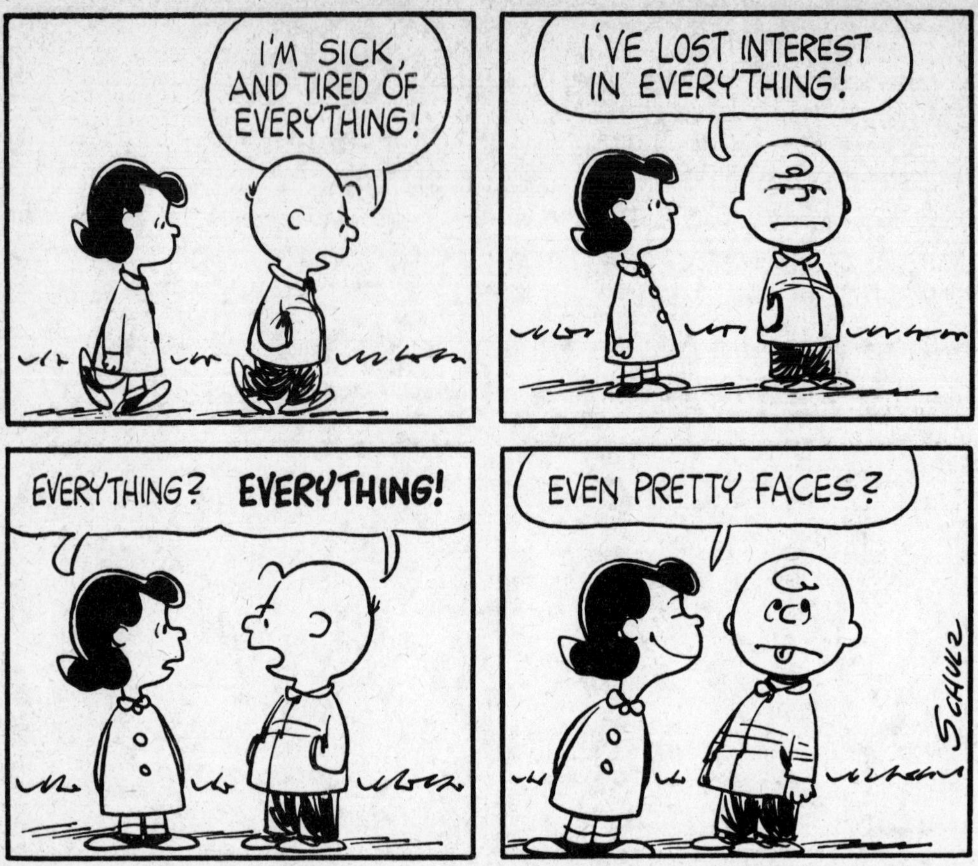
I'M SICK, AND TIRED OF EVERYTHING!
I'VE LOST INTEREST IN EVERYTHING!
EVERYTHING?
EVERYTHING!
EVEN PRETTY FACES?
SCHULZ

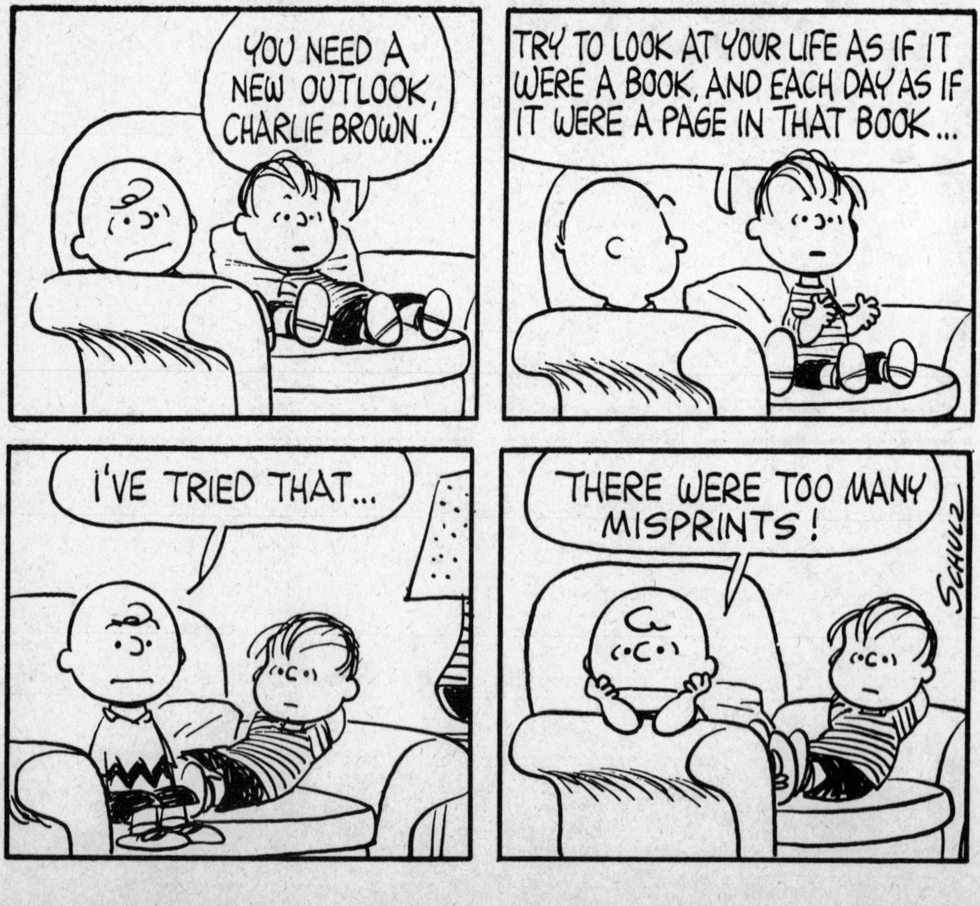
YOU NEED A NEW OUTLOOK, CHARLIE BROWN..
TRY TO LOOK AT YOUR LIFE AS IF IT WERE A BOOK, AND EACH DAY AS IF IT WERE A PAGE IN THAT BOOK...
I'VE TRIED THAT...
THERE WERE TOO MANY MISPRINTS!
SCHULZ

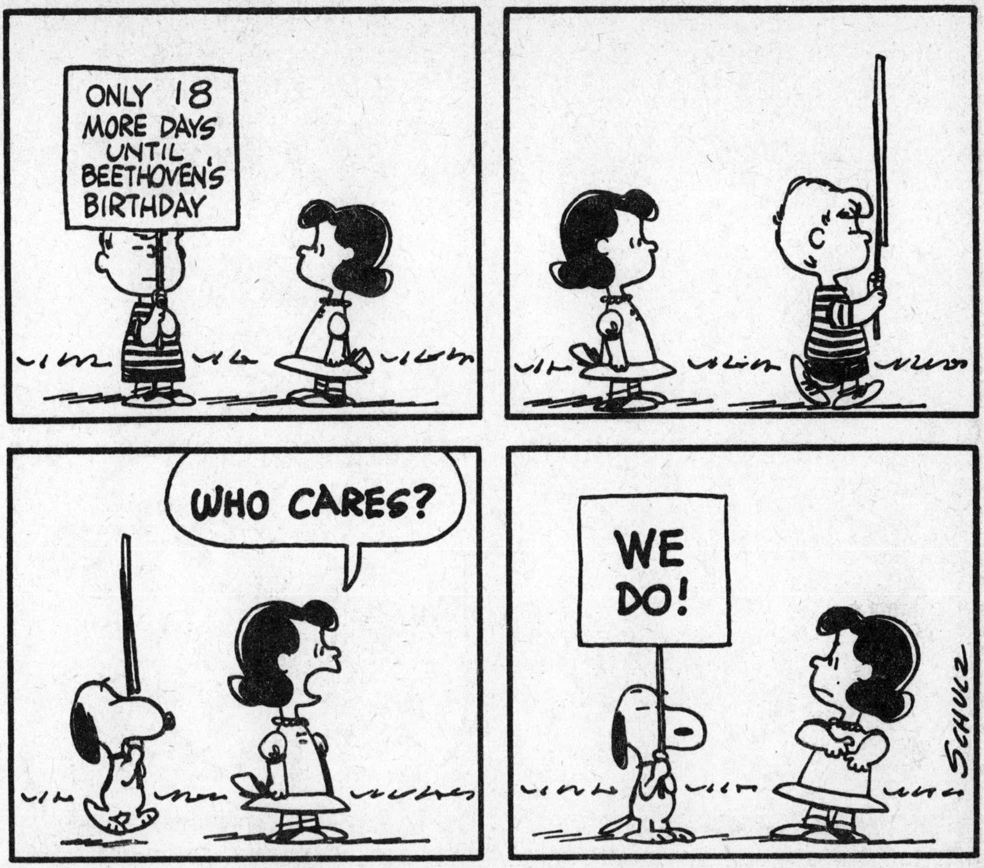
ONLY 18 MORE DAYS UNTIL BEETHOVEN'S BIRTHDAY
WHO CARES?
WE DO!
SCHULZ

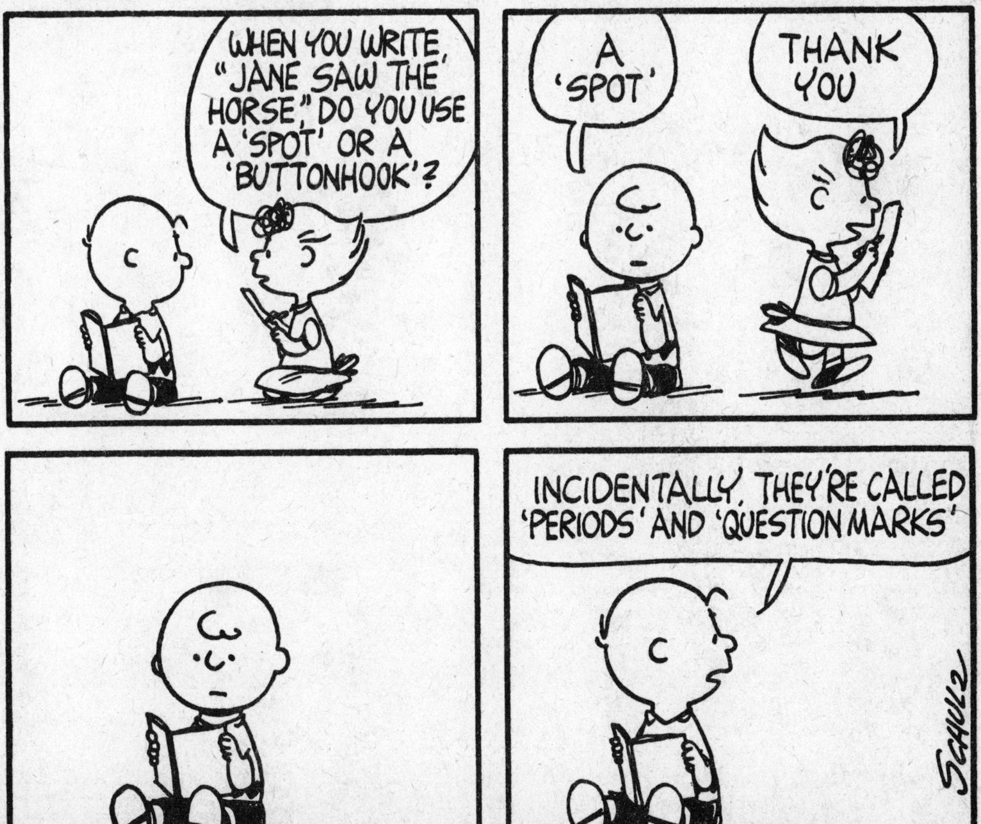
WHEN YOU WRITE, "JANE SAW THE HORSE," DO YOU USE A 'SPOT' OR A 'BUTTONHOOK'?
A 'SPOT'
THANK YOU
INCIDENTALLY, THEY'RE CALLED 'PERIODS' AND 'QUESTION MARKS'
SCHULZ

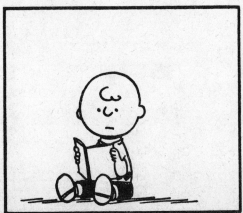

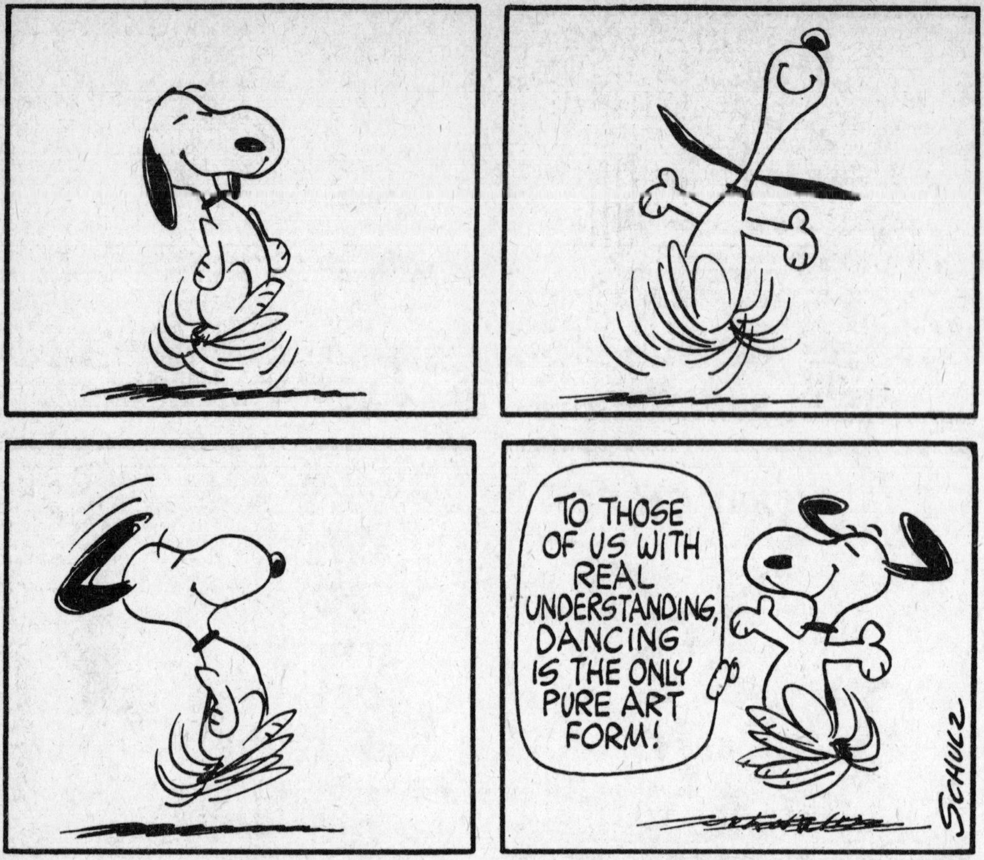
TO THOSE OF US WITH REAL UNDERSTANDING, DANCING IS THE ONLY PURE ART FORM!
SCHULZ

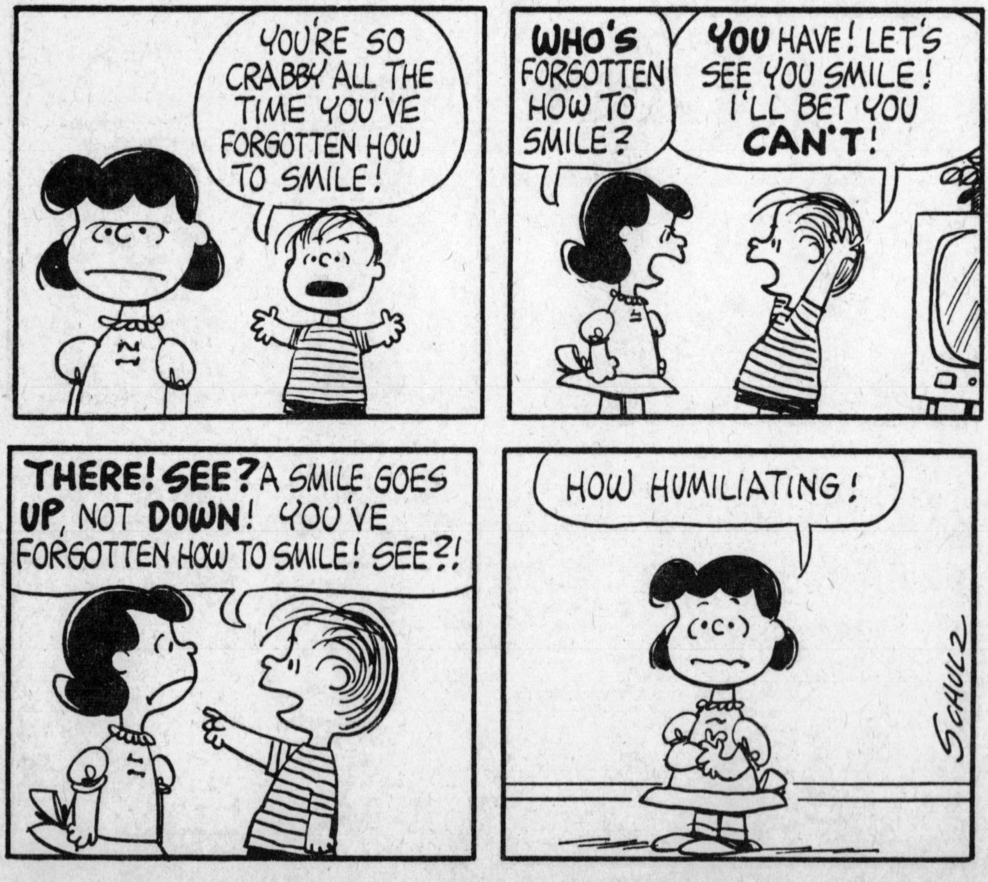
YOU'RE SO CRABBY ALL THE TIME YOU'VE FORGOTTEN HOW TO SMILE!
WHO'S FORGOTTEN HOW TO SMILE?
YOU HAVE! LET'S SEE YOU SMILE! I'LL BET YOU CAN'T!
THERE! SEE? A SMILE GOES UP, NOT DOWN! YOU'VE FORGOTTEN HOW TO SMILE! SEE?!
HOW HUMILIATING!
SCHULZ

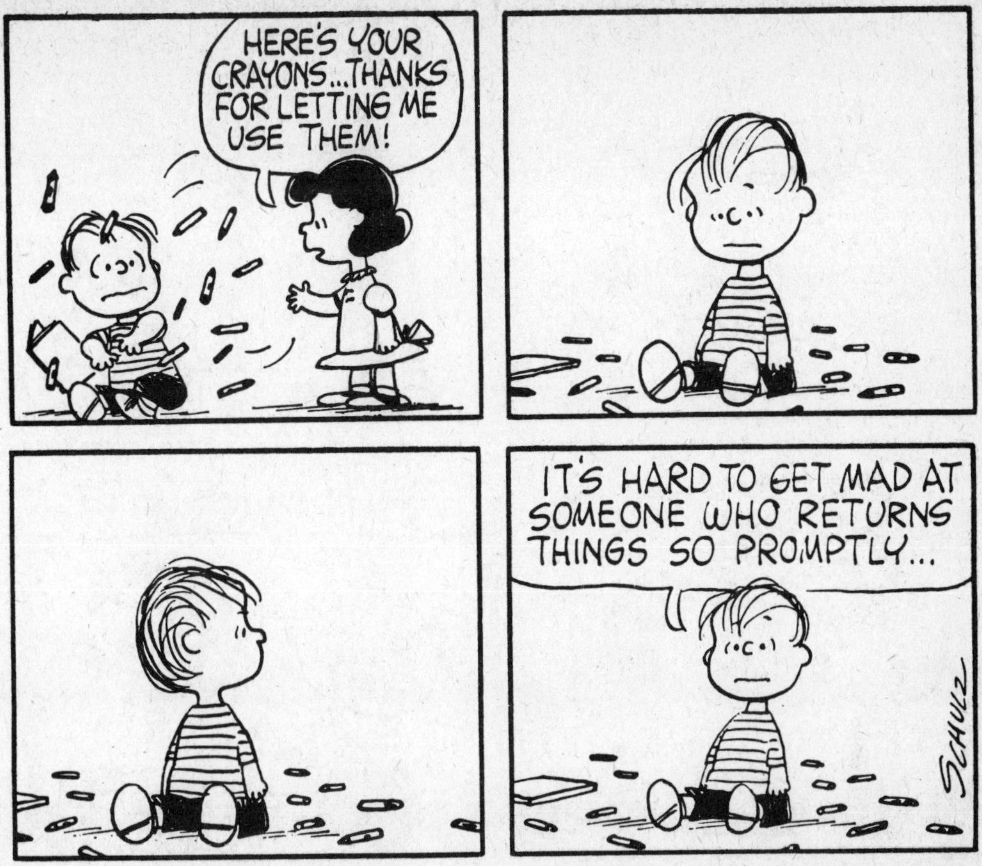
HERE'S YOUR CRAYONS...THANKS FOR LETTING ME USE THEM!
IT'S HARD TO GET MAD AT SOMEONE WHO RETURNS THINGS SO PROMPTLY...
SCHULZ

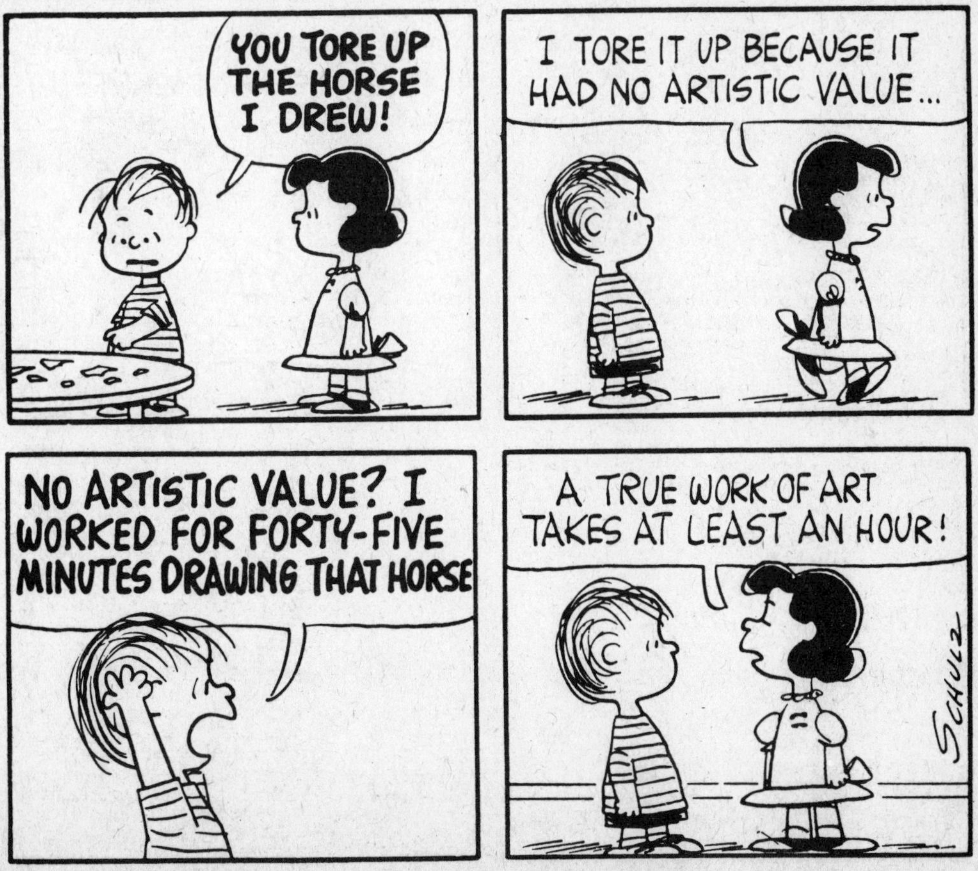
YOU TORE UP THE HORSE I DREW!
I TORE IT UP BECAUSE IT HAD NO ARTISTIC VALUE...
NO ARTISTIC VALUE? I WORKED FOR FORTY-FIVE MINUTES DRAWING THAT HORSE
A TRUE WORK OF ART TAKES AT LEAST AN HOUR!
SCHULZ

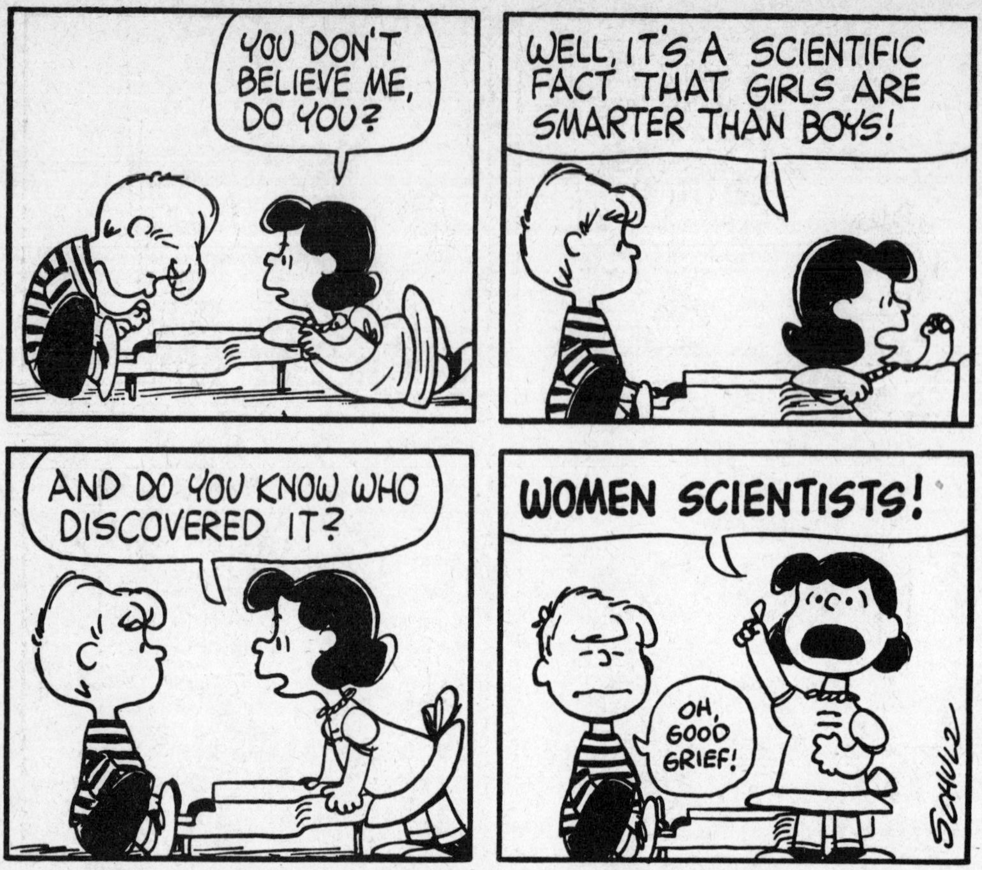
YOU DON'T BELIEVE ME, DO YOU?
WELL, IT'S A SCIENTIFIC FACT THAT GIRLS ARE SMARTER THAN BOYS!
AND DO YOU KNOW WHO DISCOVERED IT?
WOMEN SCIENTISTS!
OH, GOOD GRIEF!
SCHULZ

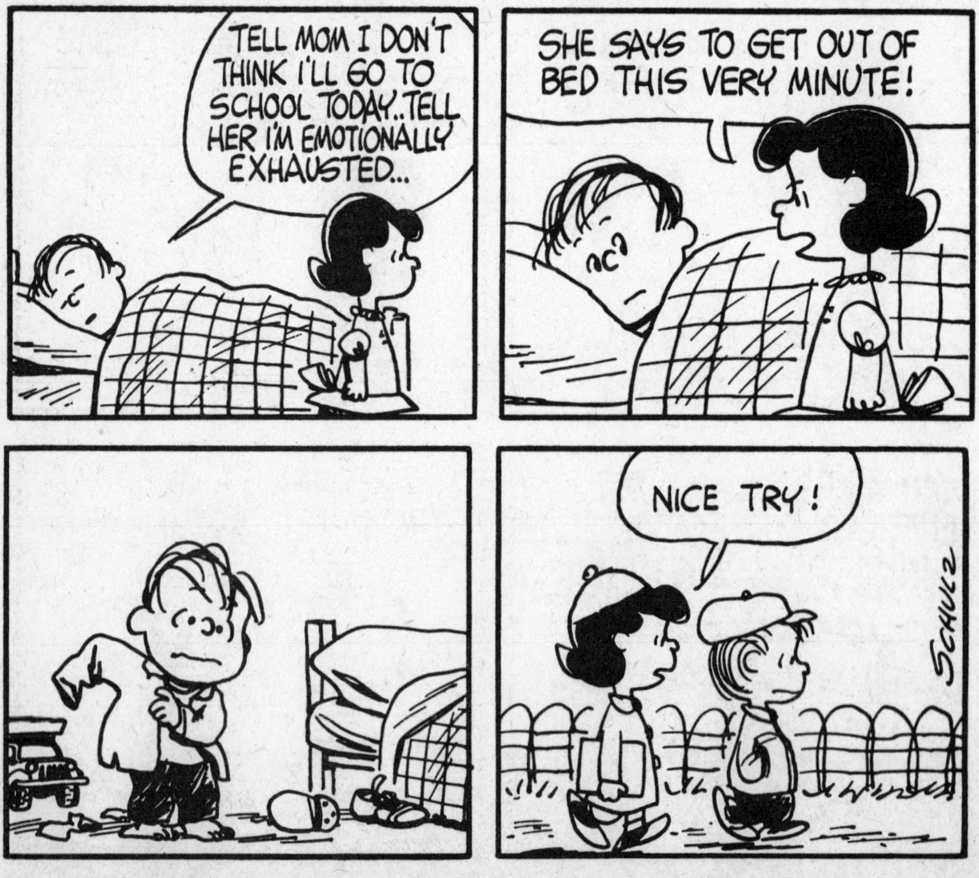
TELL MOM I DON'T THINK I'LL GO TO SCHOOL TODAY..TELL HER I'M EMOTIONALLY EXHAUSTED...
SHE SAYS TO GET OUT OF BED THIS VERY MINUTE!
NICE TRY!
SCHULZ

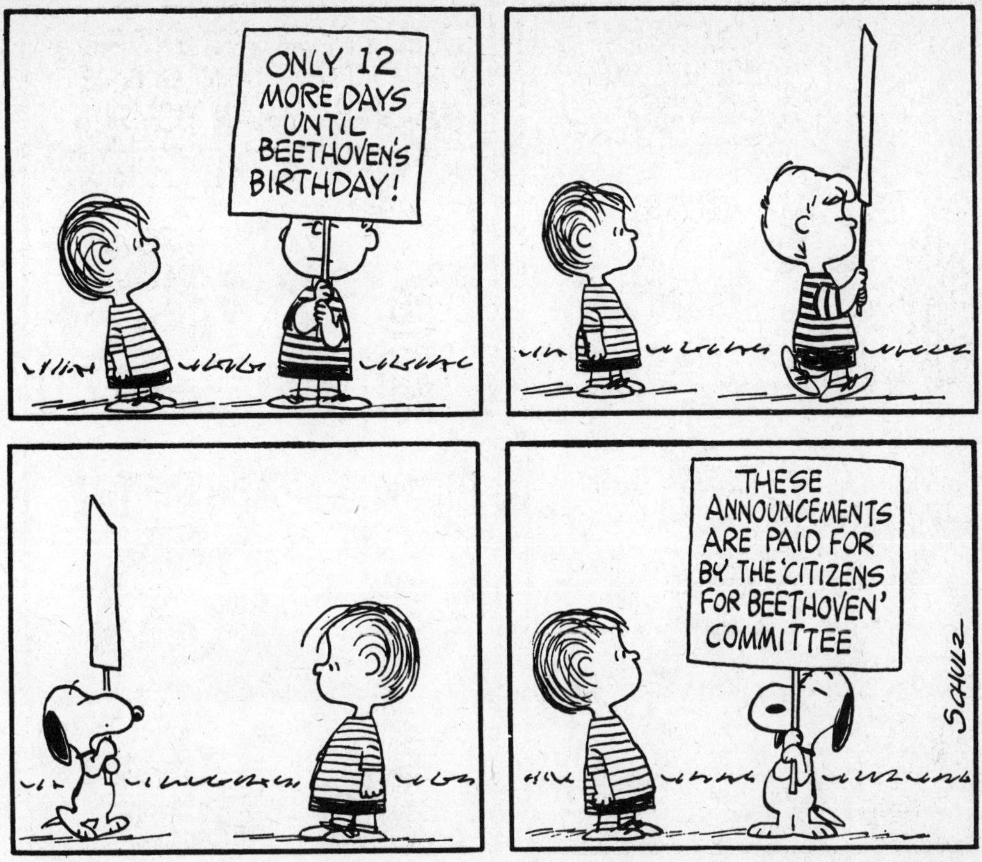
ONLY 12 MORE DAYS UNTIL BEETHOVEN'S BIRTHDAY!
THESE ANNOUNCEMENTS ARE PAID FOR BY THE 'CITIZENS FOR BEETHOVEN' COMMITTEE
SCHULZ

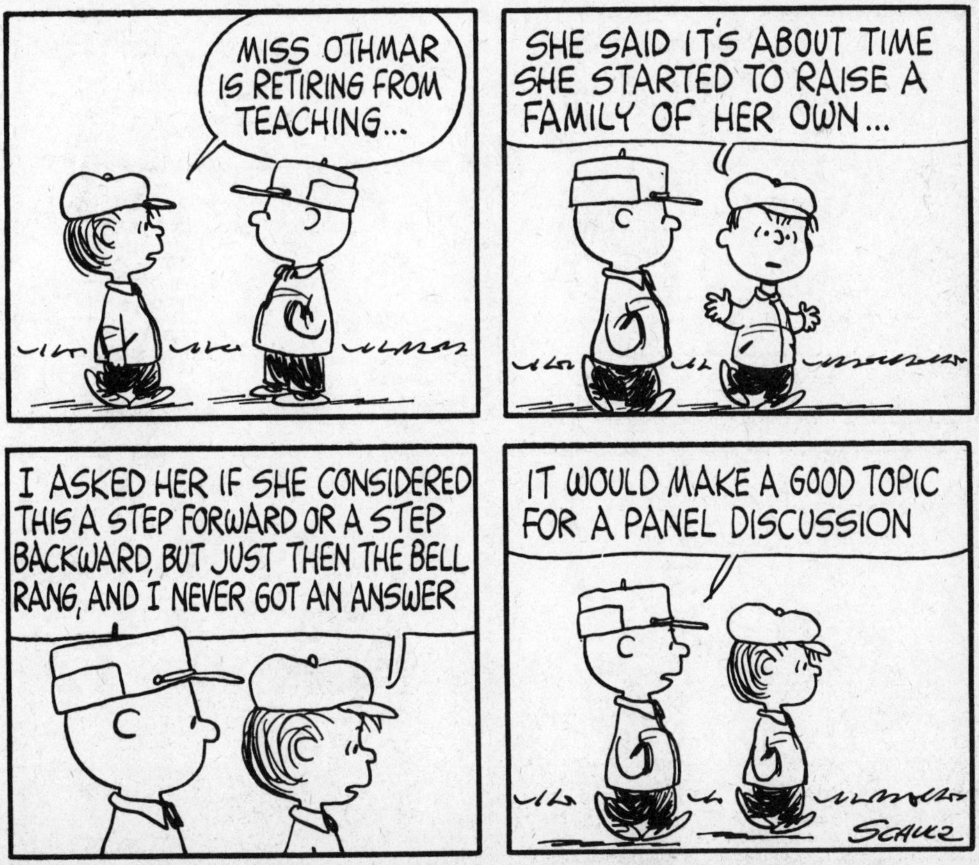
MISS OTHMAR IS RETIRING FROM TEACHING...
SHE SAID IT'S ABOUT TIME SHE STARTED TO RAISE A FAMILY OF HER OWN...
I ASKED HER IF SHE CONSIDERED THIS A STEP FORWARD OR A STEP BACKWARD, BUT JUST THEN THE BELL RANG, AND I NEVER GOT AN ANSWER
IT WOULD MAKE A GOOD TOPIC FOR A PANEL DISCUSSION
SCHULZ

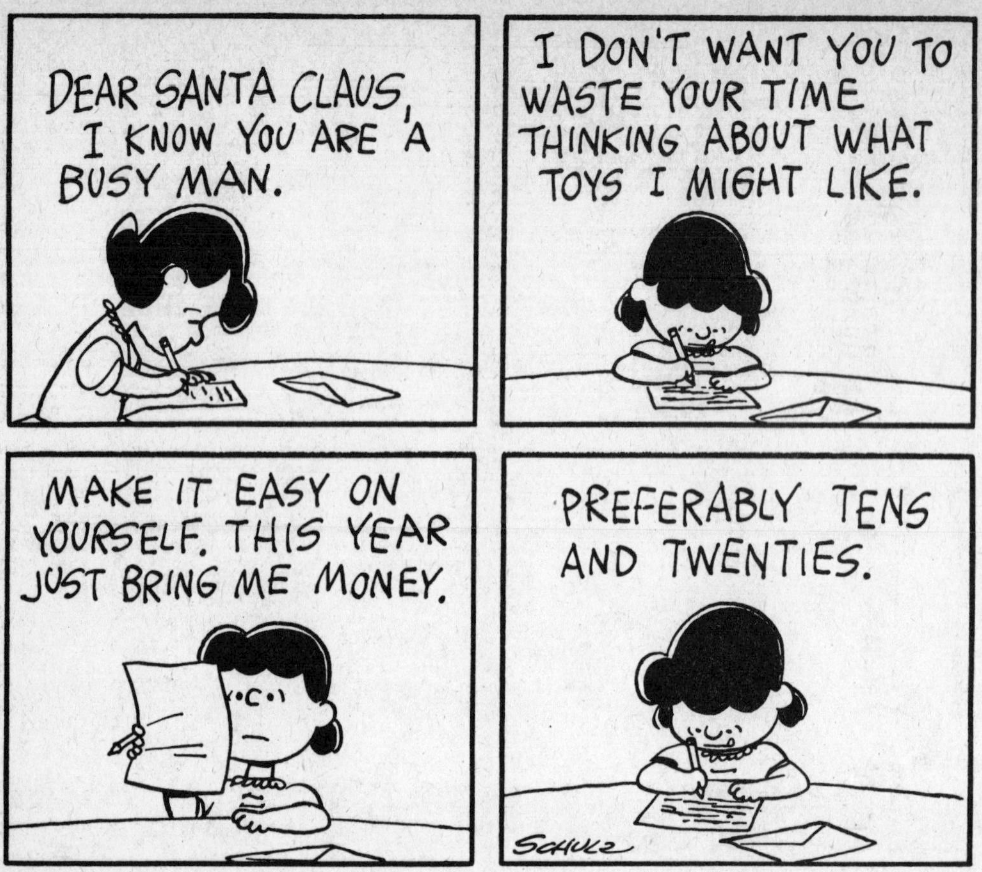
DEAR SANTA CLAUS,
I KNOW YOU ARE A BUSY MAN.
I DON'T WANT YOU TO WASTE YOUR TIME THINKING ABOUT WHAT TOYS I MIGHT LIKE.
MAKE IT EASY ON YOURSELF. THIS YEAR JUST BRING ME MONEY.
PREFERABLY TENS AND TWENTIES.
SCHULZ

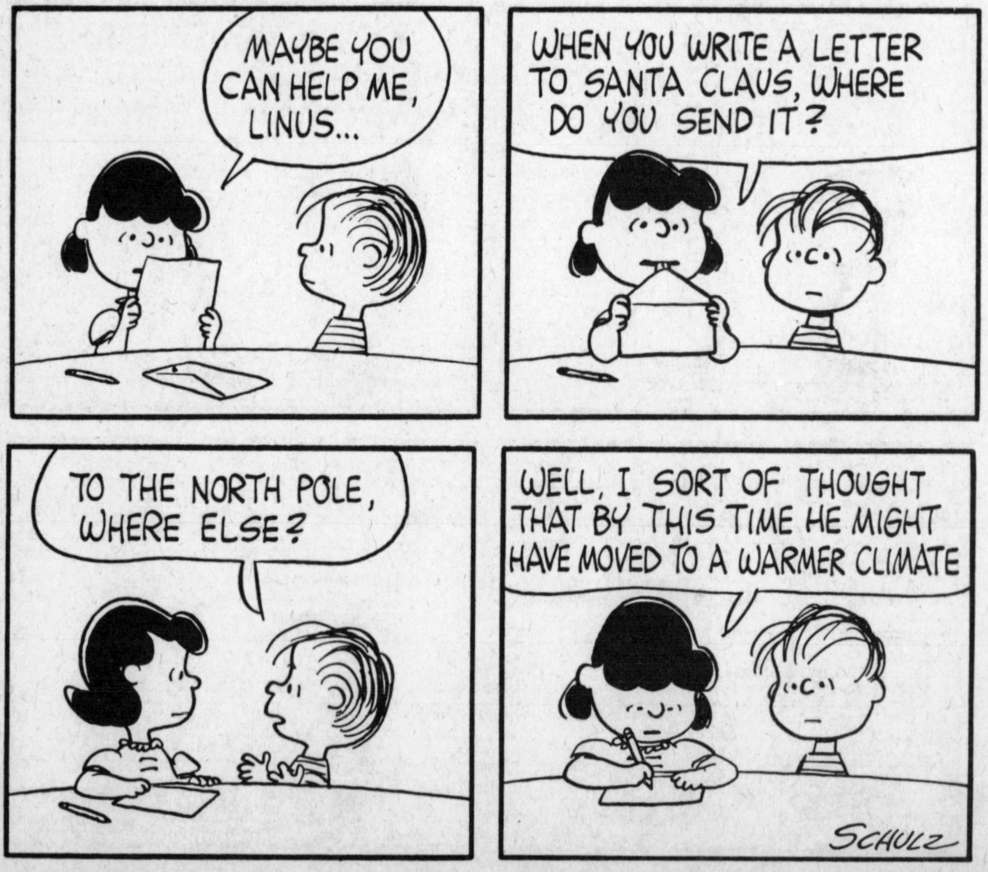
MAYBE YOU CAN HELP ME, LINUS...
WHEN YOU WRITE A LETTER TO SANTA CLAUS, WHERE DO YOU SEND IT?
TO THE NORTH POLE, WHERE ELSE?
WELL, I SORT OF THOUGHT THAT BY THIS TIME HE MIGHT HAVE MOVED TO A WARMER CLIMATE
SCHULZ

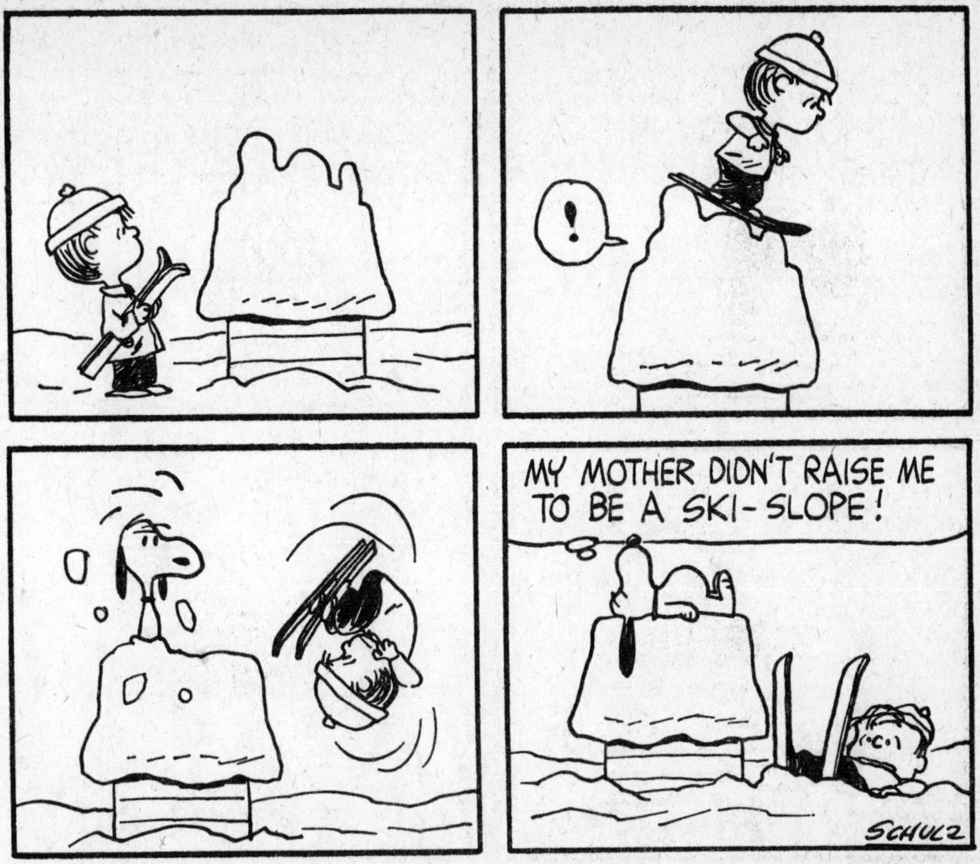
!
MY MOTHER DIDN'T RAISE ME TO BE A SKI-SLOPE!
SCHULZ

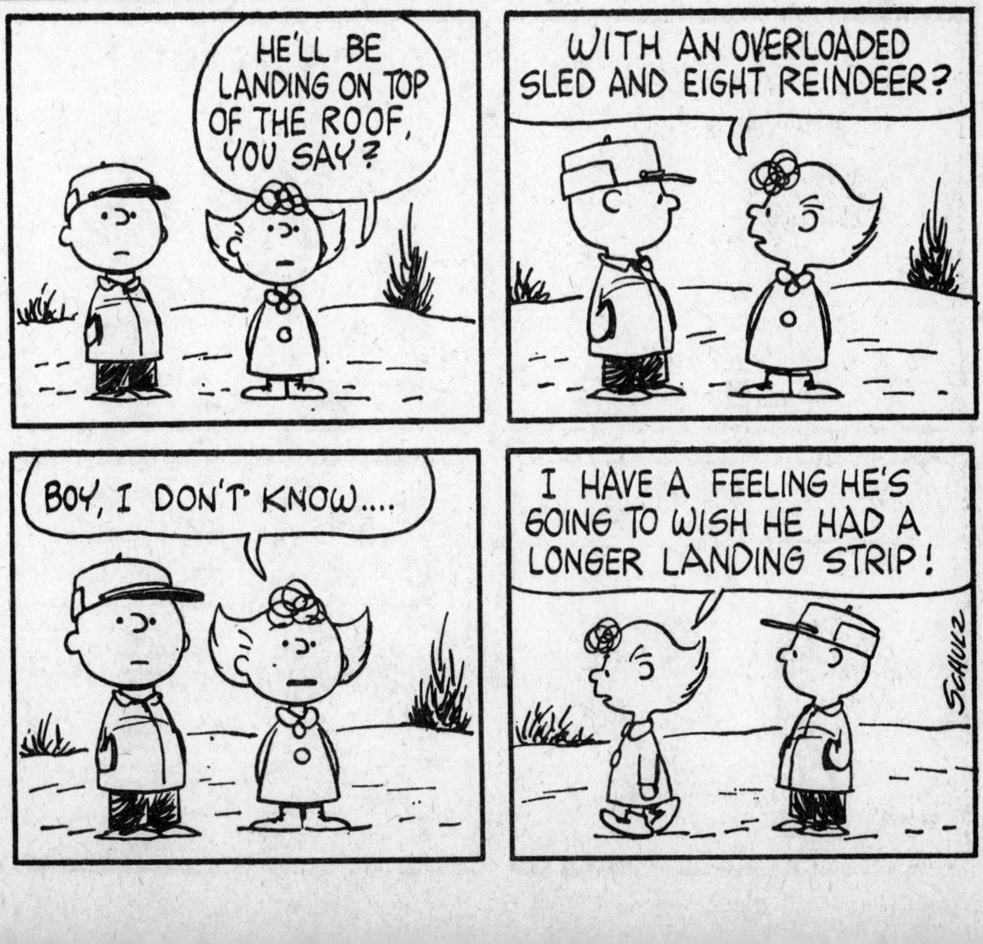
HE'LL BE LANDING ON TOP OF THE ROOF, YOU SAY?
WITH AN OVERLOADED SLED AND EIGHT REINDEER?
BOY, I DON'T KNOW....
I HAVE A FEELING HE'S GOING TO WISH HE HAD A LONGER LANDING STRIP!
SCHULZ

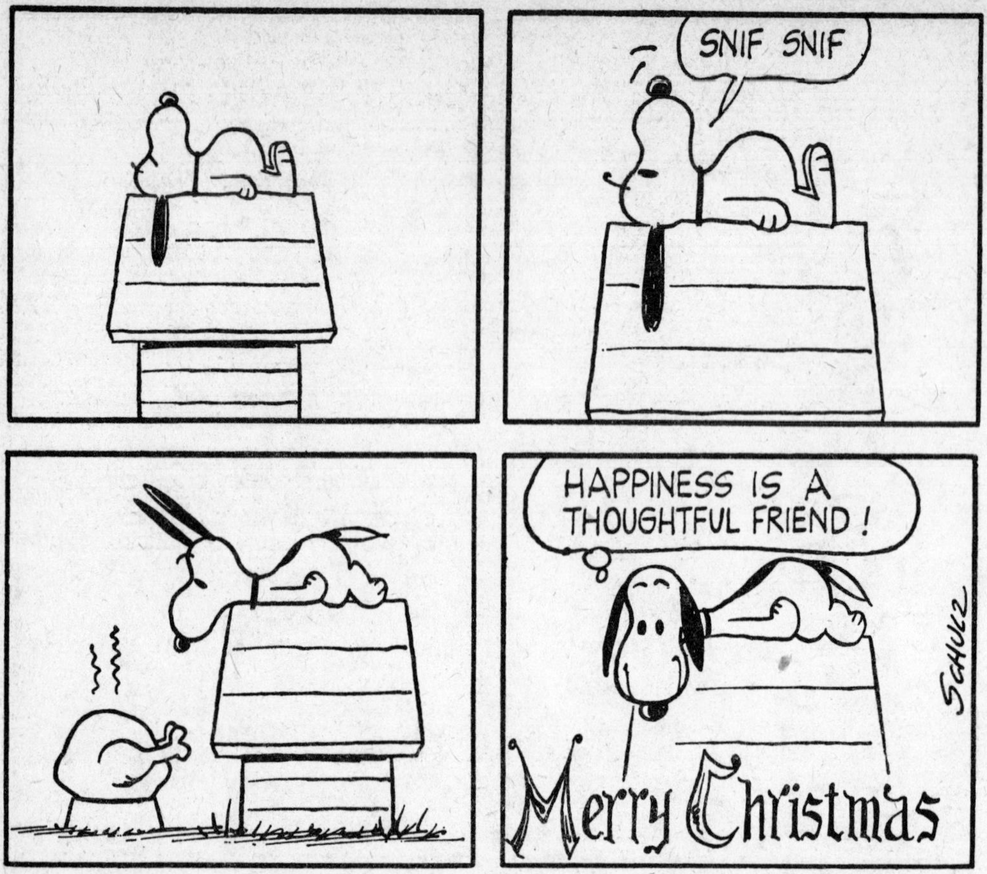
SNIF SNIF
HAPPINESS IS A THOUGHTFUL FRIEND!
Merry Christmas
SCHULZ

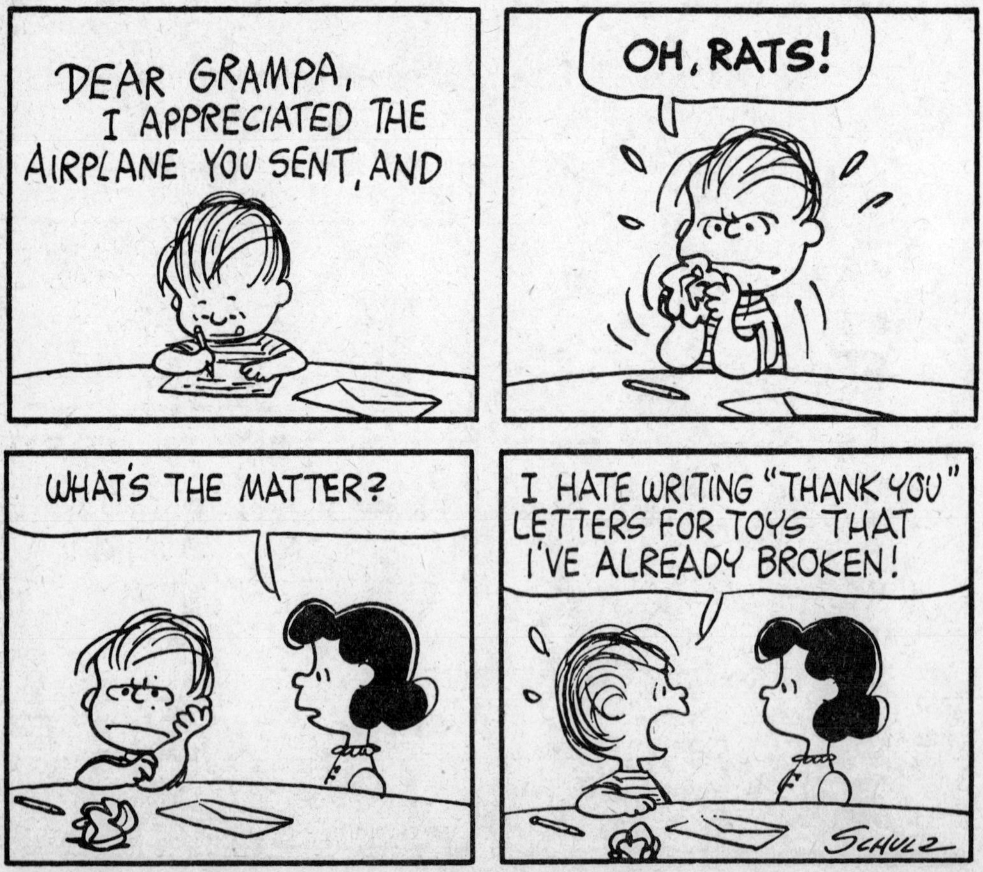
DEAR GRAMPA,
I APPRECIATED THE AIRPLANE YOU SENT, AND
OH, RATS!
WHAT'S THE MATTER?
I HATE WRITING "THANK YOU" LETTERS FOR TOYS THAT I'VE ALREADY BROKEN!
SCHULZ

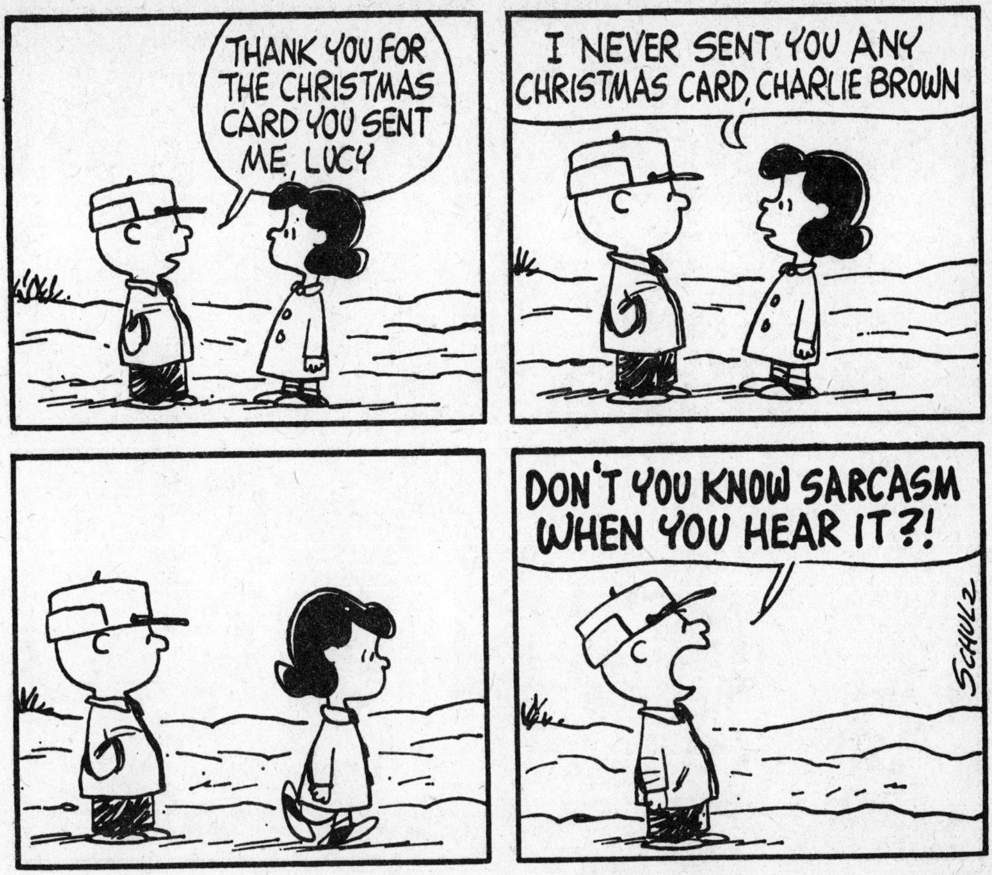
THANK YOU FOR THE CHRISTMAS CARD YOU SENT ME, LUCY
I NEVER SENT YOU ANY CHRISTMAS CARD, CHARLIE BROWN
DON'T YOU KNOW SARCASM WHEN YOU HEAR IT?!
SCHULZ

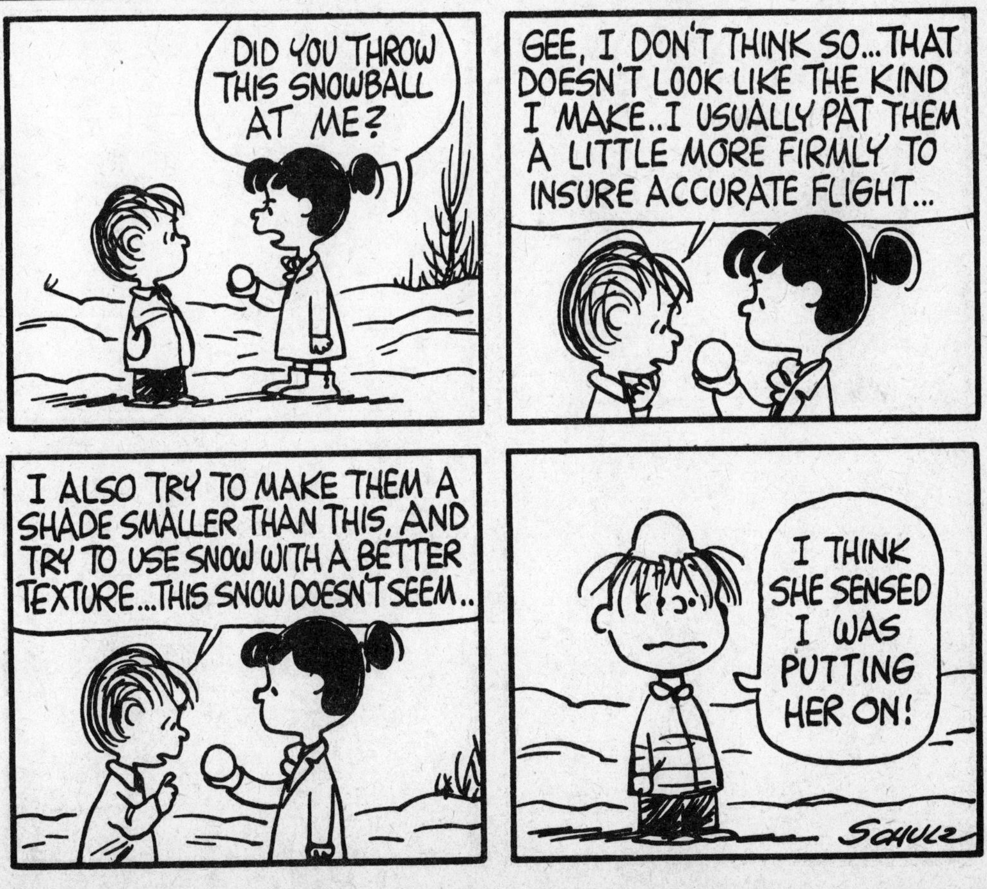
DID YOU THROW THIS SNOWBALL AT ME?
GEE, I DON'T THINK SO...THAT DOESN'T LOOK LIKE THE KIND I MAKE..I USUALLY PAT THEM A LITTLE MORE FIRMLY TO INSURE ACCURATE FLIGHT...
I ALSO TRY TO MAKE THEM A SHADE SMALLER THAN THIS, AND TRY TO USE SNOW WITH A BETTER TEXTURE...THIS SNOW DOESN'T SEEM..
I THINK SHE SENSED I WAS PUTTING HER ON!
SCHULZ

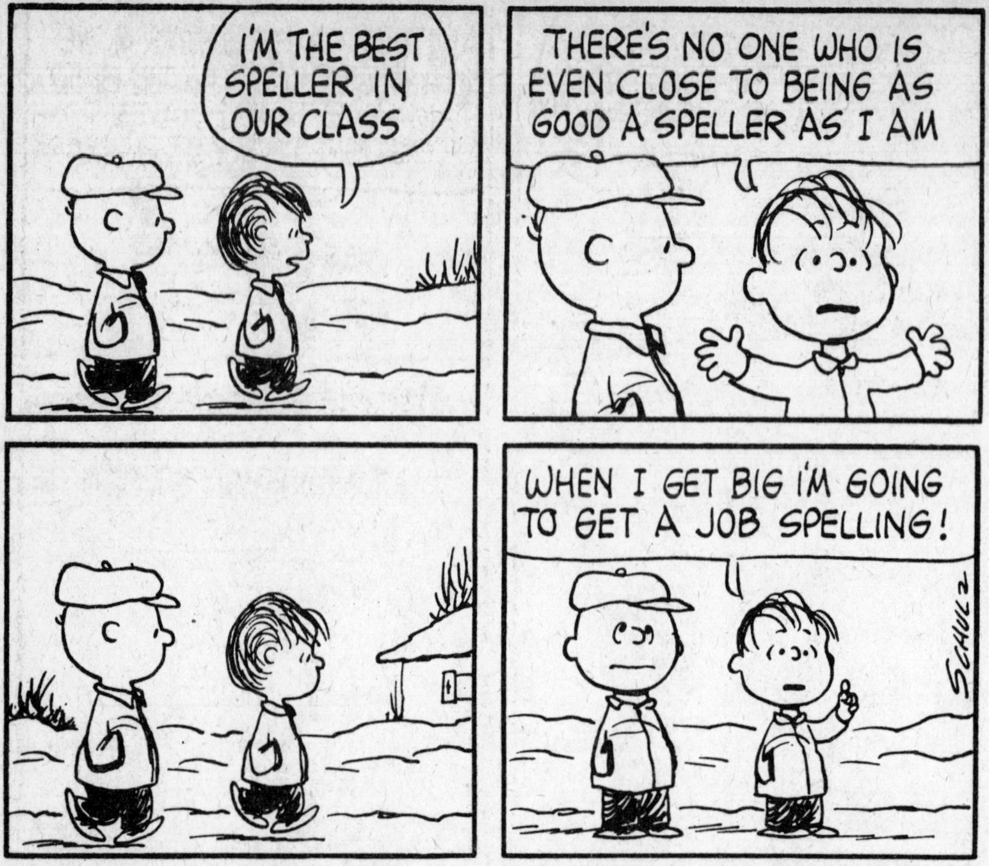
I'M THE BEST SPELLER IN OUR CLASS
THERE'S NO ONE WHO IS EVEN CLOSE TO BEING AS GOOD A SPELLER AS I AM
WHEN I GET BIG I'M GOING TO GET A JOB SPELLING!
SCHULZ

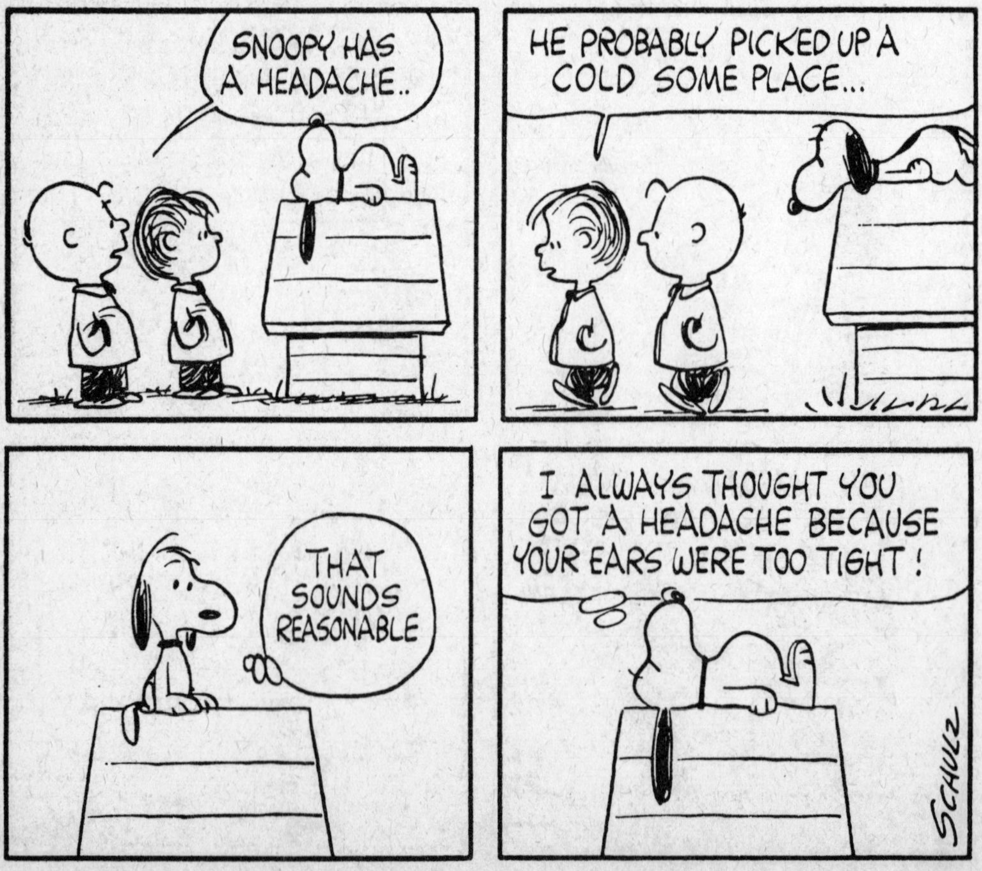
SNOOPY HAS A HEADACHE..
HE PROBABLY PICKED UP A COLD SOME PLACE...
THAT SOUNDS REASONABLE
I ALWAYS THOUGHT YOU GOT A HEADACHE BECAUSE YOUR EARS WERE TOO TIGHT!
SCHULZ

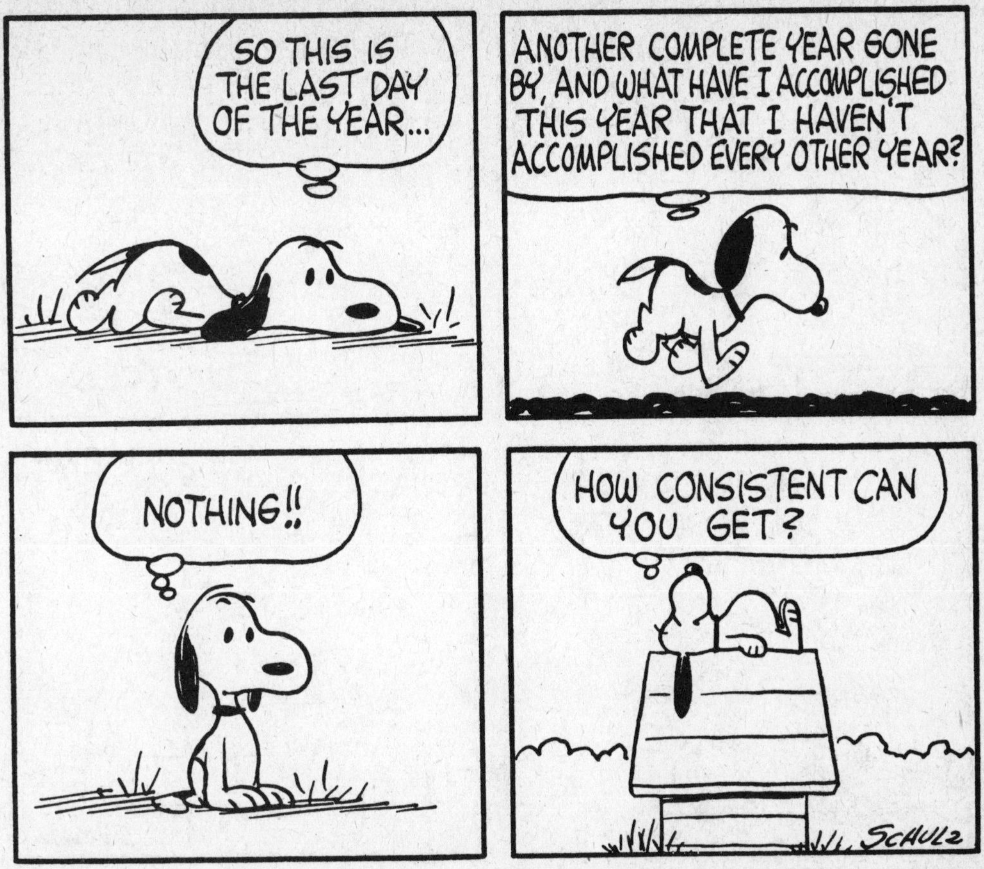
SO THIS IS THE LAST DAY OF THE YEAR...
ANOTHER COMPLETE YEAR GONE BY, AND WHAT HAVE I ACCOMPLISHED THIS YEAR THAT I HAVEN'T ACCOMPLISHED EVERY OTHER YEAR?
NOTHING!!
HOW CONSISTENT CAN YOU GET?
SCHULZ

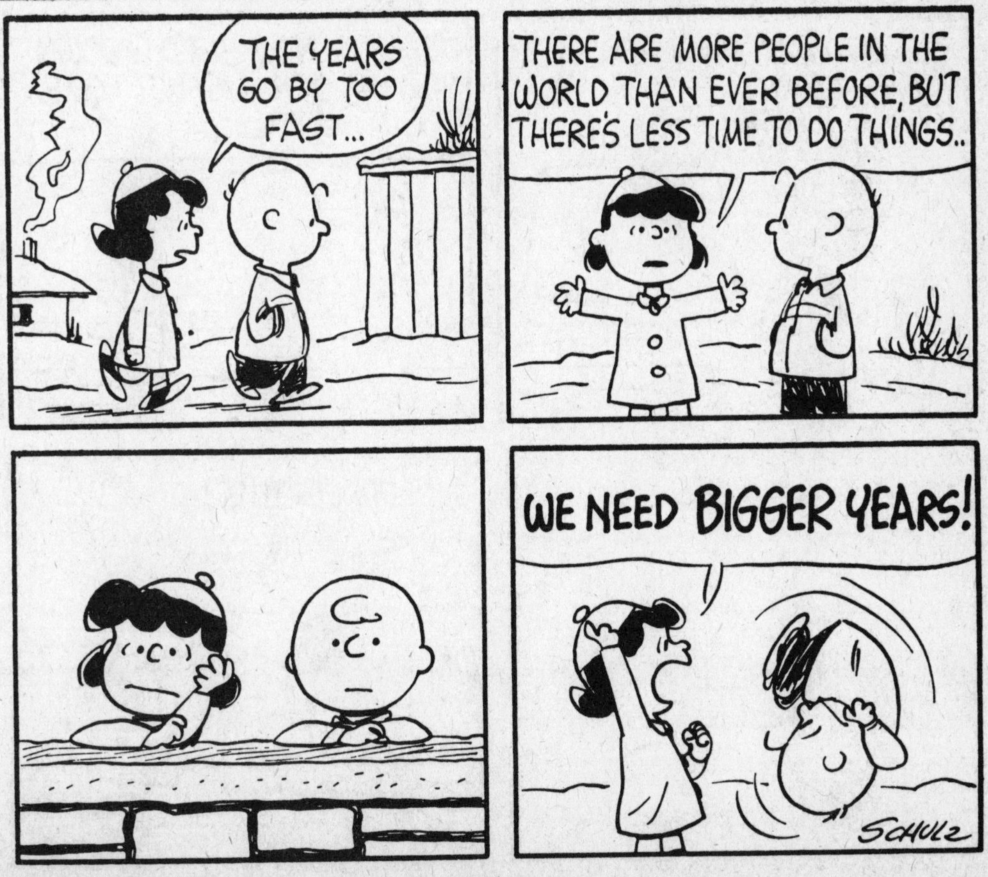
THE YEARS GO BY TOO FAST...
THERE ARE MORE PEOPLE IN THE WORLD THAN EVER BEFORE, BUT THERE'S LESS TIME TO DO THINGS..
WE NEED BIGGER YEARS!
SCHULZ

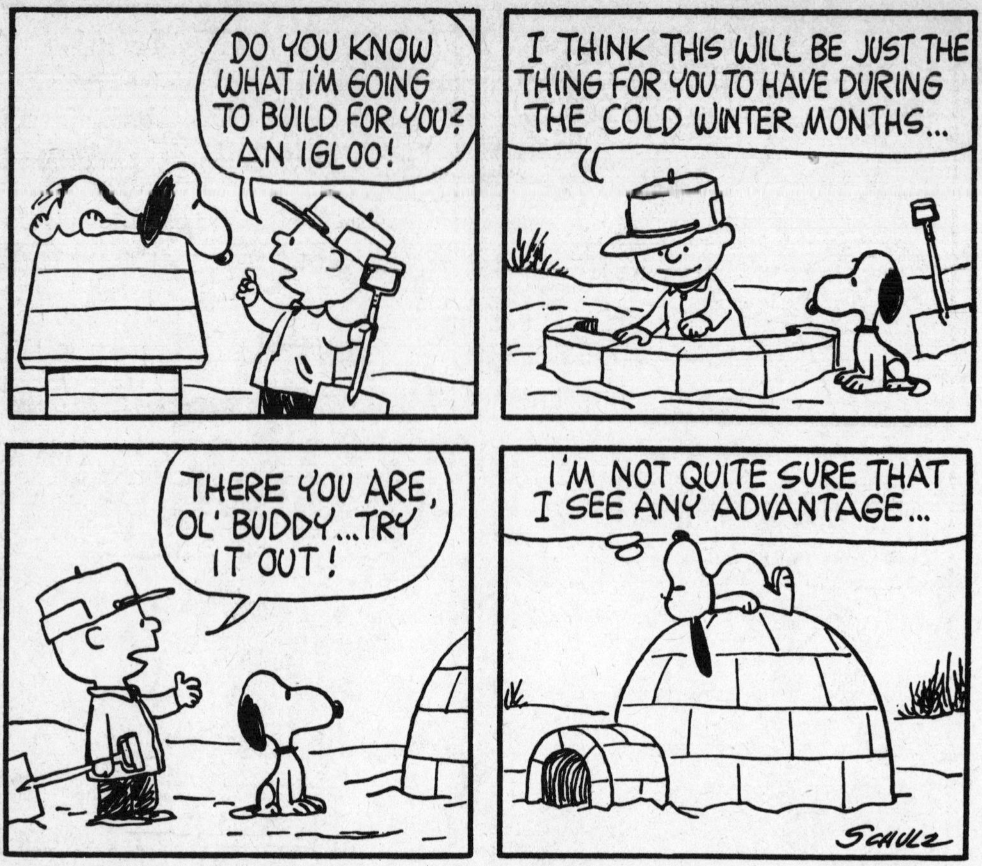
DO YOU KNOW WHAT I'M GOING TO BUILD FOR YOU? AN IGLOO!
I THINK THIS WILL BE JUST THE THING FOR YOU TO HAVE DURING THE COLD WINTER MONTHS...
THERE YOU ARE, OL' BUDDY...TRY IT OUT!
I'M NOT QUITE SURE THAT I SEE ANY ADVANTAGE...
SCHULZ

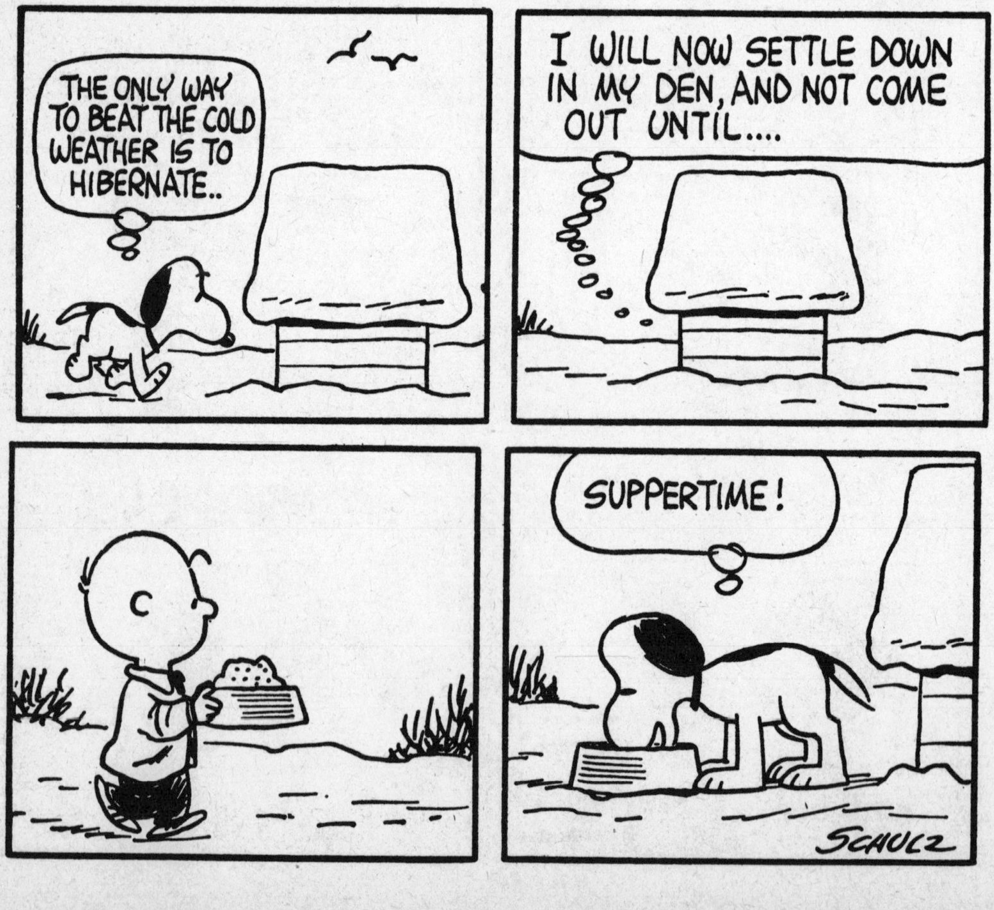
THE ONLY WAY TO BEAT THE COLD WEATHER IS TO HIBERNATE..
I WILL NOW SETTLE DOWN IN MY DEN, AND NOT COME OUT UNTIL....
SUPPERTIME!
SCHULZ

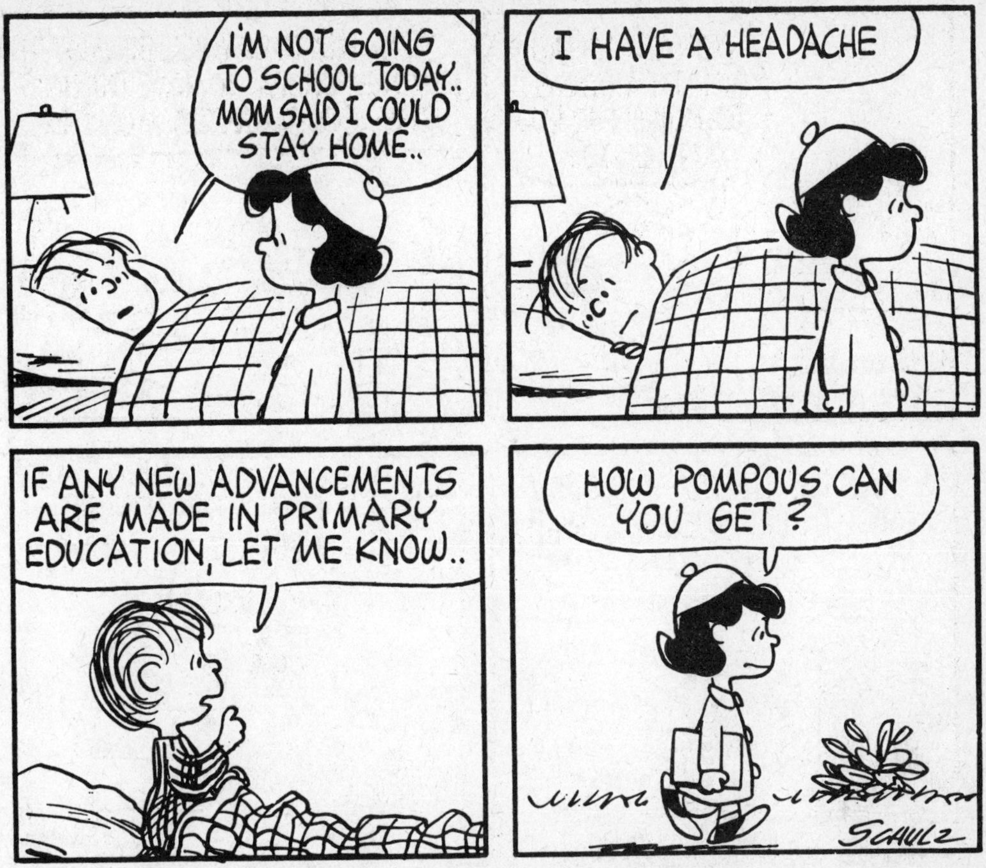
I'M NOT GOING TO SCHOOL TODAY.. MOM SAID I COULD STAY HOME..
I HAVE A HEADACHE
IF ANY NEW ADVANCEMENTS ARE MADE IN PRIMARY EDUCATION, LET ME KNOW..
HOW POMPOUS CAN YOU GET?
SCHULZ

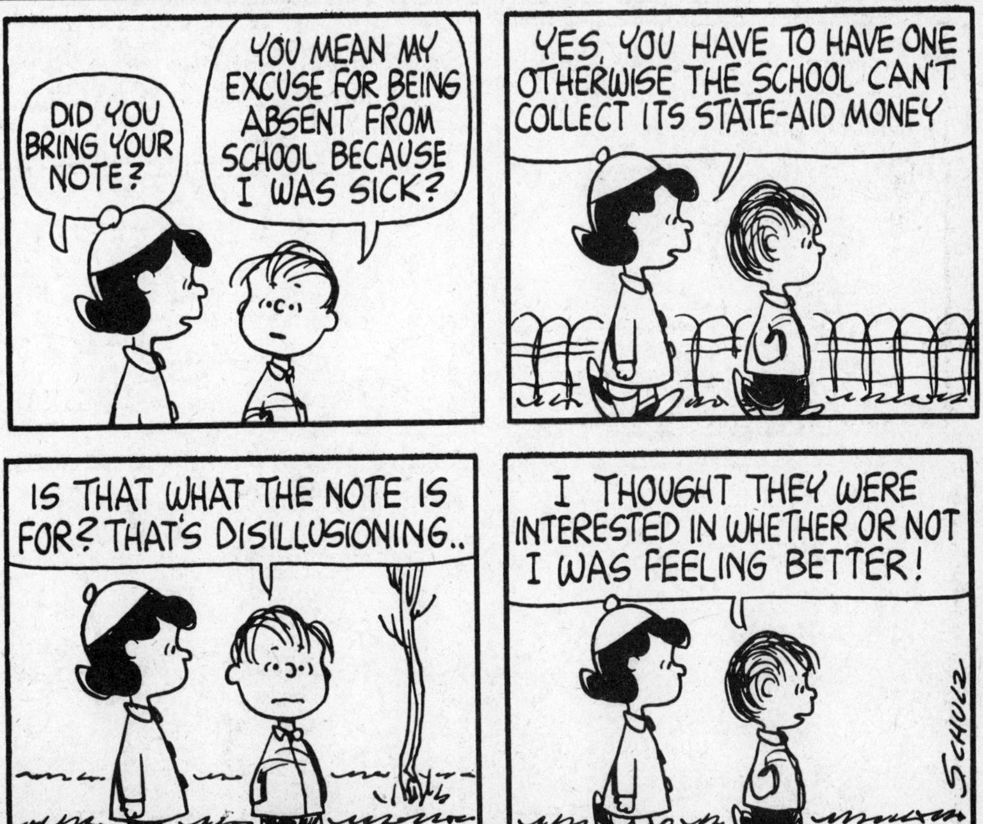
DID YOU BRING YOUR NOTE?
YOU MEAN MY EXCUSE FOR BEING ABSENT FROM SCHOOL BECAUSE I WAS SICK?
YES, YOU HAVE TO HAVE ONE OTHERWISE THE SCHOOL CAN'T COLLECT ITS STATE-AID MONEY
IS THAT WHAT THE NOTE IS FOR? THAT'S DISILLUSIONING..
I THOUGHT THEY WERE INTERESTED IN WHETHER OR NOT I WAS FEELING BETTER!
SCHULZ

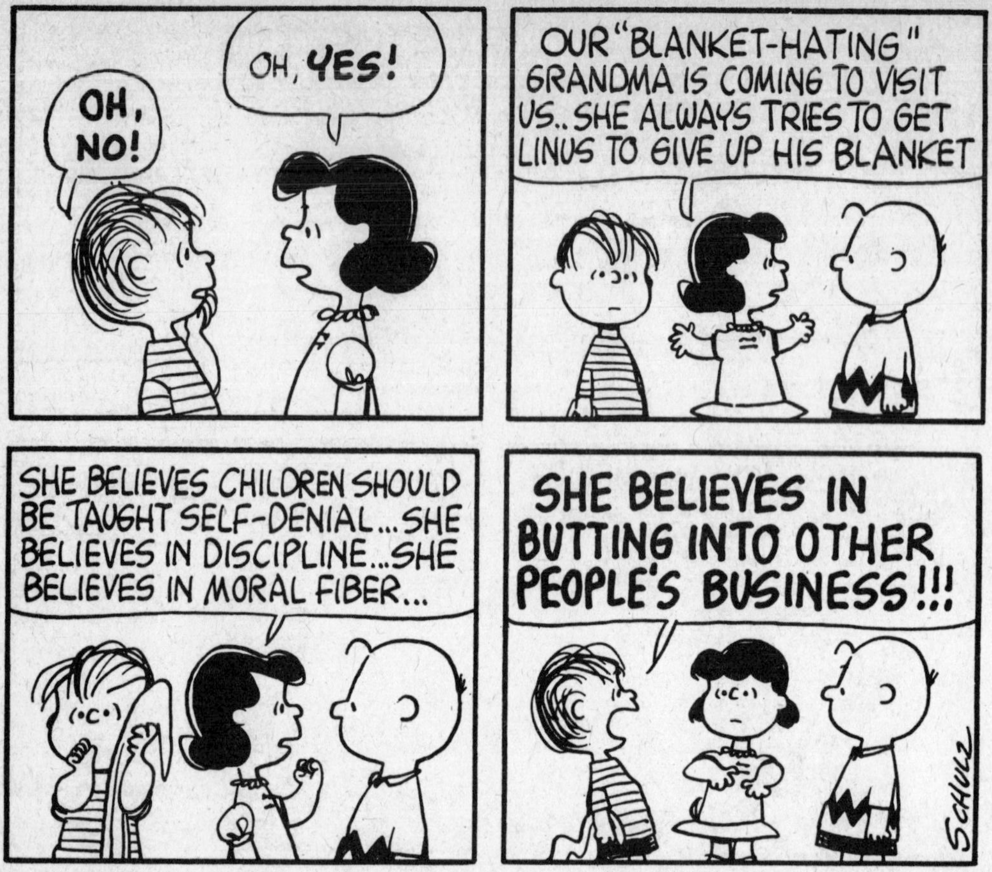
OH, NO!
OH, YES!
OUR "BLANKET-HATING" GRANDMA IS COMING TO VISIT US.. SHE ALWAYS TRIES TO GET LINUS TO GIVE UP HIS BLANKET
SHE BELIEVES CHILDREN SHOULD BE TAUGHT SELF-DENIAL...SHE BELIEVES IN DISCIPLINE...SHE BELIEVES IN MORAL FIBER...
SHE BELIEVES IN BUTTING INTO OTHER PEOPLE'S BUSINESS!!!
SCHULZ

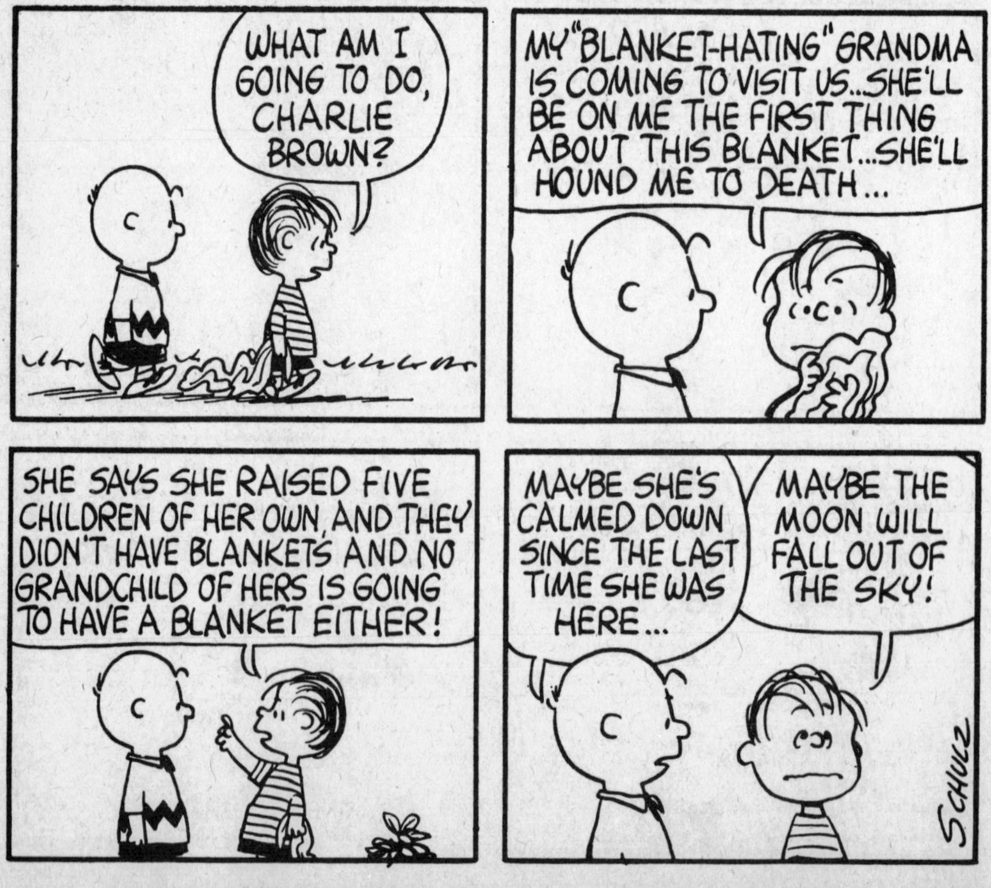
WHAT AM I GOING TO DO, CHARLIE BROWN?
MY "BLANKET-HATING" GRANDMA IS COMING TO VISIT US...SHE'LL BE ON ME THE FIRST THING ABOUT THIS BLANKET...SHE'LL HOUND ME TO DEATH...
SHE SAYS SHE RAISED FIVE CHILDREN OF HER OWN, AND THEY DIDN'T HAVE BLANKETS AND NO GRANDCHILD OF HERS IS GOING TO HAVE A BLANKET EITHER!
MAYBE SHE'S CALMED DOWN SINCE THE LAST TIME SHE WAS HERE...
MAYBE THE MOON WILL FALL OUT OF THE SKY!
SCHULZ

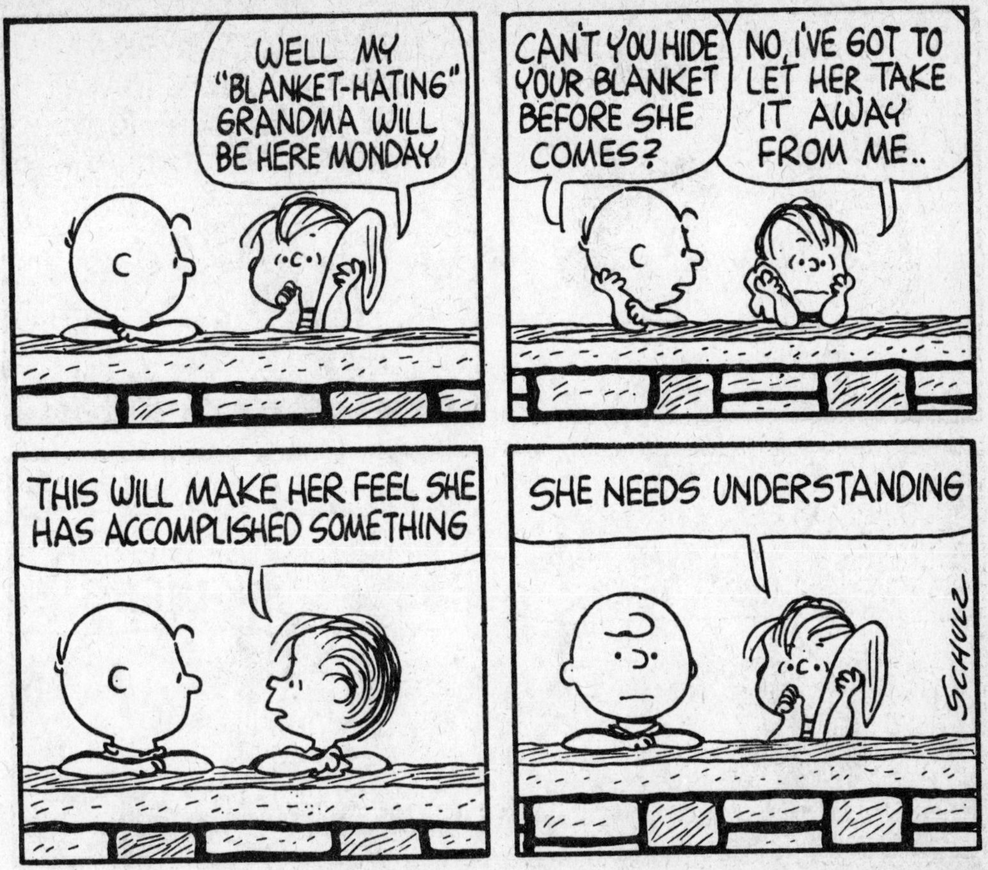
WELL MY "BLANKET-HATING" GRANDMA WILL BE HERE MONDAY
CAN'T YOU HIDE YOUR BLANKET BEFORE SHE COMES?
NO, I'VE GOT TO LET HER TAKE IT AWAY FROM ME..
THIS WILL MAKE HER FEEL SHE HAS ACCOMPLISHED SOMETHING
SHE NEEDS UNDERSTANDING
SCHULZ

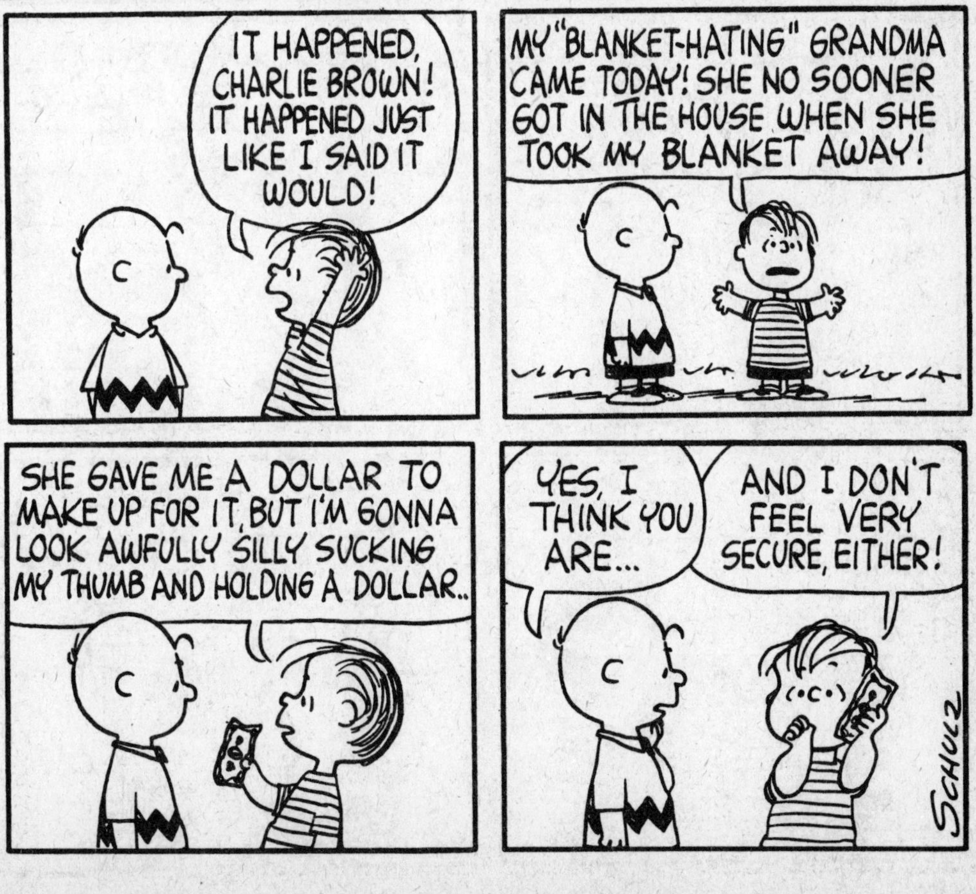
IT HAPPENED, CHARLIE BROWN! IT HAPPENED JUST LIKE I SAID IT WOULD!
MY "BLANKET-HATING" GRANDMA CAME TODAY! SHE NO SOONER GOT IN THE HOUSE WHEN SHE TOOK MY BLANKET AWAY!
SHE GAVE ME A DOLLAR TO MAKE UP FOR IT, BUT I'M GONNA LOOK AWFULLY SILLY SUCKING MY THUMB AND HOLDING A DOLLAR..
YES, I THINK YOU ARE...
AND I DON'T FEEL VERY SECURE, EITHER!
SCHULZ

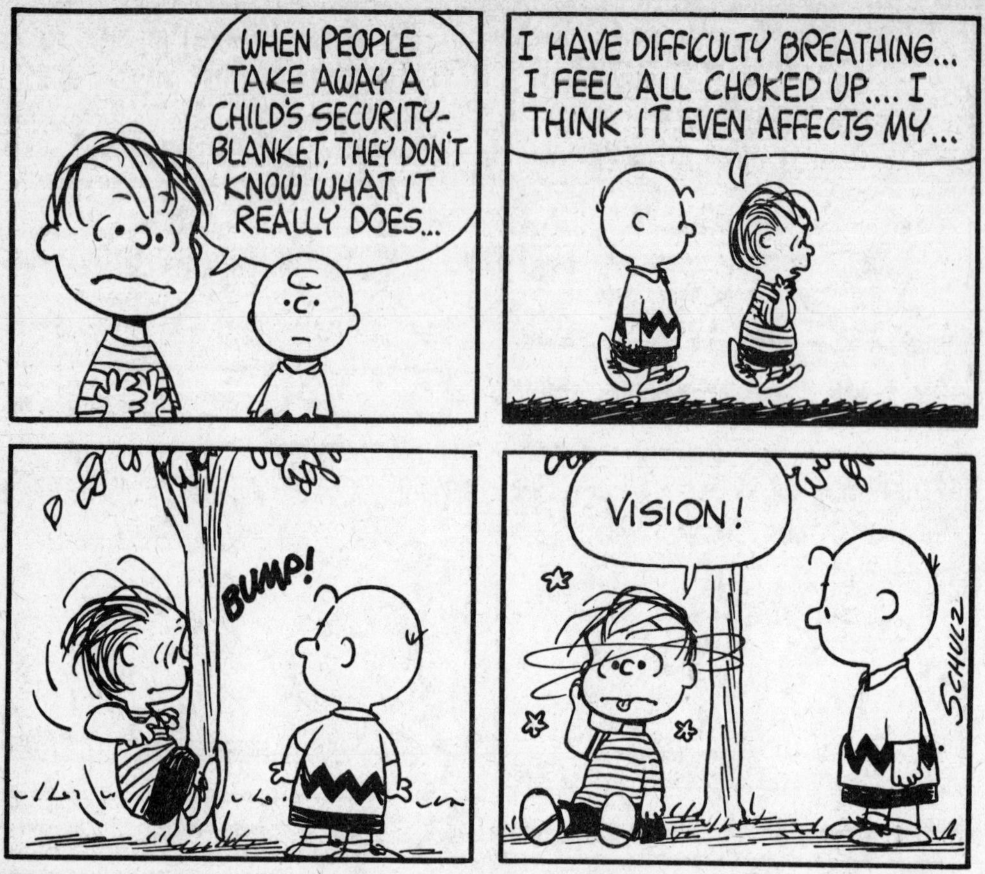
WHEN PEOPLE TAKE AWAY A CHILD'S SECURITY-BLANKET, THEY DON'T KNOW WHAT IT REALLY DOES...
I HAVE DIFFICULTY BREATHING... I FEEL ALL CHOKED UP.... I THINK IT EVEN AFFECTS MY...
BUMP!
VISION!
SCHULZ

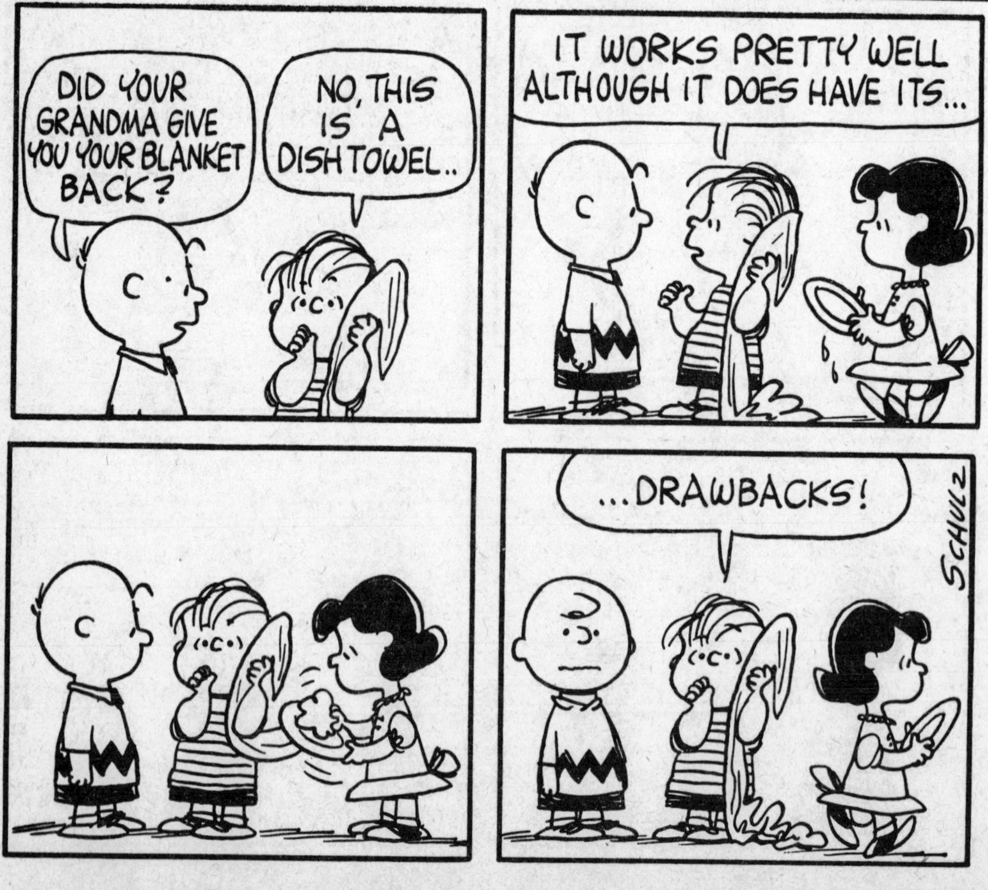
DID YOUR GRANDMA GIVE YOU YOUR BLANKET BACK?
NO, THIS IS A DISHTOWEL..
IT WORKS PRETTY WELL ALTHOUGH IT DOES HAVE ITS...
...DRAWBACKS!
SCHULZ

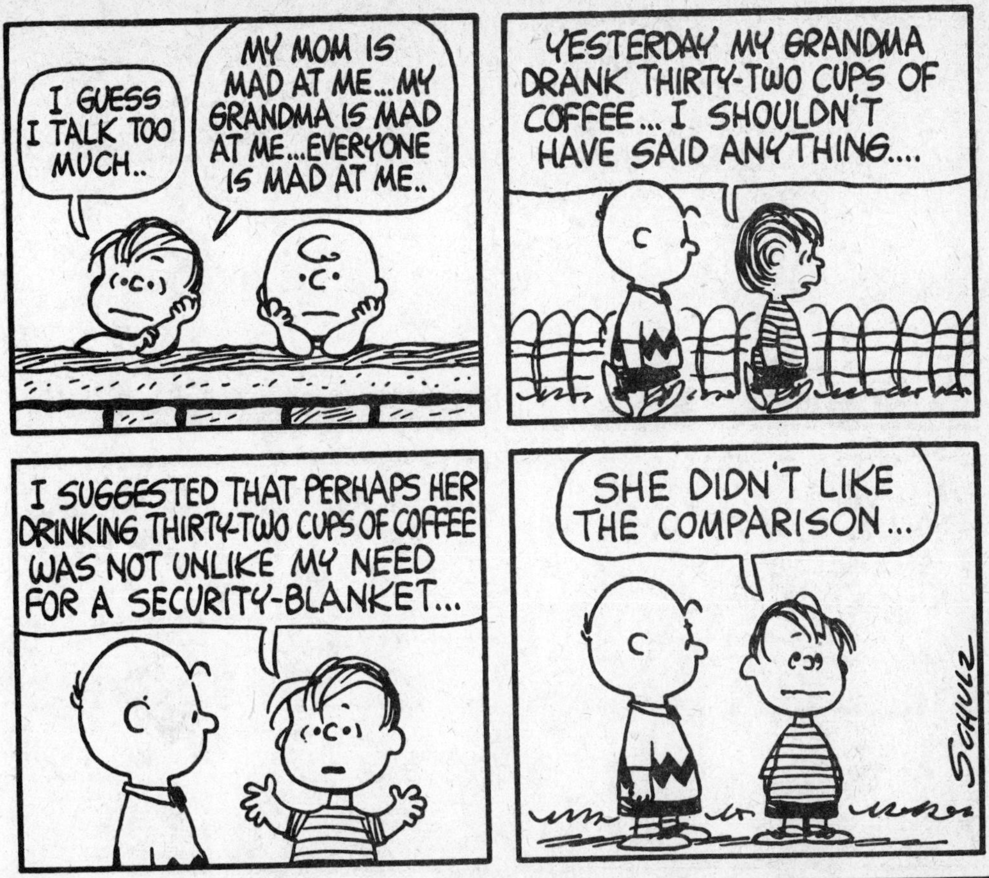
I GUESS I TALK TOO MUCH..
MY MOM IS MAD AT ME...MY GRANDMA IS MAD AT ME...EVERYONE IS MAD AT ME..
YESTERDAY MY GRANDMA DRANK THIRTY-TWO CUPS OF COFFEE... I SHOULDN'T HAVE SAID ANYTHING....
I SUGGESTED THAT PERHAPS HER DRINKING THIRTY-TWO CUPS OF COFFEE WAS NOT UNLIKE MY NEED FOR A SECURITY-BLANKET...
SHE DIDN'T LIKE THE COMPARISON...
SCHULZ

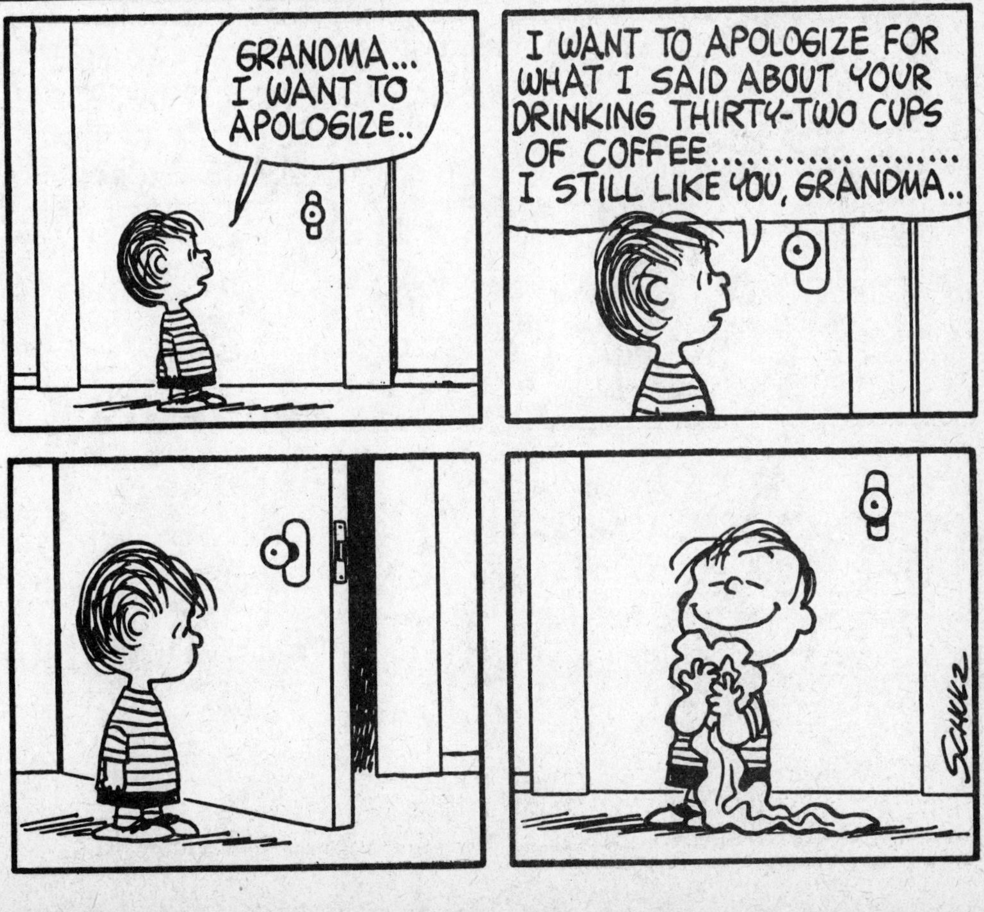
GRANDMA... I WANT TO APOLOGIZE..
I WANT TO APOLOGIZE FOR WHAT I SAID ABOUT YOUR DRINKING THIRTY-TWO CUPS OF COFFEE..................... I STILL LIKE YOU, GRANDMA..
SCHULZ

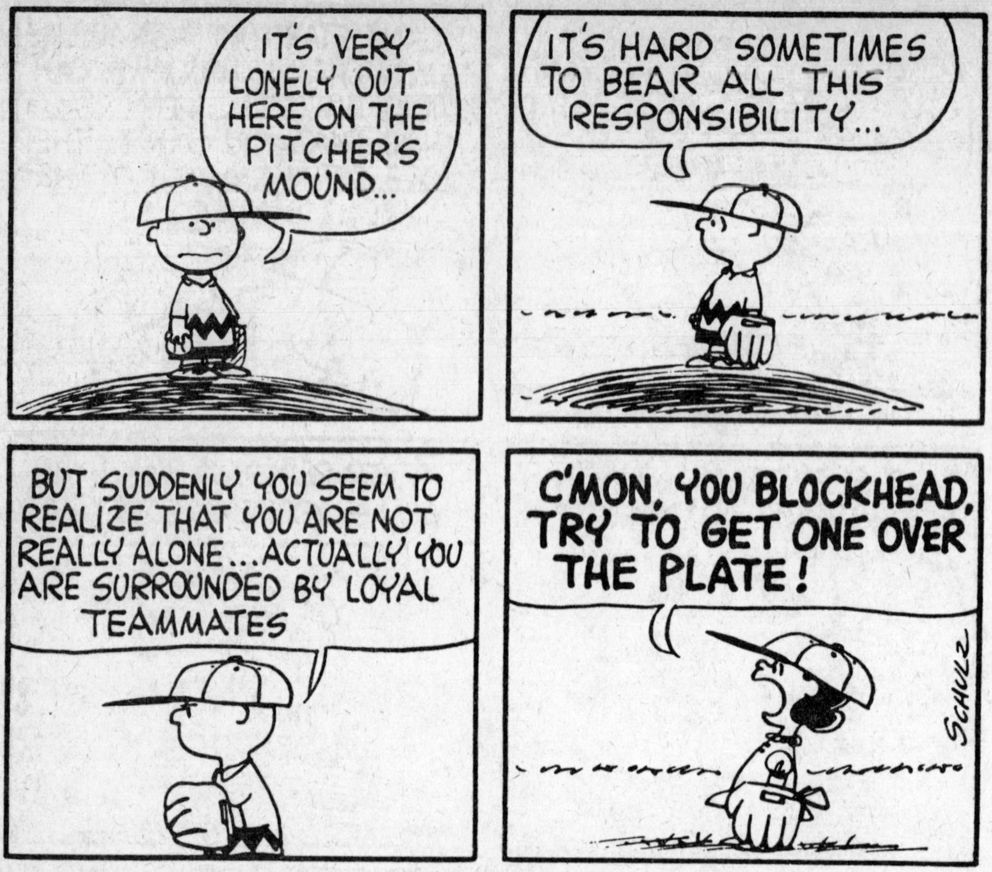
IT'S VERY LONELY OUT HERE ON THE PITCHER'S MOUND...
IT'S HARD SOMETIMES TO BEAR ALL THIS RESPONSIBILITY...
BUT SUDDENLY YOU SEEM TO REALIZE THAT YOU ARE NOT REALLY ALONE...ACTUALLY YOU ARE SURROUNDED BY LOYAL TEAMMATES
C'MON, YOU BLOCKHEAD, TRY TO GET ONE OVER THE PLATE!
SCHULZ

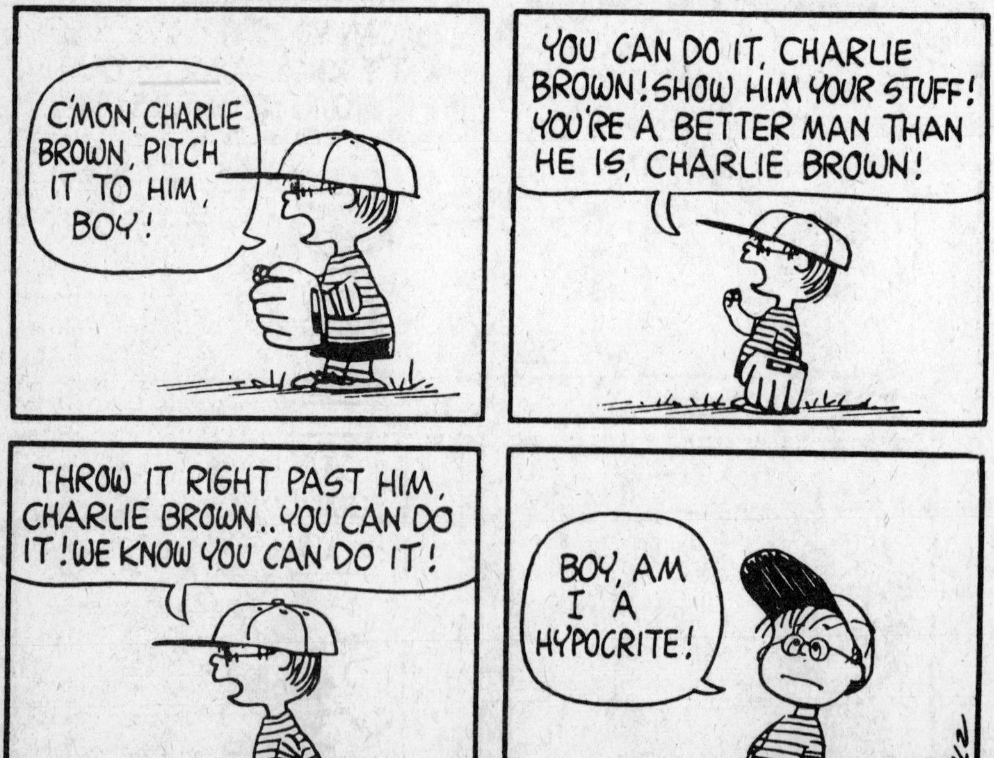
C'MON, CHARLIE BROWN, PITCH IT TO HIM, BOY!
YOU CAN DO IT, CHARLIE BROWN! SHOW HIM YOUR STUFF! YOU'RE A BETTER MAN THAN HE IS, CHARLIE BROWN!
THROW IT RIGHT PAST HIM, CHARLIE BROWN..YOU CAN DO IT! WE KNOW YOU CAN DO IT!
BOY, AM I A HYPOCRITE!
SCHULZ

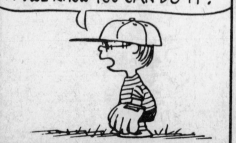

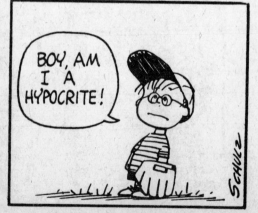

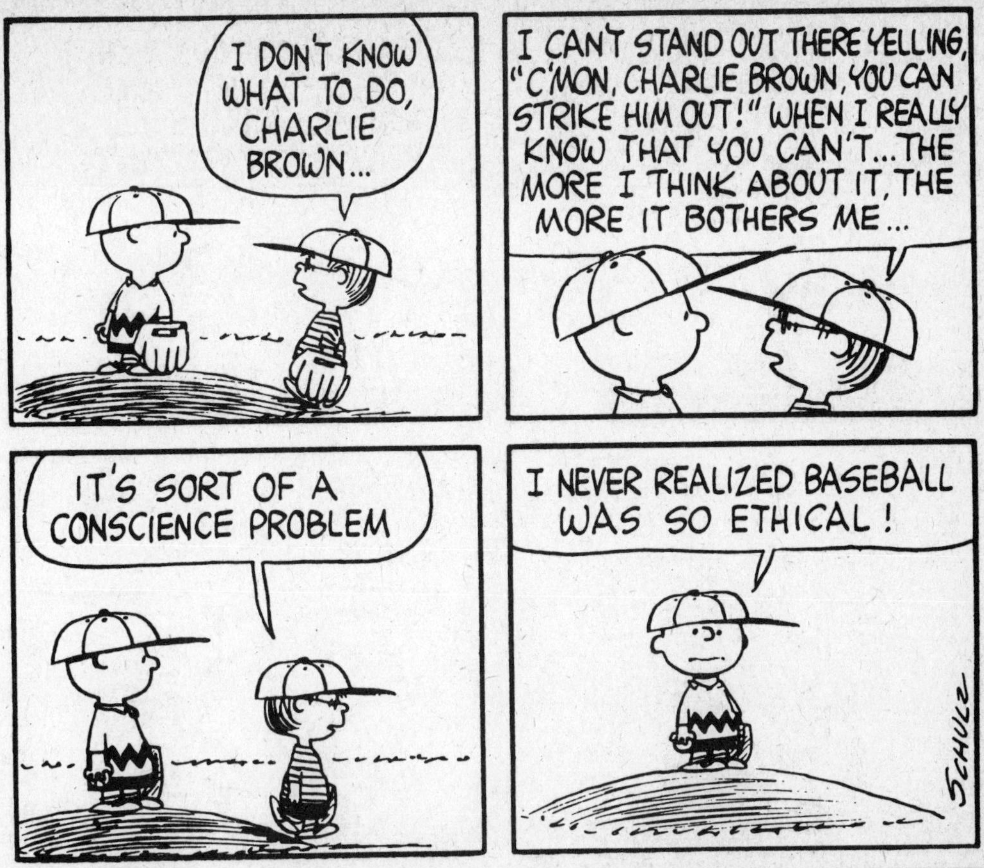
I DON'T KNOW WHAT TO DO, CHARLIE BROWN...
I CAN'T STAND OUT THERE YELLING, "C'MON, CHARLIE BROWN, YOU CAN STRIKE HIM OUT!" WHEN I REALLY KNOW THAT YOU CAN'T... THE MORE I THINK ABOUT IT, THE MORE IT BOTHERS ME...
IT'S SORT OF A CONSCIENCE PROBLEM
I NEVER REALIZED BASEBALL WAS SO ETHICAL!
SCHULZ

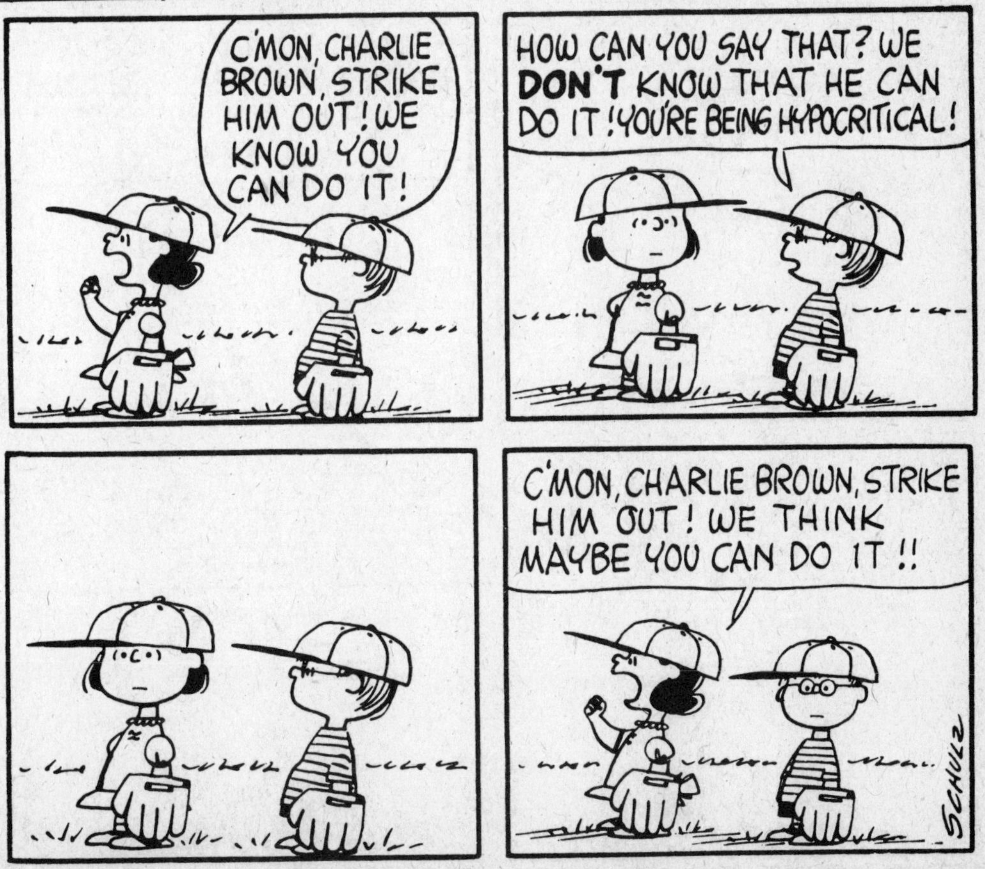
C'MON, CHARLIE BROWN, STRIKE HIM OUT! WE KNOW YOU CAN DO IT!
HOW CAN YOU SAY THAT? WE **DON'T** KNOW THAT HE CAN DO IT! YOU'RE BEING HYPOCRITICAL!
C'MON, CHARLIE BROWN, STRIKE HIM OUT! WE THINK MAYBE YOU CAN DO IT!!
SCHULZ

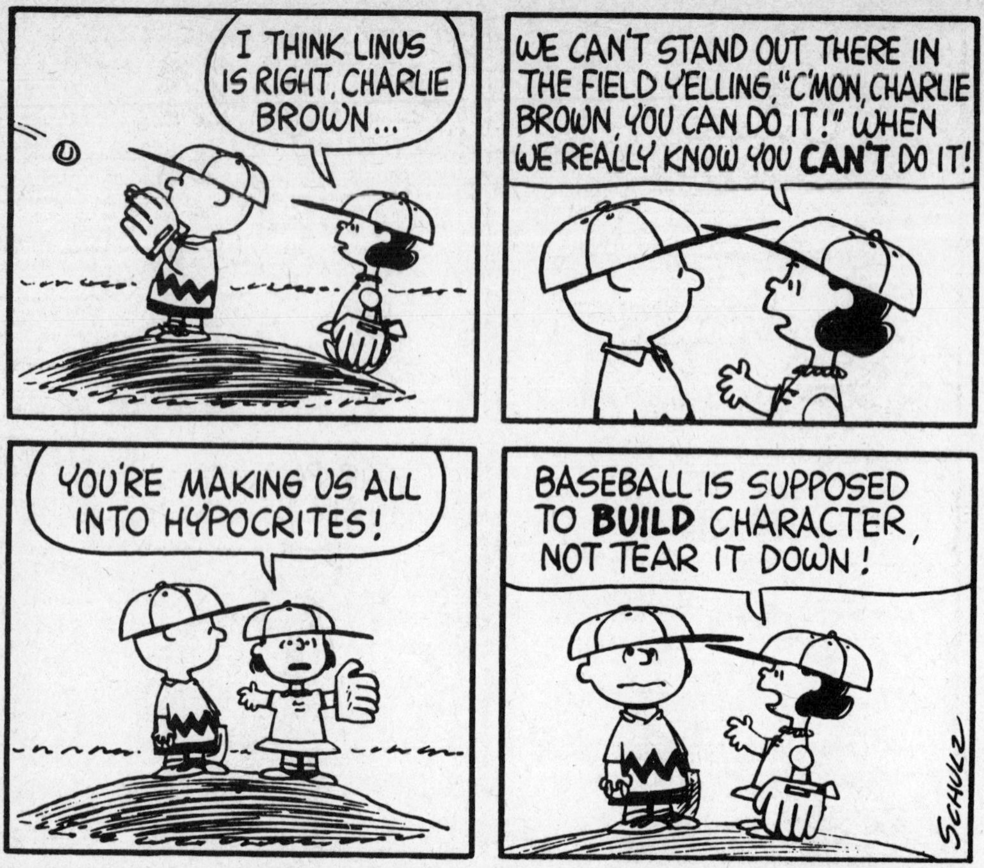

I THINK LINUS IS RIGHT, CHARLIE BROWN...
WE CAN'T STAND OUT THERE IN THE FIELD YELLING, "C'MON, CHARLIE BROWN, YOU CAN DO IT!" WHEN WE REALLY KNOW YOU **CAN'T** DO IT!
YOU'RE MAKING US ALL INTO HYPOCRITES!
BASEBALL IS SUPPOSED TO **BUILD** CHARACTER, NOT TEAR IT DOWN!
SCHULZ

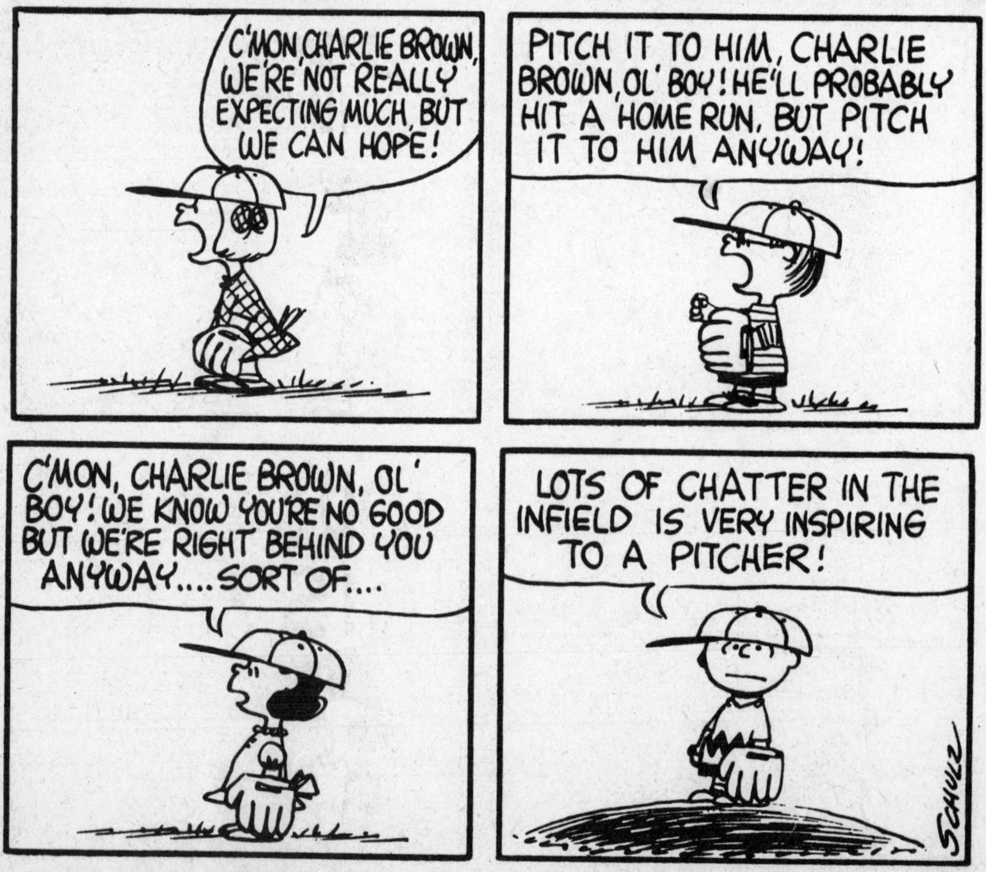

C'MON, CHARLIE BROWN, WE'RE NOT REALLY EXPECTING MUCH, BUT WE CAN HOPE!
PITCH IT TO HIM, CHARLIE BROWN, OL' BOY! HE'LL PROBABLY HIT A HOME RUN, BUT PITCH IT TO HIM ANYWAY!
C'MON, CHARLIE BROWN, OL' BOY! WE KNOW YOU'RE NO GOOD BUT WE'RE RIGHT BEHIND YOU ANYWAY.... SORT OF....
LOTS OF CHATTER IN THE INFIELD IS VERY INSPIRING TO A PITCHER!
SCHULZ

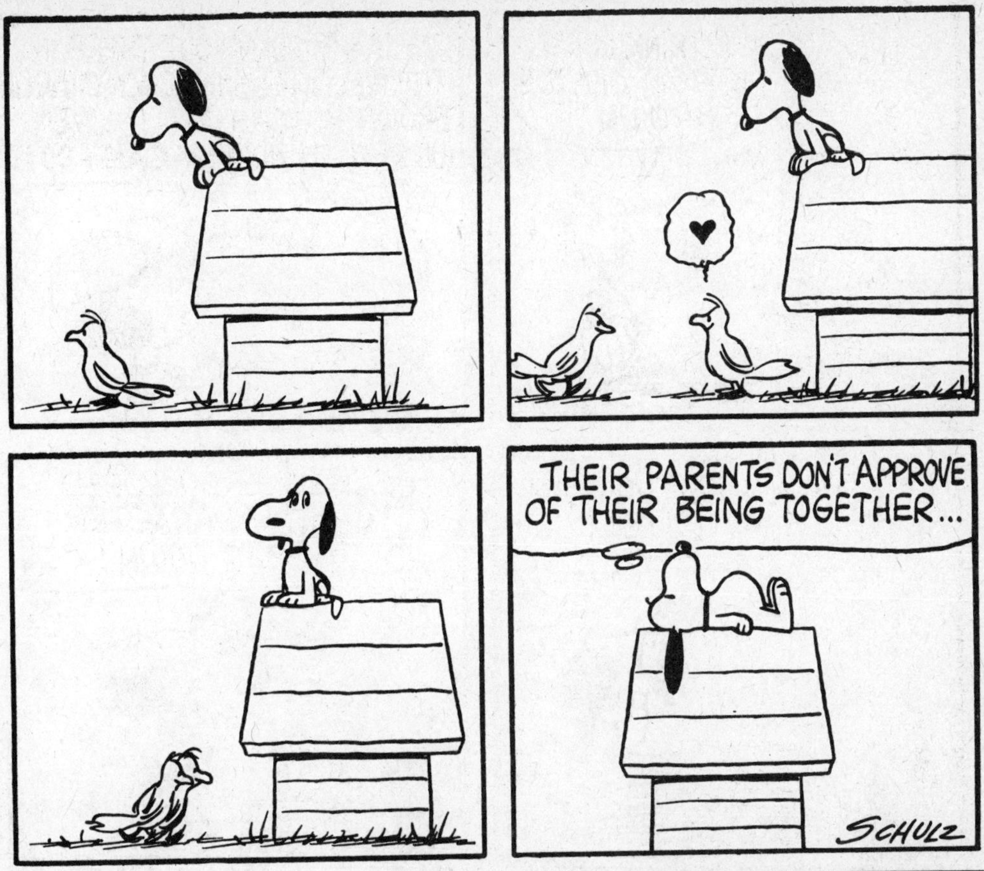
THEIR PARENTS DON'T APPROVE OF THEIR BEING TOGETHER...
SCHULZ

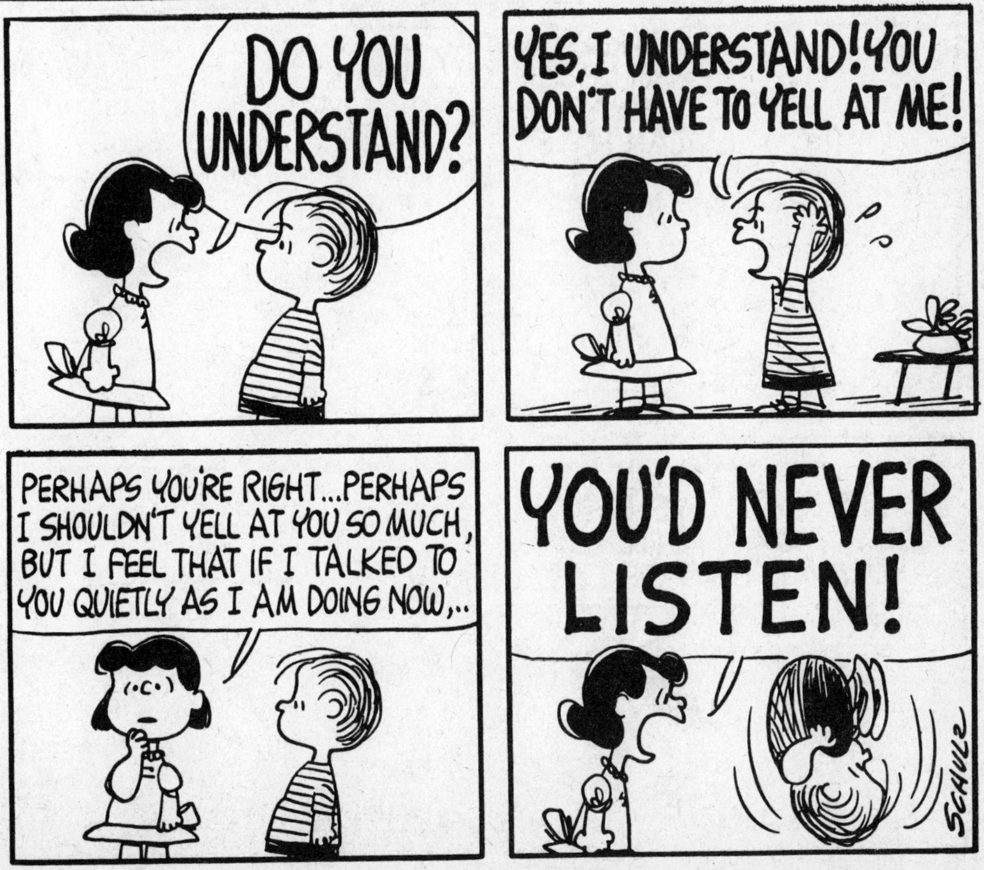
DO YOU UNDERSTAND?
YES, I UNDERSTAND! YOU DON'T HAVE TO YELL AT ME!
PERHAPS YOU'RE RIGHT...PERHAPS I SHOULDN'T YELL AT YOU SO MUCH, BUT I FEEL THAT IF I TALKED TO YOU QUIETLY AS I AM DOING NOW,..
YOU'D NEVER LISTEN!
SCHULZ

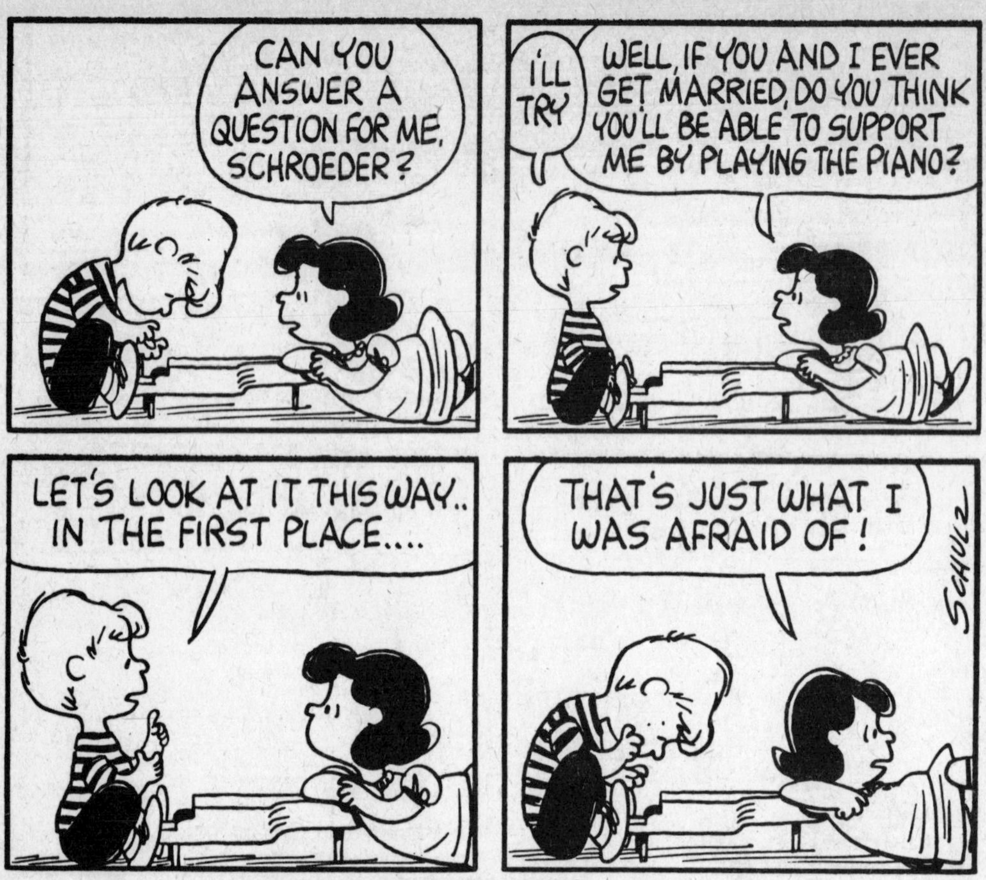
CAN YOU ANSWER A QUESTION FOR ME, SCHROEDER?
I'LL TRY
WELL, IF YOU AND I EVER GET MARRIED, DO YOU THINK YOU'LL BE ABLE TO SUPPORT ME BY PLAYING THE PIANO?
LET'S LOOK AT IT THIS WAY.. IN THE FIRST PLACE....
THAT'S JUST WHAT I WAS AFRAID OF!
SCHULZ

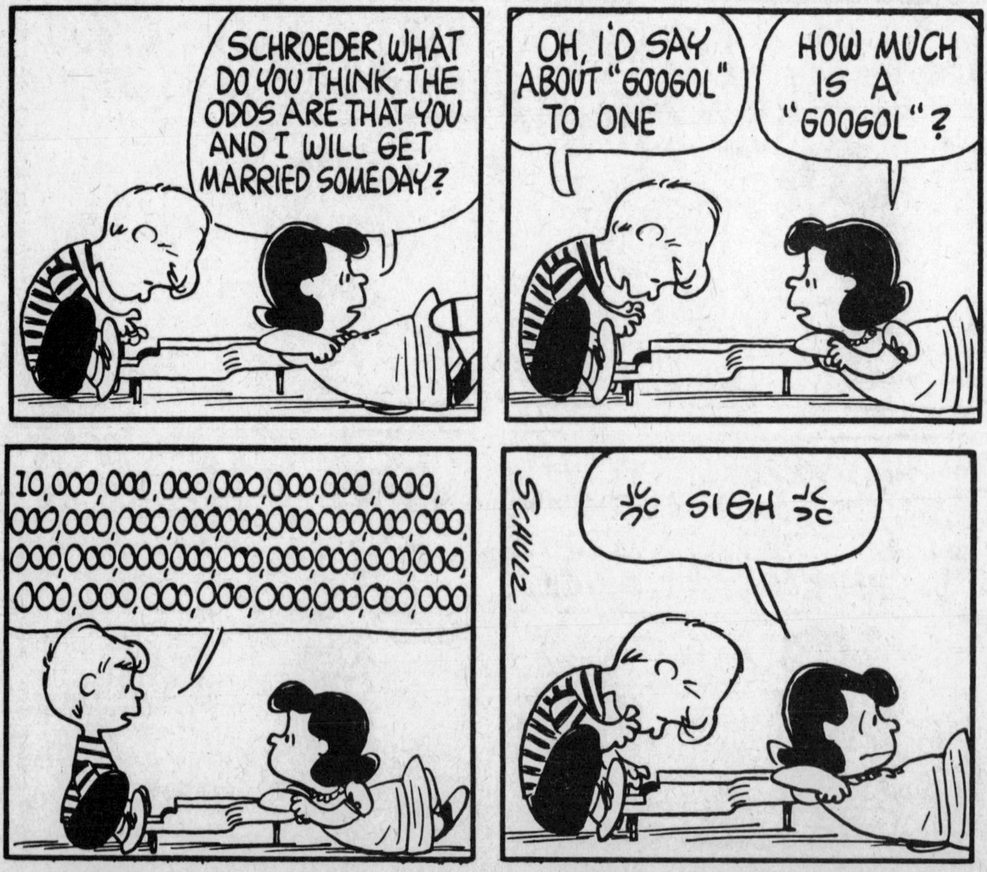
SCHROEDER, WHAT DO YOU THINK THE ODDS ARE THAT YOU AND I WILL GET MARRIED SOMEDAY?
OH, I'D SAY ABOUT "GOOGOL" TO ONE
HOW MUCH IS A "GOOGOL"?
10,000,000,000,000,000,000,000,000,
000,000,000,000,000,000,000,000,000,
000,000,000,000,000,000,000,000,000,
000,000,000,000,000,000,000,000
SCHULZ
SIGH

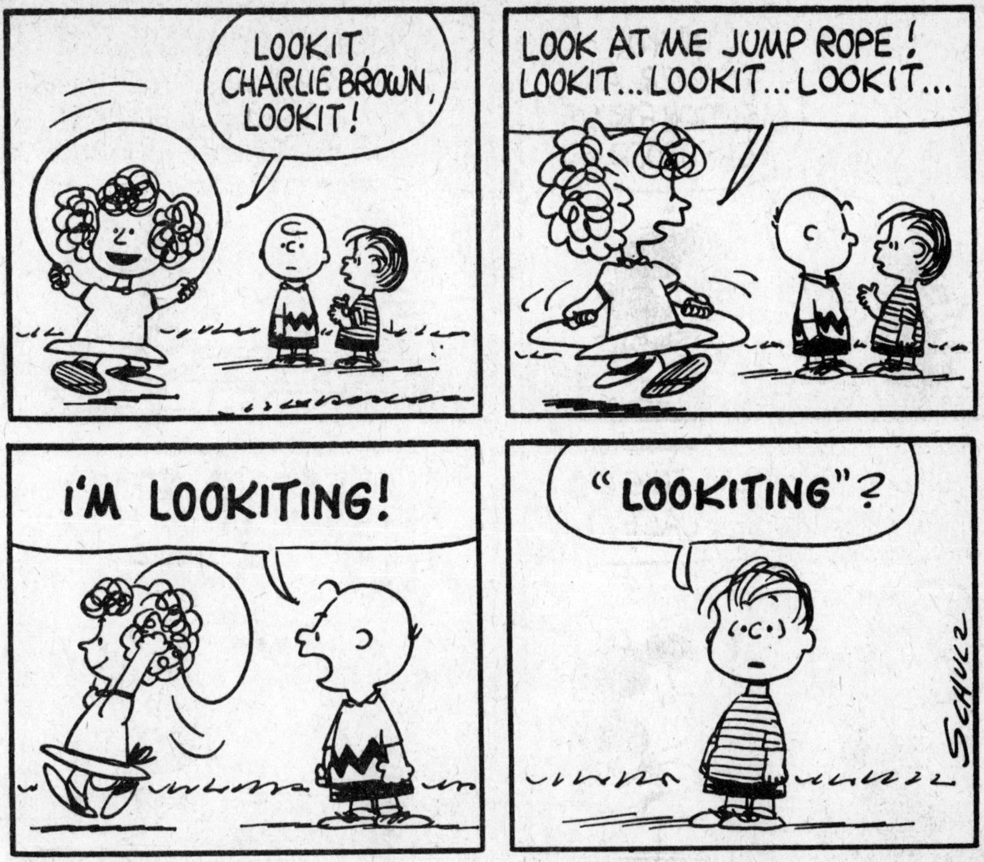
LOOKIT, CHARLIE BROWN, LOOKIT!
LOOK AT ME JUMP ROPE! LOOKIT... LOOKIT... LOOKIT...
I'M LOOKITING!
"LOOKITING"?
SCHULZ

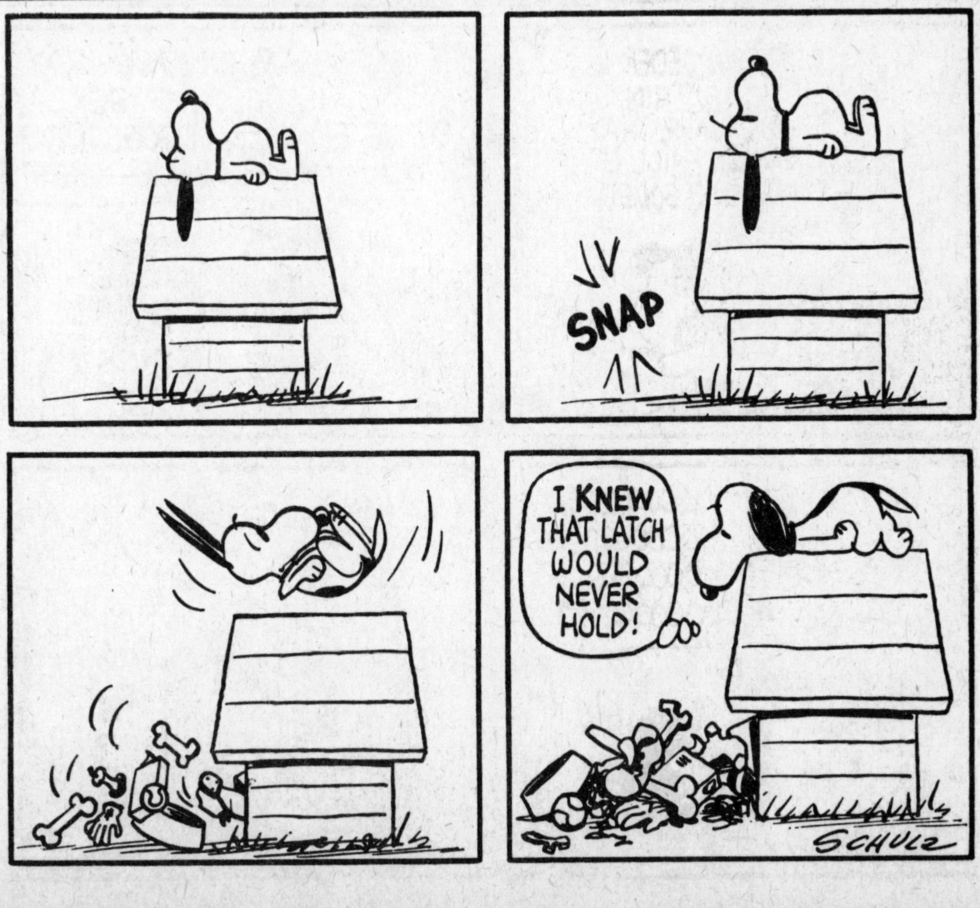
SNAP
I KNEW THAT LATCH WOULD NEVER HOLD!
SCHULZ

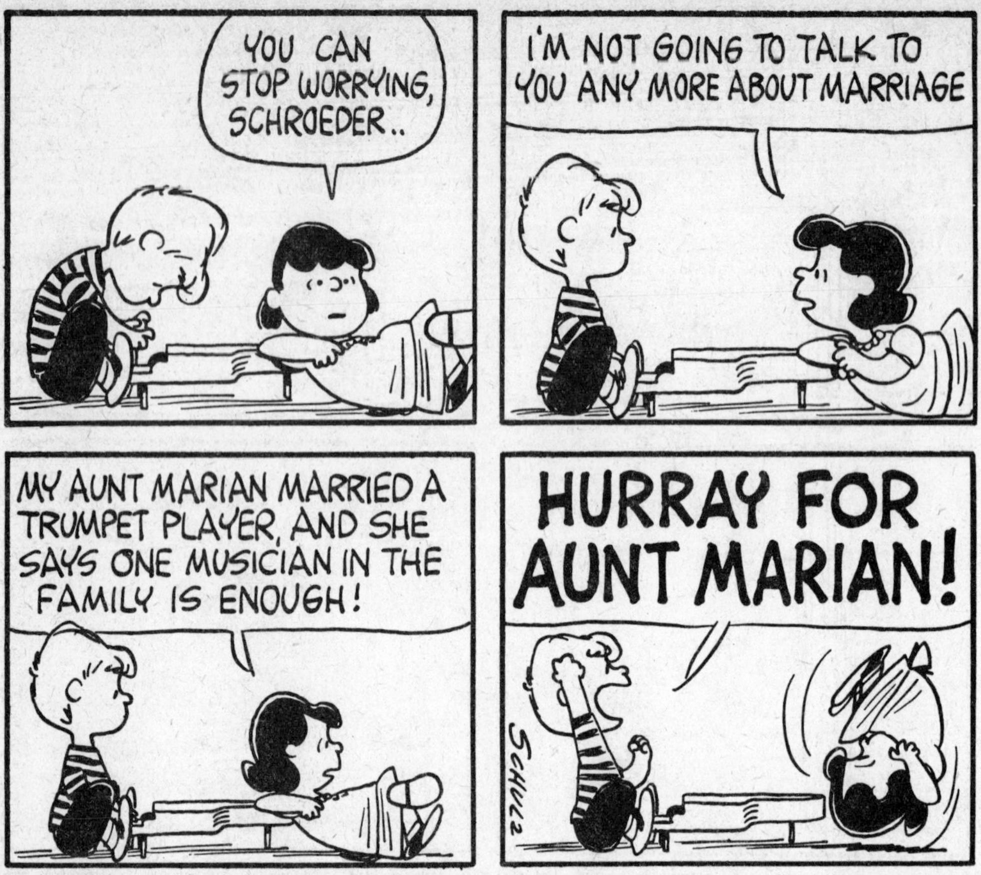
YOU CAN STOP WORRYING, SCHROEDER..
I'M NOT GOING TO TALK TO YOU ANY MORE ABOUT MARRIAGE
MY AUNT MARIAN MARRIED A TRUMPET PLAYER, AND SHE SAYS ONE MUSICIAN IN THE FAMILY IS ENOUGH!
HURRAY FOR AUNT MARIAN!
SCHULZ

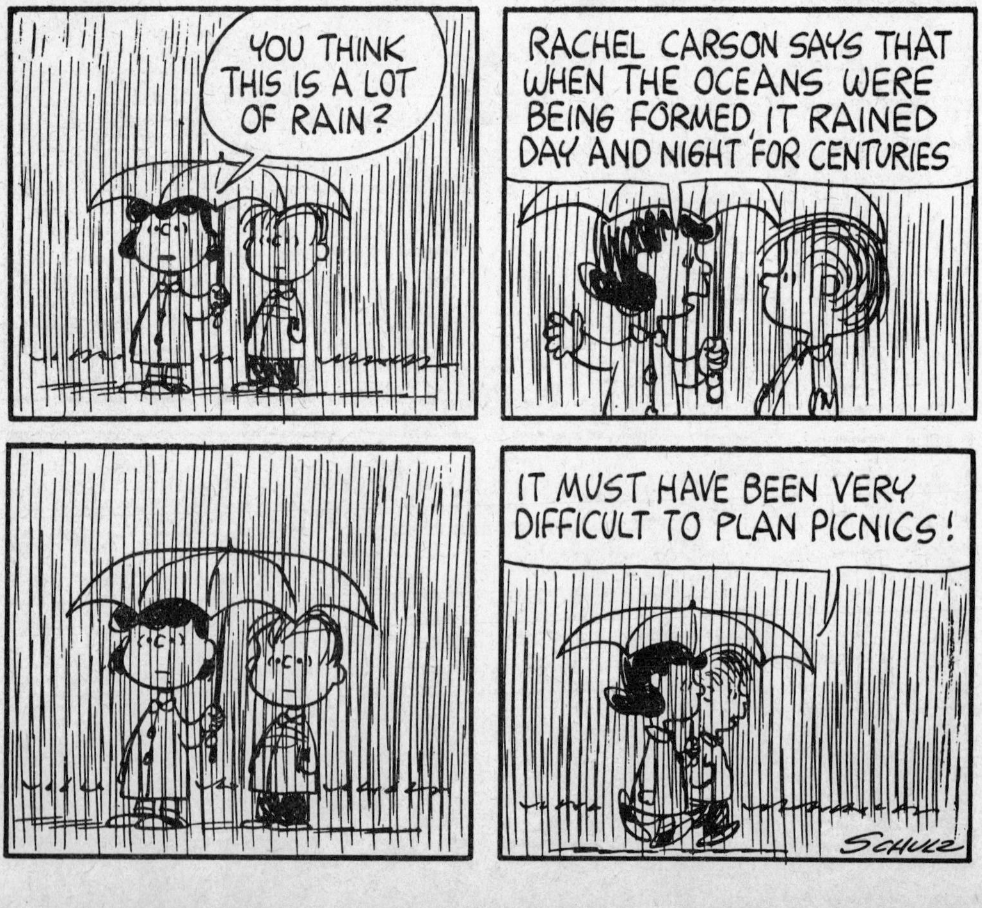
YOU THINK THIS IS A LOT OF RAIN?
RACHEL CARSON SAYS THAT WHEN THE OCEANS WERE BEING FORMED, IT RAINED DAY AND NIGHT FOR CENTURIES
IT MUST HAVE BEEN VERY DIFFICULT TO PLAN PICNICS!
SCHULZ

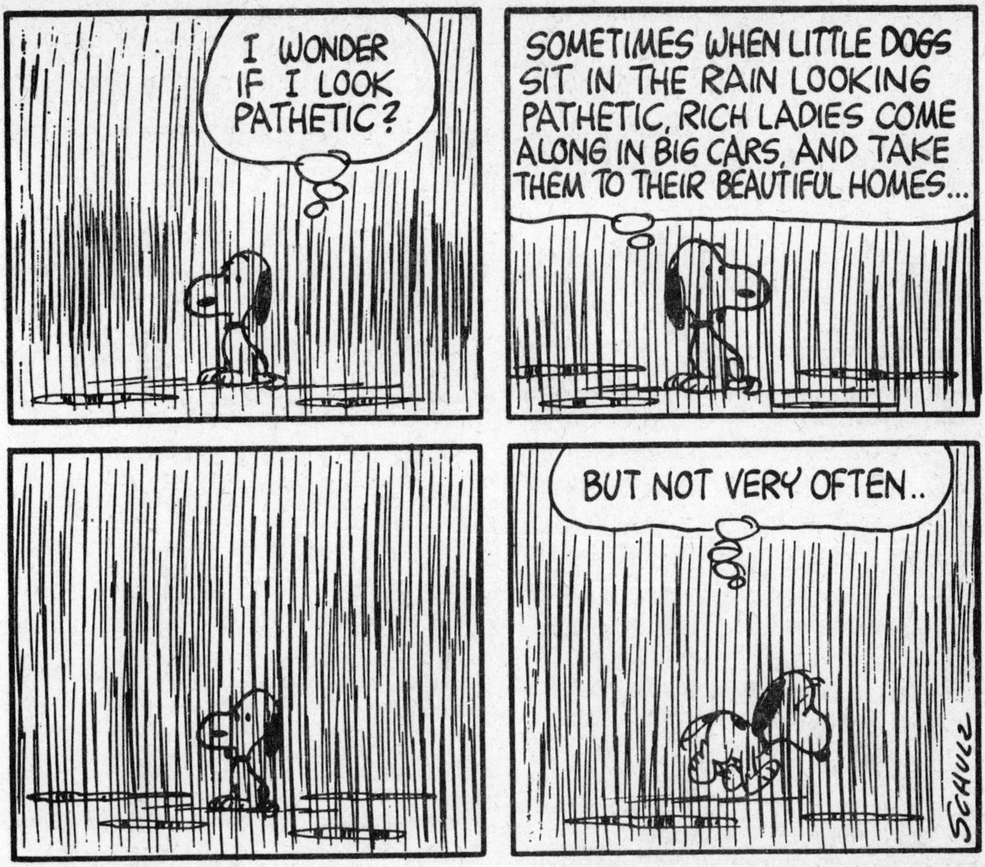
I WONDER IF I LOOK PATHETIC?
SOMETIMES WHEN LITTLE DOGS SIT IN THE RAIN LOOKING PATHETIC, RICH LADIES COME ALONG IN BIG CARS, AND TAKE THEM TO THEIR BEAUTIFUL HOMES...
BUT NOT VERY OFTEN..
SCHULZ

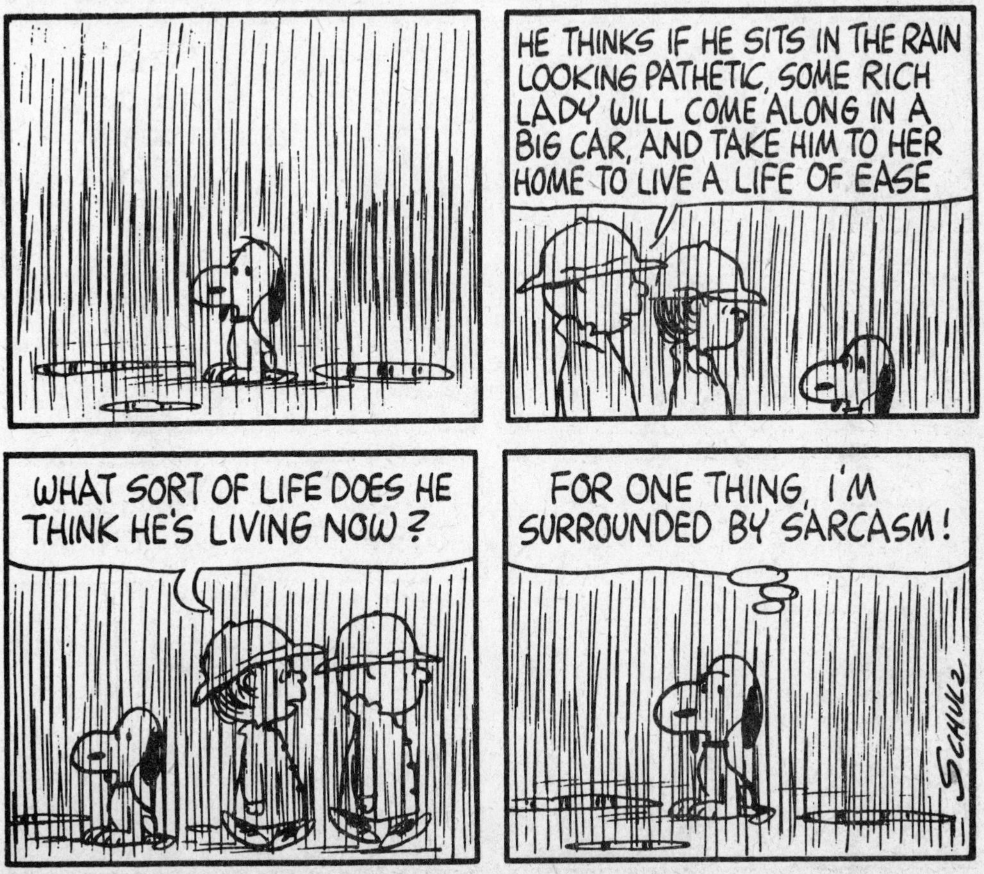
HE THINKS IF HE SITS IN THE RAIN LOOKING PATHETIC, SOME RICH LADY WILL COME ALONG IN A BIG CAR, AND TAKE HIM TO HER HOME TO LIVE A LIFE OF EASE
WHAT SORT OF LIFE DOES HE THINK HE'S LIVING NOW?
FOR ONE THING, I'M SURROUNDED BY SARCASM!
SCHULZ

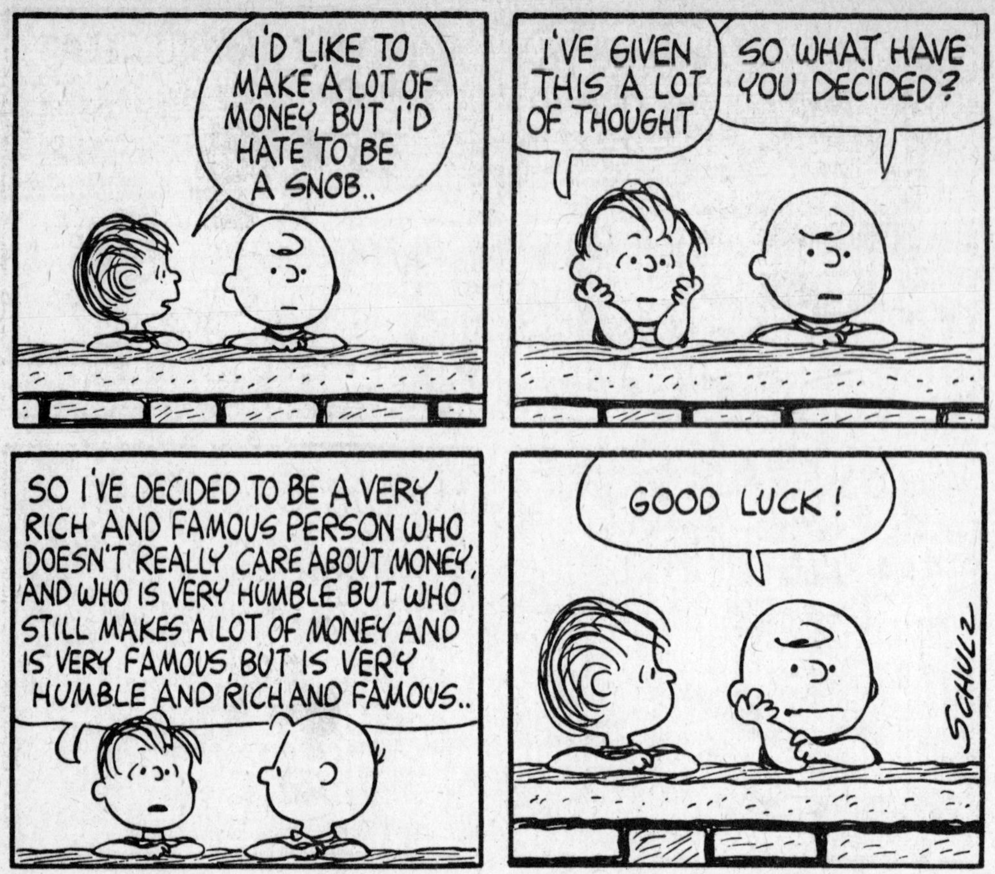
I'D LIKE TO MAKE A LOT OF MONEY, BUT I'D HATE TO BE A SNOB..
I'VE GIVEN THIS A LOT OF THOUGHT
SO WHAT HAVE YOU DECIDED?
SO I'VE DECIDED TO BE A VERY RICH AND FAMOUS PERSON WHO DOESN'T REALLY CARE ABOUT MONEY, AND WHO IS VERY HUMBLE BUT WHO STILL MAKES A LOT OF MONEY AND IS VERY FAMOUS, BUT IS VERY HUMBLE AND RICH AND FAMOUS..
GOOD LUCK!
SCHULZ

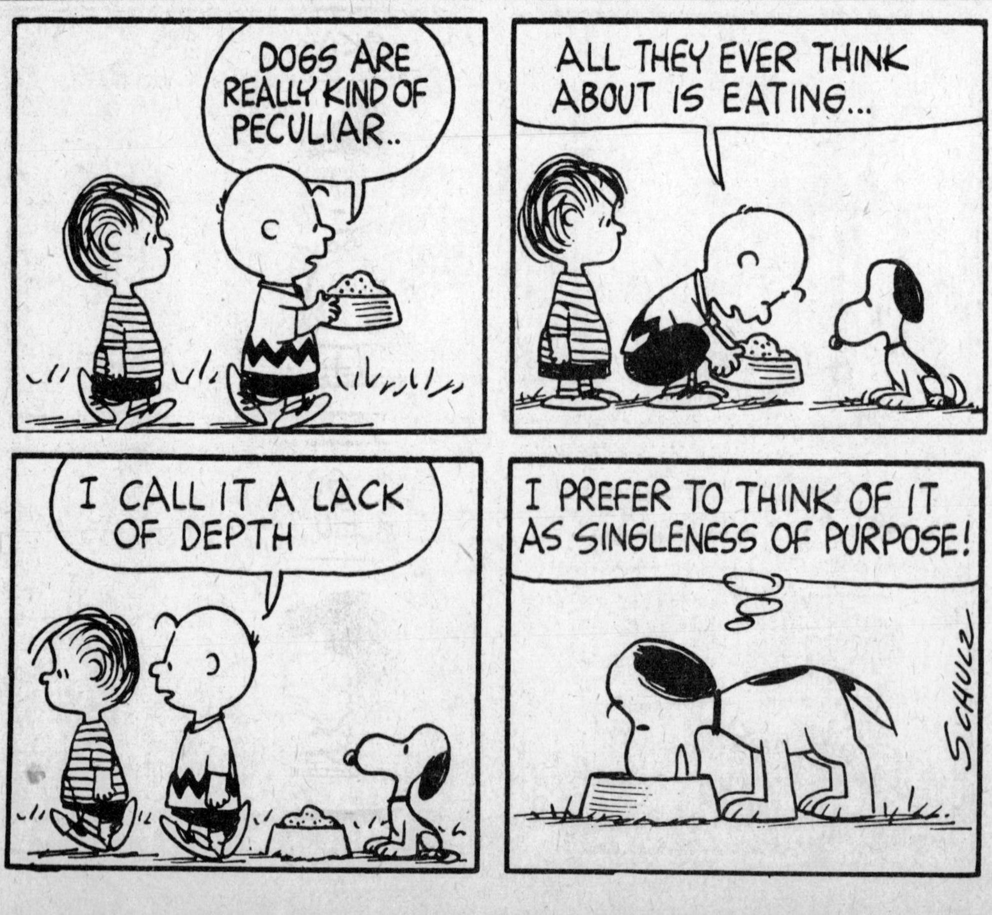
DOGS ARE REALLY KIND OF PECULIAR..
ALL THEY EVER THINK ABOUT IS EATING...
I CALL IT A LACK OF DEPTH
I PREFER TO THINK OF IT AS SINGLENESS OF PURPOSE!
SCHULZ

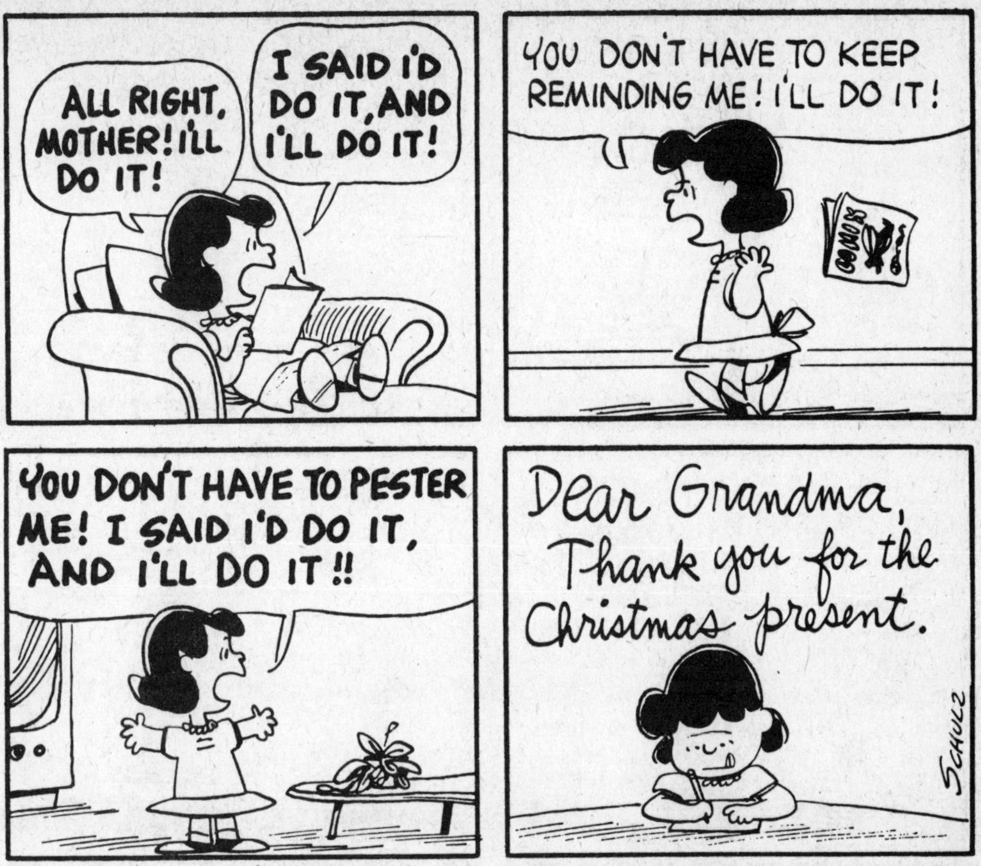
ALL RIGHT, MOTHER! I'LL DO IT!
I SAID I'D DO IT, AND I'LL DO IT!
YOU DON'T HAVE TO KEEP REMINDING ME! I'LL DO IT!
YOU DON'T HAVE TO PESTER ME! I SAID I'D DO IT, AND I'LL DO IT!!
Dear Grandma,
Thank you for the Christmas present.
SCHULZ

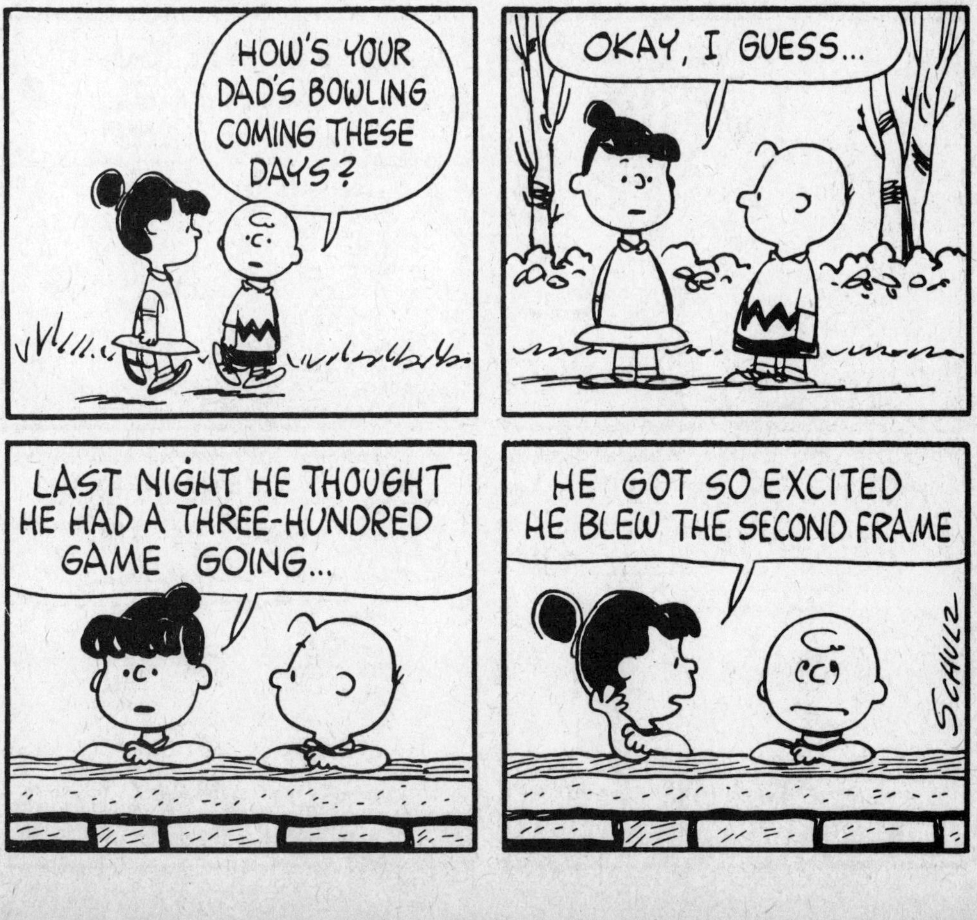
HOW'S YOUR DAD'S BOWLING COMING THESE DAYS?
OKAY, I GUESS...
LAST NIGHT HE THOUGHT HE HAD A THREE-HUNDRED GAME GOING...
HE GOT SO EXCITED HE BLEW THE SECOND FRAME
SCHULZ

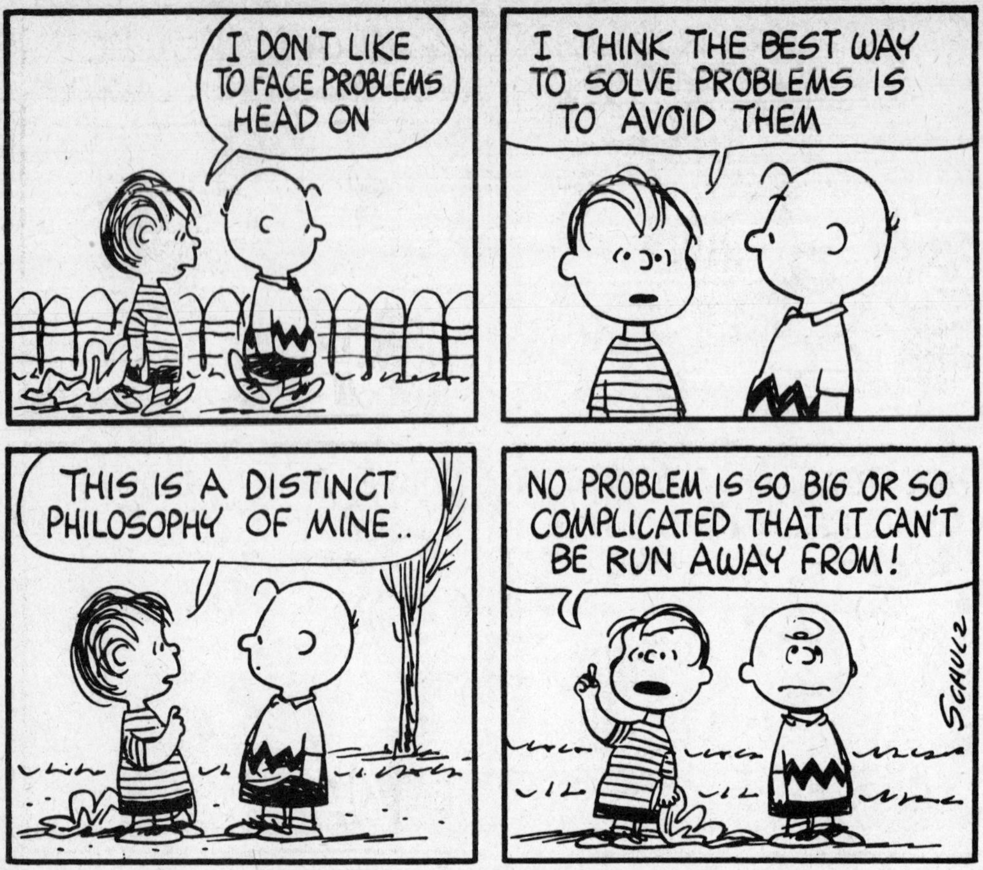
I DON'T LIKE TO FACE PROBLEMS HEAD ON
I THINK THE BEST WAY TO SOLVE PROBLEMS IS TO AVOID THEM
THIS IS A DISTINCT PHILOSOPHY OF MINE..
NO PROBLEM IS SO BIG OR SO COMPLICATED THAT IT CAN'T BE RUN AWAY FROM!
SCHULZ

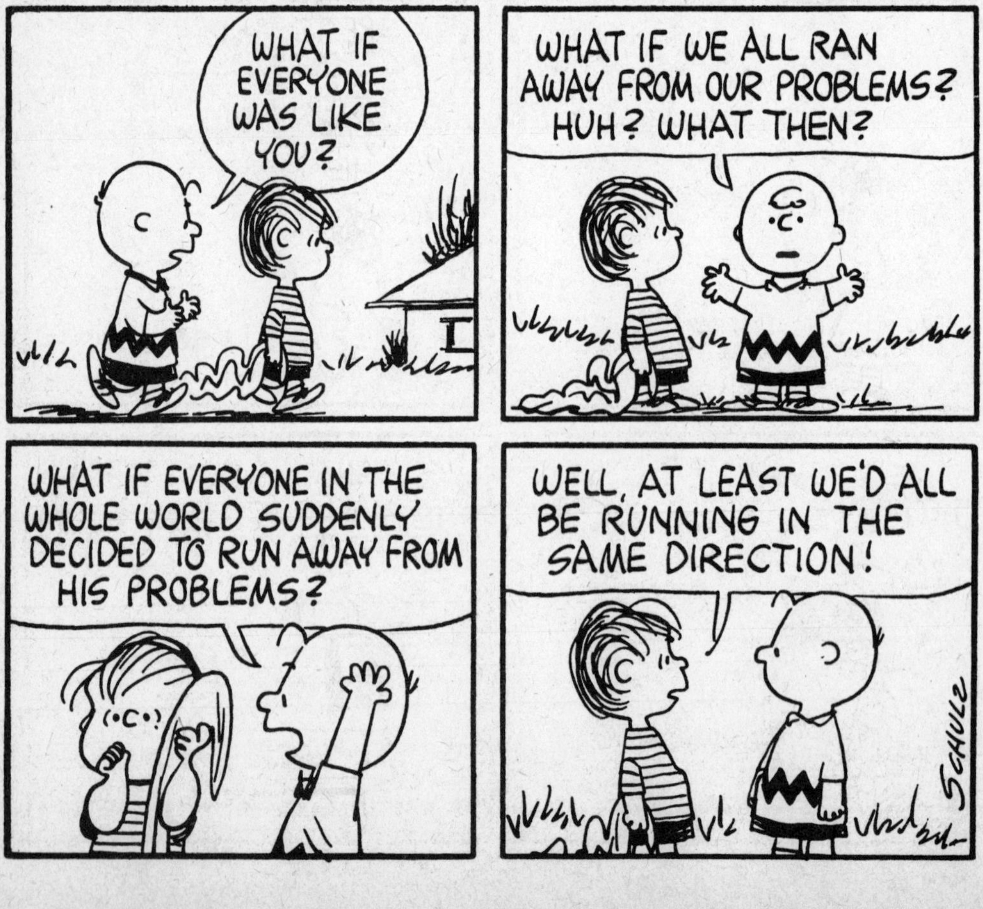
WHAT IF EVERYONE WAS LIKE YOU?
WHAT IF WE ALL RAN AWAY FROM OUR PROBLEMS? HUH? WHAT THEN?
WHAT IF EVERYONE IN THE WHOLE WORLD SUDDENLY DECIDED TO RUN AWAY FROM HIS PROBLEMS?
WELL, AT LEAST WE'D ALL BE RUNNING IN THE SAME DIRECTION!
SCHULZ

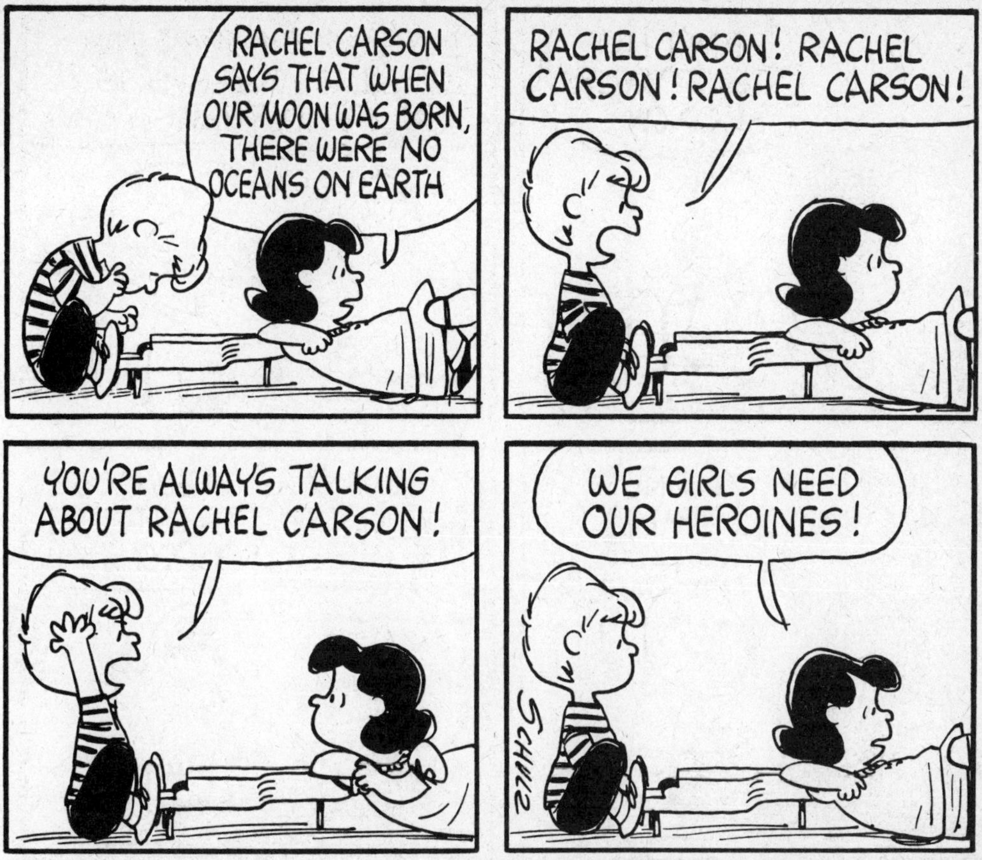
RACHEL CARSON SAYS THAT WHEN OUR MOON WAS BORN, THERE WERE NO OCEANS ON EARTH
RACHEL CARSON! RACHEL CARSON! RACHEL CARSON!
YOU'RE ALWAYS TALKING ABOUT RACHEL CARSON!
WE GIRLS NEED OUR HEROINES!
SCHULZ

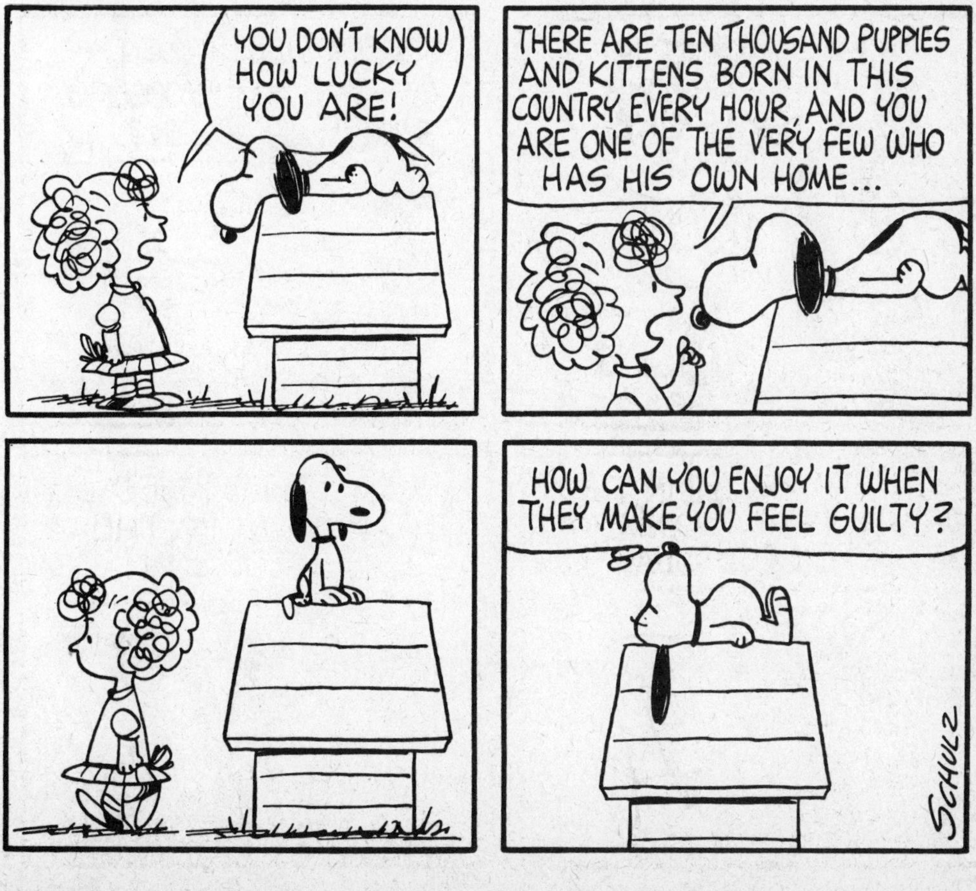
YOU DON'T KNOW HOW LUCKY YOU ARE!
THERE ARE TEN THOUSAND PUPPIES AND KITTENS BORN IN THIS COUNTRY EVERY HOUR, AND YOU ARE ONE OF THE VERY FEW WHO HAS HIS OWN HOME...
HOW CAN YOU ENJOY IT WHEN THEY MAKE YOU FEEL GUILTY?
SCHULZ

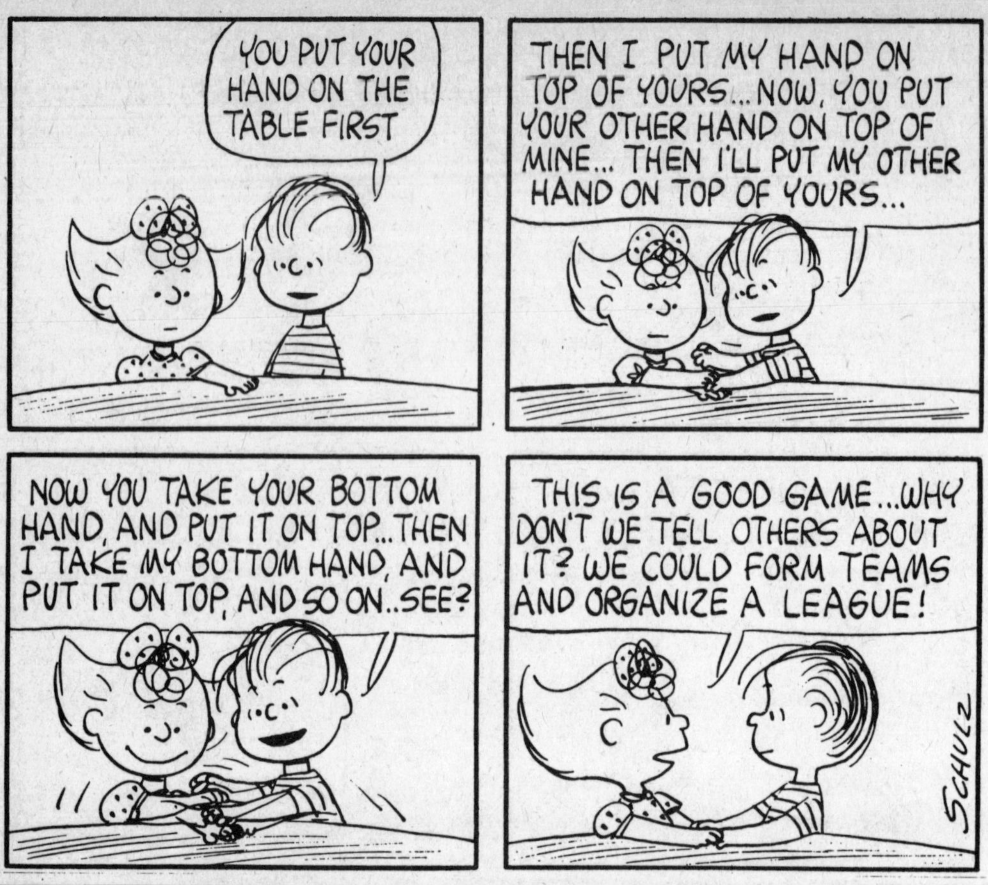
YOU PUT YOUR HAND ON THE TABLE FIRST
THEN I PUT MY HAND ON TOP OF YOURS... NOW, YOU PUT YOUR OTHER HAND ON TOP OF MINE... THEN I'LL PUT MY OTHER HAND ON TOP OF YOURS...
NOW YOU TAKE YOUR BOTTOM HAND, AND PUT IT ON TOP...THEN I TAKE MY BOTTOM HAND, AND PUT IT ON TOP, AND SO ON..SEE?
THIS IS A GOOD GAME...WHY DON'T WE TELL OTHERS ABOUT IT? WE COULD FORM TEAMS AND ORGANIZE A LEAGUE!
SCHULZ

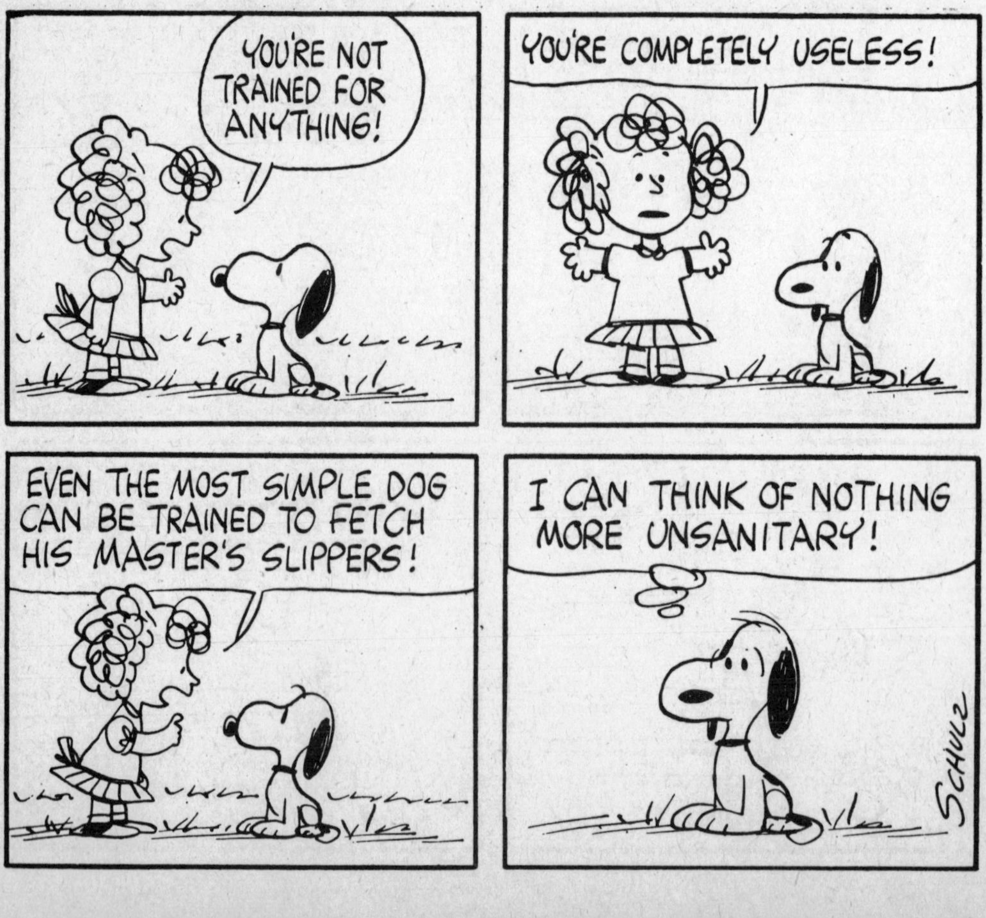
YOU'RE NOT TRAINED FOR ANYTHING!
YOU'RE COMPLETELY USELESS!
EVEN THE MOST SIMPLE DOG CAN BE TRAINED TO FETCH HIS MASTER'S SLIPPERS!
I CAN THINK OF NOTHING MORE UNSANITARY!
SCHULZ

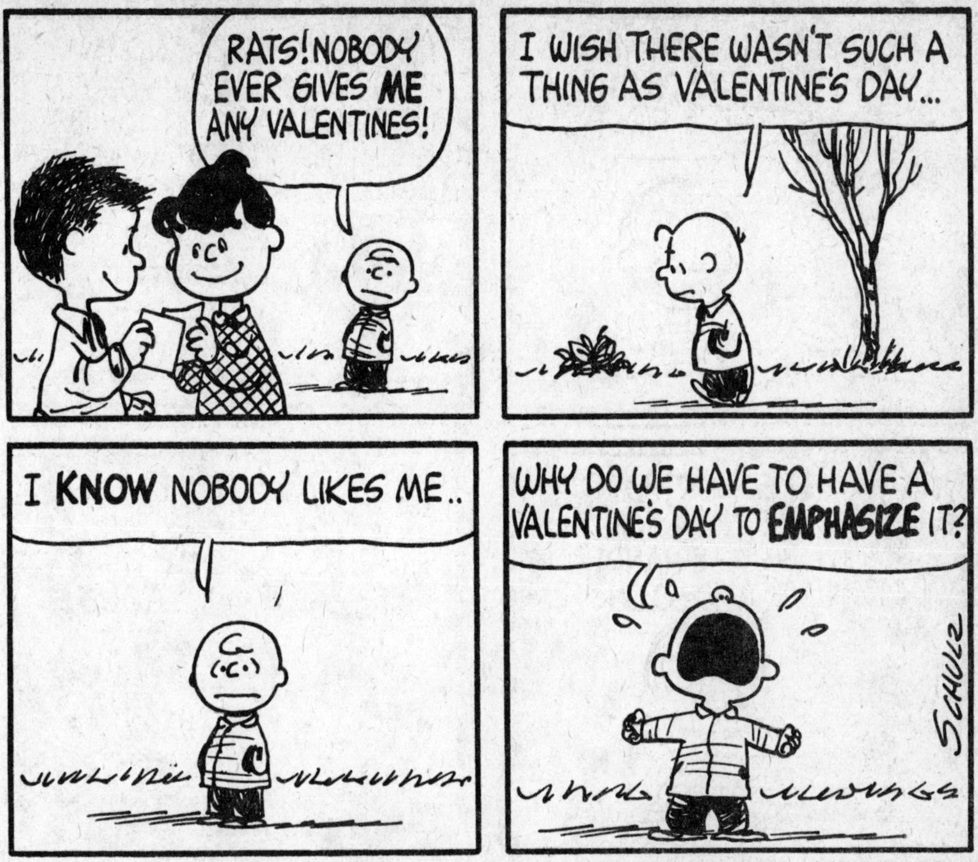
RATS! NOBODY EVER GIVES ME ANY VALENTINES!
I WISH THERE WASN'T SUCH A THING AS VALENTINE'S DAY...
I KNOW NOBODY LIKES ME..
WHY DO WE HAVE TO HAVE A VALENTINE'S DAY TO EMPHASIZE IT?
SCHULZ

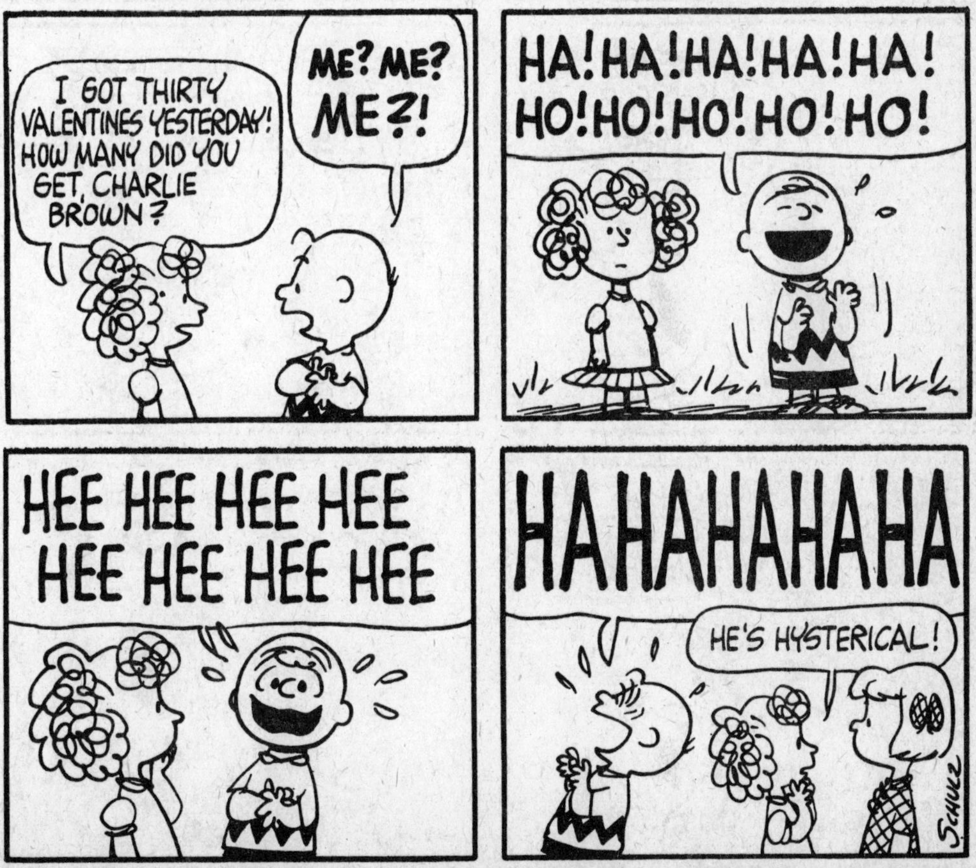
I GOT THIRTY VALENTINES YESTERDAY! HOW MANY DID YOU GET, CHARLIE BROWN?
ME? ME? ME?!
HA! HA! HA! HA! HA! HO! HO! HO! HO! HO!
HEE HEE HEE HEE HEE HEE HEE HEE
HAHAHAHAHA
HE'S HYSTERICAL!
SCHULZ

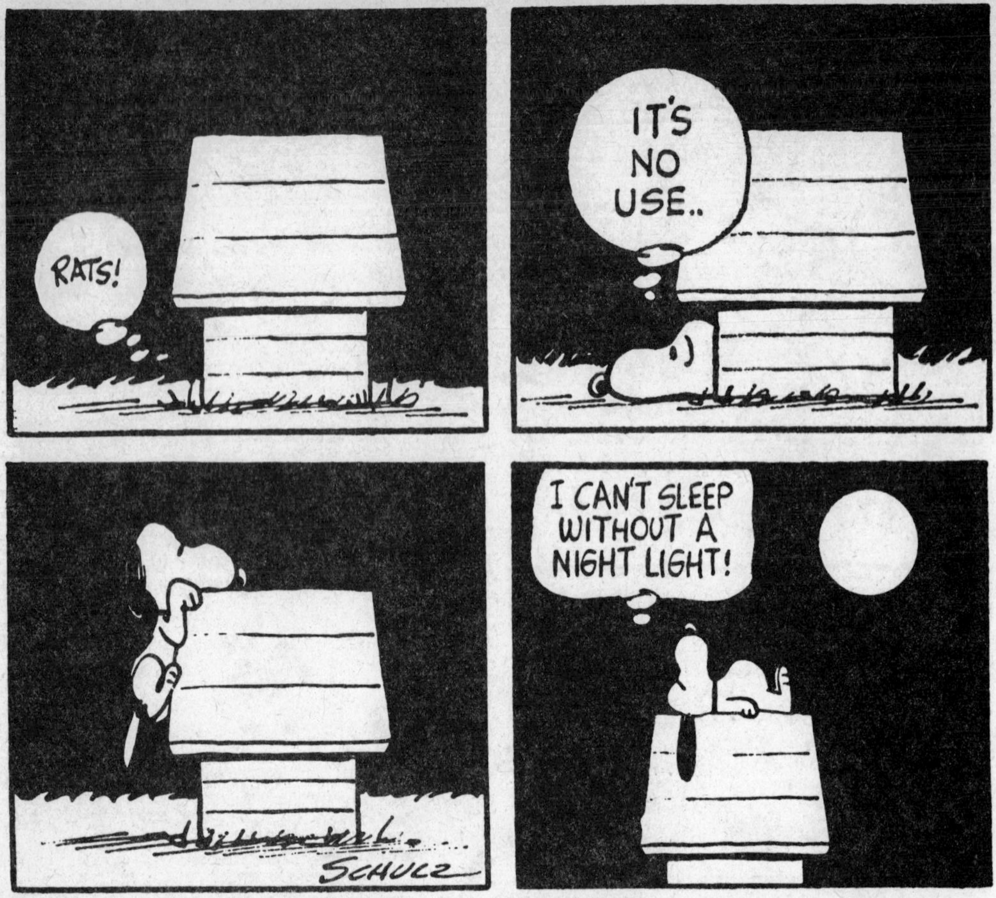
RATS!
IT'S NO USE..
I CAN'T SLEEP WITHOUT A NIGHT LIGHT!
SCHULZ

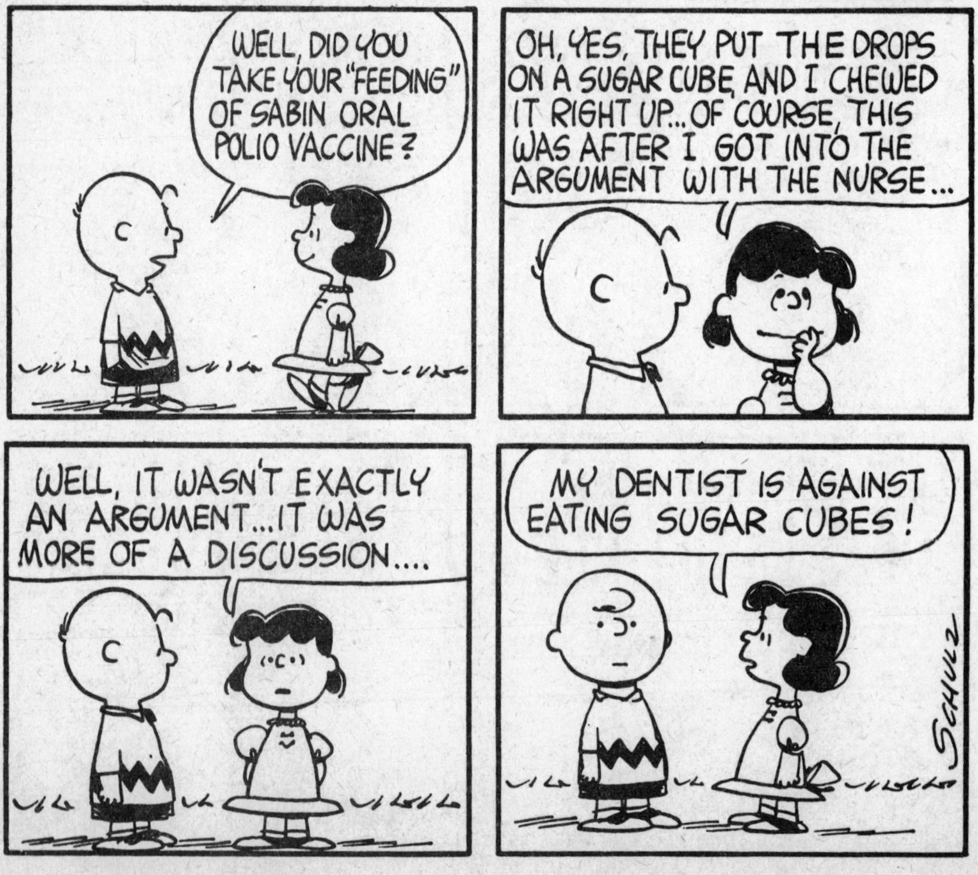
WELL, DID YOU TAKE YOUR "FEEDING" OF SABIN ORAL POLIO VACCINE?
OH, YES, THEY PUT THE DROPS ON A SUGAR CUBE, AND I CHEWED IT RIGHT UP...OF COURSE, THIS WAS AFTER I GOT INTO THE ARGUMENT WITH THE NURSE...
WELL, IT WASN'T EXACTLY AN ARGUMENT...IT WAS MORE OF A DISCUSSION....
MY DENTIST IS AGAINST EATING SUGAR CUBES!
SCHULZ

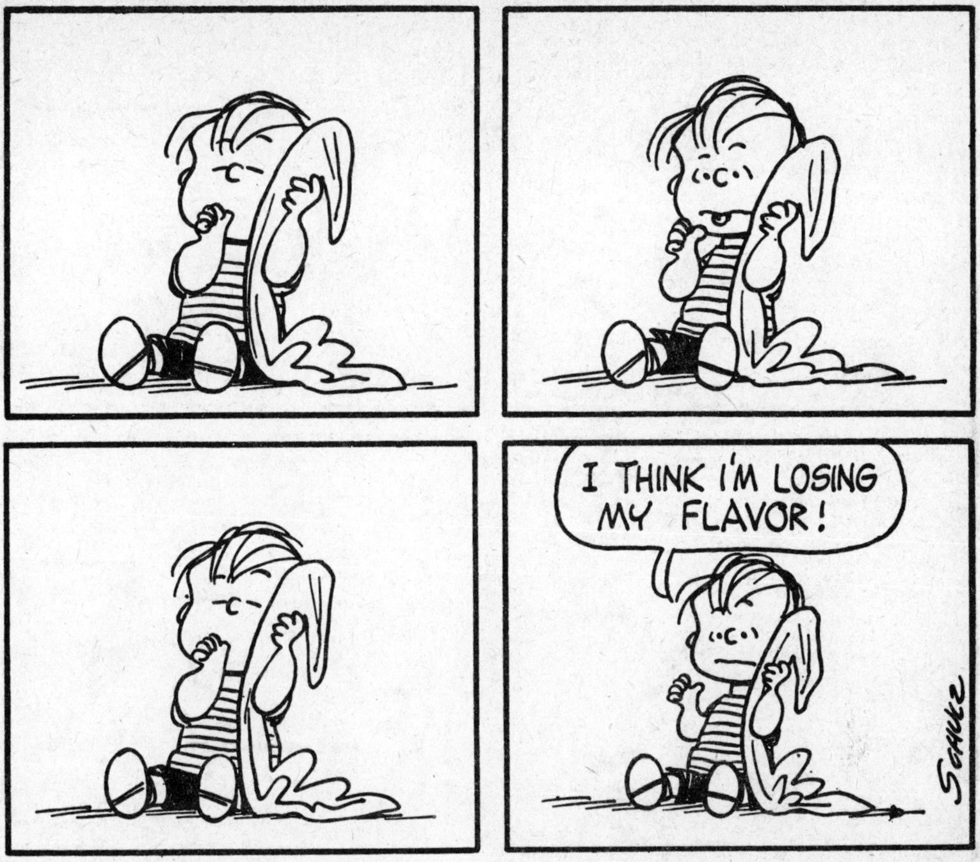
I THINK I'M LOSING MY FLAVOR!
SCHULZ

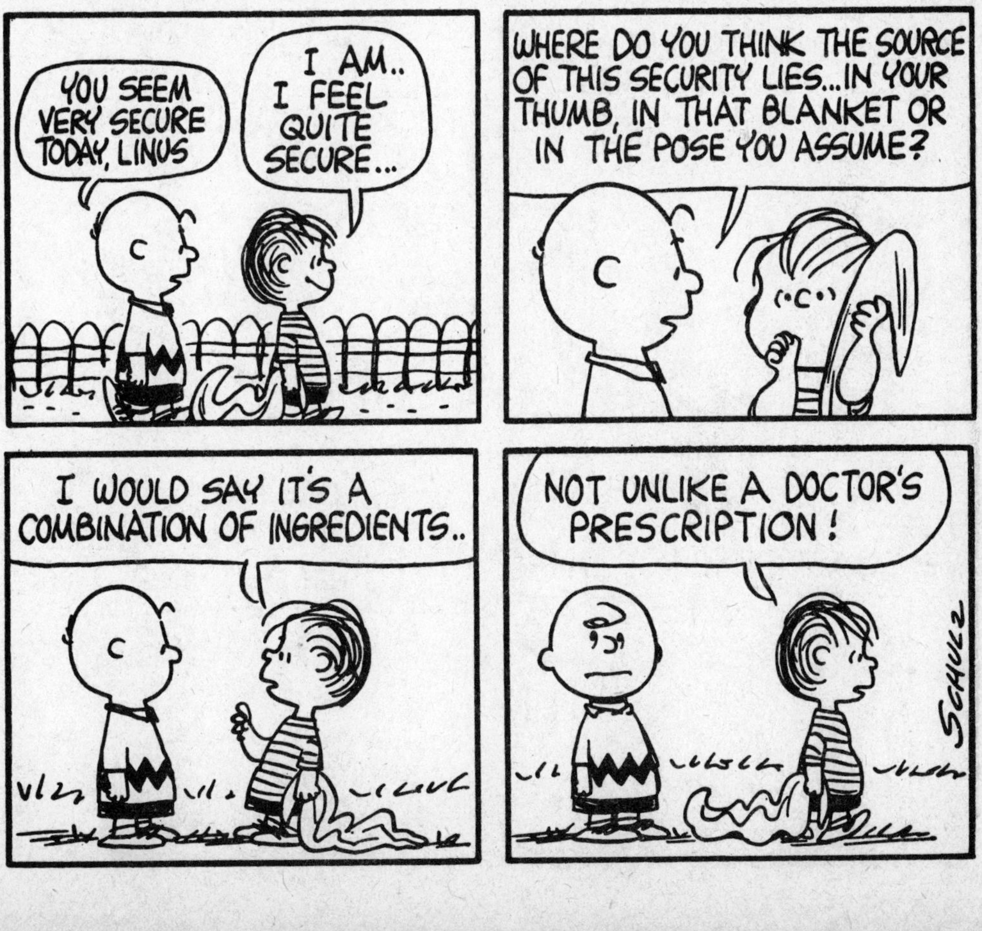
YOU SEEM VERY SECURE TODAY, LINUS
I AM.. I FEEL QUITE SECURE...
WHERE DO YOU THINK THE SOURCE OF THIS SECURITY LIES...IN YOUR THUMB, IN THAT BLANKET OR IN THE POSE YOU ASSUME?
I WOULD SAY IT'S A COMBINATION OF INGREDIENTS..
NOT UNLIKE A DOCTOR'S PRESCRIPTION!
SCHULZ

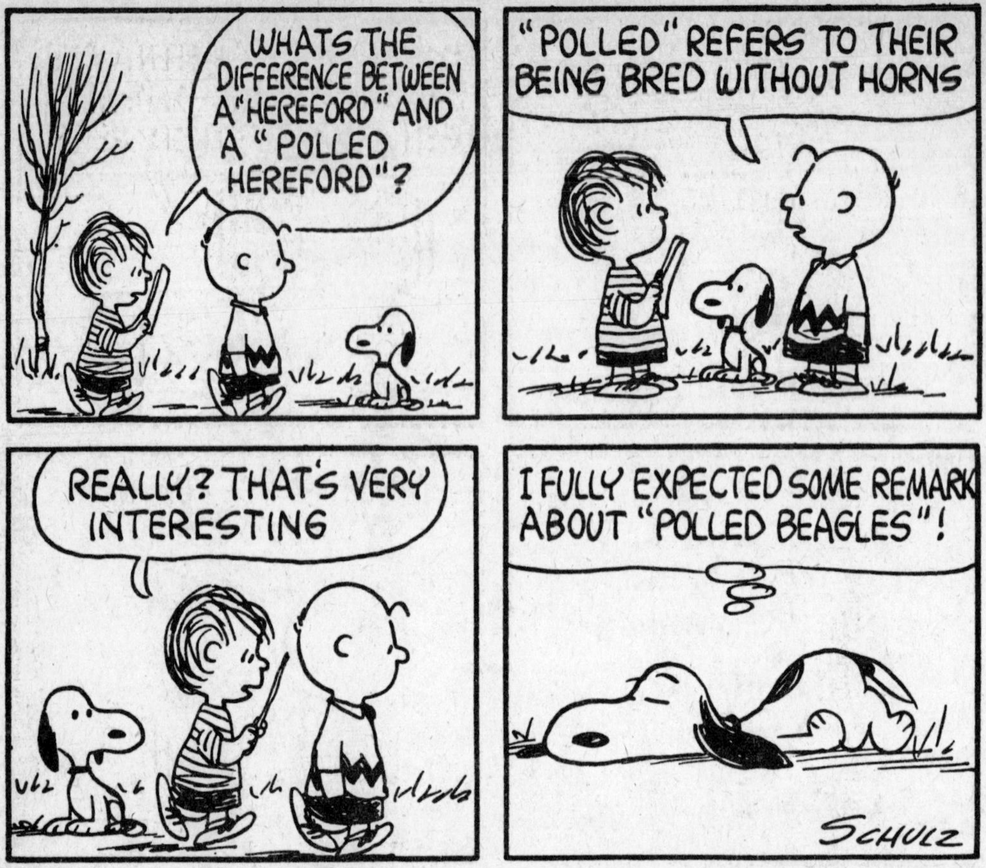
WHATS THE DIFFERENCE BETWEEN A "HEREFORD" AND A "POLLED HEREFORD"?
"POLLED" REFERS TO THEIR BEING BRED WITHOUT HORNS
REALLY? THAT'S VERY INTERESTING
I FULLY EXPECTED SOME REMARK ABOUT "POLLED BEAGLES"!
SCHULZ

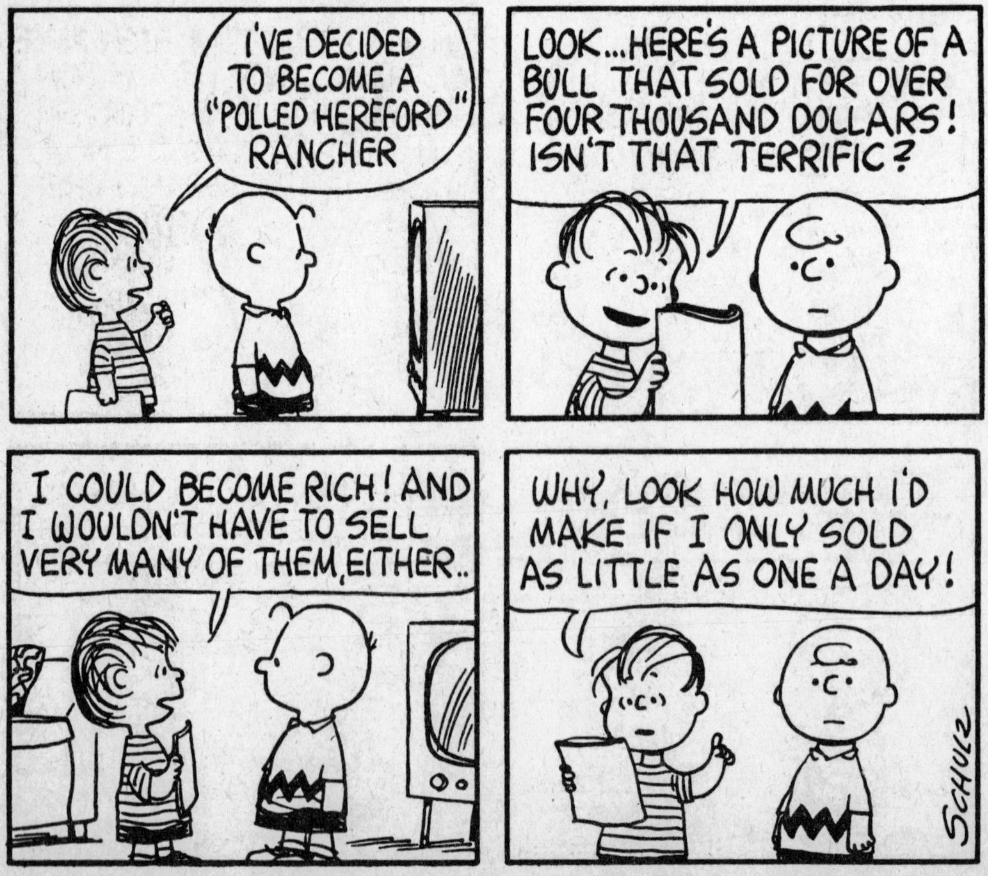
I'VE DECIDED TO BECOME A "POLLED HEREFORD" RANCHER
LOOK...HERE'S A PICTURE OF A BULL THAT SOLD FOR OVER FOUR THOUSAND DOLLARS! ISN'T THAT TERRIFIC?
I COULD BECOME RICH! AND I WOULDN'T HAVE TO SELL VERY MANY OF THEM, EITHER..
WHY, LOOK HOW MUCH I'D MAKE IF I ONLY SOLD AS LITTLE AS ONE A DAY!
SCHULZ

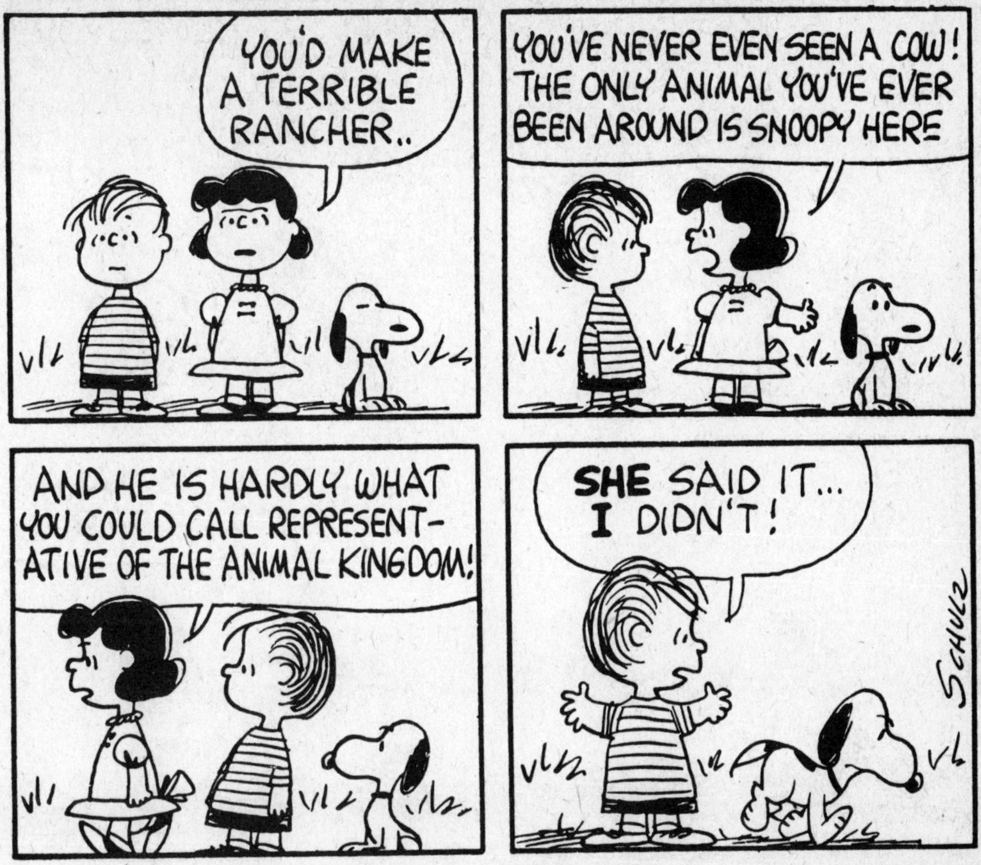
YOU'D MAKE A TERRIBLE RANCHER..
YOU'VE NEVER EVEN SEEN A COW! THE ONLY ANIMAL YOU'VE EVER BEEN AROUND IS SNOOPY HERE
AND HE IS HARDLY WHAT YOU COULD CALL REPRESENTATIVE OF THE ANIMAL KINGDOM!
SHE SAID IT... I DIDN'T!
SCHULZ

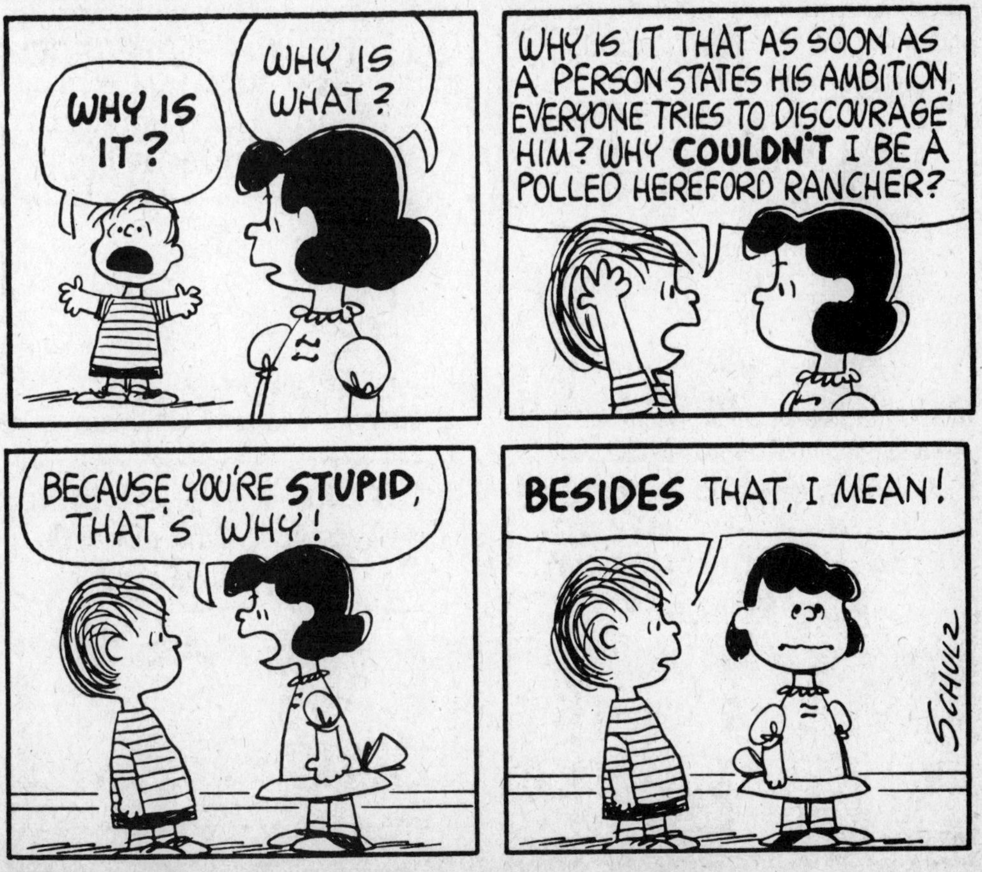
WHY IS IT?
WHY IS WHAT?
WHY IS IT THAT AS SOON AS A PERSON STATES HIS AMBITION, EVERYONE TRIES TO DISCOURAGE HIM? WHY COULDN'T I BE A POLLED HEREFORD RANCHER?
BECAUSE YOU'RE STUPID, THAT'S WHY!
BESIDES THAT, I MEAN!
SCHULZ

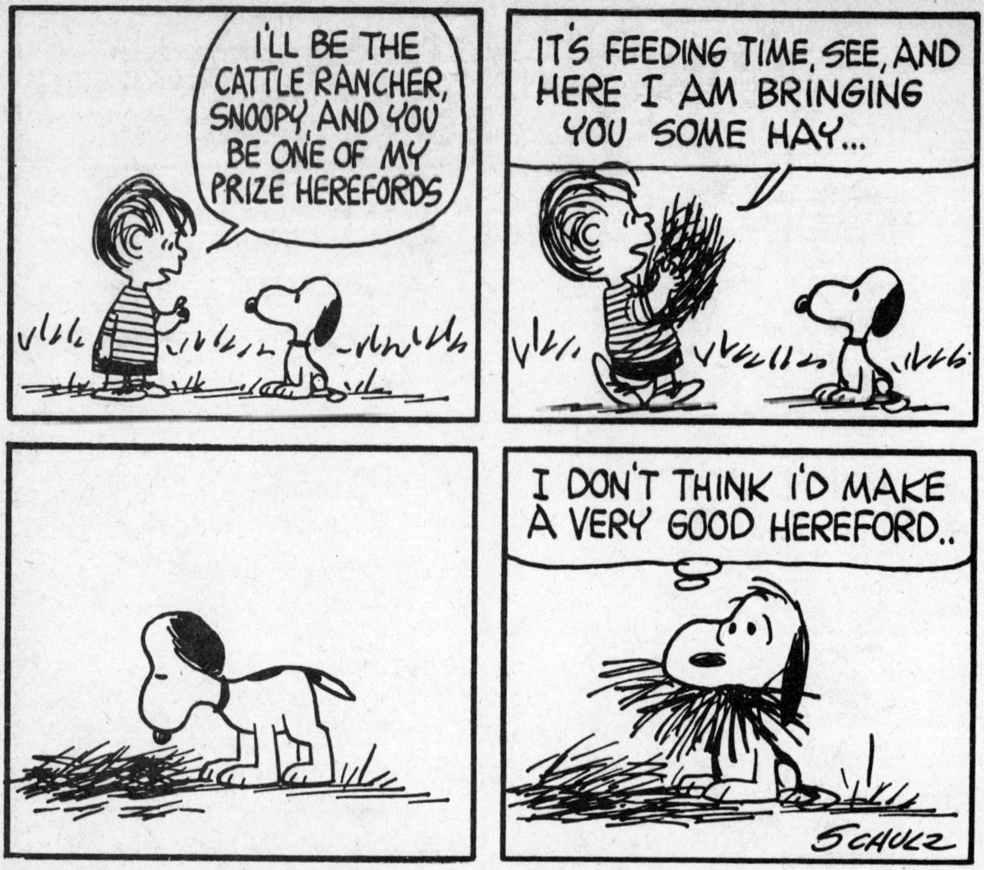
I'LL BE THE CATTLE RANCHER, SNOOPY, AND YOU BE ONE OF MY PRIZE HEREFORDS
IT'S FEEDING TIME, SEE, AND HERE I AM BRINGING YOU SOME HAY...
I DON'T THINK I'D MAKE A VERY GOOD HEREFORD..
SCHULZ

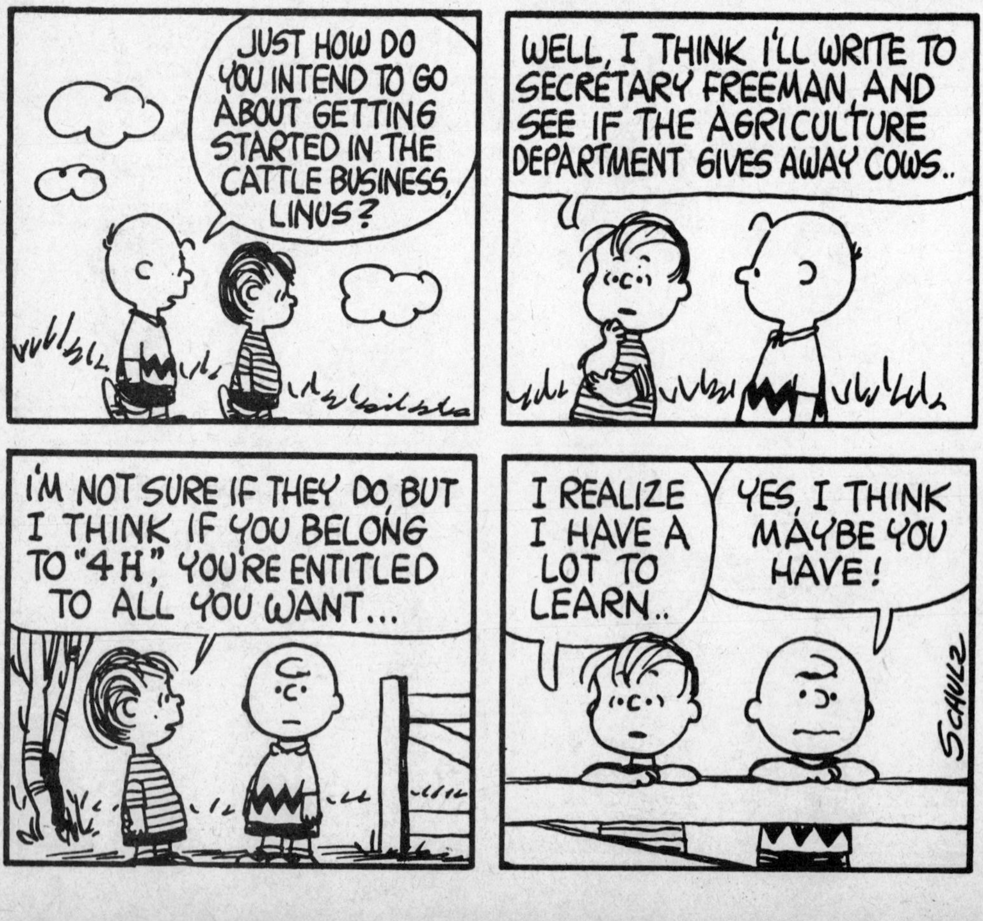
JUST HOW DO YOU INTEND TO GO ABOUT GETTING STARTED IN THE CATTLE BUSINESS, LINUS?
WELL, I THINK I'LL WRITE TO SECRETARY FREEMAN, AND SEE IF THE AGRICULTURE DEPARTMENT GIVES AWAY COWS..
I'M NOT SURE IF THEY DO, BUT I THINK IF YOU BELONG TO "4 H," YOU'RE ENTITLED TO ALL YOU WANT...
I REALIZE I HAVE A LOT TO LEARN..
YES, I THINK MAYBE YOU HAVE!
SCHULZ

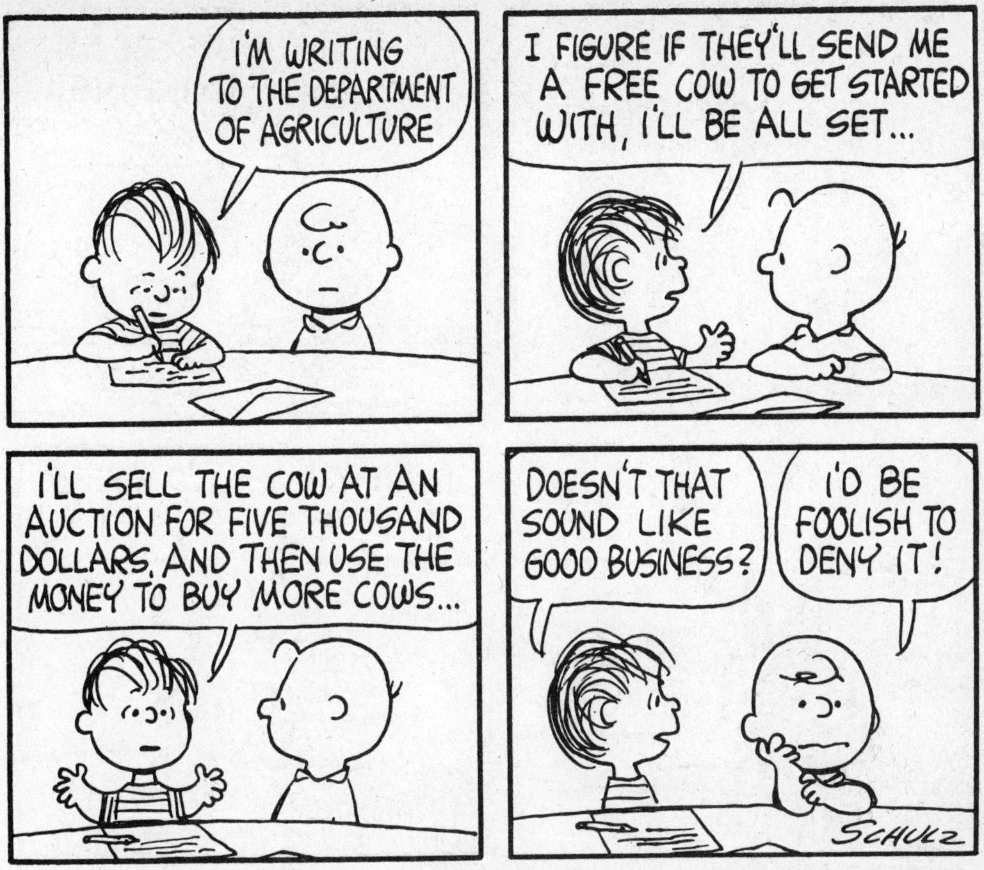
I'M WRITING TO THE DEPARTMENT OF AGRICULTURE
I FIGURE IF THEY'LL SEND ME A FREE COW TO GET STARTED WITH, I'LL BE ALL SET...
I'LL SELL THE COW AT AN AUCTION FOR FIVE THOUSAND DOLLARS, AND THEN USE THE MONEY TO BUY MORE COWS...
DOESN'T THAT SOUND LIKE GOOD BUSINESS?
I'D BE FOOLISH TO DENY IT!
SCHULZ

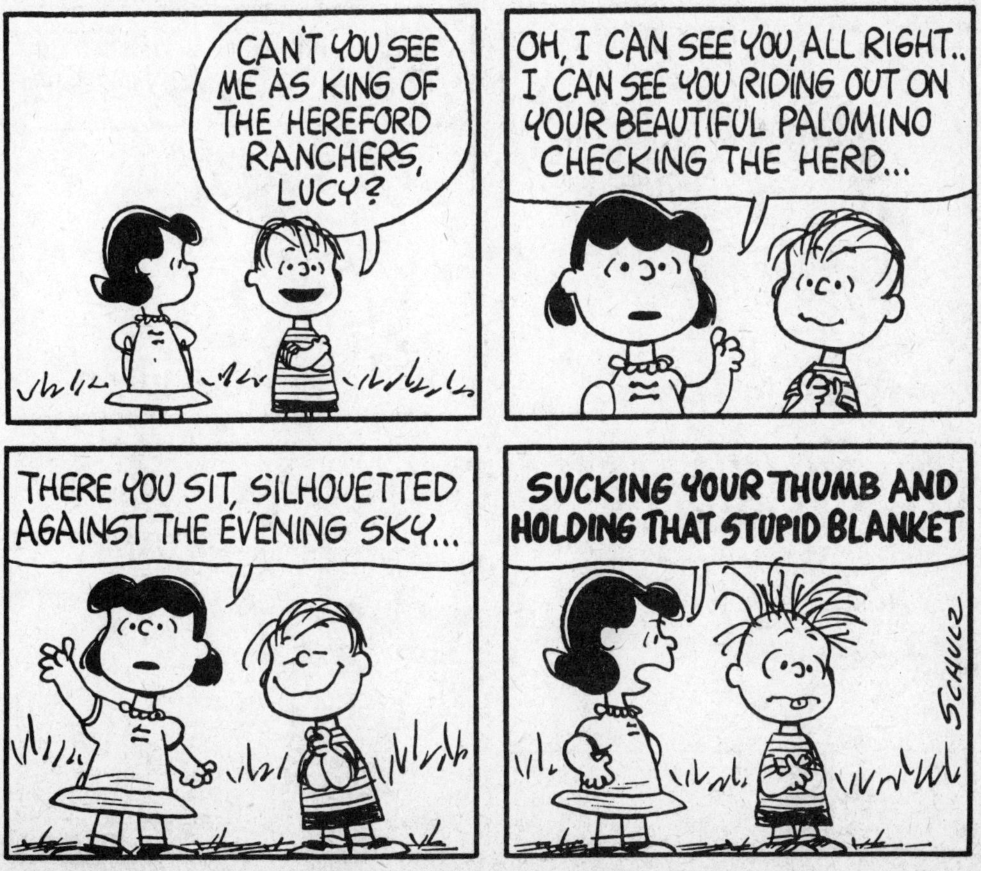
CAN'T YOU SEE ME AS KING OF THE HEREFORD RANCHERS, LUCY?
OH, I CAN SEE YOU, ALL RIGHT.. I CAN SEE YOU RIDING OUT ON YOUR BEAUTIFUL PALOMINO CHECKING THE HERD...
THERE YOU SIT, SILHOUETTED AGAINST THE EVENING SKY...
SUCKING YOUR THUMB AND HOLDING THAT STUPID BLANKET
SCHULZ

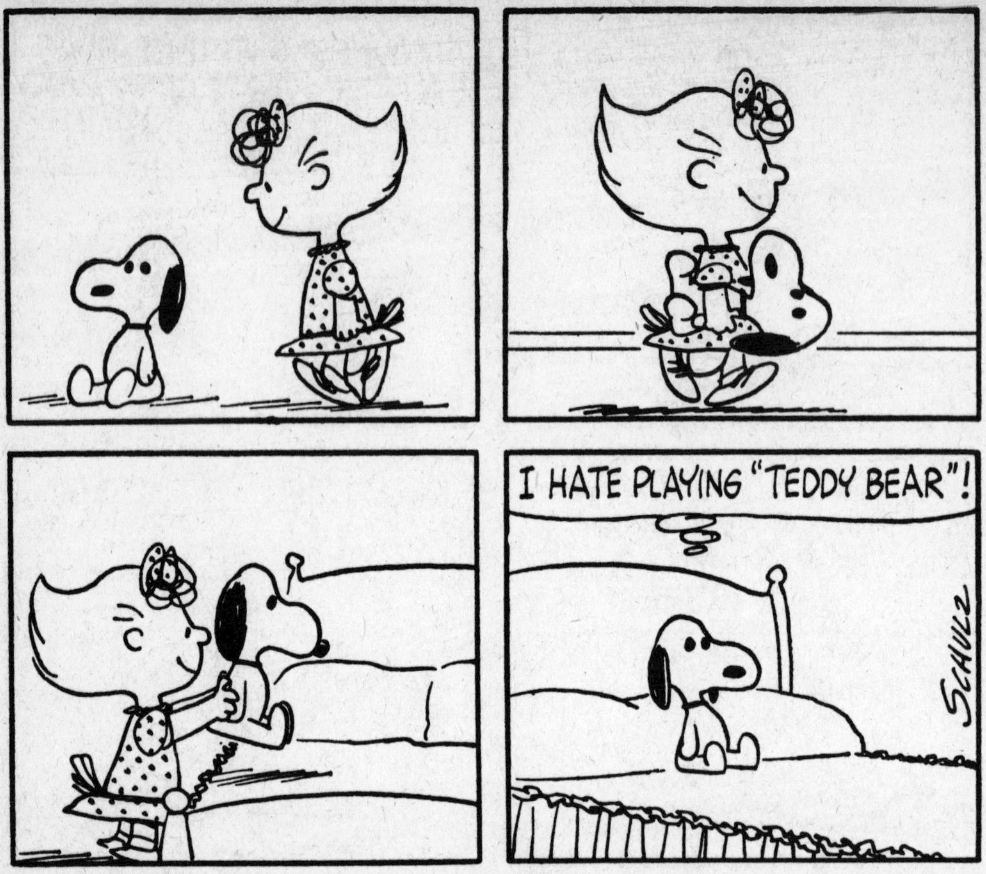
I HATE PLAYING "TEDDY BEAR"!
SCHULZ

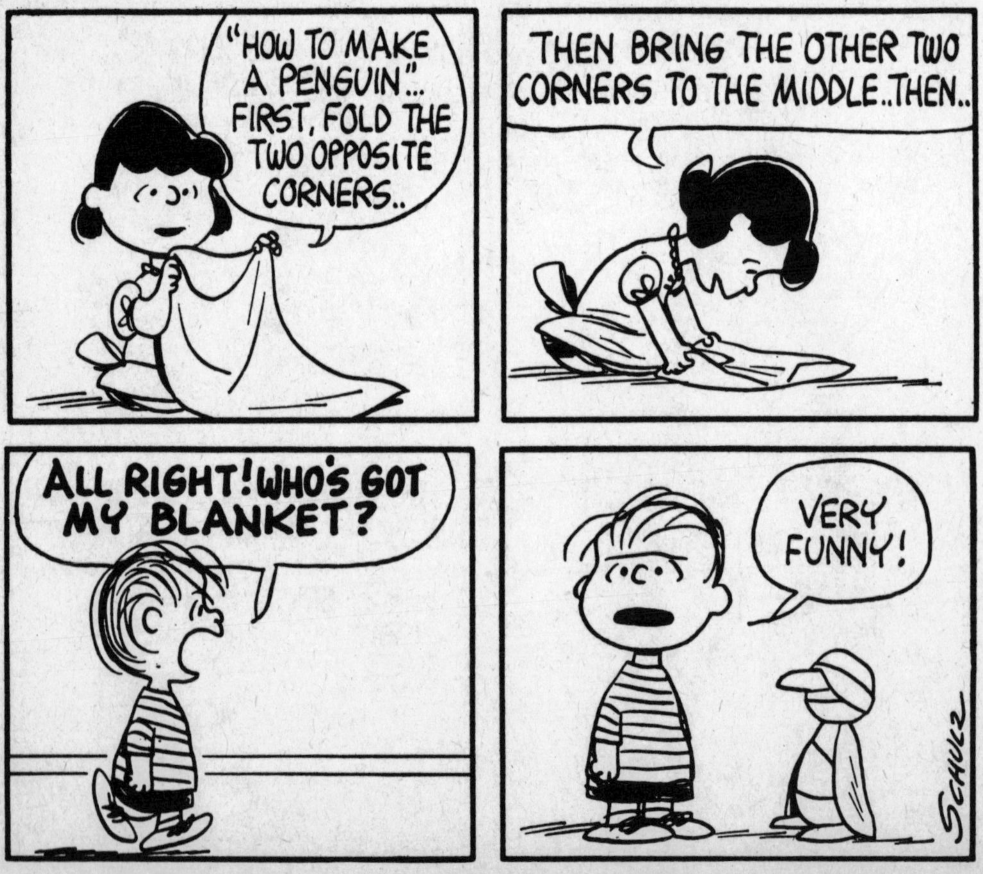
"HOW TO MAKE A PENGUIN"... FIRST, FOLD THE TWO OPPOSITE CORNERS..
THEN BRING THE OTHER TWO CORNERS TO THE MIDDLE..THEN..
ALL RIGHT! WHO'S GOT MY BLANKET?
VERY FUNNY!
SCHULZ

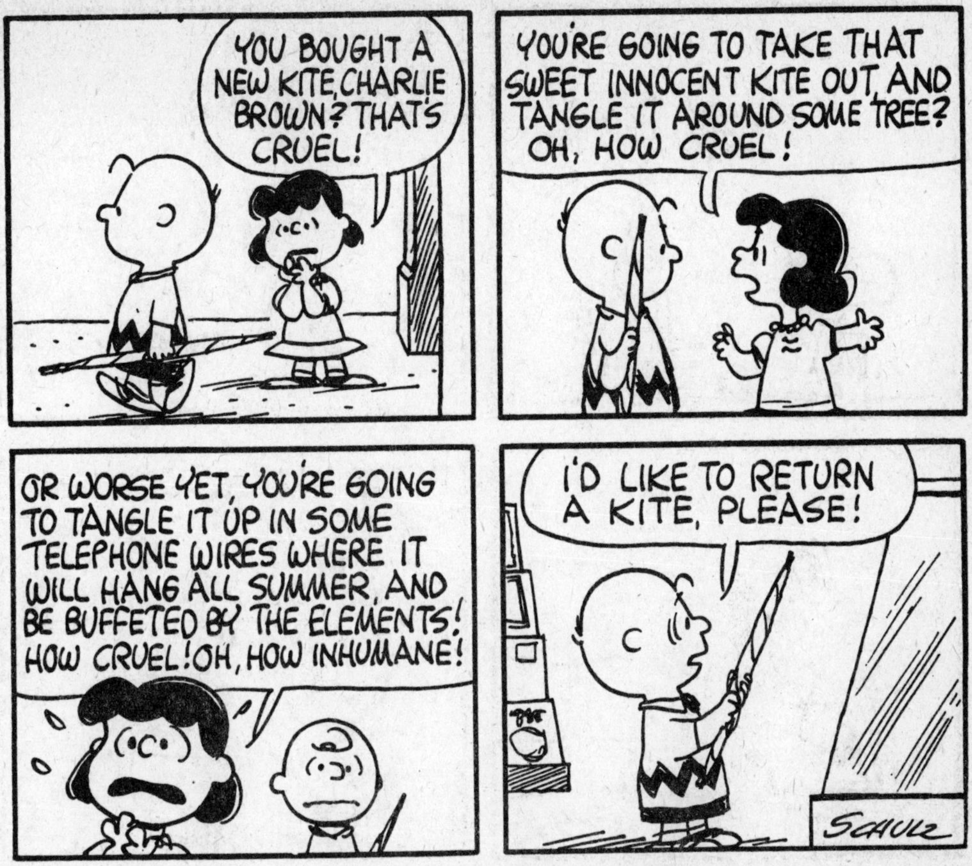
YOU BOUGHT A NEW KITE, CHARLIE BROWN? THAT'S CRUEL!
YOU'RE GOING TO TAKE THAT SWEET INNOCENT KITE OUT, AND TANGLE IT AROUND SOME TREE? OH, HOW CRUEL!
OR WORSE YET, YOU'RE GOING TO TANGLE IT UP IN SOME TELEPHONE WIRES WHERE IT WILL HANG ALL SUMMER, AND BE BUFFETED BY THE ELEMENTS! HOW CRUEL! OH, HOW INHUMANE!
I'D LIKE TO RETURN A KITE, PLEASE!
SCHULZ

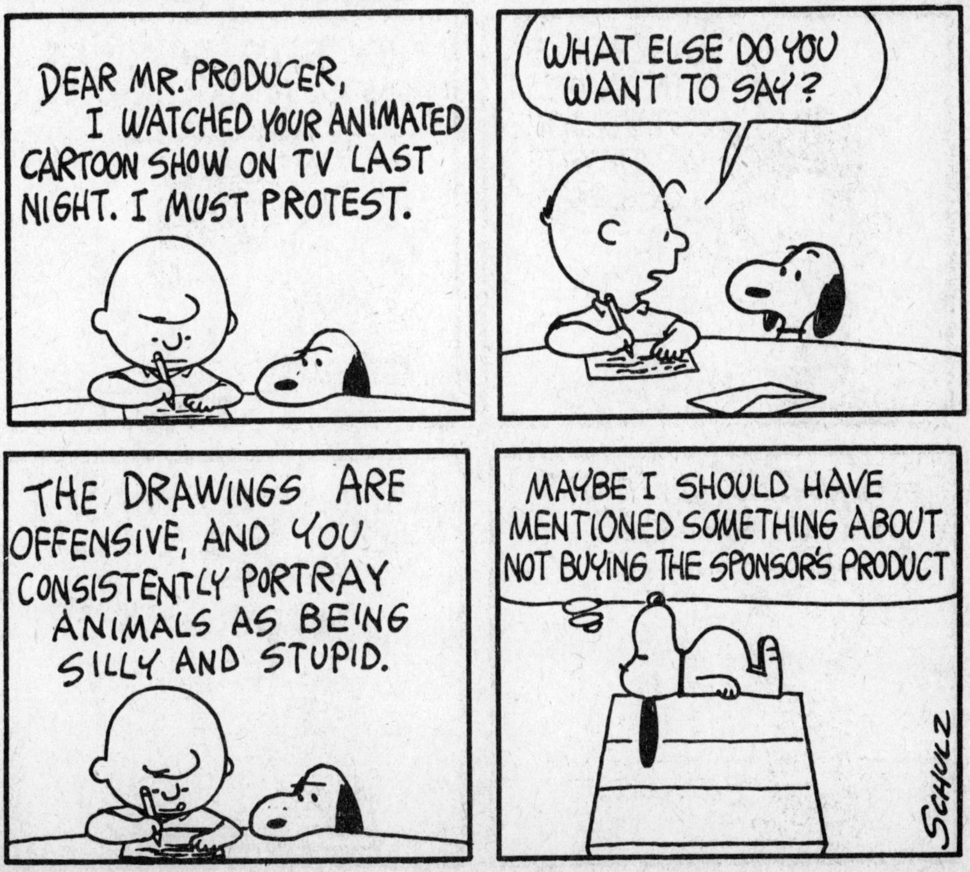
DEAR MR. PRODUCER, I WATCHED YOUR ANIMATED CARTOON SHOW ON TV LAST NIGHT. I MUST PROTEST.
WHAT ELSE DO YOU WANT TO SAY?
THE DRAWINGS ARE OFFENSIVE, AND YOU CONSISTENTLY PORTRAY ANIMALS AS BEING SILLY AND STUPID.
MAYBE I SHOULD HAVE MENTIONED SOMETHING ABOUT NOT BUYING THE SPONSOR'S PRODUCT
SCHULZ

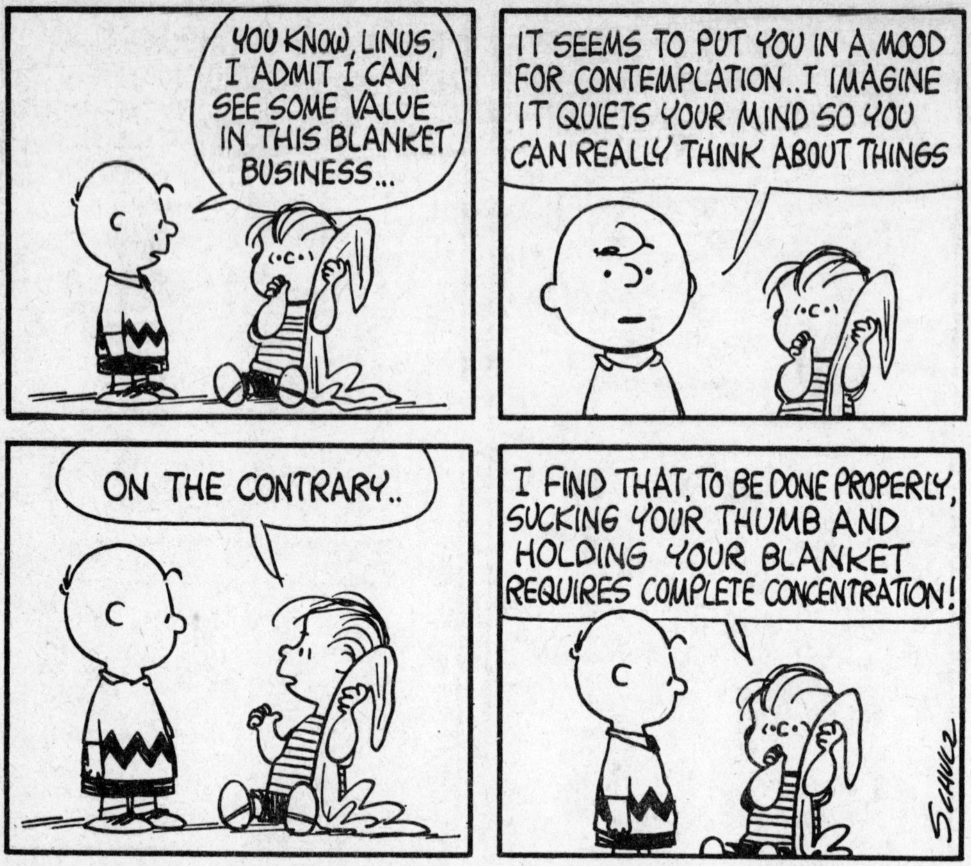
YOU KNOW, LINUS, I ADMIT I CAN SEE SOME VALUE IN THIS BLANKET BUSINESS...
IT SEEMS TO PUT YOU IN A MOOD FOR CONTEMPLATION..I IMAGINE IT QUIETS YOUR MIND SO YOU CAN REALLY THINK ABOUT THINGS
ON THE CONTRARY..
I FIND THAT, TO BE DONE PROPERLY, SUCKING YOUR THUMB AND HOLDING YOUR BLANKET REQUIRES COMPLETE CONCENTRATION!
SCHULZ

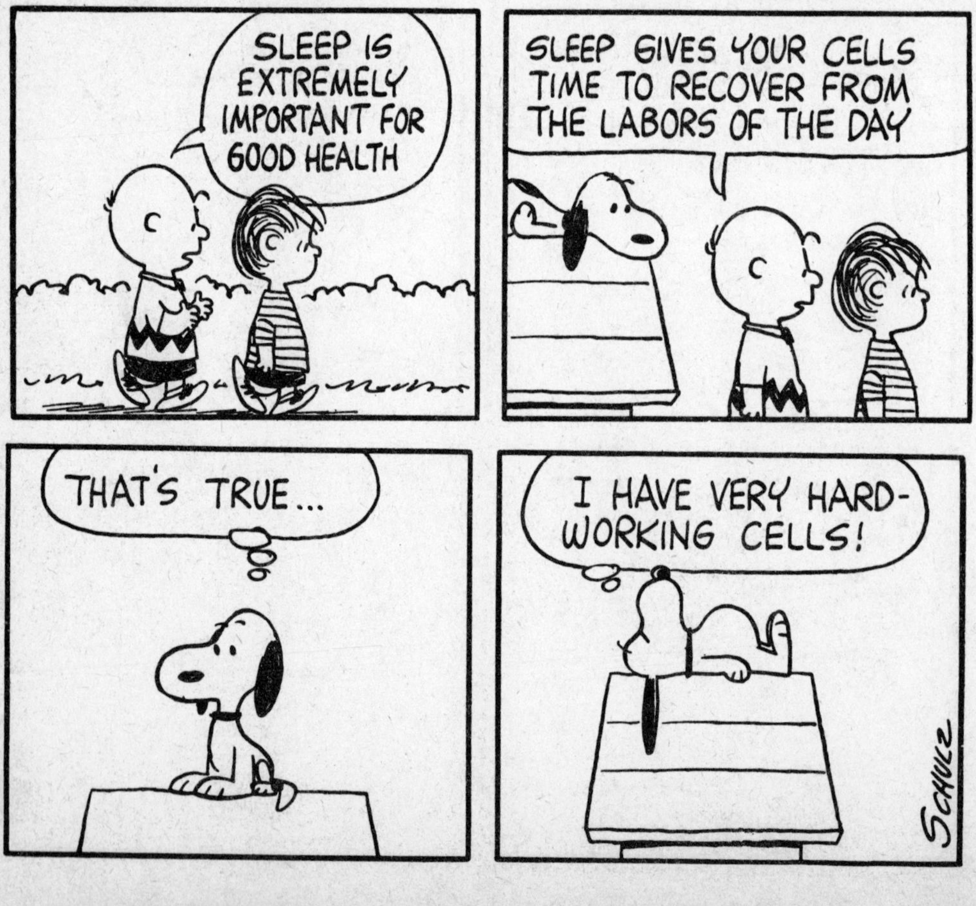
SLEEP IS EXTREMELY IMPORTANT FOR GOOD HEALTH
SLEEP GIVES YOUR CELLS TIME TO RECOVER FROM THE LABORS OF THE DAY
THAT'S TRUE...
I HAVE VERY HARD-WORKING CELLS!
SCHULZ

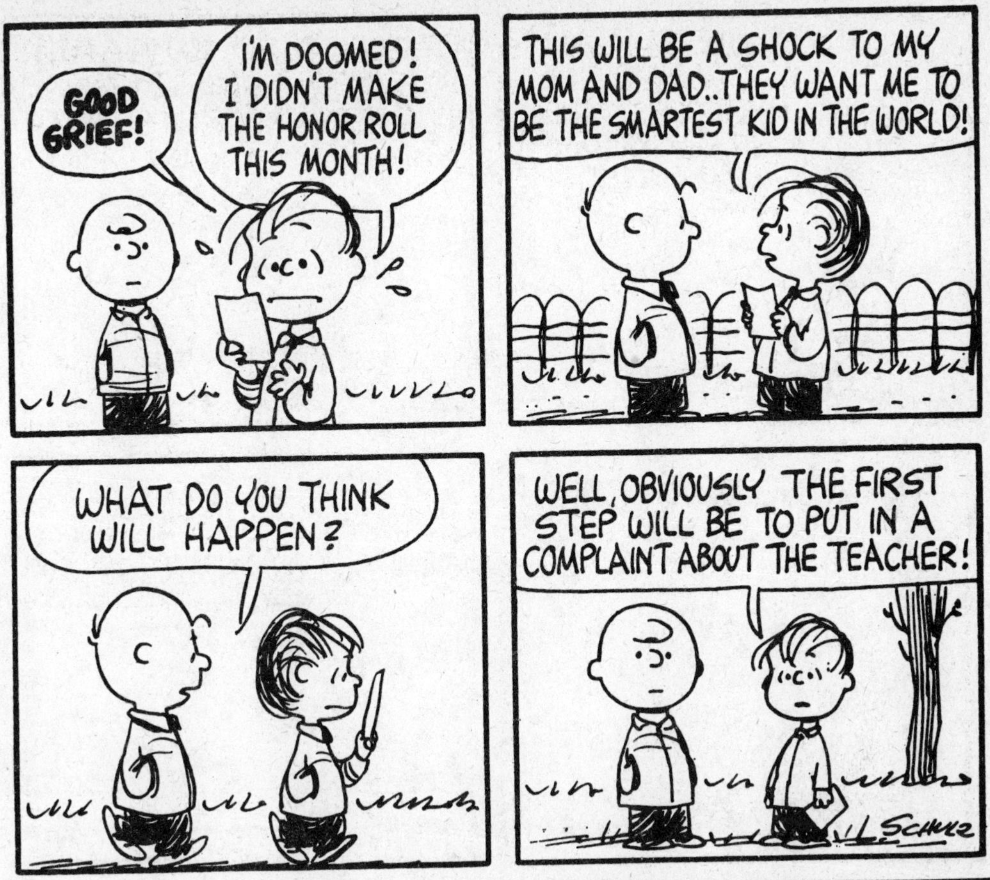
GOOD GRIEF!
I'M DOOMED! I DIDN'T MAKE THE HONOR ROLL THIS MONTH!
THIS WILL BE A SHOCK TO MY MOM AND DAD..THEY WANT ME TO BE THE SMARTEST KID IN THE WORLD!
WHAT DO YOU THINK WILL HAPPEN?
WELL, OBVIOUSLY THE FIRST STEP WILL BE TO PUT IN A COMPLAINT ABOUT THE TEACHER!
SCHULZ

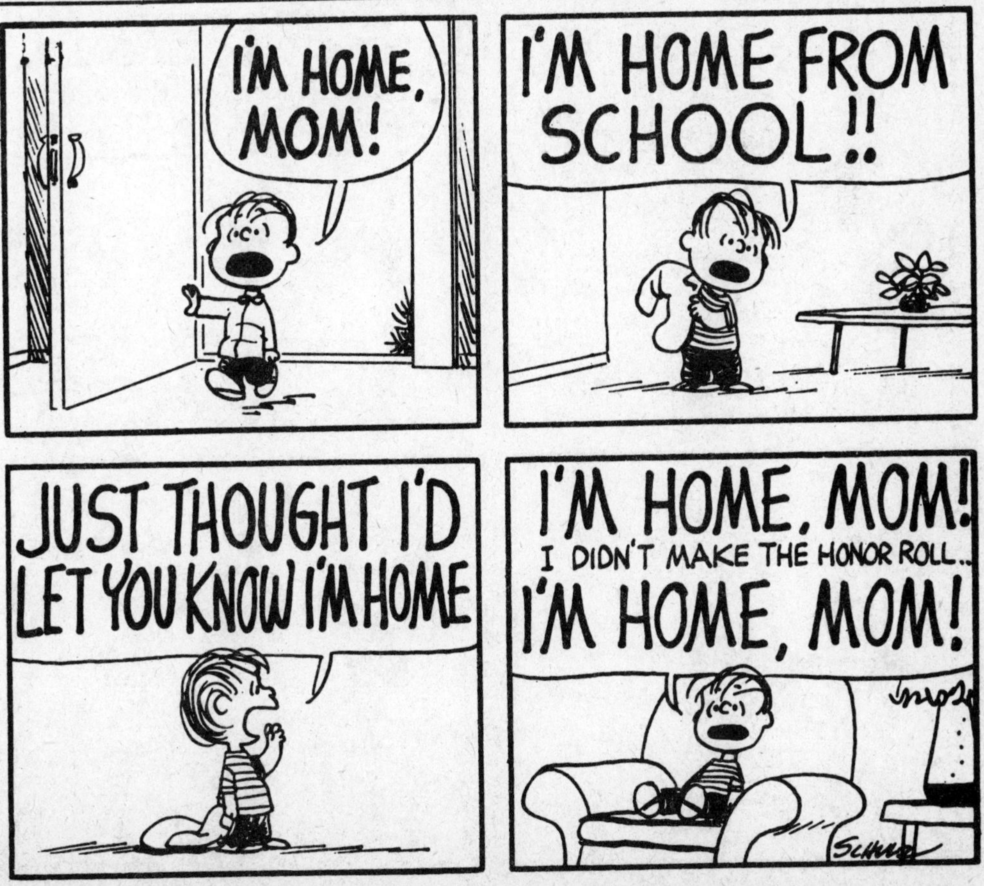
I'M HOME, MOM!
I'M HOME FROM SCHOOL!!
JUST THOUGHT I'D LET YOU KNOW I'M HOME
I'M HOME, MOM!
I DIDN'T MAKE THE HONOR ROLL..
I'M HOME, MOM!
SCHULZ

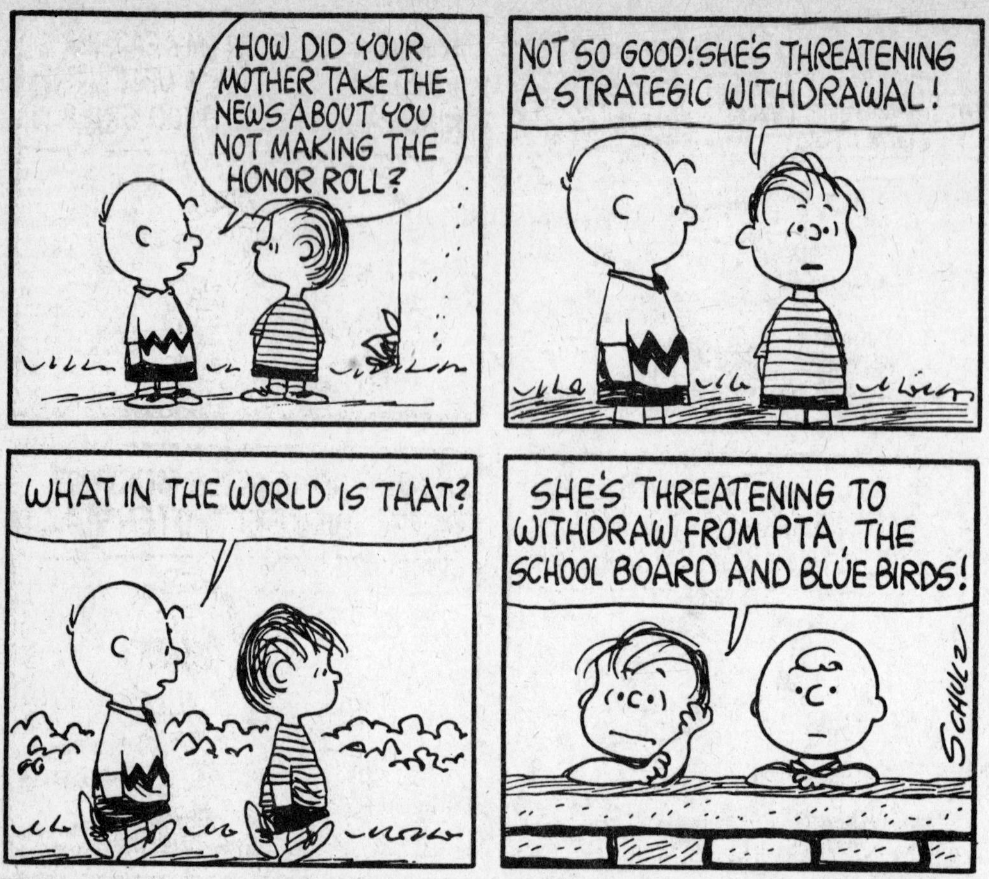
HOW DID YOUR MOTHER TAKE THE NEWS ABOUT YOU NOT MAKING THE HONOR ROLL?
NOT SO GOOD! SHE'S THREATENING A STRATEGIC WITHDRAWAL!
WHAT IN THE WORLD IS THAT?
SHE'S THREATENING TO WITHDRAW FROM PTA, THE SCHOOL BOARD AND BLUE BIRDS!
SCHULZ

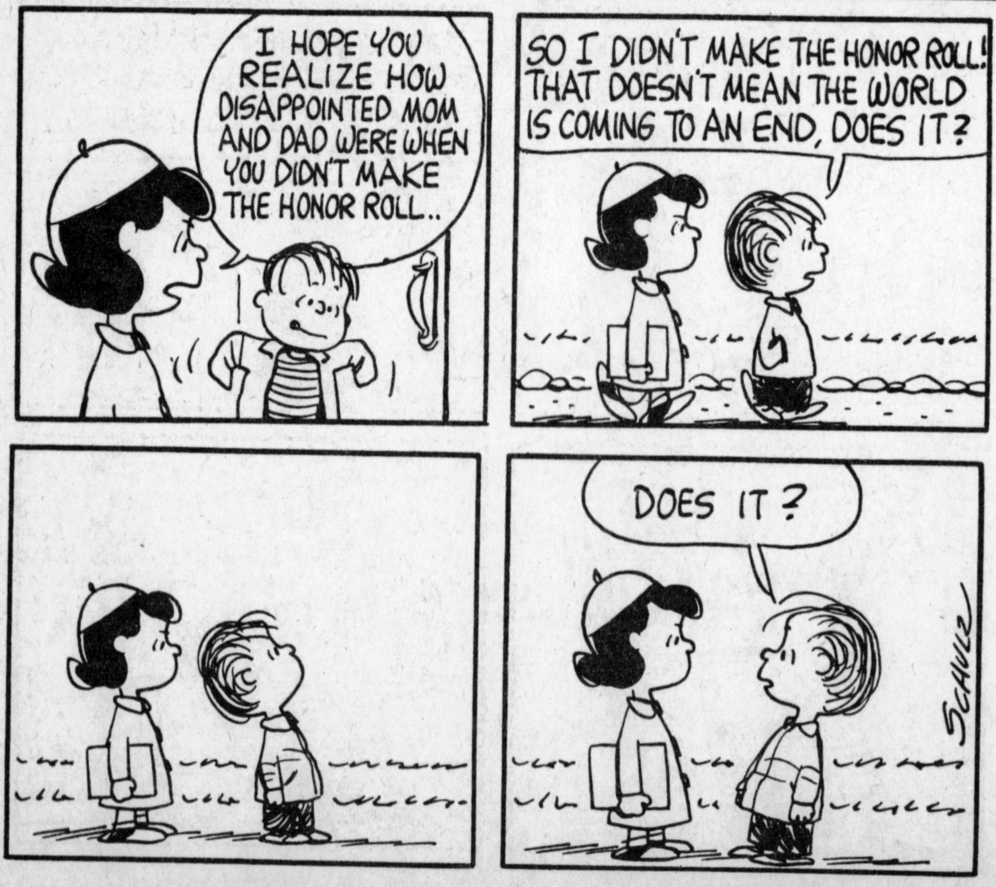
I HOPE YOU REALIZE HOW DISAPPOINTED MOM AND DAD WERE WHEN YOU DIDN'T MAKE THE HONOR ROLL..
SO I DIDN'T MAKE THE HONOR ROLL! THAT DOESN'T MEAN THE WORLD IS COMING TO AN END, DOES IT?
DOES IT?
SCHULZ

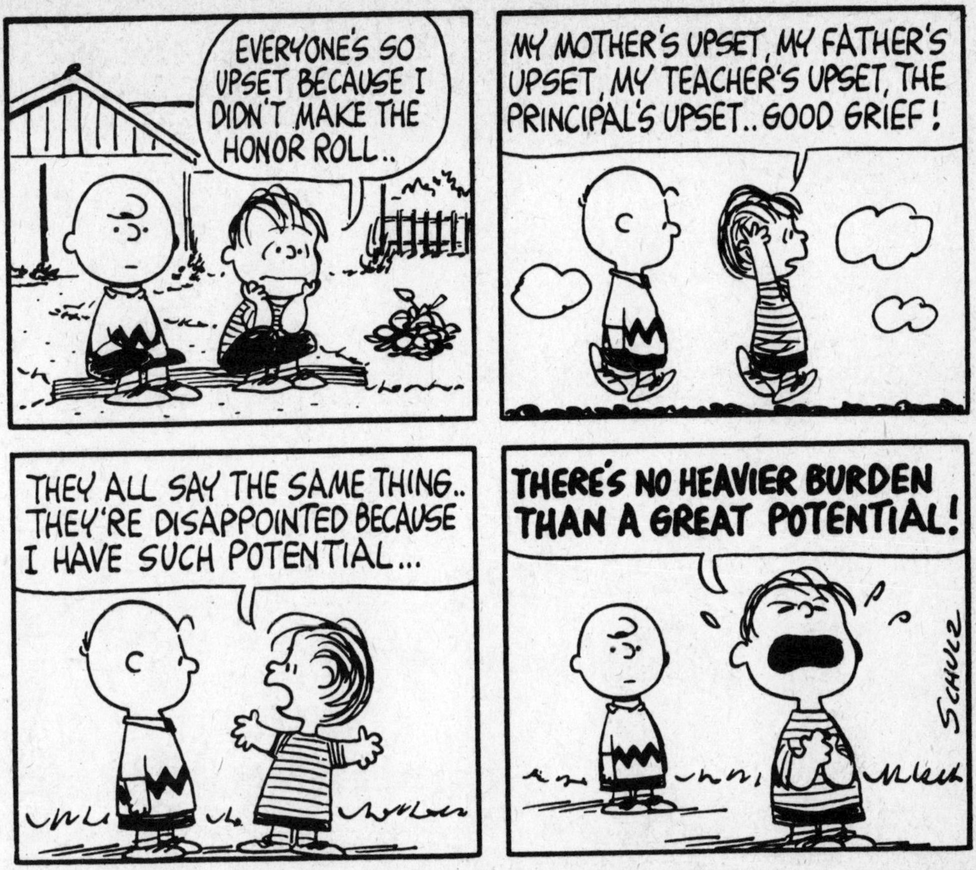
EVERYONE'S SO UPSET BECAUSE I DIDN'T MAKE THE HONOR ROLL..
MY MOTHER'S UPSET, MY FATHER'S UPSET, MY TEACHER'S UPSET, THE PRINCIPAL'S UPSET.. GOOD GRIEF!
THEY ALL SAY THE SAME THING.. THEY'RE DISAPPOINTED BECAUSE I HAVE SUCH POTENTIAL...
THERE'S NO HEAVIER BURDEN THAN A GREAT POTENTIAL!
SCHULZ

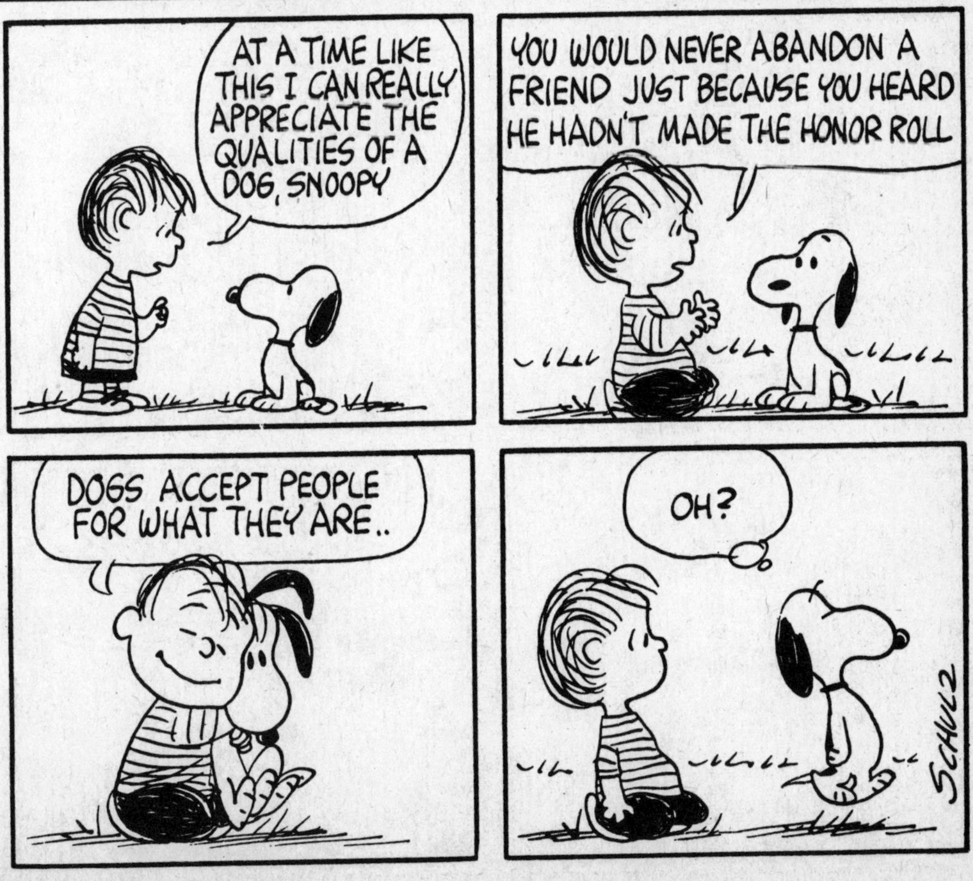
AT A TIME LIKE THIS I CAN REALLY APPRECIATE THE QUALITIES OF A DOG, SNOOPY
YOU WOULD NEVER ABANDON A FRIEND JUST BECAUSE YOU HEARD HE HADN'T MADE THE HONOR ROLL
DOGS ACCEPT PEOPLE FOR WHAT THEY ARE..
OH?
SCHULZ

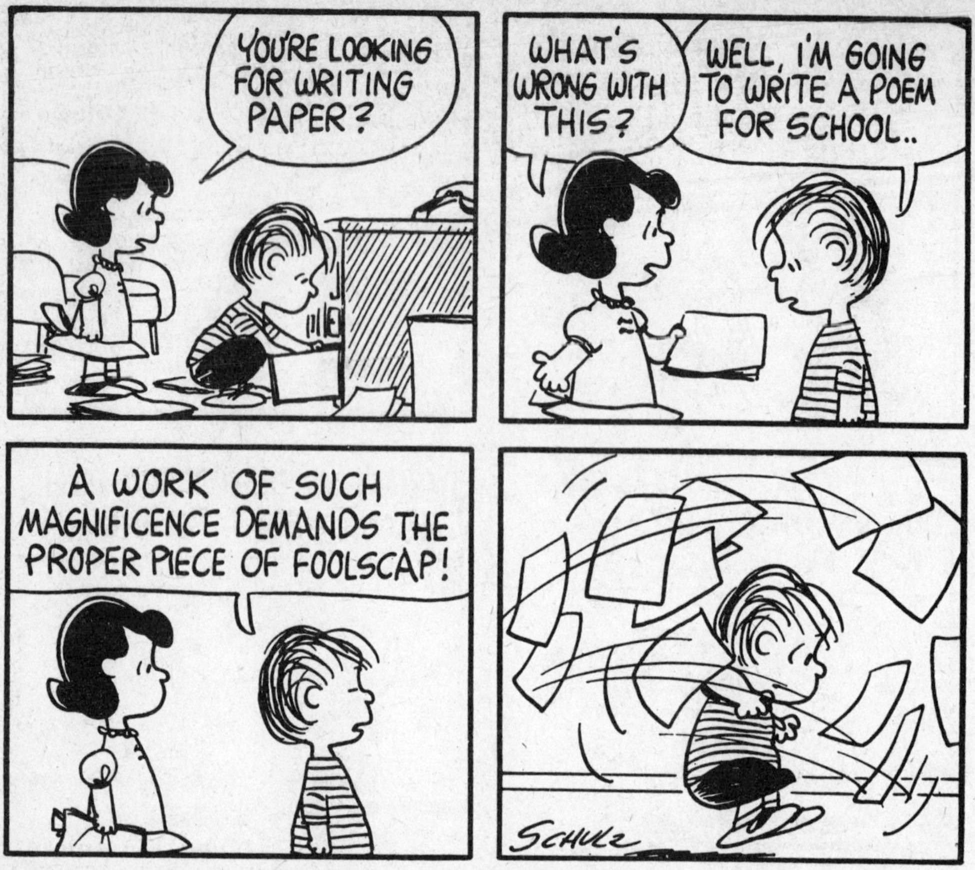
YOU'RE LOOKING FOR WRITING PAPER?
WHAT'S WRONG WITH THIS?
WELL, I'M GOING TO WRITE A POEM FOR SCHOOL..
A WORK OF SUCH MAGNIFICENCE DEMANDS THE PROPER PIECE OF FOOLSCAP!
SCHULZ

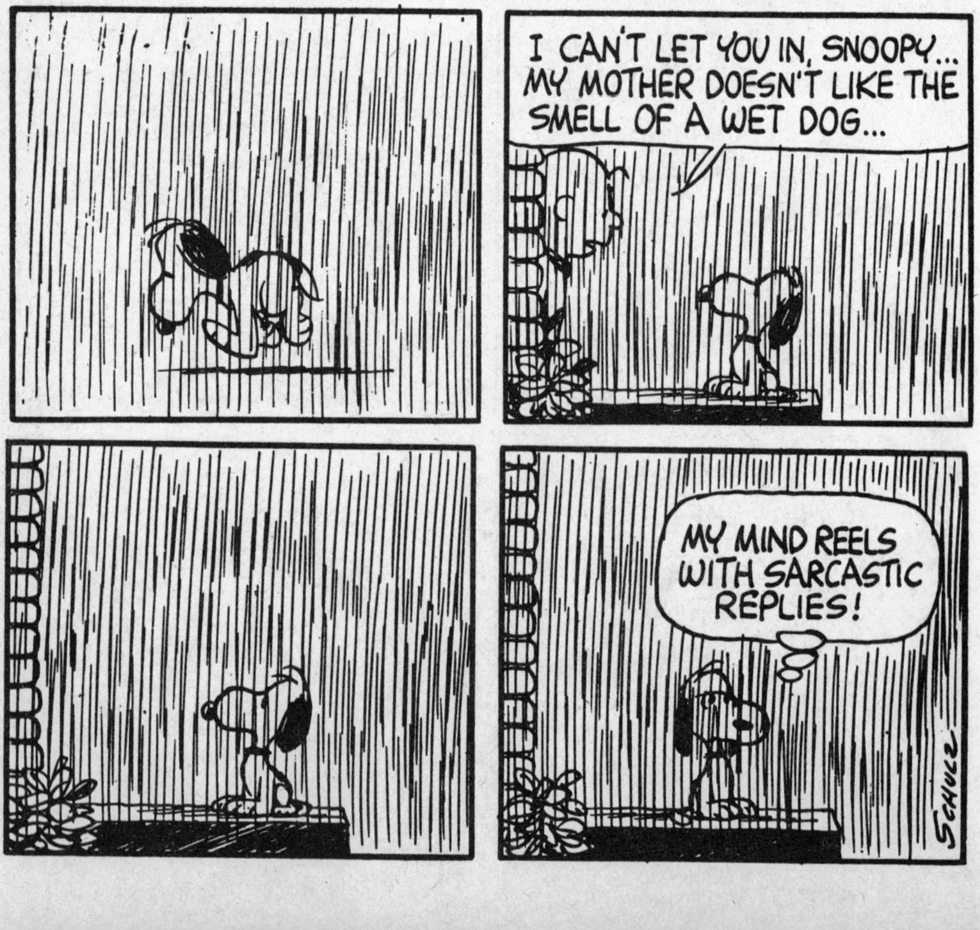
I CAN'T LET YOU IN, SNOOPY... MY MOTHER DOESN'T LIKE THE SMELL OF A WET DOG...
MY MIND REELS WITH SARCASTIC REPLIES!
SCHULZ

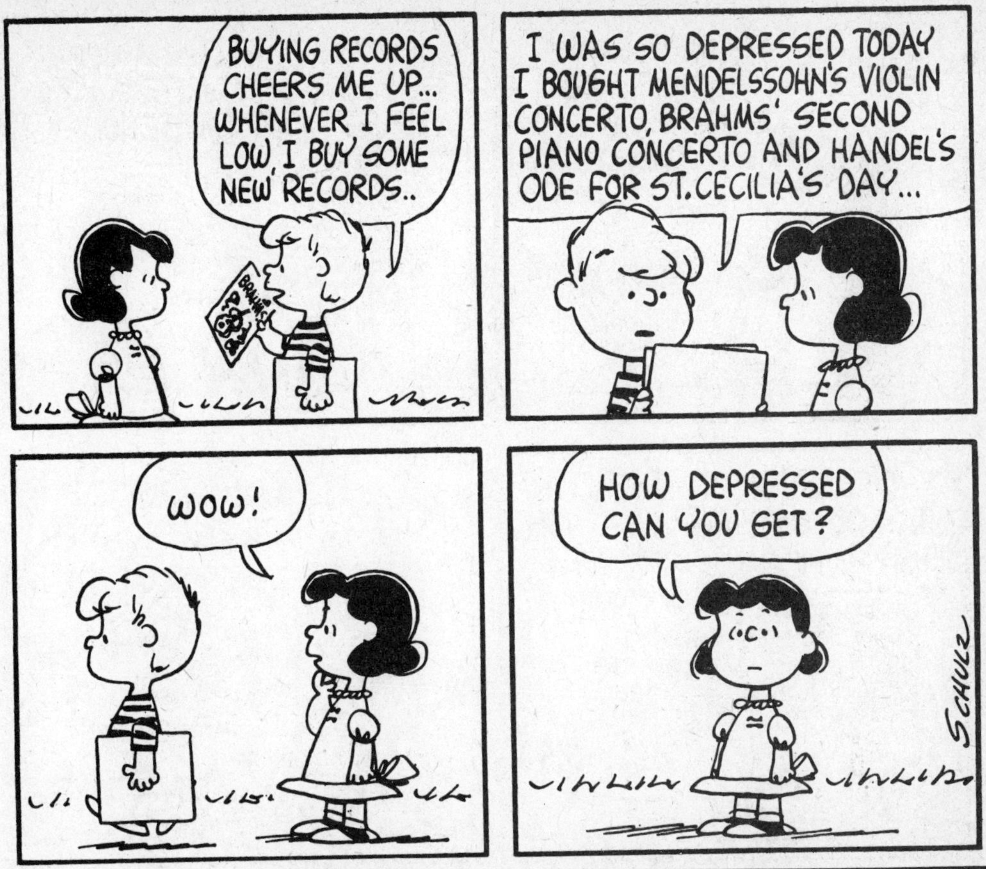
BUYING RECORDS CHEERS ME UP... WHENEVER I FEEL LOW, I BUY SOME NEW RECORDS..
I WAS SO DEPRESSED TODAY I BOUGHT MENDELSSOHN'S VIOLIN CONCERTO, BRAHMS' SECOND PIANO CONCERTO AND HANDEL'S ODE FOR ST. CECILIA'S DAY...
WOW!
HOW DEPRESSED CAN YOU GET?
SCHULZ

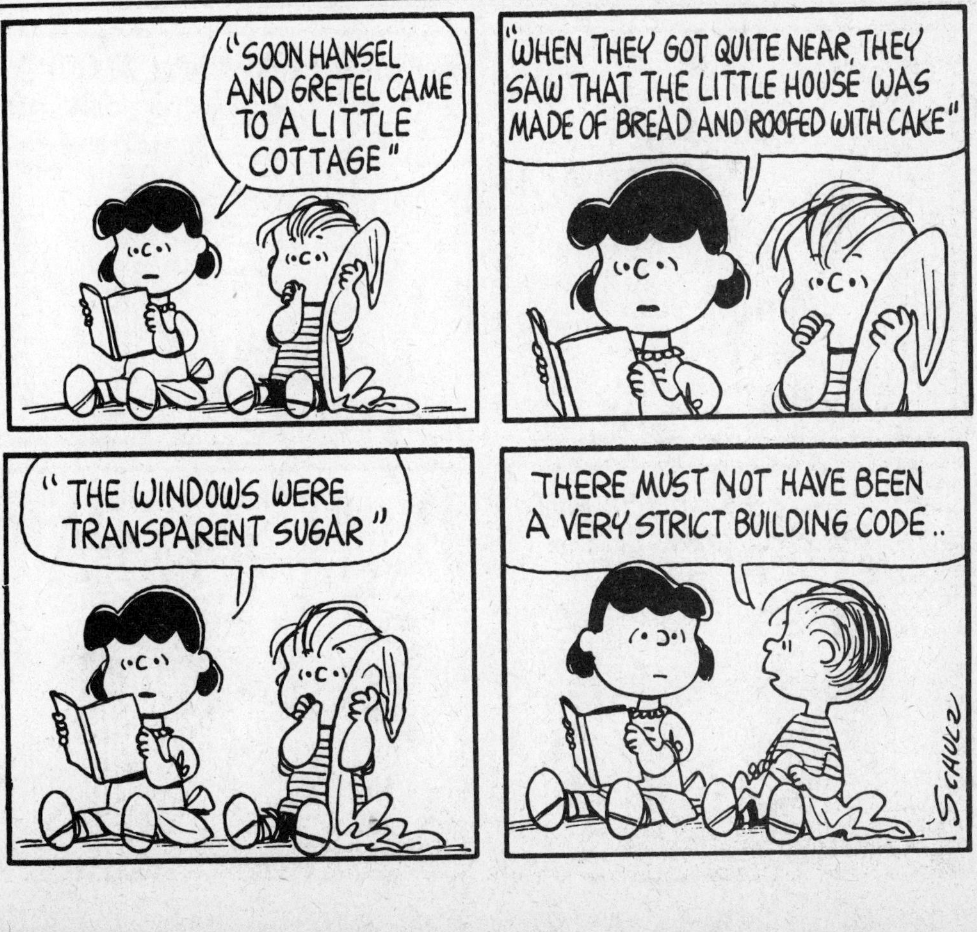
"SOON HANSEL AND GRETEL CAME TO A LITTLE COTTAGE"
"WHEN THEY GOT QUITE NEAR, THEY SAW THAT THE LITTLE HOUSE WAS MADE OF BREAD AND ROOFED WITH CAKE"
"THE WINDOWS WERE TRANSPARENT SUGAR"
THERE MUST NOT HAVE BEEN A VERY STRICT BUILDING CODE..
SCHULZ

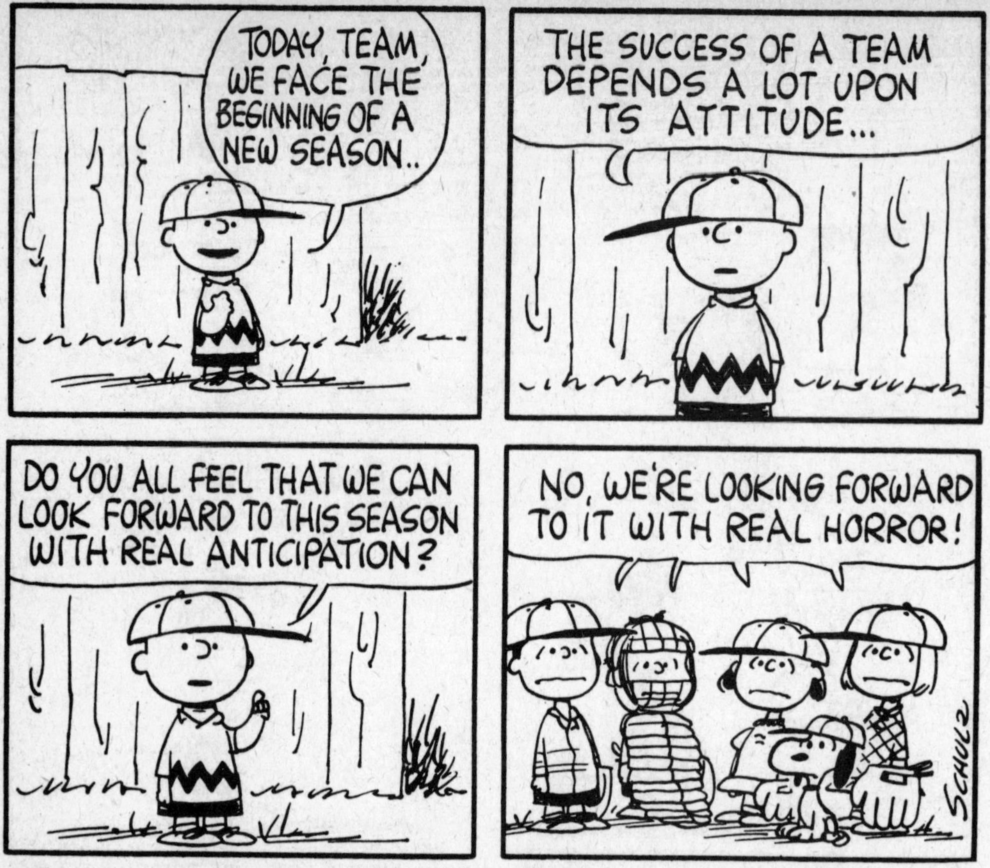
TODAY, TEAM, WE FACE THE BEGINNING OF A NEW SEASON..
THE SUCCESS OF A TEAM DEPENDS A LOT UPON ITS ATTITUDE...
DO YOU ALL FEEL THAT WE CAN LOOK FORWARD TO THIS SEASON WITH REAL ANTICIPATION?
NO, WE'RE LOOKING FORWARD TO IT WITH REAL HORROR!
SCHULZ

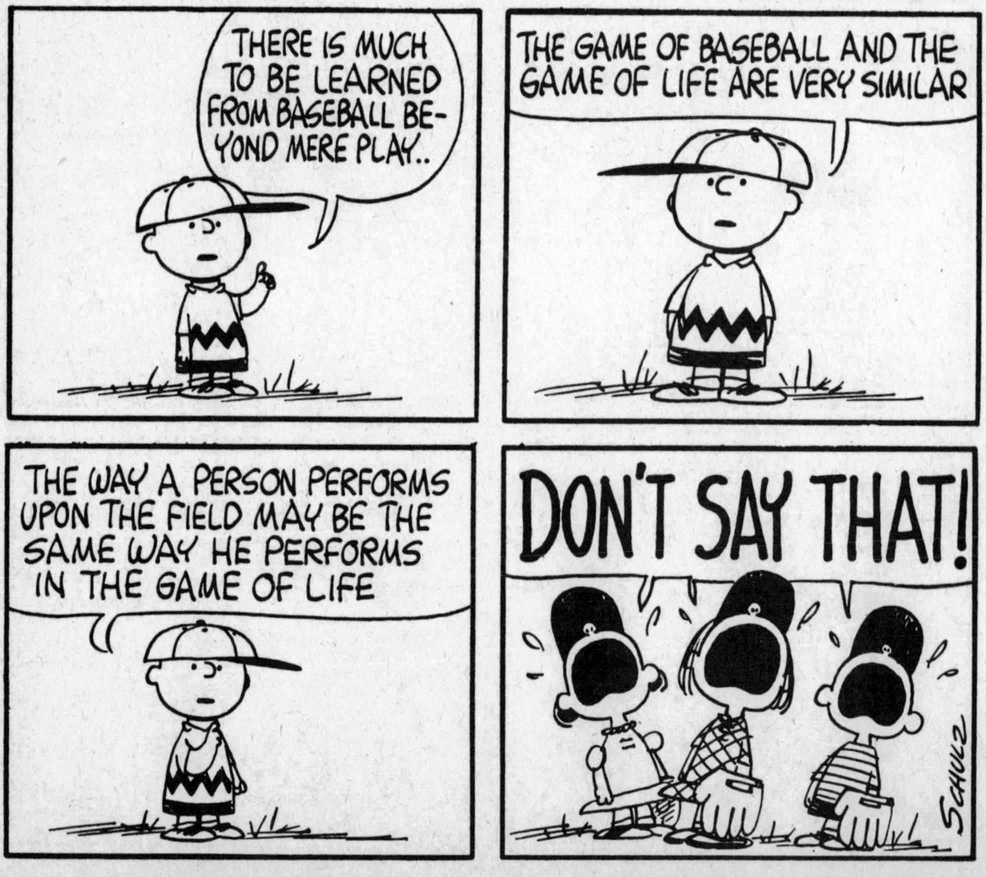
THERE IS MUCH TO BE LEARNED FROM BASEBALL BEYOND MERE PLAY..
THE GAME OF BASEBALL AND THE GAME OF LIFE ARE VERY SIMILAR
THE WAY A PERSON PERFORMS UPON THE FIELD MAY BE THE SAME WAY HE PERFORMS IN THE GAME OF LIFE
DON'T SAY THAT!
SCHULZ

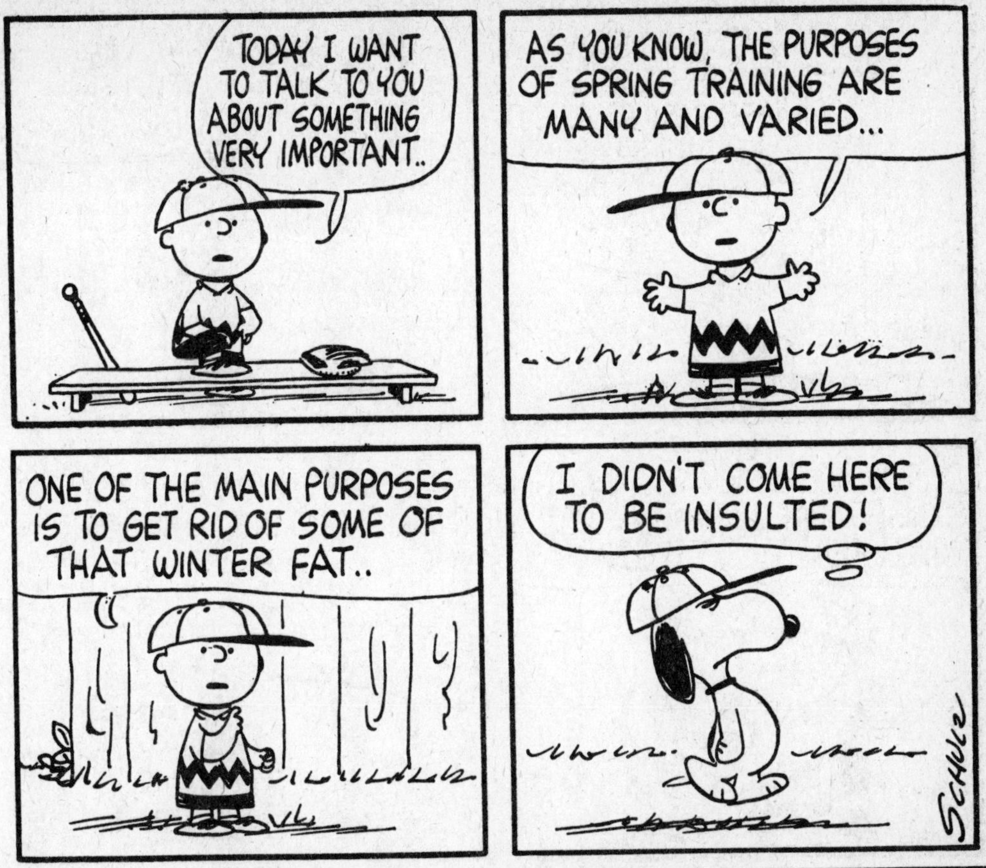
TODAY I WANT TO TALK TO YOU ABOUT SOMETHING VERY IMPORTANT..
AS YOU KNOW, THE PURPOSES OF SPRING TRAINING ARE MANY AND VARIED...
ONE OF THE MAIN PURPOSES IS TO GET RID OF SOME OF THAT WINTER FAT..
I DIDN'T COME HERE TO BE INSULTED!
SCHULZ

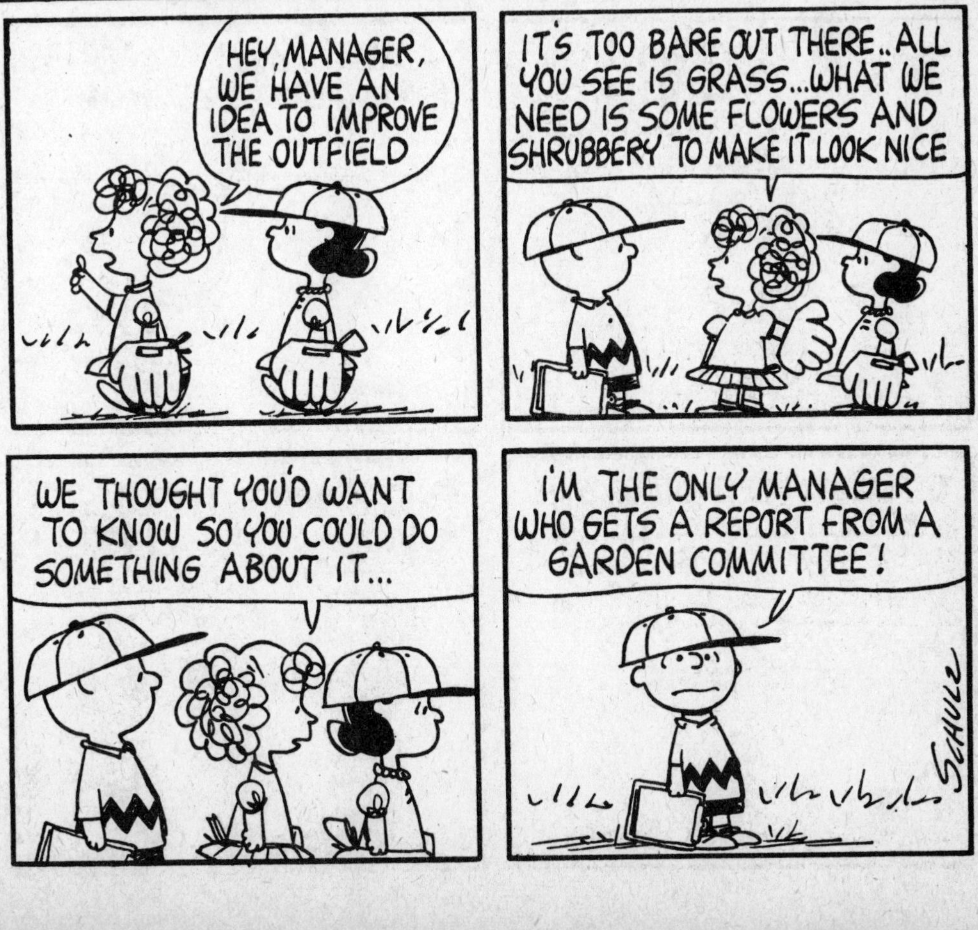
HEY, MANAGER, WE HAVE AN IDEA TO IMPROVE THE OUTFIELD
IT'S TOO BARE OUT THERE..ALL YOU SEE IS GRASS...WHAT WE NEED IS SOME FLOWERS AND SHRUBBERY TO MAKE IT LOOK NICE
WE THOUGHT YOU'D WANT TO KNOW SO YOU COULD DO SOMETHING ABOUT IT...
I'M THE ONLY MANAGER WHO GETS A REPORT FROM A GARDEN COMMITTEE!
SCHULZ

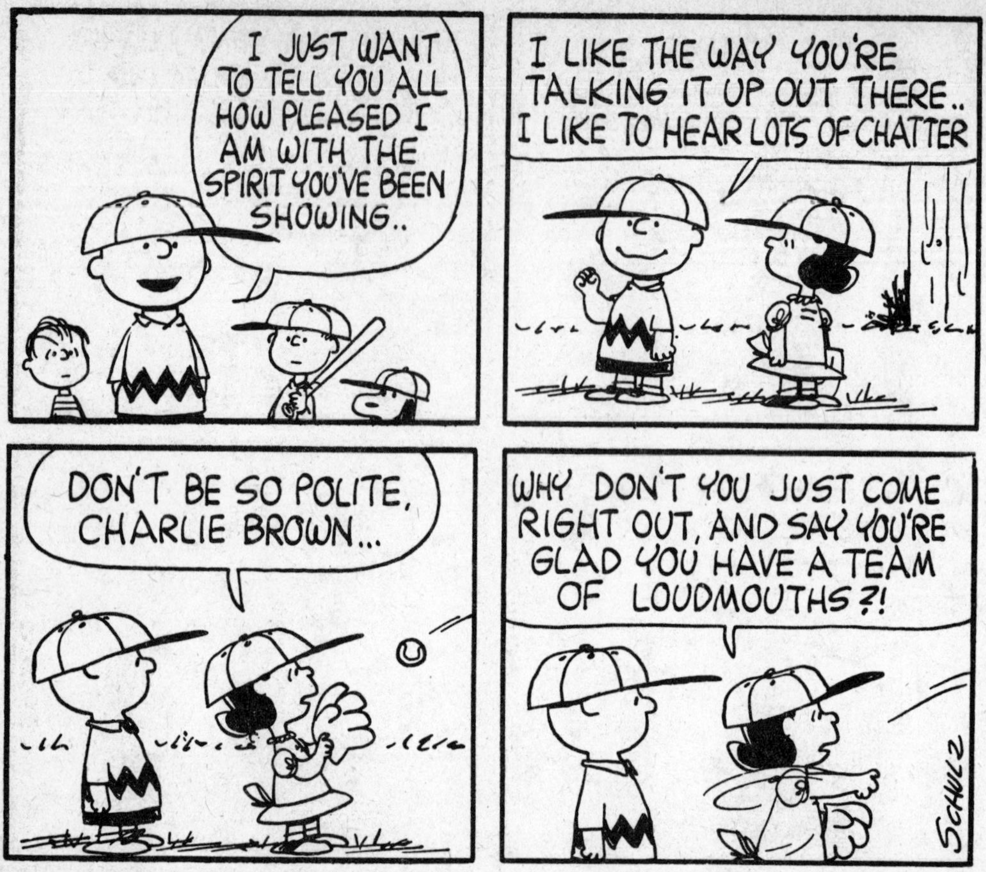
I JUST WANT TO TELL YOU ALL HOW PLEASED I AM WITH THE SPIRIT YOU'VE BEEN SHOWING..
I LIKE THE WAY YOU'RE TALKING IT UP OUT THERE.. I LIKE TO HEAR LOTS OF CHATTER
DON'T BE SO POLITE, CHARLIE BROWN...
WHY DON'T YOU JUST COME RIGHT OUT, AND SAY YOU'RE GLAD YOU HAVE A TEAM OF LOUDMOUTHS?!
SCHULZ

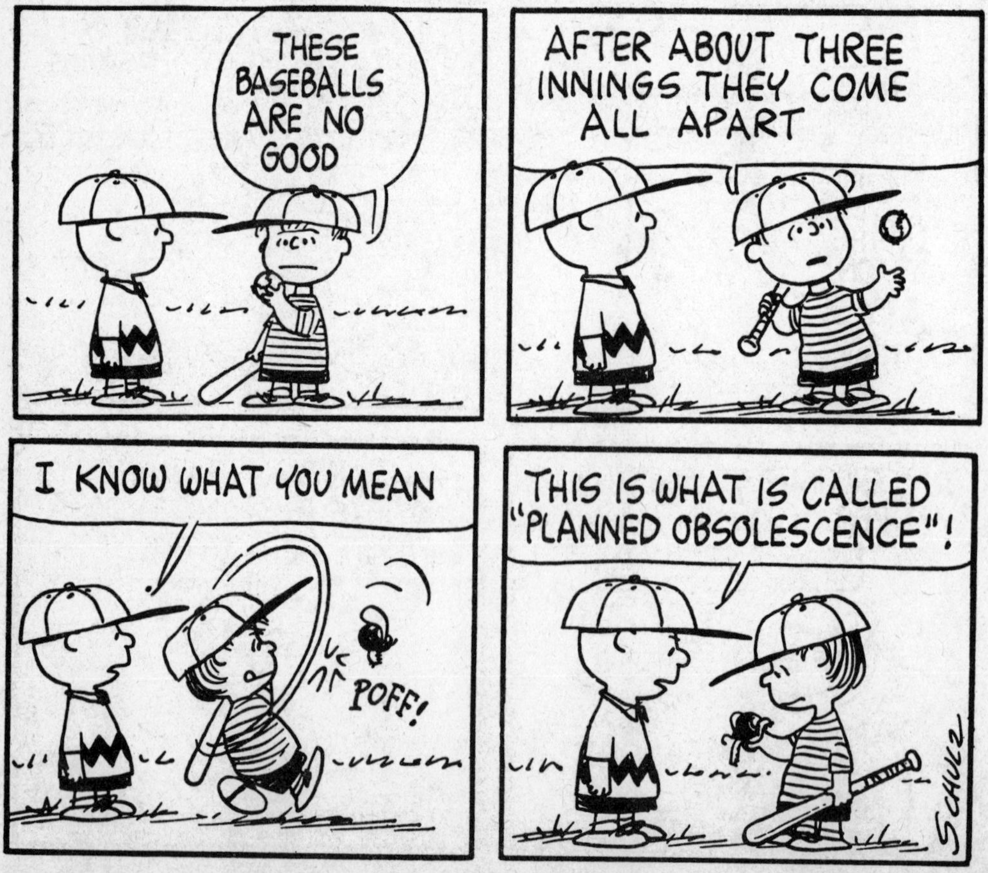
THESE BASEBALLS ARE NO GOOD
AFTER ABOUT THREE INNINGS THEY COME ALL APART
I KNOW WHAT YOU MEAN
POFF!
THIS IS WHAT IS CALLED "PLANNED OBSOLESCENCE"!
SCHULZ

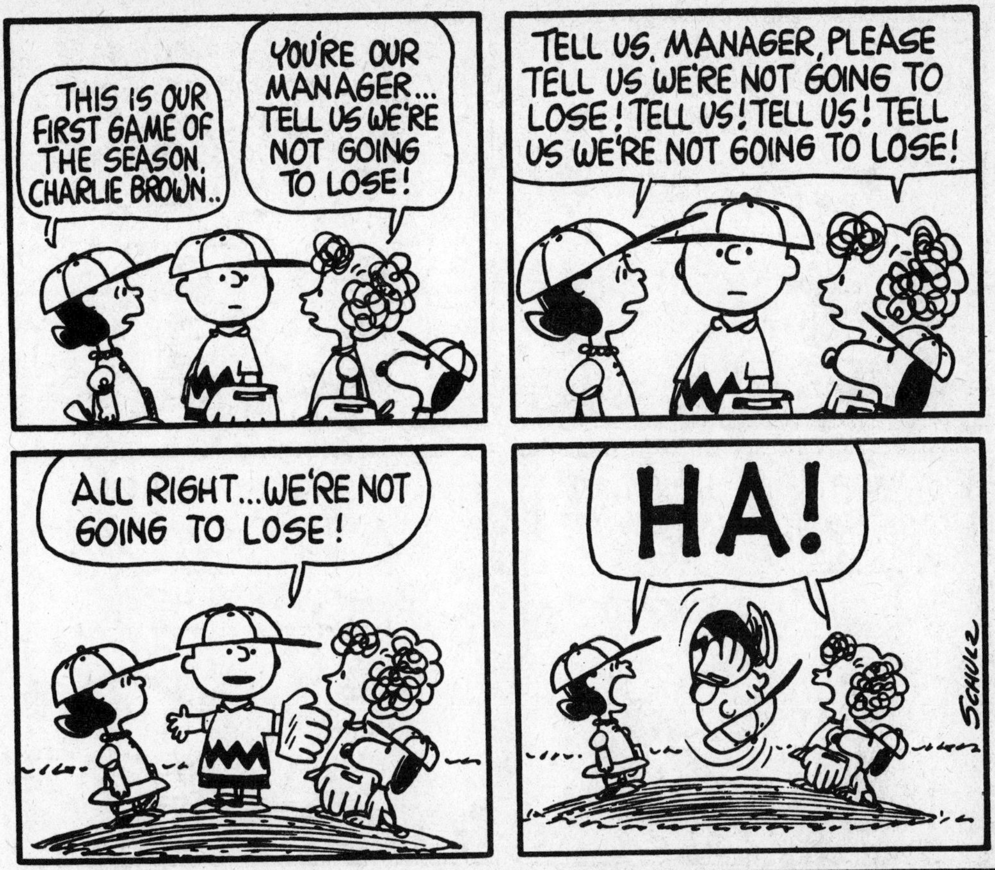
THIS IS OUR FIRST GAME OF THE SEASON, CHARLIE BROWN..
YOU'RE OUR MANAGER... TELL US WE'RE NOT GOING TO LOSE!
TELL US, MANAGER, PLEASE TELL US WE'RE NOT GOING TO LOSE! TELL US! TELL US! TELL US WE'RE NOT GOING TO LOSE!
ALL RIGHT...WE'RE NOT GOING TO LOSE!
HA!
SCHULZ

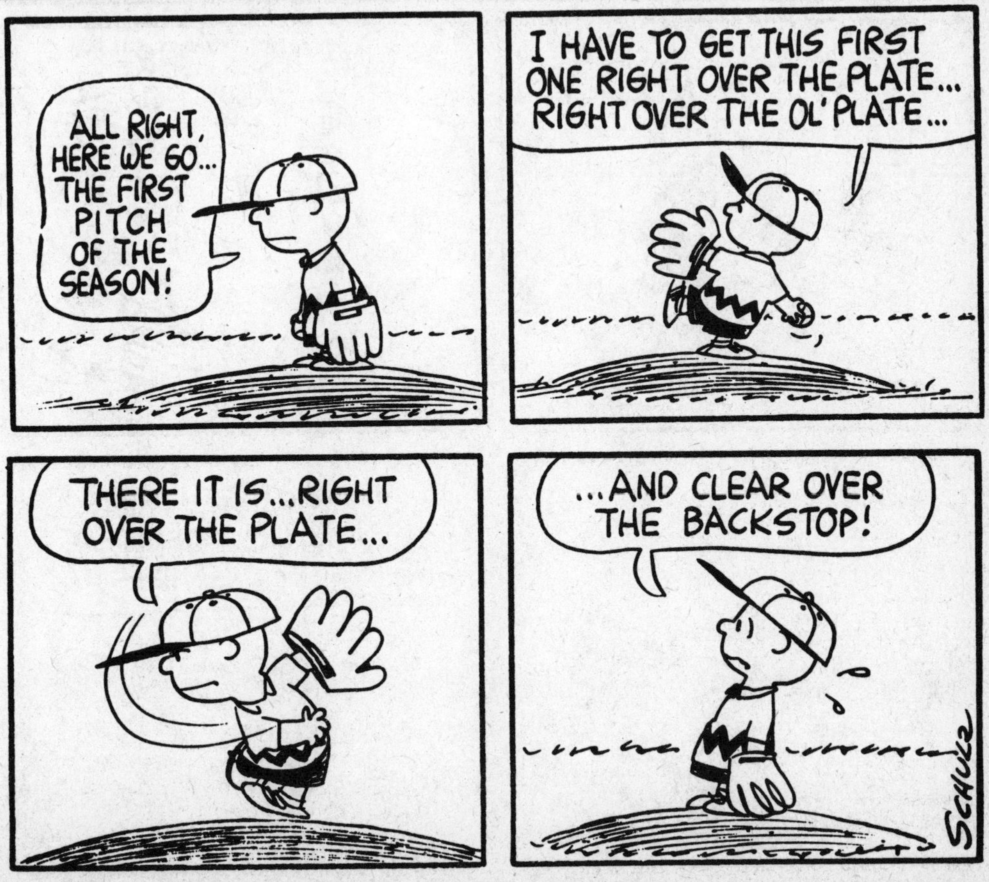
ALL RIGHT, HERE WE GO... THE FIRST PITCH OF THE SEASON!
I HAVE TO GET THIS FIRST ONE RIGHT OVER THE PLATE... RIGHT OVER THE OL' PLATE...
THERE IT IS...RIGHT OVER THE PLATE...
...AND CLEAR OVER THE BACKSTOP!
SCHULZ

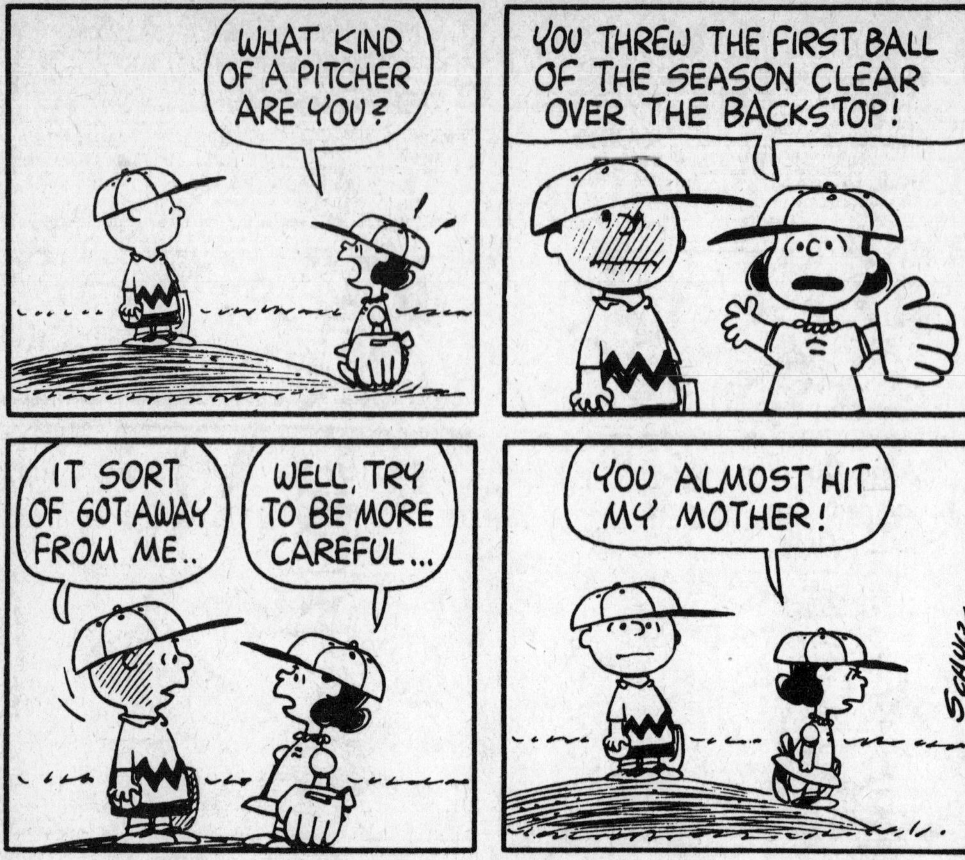
WHAT KIND OF A PITCHER ARE YOU?
YOU THREW THE FIRST BALL OF THE SEASON CLEAR OVER THE BACKSTOP!
IT SORT OF GOT AWAY FROM ME..
WELL, TRY TO BE MORE CAREFUL...
YOU ALMOST HIT MY MOTHER!
SCHULZ

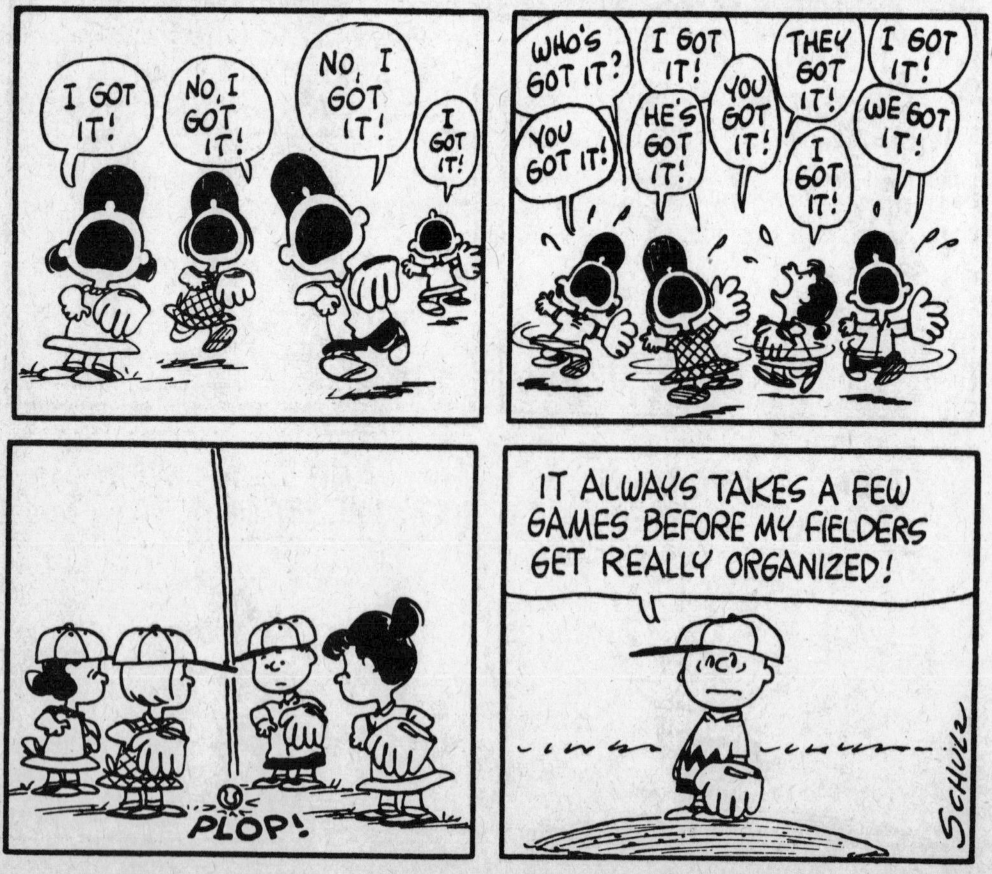
I GOT IT!
NO, I GOT IT!
NO, I GOT IT!
I GOT IT!
WHO'S GOT IT?
I GOT IT!
THEY GOT IT!
I GOT IT!
YOU GOT IT!
HE'S GOT IT!
YOU GOT IT!
I GOT IT!
WE GOT IT!
PLOP!
IT ALWAYS TAKES A FEW GAMES BEFORE MY FIELDERS GET REALLY ORGANIZED!
SCHULZ

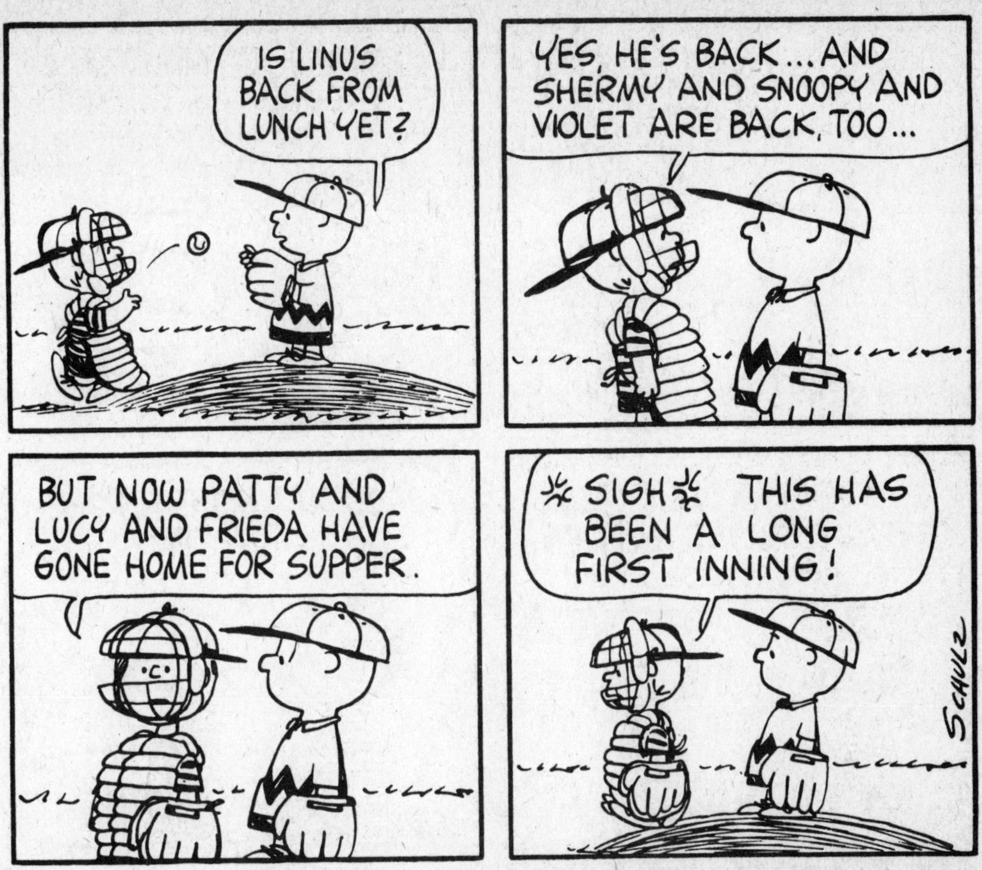
IS LINUS BACK FROM LUNCH YET?
YES, HE'S BACK... AND SHERMY AND SNOOPY AND VIOLET ARE BACK, TOO...
BUT NOW PATTY AND LUCY AND FRIEDA HAVE GONE HOME FOR SUPPER.
SIGH THIS HAS BEEN A LONG FIRST INNING!
SCHULZ

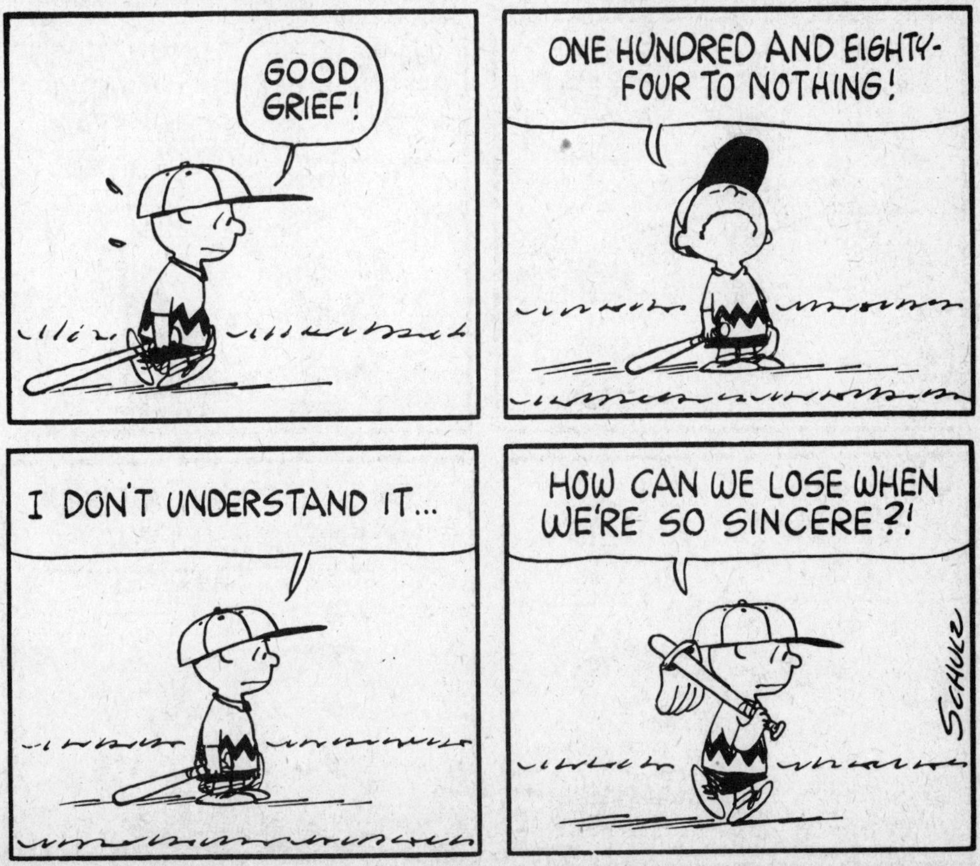
GOOD GRIEF!
ONE HUNDRED AND EIGHTY-FOUR TO NOTHING!
I DON'T UNDERSTAND IT...
HOW CAN WE LOSE WHEN WE'RE SO SINCERE?!
SCHULZ

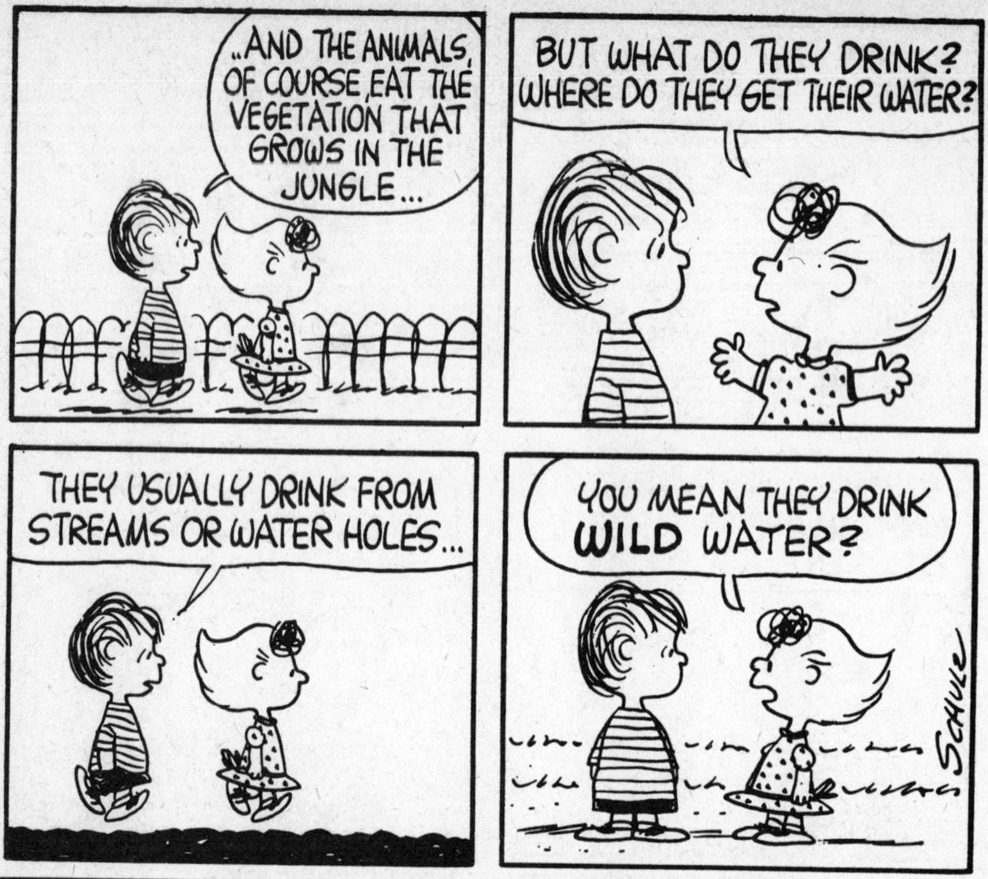
..AND THE ANIMALS, OF COURSE, EAT THE VEGETATION THAT GROWS IN THE JUNGLE...
BUT WHAT DO THEY DRINK? WHERE DO THEY GET THEIR WATER?
THEY USUALLY DRINK FROM STREAMS OR WATER HOLES...
YOU MEAN THEY DRINK **WILD** WATER?
SCHULZ

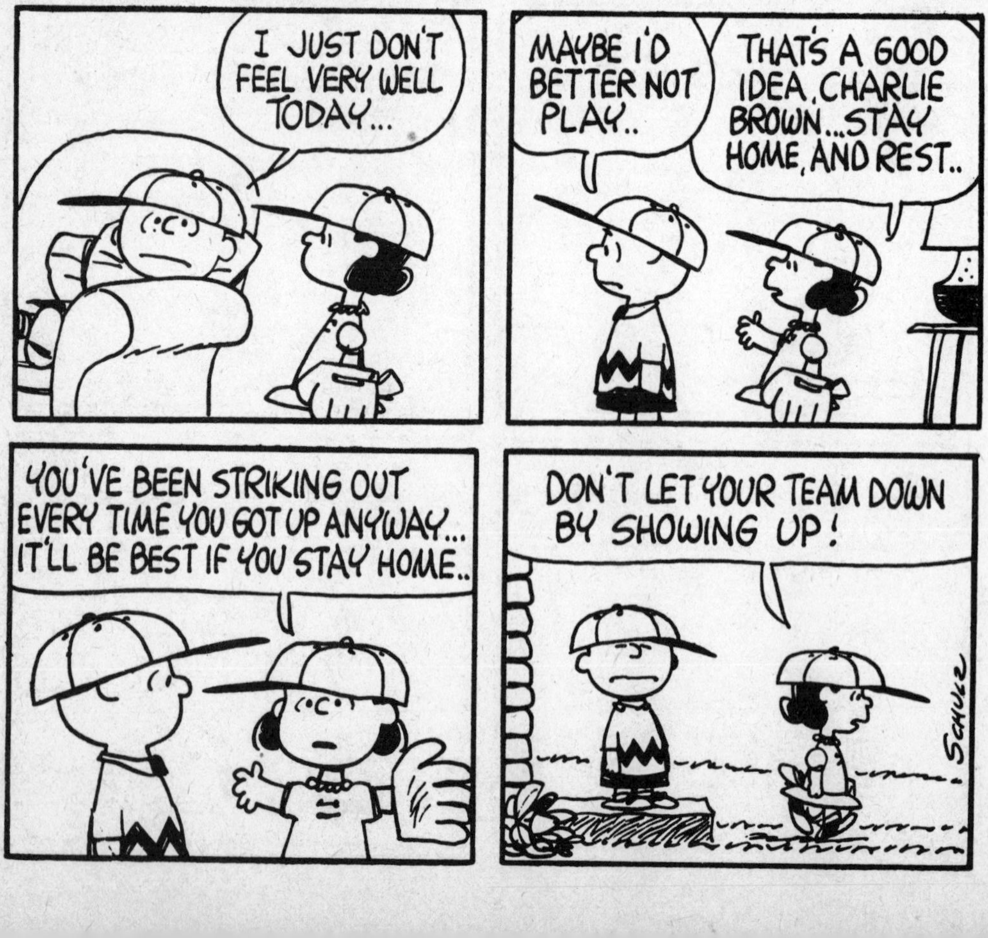
I JUST DON'T FEEL VERY WELL TODAY...
MAYBE I'D BETTER NOT PLAY..
THAT'S A GOOD IDEA, CHARLIE BROWN...STAY HOME, AND REST..
YOU'VE BEEN STRIKING OUT EVERY TIME YOU GOT UP ANYWAY... IT'LL BE BEST IF YOU STAY HOME..
DON'T LET YOUR TEAM DOWN BY SHOWING UP!
SCHULZ

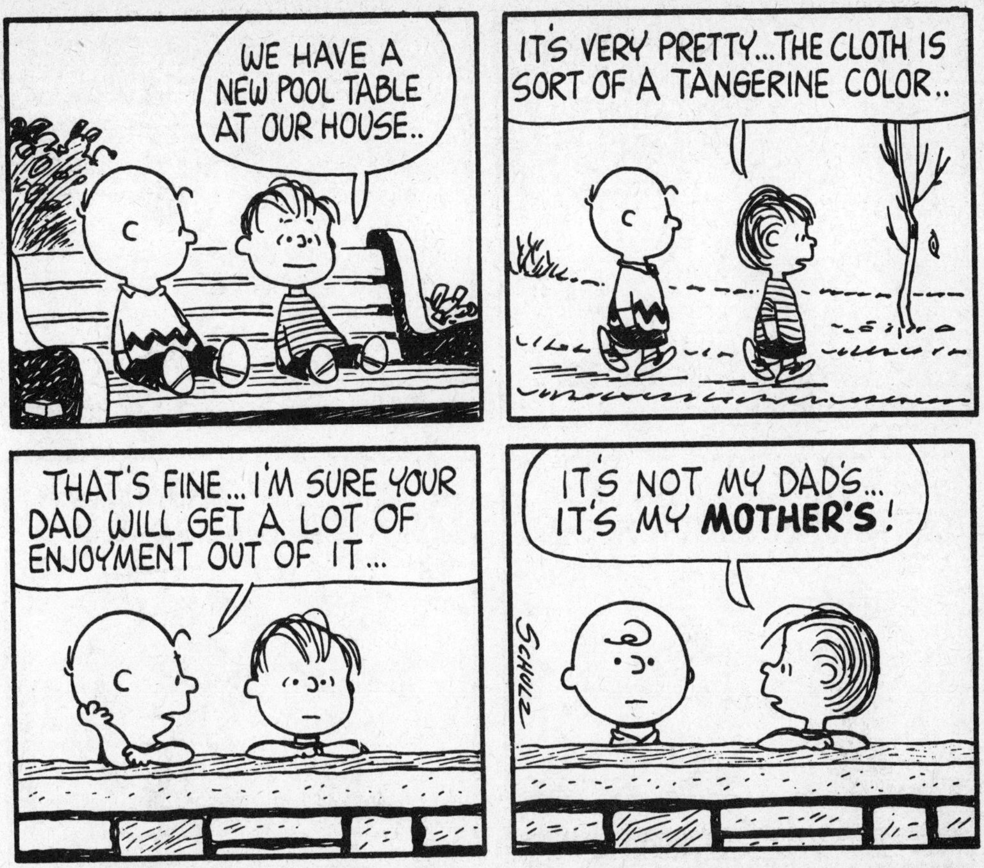

WE HAVE A NEW POOL TABLE AT OUR HOUSE..
IT'S VERY PRETTY...THE CLOTH IS SORT OF A TANGERINE COLOR..
THAT'S FINE... I'M SURE YOUR DAD WILL GET A LOT OF ENJOYMENT OUT OF IT...
IT'S NOT MY DAD'S... IT'S MY **MOTHER'S**!
SCHULZ

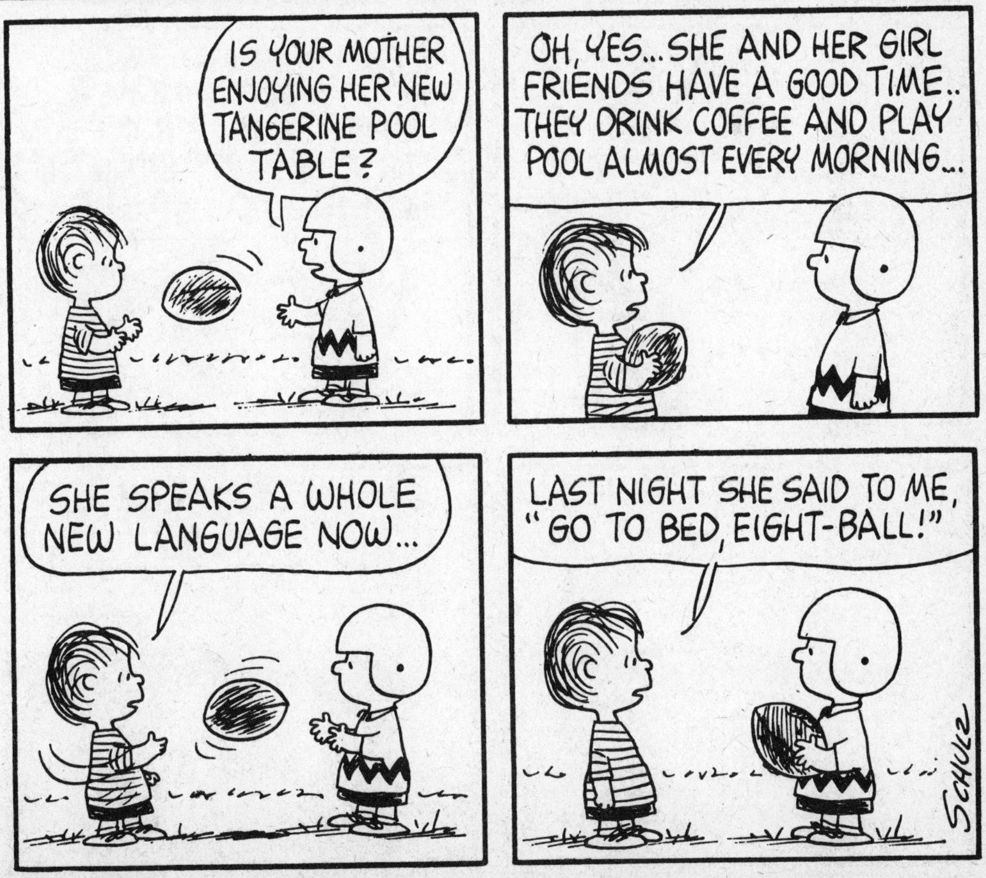

IS YOUR MOTHER ENJOYING HER NEW TANGERINE POOL TABLE?
OH, YES... SHE AND HER GIRL FRIENDS HAVE A GOOD TIME.. THEY DRINK COFFEE AND PLAY POOL ALMOST EVERY MORNING...
SHE SPEAKS A WHOLE NEW LANGUAGE NOW...
LAST NIGHT SHE SAID TO ME, "GO TO BED, EIGHT-BALL!"
SCHULZ

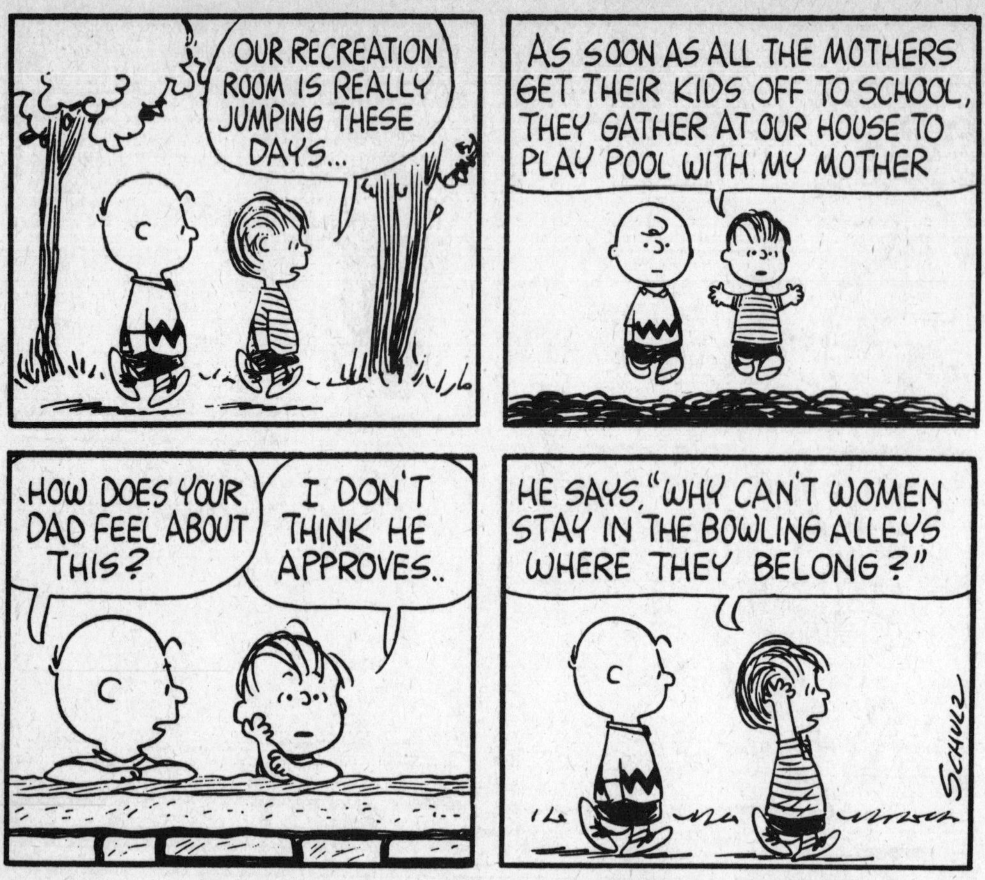
OUR RECREATION ROOM IS REALLY JUMPING THESE DAYS...
AS SOON AS ALL THE MOTHERS GET THEIR KIDS OFF TO SCHOOL, THEY GATHER AT OUR HOUSE TO PLAY POOL WITH MY MOTHER
HOW DOES YOUR DAD FEEL ABOUT THIS?
I DON'T THINK HE APPROVES..
HE SAYS, "WHY CAN'T WOMEN STAY IN THE BOWLING ALLEYS WHERE THEY BELONG?"
SCHULZ

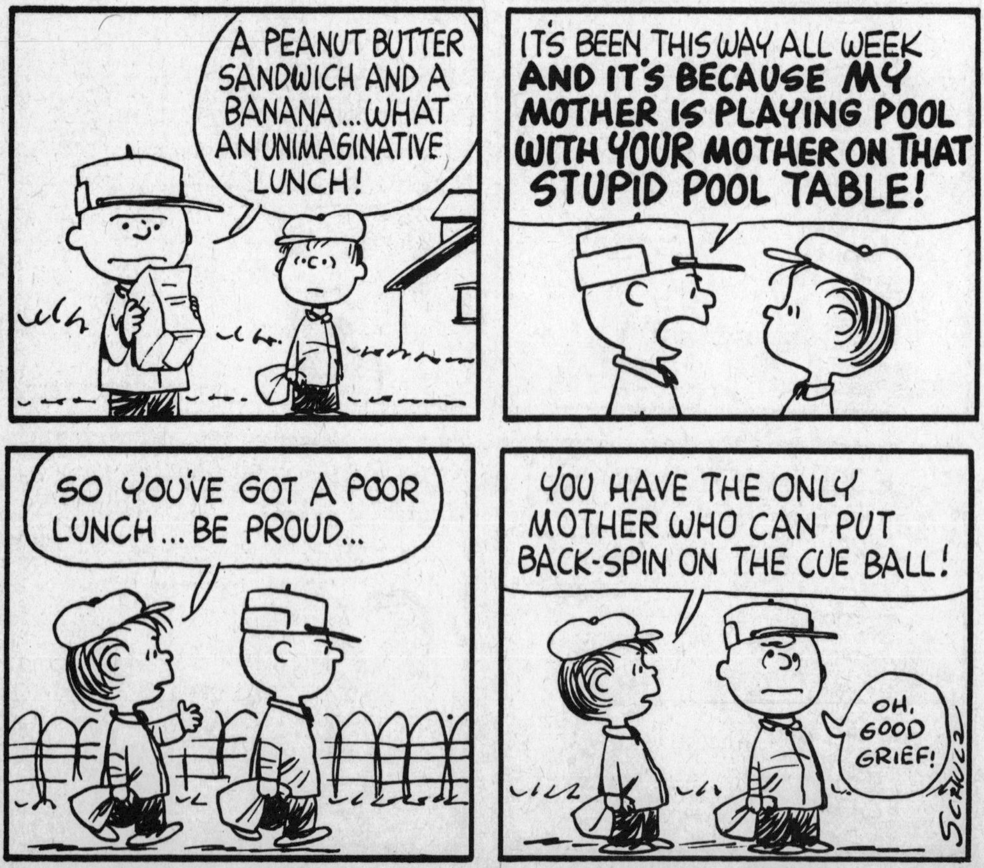
A PEANUT BUTTER SANDWICH AND A BANANA...WHAT AN UNIMAGINATIVE LUNCH!
IT'S BEEN THIS WAY ALL WEEK AND IT'S BECAUSE MY MOTHER IS PLAYING POOL WITH YOUR MOTHER ON THAT STUPID POOL TABLE!
SO YOU'VE GOT A POOR LUNCH... BE PROUD...
YOU HAVE THE ONLY MOTHER WHO CAN PUT BACK-SPIN ON THE CUE BALL!
OH, GOOD GRIEF!
SCHULZ

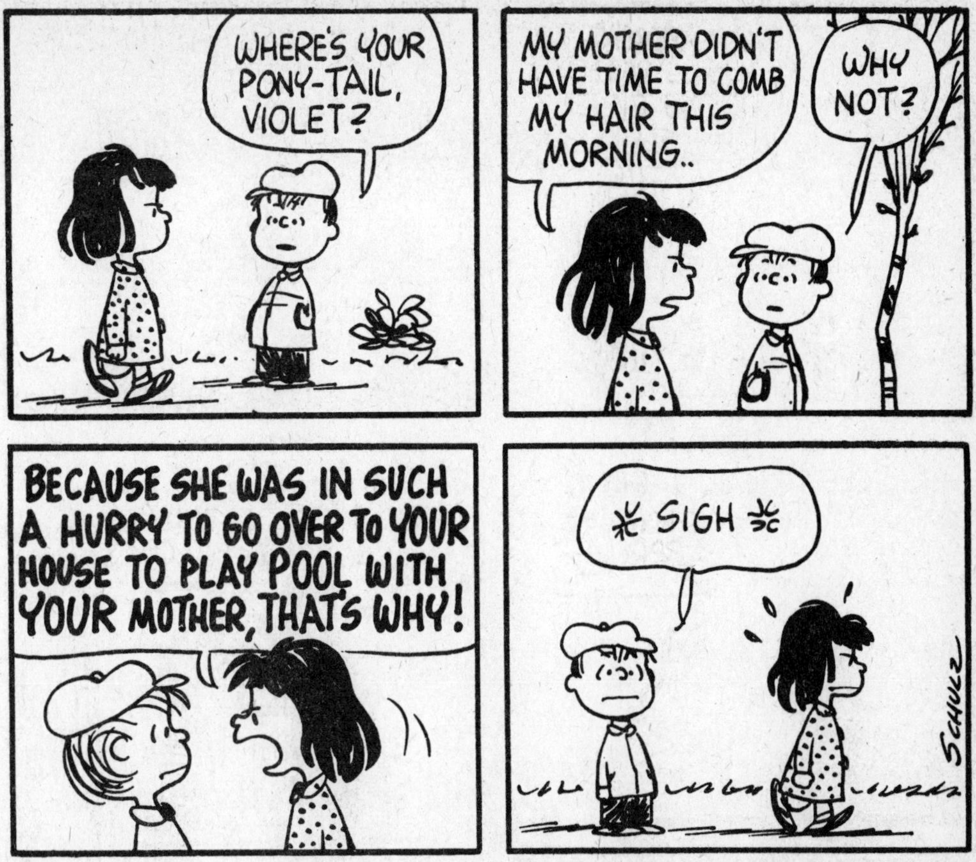
WHERE'S YOUR PONY-TAIL, VIOLET?
MY MOTHER DIDN'T HAVE TIME TO COMB MY HAIR THIS MORNING..
WHY NOT?
BECAUSE SHE WAS IN SUCH A HURRY TO GO OVER TO YOUR HOUSE TO PLAY POOL WITH YOUR MOTHER, THAT'S WHY!
SIGH
SCHULZ

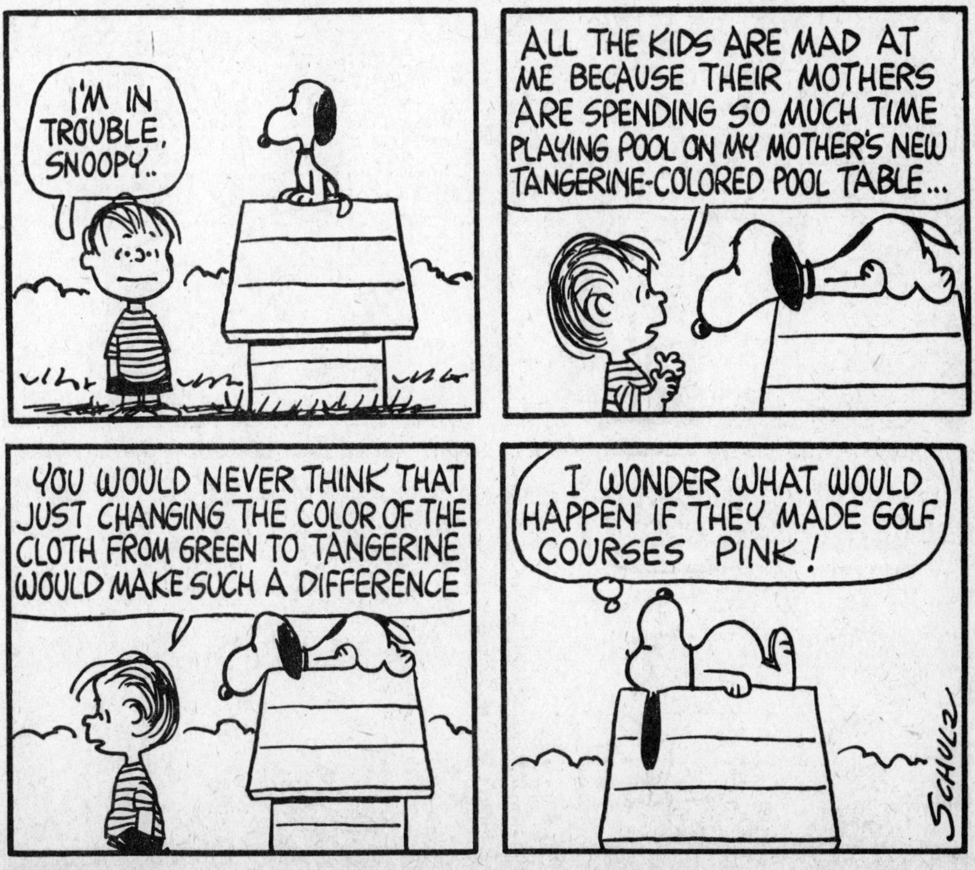
I'M IN TROUBLE, SNOOPY..
ALL THE KIDS ARE MAD AT ME BECAUSE THEIR MOTHERS ARE SPENDING SO MUCH TIME PLAYING POOL ON MY MOTHER'S NEW TANGERINE-COLORED POOL TABLE...
YOU WOULD NEVER THINK THAT JUST CHANGING THE COLOR OF THE CLOTH FROM GREEN TO TANGERINE WOULD MAKE SUCH A DIFFERENCE
I WONDER WHAT WOULD HAPPEN IF THEY MADE GOLF COURSES PINK!
SCHULZ

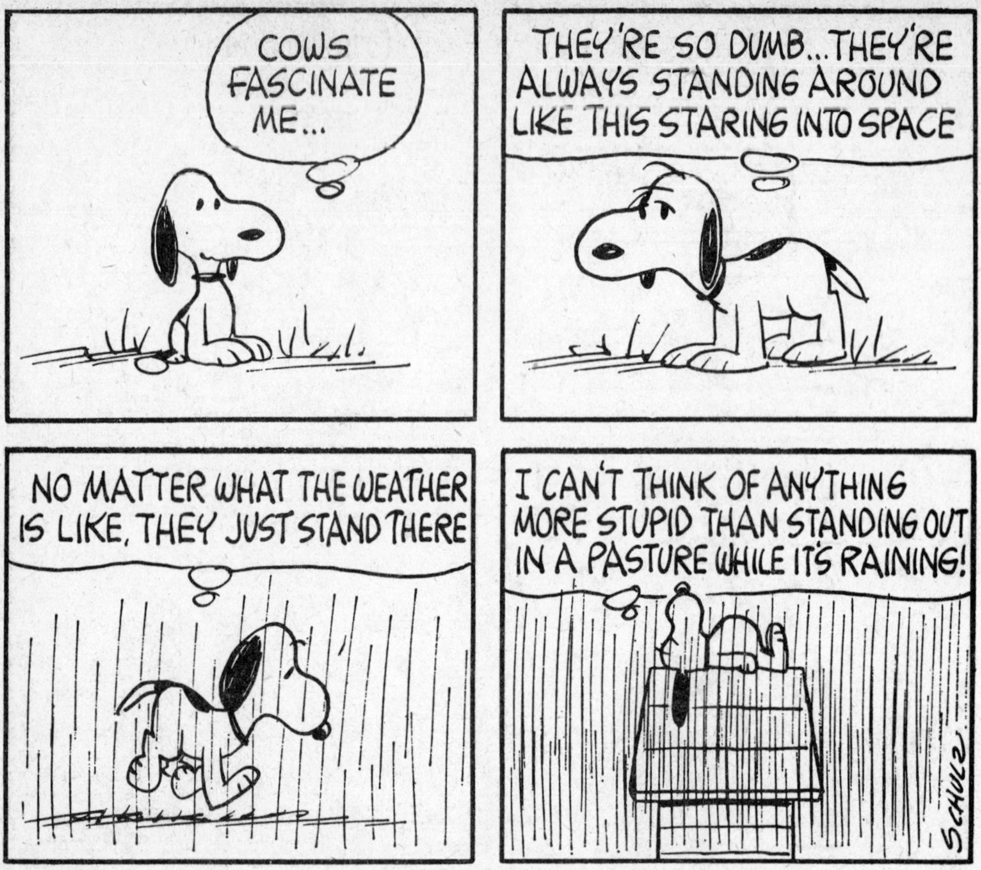
COWS FASCINATE ME...
THEY'RE SO DUMB...THEY'RE ALWAYS STANDING AROUND LIKE THIS STARING INTO SPACE
NO MATTER WHAT THE WEATHER IS LIKE, THEY JUST STAND THERE
I CAN'T THINK OF ANYTHING MORE STUPID THAN STANDING OUT IN A PASTURE WHILE IT'S RAINING!
SCHULZ

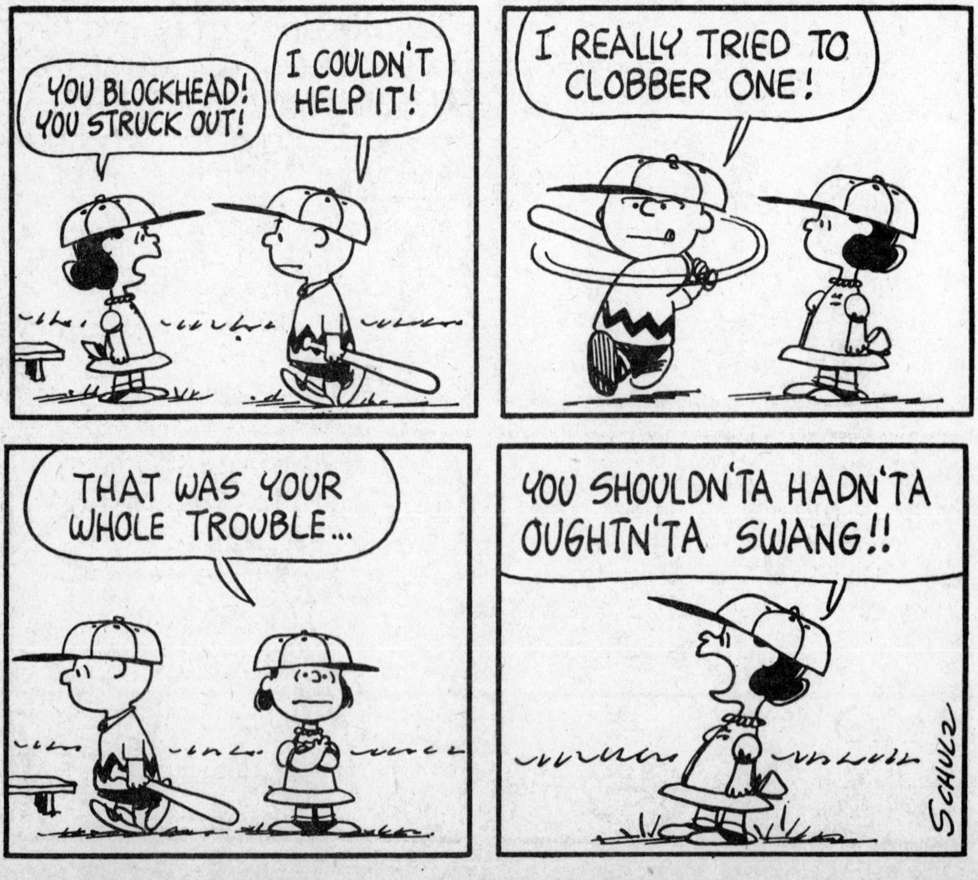
YOU BLOCKHEAD! YOU STRUCK OUT!
I COULDN'T HELP IT!
I REALLY TRIED TO CLOBBER ONE!
THAT WAS YOUR WHOLE TROUBLE...
YOU SHOULDN'TA HADN'TA OUGHTN'TA SWANG!!
SCHULZ

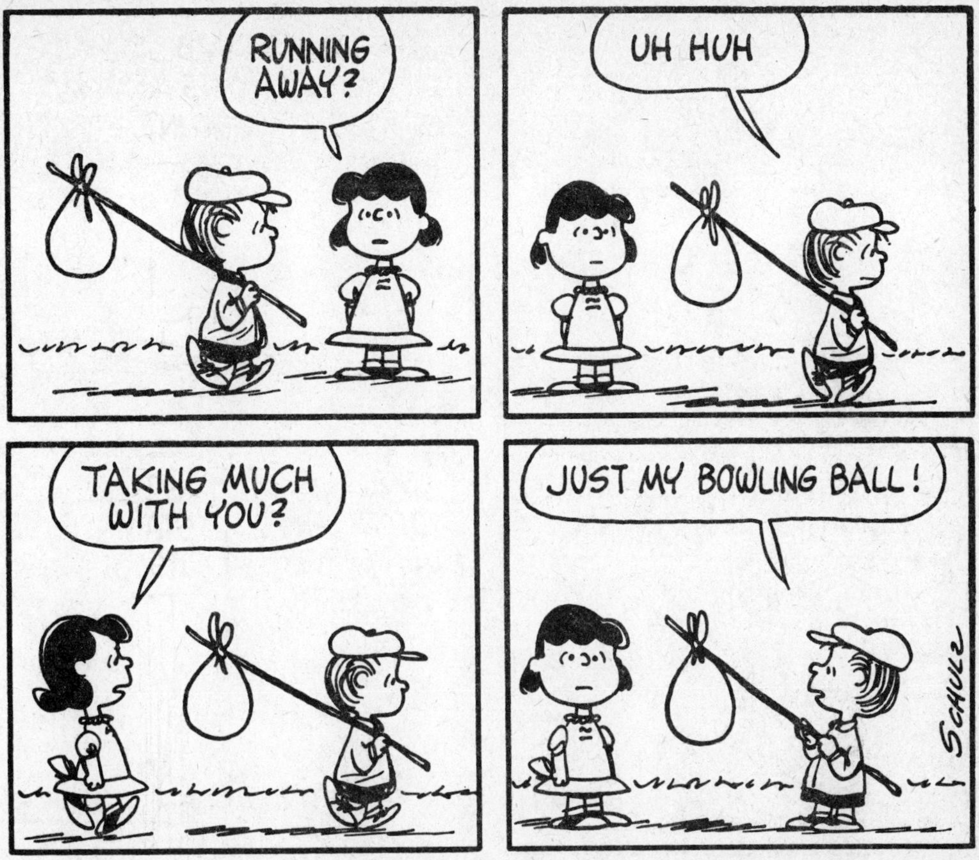
RUNNING AWAY?
UH HUH
TAKING MUCH WITH YOU?
JUST MY BOWLING BALL!
SCHULZ

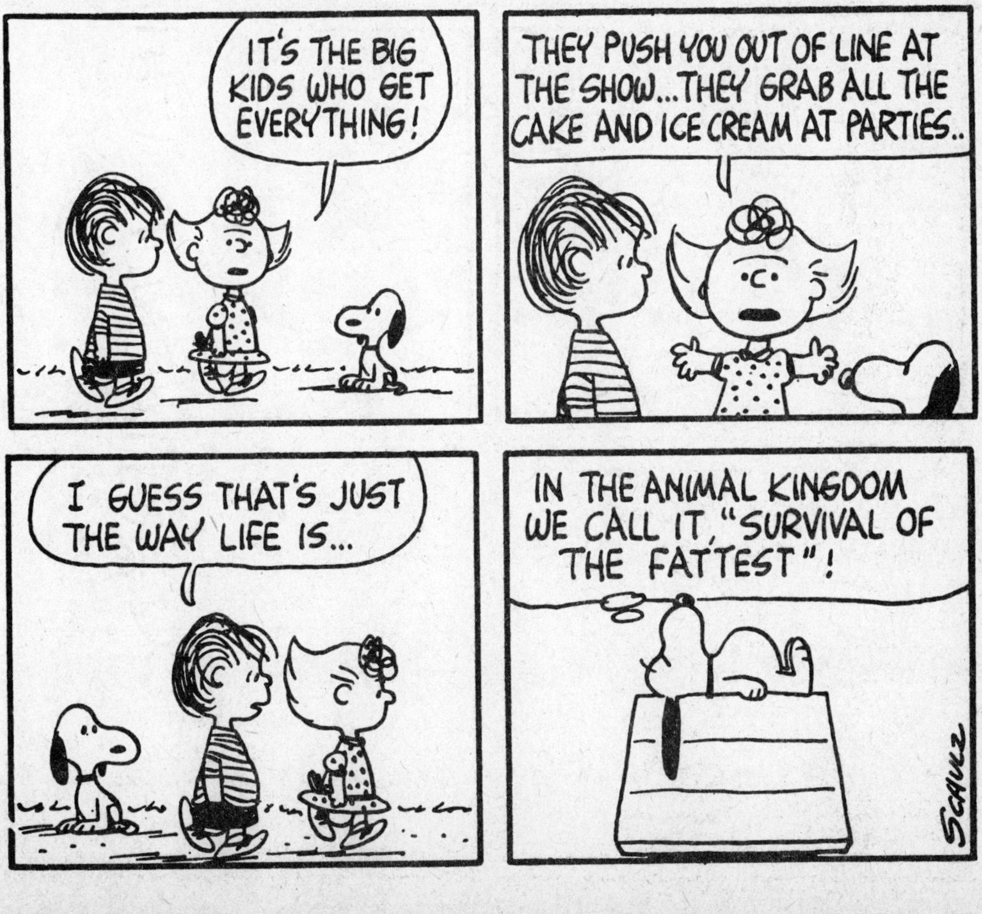
IT'S THE BIG KIDS WHO GET EVERYTHING!
THEY PUSH YOU OUT OF LINE AT THE SHOW...THEY GRAB ALL THE CAKE AND ICE CREAM AT PARTIES..
I GUESS THAT'S JUST THE WAY LIFE IS...
IN THE ANIMAL KINGDOM WE CALL IT, "SURVIVAL OF THE FATTEST"!
SCHULZ

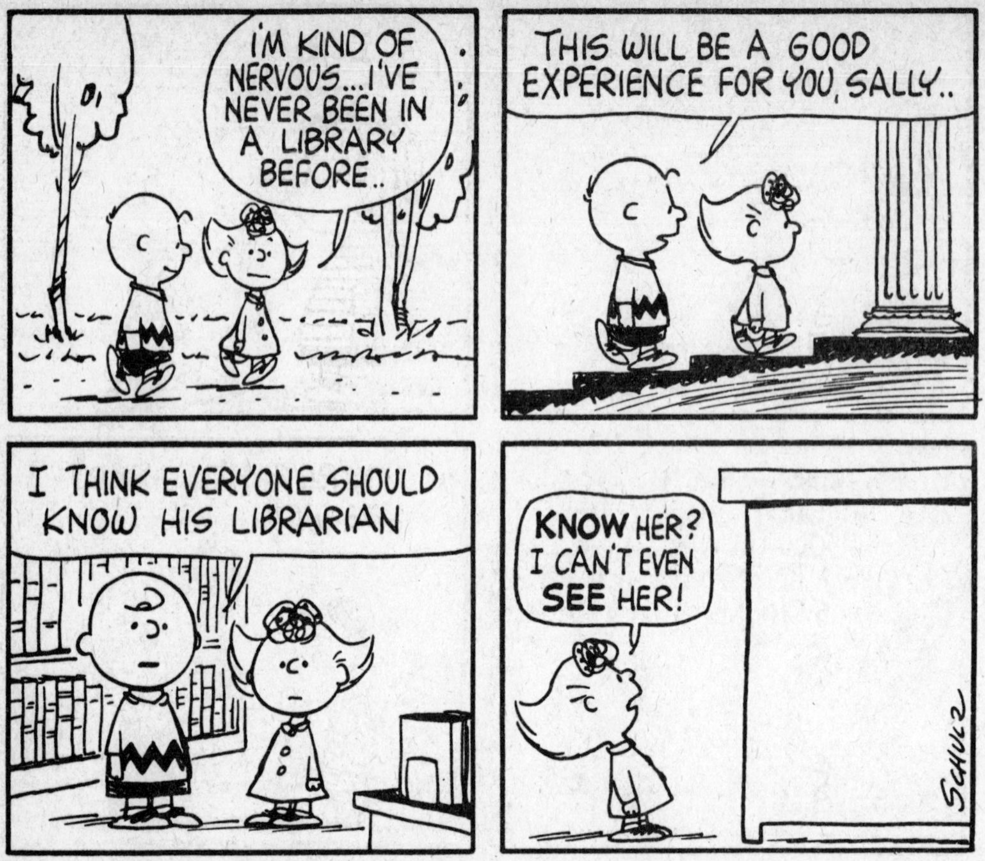
I'M KIND OF NERVOUS...I'VE NEVER BEEN IN A LIBRARY BEFORE..
THIS WILL BE A GOOD EXPERIENCE FOR YOU, SALLY..
I THINK EVERYONE SHOULD KNOW HIS LIBRARIAN
KNOW HER? I CAN'T EVEN SEE HER!
SCHULZ

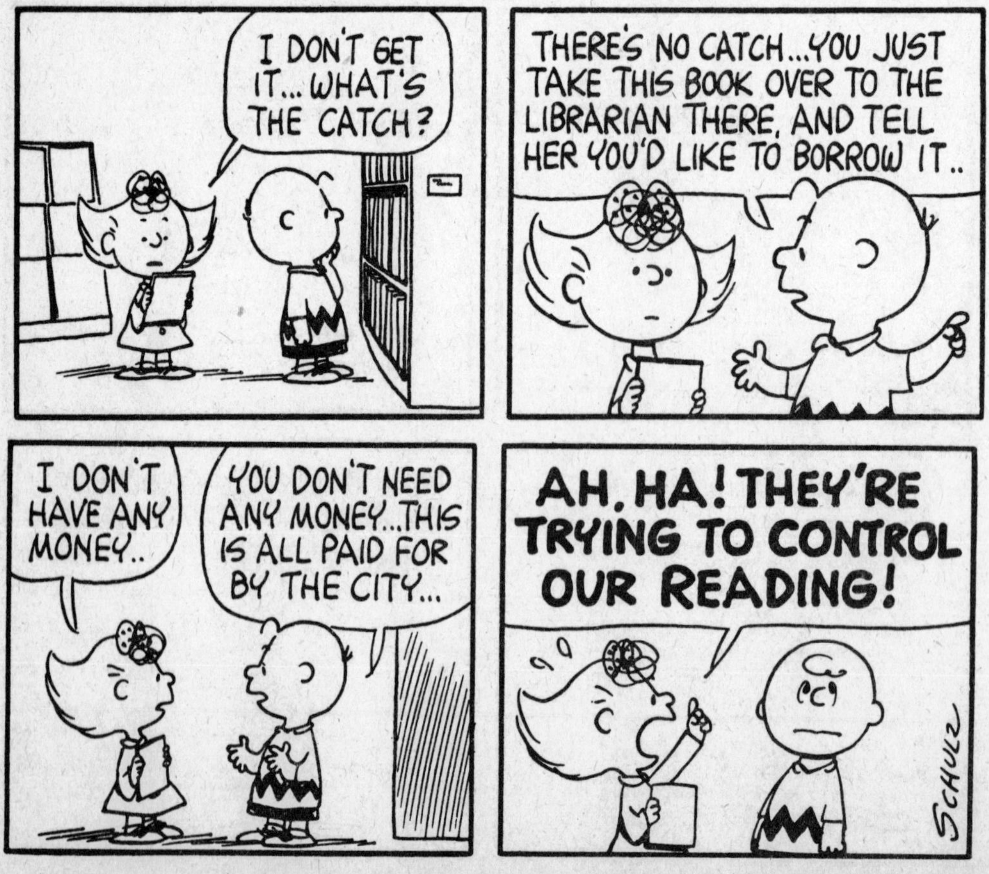
I DON'T GET IT...WHAT'S THE CATCH?
THERE'S NO CATCH...YOU JUST TAKE THIS BOOK OVER TO THE LIBRARIAN THERE, AND TELL HER YOU'D LIKE TO BORROW IT..
I DON'T HAVE ANY MONEY..
YOU DON'T NEED ANY MONEY...THIS IS ALL PAID FOR BY THE CITY...
AH, HA! THEY'RE TRYING TO CONTROL OUR READING!
SCHULZ

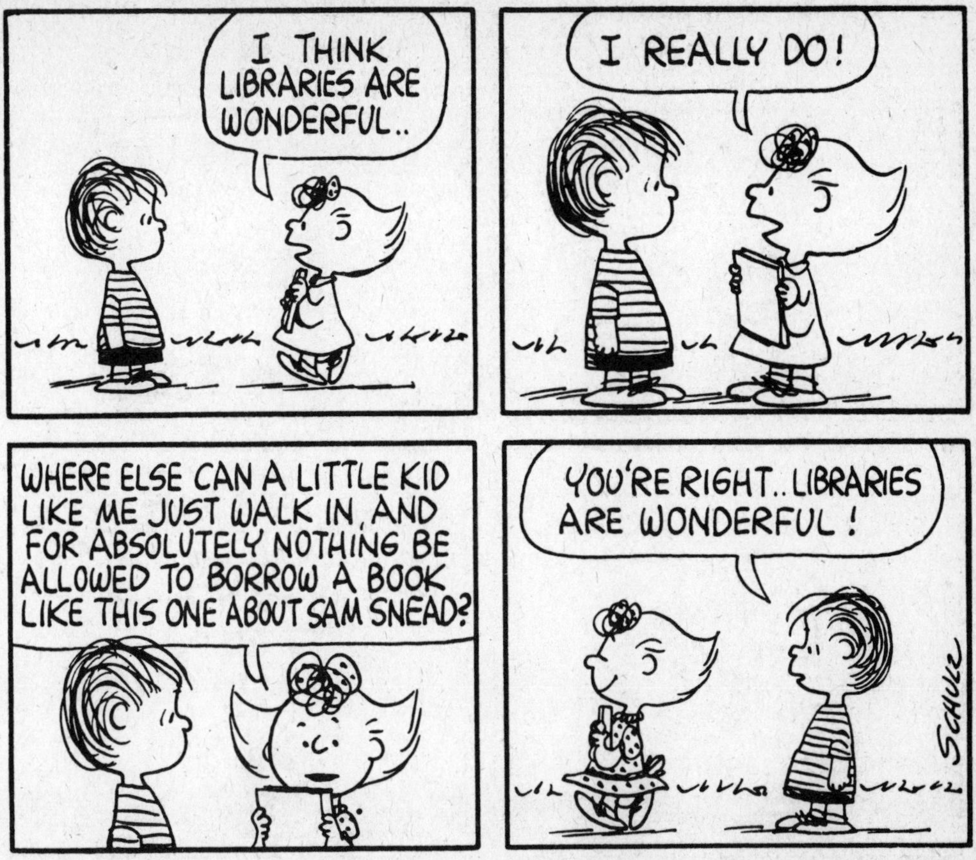
I THINK LIBRARIES ARE WONDERFUL..
I REALLY DO!
WHERE ELSE CAN A LITTLE KID LIKE ME JUST WALK IN, AND FOR ABSOLUTELY NOTHING BE ALLOWED TO BORROW A BOOK LIKE THIS ONE ABOUT SAM SNEAD?
YOU'RE RIGHT.. LIBRARIES ARE WONDERFUL!
SCHULZ

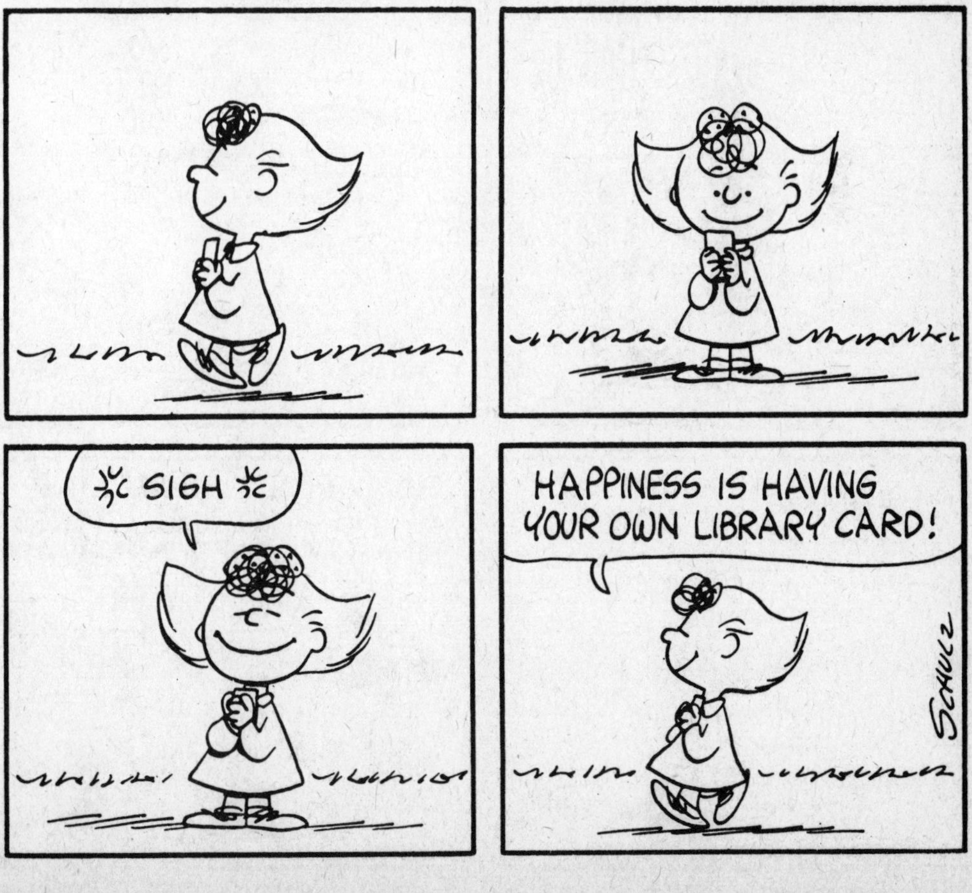
SIGH
HAPPINESS IS HAVING YOUR OWN LIBRARY CARD!
SCHULZ

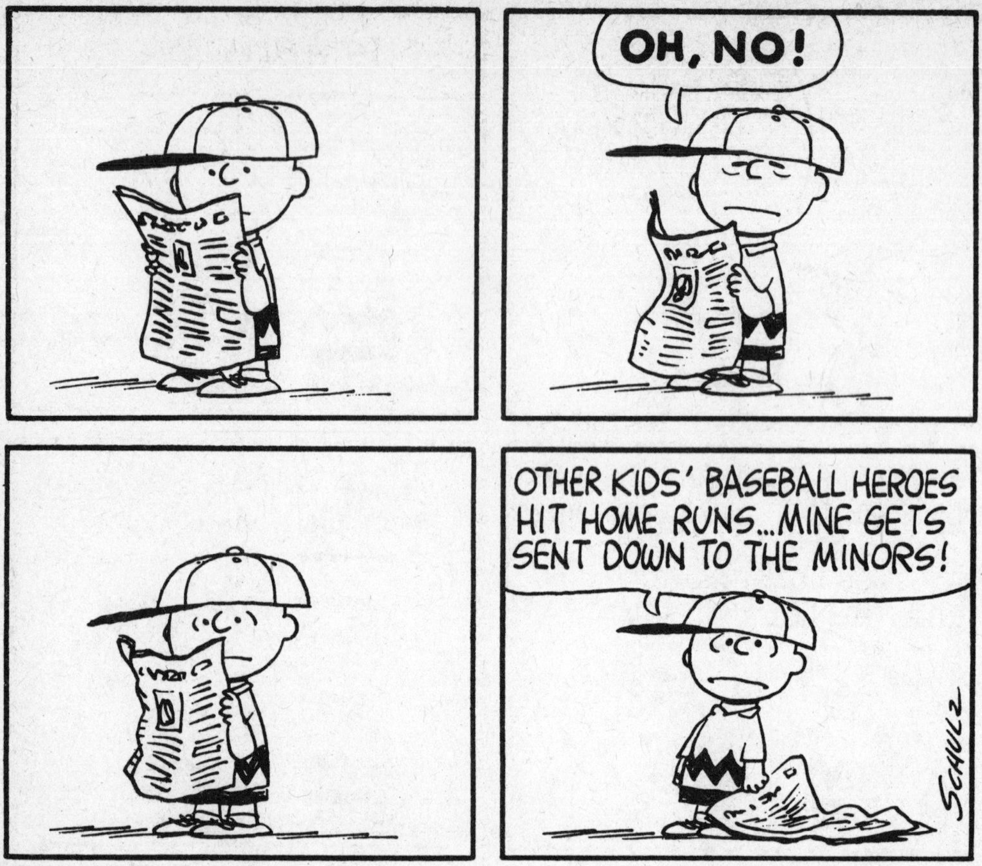
OH, NO!
OTHER KIDS' BASEBALL HEROES HIT HOME RUNS...MINE GETS SENT DOWN TO THE MINORS!
SCHULZ

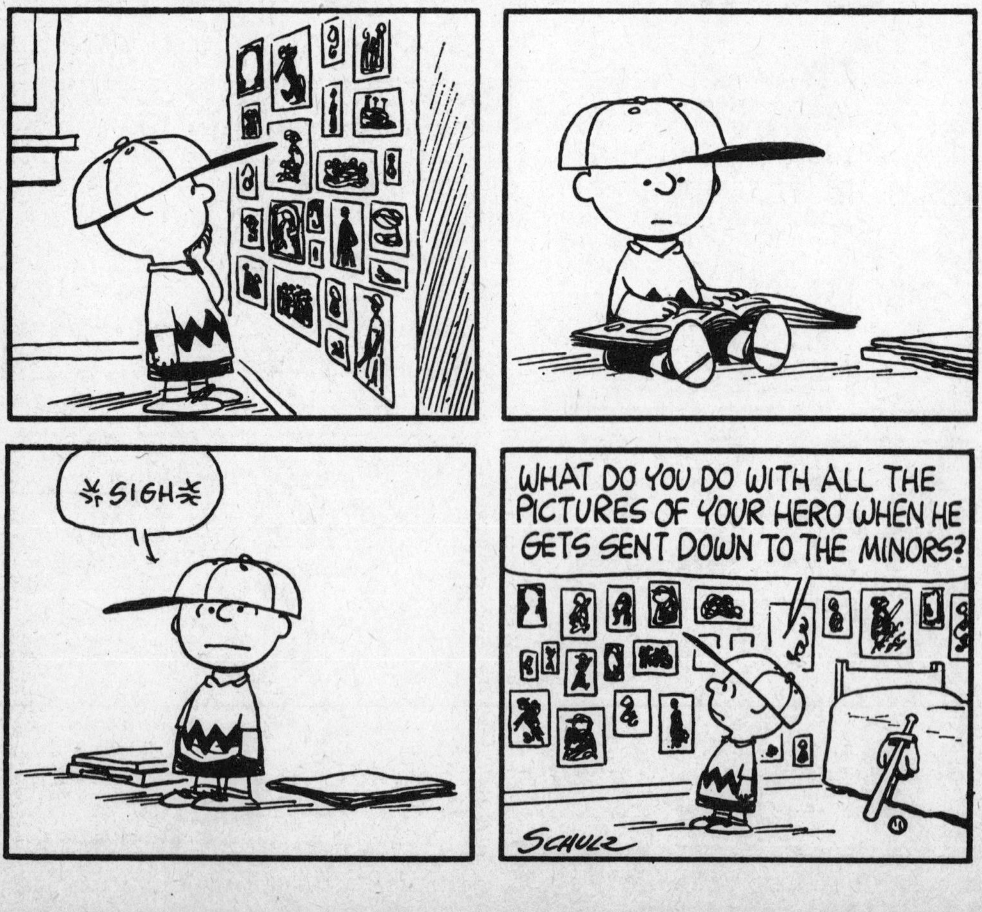
SIGH
WHAT DO YOU DO WITH ALL THE PICTURES OF YOUR HERO WHEN HE GETS SENT DOWN TO THE MINORS?
SCHULZ

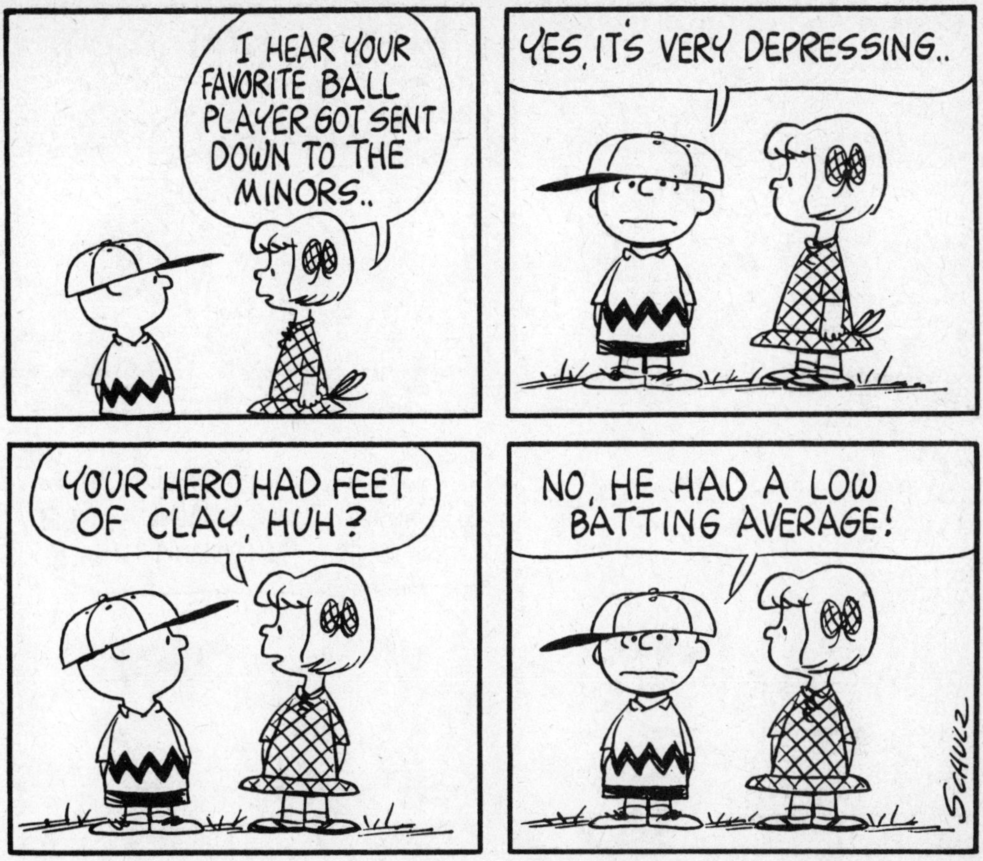
I HEAR YOUR FAVORITE BALL PLAYER GOT SENT DOWN TO THE MINORS..
YES, IT'S VERY DEPRESSING..
YOUR HERO HAD FEET OF CLAY, HUH?
NO, HE HAD A LOW BATTING AVERAGE!
SCHULZ

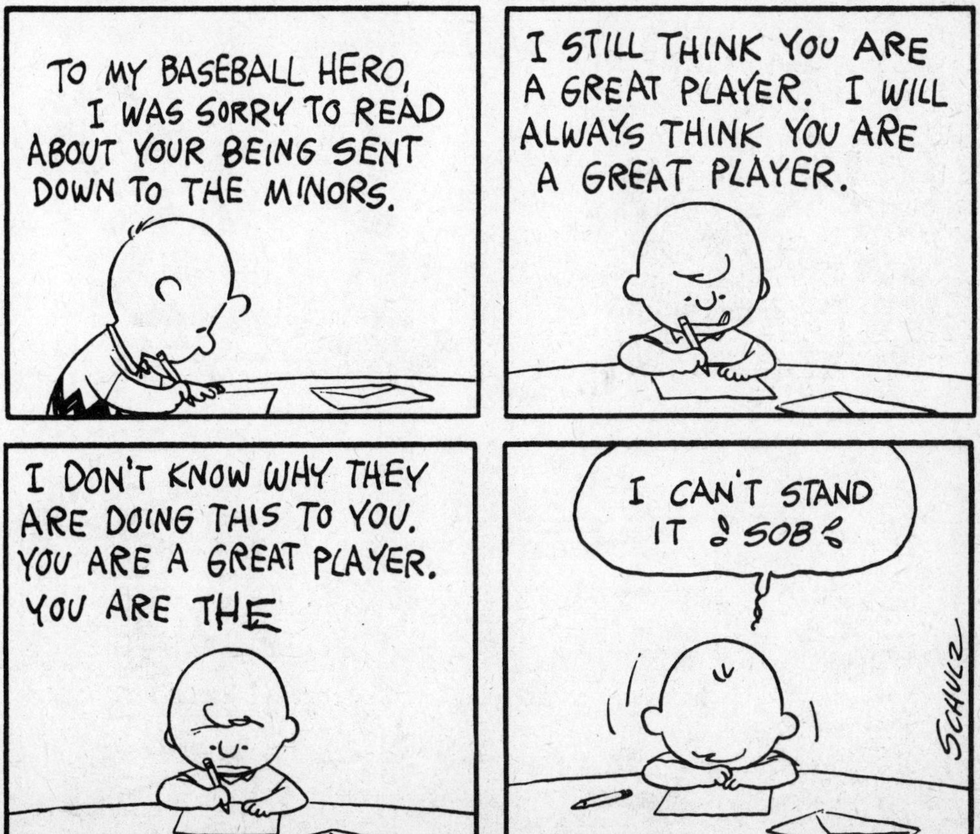
TO MY BASEBALL HERO,
I WAS SORRY TO READ ABOUT YOUR BEING SENT DOWN TO THE MINORS.
I STILL THINK YOU ARE A GREAT PLAYER. I WILL ALWAYS THINK YOU ARE A GREAT PLAYER.
I DON'T KNOW WHY THEY ARE DOING THIS TO YOU. YOU ARE A GREAT PLAYER. YOU ARE THE
I CAN'T STAND IT SOB
SCHULZ

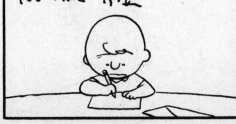

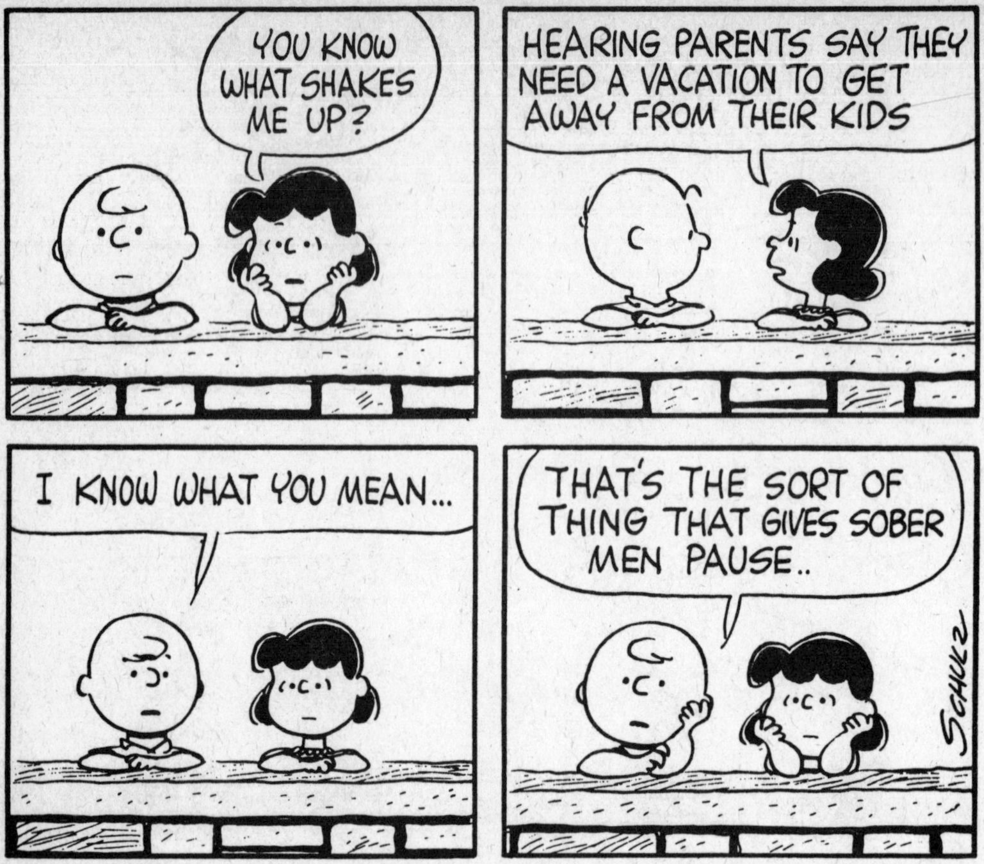
YOU KNOW WHAT SHAKES ME UP?
HEARING PARENTS SAY THEY NEED A VACATION TO GET AWAY FROM THEIR KIDS
I KNOW WHAT YOU MEAN...
THAT'S THE SORT OF THING THAT GIVES SOBER MEN PAUSE..
SCHULZ

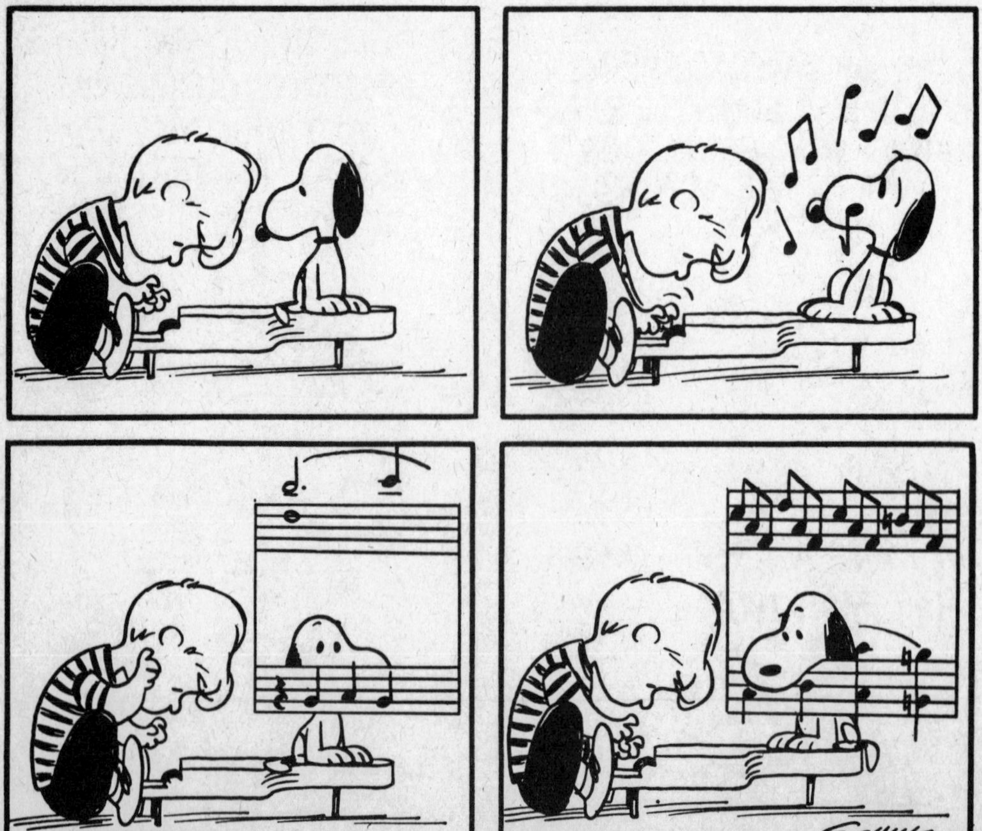
SCHULZ